twelfth canadian edition

microeconomics

Campbell R. McConnell
University of Nebraska – Emeritus

Stanley L. Brue
Pacific Lutheran University

Sean M. Flynn
Scripps College

Thomas P. Barbiero
Ryerson University

McGraw-Hill Ryerson

Connect. Learn. Succeed.

The McGraw·Hill Companies

McGraw-Hill Ryerson
Connect. Learn. Succeed.

Microeconomics
Twelfth Canadian Edition

Copyright © 2010, 2007, 2005, 2002, 1999, 1996, 1993, 1990, 1987, 1984, 1981, 1978 by McGraw-Hill Ryerson Limited, a Subsidiary of The McGraw-Hill Companies. All rights reserved. No part of this publication may be reproduced or transmitted in any form or by any means, or stored in a data base or retrieval system, without the prior written permission of McGraw-Hill Ryerson Limited, or in the case of photocopying or other reprographic copying, a license from The Canadian Copyright Licensing Agency (Access Copyright). For an Access Copyright licence, visit www.accesscopyright.ca or call toll free to 1-800-893-5777.

Statistics Canada information is used with the permission of Statistics Canada. Users are forbidden to copy this material and/or redisseminate the data, in an original or modified form, for commercial purposes, without the expressed permission of Statistics Canada. Information on the availability of the wide range of data from Statistics Canada can be obtained from Statistics Canada's Regional Offices, its World Wide Web site at http://www.statcan.gc.ca and its toll-free access number 1-800-263-1136.

ISBN-13: 978-0-07-096952-0
ISBN-10: 0-07-096952-3

1 2 3 4 5 6 7 8 9 10 WCD 1 9 8 7 6 5 4 3 2 1 0

Printed and bound in the United States of America.

Care has been taken to trace ownership of copyright material contained in this text; however, the publisher will welcome any information that enables it to rectify any reference or credit for subsequent editions.

VICE PRESIDENT AND EDITOR-IN-CHIEF: Joanna Cotton
SPONSORING EDITORS: Bruce McIntosh, James Booty
EXECUTIVE MARKETING MANAGER: Joy Armitage Taylor
DEVELOPMENTAL EDITORS: Daphne Scriabin, Andria Fogarty
EDITORIAL ASSOCIATE: Stephanie Hess
PERMISSIONS/PHOTO RESEARCHER: Lynn McIntyre
SENIOR SUPERVISING EDITOR: Joanne Limebeer
COPY EDITOR: Kelli Howey
PROOFREADER: Judy Sturrup
TEAM LEAD, PRODUCTION: Paula Brown
COVER DESIGN: Sarah Orr/ArtPlus Limited
COVER IMAGE: Richard Ross/Corbis
INTERIOR DESIGN: Sarah Orr/ArtPlus Limited
PAGE LAYOUT: Heather Brunton, Lesley Lavender/ArtPlus Limited
PRINTER: Worldcolor

Library and Archives Canada Cataloguing in Publication Data

Microeconomics / Campbell R. McConnell ... [et al.]. — 12th Canadian ed.
    Includes index.

Previous eds. by Campbell R. McConnell, Stanley L. Brue, and Thomas P. Barbiero.

ISBN 978-0-07-096952-0

    1. Microeconomics—Textbooks.   I. McConnell, Campbell R.

HB172.M516 2010   338.5   C2009-905340-3

The pages within this book were printed on paper containing 10% Post-Consumer Fiber.

Dedication

To Elsa, Marta, Emilia, Robert, and past instructors.

About the Authors

Campbell R. McConnell earned his Ph.D. from the University of Iowa after receiving degrees from Cornell College and the University of Illinois. He taught at the University of Nebraska-Lincoln from 1953 until his retirement in 1990. He is also co-author of *Contemporary Labor Economics*, seventh edition, and *Essentials of Economics*, first edition (both The McGraw-Hill Companies), and has edited readers for the principles and labour economics courses. He is a recipient of both the University of Nebraska Distinguished Teaching Award and the James A. Lake Academic Freedom Award, and is past-president of the Midwest Economics Association. Professor McConnell was awarded an honorary Doctor of Laws degree from Cornell College in 1973 and received its Distinguished Achievement Award in 1994. His primary areas of interest are labour economics and economic education. He has an extensive collection of jazz recordings and enjoys reading jazz history.

Stanley L. Brue did his undergraduate work at Augustana College (South Dakota) and received its Distinguished Achievement Award in 1991. He received his Ph.D. from the University of Nebraska–Lincoln. He is a professor at Pacific Lutheran University, where he has been honored as a recipient of the Burlington Northern Faculty Achievement Award. Professor Brue has also received the national Leavey Award for excellence in economic education. He has served as national president and chair of the Board of Trustees of Omicron Delta Epsilon International Economics Honorary. He is co-author of *Economic Scenes*, fifth edition (Prentice-Hall), *Contemporary Labor Economics*, seventh edition, *Essentials of Economics*, first edition (both The McGraw-Hill Companies), and *The Evolution of Economic Thought*, seventh edition (South-Western). For relaxation, he enjoys international travel, attending sporting events, and skiing with family and friends.

Sean M. Flynn did his undergraduate work at the University of Southern California before completing his Ph.D. at U.C. Berkeley, where he served as the head graduate student instructor for the Department of Economics after receiving the Outstanding Graduate Student Instructor Award. He teaches at Scripps College in Claremont, California, and is also the author of *Essentials of Economics*, second edition (The McGraw-Hill Companies). His research interests include finance and behavioural economics. An accomplished martial artist, he has represented the United States in international aikido tournaments and is the author of *Understanding Shodokan Aikido* (Shodokan Press). Other hobbies include running, travel, and ethnic food.

Thomas P. Barbiero received his Ph.D. from the University of Toronto after completing undergraduate studies at the same university. He is a professor at Ryerson University in Toronto. Professor Barbiero teaches an economic history course to Ryerson students in Rome during the spring semester. His research interests include the economic history of modern Italy and international institutions. He spends his summers in Fontanarosa, a small town in his native region of Campania in southern Italy.

Brief Contents

Web Site Bonus Chapters (found at www.mcgrawhill.ca/olc/mcconnell)

Contents

**WEB SITE BONUS CHAPTERS (FOUND AT
WWW.MCGRAWHILL.CA/OLC/MCCONNELL)**

CHAPTER 14W: Income Inequality, Poverty,
and Discrimination

CHAPTER 16W: Canadian Agriculture:
Economics and Policy

Preface

Welcome to the twelfth Canadian edition of *Microeconomics*. Thousands of Canadian students have studied economics from the Canadian editions of *Microeconomics* and *Macroeconomics*. An estimated 14 million students worldwide have now used a version of the McConnell textbooks, making them the world's best-selling economic principles textbooks.

A Note about the Cover and the New U.S. Co-author

We chose the cover to reference the additional material included in the twelfth Canadian edition on environmental issues such as carbon taxes, the rise in oil prices, and climate change. It is estimated that shipping by rail can help reduce your carbon footprint by up to 82 percent. Additionally, we have printed the interior of this textbook on paper containing 10 percent post-consumer fiber.

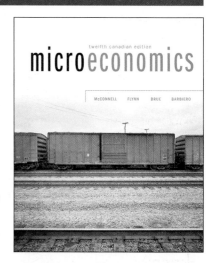

Our new co-author, Sean M. Flynn, has helped to modernize the content of the book from cover to cover. Sean did his undergraduate at the University of Southern California, received his Ph.D from U.C. Berkley (in 2002), teaches principles at Scripps College, and is the author of *Essentials of Economics*, second edition. We are greatly pleased to have Sean working on the text since he shares our commitment to present economics in a way that is understandable to all.

Fundamental Objectives

We have three main goals for *Microeconomics*, which are to:

- Help the beginning student master the principles essential for understanding economic problems, specific economic issues, and the policy alternatives.

- Help the student understand and apply the economic perspective, and reason accurately and objectively about economic matters.

- Promote a lasting student interest in economics and the economy.

What's New and Improved?

One of the benefits of writing a successful text is the opportunity to revise—to delete the outdated and install the new, to rewrite misleading or ambiguous statements, to introduce more relevant illustrations, to improve the organizational structure, and to enhance the learning aids. The more significant changes include the following:

New Chapter

There is a new chapter in the print version of *Microeconomics*. Our common purpose for the new chapter is to incorporate contemporary analytical themes and address current economic issues.

CHAPTER 14: NATURAL RESOURCE AND ENERGY ECONOMICS

This new micro chapter—brought from our Web site for the eleventh edition—is now in Part 3 (The Microeconomics of Resource Markets). This chapter addresses the question of whether the world is becoming overpopulated and rapidly running out of resources. It covers topics such as declining fertility rates, the optimal rate of resource extraction, resource substitution, resource sustainability, oil prices, and alternative energy sources. An understanding of the basic economic principles of natural resource economics will be critical to future citizens and leaders. This micro treatment of natural resources and energy topics is particularly timely since many students are regularly exposed to alarmist views on these subjects.

Two New Appendixes

Two additional chapter appendixes are available for optional assignment in this edition. All are supported by the supplementary materials. The concise new appendixes are:

CHAPTER 3: ADDITIONAL EXAMPLES OF SUPPLY AND DEMAND

At the end of Chapter 3 we provide several additional examples of supply and demand, including concrete examples of simultaneous shifts in supply and demand curves. Products covered include lettuce, corn and ethanol, pink salmon, gasoline, and sushi. We also use the Olympic Games to illustrate examples of pre-set prices, shortages, and surpluses.

CHAPTER 11: ADDITIONAL GAME THEORY APPLICATIONS

We placed several applications of game theory in a new appendix at the end of the chapter on monopolistic competition and oligopoly. Instructors who like to stress game theory in dealing with oligopoly now have strong backup support from the textbook for their efforts. The appendix discusses concepts such as dominant strategies, Nash equilibrium, repeated games, and first-mover advantages.

New (or Relocated) "Consider This" and "Last Word" Boxes

Our **Consider This** boxes are used to provide analogies, examples, or stories that help drive home central economic ideas in a student-oriented, real-world manner. For instance "Market Failure and the Need for Government" demonstrates that while markets are generally efficient, they sometimes fail and government intervention is needed. These brief vignettes, each accompanied by a photo, illustrate key points in a lively, colourful, and easy-to-remember way.

New or relocated Consider This boxes include such disparate topics as an economic comparison of the two Koreas (Chapter 2), the similarity between the concept of elasticity and a Bungee cord (Chapter 4), government policies and birth rates (Chapter 14), turning entrails into oil (Chapter 14), and consumption inequality (Chapter 14W).

Our **Last Word** pieces are lengthier applications and case studies located toward the end of chapters. New or relocated Last Words include insights from behavioural economics (Chapter 5), the economic growth-environmental protection link (Chapter 14), and on fair trade products (Chapter 17).

Contemporary Discussions and Examples

The twelfth Canadian edition refers to and discusses many current topics. Examples include the surpluses and shortages of tickets at the Olympics, aspects of behavioural economics, game theory, impacts of ethanol subsidies, oil and gasoline prices, climate change, consumption versus income inequality, and many more. Also new to this edition is an intuitive discussion of compound interest and the time value of money. We have located this new content in Chapter 13 on rent, interest, and profit.

Integrated Text and Web Site

We continue to integrate the book and our Web site by including icons in the text margin that direct readers to additional content. **Worked Problems** are now available at the McConnell Web site and provide students with a step-by-step illustration of how to solve a problem. These pieces consist of side-by-side computational questions and the computational procedures used to derive the answers. In essence, they extend the textbook's explanations involving computations—for example, of real GDP, real GDP per capita, the unemployment rate, the inflation rate, per-unit production costs, and more. At relevant points in the text, the worked problem icon directs the student to the Web site for additional support.

For those students who want to explore the mathematical details of the theoretical concepts covered in the text, **Math** icons direct the students to the McConnell Web site.

Also on the Web site are **Origin** articles. These brief histories examine the origins of 70 major ideas identified in the book. Students will find it interesting to learn about economists who first developed such ideas as opportunity cost, equilibrium price, the multiplier, and comparative advantage and elasticity. The Origin icon directs students to the McConnell Web site for this extension material.

For selected Key Graphs, **interactive graphs** are available on the McConnell Web site (**www. mcgrawhill.ca/olc/mcconnell**). Developed under the supervision of Norris Peterson of Pacific Lutheran University, this interactive feature depicts major graphs and instructs students to shift the curves, observe the outcomes, and derive relevant generalizations.

Web Chapters

Bonus Web chapters are available in PDF format for easy download at **www.mcgrawhill.ca/olc/mcconnell**. They are: Chapter 14W, Income Inequality, Poverty, and Discrimination, and Chapter 16W, Canadian Agriculture: Economics and Policy.

Distinguishing Features

- ***Comprehensive Explanations at an Appropriate Level***   *Microeconomics* is comprehensive, analytical, and challenging, yet fully accessible to a wide range of students. Its thoroughness and accessibility enable instructors to select topics for special classroom emphasis with confidence that students can independently read and comprehend other assigned material in the book. Where needed, an extra sentence of explanation is provided. Brevity at the expense of clarity is false economy.

- ***Fundamentals of the Market System***   Many economies throughout the world are making difficult transitions from planning systems to market systems. Our detailed description in Chapter 2 of the institutions and operation of the market system is even more relevant than before. We pay particular attention to property rights, entrepreneurship, freedom of enterprise and choice, competition, and the role of profits because these concepts are often misunderstood by beginning students.

- ***Stress on the Theory of the Firm and Technological Advance***   We have given much attention to microeconomics in general and to the theory of the firm in particular, for two reasons: First, the concepts of microeconomics are difficult for most beginning students; abbreviated expositions usually compound these difficulties by raising more questions than they answer. Second, we wanted to couple analysis of the various market structures with a discussion of the impact of each market arrangement on price, output levels, resource allocation, and the rate of technological advance.

- ***Focus on Economic Issues***   For many students, the macro chapters on fiscal policy, monetary policy, and public debt, and the micro chapters on competition policy, agriculture, income inequality, labour issues, and health care are where the action is. We guide that action along logical lines through the application of appropriate analytical tools.

- ***Integrated Text and Web Site***   *Microeconomics* and its Web site are highly integrated through in-text Web icons, bonus Web chapters, Web newspaper articles, Web math notes, and other features. Our Web site is part and parcel of our student learning package, customized to the book.

Organizational Alternatives

Although instructors generally agree as to the content of principles of economics courses, they sometimes differ as to how to arrange the material. *Microeconomics* includes four parts, and that provides considerable organizational flexibility. Some instructors will prefer to intersperse the microeconomics of Parts 2 and 3 with the chapters of Part 4. Chapter 16W on agriculture may follow Chapter 7 on perfect competition; Chapter 10 on competition policy and regulation may follow either Chapters 8 or 9 on imperfect competition models; Chapter 14W on income inequality may follow Chapter 13 on rent, interest, and profit.

Pedagogical Aids

Microeconomics has always been student oriented. Economics is concerned with efficiency—accomplishing goals using the best methods. Therefore, we offer the student some brief introductory comments on how to improve their efficiency and hence their grades.

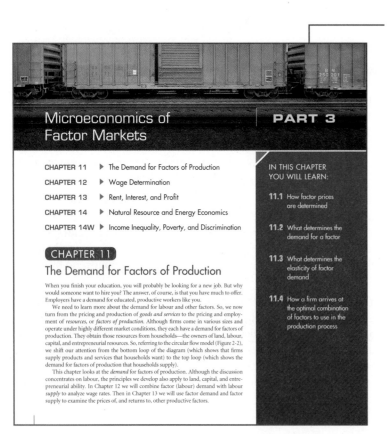

- ***In This Chapter You Will Learn***   We set out the learning objectives at the start of each chapter so the chapter's main concepts can be easily recognized. We have also tied the learning objectives to each of the numbered sections in each chapter and the Study Questions at the end of each chapter. In addition, the chapter summaries are organized by number.

- ***Terminology***   A significant portion of any introductory course is terminology. Key terms are highlighted in bold type the first time they appear in the text. Key terms are defined in the margin and a comprehensive list appears at the end of each chapter. A glossary of definitions can also be found at the end of the book and on the Web site.

- **Ten Key Concepts** Ten Key Concepts have been identified to help students organize the main principles. The Ten Key Concepts are introduced in Chapter 1 and each one is reinforced throughout the textbook by an icon.

FACING TRADEOFFS	**CONCEPT 3** ("Choosing a Little More or Less"): Choices are usually made at the margin; we choose a "little" more or a "little" less of something.
OPPORTUNITY COSTS	**CONCEPT 4** ("The Influence of Incentives"): The choices you make are influenced by incentives.
CHOOSING A LITTLE MORE OR LESS	**Interaction among Individuals**
THE INFLUENCE OF INCENTIVES	**CONCEPT 5** ("Specialization and Trade"): Specialization and trade will improve the well-being of all participants.
SPECIALIZATION & TRADE	**CONCEPT 6** ("The Effectiveness of Markets"): Markets usually do a good job of coordinating trade among individuals, groups, and nations.
THE EFFECTIVENESS OF MARKETS	**CONCEPT 7** ("The Role of Governments"): Governments can occasionally improve the coordinating function of markets.
THE ROLE OF GOVERNMENTS	**The Economy as a Whole and the Standard of Living**
PRODUCTION & THE STANDARD OF LIVING	**CONCEPT 8** ("Production and the Standard of Living"): The standard of living of the average person in a particular country is dependent on its production of goods and services. A rise in the standard of living requires a rise in the output of goods and services.
MONEY & INFLATION	**CONCEPT 9** ("Money and Inflation"): If the monetary authorities of a country annually print money in excess of the growth of output of goods and services it will eventually lead to inflation.
INFLATION– UNEMPLOYMENT TRADEOFF	**CONCEPT 10** ("Inflation–Unemployment Tradeoff"): In the short run, society faces a short-run **tradeoff** between **inflation** and its level of **unemployment**.

As you read the text, be on the lookout for the icon that alerts you that one of these concepts is being discussed. We now turn to our first topic, the economic way of thinking.

- **Key Graphs** We have labelled graphs having special relevance as Key Graphs. There is a quick quiz of four questions related to each Key Graph, with answers provided at the bottom of the graph.

- **Graphics with Supporting Data** Where possible we have tried to provide data to support our graphs. In such cases a data table now appears in the same figure with the graph.

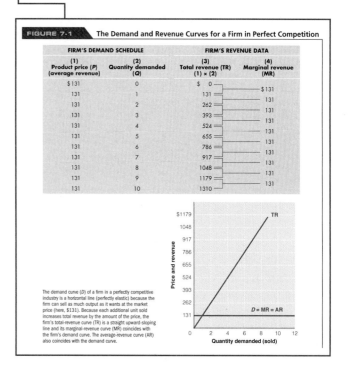

FIGURE 7-1 The Demand and Revenue Curves for a Firm in Perfect Competition

FIRM'S DEMAND SCHEDULE		**FIRM'S REVENUE DATA**	
(1) Product price (P) (average revenue)	(2) Quantity demanded (Q)	(3) Total revenue (TR) (1) × (2)	(4) Marginal revenue (MR)
$131	0	$ 0	$131
131	1	131	131
131	2	262	131
131	3	393	131
131	4	524	131
131	5	655	131
131	6	786	131
131	7	917	131
131	8	1048	131
131	9	1179	131
131	10	1310	

The demand curve (D) of a firm in a perfectly competitive industry is a horizontal line (perfectly elastic) because the firm can sell as much output as it wants at the market price (here, $131). Because each additional unit sold increases total revenue by the amount of the price, the firm's total-revenue curve (TR) is a straight upward-sloping line and its marginal-revenue curve (MR) coincides with the firm's demand curve. The average-revenue curve (AR) also coincides with the demand curve.

- **Data Updates** Data updates for selected graphs and tables can be found on the McConnell-Brue-Flynn-Barbiero Web site **www.mcgrawhill.ca/olc.mcconnell**.

@ **KEY GRAPH**

FIGURE 17-2 Trading Possibilities Lines and the Gains from Trade

As a result of international specialization and trade, Canada and Brazil both can have levels of output higher than those attainable on their domestic production possibilities curves. Panel (a): Canada can move from point A on its domestic production possibilities curve to, say, A' on its trading possibilities line. Panel (b): Brazil can move from B to B'.

(a) Canada

(b) Brazil

Quick Quiz

1. The production possibilities curves in graphs (a) and (b) imply:
   a. increasing domestic opportunity costs.
   b. decreasing domestic opportunity costs.
   c. constant domestic opportunity costs.
   d. first decreasing, then increasing, domestic opportunity costs.

2. Before specialization, the domestic opportunity cost of producing 1 unit of steel is:
   a. 1 unit of soybeans in both Canada and Brazil.
   b. 1 unit of soybeans in Canada and 2 units of soybeans in Brazil.
   c. 2 units of soybeans in Canada and 1 unit of soybeans in Brazil.
   d. 1 unit of soybeans in Canada and ½ unit of soybeans in Brazil.

3. After specialization and trade, the world output of steel and soybeans is:
   a. 20 tonnes of steel and 20 tonnes of soybeans.
   b. 45 tonnes of steel and 15 tonnes of soybeans.
   c. 30 tonnes of steel and 20 tonnes of soybeans.
   d. 10 tonnes of steel and 30 tonnes of soybeans.

4. After specialization and international trade:
   a. Canada can obtain units of soybeans at less cost than before trade.
   b. Brazil can obtain more than 20 tonnes of soybeans, if it so chooses.
   c. Canada no longer has a comparative advantage in producing steel.
   d. Brazil can benefit by prohibiting soybean imports from Canada.

Answers: 1. c; 2. b; 3. c; 4. a

Average Weekly Wages in Selected Industries, 2008

TABLE 12-3

Industry	Average weekly earnings (including overtime)
All Industries	$ 810.45
Mining, and oil and gas extraction	1527.98
Construction	1014.51
Finance, insurance, and real estate	1000.76
Manufacturing	949.54
Logging and forestry	935.84
Transportation and warehousing	883.28
Educational and related services	862.64
Real estate services	772.87
Health and social services	743.94

Source: Statistics Canada, http://www40.statcan.gc.ca/l01/cst01/labr73a-eng.htm. Adapted from Statistics Canada CANSIM database, http://cansim2.statcan.ca, Table 281-0027, June 2008.

- **Reviewing the Chapter**   Important things should be said more than once. You will find a Chapter Summary at the conclusion of every chapter as well as two or three Quick Reviews within each chapter. The summary at the end of each chapter is presented by numbered chapter section. These review statements will help you to focus on the essential ideas of each chapter and also to study for exams.

QUICK REVIEW

▶ Profit is maximized, or loss minimized, at the output at which marginal revenue (or price in pure competition) equals marginal cost.

▶ If the market price is below the minimum average variable cost, the firm will minimize its losses by shutting down.

▶ The segment of the firm's marginal-cost curve that lies above the average-variable-cost curve is its short-run supply curve.

▶ Table 7-4 summarizes the MR = MC approach to determining the competitive firm's profit-maximizing output. It also shows the equivalent analysis in terms of total revenue and total cost.

▶ Under perfect competition, equilibrium price is a given to the individual firm and simultaneously is the result of the production (supply) decisions of all firms as a group.

- **The Last Word**   The Last Word features are lengthier applications and case studies located toward the end of each chapter. In this edition, we have included photos to pique student interest. See list of Last Word features inside the front cover of the text.

The LAST WORD

M&M's, Final Exams, and Retirement Savings: Insights from Behavioural Economics

Over the past 20 years, researchers called behavioural economists have noted behaviours that differ from the predictions of standard theory and have offered interesting explanations for why they occur.

We have just discussed how diminishing marginal utility underlies demand. The key insight is that even when we like a particular good or service, we like successive units of it less and less. Basically, we get fed up with it.

But consider this. Researchers offered moviegoers a mix of M&M's chocolate candies that contained only seven colours of M&M's and then counted how many of the candies they ate. Then, with a different group of moviegoers, they offered a mix of M&M's that had 10 different colours. In both cases, the candy was free and people could take as much or as little as they desired. The result? The moviegoers who were offered more colours ate 43 percent more candy even though every colour tastes exactly the same.

So does this mean that people do not actually experience diminishing marginal utility, as economists assume? Not really. It just means that how quickly utility diminishes varies depending on context. And part of that context is *variety*. To our ancient ancestors who were constantly struggling to have enough to eat, suddenly finding a rare type of food was such an unexpected blessing that it made sense to eat it immediately, regardless of whether they had just stuffed themselves with more ordinary foods. The vitamins and minerals of the rare and different food were simply too important to pass up. Hence, the modern human's instinct for

variety—and for the fact that diminishing marginal utility sets in more slowly when people are offered a variety of products rather than just one or two.

The pressing needs of the present rather than the elusive possibilities of the future also appear to have produced human brains that have trouble making decisions involving events that will take place more than a few days or weeks in the future. For instance, suppose that at the beginning of a semester researchers ask each student in a particular class if they would be willing to pay $20 to have the final exam delayed by one day. Typically only a handful of students are willing to pay the $20 fee for the one-day postponement. However, if you ask them the day before the exam, a large majority are suddenly willing to pay the $20 fee. Behavioural economists refer to this as "time inconsistency." Although people can correctly predict how they will feel in the future—they panicked a day before the upcoming exam!—

those predicted feelings do not carry much weight when their desire to spend the $20 today on current consumption.

This sort of behaviour has important implications for retirement savings. If you ask 55-year-olds if it is important to save for retirement, they will not only say yes but will back it up by saving a lot. But if you ask 25-year-olds if it is important to save for retirement, they will also say yes, but usually will hardly save at all. Most will spend nearly all their income, and the vast majority will continue to behave this way until they are near retirement. Then, they will begin to realize that an impoverished retirement is a near-term possibility rather than a distant concern.

Recognizing the fact that young people do not take saving for retirement very seriously, governments have instituted public policies designed to counter this reality. For example, the federal government requires nearly all workers to make Old Age pension contributions (which are used to pay benefits to currently eligible retirees). No "opt out" from the payroll taxes allowed! Because retirement benefits also will become available to workers when they age and retire, the system partially makes up for the fact that the human brain fails to put enough weight on distant possibilities, even very bad ones such as living in poverty in old age.

Question

People at buffets put more on their plates and eat more the greater the variety of items they have to select from. How does this relate to the idea that diminishing marginal utility must be understood in context? Many people buy too much on their credit cards, even though they know they will be sorry when they get their credit card bill. Relate this fact to the idea of time inconsistency.

- **Global Perspective Boxes**   Each nation functions increasingly in a global economy. To help the student gain appreciation of this wider economic environment, we provide Global Perspective features, which compare Canada to other nations.

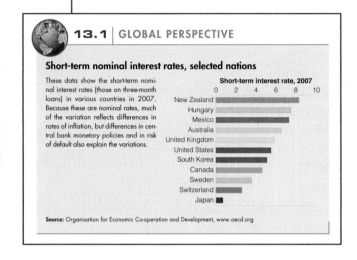

13.1 | **GLOBAL PERSPECTIVE**

Short-term nominal interest rates, selected nations

These data show the short-term nominal interest rates (those on three-month loans) in various countries in 2007. Because these are nominal rates, much of the variation reflects differences in rates of inflation, but differences in central bank monetary policies and in risk of default also explain the variations.

Source: Organisation for Economic Co-operation and Development, www.oecd.org

- **Consider This Boxes**   Consider This boxes are used to provide analogies, examples, or stories that help drive home central economic ideas in a student-oriented, real-world manner. These brief vignettes illustrate key points in a lively, colourful, and easy-to-remember way. See the list of Consider This boxes inside the front cover of the text.

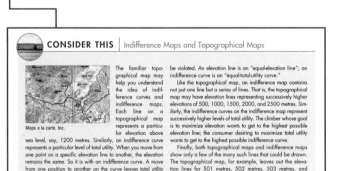

CONSIDER THIS | Indifference Maps and Topographical Maps

Maps a la carte, Inc.

The familiar topographical map may help you understand the idea of indifference curves and indifference maps. Each line on a topographical map represents a particular elevation above sea level, say, 1200 metres. Similarly, an indifference curve represents a particular level of total utility. When you move from one point on a specific elevation line to another, the elevation remains the same. So it is with an indifference curve. A move from one position to another on the curve leaves total utility unchanged. Neither elevation lines nor indifference curves can intersect. If they did, the meaning of each line or curve would

be violated. An elevation line is an "equal-elevation line"; an indifference curve is an "equal-total-utility curve."

Like the topographical map, an indifference map contains not just one line but a series of lines. That is, the topographical map may have elevation lines representing successively higher elevations of 500, 1000, 1500, 2000, and 2500 metres. Similarly, the indifference curves on the indifference map represent successively higher levels of total utility. The climber whose goal is to maximize elevation wants to get to the highest possible elevation line; the consumer desiring to maximize total utility wants to get to the highest possible indifference curve.

Finally, both topographical maps and indifference maps show only a few of the many such lines that could be drawn. The topographical map, for example, leaves out the elevation lines for 501 metres, 502 metres, 503 metres, and so on. The indifference map leaves out all the indifference curves that could be drawn between those illustrated.

- **Appendix on Graphs** Being comfortable with graphical analysis and a few related quantitative concepts will be a big advantage to students in understanding the principles of economics. The Appendix to Chapter 1, which reviews graphing, line slopes, and linear equations, should not be skipped.

- **Study Questions** A comprehensive list of questions is located at the end of each chapter. The old cliché that you "learn by doing" is very relevant to economics. Use of these questions will enhance students' understanding. We designate several of them as "Key Questions" and answer them in the Study Guide. For the twelfth Canadian edition of *Microeconomics* we have added a total of 8 new Study Questions and connected every question with a Learning Objective.

Appendix to Chapter 1

A1.1 GRAPHS AND THEIR MEANINGS

If you glance quickly through this text, you will find many graphs. Some seem simple, others more complicated. All are included to help you visualize and understand economic relationships. Physicists and chemists sometimes illustrate their theories by building arrangements of multicoloured wooden balls, representing protons, neutrons, and electrons, which are held in proper relation to one another by wires or sticks. Economists use graphs to illustrate their models. By understanding these "pictures," you can more readily make sense of economic relationships. Most of our principles or models explain relationships between just two sets of economic facts, which can be conveniently represented with two-dimensional graphs.

Construction of a Graph

A *graph* is a visual representation of the relationship between two variables. Figure A1-1 is a hypothetical illustration showing the relationship between income and consumption for the economy as a whole. Without even studying economics, we would logically expect that people would buy more goods and services when their incomes go up. Thus it is not surprising to find in Figure A1-1 that total consumption in the economy increases as total income increases.

The information in Figure A1-1 is expressed both graphically and in table form. Here is how it is done: We want to show graphically how consumption changes as income changes. We therefore represent income on the **horizontal axis** of the graph and consumption on the **vertical axis**.

Now we arrange the vertical and horizontal scales of the graph to reflect the ranges of values of consumption and income, and mark the scales in convenient increments. As you can see in Figure A1-1, the values marked on the scales cover all the values in the table. The increments on both scales are $100 for approximately each centimetre.

Because the graph has two dimensions, each point within it represents an income value and its associated consumption value. To find a point that represents one of the five income–consumption combinations shown in the table, we draw straight lines from the appropriate values on the vertical and horizontal axes. For example, to plot point *c* (the $200 income, $150 consumption), straight lines are drawn up from the horizontal (income) axis at $200 and across from the vertical (consumption) axis at $150. These straight lines intersect at point *c*, which represents this particular income–consumption combination. You should verify that the other income–consumption combinations shown in the table are properly located in the graph. Finally, by assuming

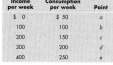

FIGURE A1-1 The Relationship between Income and Consumption

Two sets of data that are positively or directly related, such as consumption and income, graph as an upsloping line.

Income per week	Consumption per week	Point
$ 0	$ 50	a
100	100	b
200	150	c
300	200	d
400	250	e

STUDY QUESTIONS

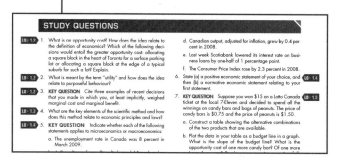

LO: 1,2   1. What is an opportunity cost? How does the idea relate to the definition of economics? Which of the following decisions would entail the greater opportunity cost: allocating a square block in the heart of Toronto for a surface parking lot or allocating a square block at the edge of a typical suburb for such a lot? Explain.

LO: 1,2   2. What is meant by the term "utility" and how does the idea relate to purposeful behaviour?

LO: 1,2   3. **KEY QUESTION** Cite three examples of recent decisions that you made in which you, at least implicitly, weighed marginal cost and marginal benefit.

LO: 1,3   4. What are the key elements of the scientific method and how does this method relate to economic principles and laws?

LO: 1,4   5. **KEY QUESTION** Indicate whether each of the following statements applies to microeconomics or macroeconomics:

    a. The unemployment rate in Canada was 8 percent in March 2009.

    d. Canadian output, adjusted for inflation, grew by 0.4 per cent in 2008.

    e. Last week Scotiabank lowered its interest rate on business loans by one-half of 1 percentage point.

    f. The Consumer Price Index rose by 2.3 percent in 2008.

LO: 1,4   6. State (a) a positive economic statement of your choice, and then (b) a normative economic statement relating to your first statement.

LO: 1,5   7. **KEY QUESTION** Suppose you won $15 on a Lotto Canada ticket at the local 7-Eleven and decided to spend all the winnings on candy bars and bags of peanuts. The price of candy bars is $0.75 and the price of peanuts is $1.50.

    a. Construct a table showing the alternative combinations of the two products that are available.

    b. Plot the data in your table as a budget line in a graph. What is the slope of the budget line? What is the opportunity cost of one more candy bar? Of one more

- **Internet Application Questions** Students are presented with questions to explore on the Internet relevant to the topic discussed in the chapter. From the McConnell Web site, **www.mcgrawhillconnect.ca**, students will find direct links to the Web sites included in these questions.

INTERNET APPLICATION QUESTIONS @

1. **Diamonds—Interested in Buying One?** Use the links on the McConnell-Brue-Flynn-Barbiero Web site (Chapter 2) to access the Internet auction site eBay. Select the category Jewelry and Watches, followed by Loose Diamonds and Gemstones, and then Loose Diamonds. How many loose diamonds are for sale at the moment? Note the wide array of sizes and prices of the diamonds. In what sense is there competition among the sellers in this market? How does that competition influence prices? In what sense is there competition among buyers? How does that competition influence prices?

2. **Barter and the Canada Revenue Agency.** Bartering occurs when goods or services are exchanged without the exchange of money. For some, barter's popularity is that it enables them to avoid paying taxes to the government. How might such avoidance occur? Use the links on the McConnell-Brue-Flynn-Barbiero Web site (Chapter 2) to access the Canada Revenue Agency's (CRA) interpretation of barter transactions. Does the CRA treat barter as taxable or nontaxable income? How is the value of a barter transaction determined?

Comprehensive Learning and Teaching Package

The twelfth Canadian edition is also accompanied by a variety of high-quality supplements that help students master the subject and help instructors implement customized courses.

For the Students

LYRYX LEARNING INC
Online Learning and Assessment
lyryx.com

Lyryx Assessment for Economics is a leading-edge online assessment system, designed to support both students and instructors. The assessment takes the form of a homework assignment called a Lab. The assessments are algorithmically generated and automatically graded so that students get instant grades and feedback. New Labs are randomly generated each time, providing the student with unlimited opportunities to try a type of question. After they submit a Lab for marking, students receive extensive feedback on their work, thus promoting their learning experience.

Lyryx for the student offers algorithmically generated and automatically graded assignments. Students get instant grades and instant feedback—no need to wait until the next class to find out how well they did! Grades are instantly recorded in a grade book that the student can view.

Students are motivated to do their labs for two reasons: first because it can be tied to assessment, and second because they can try the Lab as many times as they wish prior to the due date with only their best grade being recorded.

Instructors know from experience that if students do their economics homework, they will be successful in the course. Recent research regarding the use of Lyryx has shown that when Labs are tied to assessment, even if worth only a small percentage of the total grade of the course, students WILL do their homework—and MORE THAN ONCE!

Please contact your *i*Learning Sales Specialist for additional information on the Lyryx Assessment Economics system.

Visit http://lyryx.com

- **Online Learning Centre** This electronic learning aid, located at **www.mcgrawhill.ca/olc/mcconnell**, offers materials including chapter highlights, key terms, Origin feature, and access to the Statistics Canada free database. Highly visible Web icons in the text margins alert students to points in the book where they can springboard to the site to learn more. There also are regular news updates and an interactive glossary—all specific to *Microeconomics*. For the math-minded student, there is a "Math" section, where they can explore the mathematical details of the concepts in the text. There are also two optional bonus Web chapters.

- Developed in partnership with Youthography, a Canadian youth research company, and hundreds of students from across Canada, McGraw-Hill Connect™ embraces diverse study behaviours and preferences to maximize active learning and engagement.

  With McGraw-Hill Connect™, written by Lance Shandler of Kwantlen Polytechnic University, students complete pre- and post-diagnostic assessments that identify knowledge gaps and point them to concepts they need to learn. McGraw-Hill Connect™ provides students the option to work through recommended learning exercises and create their own personalized study plan using multiple sources of content, including a searchable e-book, multiple-choice and true/false quizzes, chapter-by-chapter learning goals, interactivities, personal notes, videos, and more. Using the copy, paste, highlight, and sticky note features, students collect, organize, and customize their study plan content to optimize learning outcomes.

For the Instructor

- **The Instructor Online Learning Centre** The Instructor Online Learning Centre (OLC) at **www.mcgrawhill.ca/olc/mcconnell** includes a password-protected Web site for instructors. The site offers downloadable Instructor supplements.

All Instructor supplements are available at the OLC:

- **Instructor's Manual** The Instructor's Manual is prepared by Thomas Barbiero of Ryerson University, and Shawn D. Knabb of Western Washington University. Available again in this edition as a Microsoft® Office Word document, the manual includes: Chapter Overview, What's New, Instructional Objectives, Comments and Teaching Suggestions, Student Stumbling Blocks, Lecture Notes, Last Word, and answers to end-of-chapter questions.

- **Microsoft® PowerPoint® Presentation Software** Prepared by Bruno Fullone of George Brown College, this presentation system is found on the Instructor's Site of the Online Learning Centre. It offers visual presentations that may be edited and manipulated to fit a particular course format.

- **Computerized Test Banks** Prepared by Nargess Kayhani, Mount St. Vincent University, Computerized Test Bank I contains about 6000 multiple-choice and true/false questions. Rob Moir, University of New Brunswick, has prepared over 30 short-answer questions with suggested answers for each chapter. Also included is U.S. Test Bank II. This test bank contains around 6300 multiple choice and true/false questions. All questions are categorized according to level and difficulty.

In addition, content cartridges are available for the course management systems **WebCT** and **Blackboard**. These platforms provide instructors with user-friendly, flexible teaching tools. Please contact your local McGraw-Hill Ryerson *i*Learning Sales Specialist for details.

- McGraw-Hill Connect™ assessment activities don't stop with students! There is material for instructors to leverage as well, including a personalized teaching plan where instructors can choose from a variety of quizzes to use in class, assign as homework, or add to exams. They can edit existing questions and add new ones; track individual student performance—by question, assignment, or in relation to the class overall—with detailed grade reports; integrate grade reports easily with Learning Management Systems such as WebCT and Blackboard; and much more. Instructors can also browse or search teaching resources and text specific supplements and organize them into customizable categories. All the teaching resources are now located in one convenient place.
  McGraw-Hill Connect™ — helping instructors and students Connect, Learn, Succeed!

Superior Service

Integrated Learning

Your **Integrated Learning Sales Specialist** is a McGraw-Hill Ryerson representative who has the experience, product knowledge, training, and support to help you assess and integrate any of the above-noted products, technology, and services into your course for optimum teaching and learning performance. Whether it's using our test bank software, helping your students improve their grades, or putting your entire course online, your *i*Learning Sales Specialist is there to help you do it. Contact your local *i*Learning Sales Specialist today to learn how to maximize all of McGraw-Hill Ryerson's resources!

*i*Learning Services Program

McGraw-Hill Ryerson offers a unique *i*Services package designed for Canadian faculty. Our mission is to equip providers of higher education with superior tools and resources required for excellence in teaching. For additional information visit **www.mcgrawhill.ca/highereducation/iservices**.

Teaching, Technology, and Learning Conference Series

The educational environment has changed tremendously in recent years, and McGraw-Hill Ryerson continues to be committed to helping you acquire the skills you need to succeed in this new milieu. Our innovative Teaching, Technology, and Learning Conference Series brings together faculty from across Canada with winners of the 3M Teaching Excellence award to share teaching and learning best practices in a collaborative and stimulating environment. Pre-conference workshops on general topics, such as teaching large classes and technology integration, will also be offered. We will also work with you at your own institution to customize workshops that best suit the needs of your faculty.

Acknowledgements

The twelfth Canadian edition of *Microeconomics* has benefitted from a number of perceptive reviewers, who were a rich source of suggestions for this revision. To each of you, and others we may have inadvertently overlooked, thank you for your considerable help in improving *Microeconomics*. Reviewers include:

Ather H. Akbari, Saint Mary's University

Morris Altman, University of Saskatchewan

Nancy Carson, Thompson Rivers University

Percy Christon-Quao, Kwantlen Polytechnic University

Carl Graham, Assiniboine Community College

David Gray, University of Ottawa

Rita Halma, Lethbridge College

Shahidul Islam, Grant MacEwan University

Geraldine Joosse, Lethbridge College

Nargess Kayhani, Mount Saint Vincent University

Joan McEachern, Kwantlen Polytechnic University

Eric Moon, Seneca College

John Newark, Athabasca University

C. Fiifi Odoom, Douglas College

Richard Schwindt, Simon Fraser University

Lance Shandler, Kwantlen Polytechnic University

Carl Weston, Mohawk College

We are greatly indebted to an all-star group of professionals at McGraw-Hill Ryerson—in particular Bruce McIntosh and James Booty, Sponsoring Editors; Daphne Scriabin and Andria Fogarty, Developmental Editors; Joy Armitage Taylor, Executive Marketing Manager; and Stephanie Hess, Editorial Associate—for their publishing and marketing expertise. We thank Kelli Howey for her thorough and sensitive editing, Jacques Cournoyer for his vivid Last Word illustrations, Sarah Orr/ArtPlus Limited for the cover and interior design, Gianluigi Pelloni of the University of Bologna (Rimini Campus) for his helpful suggestions and insights, and Michael Lindsay of Humber College Institute of Technology & Advanced Learning for his technical checks.

We also strongly acknowledge the McGraw-Hill Ryerson sales staff, who greeted this edition with wholehearted enthusiasm.

Campbell R. McConnell
Stanley L. Brue
Sean M. Flynn
Thomas P. Barbiero

An Introduction to Economics and the Economy

PART 1

CHAPTER 1

Limits, Alternatives, and Choices

(An appendix on understanding graphs follows this chapter. If you need a quick review of this mathematical tool, you might benefit by reading the appendix first.)

People's wants are numerous and varied. Biologically, people need only air, water, food, clothing, and shelter. But in modern society people also desire goods and services that provide a more comfortable or affluent standard of living. We want bottled water, soft drinks, and fruit juices, not just water from the creek. We want salads, burgers, and pizzas, not just berries and nuts. We want jeans, suits, and coats, not just woven reeds. We want apartments, condominiums, or houses, not just mud huts. And, as the saying goes, "that is not the half of it." We also want flat-panel TVs, Internet service, education, cell phones, health care, and much more.

Fortunately, society possesses productive resources, such as labour and managerial talent, tools and machinery, and land and mineral deposits. These resources, employed in the economic system (or simply the economy), help us produce goods and services that satisfy many of our economic wants. But the blunt reality is that our economic wants far exceed the productive capacity of our scarce (limited) resources. We are forced to make choices. This unyielding truth underlies the definition of **economics,** which is the social science concerned with how individuals, institutions, and society make optimal (best) choices under conditions of scarcity.

Numerous problems and issues arise from the challenge of making optimal choices under conditions of scarcity. Although it is tempting to plunge into them, that sort of analysis must wait until we discuss some important preliminaries.

IN THIS CHAPTER YOU WILL LEARN:

1.1 Ten key concepts to retain for a lifetime

1.2 The features of the economic way of thinking

1.3 The role of theories, principles, and models in economics

1.4 The distinction between microeconomics and macroeconomics

1.5 The nature of the economic problem and the categories of scarce resources

1.6 The production possibilities model and the nature of increasing opportunity costs

1.7 What economic growth is, and how present choices determine future production possibilities

A1.1 (Appendix) About graphs, curves, and slopes as they relate to economics

ORIGIN 1.1
Economics

economics
The social science concerned with how individuals, institutions, and society make optimal (best) choices under conditions of scarcity.

Economics is concerned with the efficient use of scarce resources to obtain the maximum satisfaction of society's unlimited wants.

 FACING TRADEOFFS

 OPPORTUNITY COSTS

 CHOOSING A LITTLE MORE OR LESS

 THE INFLUENCE OF INCENTIVES

 SPECIALIZATION & TRADE

 THE EFFECTIVENESS OF MARKETS

 THE ROLE OF GOVERNMENTS

 PRODUCTION & THE STANDARD OF LIVING

 MONEY & INFLATION

 INFLATION– UNEMPLOYMENT TRADEOFF

1.1 | Ten Key Concepts to Retain for a Lifetime

Suppose you unexpectedly meet your introductory economics professor on the street five or ten years after you complete this course. What will you be able to tell her you retained from the course? More than likely you will not be able to remember very much. To help you retain the main ideas that economics has to offer, we have come up with **10 key concepts** we believe are essential to understand the world around you and will help you in your chosen career. These key concepts will be reinforced throughout the textbook so that you will hopefully retain them long after the course is over. When a key concept is about to be discussed you will be alerted with an icon and the concept description.

The 10 key concepts are simply listed here; you will find elaboration on each key concept as we progress through the textbook. At the end of the course you should review these 10 key concepts. They will help you organize and better understand the materials you have studied. We have divided the 10 key concepts into three categories: (a) concepts that pertain to the individual; (b) concepts that explain the interaction among individuals; and (c) concepts that deal with the economy as a whole and the standard of living.

The Individual

CONCEPT 1 ("Facing Tradeoffs"): Scarcity in relation to wants means you face **tradeoffs;** therefore, you have to make choices.

CONCEPT 2 ("Opportunity Costs"): The cost of the choice you make is what you give up for it, or the **opportunity cost.**

CONCEPT 3 ("Choosing a Little More or Less"): Choices are usually made at the margin; we choose a "little" more or a "little" less of something.

CONCEPT 4 ("The Influence of Incentives"): The choices you make are influenced by incentives.

Interaction among Individuals

CONCEPT 5 ("Specialization and Trade"): Specialization and trade will improve the well-being of all participants.

CONCEPT 6 ("The Effectiveness of Markets"): Markets usually do a good job of coordinating trade among individuals, groups, and nations.

CONCEPT 7 ("The Role of Governments"): Governments can occasionally improve the coordinating function of markets.

The Economy as a Whole and the Standard of Living

CONCEPT 8 ("Production and the Standard of Living"): The standard of living of the average person in a particular country is dependent on its production of goods and services. A rise in the standard of living requires a rise in the output of goods and services.

CONCEPT 9 ("Money and Inflation"): If the monetary authorities of a country annually print money in excess of the growth of output of goods and services it will eventually lead to inflation.

CONCEPT 10 ("Inflation–Unemployment Tradeoff"): In the short run, society faces a short-run **tradeoff** between **inflation** and its level of **unemployment.**

As you read the text, be on the lookout for the icon that alerts you that one of these concepts is being discussed. We now turn to our first topic, the economic way of thinking.

1.2 | The Economic Way of Thinking

Close your eyes for a minute and pretend you are in paradise, a place where you can have anything you want whenever you desire it. On a particular day you may decide you want a new pair of jeans, a new notebook computer, a cellular phone, tickets to see Avril Lavigne, and a new red Ferrari sports car to cruise around in. Your friends may have a completely different list of wants, but in paradise all of their desires also will be satisfied. Indeed, everyone's desires are satisfied. The following day you can start all over and make any request you have, and it will be fulfilled. And so it will continue, forever. Your body will never get old or sick, you will have all the friends and love you want, etc., etc.

Of course, paradise may be waiting for us in the afterlife, but in this world our wants greatly outstrip our ability to satisfy them. Anytime there is a situation in which wants are greater than the resources to meet those desires, we have an economic problem. It is this reality that gives economists their unique perspective. This **economic perspective** or *economic way of thinking* has several critical and closely interrelated features.

economic perspective
A viewpoint that envisions individuals and institutions making rational decisions by comparing the marginal benefits and marginal costs associated with their actions.

Scarcity and Choice

From our definition of economics, it is easy to see why economists view the world through the lens of scarcity. Since resources are scarce (limited), it follows that the goods and services we produce must also be limited. Scarcity limits our options and necessitates that we make choices. Because we "can't have it all," we must decide what we will have, and what we must forgo.

At the core of economics is the idea that "there is no free lunch." You may get treated to lunch, making it "free" to you, but there is a cost to someone—ultimately, society (see the Consider This box). Scarce inputs of land, equipment, farm labour, the labour of cooks and waiters, and managerial talent are required. Because these resources could be used in other production activities, they and the other goods and services they could have produced are sacrificed in making the lunch available. Economists call these sacrifices **opportunity costs.** To get more of one thing, you forgo the opportunity of getting the next best thing. That sacrifice is the opportunity cost of the choice. For example, you have $100 that you can spend on a pair of jeans or shoes. The opportunity cost of buying the shoes is the jeans you could have purchased, and vice versa.

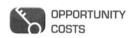 OPPORTUNITY
COSTS

opportunity cost
The amount of other products that must be forgone or sacrificed to produce a unit of a product.

CONSIDER THIS | Free for All?

Free products are seemingly everywhere. Sellers from time to time offer free software, free cell phones, and no-fee chequing accounts. Dentists give out free toothbrushes. At provincial visitors' centres, there are free brochures and maps.

Does the presence of so many free products contradict the economist's assertion that "there is no free lunch"? No! Scarce resources are used to produce each of these products, and because those resources have alternative uses, society gives up something else to get the "free" good. Where resources are used to produce goods and services, there is no free lunch.

So why are these goods offered for free? In a word: marketing. Firms sometimes offer free products to entice people to try them, hoping they will then purchase them later. The free version of software may eventually entice you to buy the next upgraded version, in other instances free brochures contain advertising for shops and restaurants, and free access to the Internet is filled with ads. In still other cases, the product is free only in conjunction with a purchase. To get the soft drink you must buy the large pizza. To get the free cell phone you need to sign up for a year (or more) of cell phone service.

So free products may or may not be truly free to individuals. They are never free to society.

ORIGIN 1.2
Utility

utility
The satisfaction a person gets from consuming a good or service.

Purposeful Behaviour

Economics assumes that human behaviour reflects "rational self-interest." Individuals look for and pursue opportunities to increase their **utility**—the pleasure, happiness, or satisfaction obtained from consuming a good or service. They allocate their time, energy, and money to maximize their satisfaction. Because they weigh costs and benefits, their decisions are purposeful or rational, not random or chaotic.

Consumers are purposeful in deciding what goods and services to buy. Business firms are purposeful in deciding what products to produce and how to produce them. Government entities are purposeful in deciding what public services to provide and how to finance them.

"Purposeful behaviour" does not assume that people and institutions are immune from faulty logic and therefore are perfect decision makers. They sometimes make mistakes. Nor does it mean that people's decisions are unaffected by emotion or the decisions of those around them. "Purposeful behaviour" simply means that people make decisions with some desired outcome in mind.

Rational self-interest is not the same as selfishness. In the economy, increasing one's own wage, rent, interest, or profit normally requires identifying and satisfying *somebody else's* wants! Also, people make personal sacrifices for others. They contribute time and money to charities because they derive pleasure from doing so. Parents help pay for their children's education for the same reason. These self-interested, but unselfish, acts help maximize the giver's satisfaction as much as any personal purchase of goods or services. Self-interested behaviour is simply behaviour designed to increase personal satisfaction, however it may be derived.

ORIGIN 1.3
Marginal Analysis

marginal analysis
The comparison of marginal ("extra" or "additional") benefits and marginal costs, usually for decision making.

Marginal Analysis: Benefits and Costs

The economic perspective focuses largely on **marginal analysis**—comparisons of *marginal benefits* and *marginal costs*. To economists, "marginal" means "extra," "additional," or "a change in." Most choices or decisions involve changes in the status quo (the existing state of affairs). Should you attend school for another year or not? Should you study an extra hour for an exam? Should you add fries to your fast-food order? Similarly, should a business expand or reduce its output? Should government increase or decrease health care funding?

CONSIDER THIS | Fast Food Lines

The economic perspective is useful in analyzing all sorts of behaviours. Consider an everyday example: the behaviour of customers at a fast-food restaurant. When customers enter the restaurant, they go to the shortest line, believing that line will minimize their time cost of obtaining food. They are acting purposefully; time is limited, and people prefer using it in some way other than standing in line.

If one fast-food line is temporarily shorter than other lines, some people will move to that line. These movers apparently view the time saving from the shorter line (marginal benefit) as exceeding the cost of moving from their present line (marginal cost). The line switching tends to equalize line lengths. No further movement of customers between lines occurs once all lines are about equal.

Fast-food customers face another cost-benefit decision when a clerk opens a new station at the counter. Should they move to the new station or stay put? Those who shift to the new line decide that the time saving from the move exceeds the extra cost of physically moving. In so deciding, customers

must also consider just how quickly they can get to the new station compared with others who may be contemplating the same move. (Those who hesitate in this situation are lost!)

Customers at the fast-food establishment do not have perfect information when they select lines. Thus, not all decisions turn out as expected. For example, you might enter a short line and find someone in front of you is ordering hamburgers and fries for 40 people in the Greyhound bus parked out back (and the employee is a trainee!). Nevertheless, at the time you made your decision, you thought it was optimal.

Finally, customers must decide what food to order when they arrive at the counter. In making their choices, they again compare marginal costs and marginal benefits in attempting to obtain the greatest personal satisfaction for their expenditure.

Economists believe that what is true for the behaviour of customers at fast-food restaurants is true for economic behaviour in general. Faced with an array of choices, consumers, workers, and businesses rationally compare marginal costs and marginal benefits in making decisions.

CHOOSING A LITTLE MORE OR LESS

Each option will have marginal benefits and marginal costs. In making choices, the decision maker will compare those two amounts. Example: You and your fiancé are shopping for an engagement ring. Should you buy a ¼-carat diamond, a ½-carat diamond, a ¾-carat diamond, or a larger one? The marginal cost of the larger diamond is the added expense beyond the smaller diamond. The marginal benefit is the greater lifetime pleasure (utility) from the larger stone. If the marginal benefit of the larger diamond exceeds its marginal cost, you buy the larger stone. But if the marginal cost is more than the marginal benefit, buy the smaller diamond instead, even if you can afford the larger stone.

In a world of scarcity, the marginal benefit associated with some specific option always includes the marginal cost of forgoing something else. Spending money on the larger diamond may mean forgoing a honeymoon to an exotic location. Opportunity costs, the value of the next best thing forgone, is always present whenever a choice is made. *(Key Question 3)*

1.3 | Theories, Principles, and Models

scientific method
The systematic pursuit of knowledge through formulating a problem, collecting data, and formulating and testing hypotheses to obtain theories, principles, and laws.

Like the physical and life sciences, as well as other social sciences, economics relies on the **scientific method.** That procedure consists of several elements:

- Observing real-world behaviour and outcomes.

- Based on those observations, formulating a possible explanation of cause and effect (hypothesis).

- Testing this explanation by comparing the outcomes of specific events to the outcome predicted by the hypothesis.

- Accepting, rejecting, or modifying the hypothesis based on these comparisons.

- Continuing to test the hypothesis against the facts. As favourable results accumulate, the hypothesis evolves into a theory. A very well tested and widely accepted theory is referred to as an economic law or an **economic principle**—a statement about economic behaviour or the economy that enables prediction of the probable effects of certain actions. Combinations of such laws or principles are incorporated into models, which are simplified representations of how parts of the economy work, such as a market or segment of the economy.

economic principle
A statement about economic behaviour or the economy that enables prediction of the probable effects of certain actions.

Economists develop theories of the behaviour of individuals (consumers, workers) and institutions (businesses, governments) engaged in the production, exchange, and consumption of goods and services. Theories, principles, and models are "purposeful simplifications." The full scope of economic reality itself is too complex and bewildering to be understood as a whole. In developing theories, principles, and models, economists remove the clutter and simplify.

Economic principles and models are highly useful in analyzing economic behaviour and understanding how the economy operates. They are the tools for ascertaining cause and effect (or action and outcome) within the economic system. Good theories do a good job of explaining and predicting. They are supported by facts concerning how individuals and institutions actually behave in producing, exchanging, and consuming goods and services.

There are some other things you should know about economic principles.

- *Generalizations* Economic principles are generalizations relating to economic behaviour or to the economy itself. Economic principles are expressed as the tendencies of typical or average consumers, workers, or business firms. For example, economists say that consumers buy more of a particular product when its price falls. Economists recognize that some consumers may increase their purchases by a large amount, others by a small amount, and a few not at all. This "price–quantity" principle, however, holds for the typical consumer and for consumers as a group.

ORIGIN 1.4
Ceteris Paribus

other-things-equal assumption
The assumption that factors other than those being considered are held constant.

- *Other-Things-Equal Assumption* In constructing their theories, economists use the *ceteris paribus* or **other-things-equal assumption**—the assumption that factors other than those being considered do not change. They assume that all variables except those under immediate consideration are held constant for a particular analysis. For example, consider the relationship

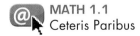

MATH 1.1
Ceteris Paribus

between the price of Pepsi and the amount of it purchased. Assume that of all the factors that might influence the amount of Pepsi purchased (for example, the price of Pepsi, the price of Coca-Cola, and consumer incomes and preferences), only the price of Pepsi varies. This is helpful because the economist can then focus on the relationship between the price of Pepsi and purchases of Pepsi in isolation without being confused by changes in other variables.

- **Graphical Expression** Many economic models are expressed graphically. Be sure to read the appendix at the end of this chapter as a review of graphs.

1.4 | Microeconomics and Macroeconomics

Economists develop economic principles and models at two levels, microeconomics and macroeconomics.

Microeconomics

microeconomics
The part of economics concerned with such individual units as industries, firms, and households.

Microeconomics is the part of economics concerned with individual units such as a household, a firm, or an industry. At this level of analysis, the economist observes the details of an economic unit, or very small segment of the economy, under a figurative microscope. In microeconomics we look at decision making by individual customers, workers, households, and business firms. We measure the price of a specific product, the number of workers employed by a single firm, the revenue or income of a particular firm or household, or the expenditures of a specific firm, government entity, or family. In microeconomics, we examine the grains of sand, the rocks, and the shells, not the beach.

Macroeconomics

macroeconomics
The part of economics concerned with the economy as a whole.

aggregate
A collection of specific economic units treated as if they were one unit.

Macroeconomics examines either the economy as a whole or its basic subdivisions or aggregates, such as the government, household, and business sectors. An **aggregate** is a collection of specific economic units treated as if they were one unit. Therefore, we might lump together the millions of consumers in the Canadian economy and treat them as if they were one huge unit called "consumers."

In using aggregates, macroeconomics seeks to obtain an overview, or general outline, of the structure of the economy and the relationships of its major aggregates. Macroeconomics speaks of such economic measures as total output, total employment, total income, aggregate expenditures, and the general level of prices in analyzing various economic problems. No or very little attention is given to specific units making up the various aggregates. Figuratively, macroeconomics looks at the beach, not the grains of sand, the rocks, and the shells.

The micro–macro distinction does not mean that economics is so highly compartmentalized that every topic can be readily labelled as either macro or micro; many topics and subdivisions of economics are rooted in both. Example: While the problem of unemployment is usually treated as a macroeconomic topic (because unemployment relates to aggregate production), economists recognize that the decisions made by *individual* workers on how long to search for jobs and the way *specific* labour markets encourage or impede hiring are also critical in determining the unemployment rate. **(Key Question 5)**

Positive and Normative Economics

positive economics
The analysis of facts to establish cause-and-effect relationships.

normative economics
The part of economics involving value judgments about what the economy should be like.

Both microeconomics and macroeconomics contain elements of positive economics and normative economics. **Positive economics** focuses on facts and cause-and-effect relationships. It includes description, theory development, and theory testing (theoretical economics). Positive economics avoids value judgments, tries to establish scientific statements about economic behaviour, and deals with what the economy is actually like. Such scientific-based analysis is critical to good policy analysis.

Economic policy, on the other hand, involves **normative economics,** which incorporates value judgments about what the economy *should* be like or what particular policy actions *should* be recommended to achieve a desirable goal (policy economics). Normative economics looks at the desirability of certain aspects of the economy. It underlies expressions of support for particular economic policies.

Positive economics concerns *what is,* while normative economics embodies subjective feelings about *what ought to be.* Examples: Positive statement: "The unemployment rate in France is higher than that in Canada." Normative statement: "France ought to undertake policies to make its labour market more flexible to reduce unemployment rates." When you see words such as "ought" or "should" in a sentence, there is a strong chance you are encountering a normative statement.

Most of the disagreement among economists involves normative, value-based policy questions. Of course, there is often some disagreement about which theories or models best represent the economy and its parts. But economists agree on a full range of economic principles. Most economic controversy thus reflects differing opinions or value judgments about what society should be like.

QUICK REVIEW

▶ Economics examines how individuals, institutions, and society make choices under conditions of scarcity.

▶ The economic way of thinking stresses (a) resource scarcity and the necessity of making choices, (b) the assumption of purposeful (or rational) behaviour, and (c) comparisons of marginal benefit and marginal cost. In choosing among alternatives, people incur opportunity costs.

▶ Economists use the scientific method to establish economic theories—cause–effect generalizations about the economic behaviour of individuals and institutions.

▶ Microeconomics focuses on specific units of the economy; macroeconomics examines the economy as a whole.

▶ Positive economics deals with factual statements ("what is"); normative economics involves value judgments ("what ought to be").

1.5 | The Economic Problem

economic problem
The need to make choices because society's material wants for goods and services are unlimited but the resources available to satisfy these wants are limited (scarce).

Both individuals and society face an **economic problem,** which is the need to make choices because economic wants are virtually unlimited but the means (income, time, resources) for satisfying those wants are limited. We will construct a simple microeconomic model to look at the general economic problem faced by an individual.

Limited Income

We all have a finite amount of income, even the wealthiest among us. Even members of the Thompson and Weston families—Canada's richest—have to decide how to spend their money! And the majority of us have much more limited means. Our income comes to us in the form of wages, interest, rent, and profit, although we may also receive money from government programs or from family members. As Global Perspective 1.1 shows, the average income of Canadians in 2007 was $39,420 ($US). In the poorest nations, it was less than $500.

Unlimited Wants

For better or worse, most people have virtually unlimited wants. We desire various goods and services that provide utility. Our wants extend over a wide range of products, from *necessities* (food, shelter, clothing) to *luxuries* (perfumes, yachts, sports cars). Some wants such as basic food, shelter, and clothing have biological roots. Other wants—for example, specific kinds of food, shelter, and clothing—arise from the conventions and customs of society.

1.1 | GLOBAL PERSPECTIVE

Average Income, Selected Nations

Average income (total income/population) and therefore typical individual budget constraints vary greatly among nations.

Source: World Bank, www.worldbank.org.

Country	Per Capita Income, 2007 (U.S. dollars, based on exchange rates)
Switzerland	59,880
United States	46,040
Canada	39,420
France	38,500
Japan	37,670
South Korea	19,690
Mexico	8,340
Brazil	5,910
China	2,360
Nigeria	930
Pakistan	870
Rwanda	320
Liberia	150

Over time, as new and improved products are introduced, economic wants tend to change and multiply, fuelled by new products. Only recently have people wanted iPods, Internet service, digital cameras, or camera phones, because those products did not exist a few decades ago. Also, the satisfaction of certain wants may trigger others: the acquisition of a Ford Focus or a Honda Civic has been known to whet the appetite for a Lexus or a Mercedes.

Services, as well as goods, satisfy our wants. Car repair work, the removal of an inflamed appendix, legal and accounting advice, and haircuts all satisfy human wants. Actually, we buy many goods, such as automobiles and washing machines, for the services they render. The differences between goods and services are often smaller than they appear to be.

For most people, the desires for goods and services cannot be fully satisfied. Bill Gates may have all that he wants for himself but it is clear from his massive charitable giving that he keenly wants better health care for the world's poor. Our desires for a particular good or service can be satisfied; over a short period of time we can surely get enough toothpaste or pasta. And one appendectomy is plenty. But our broader desire for more goods and services and higher-quality goods and services seems to be another story.

Because we have only limited income (usually through our work) but seemingly insatiable wants, it is in our self-interest to pick and choose goods and services that maximize our satisfaction.

The Budget Line

budget line
A schedule or curve that shows various combinations of two products a consumer can purchase with a specific money income.

We can depict the economic problem facing individuals via a **budget line** (or, more technically, *budget constraint*). It is a schedule or curve that shows various combinations of two products a consumer can purchase with a specific money income.

To understand this idea, suppose that you received a Chapters (or Indigo) gift card as a birthday present. The $120 card is soon to expire. You take the card to the store and confine your purchase decisions to two alternatives: DVDs and paperback books. DVDs are $20 each and paperback books are $10 each. Your purchase options are shown in the table in Figure 1-1.

FIGURE 1-1   A Consumer's Budget Line ✓

The budget line (or budget constraint) shows all the combinations of any two products that can be purchased, given the prices of the products and the consumer's money income.

Units of DVDs (Price = $20)	Units of Books (Price = $10)	Total Expenditure
6	0	($120 = $120 + $0)
5	2	($120 = $100 + $20)
4	4	($120 = $80 + $40)
3	6	($120 = $60 + $60)
2	8	($120 = $40 + $80)
1	10	($120 = $20 + $100)
0	12	($120 = $0 + $120)

THE BUDGET LINE: WHOLE-UNIT COMBINATIONS OF DVDS AND PAPERBACK BOOKS ATTAINABLE WITH AN INCOME OF $120

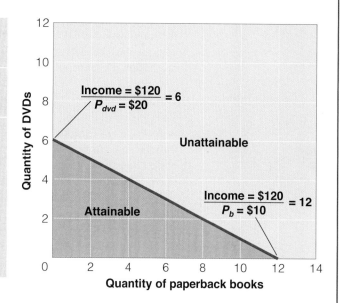

At one extreme, you might spend all of your $120 "income" on 6 DVDs at $20 each and have nothing left to spend on books. Or, by giving up 2 DVDs and thereby gaining $40, you can have 4 DVDs at $20 each and 4 books at $10 each. And so on to the other extreme, at which you could buy 12 books at $10 each, spending your entire gift card on books with nothing left to spend on DVDs.

The graph in Figure 1-1 shows the budget line. Note that the graph is not restricted to whole units of DVDs and books as is the table. Every point on the graph represents a possible combination of DVDs and books, including fractional quantities. The slope of the graphed budget line measures the ratio of the price of books (P_b) to the price of DVDs (P_{dvd}); more precisely, the slope is $P_b/P_{dvd} = \$-10/\$+20 = -\frac{1}{2}$ or −0.5. So you must forgo 1 DVD (measured on the vertical axis) to buy 2 books (measured on the horizontal axis). This yields a slope of −½ or −0.5.

The budget line illustrates several ideas.

ATTAINABLE AND UNATTAINABLE COMBINATIONS

All the combinations of DVDs and books on or inside the budget line are *attainable* from the $120 of money income. You can afford to buy, for example, 3 DVDs at $20 each and 6 books at $10 each. You also can obviously afford to buy 2 DVDs and 5 books, if you so desire, and not use up the value on the gift card. But, to achieve maximum utility you will want to spend the full $120.

In contrast, all combinations beyond the budget line are *unattainable*. The $120 limit simply does not allow you to purchase, for example, 5 DVDs at $20 each and 5 books at $10 each. That $150 expenditure would clearly exceed the $120 limit. In Figure 1-1 the attainable combinations are on and within the budget line; the unattainable combinations are beyond the budget line.

TRADEOFFS AND OPPORTUNITY COSTS

The budget line in Figure 1-1 illustrates the idea of tradeoffs arising from limited income. To obtain more DVDs, you have to give up some books. For example, to obtain the first DVD you trade off 2 books. So the opportunity cost of the first DVD is 2 books. To obtain the second DVD the opportunity cost is also 2 books. The straight-line budget constraint, with its constant slope, indicates

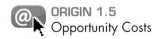

ORIGIN 1.5
Opportunity Costs

constant opportunity cost. That is, the opportunity cost of 1 extra DVD remains the same (= 2 books) as more DVDs are purchased. And, in reverse, the opportunity cost of 1 extra book does not change (= ½ DVD) as more books are bought.

CHOICE

Limited income forces people to choose what to buy and what to forgo to fulfill wants. You will select the combination of DVDs and paperback books that you think is "best." That is, you will evaluate your marginal benefits and marginal costs (here, product price) to make choices that maximize your satisfaction. Other people, with the same $120 gift card, would undoubtedly make different choices.

INCOME CHANGES

WORKED PROBLEM 1.1
Budget Line

The location of the budget line varies with money income. An increase in money income shifts the budget line to the right; a decrease in money income shifts it to the left. To verify this, recalculate the table in Figure 1-1, assuming the card value (income) is (a) $240 and (b) $60, and plot the new budget lines in the graph. No wonder people like to have more income: that shifts their budget lines outward and enables them to buy more goods and services. But even with more income, people will still face spending tradeoffs, opportunity costs, and choices. *(Key Question 7)*

Society's Economic Problem

Society must also make choices under conditions of scarcity. It, too, faces the economic problem. Should it devote more of its limited resources to the criminal justice system (police, courts, and prisons) or to education (teachers, books, and schools)? If it decides to devote more resources to both, what other goods and services does it forgo? Health care? Energy development?

Scarce Resources

economic resources
The land, labour, capital, and entrepreneurial ability that are used in the production of goods and services.

Society has limited or scarce **economic resources**, meaning all natural, human, and manufactured resources that go into the production of goods and services. That includes the entire set of factory and farm buildings and all the equipment, tools, and machinery used to produce manufactured goods and agricultural products; all transportation and communication facilities; all types of labour; and land and mineral resources.

Resource Categories

Economists classify economic resources into four general categories.

LAND

land
Natural resources used to produce goods and services.

Land means much more to the economist than it does to most people. To the economist, **land** includes all natural resources ("gifts of nature") used in the production process, such as arable land, forests, mineral and oil deposits, and water resources.

LABOUR

labour
The physical and mental talents of individuals used in producing goods and services.

The resource **labour** consists of the physical and mental talents of individuals used in producing goods and services. The services of a logger, retail clerk, machinist, teacher, professional hockey player, and nuclear physicist all fall under the general heading "labour."

CAPITAL

capital
Human-made resources (buildings, machinery, and equipment) used to produce goods and services.

For economists, **capital** (or capital goods) includes all manufactured aids used in producing consumer goods and services: tools and machinery, as well as all factory, storage, transportation, and distribution facilities. Note that the term "capital" does not refer to money; because money produces nothing, economists do not include it as an economic resource. Money (or money capital or financial capital) is simply a means for purchasing capital goods.

investment
Spending for the production and accumulation of capital.

Economists refer to the purchase of capital goods as **investment.** The amount of training and education that a person acquires through his or her lifetime is referred to as *human capital*, since it is similar to an investment in capital goods in that it can enhance output. But you should note that human capital is normally categorized under labour resources.

Capital goods differ from consumer goods because consumer goods satisfy wants directly, while capital goods do so indirectly by aiding the production of consumer goods.

ENTREPRENEURIAL ABILITY

entrepreneurial ability
The human talents that combine the other resources to produce a product, make non-routine decisions, innovate, and bear risks.

Finally, there is the special human resource, distinct from labour, called **entrepreneurial ability.** The entrepreneur performs several functions:

- The entrepreneur takes the initiative in combining the resources of land, labour, and capital to produce a good or a service. Both a sparkplug and a catalyst, the entrepreneur is the driving force behind production and the agent who combines the other resources in what is hoped will be a successful business venture.

- The entrepreneur makes the strategic business decisions that set the course of an enterprise.

- The entrepreneur is an innovator. He or she commercializes new products, new production techniques, or even new forms of business organization.

- The entrepreneur is a risk bearer. He or she has no guarantee of profit. The reward for the entrepreneur's time, efforts, and abilities may be profits or losses. The entrepreneur risks not only his or her invested funds but those of associates and shareholders as well.

factors of production
Economic resources: land, labour, capital, and entrepreneurial ability.

Because land, labour, capital, and entrepreneurial ability are combined to produce goods and services, they are called the **factors of production,** or simply "inputs."

QUICK REVIEW

- ▶ Because wants exceed incomes, individuals face an economic problem: they must decide what to buy and what to forgo.

- ▶ A budget line (budget constraint) shows the various combinations of two goods that a consumer can purchase with a specific money income.

- ▶ Straight-line budget constraints imply constant opportunity costs associated with obtaining more of either of the two goods.

- ▶ Economists categorize economic resources as land, labour, capital, and entrepreneurial ability.

1.6 Production Possibilities Model and Increasing Opportunity Costs

Society uses its scarce resources to produce goods and services. The alternatives and choices it faces can best be understood through a macroeconomic model of production possibilities. To keep things simple, let's initially assume:

- *Full Employment*   The economy is employing all its available resources.

- *Fixed Resources*   The quantity and quality of the factors of production are fixed.

- *Fixed Technology*   The state of technology (the methods used to produce output) is constant.

consumer goods
Products and services that satisfy human wants directly.

capital goods
Goods that do not directly satisfy human wants.

- *Two Goods*   The economy is producing only two goods: pizzas and industrial robots. Pizzas symbolize **consumer goods,** products that satisfy our wants directly; industrial robots (for example, the kind used to weld automobile frames) symbolize **capital goods,** products that satisfy our wants indirectly by making possible more efficient production of consumer goods.

TABLE 1-1	Production Possibilities of Pizzas and Robots with Full Employment and Productive Efficiency				
	PRODUCTION ALTERNATIVES				
Type of Product	**A**	**B**	**C**	**D**	**E**
Pizzas (in hundred thousands)	0	1	2	3	4
Robots (in thousands)	10	9	7	4	0

Production Possibilities Table

A production possibilities table lists the different combinations of two products that can be produced with a specific set of resources, assuming full employment. Table 1-1 contains such a simple economy that is producing pizzas and industrial robots; the data are, of course, hypothetical. At alternative A, this economy would be devoting all its available resources to the production of industrial robots (capital goods); at alternative E, all resources would go to pizza production (consumer goods). Those alternatives are unrealistic extremes; an economy typically produces both capital goods and consumer goods, as in B, C, and D. As we move from alternative A to E, we increase the production of pizzas at the expense of the production of industrial robots.

Because consumer goods satisfy our wants directly, any movement toward E looks tempting. In producing more pizzas, society increases the current satisfaction of its wants. But there is a cost: More pizzas mean fewer industrial robots. This shift of resources to consumer goods catches up with society over time because the stock of capital goods does not expand, with the result that some potential for greater future production is lost. By moving toward alternative E, society chooses "more now" at the expense of "much later."

By moving toward A, society chooses to forgo current consumption, thereby freeing up resources that can be used to increase the production of capital goods. By building up its stock of capital this way, society will have greater future production and, therefore, greater future consumption. By moving toward A, society is choosing "more later" at the cost of "less now."

Generalization: At any point in time, a fully employed economy must sacrifice some of one good to obtain more of another good. Scarce resources prohibit such an economy from having more of both goods. Society must choose among alternatives. There is no such thing as a free pizza, or a free industrial robot. Having more of one thing means having less of something else. For example, if Canadians want more spending on health care, they will have to be satisfied with less spending on education.

Production Possibilities Curve

production possibilities curve
A curve showing the different combinations of goods or services that can be produced in a full-employment, full-production economy where the available supplies of resources and technology are fixed.

The data presented in a production possibilities table are shown graphically as a **production possibilities curve.** Such a curve displays the different combinations of goods and services that society can produce in a fully employed economy, assuming a fixed availability of supplies of resources and constant technology. We arbitrarily represent the economy's output of capital goods (here, industrial robots) on the vertical axis and the output of consumer goods (here, pizzas) on the horizontal axis, as shown in **Figure 1-2 (Key Graph).**

Each point on the production possibilities curve represents some maximum output of the two products. The curve is a "constraint" because it shows the limit of attainable outputs. Points on the curve are attainable as long as the economy uses all its available resources. Points lying inside the curve are also attainable, but they reflect less total output and therefore are not as desirable as points on the curve. Points inside the curve imply that the economy could have more of both industrial robots and pizzas if it achieved full employment. Points lying beyond the production possibilities curve, like *W*, would represent a greater output than the output at any point on the curve. Such points, however, are unattainable with the current availability of resources and technology.

KEY GRAPH

FIGURE 1-2 The Production Possibilities Curve

Each point on the production possibilities curve represents some maximum combination of two products that can be produced if full employment and full production are achieved. When operating on the curve, more robots means fewer pizzas, and vice versa. Limited resources and a fixed technology make any combination of robots and pizzas lying outside the curve (such as at W) unattainable. Points inside the curve are attainable, but they indicate that full employment and productive efficiency are not being realized.

PRODUCTION ALTERNATIVES

Type of Product	A	B	C	D	E
Pizzas (in hundred thousands)	0	1	2	3	4
Robots (in thousands)	10	9	7	4	0

Quick Quiz

1. **Production possibilities curve _ABCDE_ is bowed out from the origin because:**
   a. the marginal benefit of pizzas declines as more pizzas are consumed.
   b. the curve gets steeper as we move from _E_ to _A_.
   c. it reflects the law of increasing opportunity costs.
   d. resources are scarce.

2. **The marginal opportunity cost of the second unit of pizzas is:**
   a. 2 units of robots.
   b. 3 units of robots.
   c. 7 units of robots.
   d. 9 units of robots.

3. **The total opportunity cost of 7 units of robots is:**
   a. 1 unit of pizzas.
   b. 2 units of pizzas.
   c. 3 units of pizzas.
   d. 4 units of pizzas.

4. **All points on this production possibilities curve necessarily represent:**
   a. society's optimal choice.
   b. less than full use of resources.
   c. unattainable levels of output.
   d. full employment.

Law of Increasing Opportunity Costs

Figure 1-2 clearly shows that more pizzas mean fewer industrial robots. The number of units of industrial robots that must be given up to obtain another unit of pizzas, of course, is the opportunity cost of that unit of pizzas.

In moving from alternative A to alternative B in Table 1-1, the cost of 1 additional unit of pizzas is 1 less unit of industrial robots. But when additional units are considered—B to C, C to D, and D to E—an important economic principle is revealed: For society, the opportunity cost of each additional unit of pizzas is greater than the opportunity cost of the preceding one. When we move from A to B, just 1 unit of industrial robots is sacrificed for 1 more unit of pizzas; but in going from B to C we sacrifice 2 additional units of industrial robots for 1 more unit of pizzas; then 3 more of industrial robots for 1 more of pizzas; and finally 4 for 1. Conversely, confirm that as we move from E to A, the cost of an additional unit of industrial robots (on average) is ¼, ⅓, ½, and 1 unit of pizzas, respectively, for the four successive moves.

law of increasing opportunity costs
As the production of a good increases, the opportunity cost of producing an additional unit rises.

Our example illustrates the **law of increasing opportunity costs.** As the production of a particular good increases, the opportunity cost of producing an additional unit rises.

SHAPE OF THE CURVE

The law of increasing opportunity costs is reflected in the shape of the production possibilities curve: The curve is bowed out from the origin of the graph. Figure 1-2 shows that when the economy moves from *A* to *E*, it must give up successively larger amounts of industrial robots (1, 2, 3, and 4) to acquire equal increments of pizzas (1, 1, 1, and 1). This is shown in the slope of the production possibilities curve, which becomes steeper as we move from *A* to *E*.

ECONOMIC EXPLANATION

The economic explanation for the law of increasing opportunity costs is that *economic resources are not completely adaptable to alternative uses.* Many resources are better at producing one type of good than at producing others. Some land is highly suited to growing the ingredients necessary for pizza production, but as pizza production expands society has to start using land that is less bountiful for farming. Other land is rich in mineral deposits and therefore well-suited to producing the materials needed to make industrial robots. As society steps up the production of robots, it must use land that is less and less adaptable to making their components.

If we start at *A* and move to *B* in Figure 1-2, we can shift resources whose productivity is relatively high in pizza production and low in industrial robots. But as we move from *B* to *C, C* to *D,* and so on, resources highly productive of pizzas become increasingly scarce. To get more pizzas, resources whose productivity in industrial robots is relatively great will be needed. It will take increasingly more of such resources, and hence greater sacrifices of industrial robots, to achieve each 1-unit increase in pizzas. This lack of perfect flexibility, or interchangeability, on the part of resources is the cause of increasing opportunity costs for society. *(Key Question 10)*

WORKED PROBLEM 1.2
Production Possibilities

Optimal Allocation

Of all the attainable combinations of pizzas and industrial robots on the curve in Figure 1-2, which is optimal (best)? That is, what specific quantities of resources should be allocated to pizzas and what specific quantities to industrial robots in order to maximize satisfaction?

Recall that economic decisions centre on comparisons of marginal benefit (MB) and marginal cost (MC). Any economic activity should be expanded as long as marginal benefit exceeds marginal cost and should be reduced if marginal cost exceeds marginal benefit. The optimal amount of the activity occurs where MB = MC. Society needs to make a similar assessment about its production decision.

Consider pizzas. We already know from the law of increasing opportunity costs that the marginal costs of additional units of pizzas will rise as more units are produced. At the same time, we need to recognize that the extra or marginal benefits that come from producing and consuming pizza decline with each successive unit of pizza. Consequently, each successive unit of pizza brings with it both increasing marginal costs and decreasing marginal benefits.

FIGURE 1-3 ### Optimal Allocation: MB = MC

Optimal allocation requires the expansion of a good's output until its marginal benefit (MB) and marginal cost (MC) are equal. No resources beyond that point should get allocated to the product. Here, allocative efficiency occurs when 200,000 pizzas are produced.

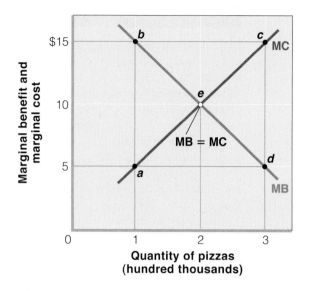

The optimal quantity of pizza production is indicated by point *e* at the intersection of the MB and MC curves: 200,000 units in Figure 1-3. Why is this amount the optimal quantity? If only 100,000 units of pizzas were produced, the marginal benefit of an extra unit of them (point *a*) would exceed its marginal cost (point *b*). In money terms, MB is $15, while MC is only $5. When society gains something worth $15 at a marginal cost of only $5, it is better off. In Figure 1-3, net gains can continue to be realized until pizza-product production has been increased to 200,000.

In contrast, the production of 300,000 units of pizzas is excessive. There the MC of an added unit is $15 (point *c*) and its MB is only $5 (point *d*). This means that 1 unit of pizzas is worth only $5 to society but costs it $15 to obtain. This is a losing proposition for society!

So resources are being efficiently allocated to any product when the marginal benefit and marginal cost of its output are equal (MB = MC). Suppose that by applying the above analysis to industrial robots, we find its optimal (MB = MC) output is 7000. This would mean that alternative *C* (200,000 units of pizzas and 7000 units of industrial robots) on the production possibilities curve in Figure 1-2 would be optimal for this economy. *(Key Question 11)*

QUICK REVIEW

▶ The production possibilities curve illustrates (a) scarcity of resources, implied by the area of unattainable combinations of output lying outside the production possibilities curve; (b) choice among outputs, reflected in the variety of attainable combinations of goods lying along the curve; (c) opportunity cost, illustrated by the downward slope of the curve; and (d) the law of increasing opportunity costs, implied by the bowed-outward shape of the curve.

▶ A comparison of marginal benefits and marginal costs is needed to determine the best or optimal output mix on a production possibilities curve.

1.7 | Economic Growth, Present Choices, and Future Possibilities

In the depths of the Great Depression of the 1930s, almost 20 percent of workers were unemployed and one-quarter of Canadian production capacity was idle. Canada has suffered a number of considerably milder downturns since then, one occurring in 1991. Almost all nations have experienced widespread unemployment and unused production capacity from business downturns at one time or another. Since 1995, for example, several nations—including Argentina, Japan, Mexico, Germany, and South Korea—have had economic downturns and unemployment.

How do these realities relate to the production possibilities model? Our analysis and conclusions change if we relax the assumption that all available resources are fully employed. The five alternatives in Table 1-1 represent maximum outputs; they illustrate the combinations of pizzas and industrial robots that can be produced when the economy is operating at full employment. With unemployment, this economy would produce less than each alternative shown in the table.

Graphically, we represent situations of unemployment by points inside the original production possibilities curve (reproduced here in Figure 1-4). Point *U* is one such point. Here the economy is falling short of the various maximum combinations of pizzas and industrial robots represented by the points on the production possibilities curve. The arrows in Figure 1-4 indicate three possible paths back to full employment. A move toward full employment would yield a greater output of one or both products.

A Growing Economy

When we drop the assumptions that the quantity and quality of resources and technology are fixed, the production possibilities curve shifts position and the potential maximum output of the economy changes.

INCREASES IN FACTOR SUPPLIES

Although factor supplies are fixed at any specific moment, they change over time via more education and training. Historically, the economy's stock of capital has increased at a significant, though

FIGURE 1-4

Unemployment, Productive Inefficiency, and the Production Possibilities Curve

Any point inside the production possibilities curve, such as U, represents unemployment or a failure to achieve productive efficiency. The arrows indicate that, by realizing full employment and productive efficiency, the economy could operate on the curve. This means it could produce more of one or both products than it is producing at point U.

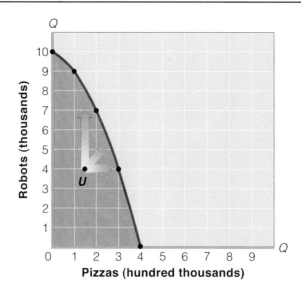

unsteady, rate. And although some of our energy and mineral resources are being depleted, new sources are also being discovered. The development of irrigation programs, for example, adds to the supply of arable land.

The net result of these increased supplies of the factors of production is the ability to produce more of both consumer goods and capital goods. Thus, 20 years from now the production possibilities may supersede those shown in Table 1-1. The new production possibilities might look like those in the table in Figure 1-5. The greater abundance of resources will result in a greater potential output of one or both products at each alternative. The economy will have achieved economic growth in the form of expanded potential output. Thus, when an increase in the quantity or quality of resources occurs, the production possibilities curve shifts outward and to the right, as illustrated by the move from the inner curve to curve A′B′C′D′E′ in Figure 1-5. This sort of shift represents growth of economic capacity, which when used means **economic growth:** a larger total output.

economic growth
An outward shift in the production possibilities curve that results from an increase in factor supplies or quality or an improvement in technology

ADVANCES IN TECHNOLOGY

An advancing technology brings both new and better goods and improved ways of producing them. For now, let's think of technological advance as being only improvements in the methods of production; for example, the introduction of computerized systems to manage inventories and schedule production. These advances alter our previous discussion of the economizing problem by allowing society to produce more goods with available resources. As with increases in resource supplies, technological advances make possible the production of more industrial robots and more pizzas.

A real-world example of improved technology is the recent surge of new technologies relating to computers, communications, and biotechnology. Technological advances have dropped the prices of computers and greatly increased their speed. Improved software has greatly increased the everyday usefulness of computers. Cellular phones and the Internet have increased communications capacity, enhancing production and improving the efficiency of markets. Advances in biotechnology have

---

FIGURE 1·5   ## Economic Growth and the Production Possibilities Curve

The increase in supplies of resources, the improvements in resource quality, and the technological advances that occur in a dynamic economy move the production possibilities curve outward and to the right, allowing the economy to have larger quantities of both types of goods.

PRODUCTION ALTERNATIVES					
Type of Product	**A′**	**B′**	**C′**	**D′**	**E′**
Pizzas (in hundred thousands)	0	2	4	6	8
Robots (in thousands)	14	12	9	5	0

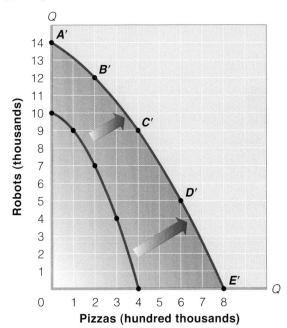

resulted in important agricultural and medical discoveries. These and other new and improved technologies have contributed to both global and Canadian economic growth (outward shifts of the nation's production possibilities curve).

Conclusion: Economic growth is the result of (1) increases in supplies of factors of production, (2) improvements in factor quality, and (3) technological advances. The consequence of growth is that a full-employment economy can enjoy a greater output of both consumption goods and capital goods. While static, no-growth economies must sacrifice some of one good to obtain more of another, dynamic, growing economies can have larger quantities of both goods. *(Key Question 13)*

Present Choices and Future Possibilities

An economy's current choice of positions on its production possibilities curve helps determine the future location of that curve. Let's designate the two axes of the production possibilities curve as "goods for the future" and "goods for the present," as in Figure 1-6. Goods for the future are such things as capital goods, research and education, and preventive medicine. They increase the quantity and quality of property resources, enlarge the stock of technological information, and improve the quality of human resources. As we have already seen, goods for the future, such as capital goods, are the ingredients of economic growth. Goods for the present are consumer goods, such as food, clothing, and entertainment.

Now suppose there are two hypothetical economies, Presentville and Futureville, which are initially identical in every respect except one: Presentville's current choice of positions on its production possibilities curve strongly favours present goods over future goods. Point *P* in Figure 1-6a indicates that choice. It is located quite far down the curve to the right, indicating a high priority for goods for the present, at the expense of fewer goods for the future. Futureville, in contrast, makes a current choice that stresses larger amounts of future goods and smaller amounts of present goods, as shown by point *F* in Figure 1-6b.

Now, other things equal, we can expect the future production possibilities curve of Futureville to be farther to the right than Presentville's curve. By currently choosing an output more favourable to technological advances and to increases in the quantity and quality of resources, Futureville will achieve greater economic growth than Presentville. In terms of capital goods, Futureville is choosing to make larger current additions to its "national factory" by devoting more of its current output to capital than Presentville. The payoff from this choice for Futureville is greater future production capacity and economic growth. The opportunity cost is fewer consumer goods in the present for Futureville to enjoy.

Is Futureville's choice thus necessarily "better" than Presentville's? That, we cannot say. The different outcomes simply reflect different preferences and priorities in the two countries. But each country will have to live with the economic consequences of its choice. *(Key Question 14)*

 CONSIDER THIS | Women, the Workforce, and Production Possibilities

We have seen that more factors of production and better-quality factors and improved technology shift a nation's production possibilities curve outward. An example of more resources is the large increase in the number of employed women in Canada in the past 40 years. Sixty percent of adult Canadian women work full-time or part-time in paid jobs today, compared to only 40 percent in 1965.

Over recent decades, women have greatly increased their productivity in the workplace, mostly by becoming better educated and professionally trained. As a result, they can earn higher wages. Because those higher wages have increased the opportunity cost—the forgone wage earnings—of staying at home, women have substituted employment in the labour market for the now more "expensive" traditional home activities. This substitution has been particularly pronounced among married women. Along with other factors such as changing attitudes and expanded job access, the rising earnings of women have produced a substantial increase in the number of women workers in Canada. This increase in the quantity of available resources has helped push the Canadian production possibilities curve outward.

KEY GRAPH

FIGURE 1-6   Present Choices and Future Locations of a Production Possibilities Curve

A nation's current choice favouring "present goods," as made by Presentville in (a), will cause a modest outward shift of the curve in the future. A nation's current choice favouring "future goods," as made by Futureville in (b), will result in a greater outward shift of the curve in the future.

A Qualification: International Trade

Production possibilities analysis implies that an individual nation is limited to the combinations of output indicated by its production possibilities curve. But we must modify this principle when international specialization and trade exist.

You will see in later chapters that an economy can circumvent, through international specialization and trade, the output limits imposed by its domestic production possibilities curve. *International specialization* means directing domestic resources to output that a nation is highly efficient at producing. *International trade* involves the exchange of these goods for goods produced abroad. Specialization and trade enable a nation to get more of a desired good at less sacrifice of some other good. Rather than sacrifice three units of robots to get a third unit of pizza, as in Table 1-1, a nation might be able to obtain the third unit of pizza by trading only two units of robots for it. Specialization and trade have the same effect as having more and better resources or discovering improved production techniques; both increase the quantities of capital and consumer goods available to society. Expansion of domestic production possibilities and international trade are two separate routes for obtaining greater output.

 QUICK REVIEW

▶ Unemployment causes an economy to operate at a point inside its production possibilities curve.

▶ Increases in resource supplies, improvements in resource quality, and technological advances cause economic growth, which is depicted as an outward shift of the production possibilities curve.

▶ An economy's present choice of capital and consumer goods helps determine the future location of its production possibilities curve.

▶ International specialization and trade enable a nation to obtain more goods than its production possibilities curve indicates.

The **LAST WORD**   Pitfalls to Sound Economic Reasoning

Because they affect us so personally, we often have difficulty thinking
accurately and objectively about economic issues.

Here are some common pitfalls to avoid in successfully applying the economic perspective.

Biases Most people bring a bundle of biases and preconceptions to the field of economics. For example, some might think that corporate profits are excessive or that lending money is always superior to borrowing money. Others might believe that government is necessarily less efficient than businesses, or that more government regulation is always better than less. Biases cloud thinking and interfere with objective analysis. All of us must be willing to shed biases and preconceptions that are not supported by facts.

Loaded Terminology The economic terminology used in newspapers and broadcast media is sometimes emotionally biased, or loaded. The writer or spokesperson may have a cause to promote or an axe to grind and may slant comments accordingly. High profits may be labelled "obscene," low wages may be called "exploitive," or self-interested behaviour may be identified as "greed." Government workers may be referred to as "mindless bureaucrats" and those favouring stronger government regulations may be called "socialists." To objectively analyze economic issues, you must be prepared to reject or discount such terminology.

Fallacy of Composition Another pitfall in economic thinking is the assumption that what is true for one individual or part of a whole is necessarily true for a group of individuals or the whole. This is a logical fallacy called the *fal-*

lacy of composition; the assumption is not correct. A statement that is valid for an individual or part is not necessarily valid for the larger group or whole. As an example, you may see the action better if you leap to your feet to see an outstanding play at a football game. But if everyone leaps to their feet at the same time, nobody—including you—will have a better view than when all remained seated.

Here are two economic examples: An individual shareholder can sell shares of, say, Research In Motion (RIM, the maker of the BlackBerry) stock without affecting the price of the stock. The individual's sale will not noticeably reduce the share price because the sale is a negligible fraction of the total shares of RIM being bought and sold. But if all the RIM shareholders decide to sell their shares on the same day, the market will be flooded with shares and the stock price will fall precipitously. Similarly, a single cattle ranch can increase its revenue by expanding the size of its livestock herd. The extra cattle will not affect the price of cattle when they are brought to market. But if all ranchers as a group expand their herds, the total output of cattle will increase so much that the price of cattle will decline when the cattle are sold. If the price reduction

is relatively large, ranchers as a group might find that their income has fallen despite their having sold a greater number of cattle because the fall in price overwhelms the increase in quantity.

Post Hoc Fallacy You must think very carefully before concluding that because event A precedes event B, A is the cause of B. This kind of faulty reasoning is known as the *post hoc, ergo propter hoc,* or "after this, therefore because of this" fallacy. To give a noneconomic example: The Calgary Flames team hires a new coach and the team's record improves. Is the new coach the cause? Maybe. Perhaps the presence of more experienced and talented players or an easier schedule is the true cause. Another example is that the rooster crows before dawn, but does not cause the sunrise.

Correlation But Not Causation Do not confuse correlation, or connection, with causation. Correlation between two events or two sets of data indicates only that they are associated in some systematic and dependable way. For example, we may find that when variable X increases, Y also increases. But this correlation does not necessarily mean that there is causation—that increases in X cause increases in Y. The relationship could be purely coincidental or dependent on some other factor, Z, not included in the analysis.

Here is an example: Economists have found a positive correlation between education and income. In general, people with more education earn higher incomes than those with less education.

Common sense suggests education is the cause and higher incomes are the effect; more education implies a more knowledgeable and productive worker, and such workers receive larger salaries.

But causation could also partly run the other way. People with higher incomes could buy more education, just as they buy more furniture and steaks. Or is part of the relationship explainable in still other ways? Are education and income correlated because the characteristics required for succeeding in education—ability and motivation—are the same ones required to be a productive and highly paid worker? If so, then people with those traits will probably both obtain more education and earn higher incomes. But greater education will not be the sole cause of the higher income.

Question

Studies indicate that married men on average earn more income than unmarried men of the same age and education level. Why must we be cautious in concluding that marriage is the cause and higher income is the effect?

CHAPTER SUMMARY

1.1 ▶ TEN KEY CONCEPTS TO RETAIN FOR A LIFETIME

- There are 10 key concepts to remember: four deal with the individual, three with the interaction among individuals, and three with the economy as a whole.

1.2 ▶ THE ECONOMIC WAY OF THINKING

- Economics is the social science that examines how individuals, institutions, and society make choices under conditions of scarcity. Central to economics is the idea of opportunity cost: the value of the good, service, or time forgone to obtain something else.

- The economic perspective includes three elements: scarcity and choice, purposeful behaviour, and marginal analysis. It sees individuals and institutions making rational decisions based on comparisons of marginal benefits and marginal costs.

1.3 ▶ THEORIES, PRINCIPLES, AND MODELS

- Economists employ the scientific method, in which they form and test hypotheses of cause-and-effect relationships to generate theories, principles, and laws. Economists often combine principles and laws into representations called models.

1.4 ▶ MICROECONOMICS AND MACROECONOMICS

- Microeconomics examines specific economic units or institutions. Macroeconomics looks at the economy as a whole or its major aggregates.

- Positive economics deals with facts; normative economics reflects value judgments.

1.5 ▶ THE ECONOMIC PROBLEM

- Individuals face an economic problem. Because their wants exceed their incomes, they must decide what to purchase and what to forgo. Society also faces the economic problem. Societal wants exceed the available resources necessary to fulfill them. Society therefore must decide what to produce and what to forgo.

- Graphically, a budget line (or budget constraint) illustrates the economic problem for individuals. The line shows the various combinations of two products that a consumer can purchase with a specific money income, given the prices of the two products.

- Economic resources are inputs into the production process and can be classified as land, labour, capital, and entrepreneurial ability. Economic resources are also known as factors of production or inputs.

1.6 ▶ PRODUCTION POSSIBILITIES MODEL AND INCREASING OPPORTUNITY COSTS

- Economists illustrate society's economic problem through production possibilities analysis. Production possibilities tables and curves show the different combinations of goods and services that can be produced in a fully employed economy, assuming that resource quantity, resource quality, and technology are fixed.

- An economy that is fully employed and thus operating on its production possibilities curve must sacrifice the output of some types of goods and services to increase the production of others. The gain of one type of good or service is always accompanied by an opportunity cost in the form of the loss of some of the other type.

- Because resources are not equally productive in all possible uses, shifting resources from one use to another creates increasing opportunity costs. The production of additional units of one product requires the sacrifice of increasing amounts of the other product.

- The optimal (best) point on the production possibilities curve represents the most desirable mix of goods and is determined by expanding the production of each good until its marginal benefit (MB) equals its marginal cost (MC).

1.7 ▸ ECONOMIC GROWTH, PRESENT CHOICES, AND FUTURE POSSIBILITIES

- Over time, technological advances and increases in the quantity and quality of resources enable the economy to produce more of all goods and services; that is, to experience economic growth. Society's choice as to the mix of consumer goods and capital goods in current output is a major determinant of the future location of the production possibilities curve and thus of the extent of economic growth. International trade enables nations to obtain more goods from their limited resources than their production possibilities curve indicates.

TERMS AND CONCEPTS

economics, p. 2
economic perspective, p. 3
opportunity cost, p. 3
utility, p. 4
marginal analysis, p. 4
scientific method, p. 5
economic principle, p. 5
other-things-equal assumption, p. 5
microeconomics, p. 6

macroeconomics, p. 6
aggregate, p. 6
positive economics, p. 6
normative economics, p. 6
economic problem, p. 7
budget line, p. 8
economic resources, p. 10
land, p. 10
labour, p. 10

capital, p. 10
investment, p. 11
entrepreneurial ability, p. 11
factors of production, p. 11
consumer goods, p. 11
capital goods, p. 11
production possibilities curve, p. 12
law of increasing opportunity costs, p. 14
economic growth, p. 17

STUDY QUESTIONS

LO 1.2 1. What is an opportunity cost? How does the idea relate to the definition of economics? Which of the following decisions would entail the greater opportunity cost: allocating a square block in the heart of Toronto for a surface parking lot or allocating a square block at the edge of a typical suburb for such a lot? Explain.

LO 1.2 2. What is meant by the term "utility" and how does the idea relate to purposeful behaviour?

LO 1.2 3. **KEY QUESTION** Cite three examples of recent decisions that you made in which you, at least implicitly, weighed marginal cost and marginal benefit.

LO 1.3 4. What are the key elements of the scientific method and how does this method relate to economic principles and laws?

LO 1.4 5. **KEY QUESTION** Indicate whether each of the following statements applies to microeconomics or macroeconomics:

   a. The unemployment rate in Canada was 8 percent in March 2009.

   b. A Canadian software firm discharged 15 workers last month and transferred the work to India.

   c. An unexpected freeze in central Florida reduced the citrus crop and caused the price of oranges to rise.

   d. Canadian output, adjusted for inflation, grew by 0.4 percent in 2008.

   e. Last week Scotiabank lowered its interest rate on business loans by one-half of 1 percentage point.

   f. The Consumer Price Index rose by 2.3 percent in 2008.

6. State (a) a positive economic statement of your choice, and **LO** then (b) a normative economic statement relating to your first statement.

7. **KEY QUESTION** Suppose you won $15 on a Lotto Canada **LO 1** ticket at the local 7-Eleven and decided to spend all the winnings on candy bars and bags of peanuts. The price of candy bars is $0.75 and the price of peanuts is $1.50.

   a. Construct a table showing the alternative combinations of the two products that are available.

   b. Plot the data in your table as a budget line in a graph. What is the slope of the budget line? What is the opportunity cost of one more candy bar? Of one more bag of peanuts? Do these opportunity costs rise, fall, or remain constant as each additional unit of the product is purchased?

c. How, in general, would you decide which of the available combinations of candy bars and bags of peanuts to buy?

d. Suppose that you had won $30 on your ticket, not $15. Show the $30 budget line in your diagram. Why would this budget line be preferable to the old one?

1.5 8. What are economic resources? What categories do economists use to classify them? Why are resources also called factors of production? Why are they called inputs?

1.5 9. Why is money not considered to be a capital resource in economics? Why is entrepreneurial ability considered a category of economic resource, distinct from labour? What are the major functions of the entrepreneur?

1.6 10. **KEY QUESTION**   Below is a production possibilities table for consumer goods (automobiles) and capital goods (forklifts):

PRODUCTION ALTERNATIVES

Type of production	A	B	C	D	E
Automobiles	0	2	4	6	8
Forklifts	30	27	21	12	0

a. Show these data graphically. Upon what specific assumptions is this production possibilities curve based?

b. If the economy is at point C, what is the cost of one more automobile? Of one more forklift? Explain how the production possibilities curve reflects the law of increasing opportunity costs.

c. If the economy characterized by this production possibilities table and curve were producing 3 automobiles and 20 forklifts, what could you conclude about its use of its available resources?

d. What would production at a point outside the production possibilities curve indicate? What must occur before the economy can attain such a level of production?

11. **KEY QUESTION**   Specify and explain the typical shapes **1.6** of marginal benefit and marginal cost curves. How are these curves used to determine the optimal allocation of resources to a particular product? If current output is such that marginal cost exceeds marginal benefit, should more or fewer resources be allocated to this product? Explain.

12. Explain how (if at all) each of the following events affects **1.6** the location of a country's production possibilities curve:

a. The quality of education increases. *increase*

b. The number of unemployed workers increases. *no change*

c. A new technique improves the efficiency of extracting iron from ore. *increase*

d. A devastating earthquake destroys numerous production facilities. *decrease*

13. **KEY QUESTION**   Suppose improvement occurs in the **1.6** technology of producing forklifts but not in the technology of producing automobiles. Draw the new production possibilities curve. Now assume that a technological advance occurs in producing automobiles but not in producing forklifts. Draw the new production possibilities curve. Now draw a production possibilities curve that reflects technological improvement in the production of both goods.

14. **KEY QUESTION**   On average, households in China save **1.7** 40 percent of their annual income each year, whereas households in Canada save less than 5 percent. Production possibilities are growing at roughly 9 percent annually in China and 3.5 percent in Canada. Use graphical analysis of "present goods" versus "future goods" to explain the difference in growth rates.

15. Suppose that, on the basis of a nation's production possibilities **1.7** curve, an economy must sacrifice 10,000 pizzas domestically to get the 1 additional industrial robot it desires, but that it can get the robot from another country in exchange for 9000 pizzas. Relate this information to the following statement: "Through international specialization and trade, a nation can reduce its opportunity cost of obtaining goods and thus move outside its production possibilities curve."

INTERNET APPLICATION QUESTIONS @

1. **More Labour Resources—What Is the Evidence for Canada and France?** Use the links on the McConnell-Brue-Flynn-Barbiero Web site (Chapter 1) to compare the growth in employment in Canada and France. In which of the two countries did "more labour resources" (in percentage terms) have the greatest impact in shifting the nation's production possibilities curve outward over the 10-year period?

2. **Normative Economics—Canadian Politics.** Many economic policy statements made by the Liberal Party, the Conservative Party, and the New Democratic Party can be considered normative rather than positive economic statements. Use the links on the McConnell-Brue-Flynn-Barbiero Web site (Chapter 1) and compare and contrast their views on how to achieve economic goals. How much of the disagreement is based on positive statements and how much on normative statements? Give an example of loaded terminology from each site.

Appendix to Chapter 1

If you glance quickly through this text, you will find many graphs. Some seem simple, others more complicated. All are included to help you visualize and understand economic relationships. Physicists and chemists sometimes illustrate their theories by building arrangements of multicoloured wooden balls, representing protons, neutrons, and electrons, which are held in proper relation to one another by wires or sticks. Economists use graphs to illustrate their models. By understanding these "pictures," you can more readily make sense of economic relationships. Most of our principles or models explain relationships between just two sets of economic facts, which can be conveniently represented with two-dimensional graphs.

Construction of a Graph

A *graph* is a visual representation of the relationship between two variables. Figure A1-1 is a hypothetical illustration showing the relationship between income and consumption for the economy as a whole. Without even studying economics, we would logically expect that people would buy more goods and services when their incomes go up. Thus it is not surprising to find in Figure A1-1 that total consumption in the economy increases as total income increases.

The information in Figure A1-1 is expressed both graphically and in table form. Here is how it is done: We want to show graphically how consumption changes as income changes. We therefore represent income on the **horizontal axis** of the graph and consumption on the **vertical axis**.

Now we arrange the vertical and horizontal scales of the graph to reflect the ranges of values of consumption and income, and mark the scales in convenient increments. As you can see in Figure A1-1, the values marked on the scales cover all the values in the table. The increments on both scales are $100 for approximately each centimetre.

Because the graph has two dimensions, each point within it represents an income value and its associated consumption value. To find a point that represents one of the five income–consumption combinations in the table, we draw straight lines from the appropriate values on the vertical and horizontal axes. For example, to plot point *c* (the $200 income, $150 consumption), straight lines are drawn up from the horizontal (income) axis at $200 and across from the vertical (consumption) axis at $150. These straight lines intersect at point *c*, which represents this particular income–consumption combination. You should verify that the other income–consumption combinations shown in the table are properly located in the graph. Finally, by assuming

Two sets of data that are positively or directly related, such as consumption and income, graph as an upsloping line.

Income per week	Consumption per week	Point
$ 0	$ 50	a
100	100	b
200	150	c
300	200	d
400	250	e

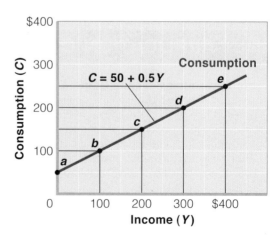

that the same general relationship between income and consumption prevails for all other incomes, we draw a line or smooth curve to connect these points. That line or curve represents the income–consumption relationship.

If the curve is a straight line, as in Figure A1-1, we say the relationship is *linear*. (It is permissible, and even customary, to call straight lines in graphs "curves.")

Direct and Inverse Relationships

The line in Figure A1-1 slopes upward to the right, depicting a direct relationship between income and consumption. By a **direct relationship** (or positive relationship) we mean that two variables—in this case, consumption and income—change in the *same* direction. An increase in consumption is associated with an increase in income; a decrease in consumption accompanies a decrease in income. When two sets of data are positively or directly related, they always graph as an *upward-sloping* line, as in Figure A1-1.

In contrast, two sets of data may be inversely related. Consider Figure A1-2, which shows the relationship between the price of basketball tickets and game attendance at Informed University (IU). Here we have an **inverse relationship** (or negative relationship) because the two variables change in *opposite* directions. When ticket prices decrease, attendance increases. When ticket prices increase, attendance decreases. The six data points in the table are plotted in the graph. Observe that an inverse relationship always graphs as a *downward-sloping* line.

Dependent and Independent Variables

Although it is not always easy, economists seek to determine which variable is the "cause" and which is the "effect." Or, more formally, they seek the independent variable and the dependent variable. The **independent variable** is the cause or source; it is the variable that changes first. The **dependent variable** is the effect or outcome; it is the variable that changes because of the change in the independent variable. As in our income–consumption example, income generally is the independent variable and consumption the dependent variable. Income causes consumption to be what it is rather than the other way around. Similarly, ticket prices (set in advance of the season and printed on the ticket) determine attendance at Informed University basketball games; attendance at games does not determine the printed ticket prices for those games. Ticket price is the independent variable, and the quantity of tickets purchased is the dependent variable.

You may recall from your high school courses that mathematicians put the independent variable (cause) on the horizontal axis and the dependent variable (effect) on the vertical axis. Economists are less tidy; their graphing of independent and dependent variables is more arbitrary. Their conventional graphing of the income–consumption relationship is consistent with mathematical presentation, but economists put price and cost data on the vertical axis. Hence, economists' graphing of IU's ticket price–attendance data differs from the normal mathematical procedure. This does not present a problem, but we want you to be aware of this fact to avoid possible confusion.

FIGURE A1-2   **The Relationship between Ticket Prices and Attendance**

Two sets of data that are negatively or inversely related, such as ticket price and the attendance at basketball games, graph as a downward-sloping line.

Ticket price	Attendance, thousands	Point
$ 50	0	a
40	4	b
30	8	c
20	12	d
10	16	e
0	20	f

$P = 50 - 2.5Q$

Other Things Equal

Our simple two-variable graphs purposely ignore many other factors that might affect the amount of consumption occurring at each income level or the number of people who attend IU basketball games at each possible ticket price. When economists plot the relationship between any two variables, they employ the *ceteris paribus* (other-things-equal) assumption. Thus, in Figure A1-1 all factors other than income that might affect the amount of consumption are held constant. Similarly, in Figure A1-2 all factors other than ticket price that might influence attendance at IU basketball games are assumed constant. In reality, "other things" are not equal; they often change and when they do, the relationship represented in our two tables and graphs will change. Specifically, the lines we have plotted will shift to new locations.

Consider a stock market "crash." The dramatic drop in the value of stocks might cause people to feel less wealthy and therefore less willing to consume at each level of income. The result might be a downward shift of the consumption line. To see this, you should plot a new consumption line in Figure A1-1, assuming that consumption is, say, $20 less at each income level. Note that the relationship remains direct; the line merely shifts downward to reflect less consumption spending at each income level.

Similarly, factors other than ticket prices might affect IU game attendance. If IU loses most of its games, attendance at IU games might fall at each ticket price. To see this, redraw the graph in Figure A1-2, assuming that 2000 fewer fans attend IU games at each ticket price. ***(Key Appendix Question 2)***

Slope of a Line

Lines can be described in terms of their slopes and their intercepts. The **slope of a straight line** is the ratio of the vertical change (the rise or drop) to the horizontal change (the run) between any two points of the line, or "rise" over "run."

POSITIVE SLOPE

Between point *c* and point *d* in Figure A1-1 the rise or vertical change (the change in consumption) is +$50 and the run or horizontal change (the change in income) is +$100. Therefore

$$\text{Slope} = \frac{\text{vertical change}}{\text{horizontal change}} = \frac{+50}{+100} = \frac{1}{2} = 0.5$$

Note that our slope of ½ or 0.5 is positive because consumption and income change in the same direction; that is, consumption and income are directly or positively related.

The slope of 0.5 tells us there will be a $1 increase in consumption for every $2 increase in income. Similarly, it indicates that for every $2 decrease in income there will be a $1 decrease in consumption.

NEGATIVE SLOPE

Between any two of the identified points in Figure A1-2, say point *c* and point *d*, the vertical change is −10 (the drop) and the horizontal change is +4 (the run). Therefore

$$\text{Slope} = \frac{\text{vertical change}}{\text{horizontal change}} = \frac{-10}{+4} = -2\frac{1}{2} = -2.5$$

This slope is negative because ticket price and attendance have an inverse or negative relationship.

Note that on the horizontal axis attendance is stated in thousands of people. So the slope of −10/+4 or −2.5 means that lowering the price by $10 will increase attendance by 4000 people. This is the same as saying that a $2.50 price reduction will increase attendance by 1000 people.

SLOPES AND MEASUREMENT UNITS

The slope of a line will be affected by the choice of units for either variable. If, in our ticket-price illustration, we had chosen to measure attendance in individual people, our horizontal change would have been 4000 and the slope would have been

$$\text{Slope} = \frac{-10}{+4000} = \frac{-1}{+400} = -0.0025$$

The slope depends on the units by which variables are measured.

SLOPES AND MARGINAL ANALYSIS

Recall that economics largely deals with changes from the status quo. The concept of slope is important in economics because it reflects marginal changes—those involving one more (or one less) unit. For example, in Figure A1-1 the 0.5 slope shows that $0.50 of extra or marginal consumption is associated with each $1 change in income. In this example, people collectively will consume $0.50 of any $1 increase in their incomes and reduce their consumption by $0.50 for each $1 decline in income.

INFINITE AND ZERO SLOPES

Many variables are unrelated or independent of one another. For example, the quantity of digital cameras purchased is not related to the price of bananas. In Figure A1-3a we represent the price of bananas on the vertical axis and the quantity of digital cameras demanded on the horizontal axis. The graph of their relationship is the line parallel to the vertical axis, indicating that the same quantity of cameras is purchased no matter what the price of bananas. The slope of such a line is *infinite*.

Similarly, aggregate consumption is completely unrelated to the nation's divorce rate. In Figure A1-3b we put consumption on the vertical axis and the divorce rate on the horizontal axis. The line parallel to the horizontal axis represents this lack of relatedness. This line has a slope of *zero*.

FIGURE A1-3   Infinite and Zero Slopes

(a) A line parallel to the vertical axis has an infinite slope. Here, purchases of digital cameras remain the same no matter what happens to the price of bananas.

(b) A line parallel to the horizontal axis has a slope of zero. In this case, consumption remains the same no matter what happens to the divorce rate. In both (a) and (b), the two variables are totally unrelated to one another.

(a)   **(b)**

Vertical Intercept

A line can be located on a graph (without plotting points) if we know its slope and its vertical intercept. The **vertical intercept** of a line is the point where the line meets the vertical axis. In Figure A1-1 the intercept is $50. This intercept means that if current income were zero, consumers would still spend $50. They might do this through borrowing or by selling some of their assets. Similarly, the $50 vertical intercept in Figure A1-2 shows that at a $50 ticket price, IU's basketball team would be playing in an empty arena.

Equation of a Linear Relationship

If we know the vertical intercept and slope, we can describe a line succinctly in equation form. In its general form the equation of a straight line is

$$y = a + bx$$

where y = dependent variable

a = *vertical* intercept

b = slope of line

x = independent variable

For our income–consumption example, if C represents consumption (the dependent variable) and Y represents income (the independent variable), we can write $C = a + bY$. By substituting the known values of the intercept and the slope, we get

$$C = 50 + 0.5Y$$

This equation also allows us to determine the amount of consumption C at any specific level of income. You should use it to confirm that at the $250 income level, consumption is $175.

When economists reverse mathematical convention by putting the independent variable on the vertical axis and the dependent variable on the horizontal axis, then y stands for the independent variable, rather than the dependent variable in the general form. We noted previously that this case is relevant for our IU ticket price–attendance data. If P represents the ticket price (independent variable) and Q represents attendance (dependent variable), their relationship is given by

$$P = 50 - 2.5Q$$

where the vertical intercept is 50 and the negative slope is $-2\frac{1}{2}$ or -2.5. Knowing the value of P lets us solve for Q, our dependent variable. You should use this equation to predict IU ticket sales when the ticket price is $15. *(Key Appendix Question 3)*

Slope of a Non-linear Curve

We now move from the simple world of linear relationships (straight lines) to the more complex world of non-linear relationships. The slope of a straight line is the same at all its points. The slope of a line representing a non-linear relationship changes from one point to another. Such lines are always referred to as *curves*.

Consider the downward-sloping curve in Figure A1-4. Its slope is negative throughout, but the curve flattens as we move down along it. Thus, its slope constantly changes; the curve has a different slope at each point.

To measure the slope at a specific point, we draw a straight line tangent to the curve at that point. A line is *tangent* at a point if it touches, but does not intersect, the curve at that point. Thus line aa' is tangent to the curve in Figure A1-4 at point A. The slope of the curve at that point is equal to the slope of the tangent line. Specifically, the total vertical change (drop) in the tangent line aa' is -20 and the total horizontal change (run) is $+5$. Because the slope of the tangent line aa' is $-20/+5$, or -4, the slope of the curve at point A is also -4.

Line bb' in Figure A1-4 is tangent to the curve at point B. Following the same procedure, we find the slope at B to be $-5/+15$, or $-\frac{1}{3}$. Thus, in this flatter part of the curve, the slope is less negative. *(Key Appendix Question 7)*

MATH A1.1
Slope of a Nonlinear Curve

KEY GRAPH

FIGURE A1-4 Determining the Slopes of Curves

The slope of a non-linear curve changes from point to point on the curve. The slope at any point (say, B) can be determined by drawing a straight line that is tangent to that point (line bb') and calculating the slope of that line.

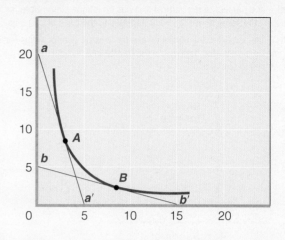

APPENDIX | SUMMARY

A1.1 GRAPHS AND THEIR MEANING

- Graphs are a convenient and revealing way to represent economic relationships.

- Two variables are positively or directly related when their values change in the same direction. The line (curve) representing two directly related variables slopes upward.

- Two variables are negatively or inversely related when their values change in opposite directions. The curve representing two inversely related variables slopes downward.

- The value of the dependent variable (the "effect") is determined by the value of the independent variable (the "cause").

- When the "other factors" that might affect a two-variable relationship are allowed to change, the graph of the relationship will likely shift to a new location.

- The slope of a straight line is the ratio of the vertical change to the horizontal change between any two points. The slope of an upward-sloping line is positive; the slope of a downward-sloping line is negative.

- The slope of a line or curve depends on the units used in measuring the variables. It is especially relevant for economics because it measures marginal changes.

- The slope of a horizontal line is zero; the slope of a vertical line is infinite.

- The vertical intercept and slope of a line determine its location; they are used in expressing the line—and the relationship between the two variables—as an equation.

- The slope of a curve at any point is determined by calculating the slope of a straight-line tangent to the curve at that point.

APPENDIX | TERMS AND CONCEPTS

horizontal axis   The "left-right" or "west-east" axis on a graph or grid. (p. 24)

vertical axis   The "up-down" or "north-south" axis on a graph or grid. (p. 24)

direct relationship   The (positive) relationship between two variables that change in the same direction, for example, product price and quantity supplied. (p. 25)

inverse relationship   The (negative) relationship between two variables that change in opposite directions, for example, product price and quantity demanded. (p. 25)

independent variable   The variable causing a change in some other (dependent) variable. (p. 25)

dependent variable   A variable that changes as a consequence of a change in some other (independent) variable; the "effect" or outcome. (p. 25)

slope of a line   The ratio of the vertical change (the rise or fall) to the horizontal change (the run) between any two points on a line. The slope of an upward sloping line is positive, reflecting a direct relationship between two variables; the slope of a downward sloping line is negative, reflecting an inverse relationship between two variables. (p. 26)

vertical intercept   The point at which a line meets the vertical axis of a graph. (p. 27)

APPENDIX | STUDY QUESTIONS

A1.1 1. Briefly explain the use of graphs as a way to represent economic relationships. What is an inverse relationship? How does it graph? What is a direct relationship? How does it graph? Graph and explain the relationships you would expect to find between (a) the number of centimetres of rainfall per month and the sale of umbrellas, (b) the amount of tuition and the level of enrollment at a college or university, and (c) the popularity of a music artist and the price of her concert tickets.

In each case cite and explain how variables other than those specifically mentioned might upset the expected relationship. Is your graph in part (b), above, consistent with the fact that, historically, enrollments and tuition have both increased? If not, explain any difference.

A1.1 2. **KEY APPENDIX QUESTION**   Indicate how each of the following might affect the data shown in Figure A1-2 of this appendix:

a. IU's athletic director schedules higher-quality opponents.

b. A National Basketball Association (NBA) team locates in the city where IU also plays.

c. IU contracts to have all its home games televised.

A1.1 3. **KEY APPENDIX QUESTION**   The following table contains data on the relationship between saving and income. Rearrange these data into a meaningful order and graph them on the accompanying grid. What is the slope of the line? The vertical intercept? Interpret the meaning of both the slope and the intercept. Write the equation that represents this line. What would you predict saving to be at the $12,500 level of income?

Income (per year)	Saving (per year)
$15,000	$1,000
0	−500
10,000	500
5,000	0
20,000	1,500

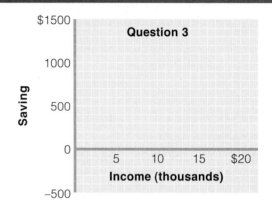

4. Construct a table from the data shown on the graph below. **LO A1.1** Which is the dependent variable and which the independent variable? Summarize the data in equation form.

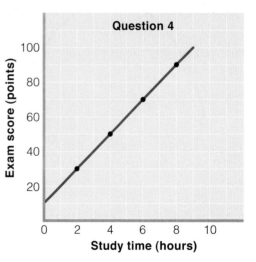

5. Suppose that when the interest rate on loans is 16 percent, **LO A1.1** businesses find it unprofitable to invest in machinery and equipment. However, when the interest rate is 14 percent, $5 billion worth of investment is profitable. At 12 percent interest, a total of $10 billion of investment is profitable. Similarly, total investment increases by $5 billion for each successive 2-percentage-point decline in the interest rate.

Describe the relevant relationship between the interest rate and investment in words, in a table, graphically, and as an equation. Put the interest rate on the vertical axis and investment on the horizontal axis. In your equation use the form $i = a - bI$, where i is the interest rate, a is the vertical intercept, $-b$ is the slope of the line (which is negative), and I is the level of investment. Comment on the advantages and disadvantages of the verbal, tabular, graphical, and equation forms of description.

LO A1.1 6. Suppose that $C = a + bY$, where C = consumption, a = consumption at zero income, b = slope, and Y = income.

   a. Are C and Y positively related or are they negatively related?

   b. If graphed, would the curve for this equation slope upward or slope downward?

   c. Are the variables C and Y inversely related or directly related?

   d. What is the value of C if $a = 10$, $b = 0.50$, and $Y = 200$?

   e. What is the value of Y if $C = 100$, $a = 10$, and $b = 0.25$?

LO A1.1 7. **KEY APPENDIX QUESTION**   The accompanying graph shows curve XX′ and tangents at points A, B, and C. Calculate the slope of the curve at these three points.

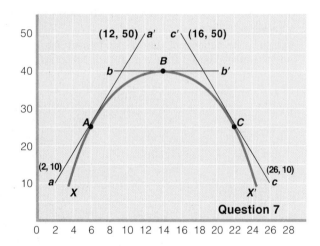

Question 7

8. In the accompanying graph, is the slope of curve AA′ positive **LO** or negative? Does the slope increase or decrease as we move along the curve from A to A′? Answer the same two questions for curve BB′.

Question 8

CHAPTER 2

The Market System and the Circular Flow

You are at a mall in Halifax. Suppose you were assigned to compile a list of all the individual goods and services there, including the different brands and variations of each type of product. That task would be daunting and the list would be long! And even though a single shopping mall in Vancouver contains a remarkable quantity and variety of goods, it is only a tiny part of the Canadian economy.

Who decided that the particular goods and services available at the mall and in the broader Canadian economy should be produced? How did the producers determine which technology and types of factors to use in producing these particular goods? Who will obtain these products? What accounts for the new and improved products among these goods? This chapter will answer these and related questions.

2.1 | Economic Systems

Every society needs to develop an **economic system**—a particular set of institutional arrangements and a coordinating mechanism—to respond to the economic problem. The economic system determines what goods are produced, how they are produced, who gets them, how to accommodate change, and how to promote technological progress.

Economic systems differ as to (1) who owns the factors of production and (2) the method used to motivate, coordinate, and direct economic activity. There are two general types of economic systems: the command system and the market system.

The Command System

The **command system** is also known as *socialism* or *communism*. In that system, government owns most property resources and economic decision making occurs through a central economic plan. A central planning board appointed by the government makes nearly all the major decisions concerning the use of resources, the composition and distribution of output, and the organization of production. The government owns most of the business firms, which produce according to government directives. The central planning

economic system
A particular set of institutional arrangements and a coordinating mechanism for producing goods and services.

command system
An economic system in which most property resources are owned by the government and economic decisions are made by a central government body.

board determines production goals for each enterprise and specifies the amount of resources to be allocated to each enterprise so that it can reach its production goals. The division of output between capital and consumer goods is centrally decided, and capital goods are allocated among industries on the basis of the central planning board's long-term priorities.

A pure command economy would rely exclusively on a central plan to allocate the government-owned property resources. But, in reality, even the pre-eminent command economy—the Soviet Union—tolerated some private ownership and incorporated some markets before its collapse in 1992. Recent reforms in Russia and most of the eastern European nations have to one degree or another transformed their command economies to market-oriented systems. China's reforms have not gone as far, but they have greatly reduced the reliance on central planning. Although there is still extensive government ownership of resources and capital in China, the nation has increasingly relied on free markets to organize and coordinate its economy. North Korea and Cuba are the last remaining examples of largely centrally planned economies. Later in this chapter, we will explore the main reasons for the general demise of the command systems.

The Market System

market system
An economic system in which property resources are privately owned and markets and prices are used to direct and coordinate economic activities.

The polar alternative to the command system is the **market system,** or *capitalism.* The system is characterized by the private ownership of resources and the use of markets and prices to coordinate and direct economic activity. Participants act in their own self-interest. Individuals and businesses seek to achieve their economic goals through their own decisions regarding work, consumption, or production. The system allows for the private ownership of capital, communicates through prices, and coordinates economic activity through *markets*—places where buyers and sellers come together. Goods and services are produced and resources are supplied by whoever is willing and able to do so at the prevailing prices. The result is competition among independently acting buyers and sellers of each product and resource. Thus, economic decision making is widely dispersed. Also, the high potential for monetary rewards creates powerful incentives for existing firms to innovate and entrepreneurs to pioneer new products and processes.

 ORIGIN 2.1
Laissez-faire

In *pure* capitalism—or *laissez-faire* capitalism—government's role is limited to protecting private property and establishing an environment appropriate to the operation of the market system. The term "laissez-faire" means "let it be"; that is, keep government from interfering with the economy. The idea is that such interference will inhibit the efficient working of the market system.

But in the capitalism practised in Canada and most other countries, government plays a significant role in the economy. It not only provides the rules for economic activity but also attempts to promote economic stability and growth, provides certain goods and services that would otherwise be underproduced or not produced at all, and modifies the distribution of income. The government, however, is not the dominant economic force in deciding what to produce, how to produce it, and who will get it. That force is the market.

2.2 | Characteristics of the Market System

An examination of some of the key features of the market system in detail will be instructive.

Private Property

private property
The right of private persons and firms to obtain, own, control, employ, dispose of, and bequeath land, capital, and other property.

In a market system, private individuals and firms, not the government, own most of the property resources (land and capital). It is this extensive private ownership of capital that gives capitalism its name. This right of **private property,** coupled with the freedom to negotiate binding legal contracts, enables individuals and businesses to obtain, use, and dispose of property resources as they see fit. The right of property owners to designate who will receive their property when they die sustains the institution of private property.

Property rights encourage investment, innovation, exchange, maintenance of property, and economic growth. No one would stock a store, build a factory, or clear land for farming if someone else, or the government itself, could take that property for his or her own benefit.

Property rights also extend to intellectual property through patents, copyrights, and trademarks. Such long-term protection encourages people to write books, music, and computer programs and to invent new products and production processes without fear that others will steal them and the rewards they may bring.

Moreover, property rights facilitate exchange. The title to an automobile or the deed to a cattle ranch assures the buyer that the seller is the legitimate owner. Also, property rights encourage owners to maintain or improve their property so as to preserve or increase its value. Finally, property rights enable people to use their time and resources to produce more goods and services, rather than using them to protect and retain the property they have already produced or acquired.

Freedom of Enterprise and Choice

freedom of enterprise
The freedom of firms to obtain economic resources, to use these resources to produce products of the firm's own choosing, and to sell their products in markets of their choice.

freedom of choice
The freedom of owners of property resources to employ or dispose of them as they see fit, and of consumers to spend their incomes in a manner that they think is appropriate.

Closely related to private ownership of property is freedom of enterprise and choice. The market system requires that various economic units make certain choices, which are expressed and implemented in the economy's markets:

- **Freedom of enterprise** ensures that entrepreneurs and private businesses are free to obtain and use economic resources to produce their choice of goods and services and to sell them in their chosen markets.

- **Freedom of choice** enables owners to employ or dispose of their property and money as they see fit. It also allows workers to enter any line of work for which they are qualified. Finally, it ensures that consumers are free to buy the goods and services that best satisfy their wants.

These choices are free only within broad legal limitations, of course. Illegal choices such as selling human organs or buying illicit drugs are punished through fines and imprisonment. (Global Perspective 2.1 reveals that the degree of economic freedom varies greatly from economy to economy.)

Self-Interest

 ORIGIN 2.2
Self-Interest

self-interest
That which each firm, property owner, worker, and consumer believes is best for itself.

In the market system, **self-interest** is the motivating force of the various economic units as they express their free choices. Self-interest simply means that each economic unit tries to achieve its own particular goal, which usually requires delivering something of value to others. Entrepreneurs try to maximize profit or minimize loss. Property owners try to get the highest price for the sale or rent of their resources. Workers try to maximize their utility (satisfaction) by finding jobs that offer the best combination of wages, hours, fringe benefits, and working conditions. Consumers try to obtain the products they want at the lowest possible price and apportion their expenditures to maximize their utility. The motive of self-interest gives direction and consistency to what might otherwise be a chaotic economy.

Competition

competition
The presence in a market of a large number of independent buyers and sellers competing with one another and the freedom of buyers and sellers to enter and leave the market.

The market system depends on **competition** among economic units. The basis of this competition is freedom of choice exercised in pursuit of a monetary return. Very broadly defined, competition requires:

- independently acting sellers and buyers operating in a particular product or factor market

- freedom of sellers and buyers to enter or leave markets, on the basis of their economic self-interest

Competition among buyers and sellers diffuses economic power within the businesses and households that make up the economy. When there are independently acting sellers and buyers in a market, no one buyer or seller is able to dictate the price of the product or factor because others can undercut that price.

2.1 | GLOBAL PERSPECTIVE

Index of Economic Freedom, Selected Nations

The Index of Economic Freedom measures economic freedom using 10 broad categories, such as trade policy, property rights, and government intervention, with each category containing more than 50 specific criteria. The Index then ranks 157 nations according to the degree of economic freedom. A few selected rankings for 2009 are listed here.

FREE
1 Hong Kong
3 Australia
6 United States
7 Canada

MOSTLY FREE
20 Belgium
29 Spain
64 France

MOSTLY UNFREE
105 Brazil
132 China
146 Russia

REPRESSED
174 Venezuela
177 Cuba
179 North Korea

Source: Heritage Foundation (www.heritage.org) and the *Wall Street Journal*.

Competition also implies that producers can enter or leave an industry; there are no insurmountable barriers to an industry's expanding or contracting. This freedom of an industry to expand or contract provides the economy with the flexibility needed to remain efficient over time. Freedom of entry and exit enables the economy to adjust to changes in consumer tastes, technology, and factor availability.

The diffusion of economic power inherent in competition limits the potential abuse of that power. A producer that charges more than the competitive market price will lose sales to other producers. An employer who pays less than the competitive market wage rate will lose workers to other employers. A firm that fails to exploit new technology will lose profits to firms that do. Competition is the basic regulatory force in the market system.

Markets and Prices

We may wonder why an economy based on self-interest does not collapse in chaos. If consumers want breakfast cereal but businesses choose to produce running shoes and resource suppliers decide to make computer software, production would seem to be deadlocked by the apparent inconsistencies of free choices.

In reality, the millions of decisions made by households and businesses are highly coordinated with one another. Markets and prices are key components of the market system. They give the system its ability to coordinate millions of daily economic decisions. A **market** is an institution or mechanism that brings buyers ("demanders") and sellers ("suppliers") into contact. A market system conveys the decisions made by buyers and sellers of products and factors. The decisions made on each side of the market determine a set of product and factor prices that guide resource owners, entrepreneurs, and consumers as they make and revise their choices and pursue their self-interest.

market
Any institution or mechanism that brings together buyers and sellers of particular goods, services, or resources for the purpose of exchange.

Just as competition is the regulatory mechanism of the market system, the market system itself is the organizing and coordinating mechanism. It is an elaborate communication network through which innumerable individual free choices on the part of consumers and producers are recorded, summarized, and balanced. Those who respond to market signals and heed market dictates are rewarded with greater profit and income; those who do not respond to those signals and choose to ignore market dictates are penalized. Through this mechanism society decides what the economy should produce, how production can be organized efficiently, and how the fruits of production are to be distributed among the various units that make up the economy.

QUICK REVIEW

▸ The market system rests on the private owner-ship of property and on freedom of enterprise and freedom of choice.

▸ The market system permits consumers, resource suppliers, and businesses to pursue and further their self-interest.

▸ Competition diffuses economic power and limits the actions of any single seller or buyer.

▸ The coordinating mechanism of capitalism is a system of markets and prices.

Technology and Capital Goods

In the market system, competition, freedom of choice, self-interest, and personal reward provide the opportunity and motivation for technological advance. The monetary rewards for new products or production techniques accrue directly to the innovator. The market system therefore encourages extensive use and rapid development of complex capital goods: tools, machinery, large-scale factories, and facilities for storage, communication, transportation, and marketing.

Advanced technology and capital goods are important because the most direct methods of pro-duction are often the least efficient. The only way to avoid that inefficiency is to rely on capital goods. It would be ridiculous for a farmer to go at production with bare hands. There are huge benefits to be derived from creating and using such capital equipment as plows, tractors, storage bins, and so on. More efficient production means much more abundant output.

Specialization

specialization
The use of the resources of an individual, a firm, a region, or a nation to produce one or a few goods and services.

The extent to which market economies rely on **specialization** is astonishing. Specialization is the use of resources of an individual, region, or nation to produce one or a few goods or services rather than the entire range of goods and services. Those goods and services are then exchanged for a full range of desired products. The majority of consumers produce virtually none of the goods and services they consume, and they consume little or nothing of the items they produce. The person working nine-to-five installing windows in commercial aircraft may rarely fly. Many farmers sell their milk to the local dairy and then buy margarine at the local grocery store. Society learned long ago that self-sufficiency breeds inefficiency. The jack-of-all-trades may be a very colourful indi-vidual but is certainly not an efficient producer.

DIVISION OF LABOUR

division of labour
Dividing the work required to produce a product into a number of different tasks that are performed by different workers.

Human specialization—called the **division of labour**—contributes to a society's output in several ways:

- ***Specialization Makes Use of Differences in Ability***   Specialization enables individuals to take advantage of existing differences in their abilities and skills. If Peyton is strong, athletic, and good at throwing a football and Beyoncé is beautiful, agile, and can sing, their distribution of talents can be most efficiently used if Peyton plays professional football and Beyoncé records songs and gives concerts.

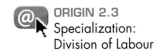

ORIGIN 2.3
Specialization:
Division of Labour

- **Specialization Fosters Learning by Doing**   Even if the abilities of two people are identical, specialization may still be advantageous. By devoting time to a single task, a person is more likely to develop the skills required and to improve techniques than by working at a number of different tasks. You learn to be a good lawyer by studying and practising law.

- **Specialization Saves Time**   By devoting time to a single task, a person avoids the loss of time incurred in shifting from one job to another. Also, time is saved by not "fumbling around" with a task that one is not trained to do.

For all these reasons, specialization increases the total output society derives from limited resources.

GEOGRAPHIC SPECIALIZATION

Specialization also works on a regional and international basis. It is conceivable that apples could be grown in Saskatchewan, but because of the unsuitability of the land, rainfall, and temperature, the costs would be very high. And it is conceivable that wheat could be grown in British Columbia, but such production would be costly for similar geographical reasons. So, Saskatchewan farmers produce products—wheat in particular—for which their resources are best suited, and British Columbians (especially in the Okanagan Valley) do the same, producing apples and other fruits. By specializing, both regional economies produce more than is needed locally. Then, very sensibly, Saskatchewan and British Columbia exchange some of their surpluses—wheat for apples, apples for wheat.

Similarly, on an international scale, Canada specializes in producing such items as commercial aircraft (Bombardier) and communication equipment (Research In Motion), which it sells abroad in exchange for digital video recorders from China, bananas from Honduras, and woven baskets from Thailand. Both human specialization and geographic specialization are needed to achieve efficiency in the use of limited resources.

Use of Money

A rather obvious characteristic of any economic system is the extensive use of money. Money performs several functions, but first and foremost it is a **medium of exchange.** It makes trade easier.

medium of exchange
Items sellers generally accept and buyers generally use to pay for a good or service.

Specialization requires exchange. Exchange can, and sometimes does, occur through **barter**—swapping goods for goods; say, exchanging wheat for apples. But barter poses serious problems because it requires a *coincidence of wants* between the buyer and the seller. In our example, we assumed that Saskatchewan had excess wheat to trade and wanted apples. And we assumed that British Columbia had excess apples to trade and wanted wheat. So an exchange occurred. But if such a coincidence of wants is missing, trade will not occur.

barter
The exchange of one good or service for another good or service.

Suppose that Saskatchewan has no interest in British Columbia's apples but wants potatoes from Prince Edward Island. And suppose that Prince Edward Island wants British Columbia's apples but not Saskatchewan's wheat. And, to complicate matters, suppose that British Columbia wants some of Saskatchewan's wheat but none of Prince Edward Island's potatoes. We summarize the situation in Figure 2-1.

In none of the cases shown in the figure is there a coincidence of wants. Trade by barter would obviously be difficult. Instead, people in each province use **money,** which is simply a convenient social invention to facilitate exchanges of goods and services. Historically, people have used cattle, cigarettes, shells, stones, pieces of metal, and many other commodities, with varying degrees of success, as a medium of exchange. But to serve as money, an item needs to pass only one test: It must be generally acceptable to sellers in exchange for their goods and services. Money is socially defined: whatever society accepts as a medium of exchange *is* money.

money
Any item that is generally acceptable to sellers in exchange for goods and services.

Today, most economies use pieces of paper as money. The use of paper dollars (currency) as a medium of exchange is what enables Saskatchewan, British Columbia, and Prince Edward Island to overcome their trade stalemate, as demonstrated in Figure 2-1.

FIGURE 2·1   **Money Facilitates Trade When Wants Do Not Coincide**

The use of money as a medium of exchange permits trade to be accomplished despite a non–coincidence of wants. (1) Saskatchewan trades the wheat that B.C. wants for money; (2) Saskatchewan trades the money it receives from B.C. for the potatoes it wants from P.E.I.; (3) P.E.I. trades the money it receives from Saskatchewan for the apples it wants from B.C.

On a global basis different nations have different currencies, which complicates specialization and exchange. But swapping dollars, yen, euros, pounds, and pesos for one another in markets in which currencies are bought and sold makes it possible for Canadians, Japanese, Germans, Britons, and Mexicans to exchange goods and services without resorting to barter.

Active, But Limited, Government

An active, but limited, government is the final characteristic of market systems in modern advanced industrial economies. Although a market system promotes a high degree of efficiency in the use of its resources, it has certain inherent shortcomings called "market failures." We will discover in subsequent chapters that government can increase the overall efficiency of the economic system in several ways.

QUICK REVIEW

▸ The market systems of modern industrial economies are characterized by extensive use of technologically advanced capital goods. Such goods help these economies achieve greater efficiency in production.

▸ Specialization is extensive in market systems; it enhances efficiency and output by enabling individuals, regions, and nations to produce the goods and services for which their resources are best suited.

▸ The use of money in market systems facilitates the exchange of goods and services that specialization requires.

2.3 | Five Fundamental Questions

The key features of the market system help explain how market economies respond to five fundamental questions:

- What goods and services will be produced?
- How will the goods and services be produced?
- Who will get the goods and services?
- How will the system accommodate change?
- How will the system promote progress?

These five questions highlight the economic choices underlying the production possibilities curve discussed in Chapter 1. They reflect the reality of scarce resources in a world of unlimited wants. All economies, whether market or command, must address these five questions.

What Will Be Produced?

How will a market system decide on the specific types and quantities of goods and services to be produced? The simple answer is this: The goods and services produced at a continuing profit will be produced, and those produced at a continuing loss will not. Profits and losses are the difference between the total revenue (TR) a firm receives from the sale of its products and the total cost (TC) of producing those products. (For economists, economic costs include not only wage and salary payments to labour, and interest and rental payments for capital and land, but also payments to the entrepreneur for organizing and combining the other resources to produce a commodity.)

Continuing economic profit (TR > TC) in an industry results in expanded production and the movement of resources toward that industry. Existing firms grow and new firms enter. The industry expands. Continuing losses (TC > TR) in an industry leads to reduced production and the departure of resources from that industry. Some existing firms shrink in size; others go out of business. The industry contracts.

consumer sovereignty
Determination by consumers of the types and quantities of goods and services that will be produced with the scarce resources of the economy.

In the market system, consumers are sovereign (in command). **Consumer sovereignty** is crucial in determining the types and quantities of goods produced. Consumers spend their income on the goods they are most willing and able to buy. Through these "**dollar votes**" they register their wants in the market. If the dollar votes for a certain product are large enough to create a profit, businesses will produce that product and offer it for sale. In contrast, if the dollar votes do not create sufficient revenues to cover costs, businesses will not produce the product. So the consumers are sovereign. Through their dollar votes they collectively direct resources to industries that are meeting consumer wants and away from industries that are not meeting consumer wants.

dollar votes
The "votes" that consumers and entrepreneurs cast for the production of consumer and capital goods, respectively, when they purchase them in product and resource markets.

The dollar votes of consumers determine not only which industries will continue to exist but also which products will survive or fail. Only profitable industries, firms, and products survive. So firms are not as free to produce whatever products they want. Consumers' buying decisions make the production of some products profitable and the production of other products unprofitable, thus restricting the choice of businesses in deciding what to produce. Businesses must match their production choices with consumer choices or else face losses and eventual bankruptcy.

The same holds true for resource (factor) suppliers. The employment of resources derives from the sale of the goods and services that the resources help produce. Autoworkers are employed because automobiles are sold. There are few remaining professors of early Latin because there are few people who want to learn the Latin language. Resource suppliers that want to earn income are not truly free to allocate their resources to the production of goods or services that consumers do not value highly. Consumers register their preferences in the market; producers and resource suppliers, prompted by their own self-interest, try to satisfy those preferences. *(Key Question 8)*

How Will the Goods and Services Be Produced?

What combinations of resources and technologies will be used to produce goods and services? How will the production be organized? The answer: in combinations and ways that minimize the cost per unit of output. Because competition eliminates high-cost producers, profitability for firms requires that they produce their output at minimum cost per unit. Achieving this least-cost production necessitates that firms use the right mix of labour and capital, given the prices and productivity of those resources. It also means locating production facilities in such a way as to minimize production and transportation costs.

Least-cost production also means that firms must employ the most economically efficient technique of production in producing their output. The most efficient production technique depends on:

- The available technology; that is, the various combinations of resources that will produce the most output.

- The prices of the needed resources.

WORKED PROBLEM 2.1
Least Cost Production

A technique that requires just a few inputs of resources to produce a specific output may be highly inefficient economically if those resources are valued very highly in the market. Economic efficiency requires obtaining a particular output of product with the least input of scarce resources, when both output and resource inputs are measured in dollars and cents.

Who Will Get the Output?

The market system enters the picture in two ways when determining the distribution of total output. Generally, any product will be distributed to consumers on the basis of their ability and willingness to pay its existing market price. If the price of some product, say a small sailboat, is $3000, then buyers who are willing and able to pay that price will get it; those unwilling or unable to pay the price will not.

The ability to pay the prices for sailboats and other products depends on the amount of income that consumers have, along with the prices of, and preferences for, various goods. If consumers have sufficient income and want to spend their money on a particular good, they can have it. And the amount of income they have depends on (1) the quantities of the property and human resources they supply and (2) the prices those resources command in the factor market. Factor prices (wages, interest, rent, profit) are crucial in determining the size of each person's income and therefore each person's ability to buy part of the economy's output. If a lawyer earning $300 an hour and a recreational worker earning $10 an hour both work the same number of hours each year, the lawyer will be able to take possession of 30 times as much of society's output as the recreational worker that year.

How Will the System Accommodate Change?

Market systems are dynamic: consumer preferences, technology, and supplies of resources can all change at the same time. This means that the particular allocation of resources that is now the most efficient for a specific pattern of consumer tastes, range of technological alternatives, and amount of available resources will become obsolete and inefficient as consumer preferences change, new techniques of production are discovered, and resource supplies change over time. Can the market economy adjust to such changes?

Suppose consumer tastes change. For instance, assume that consumers decide they want more fruit juice and less milk than the economy currently provides. Those changes in consumer tastes will be communicated to producers through an increase in spending on fruit juice and a decline in spending on milk. Other things equal, prices and profits in the fruit juice industry will rise and those in the milk industry will fall. Self-interest will induce existing competitors to expand output and entice new competitors to enter the prosperous fruit juice industry and will in time force firms to scale down—or even exit—the depressed milk industry.

The higher prices and greater economic profit in the fruit juice industry not only will induce that industry to expand but also will give it the revenue needed to obtain the resources necessary to its growth. Higher prices and profits will permit fruit juice producers to draw more resources from less urgent alternative employment. The reverse occurs in the milk industry, where fewer workers and other resources are employed. These adjustments in the economy are automatic responses to the changes in consumer tastes. This is consumer sovereignty at work.

The market system is a gigantic communications system. Through changes in prices and profits it communicates changes in consumer demand and elicits appropriate responses from businesses and resource suppliers. By affecting price and profits, changes in consumer demand direct the expansion of some industries and the contraction of others. Those adjustments are conveyed to the factor market. As expanding industries employ more factors of production and contracting industries employ fewer, the resulting changes in factor prices (wages and salaries, for example) and income flows steer resources from the contracting industries to the expanding industries.

This *directing* or guiding function of prices and profits is a core element of the market system. Without such a system, a government planning board or some other administrative agency would have to direct businesses and resources into the appropriate industries. A similar analysis shows that the system can and does adjust to other fundamental changes—for example, to changes in technology and in the prices of various resources.

How Will the System Promote Progress?

Society desires economic growth (greater output) and higher standards of living (greater income per person). How does the market system promote technological improvements and capital accumulation, both of which contribute to a higher standard of living for society?

TECHNOLOGICAL ADVANCE

The market system provides a strong incentive for technological advance and enables better products and processes to supplant inferior ones. An entrepreneur or firm that introduces a popular new product will gain revenue and economic profit at the expense of rivals.

Technological advance also includes new and improved methods that reduce production or distribution costs. By passing on part of its cost reduction to the consumer through a lower product price, the firm can increase sales and obtain economic profit at the expense of rival firms.

Moreover, the market system promotes the *rapid spread* of technological advance throughout an industry. Rival firms must follow the lead of the most innovative firm or else suffer immediate losses and eventual failure. In some cases, the result is **creative destruction**: the creation of new products and production methods completely destroys the market positions of firms that are wedded to existing products and older ways of doing business. For example, the advent of compact discs largely demolished long-play vinyl records, and iPods and other digital technologies are now supplanting CDs.

creative destruction
The hypothesis that the creation of new products and production methods simultaneously destroys the market power of firms that are wedded to existing products and older ways of doing business.

CAPITAL ACCUMULATION

Most technological advances require additional capital goods. The market system provides the resources necessary to produce those goods through increased dollar votes for capital goods.

But who will register votes for capital goods? Answer: entrepreneurs and owners of businesses. As receivers of profit income, they often use part of that income to purchase capital goods. Doing so yields even greater profit income in the future if the technological innovation is successful. Also, by paying interest or selling ownership shares, the entrepreneur and firm can attract some of the income of households to cast dollar votes for the production of more capital goods. (*Key Question 9*)

QUICK REVIEW

▶ The output mix of the market system is determined by profits, which in turn depend heavily on consumer preferences. Economic profits cause industries to expand; losses cause industries to contract.

▶ Competition forces industries to use the least costly production methods.

▶ In a market economy, consumer income and product prices determine how output will be distributed.

▶ Competitive markets reallocate resources in response to changes in consumer tastes, technological advances, and changes in availability of resources.

▶ Competitive markets create incentives for technological advance and capital accumulation, both of which contribute to increases in standards of living.

The "Invisible Hand"

In his 1776 book *The Wealth of Nations,* Adam Smith first noted that the operation of a market system creates a curious unity between private interests and social interests. Firms and resource suppliers, seeking to further their own self-interest and operating within the framework of a highly competitive market system, will simultaneously, as though guided by an "**invisible hand**," promote the public or social interest. For example, we have seen that in a competitive environment, businesses seek to build new and improved products to increase profits. Those enhanced products increase society's well-being. Businesses also use the least costly combination of resources to produce a specific output because it is in their self-interest to do so. To act otherwise would be to forgo profit or even to risk business failure. But, at the same time, to use scarce resources in the least costly way is clearly in the social interest as well. It "frees up" resources to produce something else that society desires.

Self-interest, awakened and guided by the competitive market system, is what induces responses appropriate to the changes in society's wants. Businesses seeking to make higher profits and to avoid losses, and resource suppliers pursuing greater monetary rewards, negotiate changes in the allocation of resources and end up with the output that society wants. Competition guides self-interest such that self-interest automatically and quite unintentionally furthers the best interest of society. The invisible hand ensures that when firms maximize their profits and resource suppliers maximize their incomes, these groups also help maximize society's output and income.

Of the various virtues of the market system, three merit re-emphasis:

- **Efficiency**　The market system promotes the efficient use of resources, by guiding them into the production of the goods and services most wanted by society. It forces the use of the most efficient techniques in organizing resources for production, and it encourages the development and adoption of new and more efficient production techniques.

- **Incentives**　The market system encourages skill acquisition, hard work, and innovation. Greater work skills and effort mean greater production and higher incomes, which usually translate into a higher standard of living. Similarly, the assumption of risks by entrepreneurs can result in substantial profit incomes. Successful innovations generate economic rewards.

- **Freedom**　The major noneconomic argument for the market system is its emphasis on personal freedom. In contrast to central planning, the market system coordinates economic activity without coercion. The market system permits—indeed, it thrives on—freedom of enterprise and choice. Entrepreneurs and workers are free to further their own self-interest, subject to the rewards and penalties imposed by the market system itself.

Of course, no economic system, including the market system, is flawless. The global financial crisis that gripped most economies in 2008–09 highlighted some of the shortcomings of unfettered financial markets. In Chapter 15 of *Microeconomics* we will explain several well-known shortcomings of the market system and examine the government policies that try to remedy them.

invisible hand
The tendency of firms and resource suppliers seeking to further their own self-interests in competitive markets to also promote the interest of society as a whole.

2.4 | The Demise of the Command System

Our discussion of how a market system answers the five fundamental questions provides insights on why command systems of the Soviet Union, eastern Europe, and China (prior to its market reforms) failed. Those systems encountered two insurmountable problems.

The Coordination Problem

The first difficulty was the coordination problem. The central planners had to coordinate the millions of individual decisions by consumers, resource suppliers, and businesses. Consider the setting up of a factory to produce tractors. The central planners had to establish a realistic annual production target; for example, 1000 tractors. They then had to make available all the necessary inputs—labour, machinery, electric power, steel, tires, glass, paint, transportation—for the production and delivery of those 1000 tractors.

Because the outputs of many industries serve as inputs to other industries, the failure of any single industry to achieve its output target caused a chain reaction of repercussions. For example, if iron mines, for want of machinery or labour or transportation, did not supply the steel industry with the required inputs of iron ore, the steel mills were unable to fulfill the input needs of the many industries that depended on steel. Steel-using industries that produced capital goods (such as factory equipment and modes of transportation) were unable to fulfill their planned production goals. Eventually the chain reaction spread to all firms that used steel as an input and from there to other input buyers or final consumers.

The coordination problem became more difficult as the economies expanded. Products and production processes grew more complex, and the number of industries requiring planning increased. Planning techniques that worked for the simpler economy proved highly inadequate and inefficient for the larger economy. Bottlenecks and production stoppages became the norm, not the exception. In trying to cope, planners further suppressed product variety, focusing on one or two products in each product category.

A lack of a reliable success indicator added to the coordination problem in the Soviet Union and China (prior to its market reforms). We have seen that market economies rely on profit as a success indicator. Profit depends on consumer demand, production efficiency, and product quality. In contrast, the major success indicator for the command economies usually was a quantitative production target that the central planners assigned. Production costs, product quality, and product mix were secondary considerations. Managers and workers often sacrificed product quality because

CONSIDER THIS | The Two Koreas

North Korea is one of the few command economies still standing. After the Second World War, Korea was divided into North Korea and South Korea. North Korea, under the influence of the Soviet Union, established a command economy that emphasized government ownership and central government planning. South Korea established a market economy based upon private ownership and the profit motive. Today, the differences in the economic outcomes of the two systems are striking:

	North Korea	**South Korea**
GDP	$40 billion*	$1.2 trillion*
GDP per capita	$1,800*	$24,500*
Exports	$1.3 billion	$326 billion
Imports	$2.7 billion	$309.3 billion
Agriculture as % of GDP	30 %	3 %

*Based on purchasing power equivalencies to the U.S. dollar.

Source: *CIA World Fact Book*, 2008, www.cia.gov.

they were being awarded bonuses for meeting quantitative, not qualitative, targets. If meeting production goals meant sloppy assembly work, so be it.

It was difficult at best for planners to assign quantitative production targets without unintentionally producing distortions in output. If the plan specified a production target for producing nails in terms of *weight* (tons of nails), the enterprise made only large nails. But if it specified the target as a *quantity* (thousands of nails), the firm made all small nails, and lots of them! That is precisely what happens in centrally planned economies.

The Incentive Problem

The command economies also faced an incentive problem. Central planners determined the output mix. When they misjudged how many automobiles, shoes, shirts, and chickens were wanted at the government-determined prices, persistent shortages and surpluses of those products often arose. But as long as the managers who oversaw the production of those goods were rewarded for meeting their assigned production goals, they had no incentive to adjust production in response to the shortages and surpluses. And there were no fluctuations in prices and profitability to signal that more or less of certain products was desired. Thus, many products were unavailable or in short supply, while other products were overproduced and sat for months or years in warehouses.

CONSIDER THIS | Market Failure and the Need for Government

Suppose a municipality, say Brandon, Manitoba, requires a new road. In the absence of a government request that a private firm build it, it is unlikely that a private firm will build the required road on its own initiative. Or, to express it in another way, private markets will not make available public goods. The citizens of Brandon have to elect a government to either direct a private firm to build the road, or hire the people and buy the capital equipment needed to construct the road on its own.

Why would a private firm not undertake to build a road on its own? The obstacle is common property rights. The land on which the road is to be built must be owned by the firm before it would consider building the road. Lands used by all citizens are most often held publicly. The firm would thus need to get the consent of all the citizens affected. Such unanimity would be difficult to achieve. Indeed, it is the difficulty of making collective decisions that makes government action essential in the creation of an infrastructure—such as roads and airports—necessary to facilitate the functioning of markets. Not only must a decision be made to build the road, but then the decision must be made as to who should bear the cost. The free-rider problem arises here. Every individual hopes someone will pay for the needed road. This way he or she can have the benefits without contributing to its cost. The free-rider problem can potentially arise in all situations where collective action must be taken. Unless we have a central authority—government—with the monopoly power to impose costs on all members of a society, many socially useful projects will not be undertaken.

In a pathbreaking book, *The Logic of Collective Action*,[1] Mancur Olson pointed out 40 years ago that contrary to popular belief, groups of individuals with common interest do not necessarily attempt to further those common interests. In many instances group members attempt to further their own personal interests. A few years later, the political scientist Garrett Hardin popularized the term "the tragedy of the commons"[2] to describe the problems that arise when there are common property rights. For example, where there are common property rights to a natural resource, it is typically overexploited. The cod stocks on Canada's east coast have suffered just that fate.

Where collective action is required, or where there are common property rights, governments are needed because markets fail to bring together the interests of the individual and those of society. The federal government has had to impose mandatory fishing restrictions to save the cod stocks from dwindling further. Similarly, governments must make decisions to construct a road, otherwise the road might never get built.

But we do not want to leave the impression that all government interventions to rectify market failure succeed. Some individuals point to the failure of the Canadian federal government to properly manage the cod stocks off the eastern seaboard as a case in point.

[1] Mancur Olson, *The Logic of Collective Action* (Cambridge: Cambridge University Press, 1965).

[2] Garrett Hardin, "The Tragedy of the Commons," *Science* 162 (1968): 1243–48.

The command systems of the Soviet Union and China before its market reforms also lacked entrepreneurship. Central planning did not trigger the profit motive, nor did it reward innovation and enterprise. The route for getting ahead was through participation in the political hierarchy of the Communist Party. Moving up the hierarchy meant better housing, better access to health care, and the right to shop in special stores. Meeting production targets and manoeuvring through the minefields of party politics were measures of success in "business." But a definition of business success based solely on political savvy is not conducive to technological advance, which is often disruptive to existing products, production methods, and organizational structures.

| 2.5 | The Circular Flow Model |

ORIGIN 2.4
Circular Flow
Diagram

circular flow diagram
The flow of resources from households to firms and of products from firms to households. These flows are accompanied by reverse flows of money from firms to households and from households to firms.

factor market
A market in which households sell and firms buy factors of production.

product market
A market in which products are sold by firms and bought by households.

The dynamic market economy creates continuous, repetitive flows of goods and services, resources, and money. The **circular flow diagram,** shown in **Figure 2-2 (Key Graph),** illustrates those flows. Observe that in the diagram we group private decision makers into *businesses* and *households* and group markets into the *factor market* and the *product market*.

Factor Market

The upper part of the circular flow diagram represents the **factor market:** the place where resources or the services of resource suppliers are bought and sold. In the factor market, households sell resources and businesses buy them. Households (that is, people) own all economic resources either directly as workers or entrepreneurs or indirectly through their ownership of business corporations. They sell their resources to businesses, which buy them because they are necessary for producing goods and services. The funds that businesses pay for resources are costs to businesses but are flows of wage, rent, interest, and profit income to the households. Productive resources therefore flow from households to businesses, and money flows from businesses to households.

Product Market

Next consider the lower part of the diagram, which represents the **product market:** the place where goods and services produced by businesses are bought and sold. In the product market, businesses combine resources to produce and sell goods and services. Households use the (limited) income they have received from the sale of resources to buy goods and services. The monetary flow of consumer spending on goods and services yields sales revenues for businesses. Businesses compare those revenues to their costs in determining profitability and whether or not a particular good or service should continue to be produced.

The circular flow model depicts a complex, interrelated web of decision making and economic activity involving businesses and households. For the economy, it is the circle of life. Businesses and households are both buyers and sellers. Businesses buy resources and sell products. Households buy products and sell resources. As shown in Figure 2-2, there is a counterclockwise *real flow* of economic resources and finished goods and services and a clockwise *money flow* of income and consumption expenditures.

KEY GRAPH

FIGURE 2-2
The Circular Flow Diagram

Factors of production flow from households to businesses through the factor market and products flow from businesses to households through the product market. Opposite these real flows are monetary flows. Households receive income from businesses (their costs) through the factor market and businesses receive revenue from households (their expenditures) through the product market.

Quick Quiz

1. The factor market is where:
  a. households sell products and businesses buy products.
  b. businesses sell factors of production and households sell products.
  c. households sell factors of production and businesses buy factors of production (or the services of factors).
  d. businesses sell factors of production and households buy factors of production (or the services of factors).

2. Which of the following would be determined in the product market?
  a. a manager's salary
  b. the price of equipment used in a bottling plant
  c. the price of 80 hectares of farmland
  d. the price of a new pair of athletic shoes

3. In this circular flow diagram:
  a. money flows counterclockwise.
  b. resources flow counterclockwise.
  c. goods and services flow clockwise.
  d. households are on the selling side of the product market.

4. In this circular flow diagram:
  a. households spend income in the product market.
  b. firms sell resources to households.
  c. households receive income through the product market.
  d. households produce goods.

Answers: 1. c; 2. d; 3. b; 4. a

The **LAST WORD**   Shuffling the Deck

Economist Donald Boudreaux marvels at the way the market system systematically and purposefully arranges the world's tens of billions of individual resources.

In *The Future and Its Enemies*, Virginia Postrel notes the astonishing fact that if you thoroughly shuffle an ordinary deck of 52 playing cards, chances are practically 100 percent that the resulting arrangement of cards has never before existed. Never. Every time you shuffle a deck, you produce an arrangement of cards that exists for the first time in history.

The arithmetic works out that way. For a very small number of items, the number of possible arrangements is small. Three items, for example, can be arranged only six different ways. But the number of possible arrangements grows very quickly. The number of different ways to arrange five items is 120...for ten items it's 3,628,800...for fifteen items it's 1,307,674,368,000.

The number of different ways to arrange 52 items is 8.066×10^{67}. This is a big number. No human can comprehend its enormousness. By way of comparison, the number of possible ways to arrange a mere 20 items is 2,432,902,008,176,640,000—a number larger than the total number of seconds that have elapsed since the beginning of time ten billion years ago—and this number is Lilliputian compared to 8.066×10^{67}.

What's the significance of these facts about numbers? Consider the number of different resources available in the world—my labour, your labour, your land, oil, tungsten, cedar, coffee beans, chickens, rivers, the Empire State Build-ing, [Microsoft] Windows, the wharves at Houston, the classrooms at Oxford, the airport at Miami, and on and on and on. No one can possibly count all of the different, productive resources available for our use. But we can be sure that this number is at least in the tens of billions.

When you reflect on how incomprehensibly large is the number of ways to arrange a deck containing a mere 52 cards, the mind boggles at the number of different ways to arrange all the world's resources.

If our world were random—if resources combined together haphazardly, as if a giant took them all into his hands and tossed them down like so many [cards]—it's a virtual certainty that the resulting combination of resources would be useless. Unless this chance arrangement were quickly rearranged according to some productive logic, nothing worthwhile would be produced. We would all starve to death. Because only a tiny fraction of possible arrangements serves human

ends, any arrangement will be useless if it is chosen randomly or with inadequate knowledge of how each and every resource might be productively combined with each other.

And yet, we witness all around us an arrangement of resources that's productive and serves human goals. Today's arrangement of resources might not be perfect, but it is vastly superior to most of the trillions upon trillions of other possible arrangements.

How have we managed to get one of the minuscule number of arrangements that works? The answer is private property—a social institution that encourages mutual accommodation.

Private property eliminates the possibility that resource arrangements will be random, for each resource owner chooses a course of action only if it promises rewards to the owner that exceed the rewards promised by all other available courses.

[The result] is a breathtakingly complex and productive arrangement of countless resources. This arrangement emerged over time (and is still emerging) as the result of billions upon billions of individual, daily, small decisions made by people seeking to better employ their resources and labor in ways that other people find helpful.

Source: Abridged from Donald J. Boudreaux, "Mutual Accommodation," *Ideas on Liberty*, May 2000, pp. 4–5. Reprinted with permission.

Question

What explains why millions of economic resources tend to get arranged logically and productively rather than haphazardly and unproductively?

CHAPTER SUMMARY

2.1 ▶ ECONOMIC SYSTEMS

- The command system and the market system are the two broad types of economic systems used to address the economic problem. In the command system (or socialism or communism), government owns most resources, and central planners coordinate most economic activity. In the market system (or capitalism), private individuals own most resources, and markets coordinate most economic activity.

2.2 ▶ CHARACTERISTICS OF THE MARKET SYSTEM

- The market system is characterized by the private ownership of resources, including capital, and the freedom of individuals to engage in economic activities of their choice to advance their material well-being. Self-interest is the driving force of such an economy, and competition functions as a regulatory or control mechanism.

- In the market system, markets, prices, and profits organize and make effective the many millions of individual economic decisions that occur daily.

- The use of advanced technology, specialization, and the extensive use of capital goods are common features of market systems. Functioning as a medium of exchange, money eliminates the problems of bartering and permits easy trade and greater specialization, both domestically and internationally.

2.3 ▶ FIVE FUNDAMENTAL QUESTIONS

- Every economy faces five fundamental questions: (1) What goods and services will be produced? (2) How will the goods and services be produced? (3) Who will get the goods and services? (4) How will the system accommodate change? (5) How will the system promote progress?

- The market system produces products whose production and sale yield total revenue sufficient to cover total cost. It does not produce products for which total revenue continuously falls short of total cost. Competition forces firms to use the lowest-cost production techniques.

- Positive economic profit (total revenue minus total cost) indicates that an industry is prosperous and promotes its expansion. Losses signify that an industry is not prosperous and hasten its contraction.

- Consumer sovereignty means that both businesses and resource suppliers are subject to the wants of consumers. Through their dollar votes, consumers decide on the composition of output.

- The prices that a household receives for the resources it supplies to the economy determine that household's income. This income determines the household's claim on the economy's output. Those who have income to spend get the products produced in the market system.

- By communicating changes in consumer tastes to entrepreneurs and resource suppliers, the market system prompts appropriate adjustments in the allocation of the economy's resources. The market system also encourages technological advance and capital accumulation, both of which raise a nation's standard of living.

- Competition, the primary mechanism of control in the market economy, promotes a unity of self-interest and social interests. As directed by an invisible hand, competition harnesses the self-interest motives of businesses and resource suppliers to further the social interest.

2.4 ▶ THE DEMISE OF THE COMMAND SYSTEM

- The command systems of the Soviet Union and pre-reform China met their demise because of coordination difficulties under central planning and the lack of profit incentives that encourage product improvement, produce new products, and give rise to entrepreneurship.

2.5 ▶ THE CIRCULAR FLOW MODEL

- The circular flow model illustrates the flows of resources and products from households to businesses and from businesses to households, along with the corresponding monetary flows. Businesses are on the buying side of the resource market and the selling side of the product market. Households are on the selling side of the resource market and the buying side of the product market.

TERMS AND CONCEPTS

economic system, p. 32
command system, p. 32
market system, p. 32
private property, p. 32
freedom of enterprise, p. 33
freedom of choice, p. 33
self-interest, p. 33

competition, p. 33
market, p. 34
specialization, p. 35
division of labour, p. 35
medium of exchange, p. 36
barter, p. 36
money, p. 36

consumer sovereignty, p. 38
dollar votes, p. 38
creative destruction, p. 40
invisible hand, p. 41
circular flow diagram, p. 44
factor market, p. 44
product market, p. 44

STUDY QUESTIONS

LO 2.1 1. Contrast how a market system and a command economy try to cope with economic scarcity.

LO 2.2 2. How does self-interest help achieve society's economic goals? Why is there such a wide variety of desired goods and services in a market system? In what way are entrepreneurs and businesses at the helm of the economy but commanded by consumers?

LO 2.2 3. Why is private property, and the protection of property rights, so critical to the success of the market system?

LO 2.2 4. What are the advantages of using capital in the production process? What is meant by the term "division of labour"? What are the advantages of specialization in the use of human and material resources? Explain why exchange is the necessary consequence of specialization.

LO 2.2 5. What problem does barter entail? Indicate the economic significance of money as a medium of exchange. What is meant by the statement "We want money only to part with it"?

LO 2.2 6. Evaluate and explain the following statements:

   a. The market system is a profit-and-loss system.

   b. Competition is the disciplinarian of the market economy.

LO 2.3 7. In the 1990s thousands of dot-com companies emerged with great fanfare to take advantage of the Internet and new information technologies. A few, like Yahoo, eBay, and Amazon, have generally thrived and prospered, but many others struggled and eventually failed. Explain these varied outcomes in terms of how the market system answers the question "What goods and services will be produced?"

LO 2.3 8. **KEY QUESTION** With current technology, suppose a firm is producing 400 loaves of banana bread daily. Also, assume that the least-cost combination of resources in producing those loaves is 5 units of labour, 7 units of land, 2 units of capital, and 1 unit of entrepreneurial ability, selling at prices of $40, $60, $60, and $20, respectively. If the firm can sell these 400 loaves at $2 per unit, will it continue to produce banana bread? If this firm's situation is typical for the other makers of banana bread, will factors of production flow to or away from this bakery good?

9. **KEY QUESTION** Some large hardware stores such as **LO** Canadian Tire boast of carrying as many as 20,000 different products in each store. What motivated the producers of those individual products to make them and offer them for sale? How did the producers decide on the best combinations of factors to use? Who made those factors available, and why? Who decides whether these particular hardware products should continue to be produced and offered for sale?

10. What is meant by the term "creative destruction"? How does **LO** the emergence of MP3 (iPod) technology relate to this idea?

11. In a sentence, describe the meaning of the phrase "invisible **LO** hand."

12. In market economies, firms rarely worry about the availability of inputs to produce their products, whereas in a **LO** command economies input availability is a constant concern. Why the difference?

13. Distinguish between the factor market and the product market in the circular flow model. In what way are businesses **LO** and households both sellers and buyers in this model? What are the flows in the circular flow model?

INTERNET APPLICATION QUESTIONS @

1. **Diamonds—Interested in Buying One?** Use the links on the McConnell-Brue-Flynn-Barbiero Web site (Chapter 2) to access the Internet auction site eBay. Select the category Jewelry and Watches, followed by Loose Diamonds and Gemstones, and then Loose Diamonds. How many loose diamonds are for sale at the moment? Note the wide array of sizes and prices of the diamonds. In what sense is there competition among the sellers in this market? How does that competition influence prices? In what sense is there competition among buyers? How does that competition influence prices?

2. **Barter and the Canada Revenue Agency.** Bartering occurs when goods or services are exchanged without the exchange of money. For some, barter's popularity is that it enables them to avoid paying taxes to the government. How might such avoidance occur? Use the links on the McConnell-Brue-Flynn-Barbiero Web site (Chapter 2) to access the Canada Revenue Agency's (CRA) interpretation of barter transactions. Does the CRA treat barter as taxable or nontaxable income? How is the value of a barter transaction determined?

CHAPTER 3
Demand, Supply, and Market Equilibrium

According to an old joke, if you teach a parrot to say "demand and supply," you have an economist. There is much truth in this quip. The tools of demand and supply can take us far in understanding both specific economic issues and how individual markets work.

Markets bring together buyers ("demanders") and sellers ("suppliers"), and exist in many forms. The corner gas station, an e-commerce site, the local music store, a farmer's roadside stand—all are familiar markets. The Toronto Stock Exchange and the Chicago Board of Trade are markets where buyers and sellers of stocks and bonds and farm commodities from all over the world communicate with one another to buy and sell. Auctioneers bring together potential buyers and sellers of art, livestock, used farm equipment, and, sometimes, real estate. In labour markets, new college or university graduates "sell" and employers "buy" specific labour services.

Some markets are local, while others are national or international. Some are highly personal, involving face-to-face contact between demander and supplier; others are faceless, with buyer and seller never seeing or knowing each other.

To keep things simple, we will focus in this chapter on markets consisting of large numbers of buyers and sellers of standardized products. These are the highly competitive markets such as a central grain exchange, a stock market, or a market for foreign currencies in which the price is "discovered" through the interacting decisions of buyers and sellers. All such markets involve demand, supply, price, and quantity.

3.1 | Demand

Demand is a schedule or a curve that shows the various amounts of a product that consumers are willing and able to purchase at each of a series of possible prices during a specified period of time.[1] Demand shows the quantities of a product that will be purchased at various possible prices, other things equal. Demand can easily be shown in table form. Figure 3-1 shows a hypothetical demand schedule for a single consumer purchasing bushels of corn.

---

[1] This definition obviously is worded to apply to product markets. To adjust it to apply to factor markets, substitute the word *factor* for *product* and the word *businesses* for *consumers*.

FIGURE 3-1 **An Individual Buyer's Demand for Corn**

Because price and quantity demanded are inversely related, an individual's demand schedule graphs as a downward-sloping curve such as D. Specifically, the law of demand says that, other things equal, consumers will buy more of a product as its price declines. Here and in later figures, P stands for price, and Q stands for quantity (either demanded or supplied).

Price per bushel	Quantity demanded (bushels per week)
$5	10
4	20
3	35
2	55
1	80

ORIGIN 3.1
Demand
and Supply

demand
A schedule or curve that shows the various amounts of a product that consumers are willing and able to purchase at each of a series of possible prices during a specified period of time.

As price falls, the quantity demanded rises, and as price rises, the quantity demanded falls.

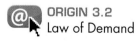

ORIGIN 3.2
Law of Demand

law of demand
Other things equal, as price falls the quantity demanded rises, and vice versa.

The table in Figure 3-1 reveals the relationship between the various prices of corn and the quantity of corn a particular consumer would be willing *and able* to purchase at each of these prices. We say willing *and able* because willingness alone is not effective in the market. You may be willing to buy a plasma television set, but if that willingness is not backed by the necessary dollars, it will not be effective and, therefore, will not be reflected in the market. If the price of corn were $5 per bushel, our consumer would be willing and able to buy 10 bushels per week; if it were $4, the consumer would be willing and able to buy 20 bushels per week, and so forth.

The table in Figure 3-1 does not tell us which of the five possible prices will actually exist in the corn market. That depends on the interaction between demand and supply. Demand is simply a statement of a buyer's plans, or intentions, with respect to the purchase of a product.

To be meaningful, the quantities demanded at each price must relate to a specific period—a day, a week, a month. Saying "a consumer will buy 10 bushels of corn at $5 per bushel" is meaningless. Unless a specific time period is stated, we do not know whether the demand for a product is large or small.

Law of Demand

A fundamental characteristic of demand is this: *Other things equal, as price falls the quantity demanded rises, and as price rises the quantity demanded falls.* There is a negative or *inverse* relationship between price and quantity demanded. This inverse relationship is called the **law of demand.**

The "other-things-equal" assumption is critical here (see Chapter 1). Many factors other than the price of the product being considered affect the amount purchased. The quantity of Nikes purchased will depend not only on the price of Nikes but also on the prices of substitutes such as Reeboks, Adidas, and New Balances. The law of demand in this case says that fewer Nikes will be purchased if the price of Nikes rises *and if the prices of Reeboks, Adidas, and New Balances all remain constant.* Another way of stating it is that if the *relative price* of Nikes rises, fewer Nikes will be bought.

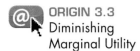

ORIGIN 3.3
Diminishing
Marginal Utility

diminishing marginal utility
As a consumer increases
the consumption of a good
or service, the marginal
utility obtained from each
additional unit of the good
or service decreases.

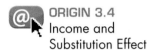

ORIGIN 3.4
Income and
Substitution Effect

income effect
A change in the price of a
product changes a consumer's
real income (purchasing
power) and thus the quantity
of the product purchased.

substitution effect
A change in the price of a
product changes the relative
expensiveness of that good
and hence changes the
willingness to buy it rather
than other goods.

MATH 3.1
The Demand
Function

demand curve
A curve illustrating the inverse
(negative) relationship between
the quantity demanded of a
good or service and its price,
other things equal.

Why the inverse relationship between price and quantity demanded? Let's look at two explanations:

- In any specific time period, each buyer of a product will derive less satisfaction (or benefit, or utility) from each successive unit of the product consumed. The second Big Mac will yield less additional satisfaction to the consumer than the first, and the third still less than the second. That is, consumption is subject to **diminishing marginal utility.** And because successive units of a particular product yield less and less marginal utility, consumers will buy additional units only if the price of those units is progressively reduced.

- We can also explain the law of demand in terms of *income* and *substitution* effects. The **income effect** indicates that a lower price increases the purchasing power of a buyer's money income, enabling the buyer to purchase more of the product than she or he could buy before. A higher price has the opposite effect. The **substitution effect** suggests that at a lower price, buyers have the incentive to substitute what is now a less expensive product for similar products that are now *relatively* more expensive. The product whose price has fallen is now "a better deal" relative to the other products.

For example, a decline in the price of chicken will increase the purchasing power of consumer incomes, enabling them to buy more chicken (the income effect). At a lower price, chicken is relatively more attractive and consumers tend to substitute it for pork, beef, and fish (the substitution effect). The income and substitution effects combine to make consumers able and willing to buy more of a product at a low price than at a high price.

The Demand Curve

The inverse relationship between price and quantity demanded for any product can be represented on a simple graph, in which, by convention, we measure *quantity demanded* on the horizontal axis and *price* on the vertical axis. In Figure 3-1 we have plotted the five price–quantity data points listed in the table and connected the points with a smooth curve, labelled *D*. Such a curve is called a **demand curve.** Its downward slope reflects the law of demand—people buy more of a product, service, or factor as its price falls. The relationship between price and quantity demanded is inverse (or negative). We also refer to the demand curve as the *marginal benefit curve*, a concept first introduced in Chapter 1. The demand curve tells us the extra benefit the consumer derives from one more unit of a good or service.

The table and the graph in Figure 3-1 contain exactly the same data and reflect the same relationship between price and quantity demanded. But the graph shows that relationship more simply and clearly than a table or a description in words.

Market Demand

So far, we have concentrated on just one consumer. By adding the quantities demanded by all consumers at each of the various possible prices, we can get from *individual* demand to *market* demand. If there are just three buyers in the market, as represented in Figure 3-2, it is relatively easy to determine the total quantity demanded at each price. Figure 3-2 shows the graphical summing procedure: At each price we sum horizontally the individual quantities demanded to obtain the total quantity demanded at that price; we then plot the price and the total quantity demanded as one point of the market demand curve.

Competition, of course, ordinarily entails many more than three buyers of a product. To avoid hundreds or thousands or millions of additions, we suppose that all the buyers in a market are willing and able to buy the same amounts at each of the possible prices. Then we just multiply those amounts by the number of buyers to obtain the market demand. This is how we arrived at the demand schedule and demand curve D_1, in Figure 3-3, for a market with 200 corn buyers. The table in Figure 3-3 shows the calculations for 200 corn buyers.

FIGURE 3-2
Market Demand for Corn, Three Buyers

The market demand curve D is the horizontal summation of the individual demand curves (D_1, D_2, and D_3) of all the consumers in the market. At the price of \$3, for example, the three individual curves yield a total quantity demanded of 100 bushels.

Price per bushel	Quantity demanded							Total quantity demanded per week
	Joe		Jen		Jay			
\$5	10	+	12	+	8	=		30
4	20	+	23	+	17	=		60
3	35	+	39	+	26	=		100
2	55	+	60	+	39	=		154
1	80	+	87	+	54	=		221

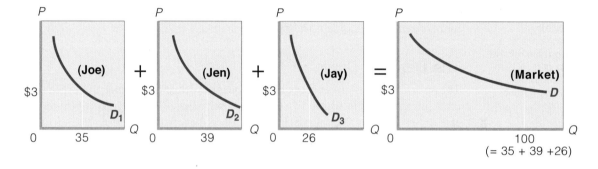

Determinants of Demand

determinants of demand
Factors other than price that determine the quantities demanded of a good or service.

In constructing a demand curve such as D_1 in Figure 3-3, we assume that price is the most important influence on the amount of any product purchased, even though other factors can and do affect purchases. These factors, called **determinants of demand,** are assumed to be constant when a demand curve like D_1 is drawn. They are the "other things equal" in the relationship between price and quantity demanded. When any of these determinants changes, the demand curve will shift to the right or left.

The basic determinants of demand are (1) consumers' tastes (preferences), (2) the number of consumers in the market, (3) consumers' incomes, (4) the prices of related goods, and (5) consumers' expectations.

Changes in Demand

A change in one or more of the determinants of demand will change the demand data (the demand schedule) in the table accompanying Figure 3-3, and therefore the location of the demand curve there. A change in the demand schedule—or, graphically, a shift in the demand curve—is called a *change in demand.*

If consumers desire to buy more corn at each possible price than is reflected in column 2 of the table in Figure 3-3, that *increase in demand* is shown as a shift of the demand curve to the right, say from D_1 to D_2. Conversely, a *decrease in demand* occurs when consumers buy less corn at each possible price than is indicated in column 2 of the table in Figure 3-3. The leftward shift of the demand curve from D_1 to D_3 in Figure 3-3 shows that situation.

Now let's see how changes in each determinant affect demand.

| FIGURE 3-3 | Changes in the Demand for Corn |

A change in one or more of the determinants of demand causes a change in demand. An increase in demand is shown as a shift of the demand curve to the right, as from D_1 to D_2. A decrease in demand is shown as a shift of the demand curve to the left, as from D_1 to D_3. These changes in demand are to be distinguished from a change in quantity demanded, which is caused by a change in the price of the product, as shown by a movement from, say, point *a* to point *b* on fixed demand curve D_1.

Market Demand for Corn, 200 Buyers, D_1	
(1) Price per bushel	(2) Total quantity demanded per week
$5	2,000
4	4,000
3	7,000
2	11,000
1	16,000

TASTES

A favourable change in consumer tastes (preferences) for a product—a change that makes the product more desirable—means that more of it will be demanded at each price. Demand will increase; the demand curve will shift rightward. An unfavourable change in consumer preferences will decrease demand, shifting the demand curve to the left.

New products may affect consumer tastes; for example, the introduction of digital cameras has greatly decreased demand for film cameras. Consumers' concern over the health hazards of cholesterol and obesity have increased the demand for broccoli, low-calorie sweeteners, and fresh fruit, while decreasing the demand for beef, veal, eggs, and whole milk. Over the past several years, the demand for coffee drinks and table wine has greatly increased, driven by changes in tastes. So, too, has the demand for DVDs and iPhones.

NUMBER OF BUYERS

An increase in the number of buyers in a market increases product demand; a decrease in the number of buyers decreases demand. For example, the rising number of older persons in Canada in recent years has increased the demand for motor homes, medical care, and retirement communities.

Immigration to Canada from many parts of the world has greatly increased the demand for a whole range of ethnic goods and services in southern Ontario and British Columbia. Improvements in communications have given financial markets international range and have thus increased the demand for stocks and bonds. International trade agreements have reduced foreign trade barriers to Canadian farm commodities, increasing the number of buyers and the demand for those products.

In contrast, the emigration (out-migration) from many small rural communities has reduced the population and thus the demand for housing, home appliances, and auto repair in those towns.

INCOME

How changes in income affect demand is more complex. For most products, a rise in income causes an increase in demand. Consumers typically buy more steaks, furniture, and electronic equipment as their incomes increase. Conversely, the demand for such products declines as income falls. Products for which demand varies directly with money income are called **normal goods.**

Although most products are normal goods, there are some exceptions. As incomes increase beyond some point, the demand for used clothing, retread tires, and third-hand automobiles may decrease, because the higher incomes enable consumers to buy new versions of those products. Similarly, rising incomes may cause the demand for charcoal grills to decline as wealthier consumers switch to gas grills. Goods for which demand varies *inversely* with money income are called **inferior goods.**

PRICES OF RELATED GOODS

A change in the price of a related good may either increase or decrease the demand for a product, depending on whether the related good is a substitute or a complement. A **substitute good** is one that can be used in place of another good. A **complementary good** is one that is used together with another good.

- *Substitutes*   Häagen-Dazs ice cream and Ben & Jerry's ice cream are substitute goods or, simply, *substitutes*. When two products are substitutes, an increase in the price of one will increase the demand for the other. Conversely, a decrease in the price of one will decrease the demand for the other. For example, when the price of Häagen-Dazs ice cream rises, consumers will demand less of it and increase their demand for Ben & Jerry's ice cream. When the price of Colgate toothpaste declines, the demand for Crest declines. So it is with other product pairs such as Nikes and Reeboks, Molson and Labatt beer, or Chevrolet and Ford pickup trucks. They are *substitutes in consumption*.

- *Complements*   Because complementary goods (or, simply, *complements*) are used together, they are typically demanded jointly. Examples include computers and software, cell phones and cellular service, and snowboards and lift tickets. If the price of a complement (for example, lettuce) goes up, the demand for the related good (salad dressing) will decline. Conversely, if the price of a complement (for example, tuition) falls, the demand for a related good (textbooks) will increase.

- *Unrelated Goods*   The vast majority of goods that are not related to one another are called *independent goods*. Examples are butter and golf balls, potatoes and automobiles, and bananas and wristwatches. A change in the price of one does not affect the demand for the other.

CONSUMER EXPECTATIONS

Changes in consumer expectations may shift demand. A newly formed expectation of higher future prices may cause consumers to buy now in order to "beat" the anticipated price rises, thus increasing current demand. That is often what happens in so-called hot real estate markets. Buyers rush in because they think the price of new homes will continue to escalate rapidly. Some buyers fear being "priced out of the market" and therefore not obtaining the home they desire. Other buyers—speculators—believe they will be able to sell the houses later at a higher price. Whichever their motivation, these buyers increase the demand for houses.

Similarly, a change in expectations concerning future income may prompt consumers to change their current spending. For example, first-round NHL draft choices may splurge on new luxury cars in anticipation of a lucrative professional hockey contract. Or workers who become fearful of losing their jobs may reduce their demand for, say, vacation travel.

---

normal good
A good or service whose consumption rises when income increases and falls when income decreases, price remaining constant.

inferior good
A good or service whose consumption declines as income rises (and conversely).

substitute goods
Products or services that can be used in place of each other.

complementary goods
Products and services that are used together.

TABLE 3-1	Determinants of Demand Curve Shifts

Determinant	Examples
Change in buyer tastes	Physical fitness rises in popularity, increasing the demand for jogging shoes and bicycles; cell phone popularity rises, reducing the demand for traditional phones.
Change in number of buyers	A decline in the birthrate reduces the demand for children's toys.
Change in income	A rise in incomes increases the demand for such normal goods as restaurant meals, sports tickets, and MP3 players while reducing the demand for such inferior goods as cabbage, turnips, and inexpensive wine.
Change in the prices of related goods	A reduction in airfares reduces the demand for bus transportation (substitute goods); a decline in the price of DVD players increases the demand for DVD movies (complementary goods).
Change in consumer expectations	Political instability in South America creates an expectation of higher future prices of coffee beans, thereby increasing today's demand for coffee beans.

In summary, an *increase* in demand—the decision by consumers to buy larger quantities of a product at each possible price—may be caused by:

- a favourable change in consumer tastes
- an increase in the number of buyers
- rising incomes if the product is a normal good
- falling incomes if the product is an inferior good
- an increase in the price of a substitute good
- a decrease in the price of a complementary good
- a new consumer expectation that prices and income will be higher in the future

You should "reverse" these generalizations to explain a *decrease* in demand. Table 3-1 provides additional illustrations of the determinants of demand. *(Key Question 3)*

Changes in Quantity Demanded

change in demand
A change in the quantity demanded of a good or service at every price.

change in quantity demanded
A movement from one point to another on a demand curve.

A *change in demand* must not be confused with a *change in quantity demanded*. A **change in demand** is a shift of the entire demand curve to the right (an increase in demand) or to the left (a decrease in demand). It occurs because the consumer's state of mind about purchasing the product has been altered in response to a change in one or more of the determinants of demand. Recall that *demand* is a schedule or a curve; therefore, a *change in demand* means a change in the schedule and a shift of the curve.

In contrast, a **change in quantity demanded** is a movement from one point to another point— from one price–quantity combination to another—on a fixed demand schedule or demand curve. The cause of such a change is an increase or decrease in the price of the product under consideration. In Figure 3-3, for example, a decline in the price of corn from $5 to $4 will increase the quantity of corn demanded from 2000 to 4000 bushels.

In Figure 3-3, the shift of the demand curve D_1 to either D_2 or D_3 is a change in demand. But the movement from point *a* to point *b* on curve D_1 represents a change in quantity demanded: Demand has not changed; it is the entire curve, and it remains fixed in place.

3.2 | Supply

supply
A schedule or curve that shows the amounts of a product that producers are willing and able to make available for sale at each of a series of possible prices during a specific period.

Supply is a schedule or curve that shows the amounts of a product that producers are willing and able to make available for sale at each of a series of possible prices during a specific period.[2] Figure 3-4 is a hypothetical supply schedule for a single producer of corn. It shows the quantities of corn that will be supplied at various prices, other things equal. We also refer to the supply curve as the *marginal cost curve,* a concept first introduced in Chapter 1. The supply curve tells us the extra cost incurred by a producer in producing one more unit of a good or service.

✓ Law of Supply

law of supply
The principle that, other things equal, an increase in the price of a product will increase the quantity of it supplied, and conversely for a price decrease.

The table in Figure 3-4 shows a direct relationship between price and quantity supplied. As price rises, the quantity supplied rises; as price falls, the quantity supplied falls. This relationship is called the **law of supply**. A supply schedule tells us that, other things equal, firms will produce and offer for sale more of their product at a high price than at a low price. The higher the price, the greater the incentive and the greater the quantity supplied.

Price is an obstacle from the standpoint of the consumer, who is on the paying end. The higher the price, the less the consumer will buy. But the supplier is on the receiving end of the product's price. To the supplier, price represents revenue, which serves as an incentive to produce and sell a product. The higher the price, the greater is the incentive and greater the quantity supplied.

Consider a farmer in Ontario who is deciding on how much corn to plant. As corn prices rise, as shown in the table in Figure 3-4, the farmer finds it profitable to plant more. And the higher corn prices enable the Ontario farmer to cover the increased costs associated with more intensive cultivation and the use of more seed, fertilizer, and pesticides. The overall result is more corn.

Now consider a manufacturer. Beyond some quantity of production, manufacturers usually encounter increasing *marginal cost*—the added cost of producing one more unit of output. Certain productive resources—in particular, the firm's plant and machinery—cannot be expanded quickly, so the firm uses more of other resources, such as labour, to produce more output. But as labour becomes more abundant relative to the fixed plant and equipment, the additional workers have relatively less space and access to equipment. For example, the added workers may have to wait to gain access to machines. As a result, each added worker produces less added output, and the marginal cost of successive units of output rises accordingly. The firm will not produce the more costly units unless it receives a higher price for them. Again, price and quantity supplied are directly related.

---

[2] This definition is worded to apply to product markets. To adjust it to apply to factor markets, substitute the word *factor* for *product* and the word *owner* for *producer.*

| FIGURE 3-4 | An Individual Producer's Supply of Corn |

Because price and quantity supplied are positively related, a firm's supply schedule is an upward-sloping curve such as S. Specifically, the law of supply says that, other things equal, firms will supply more of a product as its price rises.

Price per bushel	Quantity supplied (bushels per week)
$5	60
4	50
3	35
2	20
1	5

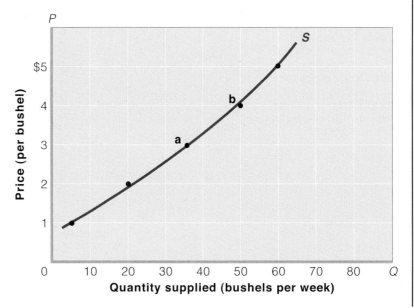

The Supply Curve

supply curve
A curve illustrating the positive (direct) relationship between the quantity supplied of a good or service and its price, other things equal.

As with demand, it is convenient to represent individual supply graphically. In Figure 3-4, curve S is the **supply curve** that corresponds with the price–quantity data in the accompanying table. The upward slope of the curve reflects the law of supply—a producer will offer more of a good, service, or factor for sale as its price rises. The relationship between price and quantity supplied is positive or direct.

MATH 3.2
The Supply
Function

Market Supply

Market supply is derived from individual supply in exactly the same way that market demand is derived from individual demand. We sum the quantities supplied by each producer at each price. That is, we obtain the market supply curve by "horizontally adding" the supply curves of the individual producers. The price–quantity supplied data in the table in Figure 3-5 are for an assumed 200 identical producers in the market, each willing to supply corn according to the supply schedule shown in Figure 3-4. Curve S_1 in Figure 3-5 is a graph of the market supply data. Note that the axes in Figure 3-5 are the same as those used in our graph of market demand (Figure 3-2). The only difference is that we change the label on the horizontal axis from "quantity demanded" to "quantity supplied."

Determinants of Supply

In constructing a supply curve, we assume that price is the most significant influence on the quantity supplied of any product. But other factors (the "other things equal") can and do affect supply. The supply curve is drawn on the assumption that these other things are fixed and do not change. If one of them does change, a *change in supply* will occur, meaning that the entire supply curve will shift.

determinants of supply
Causes other than price that determine the quantities supplied of a good or service.

The basic **determinants of supply** are (1) factor prices, (2) technology, (3) taxes and subsidies, (4) prices of other goods, (5) price expectations, and (6) the number of sellers in the market. A change in any one or more of these determinants of supply will move the supply curve for a product

FIGURE 3-5 **Changes in the Supply of Corn**

A change in one or more of the determinants of supply causes a shift in supply. An increase in supply is shown as a rightward shift of the supply curve, as from S_1 to S_2. A decrease in supply is depicted as a leftward shift of the curve, as from S_1 to S_3. In contrast, a change in the quantity supplied is caused by a change in the product's price and is shown by a movement from one point to another, as from *a* to *b*, on a fixed supply curve.

Market Supply of Corn, 200 Producers, S_1	
(1) Price per bushel	**(2) Total quantity supplied per week**
$5	12,000
4	10,000
3	7,000
2	4,000
1	1,000

either to the right or to the left. A shift to the *right*, as from S_1 to S_2 in Figure 3-5, signifies an *increase* in supply: Producers supply larger quantities of the product at each possible price. A shift to the *left*, as from S_1 to S_3, indicates a *decrease* in supply.

Changes in Supply

Let's consider how changes in each of the determinants affect supply. The key idea is that costs are a major factor underlying supply curves; anything that affects costs (other than changes in output itself) usually shifts the supply curve.

FACTOR PRICES

The prices of the factors used as inputs in the production process determine the costs of production. Higher *factor* prices raise production costs and, assuming a particular *product* price, squeeze profits. That reduction in profits reduces the incentive for firms to supply output at each product price. For example, an increase in the prices of iron ore and coke will increase the cost of producing steel for Dofasco and reduce its supply.

In contrast, lower *factor* prices reduce production costs and increase profits. So, when input prices fall, firms supply greater output at each product price. For example, a decrease in the prices of flat-panel glass will increase the supply of big-screen television sets.

TECHNOLOGY

Improvements in technology (techniques of production) enable firms to produce units of output with fewer inputs. Because inputs are costly, using fewer of them lowers production costs and increases supply. Example: Technological advances in producing flat-panel LCD (liquid crystal display) computer monitors have greatly reduced their cost. The manufacturers will now offer more such monitors than previously at various prices: the supply of flat-panel LCD monitors has increased.

TAXES AND SUBSIDIES

Businesses treat most taxes as costs. An increase in sales or property taxes will increase production costs and reduce supply. In contrast, subsidies are "taxes in reverse." If the government subsidizes the production of a good, it in effect lowers the producers' costs and increases supply. Government subsidies will, for example, help increase the number of rural medical practitioners.

PRICES OF OTHER GOODS

Firms that produce a particular product, say, soccer balls, can sometimes use their plant and equipment to produce alternative goods, say, basketballs and volleyballs. The higher prices of these "other goods" may entice soccer ball producers to switch production to those other goods to increase profits. This substitution in production results in a decline in the supply of soccer balls. Alternatively, when the prices of basketballs and volleyballs decline relative to the price of soccer balls, producers of those goods may decide to produce more soccer balls instead, increasing their supply.

PRODUCER EXPECTATIONS

Changes in expectations about the future price of a product may affect the producer's current willingness to supply that product. Ontario farmers anticipating a higher corn price in the future might withhold some of their current corn harvest from the market, thereby causing a decrease in the current supply of corn. In contrast, in many types of manufacturing industries, newly formed expectations that price will increase may induce firms to add another shift of workers or to expand their production facilities, causing current supply to increase.

NUMBER OF SELLERS

Other things equal, the larger the number of suppliers, the greater the market supply. As more firms enter an industry, the supply curve shifts to the right. Conversely, the smaller the number of firms in the industry, the less the market supply. This means that as firms leave an industry, the supply curve shifts to the left. Example: Canada and the United States have imposed restrictions on haddock fishing to replenish dwindling stocks. As part of that policy, the federal government has bought the boats of some of the haddock fishers as a way of putting them out of business and decreasing the catch. The result has been a decline in the market supply of haddock.

Table 3-2 is a checklist of the determinants of supply, along with further illustrations. *(Key Question 6)*

Changes in Quantity Supplied

change in supply
A change in the quantity supplied of a good or service at every price; a shift of the supply curve to the left or right.

The distinction between a *change in supply* and a *change in quantity supplied* mirrors the distinction between a change in demand and a change in quantity demanded. Because supply is a schedule or curve, a **change in supply** means a change in the entire schedule and a shift of the entire curve. An increase in supply shifts the curve to the right; a decrease in supply shifts it to the left. The cause of a change in supply is a change in one or more of the determinants of supply.

TABLE 3-2	Determinants of Supply Curve Shifts
Determinant	**Examples**
Change in factor prices	A decrease in the price of microchips increases the supply of computers; an increase in the price of crude oil reduces the supply of gasoline.
Change in technology	The development of more effective wireless technology increases the supply of cell phones.
Changes in taxes and subsidies	An increase in the excise tax on cigarettes reduces the supply of cigarettes; a decline in subsidies to universities reduces the supply of higher education.
Change in prices of other goods	An increase in the price of cucumbers decreases the supply of watermelons.
Change in producer expectations	An expectation of a substantial rise in future log prices decreases the supply of logs today.
Change in number of sellers	An increase in the number of Internet service providers increases the supply of such services; the formation of women's professional basketball leagues increases the supply of women's professional basketball games.

change in quantity supplied
A movement from one point to another on a fixed supply curve.

In contrast, a **change in quantity supplied** is a movement from one point to another on a fixed supply curve. The cause of such a movement is a change in the price of the specific product being considered. Consider supply curve S_1 in Figure 3-5. A decline in the price of corn from $4 to $3 decreases the quantity of corn supplied per week from 10,000 to 7000 bushels. This movement from point b to point a along S_1 is a change in quantity supplied, not a change in supply. Supply is the full schedule of prices and quantities shown, and this schedule does not change when the price of corn changes.

QUICK REVIEW

▶ A supply schedule or curve shows that, other things equal, the quantity of a good supplied varies directly with its price.

▶ The supply curve shifts because of changes in (a) factor prices, (b) technology, (c) taxes and subsidies, (d) prices of other goods, (e) producer expectations, and (f) the number of sellers.

▶ A change in supply is a shift of the supply curve; a change in quantity supplied is a movement from one point to another on a fixed supply curve.

3.3 | Market Equilibrium

With our understanding of demand and supply, we can now show how the decisions of buyers of corn interact with the decisions of the sellers to determine the price and quantity of corn. In the table in **Figure 3-6 (Key Graph)**, columns 1 and 2 repeat the market supply of corn (from Figure 3-5), and columns 2 and 3 repeat the market demand for corn (from the table in Figure 3-3). We assume this is a competitive market, so that neither buyers nor sellers can set the price.

Equilibrium Price and Quantity

equilibrium price
The price in a competitive market at which the quantity demanded and the quantity supplied are equal.

We are looking for the equilibrium price and equilibrium quantity. The **equilibrium price** (or "market-clearing price") is the price where the intentions of buyers and sellers match. It is the price where quantity demanded equals quantity supplied. The table in Figure 3-6 reveals that at $3, *and only at that price*, the number of bushels of corn that sellers wish to sell (7000) is identical to

KEY GRAPH

FIGURE 3-6
Equilibrium Price and Quantity

The intersection of the downward-sloping demand curve *D* and the upward-sloping supply curve *S* indicates the equilibrium price and quantity, here $3 and 7000 bushels of corn. The shortages of corn at below-equilibrium prices (for example, 7000 bushels at $2) drive up price. These higher prices increase the quantity supplied and reduce the quantity demanded until equilibrium is achieved. The surpluses caused by above-equilibrium prices (for example, 6000 bushels at $4) push price down. As price drops, the quantity demanded rises and the quantity supplied falls until equilibrium is established. At the equilibrium price and quantity, there are neither shortages nor surpluses of corn.

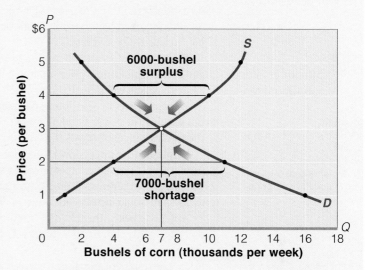

(1) Total quantity supplied per week	(2) Price per bushel	(3) Total quantity demanded per week	(4) Surplus (+) or shortage (−)
12,000	$5	2,000	+10,000↓
10,000	4	4,000	+ 6,000↓
7,000	3	7,000	0
4,000	2	11,000	− 7,000↑
1,000	1	16,000	−15,000↑

The arrows indicate the effect on price.

Quick Quiz

1. Demand curve *D* in Figure 3-6 is downward-sloping because:
   a. producers offer less product for sale as the price of the product falls.
   b. lower prices of a product create income and substitution effects, which lead consumers to purchase more of it.
   c. the larger the number of buyers in a market, the lower the product price.
   d. price and quantity demanded are directly (positively) related.

2. Supply curve *S*:
   a. reflects an inverse (negative) relationship between price and quantity supplied.
   b. reflects a direct (positive) relationship between price and quantity supplied.

   c. depicts the collective behaviour of buyers in this market.
   d. shows that producers will offer more of a product for sale at a low product price than at a high product price.

3. At the $3 price:
   a. quantity supplied exceeds quantity demanded.
   b. quantity demanded exceeds quantity supplied.
   c. the product is abundant and a surplus exists.
   d. there is no pressure on price to rise or fall.

4. At price $5 in this market:
   a. there will be a shortage of 10,000 units.
   b. there will be a surplus of 10,000 units.
   c. quantity demanded will be 12,000 units.
   d. quantity demanded will equal quantity supplied.

Answers: 1.b; 2.b; 3.d; 4.b

equilibrium quantity
The quantity demanded and supplied at the equilibrium price in a competitive market.

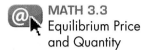

MATH 3.3
Equilibrium Price and Quantity

surplus
The amount by which the quantity supplied of a product exceeds the quantity demanded at a specific (above-equilibrium) price.

shortage
The amount by which the quantity demanded of a product exceeds the quantity supplied at a specific (below-equilibrium) price.

rationing function of prices
The ability of the competitive forces of supply and demand to establish a price at which selling and buying decisions are consistent.

productive efficiency
The production of a good in the least costly way.

allocative efficiency
The distribution of resources among firms and industries to produce the goods most wanted by society.

the number consumers want to buy (also 7000). At $3 and 7000 bushels of corn, there is neither a shortage nor a surplus of corn. So 7000 bushels of corn is the **equilibrium quantity:** the quantity demanded and quantity supplied at the equilibrium price in a competitive market.

Graphically, the equilibrium price is indicated by the intersection of the supply curve and the demand curve in Figure 3-6. (The horizontal axis now measures both quantity demanded and quantity supplied.) With neither a shortage nor a surplus at $3, the market is in equilibrium, meaning "in balance" or "at rest."

To better understand the uniqueness of the equilibrium price, let's consider other prices. At any above-equilibrium price, quantity supplied exceeds quantity demanded. For example, at the $4 price, sellers will offer 10,000 bushels of corn, but buyers will purchase only 4000. The $4 price encourages sellers to offer lots of corn but discourages many consumers from buying it. The result is a **surplus** (or *excess supply*) of 6000 bushels. If corn sellers produced them all, they would find themselves with 6000 unsold bushels of corn.

Surpluses drive prices down. Even if the $4 price existed temporarily, it could not persist. The large surplus would prompt competing sellers to lower the price to encourage buyers to take the surplus off their hands. As the price fell, the incentive to produce corn would decline and the incentive for consumers to buy corn would increase. As shown in Figure 3-6, the market would move to its equilibrium at $3.

Any price below the $3 equilibrium price would create a shortage; quantity demanded would exceed quantity supplied. Consider a $2 price, for example. We see both from column 2 of the table and from the demand curve in Figure 3-6 that quantity demanded exceeds quantity supplied at that price. The result is a **shortage** (or *excess demand*) of 7000 bushels of corn. The $2 price discourages sellers from devoting resources to corn and encourages consumers to desire more bushels than are available. The $2 price cannot persist as the equilibrium price. Many consumers who want to buy corn at this price will not obtain it. They will express a willingness to pay more than $2 to get corn. Competition among these buyers will drive up the price, eventually to the $3 equilibrium level. Unless disrupted by supply or demand changes, this $3 price of corn will continue to prevail.

Rationing Function of Prices

The ability of the competitive forces of supply and demand to establish a price at which selling and buying decisions are consistent is called the **rationing function of prices.** In our case, the equilibrium price of $3 clears the market, leaving no burdensome surplus for sellers and no inconvenient shortage for potential buyers. It is the combination of freely made individual decisions that sets this market-clearing price. In effect, the market outcome says that all buyers who are willing and able to pay $3 for a bushel of corn will obtain it; all buyers who cannot or will not pay $3 will go without corn. Similarly, all producers who are willing and able to offer corn for sale at $3 a bushel will sell it; all producers who cannot or will not sell for $3 per bushel will not sell their product. *(Key Question 8)*

Efficient Allocation

A competitive market such as that we have described not only rations goods to consumers but also allocates society's resources efficiently to the particular product. Competition among corn producers forces them to use the best technology and right mix of productive resources. Otherwise, their costs will be too high relative to the market price and they will be unprofitable. The result is **productive efficiency:** the production of any particular good in the least costly way. When society produces corn at the lowest achievable per-unit cost, it is expending the smallest amount of resources to produce that product and therefore is making available the largest amount of resources to produce other desired goods. Suppose society has only $100 worth of resources available. If it can produce a bushel of corn using $3 of those resources, then it will have available $97 of resources remaining to produce other goods. This is clearly better than producing the corn for $5 and having only $95 of resources available for the alternative uses.

Competitive markets also produce **allocative efficiency:** the *particular mix* of goods and services most highly valued by society (minimum-cost production assumed). For example, society wants land suitable for growing corn used for that purpose, not to grow dandelions. It wants diamonds to

CONSIDER THIS | Ticket Scalping: A Bum Rap!

Ticket prices for athletic events and musical concerts are usually set far in advance of the events. Sometimes the original ticket price is too low to be the equilibrium price. Lines form at the ticket window, and a severe shortage of tickets occurs at the printed price. What happens next? Buyers who are willing to pay more than the original price bid up the ticket price in resale ticket markets.

Tickets sometimes get resold for much greater amounts than the original price—in a market transaction known as "scalping." For example, an original buyer may resell a $75 ticket to a concert for $200, $250, or more. The media sometimes denounces scalpers for "ripping off" buyers by charging "exorbitant" prices.

But is scalping really a rip-off? We must first recognize that such ticket resales are voluntary transactions. If both buyer and seller did not expect to gain from the exchange, it would not occur! The seller must value the $200 more than seeing the event, and the buyer must value seeing the event at $200 or more. So there are no losers or victims

here: Both buyer and seller benefit from the transaction. The "scalping" market simply redistributes assets (game or concert tickets) from those who would rather have the money (and the other things money can buy) to those who would rather have the tickets.

Does scalping impose losses or injury on the sponsors of the event? If the sponsors are injured, it is because they initially priced tickets below the equilibrium level. Perhaps they did this to create a long waiting line and the attendant media publicity. Alternatively, they may have had a genuine desire to keep tickets affordable for lower-income, ardent fans. In either case, the event sponsors suffer an opportunity cost in the form of less ticket revenue than they might have otherwise received. But such losses are self-inflicted and quite separate and distinct from the fact that some tickets are later resold at a higher price.

So is ticket scalping undesirable? Not on economic grounds! It is an entirely voluntary activity that benefits both sellers and buyers.

---

be used for jewellery, not crushed up and used as an additive to give concrete more sparkle. It wants MP3 players and iPods, not cassette players and tapes. Moreover, society does not want to devote all its resources to corn, diamonds, and portable digital music players. It wants to assign some resources to wheat, gasoline, and cell phones. Competitive markets make those proper assignments.

MATH 3.4
Allocative
Efficiency

The equilibrium price and quantity in competitive markets usually produce an assignment of resources that is "right" from an economic perspective. Demand essentially reflects the marginal benefit (MB) of the good (the extra benefit received from consuming one more unit of a good or service) and supply reflects the marginal cost (MC) of the good (the extra cost associated with producing one more unit of a good or service). The market ensures that firms produce all units of goods for which MB exceeds MC, and no units for which MC exceeds MB. At the intersection of the demand and supply curves, MB equals MC and allocative efficiency results. As economists say, there is neither an underallocation of resources nor an overallocation of resources to the product. We say more about productive and allocative efficiency in later chapters of *Microeconomics*.

 ## Changes in Supply, Demand, and Equilibrium

We know that demand might change because of fluctuations in consumer tastes or incomes, changes in consumer expectations, or variations in the prices of related goods. Supply might change in response to changes in resource prices, technology, or taxes. What effects will such changes in supply and demand have on equilibrium price and quantity?

CHANGES IN DEMAND

Suppose that the supply for some good (for example, potatoes) is constant and demand increases, as shown in Figure 3-7a. As a result, the new intersection of the supply and demand curves is at higher values on both the price and quantity axes. An increase in demand raises both equilibrium price and equilibrium quantity. Conversely, a decrease in demand, such as that shown in Figure 3-7b, reduces

FIGURE 3-7   **Changes in Demand and Supply and the Effects on Price and Quantity**

The increase in demand from D_1 to D_2 in panel (a) increases both equilibrium price and quantity. The decrease in demand from D_1 to D_2 in panel (b) decreases both equilibrium price and quantity. The increase in supply from S_1 to S_2 in panel (c) decreases equilibrium price and increases equilibrium quantity. The decline in supply from S_1 to S_2 in panel (d) increases equilibrium price and decreases equilibrium quantity. The boxes in the top right corners summarize the respective changes and outcomes. The upward arrows in those boxes signify increases in demand (D), supply (S), equilibrium price (P), and equilibrium quantity (Q); the downward arrows signify decreases in these items.

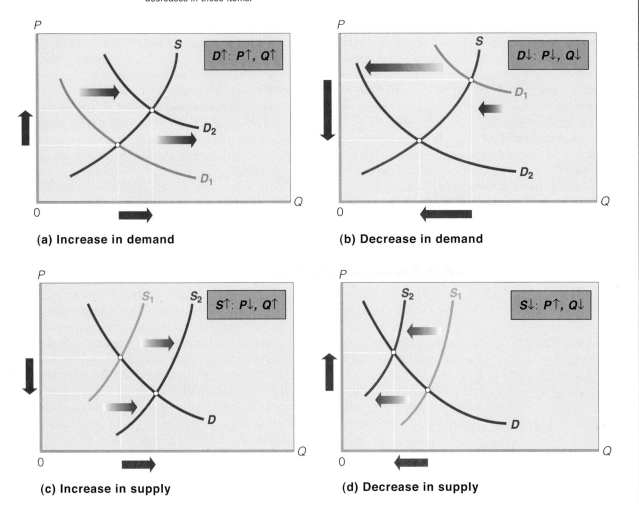

(a) Increase in demand

(b) Decrease in demand

(c) Increase in supply

(d) Decrease in supply

both equilibrium price and equilibrium quantity. (The value of graphical analysis is now apparent: We need not fumble with columns of figures to determine the outcomes; we need only compare the new and the old points of intersection on the graph.)

CHANGES IN SUPPLY

What happens if demand for some good (for example, flash drives) is constant but supply increases, as in Figure 3-7c? The new intersection of supply and demand is located at a lower equilibrium price but at a higher equilibrium quantity. An increase in supply reduces equilibrium price but increases equilibrium quantity. In contrast, if supply decreases, as in Figure 3-7d, the equilibrium price rises while the equilibrium quantity declines.

COMPLEX CASES

When both supply and demand change, the effect is a combination of the individual effects. As you study the following cases, keep in mind that each effect on the demand and supply curves has to be considered independently.

1. **Supply Increase; Demand Decrease**   What effect will a supply increase and a demand decrease for some good (for example, apples) have on equilibrium price? Both changes decrease price, so the net result is a price drop greater than that resulting from either change alone.

   What about equilibrium quantity? Here the effects of the changes in supply and demand are opposed: The increase in supply increases equilibrium quantity, but the decrease in demand reduces it. The direction of the change in quantity depends on the relative sizes of the changes in supply and demand. If the increase in supply is larger than the decrease in demand, the equilibrium quantity will increase. But if the decrease in demand is greater than the increase in supply, the equilibrium quantity will decrease.

2. **Supply Decrease; Demand Increase**   A decrease in supply and an increase in demand for some good (for example, gasoline) both increase price. Their combined effect is an increase in equilibrium price greater than that caused by either change separately. But their effect on equilibrium quantity is again indeterminate, depending on the relative sizes of the changes in supply and demand. If the decrease in supply is larger than the increase in demand, the equilibrium quantity will decrease. In contrast, if the increase in demand is greater than the decrease in supply, the equilibrium quantity will increase.

3. **Supply Increase; Demand Increase**   What if supply and demand both increase for some good (for example, cell phones)? A supply increase drops equilibrium price, while a demand increase boosts it. If the increase in supply is greater than the increase in demand, the equilibrium price will fall. If the opposite holds, the equilibrium price will rise.

   The effect on equilibrium quantity is certain: The increases in supply and in demand each raise equilibrium quantity. Therefore, the equilibrium quantity will increase by an amount greater than that caused by either change alone.

MATH 3.5
Changes in supply, demand, and equilibrium.

4. **Supply Decrease; Demand Decrease**   What about decreases in both supply and demand? If the decrease in supply is greater than the decrease in demand, equilibrium price will rise. If the reverse is true, equilibrium price will fall. Because decreases in supply and in demand each reduce equilibrium quantity, we can be sure that equilibrium quantity will fall.

CONSIDER THIS | Salsa and Coffee Beans

If you forget the other-things-equal assumption, you can encounter situations that seem to be in conflict with the laws of demand and supply. For example, suppose salsa manufacturers sell 1 million bottles of salsa at $4 a bottle in one year; 2 million bottles at $5 in the next year; and 3 million at $6 in the year thereafter. Price and quantity purchased vary directly, and these data seem to be at odds with the law of demand.

But there is no conflict here; the data do not refute the law of demand. The catch is that the law of demand's other-things-equal assumption has been violated over the three years in the example. Specifically, because of changing tastes and rising incomes, the demand for salsa has increased sharply, as in Figure 3-7a. The result is higher prices and larger quantities purchased.

Another example: The price of coffee beans occasionally has shot upward at the same time that the quantity of coffee beans harvested has declined. These events seemingly contradict the direct relationship between price and quantity denoted by supply. The other-things-equal assumption underlying the upsloping supply curve was violated. Poor coffee harvests decreased supply, as in Figure 3-7d, increasing the equilibrium price of coffee and reducing the equilibrium quantity.

The laws of demand and supply are not refuted by observations of price and quantity made over periods of time in which either demand or supply changes.

TABLE 3-3	Effects of Changes in Both Supply and Demand		
	Change in supply	Change in demand	Effect on equilibrium price	Effect on equilibrium quantity

	Change in supply	Change in demand	Effect on equilibrium price	Effect on equilibrium quantity
1	Increase	Decrease	Decrease	Indeterminate *Depend on Suply or demand*
2	Decrease	Increase	Increase	Indeterminate
3	Increase	Increase	Indeterminate	Increase
4	Decrease	Decrease	Indeterminate	Decrease

Table 3-3 summarizes these four cases. To understand them fully you should draw supply and demand diagrams for each case to confirm the effects listed in Table 3-3.

Special cases arise when a decrease in demand and a decrease in supply, or an increase in demand and an increase in supply, exactly cancel out. In both cases, the net effect on equilibrium price will be zero; price will not change. **(Key Question 9)**

The optional appendix accompanying this chapter provides examples of situations in which both supply and demand change over the same period of time.

3.4 | Application: Government-Set Prices

Prices in most markets are free to rise or fall to their equilibrium levels, no matter how high or low that might be. However, government sometimes concludes that supply and demand will produce prices that are unfairly high for buyers or unfairly low for sellers. So government may place legal limits on how high or low a price or prices may go. Is that a good idea?

Price Ceilings

price ceiling
A legally established maximum price for a good or service.

A **price ceiling** is the maximum legal price a seller may charge for a product or service. A price at or below the ceiling is legal; a price above it is not. The rationale for establishing price ceilings (or ceiling prices) on specific products is that they purportedly enable consumers to obtain some essential good or service that they could not afford at the equilibrium price. Examples are rent controls and usury laws, which specify maximum prices in the forms of rent and interest that can be charged to borrowers.

GRAPHICAL ANALYSIS

To be effective, a price ceiling on gasoline must be below the equilibrium price.

We can easily demonstrate the effects of price ceilings graphically using the example of gasoline. Let's suppose that rapidly rising world income boosts the purchase of automobiles and shifts the demand for gasoline to the right so that the equilibrium or market price reaches $1.25 per litre, shown as P_0 in Figure 3-8. The rapidly rising price of gasoline greatly burdens low-income and moderate-income households, who pressure the federal government to "do something." To keep gasoline affordable for these households, the government imposes a ceiling price, P_c, of $0.75 per litre. To be effective, a price ceiling must be below the equilibrium price. A ceiling price of $1.50, for example, would have no immediate effect on the gasoline market.

What are the effects of this $0.75 ceiling price? The rationing ability of the free market is rendered ineffective. Because the ceiling price, P_c, is below the market-clearing price, P_0, there is a shortage of gasoline. The quantity of gasoline demanded at P_c is Q_d and the quantity supplied is only Q_s; an excess demand or shortage of amount $Q_d - Q_s$ occurs.

The price ceiling, P_c, prevents the usual market adjustment in which competition among buyers bids up price, inducing more production and rationing some buyers out of the market. That process would continue until the shortage disappeared at the equilibrium price and quantity, P_0 and Q_0.

| FIGURE 3·8 | **A Price Ceiling Results in a Shortage** |

A price ceiling is a maximum legal price, such as P_c. When the ceiling price is below the equilibrium price a persistent product shortage results. Here that shortage is shown by the horizontal distance between Q_d and Q_s.

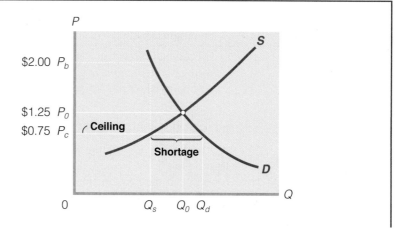

RATIONING PROBLEM

How will the government apportion the available supply, Q_s, among buyers who want the greater amount Q_d? Should gasoline be distributed on a first-come, first-served basis—that is, to those willing and able to get in line the soonest and to stay in line? Or should gas stations distribute it on the basis of favouritism? Since an unregulated shortage does not lead to an equitable distribution of gasoline, the federal government must establish some formal system for rationing it to consumers. One option is to issue ration coupons, which allow coupon-holders to purchase a fixed amount of gasoline per month. The rationing system might require the printing of coupons for Q_s litres of gasoline and then the equal distribution of the coupons among consumers so that the wealthy family of four and the poor family of four both receive the same number of coupons.

BLACK MARKETS

Ration coupons would not prevent a second problem from arising. The demand curve in Figure 3-8 tells us that many buyers are willing to pay more than the ceiling price P_c, and, of course, it is more profitable for gasoline stations to sell at prices above the ceiling. For example, at Q_s in Figure 3-8 some consumers would be willing to pay a price of up to $2.00 ($P_b$) to acquire some gasoline. Thus, despite the sizable enforcement bureaucracy that will accompany the price controls, *black markets* in which gasoline is illegally bought and sold at prices above the legal limits will flourish. Counter-feiting of ration coupons will also be a problem, and since the price of gasoline is now set by the federal government, there would be political pressure to set the price even lower.

CREDIT CARD INTEREST CEILINGS

Over the years there have been many calls in Canada for interest-rate ceilings on credit card accounts. The usual rationale for interest-rate ceilings is that the chartered banks and retail stores issuing such cards are presumably taking unfair advantage of users—and, in particular, lower-income users—by charging interest rates that average about 18 percent per year.

What might be the responses if the Canadian government imposed a below-equilibrium interest rate on credit cards? The lower interest income associated with a legal interest ceiling would require the issuers of cards to reduce their costs or enhance their revenues:

- Card issuers might tighten credit standards to reduce losses due to non-payment and collection costs. Then, low-income and young Canadians who have not yet established their creditworthi-ness would find it more difficult to obtain credit cards.

- The annual fee charged to cardholders might be increased, as might the fee charged to merchants for processing credit card sales. Similarly, card users might be charged a fee for every transaction.

- Card users now have a post-purchase grace period during which the credit provided is interest-free. That period might be shortened or eliminated.

- Certain "enhancements" that accompany some credit cards (for example, extended warranties on products bought with a card) might be eliminated.

- Oil companies, such as Petro-Canada, that issue their own cards to consumers who buy from their gasoline stations might increase their prices to help offset the decline of interest income; customers who pay cash would in effect be subsidizing customers who use credit cards.

Price Floors

price floor
A legally established price above an equilibrium price.

A **price floor** is a minimum price fixed by the government. A price at or above the price floor is legal; a price below it is not. Price floors above equilibrium prices are usually invoked when society believes that the free functioning of the market system has not provided a sufficient income for certain groups of resource suppliers or producers. Supported prices for some agricultural products and current minimum wages are two examples of price (or wage) floors. Let's analyze the results of imposing a price floor on wheat.

Suppose the equilibrium price for wheat is $3 per bushel and, because of that low price, many Prairie farmers have extremely low incomes. The federal government decides to help by establishing a legal price floor or price support of $4 per bushel.

What will be the effects? At any price above the equilibrium price, quantity supplied will exceed quantity demanded—that is, there will be an excess supply or surplus of the product. Prairie farmers will be willing to produce and offer for sale more than private buyers are willing to purchase at the price floor. As we saw with a price ceiling, an imposed legal price disrupts the rationing ability of the free market.

Supported prices for some agricultural products are an example of price floors.

GRAPHICAL ANALYSIS

Figure 3-9 illustrates the effect of a price floor on wheat. Suppose that S and D are the supply and demand curves for wheat. Equilibrium price and quantity are P_0 and Q_0, respectively. If the federal government imposes a price floor of P_f, farmers will produce Q_s, but private buyers will purchase only Q_d. The surplus is the excess of Q_s over Q_d.

FIGURE 3-9   ## A Price Floor Results in a Surplus

A price floor is a minimum legal price, such as P_f. When the price floor is above the equilibrium price, a persistent product surplus results. Here that surplus is shown by the horizontal distance between Q_s and Q_d.

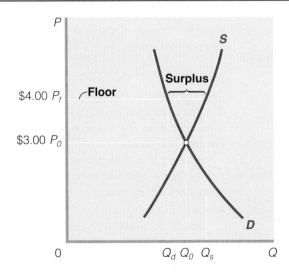

The government can cope with the surplus resulting from a price floor in only two ways:

1. It can restrict supply (for example, by asking farmers in Alberta, Saskatchewan, and Manitoba to agree to take a certain amount of land out of production) or increase demand (for example, by researching new uses for the product involved). These actions may reduce the difference between the equilibrium price and the price floor and thereby reduce the size of the resulting surplus.

2. The federal government can purchase the surplus output at the $4 price (thereby subsidizing Prairie farmers) and store or otherwise dispose of it.

ADDITIONAL CONSEQUENCES

Price floors such as P_f in Figure 3-9 not only disrupt the rationing ability of prices but also distort resource allocation. Without the price floor, the $3 equilibrium price of wheat would cause financial losses and force high-cost wheat producers to plant other crops or abandon farming altogether. But the $4 price floor allows them to continue to grow wheat and remain farmers. So society devotes too many of its scarce resources to wheat production and too few to producing other, more valuable, goods and services. It fails to achieve allocative efficiency.

That's not all. Consumers of wheat-based products pay higher prices because of the price floor. Taxpayers pay higher taxes to finance the government's purchase of the surplus. Also, the price floor causes potential environmental damage by encouraging wheat farmers to bring "marginal land" into production. The higher price also prompts imports of wheat. But, since such imports would increase the quantity of wheat supplied and thus undermine the price floor, the government needs to erect tariffs (taxes on imports) to keep the foreign wheat out. Such tariffs usually prompt other countries to retaliate with their own tariffs against Canadian agricultural or manufacturing exports.

It is easy to see why economists "sound the alarm" when politicians advocate imposing price ceilings or price floors such as price controls, interest-rate lids, or agricultural price supports. In all these cases, good intentions lead to bad economic outcomes. Government-controlled prices cause shortages or surpluses, distort resource allocation, and produce negative side effects. *(Key Question 14)*

QUICK REVIEW

▶ In competitive markets, prices adjust to the equilibrium level at which quantity demanded equals quantity supplied.

▶ The equilibrium price and quantity are those indicated by the intersection of the supply and demand curves for any product or resource.

▶ An increase in demand increases equilibrium price and quantity; a decrease in demand decreases equilibrium price and quantity.

▶ An increase in supply reduces equilibrium price but increases equilibrium quantity; a decrease in supply increases equilibrium price but reduces equilibrium quantity.

▶ Over time, equilibrium price and quantity may change in directions that seem at odds with the laws of demand and supply because the other-things-equal assumption is violated.

▶ Government-controlled prices in the form of ceilings and floors stifle the rationing functions of prices, distort resource allocations, and cause negative side effects.

The **LAST WORD**   A Legal Market for Human Organs?

A legal market might eliminate the present shortage of human organs for transplant. But many serious objections exist to turning human body parts into commodities for purchase and sale.

It has become increasingly commonplace in medicine to transplant kidneys, lungs, livers, eye corneas, pancreases, and hearts from deceased individuals to those whose organs have failed or are failing. But surgeons and many of their patients face a growing problem: Too few donated organs are available for transplant. Not everyone who needs a transplant can get one. Indeed, an inadequate supply of donated organs causes an estimated 400 Canadian deaths per year.

Why Shortages? Seldom do we hear of shortages of desired goods in market economies. What is different about organs for transplant? One difference is that no legal market exists for human organs. To understand this situation, observe the demand curve D_1 and supply curve S_1 in the accompanying figure. The downward slope of the demand curve tells us that if there were a market for human organs, the quantity of organs demanded would be greater at lower prices than at higher prices. Vertical supply curve S_1 represents the fixed quantity of human organs now donated via consent before death. Because the price of these donated organs is in effect zero, quantity demanded, Q_3, exceeds quantity supplied, Q_1. The shortage of $Q_3 - Q_1$ is rationed through a waiting list of those in medical need of transplants. Many people die while still on the waiting list.

Use of a Market A market for human organs would increase the incentive to donate organs. Such a market might work like this: An individual might specify in a legal document a willingness to sell one or more usable human organs on death or brain death. The person could specify where the money from the sale would go, for example, to family, a church, an educational institution, or a charity. Firms would then emerge to purchase organs and resell them where needed for profit. Under such a system, the supply curve of usable organs would take on the normal upward slope of typical supply curves. The higher the expected price of an organ, the greater the number of people willing to have their organs sold at death. Suppose that the supply curve is S_2 in the figure. At the equilibrium price P_1, the number of organs made available for transplant (Q_2) would equal the number purchased for transplant (also Q_2). In this generalized case, the shortage of organs would be eliminated and,

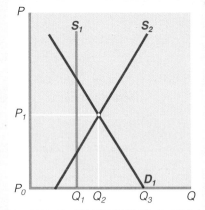

of particular importance, the number of organs available for transplanting would rise from Q_1 to Q_2. More lives would be saved and enhanced than under the present donor system.

Objections In view of this positive outcome, why is there no such market for human organs? Critics of market-based solutions have two main objections. The first is a moral objection: Critics feel that turning human organs into commodities commercializes human beings and diminishes the special nature of human life. They say there is something unseemly about selling and buying body organs as if they were bushels of wheat or ounces of gold. Moreover, critics note that the market would ration the available organs (as represented by Q_2 in the figure) to people who either can afford them (at P_1) or have health insurance for transplants. Second, a health cost objection suggests that a market for body organs would greatly increase the cost of health care. Rather than obtaining freely donated (although too few) body organs, patients would have to pay market prices for them, increasing the cost of medical care.

Rebuttal Supporters of market-based solutions to organ shortages point out that the market is simply being driven underground. Worldwide, an estimated $1 billion annual illegal market in human organs has emerged. As in other illegal markets, the unscrupulous tend to thrive.

Question

How many organ transplants were done in Canada in the latest year for which statistics are available? What is the current overall number of Canadian candidates waiting for an organ transplant? (For the answer, visit the London Health Sciences Centre Web site, www.lhsc.on.ca/About_Us/MOTP/). Do you favour the establishment of a legal market for transplant organs? Why or why not?

CHAPTER SUMMARY

3.1 ▶ DEMAND

- Demand is a schedule or curve representing the willingness of buyers in a specific period to purchase a particular product at each of various prices. The law of demand implies that consumers will buy more of a product at a low price than at a high price. Therefore, other things equal, the relationship between price and quantity demanded is negative or inverse and is graphed as a downward-sloping curve.

- Market demand curves are found by summing up (horizontally) the demand curves of the many individual consumers in the market.

- Changes in one or more of the determinants of demand (consumer tastes, the number of buyers in the market, the money incomes of consumers, the prices of related goods, and consumer expectations) shift the market demand curve. A shift to the right is an increase in demand; a shift to the left is a decrease in demand. A change in demand is different from a change in the quantity demanded, the latter being a movement from one point to another point on a fixed demand curve because of a change in the product's price.

3.2 ▶ SUPPLY

- Supply is a schedule or curve showing the amounts of a product that producers are willing to offer in the market at each possible price during a specific period. The law of supply states that, other things equal, producers will offer more of a product at a high price than at a low price. Thus, the relationship between price and quantity supplied is positive or direct, and supply is graphed as an upward-sloping curve.

- The market supply curve is the horizontal summation of the supply curves of the individual producers of the product.

- Changes in one or more of the determinants of supply (factor prices, technology, taxes and subsidies, price expectations, or the number of sellers in the market) shift the supply curve of a product. A shift to the right is an increase in supply; a shift to the left is a decrease in supply. In contrast, a change in the price of the product being considered causes a change in the quantity supplied, which is shown as a movement from one point to another point on a fixed supply curve.

3.3 ▶ MARKET EQUILIBRIUM

- The equilibrium price and quantity are established at the intersection of the supply and demand curves. The interaction of market demand and market supply adjusts the price to the point at which the quantity demanded and supplied are equal. This is the equilibrium price. The corresponding quantity is the equilibrium quantity.

- The ability of market forces to synchronize selling and buying decisions to eliminate potential surpluses and shortages is known as the rationing function of prices.

- A change in either demand or supply changes the equilibrium price and quantity. Increases in demand raise both equilibrium price and equilibrium quantity; decreases in demand lower both equilibrium price and equilibrium quantity. Increases in supply lower equilibrium price and raise equilibrium quantity; decreases in supply raise equilibrium price and lower equilibrium quantity.

- Simultaneous changes in demand and supply affect equilibrium price and quantity in various ways, depending on their direction and relative magnitudes.

3.4 ▶ APPLICATION: GOVERNMENT-SET PRICES

- A price ceiling is a maximum price set by government and is designed to help consumers.

- A price floor is a minimum price set by government and is designed to aid producers.

- Government-set prices stifle the rationing function of prices and distort the allocation of resources.

TERMS AND CONCEPTS

STUDY QUESTIONS

LO ▸ 3.1 1. Explain the law of demand. Why does a demand curve slope downward? How is a market demand curve derived from individual demand curves?

LO ▸ 3.1 2. What are the determinants of demand? What happens to the demand curve when any of these determinants change? Distinguish between a change in demand and a change in the quantity demanded, noting the cause(s) of each.

LO ▸ 3.1 3. **KEY QUESTION** What effect will each of the following have on the demand for small automobiles such as the Mini Cooper and Smart Car?

   a. Small automobiles become more fashionable.

   b. The price of large automobiles rises (with the price of small autos remaining the same).

   c. Income declines and small autos are an inferior good.

   d. Consumers anticipate that the price of small autos will greatly come down in the near future.

   e. The price of gasoline substantially drops.

LO ▸ 3.2 4. Explain the law of supply. Why does the supply curve slope upward? How is the market supply curve derived from the supply curves of individual producers?

LO ▸ 3.2 5. What are the determinants of supply? What happens to the supply curve when any of these determinants change? Distinguish between a change in supply and a change in the quantity supplied, noting the cause(s) of each.

LO ▸ 3.2 6. **KEY QUESTION** What effect will each of the following have on the supply of auto tires?

   a. A technological advance in the methods of producing tires.

   b. A decline in the number of firms in the tire industry.

   c. An increase in the price of rubber used in the production of tires.

   d. The expectation that the equilibrium price of auto tires will be lower in the future than currently.

   e. A decline in the price of the large tires used for semi-trailers and earth-hauling rigs (with no change in the price of auto tires).

   f. The levying of a per-unit tax on each auto tire sold.

   g. The granting of a subsidy of 50 cents per unit for each auto tire produced.

LO ▸ 3.3 7. "In the corn market, demand often exceeds supply and supply sometimes exceeds demand." "The price of corn rises and falls in response to changes in supply and demand." In which of these two statements are the terms "supply" and "demand" used correctly? Explain.

LO ▸ 3.3 8. **KEY QUESTION** Suppose the total demand for wheat and the total supply of wheat per month in the Winnipeg grain market are as follows:

Thousands of bushels demanded	Price per bushel	Thousands of bushels supplied	Surplus (+) or shortage (−)
85	$3.40	72	_____
80	$3.70	73	_____
75	$4.00	75	_____
70	$4.30	77	_____
65	$4.60	79	_____
60	$4.90	81	_____

   a. What is the equilibrium price? What is the equilibrium quantity? Fill in the surplus/shortage column and use it to explain why your answers are correct.

   b. Graph the demand for wheat and the supply of wheat. Be sure to label the axes of your graph correctly. Label equilibrium price P and equilibrium quantity Q.

   c. Why will $3.40 not be the equilibrium price in this market? Why not $4.90? "Surpluses drive prices up; shortages drive them down." Do you agree?

9. **KEY QUESTION** How will each of the following changes in demand and/or supply affect equilibrium price and equilibrium quantity in a competitive market; that is, do price and quantity rise, fall, or remain unchanged, or are the answers indeterminate because they depend on the magnitudes of the shifts? Use supply and demand diagrams to verify your answers.

   a. Supply decreases and demand is constant.

   b. Demand decreases and supply is constant.

   c. Supply increases and demand is constant.

   d. Demand increases and supply increases.

   e. Demand increases and supply is constant.

   f. Supply increases and demand decreases.

   g. Demand increases and supply decreases.

   h. Demand decreases and supply decreases.

10. In 2001, an outbreak of foot-and-mouth disease in Europe led to the burning of millions of cattle carcasses. What impact do you think this had on the supply of cattle hides, hide prices, the supply of leather goods, and the price of leather goods? In 2004, millions of chickens were culled in British Columbia due to the avian flu. What impact do you think this had on the supply of eggs, and the price of eggs?

11. Critically evaluate: "In comparing the two equilibrium positions in Figure 3-7b, I note that a smaller amount is actually demanded at a lower price. This refutes the law of demand."

3.3 **12.** For each stock in the stock market, the number of shares sold daily equals the number of shares purchased. That is, the quantity of each firm's shares demanded equals the quantity supplied. So, if this equality always occurs, why do the prices of stocks ever change?

3.3 **13.** Using the schedules given, plot the demand curve and the supply curve on the below graph. Label the axes and indicate for each axis the units being used to measure price and quantity. Then answer the questions.

Price	Quantity demanded (bushels of wheat)	Price	Quantity supplied (bushels of wheat)
$4.20	125,000	$4.20	230,000
4.00	150,000	4.00	220,000
3.80	175,000	3.80	210,000
3.60	200,000	3.60	200,000
3.40	225,000	3.40	190,000
3.20	250,000	3.20	180,000
3.00	275,000	3.00	170,000

a. Give the equilibrium price and quantity for wheat.

b. Indicate the equilibrium price and quantity on a graph by drawing lines from the intersection of the supply and demand curves to the price and quantity axes.

c. If the federal government decided to support the price of wheat at $4.00 per bushel, explain whether there would be a surplus or shortage and how much it would be.

d. Demonstrate your answer to part (c) on your graph being sure to label the quantity you designated as the shortage or surplus.

3.4 **14.** **KEY QUESTION** Refer to the table in Question 8. Suppose that the government establishes a price ceiling of $3.70 for wheat. What might prompt the government to establish this price ceiling? Explain carefully the main

effects. Demonstrate your answer graphically. Next, suppose that the government establishes a price floor of $4.60 for wheat. What will be the main effects of this price floor? Demonstrate your answer graphically.

15. What do economists mean when they say that "price floors and ceilings stifle the rationing function of prices and distort resource allocation"? **LO 3.4**

16. Use data in the following table to explain the economic effects of a price ceiling at $6, at $5, and at $4. **LO 3.4**

Price	Quantity demanded	Quantity supplied
$7	4500	4500
6	5000	3500
5	5500	2500
4	6000	1500

17. Use data in the following table to explain the economic effects of a price floor at $8, at $9, and at $10. **LO 3.4**

Price	Quantity demanded	Quantity supplied
$10	3000	7500
9	3500	6500
8	4000	5500
7	4500	4500

18. **Advanced analysis:** Assume that demand for a commodity is represented by the equation $P = 10 - 0.2Q_d$ and supply by the equation $P = 2 + 0.2Q_s$, where Q_d and Q_s are quantity demanded and quantity supplied, respectively, and P is price. Using the equilibrium condition $Q_s = Q_d$, solve the equations to determine equilibrium price. Now determine equilibrium quantity. Graph the two equations to substantiate your answers. **LO 3.3**

INTERNET APPLICATION QUESTIONS @

1. **Farm Commodity Prices—Supply and Demand in Action.** Use the links on the McConnell-Brue-Flynn-Barbiero Web site (Chapter 3) to access data on the prices of farm products. Choose three farm products of your choice and determine whether their prices (as measured by "prices received by farmers") have generally increased, decreased, or stayed the same over the past three years. In which of the three cases, if any, do you think that supply has increased more rapidly than demand? In which of the three cases, if any, do you think that demand has increased more rapidly than supply? Explain your reasoning.

2. **Changes in Demand—Baby Diapers and Retirement Villages.** Other things equal, an increase in the number of buyers for a product or service will increase

demand. Baby diapers and retirement villages are two products designed for different population groups. The McConnell-Brue-Flynn-Barbiero Web site (Chapter 3) provides links to population pyramids (graphs that show the distribution of population by age and sex) for countries for the current year, 2025, and 2050. View the population pyramids for Mexico, Japan, and Canada by selecting International Data Base and then Population Pyramids. Which country would you expect to have the greatest percentage increase in demand for baby diapers in the year 2050? For retirement villages? Which country would you expect to have the greatest absolute increase in demand for baby diapers? For retirement villages?

Appendix: Additional Examples of Supply and Demand

Our discussion has clearly demonstrated that supply and demand analysis is a powerful tool for understanding equilibrium prices and quantities. The information provided is fully sufficient for moving forward in the book, but you may find that additional examples of supply and demand are helpful. This optional appendix provides several concrete illustrations of changes in supply and demand. It also applies supply and demand analysis to non-priced goods (goods owned in common and not bought and sold in markets).

Your instructor may assign all, some, or none of this appendix, depending on time availability and preferences.

Changes in Supply and Demand

As Figure 3-6 demonstrates, changes in supply and demand cause changes in price, quantity, or both. The following applications illustrate this fact in several real-world markets. The simplest situations are those in which either supply changes while demand remains constant, or demand changes while supply remains constant. Let's consider two such simple cases first, before looking at more complex applications.

Lettuce

Every now and then, we hear on the news that extreme weather has severely reduced the size of some crop such as lettuce, apples, or cherries. Suppose, for example, that a severe freeze destroys a sizable portion of the lettuce crop. This unfortunate situation implies a significant decline in supply, which we represent in Figure A3-1 as a leftward shift of the supply curve from S_1 to S_2. At each price, consumers desire as much lettuce as before, so the freeze does not affect the demand for lettuce. That is, demand curve D_1 does not shift.

What are the consequences of the reduced supply of lettuce for equilibrium price and quantity? As shown in Figure A3-1, the leftward shift of the supply curve disrupts the previous equilibrium in the market for lettuce and drives the equilibrium price up from P_1 to P_2.

Consumers respond to that price hike by reducing the quantity of lettuce demanded from Q_1 to Q_2. Equilibrium in the market is restored, now at P_2 and Q_2. Consumers who are willing and able to pay price P_2 obtain lettuce; consumers unwilling or

FIGURE A3-1   **The Market for Lettuce**

The decrease in the supply of lettuce, shown here by the shift from S_1 to S_2, increases the equilibrium price of lettuce from P_1 to P_2 and reduces the equilibrium quantity from Q_1 to Q_2.

unable to pay that price do not. Some consumers continue to buy as much lettuce as before, even at the higher price. Others buy some lettuce but not as much as before, and still others forgo lettuce altogether. The latter two groups use the money they would have spent on lettuce to obtain other products, say, carrots, whose price has not gone up.

Corn and Ethanol

Between the beginning of 2006 and middle of 2007, the price of corn doubled. Did people suddenly demand more corn flakes? Not hardly! The demand for cereals, beef, and other food products that use corn as inputs was relatively stable. Instead, the driving force was a rapid increase in the price of oil and gasoline (one of our following examples). This increase boosted the demand for ethanol, an alcohol-like substance that is blended with conventional gasoline. In North America, producers refine ethanol mainly from corn, although ethanol can also be refined from sugar and other agricultural commodities. So the increase in the demand for ethanol drove up the demand for corn and raised its equilibrium price.

We depict this situation in Figure A3-2 as the rightward shift of the demand curve from D_1 to D_2. This demand increase

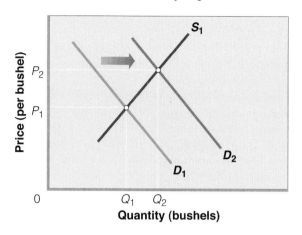

FIGURE A3-2   The Market for Corn

The increase in the demand for corn, shown here by the shift from D_1 to D_2, increases the equilibrium price of corn from P_1 to P_2 and expands the equilibrium quantity from Q_1 to Q_2.

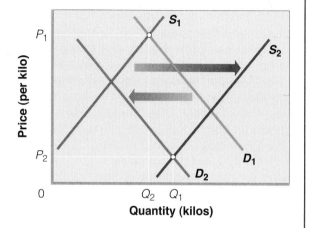

FIGURE A3-3   The Market for Pink Salmon

In the last two decades, the supply of pink salmon has increased and the demand for pink salmon has decreased. As a result, the price of pink salmon has declined, as from P_1 to P_2. Because supply has increased more than demand has decreased, the equilibrium quantity of pink salmon has increased, as from Q_1 to Q_2.

raised the equilibrium price of corn, in this case from P_1 to P_2. Producers responded accordingly by increasing the quantity of corn supplied, as from Q_1 to Q_2. At the higher price and quantity, the market achieved a new equilibrium.

Notice that the demand for corn, the price of corn, and the quantity of corn demanded and supplied all increased. But in the period depicted, the supply of corn—the entire curve S_1—remained securely fixed in place. Eventually, of course, the potential for high profits will encourage more farmers to plant more corn and therefore shift the supply curve rightward. Depending on what happens to demand, the price of corn may drop closer to P_1.

The rapid rise in the price of corn had a host of other effects that are easily understood through demand and supply analysis. The costs of producing corn-fed beef went up, which reduced the supply of beef and increased the price of hamburger and steak. The higher corn price caused the price of corn syrup (fructose) used in soft drinks to increase rapidly and led some soft-drink makers to use cane sugar instead of corn syrup in the production process. In Mexico, large numbers of angry people gathered in cities to protest the higher price of tortillas, which are made from corn and consumed in large quantities by many Mexicans.

Pink Salmon

Now let's see what happens when both supply and demand change at the same time. Several decades ago, people who caught salmon earned as much as $2 for each kilo of pink salmon—the type used mainly for canning—brought to the buyer. In Figure A3-3 that price is represented as P_1, at the intersection of supply

curve S_1 and demand curve D_1. The corresponding quantity of pink salmon is shown as Q_1 kilos. As time passed, supply and demand changed in the market for pink salmon. On the supply side, improved technology in the form of larger, more efficient fishing boats greatly increased the catch and lowered the cost of obtaining it. Also, high profits at price P_1 encouraged many new fishers to enter the industry. As a result of these changes, the supply of pink salmon greatly increased and the supply curve shifted to the right, as from S_1 to S_2 in Figure A3-3.

Over the same years, the demand for pink salmon declined, as represented by the leftward shift from D_1 to D_2 in Figure A3-3. That decrease resulted from increases in consumer income and reductions of the price of substitute products. As buyers' incomes rose, consumers shifted demand away from canned fish and toward higher-quality fresh or frozen fish, including more-valued Atlantic, Chinook, Sockeye, and Coho salmon. Moreover, the emergence of fish farming, in which salmon are raised in ocean net pens, lowered the prices of these substitute species. That, too, reduced the demand for pink salmon.

The altered supply and demand reduced the price of pink salmon to as low as $.20 per kilo, as represented by the drop in price from P_1 to P_2 in Figure A3-3. Both the supply increase and the demand decrease helped reduce the equilibrium price. However, in this particular case the equilibrium quantity of pink salmon increased, as represented by the move from Q_1 to Q_2. Both shifts of the curves reduced the equilibrium price, but equilibrium quantity increased because the increase in supply exceeded the decrease in demand.

Gasoline

The price of gasoline has increased rapidly in Canada over the past several years. For example, the average price of a litre of gasoline rose from around $.60 in 2004 to about $1.05 in 2007. What caused this more than 50 percent rise in the price of gasoline? How would we diagram this increase?

We begin in Figure A3-4 with the price of a litre of gasoline at P_1, representing the $.60 price. Simultaneous supply and demand factors disturbed this equilibrium. On the supply side, supply uncertainties relating to Middle East politics and warfare and expanded demand for oil by fast-growing countries such as China pushed up the price of a barrel of oil from $37 in 2004 to $80 in 2007. Oil is the main input for producing gasoline, so any sustained rise in its price boosts the per-unit cost of producing gasoline. Such cost rises decrease the supply of gasoline, as represented by the leftward shift of the supply curve from S_1 to S_2 in Figure A3-4. At times, refinery breakdowns in North America also contributed to this reduced supply.

While the supply of gasoline declined between 2004 and 2007, the demand for gasoline increased, as depicted by the rightward shift of the demand curve from D_1 to D_2. Incomes in general were rising over these years because the Canadian economy was rapidly expanding. Rising incomes raise demand for all normal goods, including gasoline. An increased number of low-gas-mileage SUVs and light trucks on the road also contributed to growing gas demand.

The combined decline in gasoline supply and increase in gasoline demand boosted the price of gasoline from $.60 to $1.05, as represented by the rise from P_1 to P_2 in Figure A3-4.

Because the demand increase outweighed the supply decrease, the equilibrium quantity expanded here, from Q_1 to Q_2.

In other periods the price of gasoline has *declined* as the demand for gasoline has increased. Test your understanding of the analysis by explaining how such a price decrease could occur.

Sushi

Sushi bars are springing up at a rapid rate in Canadian cities. Consumption of this raw-fish delicacy from Japan has soared in Canada in recent years. Nevertheless, the price of sushi has remained relatively constant.

Supply and demand analysis helps explain this circumstance of increased quantity and constant price. A change in tastes has increased the Canadian demand for sushi. Many first-time consumers of sushi find it highly tasty. And, as implied by the growing number of sushi bars in Canada, the supply of sushi has also expanded.

We represent these supply and demand changes in Figure A3-5 as the rightward shift of the demand curve from D_1 to D_2 and the rightward shift of the supply curve from S_1 to S_2. Observe that the equilibrium quantity of sushi increases from Q_1 to Q_2 and equilibrium price remains constant at P_1. The increase in supply, which taken alone would reduce price, has perfectly offset the increase in demand, which taken alone would raise price. The price of sushi does not change, but the equilibrium quantity greatly rises. That happens because both the increase in demand and the increase in supply expand purchases and sales.

Simultaneous increases in demand and supply can cause price to rise, fall, or remain constant, depending on the relative magnitudes of the supply and demand increases. In this case, price remained constant.

FIGURE A3-4	The Market for Gasoline

An increase in the demand for gasoline, as shown by the shift from D_1 to D_2, coupled with a decrease in supply, as shown by the shift from S_1 to S_2, boosts equilibrium price (here from P_1 to P_2). In this case, equilibrium quantity increases from Q_1 to Q_2 because the increase in demand outweighs the decrease in supply.

FIGURE A3-5	The Market for Sushi

Equal increase in the demand for sushi, as from D_1 to D_2, and in the supply of sushi, as from S_1 to S_2, expand the equilibrium quantity of sushi (here from Q_1 to Q_2), while leaving the price of sushi unchanged at P_1.

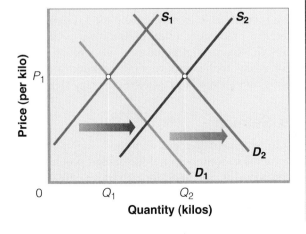

Preset Prices

In the body of this chapter we saw that an effective government-imposed price ceiling (legal maximum price) causes quantity demanded to exceed quantity supplied—a shortage. An effective government-imposed price floor (legal minimum price) causes quantity supplied to exceed quantity demanded—a surplus. Put simply: Shortages result when prices are set below equilibrium prices, and surpluses result when prices are set above equilibrium prices. We now want to establish that shortages and surpluses can occur in markets other than those in which government imposes price floors and ceilings. Such market imbalances happen when the seller or sellers set prices in advance of sales and the prices selected turn out to be below or above equilibrium prices. Consider the following two examples.

Olympic Figure Skating Finals

Tickets for the women's figure skating championship at the Olympics are among the world's hottest tickets. The popularity of this event and the high incomes of buyers translate into tremendous ticket demand. Olympic officials set the price for the tickets in advance. Invariably, the price, although high, is considerably below the equilibrium price that would equate quantity demanded and quantity supplied. A severe shortage of tickets therefore occurs in this *primary market*—the market involving the official ticket office. The shortage, in turn, creates a *secondary market* in which buyers bid for tickets held by initial purchasers rather than the original seller. Scalping tickets—selling them above the ticket price—may be legal or illegal,

depending on local laws. Figure A3-6 shows how the shortage in the primary ticket market looks in terms of supply and demand analysis. Demand curve D represents the strong demand for tickets, and supply curve S represents the supply of tickets. The supply curve is vertical because a fixed number of tickets are printed to match the capacity of the arena. At the printed ticket price of P_1, the quantity of tickets demanded, Q_2, exceeds the quantity supplied, Q_1. The result is a shortage of ab—the horizontal distance between Q_2 and Q_1 in the primary market. If the printed ticket price had been the higher equilibrium price P_2, no shortage of tickets would have occurred. But at the lower price P_1, a shortage and secondary ticket market will emerge among those buyers willing to pay more than the printed ticket price and those sellers willing to sell their purchased tickets for more than the printed price. Wherever there are shortages and secondary markets, we can safely assume that price was set below the equilibrium price.

Olympic Curling Preliminaries

Contrast the shortage of tickets for the women's figure skating finals at the Olympics to the surplus of tickets for one of the preliminary curling matches. Curling is a sport in which participants slide a heavy round object called a stone down the ice toward a target while people called sweepers use brooms to alter the course of the stone when desired. Curling is a popular spectator sport in a few nations such as Canada, but it does not draw many fans in most countries. So the demand for tickets to most of the preliminary curling events is not very strong. We demonstrate this weak demand as D in Figure A3-7. As in our previous example, the supply of tickets is fixed by the size of the arena and is shown as vertical line S.

FIGURE A3·6 ▸ **The Market for Tickets to Olympic Women's Figure Skating Finals**

The demand curve D and the supply curve S produce an equilibrium price above the P_1 price printed on the ticket. At price P_1 the quantity of tickets demanded, Q_2, greatly exceeds the quantity of tickets available (Q_1). The resulting shortage of ab (= Q_2Q_1) gives rise to a legal or illegal secondary market.

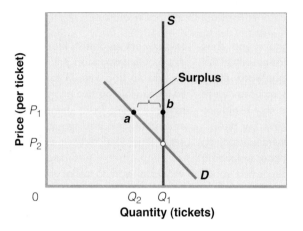

FIGURE A3-7   **The Market for Tickets to the Olympic Curling Preliminaries**

The demand curve D and the supply curve S produce an equilibrium price below the P_1 price printed on the ticket. At price P_1 the quantity of tickets demanded is less than the quantity of tickets available. The resulting surplus of ba (= Q_1Q_2) means the event is not sold out.

We represent the printed ticket price as P_1 in Figure A3-7. In this case the printed price is much higher than the equilibrium price of P_2. At the printed ticket price, quantity supplied is Q_1 and quantity demanded is Q_2. So a surplus of tickets of ba (= Q_1Q_2) occurs. No ticket scalping occurs and there are numerous empty seats. Only if Olympic officials had priced the tickets at the lower price P_2 would the event have been a sell-out. (Actually, Olympic officials try to adjust to demand realities for curling contests by holding them in smaller arenas than used for figure skating and by charging less for tickets. Nevertheless, the stands are rarely full for the preliminary contests, which compete against final events in other winter Olympic sports.)

APPENDIX | SUMMARY

- A decrease in the supply of a product increases its equilibrium price and reduces its equilibrium quantity. In contrast, an increase in the demand for a product boosts both its equilibrium price and its equilibrium quantity.

- Simultaneous changes in supply and demand affect equilibrium price and quantity in various ways, depending on the relative magnitudes of the changes in supply and demand. Equal increases in supply and demand, for example, leave equilibrium price unchanged.

- Sellers set prices of some items such as tickets in advance of the event. These items are sold in the primary market that involves the original seller and buyers. If preset prices turn out to be below the equilibrium prices, shortages occur and scalping in legal or illegal secondary markets arises. The prices in the secondary market then rise above the preset prices. In contrast, surpluses occur when the preset prices happen to exceed the equilibrium prices.

- Non-priced goods such as fish in public waters and game on public lands are owned in common and therefore not bought and sold in markets. A surplus of a non-priced good occurs when the sustainable quantity of the good exceeds the quantity demanded. A shortage of a non-priced good occurs when the quantity demanded exceeds the sustainable quantity. In this latter case, the good tends to be overconsumed and, without protection, may eventually be exhausted.

APPENDIX | STUDY QUESTIONS

A3.1 1. Suppose the supply of apples sharply increases because of perfect weather conditions throughout the growing season. Assuming no change in demand, explain the effect on the equilibrium price and quantity of apples. Explain why quantity demanded increases even though demand does not change.

A3.1 2. Assume the demand for lumber suddenly rises because of a rapid growth of demand for new housing. Assume no change in supply. *Why* does the equilibrium price of lumber rise? What would happen if the price did not rise under the demand and supply circumstances described?

A3.1 3. Suppose both the demand for olives and the supply of olives decline by equal amounts over some time period. Use graphical analysis to show the effect on equilibrium price and quantity.

A3.1 4. Assume that both the supply of bottled water and the demand for bottled water rise during the summer but that supply increases more rapidly than demand. What can you conclude about the directions of the impacts on equilibrium price and equilibrium quantity?

A3.1 5. Why are shortages or surpluses more likely with preset prices, such as those on tickets, than flexible prices, such as those on gasoline?

A3.1 6. Use this table to answer the questions that follow:

Quantity demanded, (thousands)	Price ($)	Quantity supplied, (thousands)
80	25	60
75	35	60
70	45	60
65	55	60
60	65	60
55	75	60
50	85	60

a. If this table reflects the supply of and demand for tickets to a particular World Cup soccer game, what is the stadium capacity?

b. If the preset ticket price is $45, would we expect to see a secondary market for tickets? Explain why or why not. Would the price of a ticket in the secondary market be higher than, the same as, or lower than the price in the primary (original) market?

c. Suppose for some other World Cup game the quantities of tickets demanded are 20,000 lower at each ticket price than shown in the table. If the ticket price remains $45, would the event be a sell-out? Explain why or why not.

7. Most scalping laws make it illegal to sell—but not to buy— **LO ▶ A3.1** tickets at prices above those printed on the tickets. Assuming that is the case, use supply and demand analysis to explain why the equilibrium ticket price in an illegal secondary market tends to be higher than in a legal secondary market.

8. Gasoline prices—how high (or low) now? Go to **Gasticker.** **LO ▶ A3.1** **com** or **www.garnetknight.com/gas** and follow the links to find the current retail price of gasoline in your area. How does the current price of regular gasoline compare with the price a year ago? What must have happened to either supply, demand, or both to explain the observed price change?

Math Appendix to Chapter 3

A3.1 | THE MATHEMATICS OF MARKET EQUILIBRIUM

A market equilibrium is the price and the quantity, denoted as the pair (Q^*, P^*), of a commodity bought or sold at price P^*. The following mathematical note provides an introduction of how a market equilibrium (Q^*, P^*) is derived.

The market equilibrium is found by using the market demand (buyers' behaviour), the market supply (sellers' behaviour), and the negotiating process (to find the agreed upon price and quantity, namely P^* and Q^*, on which to transact). The market equilibrium is identified by the condition reached at the end of the negotiating process that at the price they negotiated, P^*, the quantity of the commodity that buyers are willing to buy, denoted as Q_d, and the quantity sellers are willing to sell, denoted as Q_s, matches exactly.

The Demand Curve

The equation describing the downward-sloping demand when the demand curve is a straight line, in which Q_d represents the quantity demanded by buyers and P the price, is

$$P = a - bQ_d$$

The demand equation and curve below tell us that if the price is higher than a then the buyers will not buy; thus, for a transaction to occur the price must be lower. The demand equation and curve also tell us that at a price lower than a the quantity demanded by the buyers increases. Buyers' behaviour, as described by the demand equation, is that at lower prices buyers buy more quantity.

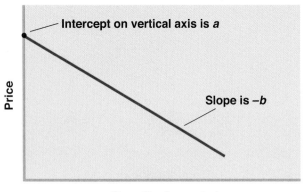

Intercept on vertical axis is a

Slope is −b

Price

Quantity demanded

The Supply Curve

The equation describing the upward-sloping market supply function when the supply curve is a straight line, in which Q_s represents the quantity supplied by sellers and P the price, is

$$P = c + dQ_s$$

If the price is lower than c then the sellers will sell nothing, as the figure below shows. If the price is c or higher, then the supply equation states that sellers facing higher prices sell more quantity. Sellers' behaviour, as described by the supply curve and equation, is that at higher prices sellers make more quantity available.

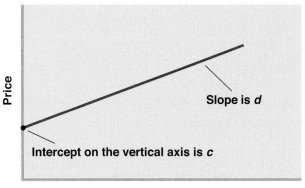

Slope is d

Price

Intercept on the vertical axis is c

Quantity supplied

The Market Equilibrium

The negotiating process (in which price and quantity or both adjust) provides the mechanism by which, eventually, buyers and sellers agree upon a price, P^*, and a quantity, Q^*, at which they can buy and sell and thus complete the transaction. At the end of the negotiating process, the quantity demanded by the buyers, Q_d, is equal to the quantity supplied by the sellers, Q_s (at the agreed-upon price), and thus the market is in equilibrium. The mathematical representation of such a negotiating process is described as follows.

At the agreed price, P^*, the equilibrium condition of the negotiating process, the equality in the quantity demanded and supplied, is

$$Q_d = Q_s$$

Having denoted Q^* as the equilibrium quantity, then it must be that $Q^* = Q_d = Q_s$. To solve for the equilibrium quantity Q^* and the equilibrium price P^* the demand and supply functions are used. With Q^* the equilibrium quantity, for the buyers

$$P^* = a - bQ^*,$$

and for the sellers

$$P^* = c + dQ^*.$$

Now, since P^* is the same agreed-upon price by both buyer and seller, then

$$a - bQ^* = c + dQ^*,$$

giving the equilibrium quantity, Q^*, as

$$Q^* = \frac{(a-c)}{(b+d)}$$

To find P^* substitute $\frac{(a-c)}{(b+d)}$ in the supply (or demand) function.

$$P^* = c + d\,\frac{(a-c)}{(b+d)}, \text{ thus}$$

$$P^* = \frac{(ad-bc)}{(b+d)}$$

The equilibrium is $(Q^*, P^*) = \left[\dfrac{(a-c)}{(b+d)}, \dfrac{(ad-bc)}{(b+d)}\right].$

The market equilibrium may also be represented diagrammatically, as shown below.

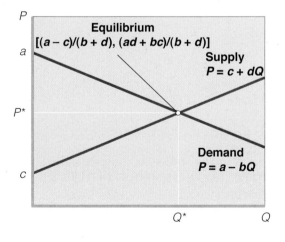

Example

Assume the demand for a pair of jeans is represented by the equation:

$$P = 100 - 0.2Q_d$$

Assume the supply of a pair of jeans is represented by the equation:

$$P = 20 + 0.2Q_s$$

Assume quantities are expressed in jeans per day, and the price in dollars.

To find the equilibrium price P^*, and equilibrium quantity Q^*, substitute Q^* for Q_d and Q_s and P^* for P in the demand and supply equations. To solve for Q^*:

$$100 - 0.2Q^* = 20 + 0.2Q^*$$
$$0.4Q^* = 80$$
$$Q^* = 200$$

To solve for P^*:

$$P^* = 100 - 0.2(200)$$
$$= 60$$

The equilibrium quantity of jeans is 200 per day, and the equilibrium price is $60 per pair of jeans.

PART 2 | Microeconomics of Product Markets

CHAPTER 4

Elasticity, Consumer Surplus, and Producer Surplus

Today's market economies rely mainly on the activities of consumers, businesses, and suppliers of factors of production to allocate resources efficiently. Those activities and their outcomes are the subject of microeconomics, to which we now turn.

In this chapter we extend our previous discussion of demand and supply by explaining significant ideas that help us answer such questions as: Why do buyers of some products (for example, ocean cruises) respond to price increases by substantially reducing their purchases, while buyers of other products (say, gasoline) respond by only slightly cutting back? Why do higher market prices for some products (for example, chicken) cause producers to greatly increase their output while price rises for other products (say, gold) cause only limited increases in output? Why does the demand for some products (for example, books) rise a great deal when household income increases while the demand for other products (say, green beans) rises just a little? How is it that most consumers obtain products at prices below the prices they actually would have been willing to pay?

How is that most producers obtain higher prices for their products than the prices they actually would have been willing to accept?

The ideas of *elasticity, consumer surplus,* and *producer surplus* help answer these questions. Let's begin by looking at elasticity.

4.1 | Price Elasticity of Demand

ORIGIN 4.1
Price Elasticity
of Demand

price elasticity of demand
A measure of the responsiveness of buyers to a change in the price of a product or resource.

MATH 4.1
Elasticity

The law of demand tells us that, other things equal, consumers will buy more of a product when its price declines and less when its price increases. But *how much* more or less will they buy?

The responsiveness (or sensitivity) of consumers to a price change is measured by a product's **price elasticity of demand.** For some products—for example, restaurant meals—consumers are highly responsive to price changes. Modest price changes cause very large changes in the quantity purchased. Economists say that the demand for such products is *relatively elastic* or simply *elastic.*

For other products—for example, toothpaste—consumers are less responsive to price changes. Substantial price changes cause only small changes in the amount purchased. The demand for such products is *relatively inelastic* or simply *inelastic.*

The Price Elasticity Coefficient and Formula

We measure the degree to which demand is elastic or inelastic with the coefficient E_d, defined as

$$E_d = \frac{\text{percentage change in quantity demanded of product X}}{\text{percentage change in price of product X}}$$

Let's look at a specific example from Table 4-1, rows 1 to 3, to see how the price elasticity of demand is calculated (don't worry about columns 4 and 5 for now; they will be discussed later). This table shows the number of movie tickets demanded (in thousands) per week at each specified price. Let's calculate E_d for, say, the $5 to $4 price range. But before we do so, let's look at how we calculate a percentage.

TABLE 4·1

Price Elasticity of Demand for Movie Tickets as Measured by the Elasticity Coefficient and the Total-Revenue Test

(1) Total quantity demanded per week (thousands)	(2) Price per unit	(3) Elasticity coefficient, E_d	(4) Total revenue (1) × (2)	(5) Total-revenue test
1	$8		$ 8,000	
		5.00		Elastic
2	7		14,000	
		2.60		Elastic
3	6		18,000	
		1.57		Elastic
4	5		20,000	
		1.00		Unit elastic
5	4		20,000	
		0.64		Inelastic
6	3		18,000	
		0.38		Inelastic
7	2		14,000	
		0.20		Inelastic
8	1		8,000	

Handwritten annotations:

Price change from $4 → $5 $= \dfrac{\frac{4-5}{5}}{\frac{5-4}{4}} = \dfrac{-20\%}{25\%} = -0.8$

CALCULATING A PERCENTAGE

To calculate the percentage change in quantity demanded between two points, we divide the change in quantity demanded (ΔQ_d)* by the original quantity demanded (Q_0) that we are considering:

$$\%\Delta Q_d = \frac{\text{change in quantity demanded of product X}}{\text{original quantity demanded of product X}} \times 100$$

For example, if the quantity demanded increases from 4 to 5 units, the percentage change in quantity demanded is calculated as follows:

$$\%\Delta Q_d = \frac{\Delta Q_d}{Q_0} = \frac{1}{4} \times 100 = 25\%$$

To calculate the percentage change in price between two points, we divide the change in price (ΔP) by the original price (P_0):

$$\%\Delta P = \frac{\text{change in price of product X}}{\text{original price of product X}} \times 100$$

For example, if the price dropped from $5 to $4, the percentage change in price is calculated as follows:

$$\%\Delta P = \frac{\Delta P}{P_0} = \frac{1}{5} \times 100 = 20\%$$

USING AVERAGES

Unfortunately, an annoying problem arises in computing the price elasticity coefficient. A price change, say, from $4 to $5 is a 25 percent (= $1/$4) increase; the quantity change from 4 to 5 units is a 20 percent (=1/5) decline in quantity, resulting in a price elasticity of .8 (20/25). But a price change from $5 to $4 is a 20 percent ($1/$5) decrease; the quantity change from 4 to 5 units is a 25 percent increase, resulting in a price elasticity of 1.25 (25/20). Which percentage change in price should we use in the denominator to compute the price elasticity coefficient? Elasticity should be the same whether price rises or falls!

midpoint formula
A method for calculating price elasticity of demand or price elasticity of supply that averages the two prices and two quantities as the reference points for competing percentages.

The simplest solution to the problem is to use the **midpoint formula** for calculating elasticity. This formula simply averages the two prices and the two quantities as the reference points for computing the percentages. That is:

$$E_d = \frac{\text{change in quantity}}{\text{sum of quantities}/2} \div \frac{\text{change in price}}{\text{sum of prices}/2}$$

In symbols, the formula becomes:

$$E_d = \frac{\Delta Q}{(Q_0 + Q_1)/2} \div \frac{\Delta P}{(P_0 + P_1)/2}$$

WORKED PROBLEM 4.1
Elasticity of Demand

For the same $5 to $4 price range, the price reference is $4.50 [= ($5 + $4)/2], and for the 4 to 5 quantity range the quantity reference is 4.5 units [= (4 + 5)/2]. The percentage change in price is now $1/$4.50, or about 22 percent, and the percentage change in quantity is 1/4.5, or also about 22 percent. So E_d is 1. This solution eliminates the "up versus down" problem. All the price elasticity coefficients that follow are calculated using this midpoint formula. *We emphasize that the midpoint formula should be used in all cases, unless you are provided with the actual price and quantity percentage changes.*

USING PERCENTAGES

Note that we use percentages rather than absolute amounts in measuring consumer responsiveness. If we use absolute changes, the choice of units will arbitrarily affect our impression of buyer responsiveness. To illustrate, if the price of a bag of popcorn at the local hockey game is reduced from $3

---

* The Greek letter delta (Δ) signifies "change in."

to $2, and consumers increase their purchases from 60 to 100 bags, it appears that consumers are quite sensitive to price changes and, therefore, that demand is elastic. After all, a price change of one unit has caused a change of 40 units in the amount demanded. But by changing the monetary unit from dollars to pennies (why not?), we find that a price change of 100 units (pennies) causes a quantity change of 40 units. This result may falsely lead us to believe that demand is inelastic. We avoid this problem by using percentage changes. This particular price decline is the same whether we measure in dollars or pennies.

Also, by using percentages, we can correctly compare consumer responsiveness to changes in the prices of different products. It makes little sense to compare the effects on quantity demanded of a $1 increase in the price of a $10,000 used car with a $1 increase in the price of a $1 soft drink. Here the price of the used car increased by 0.01 percent, while the price of the soft drink increased by 100 percent.

ELIMINATING THE MINUS SIGN

We know from the downsloping demand curve shown in Chapter 3 that price and quantity demanded are inversely related. Thus, the price elasticity coefficient of demand E_d will always be a negative number. We usually ignore the minus sign and simply present the absolute value of the elasticity coefficient to avoid an ambiguity that might otherwise arise. It can be confusing to say that an E_d of −4 is greater than one of −2. This possible confusion is avoided when we say an E_d of 4 reveals greater elasticity than one of 2. Incidentally, the ambiguity does not arise with supply because price and quantity supplied are positively related. All elasticity of supply coefficients therefore are positive numbers.

Interpretation of E_d

We interpret the coefficient of price elasticity of demand (E_d) as follows.

ELASTIC DEMAND $E_d > 1$

elastic demand
Product or resource demand with a price elasticity coefficient that is greater than one.

Demand is elastic (**elastic demand**) if a specific percentage change in price results in a larger percentage change in quantity demanded. Then E_d will be greater than one. For example, Suppose that a 2 percent decline in the price of cut flowers results in a 4 percent increase in quantity demanded. Because $E_d = 0.04/0.02 = 2$, demand for cut flowers is elastic.

INELASTIC DEMAND $E_d < 1$ weak response

inelastic demand
Product or resource demand with a price elasticity coefficient that is less than one.

If a specific percentage change in price produces a smaller percentage change in quantity demanded, demand is inelastic (**inelastic demand**). E_d will be less than one. For example, suppose that a 2 percent decline in the price of coffee leads to only a 1 percent increase in quantity demanded. Because $E_d = 0.01/0.02 = 0.5$, demand for coffee is inelastic. no response in changing price

UNIT ELASTICITY $E_d = 1$

unit elasticity
Demand or supply with a price elasticity coefficient that is equal to one.

The case separating elastic and inelastic demands occurs when a percentage change in price and the resulting percentage change in quantity demanded are the same. For example, suppose that a 2 percent drop in the price of chocolate causes a 2 percent increase in quantity demanded. This special case is termed **unit elasticity** because E_d is exactly one, or unity. In this example, $E_d = 0.02/0.02 = 1$.

EXTREME CASES   elastic demand

perfectly inelastic demand
Quantity demanded does not respond to a change in price.

When we say demand is *inelastic,* we do not mean that consumers are completely unresponsive to a price change. In that extreme situation, when a price change results in no change whatsoever in the quantity demanded, economists say that demand is **perfectly inelastic.** The price elasticity coefficient is zero because there is no response to a change in price. Approximate examples include a diabetic's demand for insulin or an addict's demand for heroin. A line parallel to the vertical axis, such as D_1 in Figure 4-1a, shows perfectly inelastic demand graphically.

CONSIDER THIS | A Bit of a Stretch

The following analogy might help you remember the distinction between "elastic" and "inelastic." Imagine two objects—one an Ace elastic bandage used to wrap injured joints and the other a relatively firm Bungee cord (rubber strap) used for securing items for transport. The Ace bandage stretches a great deal when pulled with a particular force; the Bungee cord stretches some, but not a lot.

Similar differences occur for the quantity demanded of various products when their prices change. For some products, a price change causes a substantial "stretch" of quantity demanded. When this stretch in percentage terms exceeds the percentage change in price, demand is elastic. For other products, quantity demanded stretches very little in response to

the price change. when this stretch in percentage terms is less than the percentage change in price, demand is inelastic.

In summary:

- Elastic demand displays considerable "quantity stretch" (as with the Ace bandage)

- Inelastic demand displays relatively little "quantity stretch" (as with the Bungee cord)

And by extension:

- Perfectly elastic demand has infinite quantity stretch.

- Perfectly inelastic demand has zero quantity stretch.

FIGURE 4·1   **Perfectly Inelastic and Perfectly Elastic Demand**

Demand curve D_1 in panel (a) represents perfectly inelastic demand ($E_d = 0$). A price increase does not change the quantity demanded. Demand curve D_2 in panel (b) represents perfectly elastic demand. A price increase causes quantity demanded to decline from an infinite amount to zero ($E_d = \infty$).

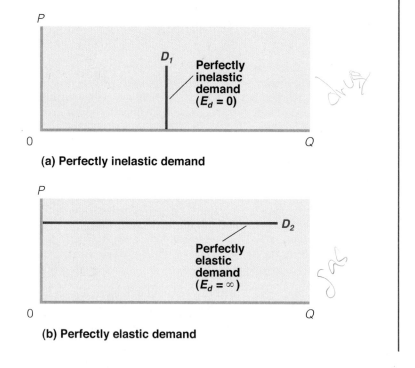

(a) Perfectly inelastic demand

(b) Perfectly elastic demand

Conversely, when we say demand is *elastic*, we do not mean that consumers are fully responsive to a price change. In that extreme situation, when a small price reduction causes buyers to increase their purchases from zero to all they can obtain, the elasticity coefficient is infinite ($= \infty$), and economists say demand is **perfectly elastic.** A line parallel to the horizontal axis, such as D_2 in Figure 4-1b, shows perfectly elastic demand. You will see in Chapter 7 that such a demand applies to a firm—say, a mining firm—that is selling in a perfectly competitive market.

perfectly elastic demand
Quantity demanded can be any amount at a particular price.

4.2 | The Total-Revenue Test

The importance of elasticity for firms is due to the effect of price changes on total revenue and thus on profits (= total revenue minus total costs).

total revenue (TR)
The total amount a seller receives from the sale of a product in a particular time period.

Total revenue (TR) is the total amount the seller receives from the sale of a product (or service) in a particular time period; it is calculated by multiplying the product price (*P*) by the quantity demanded and sold (*Q*). In equation form:

$$TR = P \times Q$$

MATH 4.2
The Total
Revenue Test

Graphically, total revenue is represented by the $P \times Q$ rectangle lying below a point on a demand curve. At point *a* in Figure 4-2a, for example, price is $2 and quantity demanded is 10 units. So total revenue is $20 (= $2 × 10), shown by the rectangle composed of the blue and purple areas under the demand curve. We know from basic geometry that the area of a rectangle is found by multiplying one side by the other. Here, one side is "price" ($2) and the other is "quantity demanded" (10 units).

total-revenue test
A test to determine elasticity of demand between any two prices, by noting what happens to total revenue when price changes.

Total revenue and the price elasticity of demand are related. In fact, the easiest way to determine whether demand is elastic or inelastic is to employ the **total-revenue test:** Note what happens to total revenue when price changes. If total revenue changes in the opposite direction from price, demand is elastic. If total revenue changes in the same direction as price, demand is inelastic. If total revenue does not change when price changes, demand is unit elastic.

FIGURE 4-2   **The Total-Revenue Test for Price Elasticity**

(a) Price declines from $2 to $1, and total revenue increases from $20 to $40. So demand is elastic. The gain in revenue (green area) exceeds the loss of revenue (blue area). (b) Price declines from $4 to $1, and total revenue falls from $40 to $20. So demand is inelastic. The gain in revenue (green area) is less than the loss of revenue (blue area). (c) Price declines from $3 to $1, and total revenue does not change. Demand is unit elastic. The gain in revenue (green area) equals the loss of revenue (blue area).

(a) Elastic

(b) Inelastic

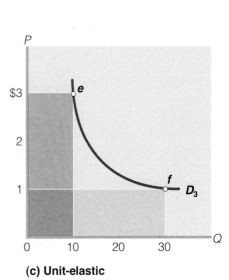

(c) Unit-elastic

Elastic Demand

If demand is elastic, a decrease in price will increase total revenue. Even though a lesser price is received per unit, enough additional units are sold to more than make up for the lower price. For example, look at demand curve D_1 in Figure 4-2a. We have already established that at point *a*, total revenue is $20 (= $2 × 10), shown as the purple plus blue area. If the price declines from $2 to $1 (point *b*), the quantity demanded becomes 40 units and total revenue is $40 (= $1 × 40). As a result of the price decline, total revenue has increased from $20 to $40. Total revenue has increased in this case because the $1 decline in price applies to 10 units, with a consequent revenue loss of $10 (the blue area). But 30 more units are sold at $1 each, resulting in a revenue gain of $30 (the green area). Visually, it is apparent that the gain of the green area exceeds the loss of the blue area. As indicated, the overall result is a net increase in total revenue of $20 (= $30 − $10).

The analysis is reversible: If demand is elastic, a price increase will reduce total revenue. The revenue gained on the higher-priced units will be more than offset by the revenue lost from the lower quantity sold. Bottom line: Other things equal, when price and total revenue move in opposite directions, demand is elastic. *Elastic demand* occurs when E_d is greater than 1, meaning the percentage change in quantity demanded is greater than the percentage change in price.

Inelastic Demand

If demand is inelastic, a price decrease will reduce total revenue. The increase in sales will not fully offset the decline in revenue per unit, and total revenue will decline. To see this, look at demand curve D_2 in Figure 4-2b. At point *c* on the curve, price is $4 and quantity demanded is 10. So, total revenue is $40, shown by the combined purple and blue rectangle. If the price drops to $1 (point *d*), total revenue declines to $20, which obviously is less than $40. Total revenue has declined because the loss of revenue (the blue area) from the lower unit price is larger than the gain in revenue (the green area) from the accompanying increase in sales. Price has fallen, and total revenue has also declined.

WORKED
PROBLEM 4.2
Total-Revenue Test

The analysis is again reversible: If demand is inelastic, a price increase will increase total revenue. So, other things equal, when price and total revenue move in the same direction, demand is inelastic. *Inelastic demand* occurs when E_d is less than 1, meaning the percentage change in quantity demanded is less than the percentage change in price.

Unit Elasticity

In the special case of unit elasticity, an increase or a decrease in price leaves total revenue unchanged. The loss in revenue from a lower unit price is exactly offset by the gain in revenue from the accompanying increase in sales. Conversely, the gain in revenue from a higher unit price is exactly offset by the revenue loss associated with the accompanying decline in the amount demanded.

In Figure 4-2c (demand curve D_3) we find that at the price of $3, 10 units will be sold, yielding total revenue of $30. At the lower $1 price, a total of 30 units will be sold, again resulting in $30 of total revenue. The $2 price reduction causes the loss of revenue shown by the blue area, but this is exactly offset by the revenue gain shown by the green area. Total revenue does not change. In fact, that would be true for all price changes along this particular curve. Other things equal, when price changes and total revenue remains constant, demand is unit elastic (or unitary). *Unit elasticity* occurs when E_d is 1, meaning the percentage change in quantity demanded equals the percentage change in price.

Price Elasticity along a Linear Demand Curve

Although the demand curves depicted in Figure 4-2 nicely illustrate the total-revenue test for elasticity, two of the graphs involve specific movements along linear (straight-line) demand curves. That presents no problem for explaining the total-revenue test. However, you need to know that elasticity typically varies over the different price ranges of the same demand curve. (The exception is the curve in Figure 4-2c, where elasticity is 1 along the entire curve.)

KEY GRAPH

FIGURE 4-3   The Relation between Price Elasticity of Demand for Movie Tickets and Total Revenue

Demand curve D in panel (a) is based on Table 4-1 and is marked to show that the hypothetical weekly demand for movie tickets is elastic at higher price ranges and inelastic at lower price ranges. The total-revenue curve TR in panel (b) is derived from demand curve D. When price falls and TR increases, demand is elastic; when price falls and TR is unchanged, demand is unit elastic; when price falls and TR declines, demand is inelastic.

(a) Demand curve

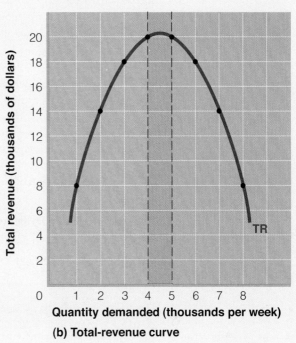

(b) Total-revenue curve

Table 4-1 and Figure 4-3 demonstrate that elasticity typically varies over the different price ranges of the same demand curve. Plotting the hypothetical data for movie tickets shown in columns 1 and 2 of Table 4-1 yields demand curve D in Figure 4-3. Observe that the demand curve is linear. But we see from column 3 of the table that the price elasticity coefficient for this demand curve declines as we move from higher to lower prices. For all downsloping straight-line and most other demand curves, demand is more price elastic toward the upper left (here, the $5 to $8 price range of D) than toward the lower right (here, the $4 to $1 price range of D).

This difference is the consequence of arithmetic properties of the elasticity measure. Specifically, in the upper left segment of the demand curve, the percentage change in quantity is large because the original reference quantity is small. Similarly, the percentage change in price is small in that segment because the original reference price is large. The relatively large percentage change in quantity divided by the relatively small change in price yields a large E_d—an elastic demand.

The reverse holds true for the lower right segment of the demand curve. Here the percentage change in quantity is small because the original reference quantity is large; similarly, the percentage change in price is large because the original reference price is small. The relatively small percentage change in quantity divided by the relatively large percentage change in price results in a small E_d—an inelastic demand.

The demand curve in Figure 4-3a also illustrates that the slope of a demand curve—its flatness or steepness—is not a sound basis for judging elasticity. The catch is that the slope of the curve is computed from *absolute* changes in price and quantity, while elasticity involves *relative* or *percentage* changes in price and quantity. The demand curve in Figure 4-3a is linear, which by definition means that the slope is constant throughout, but we have demonstrated that such a curve is elastic in its high-price ($8 to $5) range and inelastic in its low-price ($4 to $1) range. *(Key Question 2)*

Price Elasticity and the Total-Revenue Curve

In Figure 4-3b we graphed the total revenue per week to the theatre owner that corresponds to each price–quantity combination indicated along demand curve *D* in Figure 4-3a. Comparison of curves *D* and TR sharply focuses the relationship between elasticity and total revenue. Lowering the ticket price in the elastic range of demand—for example, from $8 to $5—increases total revenue. Conversely, increasing the ticket price in that range reduces total revenue. In both cases, price and total revenue change in opposite directions, confirming that demand is elastic.

The $5 to $4 price range of demand curve *D* reflects unit elasticity. When price either decreases from $5 to $4 or increases from $4 to $5, total revenue remains $20,000. In both cases, price has changed and total revenue has remained constant, confirming that demand is unit elastic when we consider these particular price changes.

In the inelastic range of demand curve *D,* lowering the price—for example, from $4 to $1—decreases total revenue, as shown in Figure 4-3b. Raising the price boosts total revenue. In both cases, price and total revenue move in the same direction, confirming that demand is inelastic.

Table 4-2 summarizes the characteristics of price elasticity of demand. You should review it carefully. *(Key Questions 4 and 5)*

Determinants of Price Elasticity of Demand

We cannot say just what will determine the price elasticity of demand in each individual situation. However, the following generalizations are often helpful.

SUBSTITUTABILITY

Generally, the larger the number of substitute goods that are available, the greater the price elasticity of demand. Various brands of candy bars are usually substitutable for one another, making the demand for one brand of candy bar, say, Snickers, highly elastic. Toward the other extreme, the demand for corrective lenses (glasses or contacts) is highly inelastic because there simply are no close substitutes.

TABLE 4-2   Price Elasticity of Demand: A Summary

Absolute value of elasticity coefficient	Demand is	Description	Impact on total revenue of a	
			Price increase	**Price decrease**
Greater than 1 ($E_d > 1$)	Elastic or relatively elastic	Quantity demanded changes by a larger percentage than does price	Total revenue decreases	Total revenue increases
Equal to 1 ($E_d = 1$)	Unit or unitary elastic	Quantity demanded changes by the same percentage as does price	Total revenue is unchanged	Total revenue is unchanged
Less than 1 ($E_d < 1$)	Inelastic or relatively inelastic	Quantity demanded changes by a smaller percentage than does price	Total revenue increases	Total revenue decreases

The elasticity of demand for a product depends on how narrowly the product is defined. Demand for Reebok sneakers is more elastic than is the overall demand for shoes. Many other brands are readily substitutable for Reebok sneakers, but there are few, if any, good substitutes for shoes.

PROPORTION OF INCOME

Other things equal, the greater the proportion of income spent on a good, the greater the price elasticity of demand for it. A 10 percent increase in the price of relatively low-priced pencils or chewing gum amounts to a very small proportion of most people's incomes, and quantity demanded will probably decline only slightly. Thus, price elasticity for such items tends to be low. But a 10 percent increase in the price of relatively high-priced automobiles or houses means additional expenditures of perhaps $3000 or $20,000, respectively. These price increases are significant fractions of the annual incomes and budgets of most families, and quantities demanded will likely diminish significantly. Price elasticity for such items tends to be high.

LUXURIES VERSUS NECESSITIES

In general, the more that a good is considered a luxury rather than a necessity, the greater is the price elasticity of demand. Electricity is generally regarded as a necessity; a price increase will not significantly reduce the amount of lighting and power used in a household. (Note the very low price elasticity coefficient of electricity in Table 4-3.) In an extreme example, a person does not decline an operation for acute appendicitis because the surgeon has found a way to extra-bill.

In general, the more a good is considered a luxury rather than a necessity, the greater is the price elasticity of demand.

However, vacation travel and jewellery are luxuries, which, by definition, can easily be forgone. If the prices of vacation travel or jewellery rise, a consumer need not buy them and will suffer no greater hardship without them. What about the demand for a common product like salt? It is highly inelastic on three counts: few good substitutes are available; salt is a negligible item in the family budget; and it is a "necessity" rather than a luxury.

TABLE 4-3   Selected Price Elasticities of Demand

Product or service	Coefficient of price elasticity of demand, E_d	Product or service	Coefficient of price elasticity of demand, E_d
Newspapers	0.10	Household appliances	0.63
Electricity (household)	0.13	Movies	0.87
Bread	0.15	Beer	0.90
Major league baseball tickets	0.23	Shoes	0.91
Telephone service	0.26	Motor vehicles	1.14
Sugar	0.30	Beef	1.27
Eggs	0.32	China, glassware, tableware	1.54
Legal services	0.37	Residential land	1.60
Automobile repair	0.40	Restaurant meals	2.27
Clothing	0.49	Lamb and mutton	2.65
Gasoline	0.60	Fresh peas	2.83
Milk	0.63		

Compiled from numerous studies and sources reporting price elasticity of demand.

TIME

Generally, product demand is more elastic the longer the period under consideration. Consumers often need time to adjust to changes in prices. When the price of a product rises, it takes time to find and experiment with other products to see whether they are acceptable. Consumers may not immediately reduce their purchases very much when the price of beef rises by 10 percent, but in time they may switch to chicken, pork, or fish.

Another consideration is product durability. Studies show that short-run demand for gasoline is more inelastic ($E_d = 0.2$) than is long-run demand ($E_d = 0.7$). In the short run, people are stuck with their present cars and trucks, but with rising gasoline prices they will eventually replace them with smaller, more fuel-efficient vehicles, or switch to mass transit.

Table 4-3 shows the estimated price elasticity coefficients for several products. Each coefficient reflects some combination of the elasticity determinants just discussed. *(Key Question 8)*

Applications of Price Elasticity of Demand

The concept of price elasticity of demand has great practical significance, as the following examples suggest.

LARGE CROP YIELDS

The demand for most farm products is highly inelastic; E_d is perhaps 0.20 or 0.25. As a result, increases in the output of farm products arising from a good growing season or from increased productivity tend to depress both the prices of farm products and the total revenues (incomes) of farmers. For farmers as a group, the inelastic demand for their product means that a large crop may be undesirable. For policymakers it means that achieving the goal of higher total farm income requires that farm output be restricted.

SALES TAXES

Both federal and provincial governments pay attention to elasticity of demand when selecting goods and services on which to levy sales taxes. If a $1 tax is levied on a product and 10,000 units are sold, tax revenue will be $10,000 (= $1 × 10,000 units sold). If the government raises the tax to $1.50 but the higher price reduces sales to 5000 because of elastic demand, tax revenue will decline to $7500 (= $1.50 × 5000 units sold). Because a higher tax on a product with elastic demand will bring in less tax revenue, legislatures seek out products that have inelastic demand—such as liquor, gasoline, and cigarettes—when levying sales tax.

DECRIMINALIZATION OF ILLEGAL DRUGS

In recent years proposals to legalize drugs have been widely debated. Proponents contend that drugs should be treated like alcohol: made legal for adults and regulated for purity and potency. Efforts to reduce consumption of illegal drugs by cracking down on users, it is argued, have been unsuccessful and the associated costs—including enlarged police forces, the construction of more prisons, an overburdened court system, and untold human costs—have increased markedly. Some contend that legalization would reduce drug trafficking significantly by taking the profit out of it. Cocaine and heroin, for example, are cheap to produce and could be sold at low prices in legal markets. Because the demand of addicts is highly inelastic, the amounts consumed at the lower prices would increase only modestly. Addicts' total expenditures for cocaine and heroin would decline and so would the street crime that finances those expenditures.

Opponents of legalization say that the overall demand for cocaine and heroin is far more elastic than proponents think. In addition to the inelastic demand of addicts, another market segment's demand is relatively elastic. This segment consists of occasional users, who use hard drugs when the prices are low but who abstain or substitute, say, alcohol when the prices are high. Thus, the lower prices associated with the legalization of hard drugs would increase consumption by occasional users. Also, removal of the legal prohibitions against using drugs might make drug use more socially acceptable, increasing the demand for cocaine and heroin.

Many economists predict that the legalization of cocaine and heroin would reduce street prices by up to 60 percent, depending on whether and how much it was taxed. According to an important study, price declines of that size would increase the number of occasional users of heroin by 54 percent and the number of occasional users of cocaine by 33 percent. The total quantity of heroin demanded would rise by an estimated 100 percent and the quantity of cocaine demanded would rise by 50 percent.[1] Assuming street prices for both heroin and cocaine rose by 60 percent, such changes in quantity demanded imply price elasticity of demand of 1.66 for heroin and 0.83 for cocaine. Many existing and first-time users might eventually become addicts. The overall result, say the opponents of legalization, would be higher social costs, possibly including an increase in street crime.

QUICK REVIEW

▶ The price elasticity of demand coefficient E_d is the ratio of the percentage change in quantity demanded to the percentage change in price. The averages of the two prices and two quantities are used as the base references in calculating the percentage changes.

▶ When E_d is greater than one, demand is elastic; when E_d is less than one, demand is inelastic; when E_d is equal to one, demand is unit elastic.

▶ When price changes, total revenue will change in the opposite direction if demand is price elastic, in the same direction if demand is price inelastic, and not at all if demand is unit elastic.

▶ Demand is typically elastic in the high-price (low-quantity) range of the demand curve and inelastic in the low-price (high-quantity) range of the curve.

▶ Price elasticity of demand is greater (a) the larger the number of substitutes available; (b) the higher the price of a product relative to one's income; (c) the greater the extent to which the product is a luxury; and (d) the longer the time period involved.

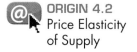
ORIGIN 4.2
Price Elasticity
of Supply

price elasticity of supply
The ratio of the percentage change in quantity supplied of a product to the percentage change in its price.

4.3 | Price Elasticity of Supply

The concept of price elasticity also applies to supply. If producers are relatively responsive to price changes, supply is elastic. If they are relatively insensitive to price changes, supply is inelastic.

We measure the degree of **price elasticity of supply** with the coefficient E_s, defined almost like E_d except that we substitute "percentage change in quantity supplied" for "percentage change in quantity demanded":

$$E_s = \frac{\text{percentage change in quantity supplied of product X}}{\text{percentage change in price of product X}}$$

For reasons explained above, the averages, or midpoints, of the before and after quantities supplied and the before and after prices are used as reference points for the percentage changes. Suppose an increase in the price of a good from $4 to $6 increases the quantity supplied from 10 units to 14 units. The percentage change in price would be 2/5, or 40 percent, and the percentage change in quantity would be 4/12, or 33 percent: $E_s = 0.33/0.40 = 0.83$. In this case supply is inelastic, since the price elasticity coefficient is less than one. If E_s is greater than one, supply is elastic. If it is equal to one, supply is unit elastic. Also, E_s is never negative, since price and quantity supplied are directly related. Thus, there are no minus signs to drop, as was necessary with elasticity of demand.

---

[1] Henry Saffer and Frank Chaloupka, "The Demand for Illegal Drugs," *Economic Inquiry*, July 1999, pp. 401–411.

The degree of price elasticity of supply depends on how easily—and therefore quickly—producers can shift resources between alternative uses. The more easily and quickly producers can shift resources, the greater the price elasticity of supply. A firm's response to, say, an increase in the price of Christmas trees depends on its ability to shift resources from the production of other products (whose prices we assume remain constant) to the production of trees. And shifting resources takes time: the longer the time available, the greater the resource "shiftability." So, we can expect a greater response, and therefore greater elasticity of supply, the longer a firm has to adjust to a price change.

In analyzing the impact of time on elasticity, we distinguish among the immediate market period, the short run, and the long run.

The Market Period

market period
A period in which producers are unable to change the quantity of a product they produce in response to a change in its price.

The **market period** is the period that occurs when the time immediately after a change in market price is too short for producers to respond with a change in quantity supplied. Suppose the owner of a small farm in southwestern Ontario brings to market one truckload of tomatoes, which is the entire season's output. The supply curve for the tomatoes is perfectly inelastic (vertical): the farmer will sell the truckload whether the price is high or low. Why? Because the farmer can offer only one truckload of tomatoes even if the price of tomatoes is much higher than anticipated. The farmer would like to offer more tomatoes, but tomatoes cannot be produced overnight. Another full growing season is needed to respond to a higher-than-expected price by producing more than one truckload. Similarly, because the product is perishable, the farmer cannot withhold it from the market. If the price is lower than anticipated, the farmer will still sell the entire truckload.

The farmer's costs of production, incidentally, will not enter into this decision to sell. Though the price of tomatoes may fall far short of production costs, the farmer will nevertheless sell out to avoid a total loss through spoilage. During the market period, our farmer's supply of tomatoes is fixed: only one truckload is offered no matter how high or low the price.

Figure 4-4a shows the farmer's vertical supply curve during the market period. Supply is perfectly inelastic because the farmer does not have time to respond to a change in demand, say from D_1 to D_2. The resulting price increase from P_0 to P_m simply determines which buyers get the fixed quantity supplied; it elicits no increase in output.

FIGURE 4-4   Time and Elasticity of Supply

The greater the amount of time producers have to adjust to a change in demand, here from D_1 to D_2, the greater will be their output response. In the immediate market period in panel (a), producers have insufficient time to change output, and so supply is perfectly inelastic. In the short run in panel (b), plant capacity is fixed, but changing the intensity of its use can alter output; supply is therefore more elastic. In the long run in panel (c), all desired adjustments, including changes in plant capacity, can be made, and supply becomes still more elastic.

(a) Immediate market period

(b) Short run

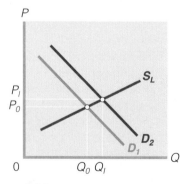

(c) Long run

However, not all supply curves need be perfectly inelastic immediately after a price change. If the product is not perishable and the price rises, producers may choose to increase quantity supplied by drawing down their inventories of unsold, stored goods, causing the market supply curve to attain some positive slope. For our tomato farmer, the market period may be a full growing season; for producers of goods that can be inexpensively stored, there may be no market period at all.

The Short Run ✓

short run
A period of time in which producers are able to change the quantities of some but not all of the resources they employ.

The **short run** in microeconomics is a period of time too short to change plant capacity but long enough to use the fixed plant capacity more or less intensively. In the short run, our farmer's plant (land and farm machinery) is fixed, but time is available to cultivate tomatoes more intensively by applying more labour and more fertilizer and pesticides to the crop. The result is a greater output in response to an increase in demand; this greater output is reflected in a more elastic supply of tomatoes, as shown by S_s in Figure 4-4b. Note that the increase in demand from D_1 to D_2 is met by an increase in quantity (from Q_0 to Q_s), so there is a smaller price adjustment (from P_0 to P_s) than in the market period. The equilibrium price is, therefore, lower in the short run than in the market period (for an explanation of equilibrium price, refer to Chapter 3).

The Long Run ✓

long run
A period of time long enough to enable producers to change the quantities of all the resources they employ.

The **long run** is a period long enough for firms to adjust their plant sizes and for new firms to enter (or existing firms to leave) the industry. In the tomato industry, for example, our farmer has time to acquire additional land and buy more machinery and equipment. Furthermore, other farmers may, over time, be attracted to tomato farming by the increased demand and higher price. Such adjustments create a larger supply response, as represented by the more elastic supply curve S_L in Figure 4-4c. The outcome is a smaller price rise (P_0 to P_1) and a larger output increase (Q_0 to Q_1) in response to the increase in demand from D_1 to D_2.

There is no total-revenue test for elasticity of supply. Supply shows a positive or direct relationship between price and amount supplied; the supply curve is upsloping. Regardless of the degree of elasticity or inelasticity, price and total revenue always move together. *(Key Question 11)*

Applications of Price Elasticity of Supply

The idea of price elasticity of supply has widespread applicability, as suggested by the following examples.

ANTIQUES AND REPRODUCTIONS

In several places across Canada, people bring antiques to a central location for appraisal by experts. Some people are pleased to learn that their old piece of furniture or funky folk art is worth a large amount, say, $30,000 or more. The high price of an antique results from strong demand and limited, highly inelastic supply. Because a genuine antique can no longer be reproduced, the quantity supplied either does not rise or rises only slightly as its price goes up. The higher price might prompt the discovery of a few more of the remaining originals and thus add to the quantity available for sale, but this quantity response is usually quite small. So the supply of antiques and other collectibles tends to be inelastic. For one-of-a-kind antiques, the supply is perfectly inelastic.

Factors such as increased population, higher income, and greater enthusiasm for collecting antiques have increased the demand for antiques over time. Because the supply of antiques is limited and inelastic, those increases in demand have greatly boosted the prices of antiques.

Contrast the inelastic supply of original antiques with the elastic supply of modern "made-to-look-old" reproductions. Such faux antiques are quite popular and widely available. When the demand for reproductions increases, the firms making them simply boost production. Because the supply of reproductions is highly elastic, increased demand raises their price only slightly.

VOLATILE GOLD PRICES

The price of gold is quite volatile, sometimes shooting upward one period and plummeting downward the next. The main sources of these fluctuations are shifts in demand and highly inelastic supply. Gold production is a costly and time-consuming process of exploration, mining, and refining. Moreover, the physical availability of gold is highly limited. For both reasons, increases in gold prices do not bring forth substantial increases in quantity supplied. Conversely, gold mining is costly to shut down and existing gold bars are expensive to store. Price decreases therefore do not produce large drops in the quantity of gold supplied. In short, the supply of gold is inelastic.

The demand for gold is partly derived from the demand for its uses such as for jewellery, dental fillings, and coins. But people also demand gold as a speculative financial investment, increasing their demand when they fear general inflation or domestic or international turmoil that might undermine the value of currency and more traditional investments, and reducing their demand when events settle down. Because of the inelastic supply of gold, even relatively small changes in demand produce relatively large changes in price.

4.4 | Cross Elasticity and Income Elasticity of Demand

Price elasticities measure the responsiveness of the quantity of a product demanded or supplied when its price changes. The consumption of a good also is affected by a change in the price of a related product or by a change in income.

Cross Elasticity of Demand

cross elasticity of demand
The ratio of the percentage change in quantity demanded of one good to the percentage change in price of some other good.

The **cross elasticity of demand** measures how responsive consumer purchases of one product (say, X) are to a change in the price of some other product (say, Y). We calculate the coefficient of cross elasticity of demand E_{xy} just as we do the coefficient of simple price elasticity, except that we relate the percentage change in the consumption of X to the percentage change in the price of Y:

$$E_{xy} = \frac{\text{percentage change in quantity demanded of product X}}{\text{percentage change in price of product Y}}$$

The concept of cross elasticity (or cross price elasticity) allows us to quantify and more fully understand substitute and complementary goods, introduced in Chapter 3.

SUBSTITUTE GOODS $E_{xy} > 0$

If cross elasticity of demand is positive, meaning that sales of X move in the same direction as a change in the price of Y, then X and Y are substitute goods. An example is photo paper for inkjet printers, such as Kodak photo paper (X) and Canon photo paper (Y). An increase in the price of Kodak photo paper causes consumers to buy more Canon photo paper, resulting in a positive cross elasticity. The larger the positive cross elasticity coefficient, the greater the substitutability between the two products.

COMPLEMENTARY GOODS $E_{xy} < 0$

When cross elasticity is negative, we know that X and Y "go together"; an increase in the price of one decreases the demand for the other. So the two are complementary goods. For example, a decrease in the price of digital cameras will increase the amount of photo paper purchased. The larger the negative cross elasticity coefficient, the greater the complementarity between the two goods.

INDEPENDENT GOODS

A zero or near-zero cross elasticity indicates that the two products being considered are unrelated or independent goods. An example is walnuts and photo paper; we would not expect a change in the price of walnuts to have any effect on purchases of photo paper, and vice versa.

normal positive

APPLICATIONS

The degree of product substitutability, measured by the cross elasticity coefficient, is important to businesses and government. Suppose Coca-Cola is considering whether to lower the price of its Sprite brand. It will want to know not only the price elasticity of demand for Sprite (will the price cut increase or decrease total revenue?), but also whether the increased sale of Sprite will come at the expense of its Coke brand. How sensitive are the sales of one of its products (Coke) to a change in the price of another of its products (Sprite)? By how much will the increased sales of Sprite reduce the sales of Coke? A low cross elasticity would indicate that Coke and Sprite are weak substitutes for each other and that a lower price for Sprite would have little effect on Coke sales.

Government also implicitly uses the concept of cross elasticity of demand in assessing whether a proposed merger between two large firms will substantially reduce competition and violate the anti-combines laws. For example, the cross elasticity between Coke and Pepsi is high, making them strong substitutes for each other. Consequently, the government would likely block a merger between the two companies because it would lessen competition. In contrast, the cross elasticity between photo paper and gasoline is low or zero. A merger between Kodak and Petro-Canada would have a minimal effect on competition, so government would be more likely to allow it. **(Key Question 14)**

Income Elasticity of Demand

income elasticity of demand
Measures the responsiveness of consumer purchases to income changes.

Income elasticity of demand measures the degree to which consumers respond to a change in their income by buying more or less of a particular good. The coefficient of income elasticity of demand, E_i, is determined with the formula

$$E_i = \frac{\text{percentage change in quantity demanded}}{\text{percentage change in income}}$$

NORMAL GOODS $E_i > 0$

For most goods, the income elasticity coefficient E_i is positive, meaning that more of them are demanded as incomes rise. Such goods are called normal goods, which we first described in Chapter 3. The value of E_i varies greatly among normal goods. For example, income elasticity of demand for automobiles is about +3.00, while income elasticity for most farm products is only about +0.20.

INFERIOR GOODS $E_i < 0$ *inferior negativ*

A negative income elasticity coefficient designates an inferior good. Retread tires, cabbage, long-distance bus tickets, and used clothing are likely candidates. Consumers decrease their purchases of inferior goods as incomes rise.

INSIGHTS TO THE ECONOMY

Coefficients of income elasticity of demand provide insights into the Canadian economy. For example, income elasticity helps to explain the expansion and contraction of industries. On average, total income in the economy has grown by 2 to 3 percent annually. As income has expanded, industries producing products for which demand is quite income elastic have expanded their outputs. Thus, automobiles (E_i = +3.0), housing (E_i = +1.5), books (E_i = +1.4), and restaurant meals (E_i = +1.4) have all experienced strong growth of output. Also, studies show that the demand for health services is income elastic. The implication of this is that the demand on the Canadian health care system will continue to outpace income growth. Meanwhile, industries producing products for which income elasticity is low or negative have tended to grow slowly or to decline. For example, agriculture (E_i = +0.20) has grown far more slowly than has the economy's total output. We do not eat twice as much when our income doubles.

As another example, when recessions occur and incomes decline, grocery stores fare relatively better than stores selling electronic equipment. People do not substantially cut back on their purchases of food when their incomes fall; income elasticity of demand for food is relatively low. But

TABLE 4-4	Cross Elasticity and Income Elasticity of Demand	
Value of coefficient	**Description**	**Type of good(s)**
Cross elasticity: Positive ($E_{wz} > 0$)	Quantity demanded of W changes in same direction as change in price of Z	Substitutes
Negative ($E_{xy} < 0$)	Quantity demanded of X changes in opposite direction from change in price of Y	Complements
Income elasticity: Positive ($E_i > 0$)	Quantity demanded of the product changes in same direction as change in income	Normal
Negative ($E_i < 0$)	Quantity demanded of the product changes in opposite direction from change in income	Inferior

they do substantially cut back on their purchases of electronic equipment; income elasticity on such equipment is relatively high. *(Key Question 16)*

Table 4-4 provides a convenient synopsis of the cross elasticity and income elasticity concepts.

4.5 | Elasticity and Real-World Applications

Demand and supply analysis and the elasticity concept are applied repeatedly in the remainder of this book. Let's strengthen our understanding of these analytical tools and their importance by examining elasticity and tax incidence.

Elasticity and Tax Incidence

In Figure 4-5, *S* and *D* represent the pre-tax market for a certain domestic wine from the Niagara Peninsula. The no-tax equilibrium price and quantity are $8 per bottle and 15 million bottles. If the Ontario government levies a tax of $2 per bottle directly on the winery for every bottle sold, who actually pays it?

DIVISION OF BURDEN

Since provincial government places the tax on the sellers (suppliers), the tax can be viewed as an addition to the cost of the product. Now sellers must get $2 more for each bottle to receive the same per-unit profit they were getting before the tax. While sellers are willing to offer, for example, 5 million bottles of untaxed wine at $4 per bottle, they must now receive $6 per bottle—$4 plus the $2 tax—to offer the same 5 million bottles. The tax shifts the supply curve upward (leftward) as shown in Figure 4-5, where S_t is the after-tax supply curve.

The after-tax equilibrium price is $9 per bottle, whereas the before-tax price was $8. So, in this case, half the $2 tax is paid by consumers as a higher price; the other half must be paid by producers in a lower after-tax per-unit revenue. That is, after paying the $2 tax per unit to the provincial government, producers receive $7, or $1 less than the $8 before-tax price. In this instance, consumers and producers share the burden of this tax equally; producers shift half the tax to consumers in a higher price and bear the other half themselves.

Note also that the equilibrium quantity decreases as a result of the tax levy and the higher price it imposes on consumers. In Figure 4-5, that decline in quantity is from 15 million bottles per month to 12.5 million bottles per month.

FIGURE 4-5   ## The Incidence of a Tax

A tax of a specified amount per unit levied on producers, here $2 per unit, shifts the supply curve upward by the amount of the tax per unit: the vertical distance between S and S_t. This shift results in a higher price (here $9) to the consumer and a lower after-tax price (here $7) to the producer. Thus, consumers and producers share the burden of the tax in some proportion (here equally at $2 per unit).

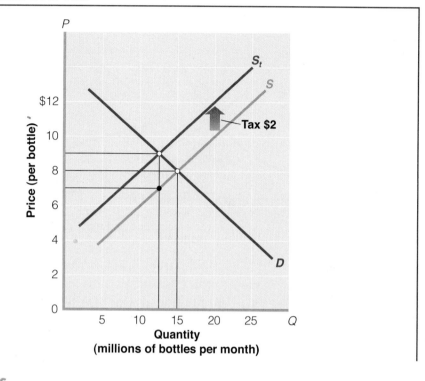

ELASTICITIES

If the elasticities of demand and supply were different from those shown in Figure 4-5, the incidence of tax would also be different. Two generalizations are relevant.

First, *with a specific supply, the more inelastic the demand for the product, the larger the portion of the tax shifted to consumers.* To verify this, sketch graphically the extreme cases where demand is perfectly elastic or perfectly inelastic. In the first case, the incidence of the tax is entirely on sellers; in the second, the tax is shifted entirely to consumers.

Figure 4-6 contrasts the more usual cases where demand is either relatively elastic or relatively inelastic in the relevant price range. With elastic demand, shown in Figure 4-6a, a small portion of the tax $(P_e - P_1)$ is shifted to consumers and most of the tax $(P_1 - P_a)$ is paid by producers. With inelastic demand, shown in Figure 4-6b, most of the tax $(P_i - P_1)$ is shifted to consumers and only a small amount $(P_1 - P_b)$ is paid by producers. In both graphs the per-unit tax is represented by the vertical distance between S_t and S.

Note also that the decline in equilibrium quantity $(Q_2 - Q_1)$ is smaller when demand is more inelastic, which is the basis of our previous applications of the elasticity concept: Revenue-seeking legislatures place heavy sales taxes on liquor, cigarettes, and other products whose demands are thought to be inelastic. Since demand for these products is relatively inelastic, the tax does not reduce sales much, so the tax revenue stays high.

The second generalization is that *with a specific demand, the more inelastic the supply, the larger the portion of the tax paid by producers.* When supply is elastic, as in Figure 4-7a, most of the tax $(P_e - P_1)$ is shifted to consumers, and only a small portion $(P_1 - P_a)$ is paid by sellers. But when supply is inelastic, as in Figure 4-7b, the reverse is true: the major portion of the tax $(P_1 - P_b)$ falls on sellers, and a relatively small amount $(P_i - P_1)$ is shifted to buyers. The equilibrium quantity also declines less with an inelastic supply than it does with an elastic supply.

Gold is an example of a product with an inelastic supply, one where the burden of a tax would mainly fall on producers. Conversely, because the supply of baseballs is elastic, producers would pass on to consumers much of a tax on baseballs. You may want to reverse the analysis and assume that the government levies a (sales) tax on consumers. *(Key Question 18)*

FIGURE 4·6 — Demand Elasticity and the Incidence of a Tax

Panel (a): If demand is elastic in the relevant price range, price rises modestly (P_1 to P_e) when a tax is levied. Hence, the producer bears most of the tax burden. Panel (b): If demand is inelastic, the price to the buyer will increase substantially (P_1 to P_i) and most of the tax will be shifted to consumers.

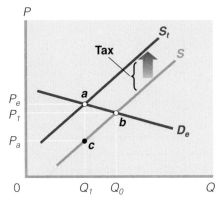

(a) Tax incidence and elastic demand

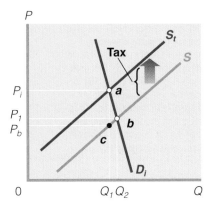

(b) Tax incidence and inelastic demand

FIGURE 4·7 — Supply Elasticity and the Incidence of a Tax

Panel (a): With an elastic supply, the sales tax results in a large price increase (P_1 to P_e), and the tax is therefore paid mainly by consumers. Panel (b): If supply is inelastic, the price rise is small (P_1 to P_i), and sellers will have to bear most of the tax.

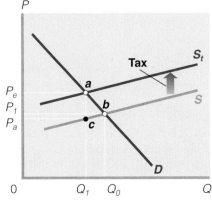

(a) Tax incidence and elastic supply

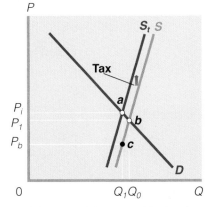

(b) Tax incidence and inelastic supply

QUICK REVIEW

▶ Price elasticity of supply measures the sensitivity of suppliers to changes in the price of a product. The price elasticity of supply coefficient E_s is the ratio of the percentage change in quantity supplied to the percentage change in price. The elasticity of supply varies directly with the amount of time producers have to respond to the price change.

▶ The cross elasticity of demand coefficient E_{xy} is computed as the percentage change in the quantity demanded of product X divided by the percentage change in the price of product Y. If the cross elasticity coefficient is positive, the two products are substitutes; if negative, they are complements.

▶ The income elasticity coefficient E_i is computed as the percentage change in quantity demanded divided by the percentage change in income. A positive coefficient indicates a normal or superior good. The coefficient is negative for an inferior good.

4.6 | Consumer and Producer Surplus

Our final goal for this chapter is to examine the reality that under usual demand and supply conditions, consumers and producers obtain "benefit surpluses" through market transactions. These surpluses vary in size among the separate buyers and sellers.

ORIGIN 4.3
Consumer Surplus

consumer surplus
The difference between the maximum price consumers are willing to pay for a product and the actual price.

Consumer Surplus

The benefit surplus received by a consumer or consumers in a market is called **consumer surplus**—the difference between the maximum price a consumer is (or consumers are) willing to pay for a product and the actual price. In nearly all markets, consumers individually and collectively gain greater total utility in dollar terms (total satisfaction) from their purchases than the amount of their expenditures (= product price × quantity). This utility surplus arises because all consumers pay the equilibrium price even though many would be willing to pay more than that price to obtain the product.

Consider Figure 4-8, where we assume the equilibrium price, P_1, of oranges is $8 per bag. The portion of the demand curve D lying above the $8 equilibrium price shows that many consumers of oranges would be willing to pay more than $8 per bag rather than go without oranges.

Table 4-5 is instructive. Column 2 reveals that Bob is willing to pay a maximum of $13 for a bag of oranges; Barb, $12; Bill, $11; Bart, $10; and Brent, $9. Betty, in contrast, is willing to pay only the $8 equilibrium price. Because all six buyers listed in Table 4-5 obtain the oranges for the $8 equilibrium price (column 3), five of them obtain a consumer surplus. Column 4 shows that Bob's consumer surplus is $5 (= $13 – $8); Barb's, $4 (= $12 – $8); Bill's, $3 (= $11 – $8); Bart's, $2 (= $10 – $8); and Brent's, $1 (= $9 – $8). Only Betty receives no consumer surplus because her maximum willingness to pay of $8 matches the $8 equilibrium price.

Obviously, most markets have more than six people. Suppose there are many other consumers besides Bob, Barb, Bill, Bart, Brent, and Betty in the market represented by Figure 4-8. It is reasonable to assume that many of these additional people are willing to pay more than $8 for a bag of oranges. By adding together the individual consumer surpluses obtained by our named and unnamed buyers, we obtain the collective consumer surplus in this specific market. To obtain the Q_1 bags of oranges represented in Figure 4-8, consumers collectively are willing to pay the total amount

---

FIGURE 4-8   **Consumer Surplus**

Consumer surplus—shown as the green triangle—is the difference between the maximum price consumers are willing to pay for a product and the lower equilibrium price, here assumed to be $8. For quantity Q_1, consumers are willing to pay the sum of the amounts represented by the green triangle and the blue rectangle. Because they need to pay only the amount shown as the blue rectangle, the green triangle shows consumer surplus.

| TABLE 4-5 | Consumer Surplus | | |

(1) Person	(2) Maximum price willing to pay	(3) Actual price (equilibrium price)	(4) Consumer surplus
Bob	$13	$8	$5 (= $13 – $8)
Barb	12	8	4 (= $12 – $8)
Bill	11	8	3 (= $11 – $8)
Bart	10	8	2 (= $10 – $8)
Brent	9	8	1 (= $9 – $8)
Betty	8	8	0 (= $8 – $8)

shown by the sum of the green triangle and blue rectangle under the demand curve and to the left of Q_1. But consumers need pay only the amount represented by the blue rectangle (= $P_1 \times Q_1$). So the green triangle is the consumer surplus in this market. It is the sum of the vertical distances between the demand curve and the $8 equilibrium price at each quantity up to Q_1. Alternatively, it is the sum of the gaps between maximum willingness to pay and actual price, such as those we calculated in Table 4-5.

Consumer surplus and price are inversely (negatively) related. Given the demand curve, higher prices reduce consumer surplus; lower prices increase it. To test this generalization, draw in an equilibrium price above $8 in Figure 4-8 and observe the reduced size of the triangle representing consumer surplus. When price goes up, the gap narrows between the maximum willingness to pay and the actual price. Next, draw in an equilibrium price below $8 and see that consumer surplus increases. When price declines, the gap widens between maximum willingness to pay and actual price.

Producer Surplus

producer surplus
The difference between the actual price producers receive for a product and the minimum acceptable price.

Like consumers, producers also receive a *benefit surplus* in markets. This **producer surplus** is the difference between the actual price a producer receives (or producers receive) and the minimum acceptable price. Sellers collectively receive a producer surplus in most markets because most sellers are willing to accept a lower-than-equilibrium price if that is required to sell the product. That lower acceptable price is shown by the portion of the supply curve in Figure 4-9 lying to the left of and below the assumed $8 equilibrium price.

Suppose that Carlos, Courtney, Chuck, Cindy, Craig, and Chad are six of the many sellers of oranges in the market. Due to differences in production costs, suppose that Carlos's minimum acceptable payment for a bag of oranges is $3, as shown in column 2 of Table 4-6, whereas Courtney's minimum acceptable payment is $4, Chuck's is $5, Cindy's is $6, Craig's is $7, and Chad's is $8. But each seller receives as payment the equilibrium price of $8. As shown in column 4, Carlos thus obtains a producer surplus of $5 (= $8 – $3); Courtney, $4 (= $8 – $4); Chuck, $3 (= $8 – $5); Cindy, $2 (= $8 – $6); Craig, $1 (= $8 – $7); and Chad, zero (= $8 – $8).

By summing the producer surpluses of these sellers along with those of other sellers, we obtain the producer surplus for the entire market for oranges. In Figure 4-9, producers collect revenues of $P_1 \times Q_1$, which is the sum of the green triangle and the blue triangle. As shown by the supply curve, however, revenues of only those illustrated by the green triangle would be required to entice producers to offer Q_1 bags of oranges for sale. The sellers therefore receive a producer surplus shown by the blue triangle. That surplus is the sum of the vertical distances between the supply curve and the $8 equilibrium price at each of the quantities to the left of Q_1.

A direct (positive) relationship exists between equilibrium price and the amount of producer surplus. Given the supply curve, lower prices reduce producer surplus; higher prices increase it. If you

WORKED PROBLEM 4.3
Consumer and Producer Surplus

FIGURE 4·9   Producer Surplus

Producer surplus—shown as the blue triangle—reflects the difference between the equilibrium price producers receive for a product (here $8) and the lower minimum payments they are willing to accept. For quantity Q_1, producers receive the sum of the amounts represented by the blue triangle plus the green triangle. Because they need receive only the amount shown by the green triangle to produce Q_1, the blue triangle represents producer surplus.

pencil in a lower equilibrium price than $8, you will see that the producer surplus triangle gets smaller. The gaps between the minimum acceptable payments and the actual prices narrow when the price falls. If you pencil in an equilibrium price above $8, the size of the producer surplus triangle increases. The gaps between minimum acceptable payments and actual prices widen when the price increases.

Efficiency Revisited

productive efficiency
The production of a good in the least costly way.

allocative efficiency
The apportionment of resources among firms and industries to produce the goods most wanted by society.

In Figure 4-10 we bring together the demand and supply curves of Figures 4-8 and 4-9 to show the equilibrium price and quantity and the previously described regions of consumer and producer surplus. All markets that have downward-sloping demand curves and upward-sloping supply curves yield consumer and producer surplus.

The equilibrium quantity in Figure 4-10 reflects economic efficiency. **Productive efficiency** is achieved because competition forces producers to use the best techniques and combinations of resources in growing and selling oranges. Production costs of each level of output are minimized. **Allocative efficiency** is achieved because the correct quantity of output—Q_1—is produced relative to other goods and services. Points on the demand curve in Figure 4-10 measure the marginal benefit

TABLE 4·6   Producer Surplus

(1) Person	(2) Minimum acceptable price	(3) Actual price (equilibrium price)	(4) Producer surplus
Carlos	$3	$8	$5 (= $8 − $3)
Courtney	4	8	4 (= $8 − $4)
Chuck	5	8	3 (= $8 − $5)
Cindy	6	8	2 (= $8 − $6)
Craig	7	8	1 (= $8 − $7)
Chad	8	8	0 (= $8 − $8)

(MB) of oranges at each level of output. Points on the supply curve measure the marginal cost (MC) of oranges at each output level. The demand and supply curves intersect at the equilibrium output Q_1, indicating that MB = MC. (For the significance of the MB = MC equality for efficiency, review the discussion relating to Figure 1-3.)

Our analysis of consumer and producer surplus provides another way of thinking about efficiency. Each point on a demand curve identifies not only the marginal benefit of the corresponding unit of output but also the *maximum willingness to pay* for it. Willingness to pay derives from the benefit that a product provides. Similarly, each point on the supply curve identifies not only the marginal cost of a good but also the *minimum acceptable price* for the good. To stay profitable, sellers must receive minimum prices that "cover" their marginal costs.

In Figure 4-10 the maximum willingness to pay for each bag of oranges up to Q_1 exceeds the corresponding minimum acceptable price. So each of these bags adds a positive amount (= maximum willingness to pay *minus* minimum acceptable price) to the *total* of consumer and producer surplus. Only at the equilibrium price Q_1, where maximum willingness to pay for the last unit equals minimum acceptable price for that unit, does society exhaust all the opportunities to add to combined consumer and producer surplus. So allocative efficiency occurs where the triangle representing "consumer surplus + producer surplus" is at its maximum size.

Other things equal, competitive markets produce equilibrium prices and quantities that maximize the sum of consumer and producer surplus. Allocative efficiency occurs at quantity levels where three conditions exist:

- MB = MC (Figure 1-3)
- maximum willingness to pay = minimum acceptable price
- combined consumer and producer surplus is at a maximum

Efficiency Losses (or Deadweight Losses)

efficiency losses
Reductions of combined consumer and producer surplus associated with underproduction or over-production of a product.

Figure 4-11 demonstrates **efficiency losses**—reductions of combined consumer and producer surplus—associated with underproduction or overproduction of a product. Suppose that output is Q_2 rather than the efficient level Q_1. The sum of consumer and producer surplus, previously *abc*, falls to *adec*. So the combined consumer and producer surplus declines by the amount of the blue triangle to the left of Q_1. That triangle represents an efficiency loss to buyers and sellers. And since buyers and sellers are members of society, it represents an efficiency loss (or a so-called "deadweight loss") to society.

| **FIGURE 4·10** | **Efficiency: Maximum Combined Consumer and Producer Surplus** |

At quantity Q_1 the combined amount of consumer surplus, shown as the green triangle, and producer surplus, shown as the blue triangle, is maximized. Efficiency occurs because, at Q_1, maximum willingness to pay, shown by the points on the demand curve, equals minimum acceptable price, shown by the points on the supply curve.

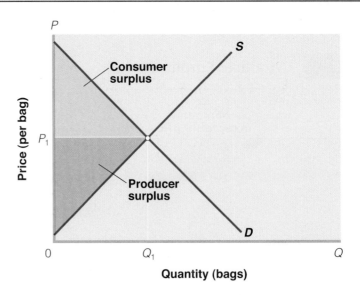

FIGURE 4-11   Efficiency: Losses (or Deadweight Losses)

Quantity levels less than or greater than the efficient quantity, Q_1, create efficiency losses. The blue triangle shows the efficiency loss associated with underproduction, Q_2, whereas the green triangle illustrates the efficiency loss associated with overproduction, Q_3.

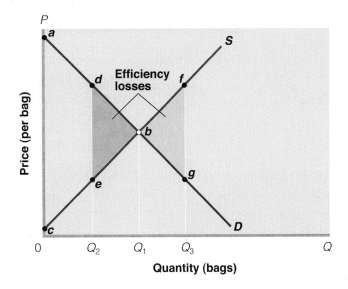

For output levels from Q_2 to Q_1, the maximum willingness to pay by consumers (as reflected by points on the demand curve) exceeds the minimum acceptable price of sellers (as reflected by points on the supply curve). By failing to produce a product for which a consumer is willing to pay, say, $10, and for which a producer is willing to accept $6, society suffers a $4 loss of net benefits. The blue triangle in Figure 4-10 shows the total loss of such net benefits due to the underproduction at Q_2.

In contrast, suppose the amount of oranges produced is Q_3 rather than the efficient level of Q_1. In Figure 4-11 the combined consumer and producer surplus therefore declines by *bfg*—the green triangle to the right of Q_1. This triangle subtracts from the total consumer and producer surplus of *abc* that would occur if the quantity had been Q_1.

For all units beyond Q_1, the consumer's maximum willingness to pay is less than the producer's minimum acceptable price. Producing an item for which the maximum willingness to pay is, say, $7 and the minimum acceptable price is $10 subtracts $3 from society's net benefits. Such production is uneconomical and creates an efficiency loss (or "deadweight loss") for society. The green triangle *bfg* to the right of Q_1 in Figure 4-11 shows the total efficiency loss from overproduction at Q_3. We are again reminded that there can be too much as well as too little of a good thing. Under most conditions, however, a competitive market ensures that the "right amount" of a particular good gets produced. *(Key Question 22)*

QUICK REVIEW

▸ Consumer surplus is the difference between the maximum price a consumer is willing to pay for a product and the lower price actually paid.

▸ Producer surplus is the difference between the minimum price a producer is willing to accept for a product and the higher price actually received.

▸ At the equilibrium price and quantity in competitive markets, marginal benefit equals marginal cost, maximum willingness to pay equals minimum acceptable price, and the total of consumer surplus and producer surplus is maximized. These individual conditions each define allocative efficiency.

▸ Quantities less than or greater than the allocatively efficient level of output create efficiency losses, also called deadweight losses.

The LAST WORD

Elasticity and Pricing Power: Why Different Consumers Pay Different Prices

Firms and nonprofit institutions often recognize and exploit differences in price elasticity of demand.

All buyers in a highly competitive market pay the same market price for the product, regardless of their individual price elasticities of demand. If the price rises, Jones may have an elastic demand and greatly reduce her purchases. Green may have a unit-elastic demand and reduce his purchases less than Jones. Lopez may have an inelastic demand and hardly curtail his purchases at all. But all three consumers will pay the single higher price regardless of their demand elasticities.

In later chapters we will find that not all sellers must passively accept a "one-for-all" price. Some firms have "market power" or "pricing power" that allows them to set their product prices in their best interests. For some goods and services, firms may find it advantageous to determine differences in price elasticity of demand and then charge different prices to different buyers.

It is extremely difficult to tailor prices for each customer on the basis of elasticity of demand, but it is relatively easy to observe differences in group elasticities. Consider airline tickets. Business travellers generally have inelastic demand for air travel. Because their time is highly valuable, they do not see slower modes of transportation as realistic substitutes. Also, their employers pay for their tickets as part of their business expenses. In contrast, leisure travellers tend to have elastic demand. They have the option to drive rather than fly or to simply not travel at all. They also pay for their tickets out of their own pockets and thus are more sensitive to price.

Airlines recognize this group difference in elasticity of demand and charge business travellers more than leisure travellers. To accomplish that, they have to dissuade business travellers from buying the less expensive round-trip tickets aimed at leisure travellers. So they place restrictions on the lower-priced tickets. For example, they make the tickets nonrefundable, require at least 2-week advance purchase, and require Saturday-night stays. These restrictions chase off most business travellers who engage in last-minute travel and want to be home for the weekend. As a result, a business traveller often pays hundreds of dollars more for a ticket than a leisure traveller on the same plane.

Discounts for children are another example of pricing based on group differences in price elasticity of demand. For many products, children have more elastic demands than adults because children have low budgets, often financed by their parents. Sellers recognize the elasticity difference and price accordingly. The barber spends as much time cutting a child's hair as an adult's but charges the child much less. A child takes up a full seat at the baseball

ADMISSION PRICES
General Admission $9.25
Bargain Matinee $7.00
Friday–Sunday and Holiday periods before 4:00 PM
Monday–Thursday during Non-Holiday periods before 6:00 PM
Children (2 -12) $6.50
Seniors (60 & Over)

game but pays a lower price than an adult. A child snowboarder occupies the same space on a chairlift as an adult snowboarder but qualifies for a discounted lift ticket.

Finally, consider pricing by colleges and universities. Price elasticities of demand for higher education are greater for prospective students from low-income families, who generally have more elastic demands for higher education than similar students from high-income families. This makes sense because tuition is a much larger proportion of household income for a low-income student or family than for his or her high-income counterpart. Desiring a diverse student body, colleges charge different *net* prices (= tuition *minus* financial aid) to the two groups on the basis of elasticity of demand. High-income students pay full tuition, unless they receive merit-based scholarships. Low-income students receive considerable financial aid in addition to merit-based scholarships and, in effect, pay a lower net price.

It is common for colleges to announce a large tuition increase and immediately cushion the news by emphasizing that they also are increasing financial aid. In effect, the college is increasing the tuition for students who have inelastic demand by the full amount and raising the net tuition of those with elastic demand by some lesser amount or not at all. Through this strategy, colleges boost revenue to cover rising costs while maintaining affordability for a wide range of students.

There are a number of other examples of dual or multiple pricing. All relate directly to price elasticity of demand.

We will revisit this topic in Chapter 8 when we discuss what economists call *price discrimination*—charging differ-

ent prices to different customers for the same product.

Question

What is the purpose of charging different groups of customers different prices? Supplement the three broad examples in the Last Word with two additional examples of your own. Hint: Think of price discounts based on group characteristics or time of purchase.

CHAPTER SUMMARY

4.1 ▶ PRICE ELASTICITY OF DEMAND

- Price elasticity of demand measures consumer response to price changes. If consumers are relatively sensitive to price changes, demand is elastic. If they are relatively unresponsive to price changes, demand is inelastic.

- The price elasticity coefficient E_d measures the degree of elasticity or inelasticity of demand. The coefficient is found by the formula

$$E_d = \frac{\text{percentage change in quantity demanded of product X}}{\text{percentage change in price of product X}}$$

The averages of prices and quantities under consideration are used as reference points in determining percentage changes in price and quantity. If E_d is greater than one, demand is elastic. If E_d is less than one, demand is inelastic. Unit elasticity is the special case in which E_d equals one.

- Perfectly inelastic demand is graphed as a line parallel to the vertical axis; perfectly elastic demand is shown by a line above and parallel to the horizontal axis.

4.2 ▶ THE TOTAL-REVENUE TEST

- Elasticity varies at different price ranges on a demand curve, tending to be elastic in the upper left segment and inelastic in the lower right segment. Elasticity cannot be judged by the steepness or flatness of a demand curve.

- If total revenue changes in the opposite direction from prices, demand is elastic. If price and total revenue change in the same direction, demand is inelastic. Where demand is of unit elasticity, a change in prices leaves total revenue unchanged.

- The number of available substitutes, the size of an item's price relative to one's income, whether the product is a luxury or a necessity, and the time given to adjust are all determinants of elasticity of demand.

4.3 ▶ PRICE ELASTICITY OF SUPPLY

- The elasticity concept also applies to supply. The coefficient of price elasticity of supply is found by the formula

$$E_s = \frac{\text{percentage change in quantity supplied of product X}}{\text{percentage change in price of product X}}$$

The averages of the price and quantities under consideration are used as reference points for computing percentage changes. Elasticity of supply depends on the ease of shifting resources between alternative uses, which in turn varies directly with the time producers have to adjust to a particular price change.

4.4 ▶ CROSS ELASTICITY AND INCOME ELASTICITY OF DEMAND

- Cross elasticity of demand indicates how sensitive the purchase of one product is to changes in the price of another product. The coefficient of cross elasticity of demand is found by the formula

$$E_{xy} = \frac{\text{percentage change in quantity demanded of product X}}{\text{percentage change in price of product Y}}$$

Positive cross elasticity of demand identifies substitute goods; negative cross elasticity identifies complementary goods.

- Income elasticity of demand indicates the responsiveness of consumer purchases to a change in income. The coefficient of income elasticity of demand is found by the formula

$$E_i = \frac{\text{percentage change in quantity demanded of product X}}{\text{percentage change in income}}$$

The coefficient is positive for normal goods and negative for inferior goods.

4.5 ▶ ELASTICITY AND REAL-WORLD APPLICATIONS

- Sales taxes affect supply and, therefore, equilibrium price and quantity. The more inelastic the demand for a product, the greater is the proportion of a sales tax that is shifted to consumers. The greater the inelasticity of supply, the larger the proportion of the tax that is paid by the seller.

4.6 ▶ CONSUMER AND PRODUCER SURPLUS

- Consumer surplus is the difference between the maximum price that a consumer is willing to pay for a product and the lower price actually paid; producer surplus is the difference between the minimum price that a producer is willing to accept for a product and the higher price actually received.

- At the equilibrium price and quantity in competitive markets, marginal benefit equals marginal cost, maximum willingness to pay equals minimum acceptable price, and the combined amount of consumer surplus and producer surplus is maximized.

- Output levels less than or greater than the equilibrium output create efficiency losses—reductions in the combined amount of consumer surplus and producer surplus. Underproduction creates efficiency losses because output is not being produced for which maximum willingness to pay exceeds minimum acceptable price. Overproduction creates efficiency losses because output is being produced for which minimum acceptable price exceeds maximum willingness to pay.

TERMS AND CONCEPTS

price elasticity of demand, p. 83
midpoint formula, p. 84
elastic demand, p. 85
inelastic demand, p. 85
unit elasticity, p. 85
perfectly inelastic demand, p. 85
perfectly elastic demand, p. 86

total revenue (TR), p. 87
total-revenue test, p. 87
price elasticity of supply, p. 93
market period, p. 94
short run, p. 95
long run, p. 95
cross elasticity of demand, p. 96

income elasticity of demand, p. 97
consumer surplus, p. 101
producer surplus, p. 102
productive efficiency, p. 103
allocative efficiency, p. 103
efficiency losses, p. 104

STUDY QUESTIONS

LO 4.1 1. Explain why the choice between discussing 1, 2, 3, 4, 5, 6, 7, and 8 units or 1000, 2000, 3000, 4000, 5000, 6000, 7000, and 8000 movie tickets makes no difference in determining elasticity in Table 4-1.

LO 4.1 2. **KEY QUESTION** Graph the accompanying demand data and then use the midpoint formula for E_d to determine price elasticity of demand for each of the four possible $1 price changes. What can you conclude about the relationship between the slope of a curve and its elasticity? Explain in a non-technical way why demand is elastic in the northwest segment of the demand curve and inelastic in the southeast segment.

Product price	Quantity demanded
$5	1
4	2
3	3
2	4
1	5

3. The following data show the relationship between price and quantity demanded at four different prices for a product: **LO**

$P = \$11,$ $Q_d = 16$

$P = \$9,$ $Q_d = 24$

$P = \$7,$ $Q_d = 32$

$P = \$5,$ $Q_d = 40$

Using the midpoint formula, what is the price elasticity of demand between:

a. $11 and $9

b. $9 and $7

c. $7 and $5

4. **KEY QUESTION** Calculate total-revenue data from the demand schedule in question 2. Graph total revenue below your demand curve. Generalize about the relationship between price elasticity and total revenue.   **LO**

5. **KEY QUESTION** How would the following changes in price affect total revenue? That is, would total revenue increase, decline, or remain unchanged?   **LO**

a. Price falls and demand is inelastic.

b. Price rises and demand is elastic.

c. Price rises and supply is elastic.

d. Price rises and supply is inelastic.

e. Price rises and demand is inelastic.

f. Price falls and demand is elastic.

g. Price falls and demand is unit elastic.

6. The president of the Micro Brewing Corporation asks you, as the company economist, to forecast changes in consumer beer purchases associated with a proposed price change. You conduct a survey and find that if the price of a six-pack increases from $5.50 to $7.50, the quantity demanded will decrease from 2200 units to 1800 units a month. Should the Micro Brewing Corporation raise its price? Explain the economic basis for this recommendation to the president. *inelastic change the price*

7. The following is a straight-line demand curve that confronts a single firm.

Price	Quantity demanded	(3)	(4)
$6	1	____	____
5	2	____	____
4	3	____	____
3	4	____	____
2	5	____	____
1	6	____	____

a. In column 3, compute total revenue. In column 4, compute the coefficient for the price elasticity of demand at each price using the midpoint formula.

b. Describe the character of elasticity across the prices based on the total-revenue test and the elasticity coefficient.

c. Does a straight-line demand curve have constant elasticity?

d. Of what practical significance is your answer to (c)?

8. **KEY QUESTION**   What are the major determinants of price elasticity of demand? Use those determinants and your own reasoning in judging whether demand for each of the following products is probably elastic or inelastic: (a) bottled water, (b) toothpaste, (c) Crest toothpaste, (d) ketchup, (e) diamond bracelet, (f) Microsoft Windows operating system.

9. What effect would a rule stating that university students must live in university or college dormitories have on the price elasticity of demand for dormitory space? What impact might this in turn have on room rates?

10. In November 1998 Vincent van Gogh's self-portrait sold at auction for $71.5 million. Portray this sale in a demand and supply diagram and comment on the elasticity of supply. Comedian George Carlin once mused, "If a painting can be forged well enough to fool some experts, why is the original so valuable?" Provide an answer.

11. **KEY QUESTION**   What is the formula for measuring the price elasticity of supply? Suppose the price of apples goes up from $20 to $22 a box. In direct response, Goldsboro Farms supplies 1200 boxes of apples instead of 1000 boxes. Compute the coefficient of price elasticity (midpoints approach) for Goldsboro's supply. Is its supply elastic, or is it inelastic?

12. Explain the perspective that tougher enforcement of drug laws may actually increase the crime rate. Use the concepts of demand, supply, and elasticity in your explanation.

13. A computer company is considering lowering the price of its laptop computer to promote sales. However, it worries that this will reduce desktop computer sales. It finds the cross elasticity of demand to be +1.5. Are its concerns legitimate? Explain.

14. **KEY QUESTION**   Suppose the cross elasticity of demand for products A and B is +3.6 and for products C and D is −5.4. What can you conclude about how products A and B are related? Products C and D?

15. Use the information in the table below to identify the type of cross elasticity relationship between products X and Y in each of the following five cases, A to E.

Cases	Percentage change in price of Y	Percentage change in quantity demanded of X	Cross elasticity type
A	5	7	____
B	9	6	____
C	5	−5	____
D	3	0	____
E	−2	10	____

16. **KEY QUESTION**   The income elasticities of demand for movies, dental services, and clothing have been estimated to be +3.4, +1.0, and +0.5, respectively. Interpret these coefficients. What does it mean if an income elasticity coefficient is negative?

17. Research has found that an increase in the price of beer would reduce the amount of marijuana consumed. Is cross elasticity of demand between the two products positive or is it negative? Are these products substitutes, or are they complements? What might be the logic behind this relationship?

18. **KEY QUESTION**   What is the incidence of a tax when demand is highly inelastic? Highly elastic? What effect does the elasticity of supply have on the incidence of a tax?

19. Refer to Table 4-5. If the six people listed in the table are the only consumers in the market and the equilibrium price is $11 (not the $8 shown), how much consumer surplus will the market generate?

LO 4.6 20. Refer to Table 4-6. If the six people listed in the table are the only producers in the market and the equilibrium price is $6 (not the $8 shown), how much producer surplus will the market generate?

LO 4.6 21. Draw a demand and supply graph and identify the areas of consumer surplus and producer surplus. Given the demand curve, what impact will an increase in supply have on the amount of consumer surplus shown in your diagram? Explain why.

22. **KEY QUESTION**   Use the ideas of consumer surplus and producer surplus to explain why economists say competitive markets are efficient. Why are below- or above-equilibrium levels of output inefficient, according to these two sets of ideas?

INTERNET APPLICATION QUESTIONS @

1. **Price Elasticity and the Price of Gold.** Go to the McConnell-Brue-Flynn-Barbiero Web site (Chapter 4) to find the latest price of gold. Compare that price to the price at the beginning of the day. What was the highest price during the last 12 months? The lowest price? Assume the price fluctuations observed resulted exclusively from changes in demand. Would the observed price changes have been greater or less if the gold supply had they been elastic rather than inelastic? Explain.

2. **Elasticity of Demand—Alcohol.** Go to the McConnell-Brue-Flynn-Barbiero Web site (Chapter 4) to access the National Bureau of Economic Research (NEBR). Select NBER Working Papers. In the Google search space, type "alcohol." Use the titles and summaries of the papers to answer the following questions relating to elasticity:

   a. Do the mentally ill have perfectly inelastic demands for cigarettes and alcohol?

   b. Does alcohol consumption increase in bad times?

   c. What is the effect of cigarette taxes (and smuggling) on the consumption of alcohol? What does that imply about the cross elasticity of demand between the two?

   d. Is binge drinking among college and university students sensitive to the price of alcohol?

CHAPTER 5

Consumer Choice and Utility Maximization

Compare the shopping carts of almost any two consumers, and you will observe striking differences. Why does Paula have potatoes, peaches, and Pepsi in her cart while Sam has sugar, saltines, and 7-Up in his? Why didn't Paula also buy pasta and plums? Why didn't Sam have soup and spaghetti on his grocery list?

In this chapter, you will see how individual consumers allocate their income among the various goods and services available to them. Given a certain budget, how does a consumer decide which goods and services to buy? As we answer this question, you will also strengthen your understanding of the law of demand.

5.1 | The Law of Diminishing Marginal Utility

The simplest theory of consumer choice rests squarely on the **law of diminishing marginal utility.** This principle, first discussed in Chapter 3, is that added satisfaction declines as a consumer acquires additional units of a given product. Although consumer wants in general may be insatiable, wants for a particular item can be satisfied. In a specific span of time over which consumers' tastes remain unchanged, consumers can get as much of a particular good or service as they can afford. But the more of that product they obtain, the less they want still more of it.

Consider durable goods, for example. Consumers' desires for an automobile, when they have none, may be very strong, but the desire for a second car is less intense, and for a third or fourth, weaker and weaker. Unless they are collectors, even the wealthiest families rarely have more than a half-dozen cars, although their income would allow them to purchase a whole fleet of vehicles.

Terminology

Evidence indicates that consumers can fulfill specific wants with succeeding units of a product but that each added unit provides less utility than the previous unit purchased. Recall that a product has utility if it can satisfy a want: **utility** is want-satisfying power.

ORIGIN 5.1
Law of Diminishing
Marginal Utility

law of diminishing marginal utility
As a consumer increases consumption of a good or service, the marginal utility obtained from each additional unit of the good or service decreases.

utility
The want-satisfying power of a good or service; the satisfaction a person gets from consuming a good or service.

total utility
The total amount of satisfaction derived from the consumption of a single product or a combination of products.

marginal utility
The extra utility a consumer obtains from the consumption of one additional unit of a product.

If successive units of a good yield smaller and smaller amounts of marginal utility, then the consumer will buy additional units only if its price falls.

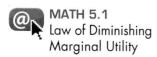

MATH 5.1
Law of Diminishing
Marginal Utility

The utility of a good or service is the satisfaction or pleasure one gets from consuming it. Keep in mind three characteristics of this concept.

1. *"Utility" and "usefulness" are not synonymous.* Paintings by Picasso may offer great utility to art connoisseurs but are useless functionally (other than for hiding a crack in a wall!).

2. *Utility is subjective.* The utility of a specific product may vary widely from person to person. A Céline Dion CD has tremendous utility for one of her fans, but no utility to someone who listens only to the Tragically Hip.

3. *Utility is difficult to quantify.* But, for purposes of illustration, we assume that people can measure satisfaction with units called *utils* (units of utility). For example, a particular consumer may get 100 utils of satisfaction from a smoothie, 10 utils of satisfaction from a candy bar, and 1 util of satisfaction from a stick of gum. These imaginary units of satisfaction are convenient for quantifying consumer behaviour for explanatory purposes.

Total Utility and Marginal Utility

Total utility and marginal utility are related but different ideas. **Total utility** is the total amount of satisfaction or pleasure a person derives from consuming some specific quantity—for example, 10 units—of a good or service. **Marginal utility** is the *extra* satisfaction a consumer gets from one additional unit of that product, for example, from the 11th unit. Alternatively, marginal utility is the change in total utility that results from the consumption of one more unit of a product.

Figure 5-1 (Key Graph) and the accompanying table demonstrate the relation between total utility and marginal utility. The curves reflect the data in the table. Column 2 shows the total utility at each level of consumption of tacos; column 3 shows the marginal utility—the change in total utility—that results from the consumption of each successive taco. Starting at the origin in Figure 5-1a, we observe that each of the first five units increases total utility (TU) but by a diminishing amount. Total utility reaches a maximum at the sixth unit and then declines.

So, in Figure 5-1b marginal utility (MU) remains positive but diminishes through the first five units (because total utility increases at a declining rate). Marginal utility is zero for the sixth unit (because that unit doesn't change total utility). Marginal utility then becomes negative with the seventh unit as the diner becomes ill (because total utility is falling). Figure 5-1b and column 3 of the table reveal that each successive taco yields less extra utility, meaning fewer utils, than the preceding taco as the consumer's want for tacos comes closer and closer to fulfillment.[1] That is, the table and the graph illustrate the law of diminishing marginal utility. (See the Consider This box for other examples of the law of diminishing marginal utility.) *(Key Question 1)*

Marginal Utility and Demand

The law of diminishing marginal utility explains why the demand curve for a given product slopes downward. If successive units of a good yield smaller and smaller amounts of marginal, or extra, utility, then the consumer will buy additional units of a product only if its price falls. The consumer for whom Figure 5-1 is relevant may buy two tacos at a price of $1 each, but because less marginal utility is obtained from additional tacos, the consumer will choose not to buy more at that price. The consumer would rather spend additional dollars on products that provide more (or equal) utility, not less utility. Therefore, additional tacos with less utility are not worth buying unless the price declines. (When marginal utility becomes negative, the restaurant would have to pay you to consume another taco!) Thus, diminishing marginal utility supports the idea that price must decrease for quantity demanded to increase. In other words, consumers behave in ways that make demand curves downward-sloping.

---

[1] In Figure 5-1b we graphed marginal utility at half-units. For example, we graphed the marginal utility of 4 utils at 3½ units because the 4 utils refers neither to the third nor the fourth unit per se but to the *addition* or *subtraction* of the fourth unit.

KEY GRAPH

FIGURE 5-1 Total and Marginal Utility

Curves TU and MU are graphed from the data in the table. Panel (a): As more of a product is consumed, total utility increases at a diminishing rate, reaches a maximum, and then declines. Panel (b): Marginal utility, by definition, reflects the changes in total utility. Thus marginal utility diminishes with increased consumption, becomes zero when total utility is at a maximum, and is negative when total utility declines. As shown by the shaded rectangles in panels (a) and (b), marginal utility is the change in total utility associated with each additional taco. Or, alternatively, each new level of total utility is found by adding marginal utility to the preceding level of total utility.

(1) Tacos consumed per meal	(2) Total utility, utils	(3) Marginal utility, utils
0	0	
		10
1	10	
		8
2	18	
		6
3	24	
		4
4	28	
		2
5	30	
		0
6	30	
		-2
7	28	

Quick Quiz

1. **Marginal utility**
   a. is the extra output a firm obtains when it adds another unit of labour.
   b. explains why product supply curves slope upward.
   c. typically rises as successive units of a good are consumed.
   d. is the extra satisfaction from the consumption of one more unit of some good or service.

2. **Marginal utility in Figure 5-1b is positive, but declining, when total utility in Figure 5-1a is positive and**
   a. rising at an increasing rate.
   b. falling at an increasing rate.
   c. rising at a decreasing rate.
   d. falling at a decreasing rate.

3. **When marginal utility is zero in panel (b), total utility in panel (a) is**
   a. also zero.
   b. neither rising nor falling.
   c. negative.
   d. rising but at a declining rate.

4. **Suppose the person represented by these graphs experienced a diminished taste for tacos. As a result the**
   a. TU curve would get steeper.
   b. MU curve would get flatter.
   c. TU and MU curves would shift downward.
   d. MU curve, but not the TU curve, would collapse to the horizontal axis.

(a) Total utility

(b) Marginal utility

Answers: 1. d; 2. c; 3. b; 4. c

CONSIDER THIS | Vending Machines and Diminishing Marginal Utility

Newspaper dispensing devices and soft-drink vending machines are similar in their basic operations. Both allow consumers to buy a product by inserting coins. But there is an important difference in the two devices. The newspaper dispenser opens to the full stack of papers and seemingly "trusts" the customer to take only a single copy, whereas the vending machine displays no such "trust," requiring the consumer to buy one can at a time. Why the difference?

The idea of diminishing marginal utility is key to solving this puzzle. Most consumers take only single copies from the newspaper box because the marginal utility of a second newspaper is nearly zero. They could grab a few extra papers and try to sell them on the street, but the revenue obtained would be small relative to their time and effort. So, in selling their product newspaper publishers rely on "zero marginal utility of the second unit," not on consumer honesty.

Also, newspapers have little "shelf life"; they are obsolete the next day. In contrast, soft-drink sellers do not allow buyers to make a single payment and then take as many cans as they want. If they did, consumers would clean out the machine because the marginal utility of successive cans of pop diminishes slowly, so buyers could take extra cans and consume them later. As a result, soft-drink firms sell their products on a pay-per-can basis.

In summary, newspaper publishers and soft-drink firms use alternative vending techniques because of the very different rates of decline in marginal utility for their products. The newspaper seller uses inexpensive dispensers that open to the full stack of papers. The soft drink seller uses expensive vending machines that limit the consumer to a single can at a time. Each vending technique is optimal under the particular economic circumstance.

QUICK REVIEW

▸ The law of diminishing marginal utility indicates that gains in satisfaction become smaller as successive units of a specific product are consumed.

▸ Utility is the benefit or satisfaction a person receives from consuming a good or a service.

▸ Diminishing marginal utility provides a simple rationale for the law of demand.

5.2 | The Theory of Consumer Choice

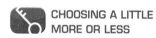

CHOOSING A LITTLE MORE OR LESS

In addition to explaining the law of demand, the idea of diminishing marginal utility explains how consumers allocate their money income among the many goods and services available for purchase.

Consumer Choice and Budget Constraint

For simplicity, we will assume that the situation for the typical consumer has the following dimensions.

rational behaviour
Human behaviour that seeks to maximize total utility.

- *Rational Behaviour*   The consumer is a rational person who tries to use his or her money income to get the greatest amount of satisfaction, or utility, from it. Consumers want to get the most for their money or, technically, to maximize their total utility. They engage in **rational behaviour.**

- *Preferences*   Each consumer has clear-cut preferences for certain goods and services of those available in the market. Buyers also have a good idea of how much marginal utility they will get from successive units of the various products they purchase.

budget constraint
The limit that a consumer's income (and the prices that must be paid for goods and services) imposes on the ability of that consumer to obtain goods and services.

- *Budget Constraints*   At any point in time the consumer has a fixed, limited amount of money income. Since each consumer supplies a finite amount of human and property resources to society, he or she earns only limited income. Thus, as noted in Chapter 1, every consumer faces a **budget constraint,** even consumers who can earn millions of dollars a year. Of course, those budget constraints are more severe for consumers with average incomes than for those with extraordinarily high incomes.

- *Prices*   Goods are scarce relative to the demand for them, so every good carries a price tag. We assume those price tags are not affected by the amounts of specific goods each person buys. After all, each person's purchase is only a tiny part of total demand. Also, because the consumer has a limited number of dollars, he or she cannot buy everything wanted. This point drives home the reality of scarcity to each consumer.

So consumers must compromise and choose the most satisfying affordable combination of goods and services. Different individuals will choose different mixes.

Utility-Maximizing Rule

utility-maximizing rule
To obtain the greatest utility, the consumer should allocate money income so that the last dollar spent on each good or service yields the same marginal utility.

To maximize satisfaction, consumers should allocate their money income so that the last dollar spent on each product yields the same amount of extra (marginal) utility. We call this the **utility-maximizing rule.** When the consumer has balanced his or her margins using this rule, no incentive exists to alter the expenditure pattern. The consumer is in equilibrium and would be worse off—total utility would decline—if any revision occurred in the bundle of goods purchased, providing no change occurs in taste, income, products, or prices.

A Numerical Example

An illustration will help explain the utility-maximizing rule. For simplicity we limit our example to two products, but the analysis also applies if there are more. Suppose consumer Holly is analyzing which combination of two products—apples and oranges—she should purchase with her fixed daily income of $10.

Holly's preferences for apples and oranges, their prices, and her income are the basic data determining the combination that will maximize her satisfaction. Table 5-1 summarizes those data, with column 2a showing the amount of marginal utility Holly will get from each successive apple and column 3a showing the same thing for oranges. Both columns reflect the law of diminishing marginal utility, which is assumed to begin with the second unit of each product purchased.

TABLE 5-1

The Utility-Maximizing Combinations of Apples and Oranges Obtainable with an Income of $10

(1) Unit of product	(2) Apple (Product A): Price = $1		(3) Oranges (Product B): Price = $2	
	(a) Marginal utility, utils	(b) Marginal utility per dollar (MU/price)	(a) Marginal utility, utils	(b) Marginal utility per dollar (MU/price)
First	10	10	24	12
Second	8	8	20	10
Third	7	7	18	9
Fourth	6	6	16	8
Fifth	5	5	12	6
Sixth	4	4	6	3
Seventh	3	3	4	2

It is assumed in this table that the amount of marginal utility received from additional units of each of the two products is independent of the quantity of the other product. For example, the marginal-utility schedule for apples is independent of the number of oranges obtained by the consumer.

MARGINAL UTILITY PER DOLLAR

To see how the utility-maximizing rule works, we must put the marginal utility information in columns 2a and 3a on a per-dollar-spent basis. Holly's choices are influenced not only by the extra utility that successive units of apples will yield, but also by how many dollars (and therefore how many oranges) she must give up to obtain additional apples.

The rational consumer compares the extra utility from each product with its added cost (that is, its price). Switching examples for a moment, suppose that you prefer a pizza whose marginal utility is, say, 36 utils to a movie whose marginal utility is 24 utils. But if the pizza's price is $12 and the movie costs only $6, you would choose the movie rather than the pizza! Why? Because the marginal utility per dollar spent would be 4 utils for the movie (= 24 utils ÷ $6) compared to only 3 utils for the pizza (= 36 utils ÷ $12). You could buy two movies for $12 and, assuming that the marginal utility of the second movie is, say, 16 utils, your total utility would be 40 utils. Clearly, 40 units of satisfaction from two movies is superior to 36 utils from the same $12 expenditure on one pizza.

To make the amounts of extra utility derived from differently priced goods comparable, marginal utilities must be put on a per-dollar-spent basis. We do this in columns 2b and 3b by dividing the marginal utility data of columns 2a and 3a by the prices of apples and oranges, $1 and $2, respectively.

DECISION-MAKING PROCESS

In Table 5-1 we show Holly's preferences on a unit basis and a per-dollar basis, as well as the price tags of apples and oranges. With $10 to spend, in what order will Holly allocate her dollars on apples and oranges to achieve the highest degree of utility within the $10 limit imposed by her income? What specific combination of the two products will she purchase to get the most from her $10?

Concentrating on columns 2b and 3b in Table 5-1, we find that Holly should begin by spending $2 on the first orange, because its marginal utility per dollar of 12 utils is higher than the first apple's 10 utils. Now Holly finds herself indifferent about whether she should buy a second orange or the first apple because the marginal utility per dollar of both is 10 utils. So she buys both of them. Holly now has one apple and two oranges. Also, the last dollar she spent on each good yielded the same marginal utility per dollar (10 utils), but this combination of apples and oranges does not represent the maximum amount of utility that Holly can obtain. It cost her only $5 [= (1 × $1) + (2 × $2)], so she has $5 remaining, which she can spend to achieve a still higher level of total utility.

Examining columns 2b and 3b again, we find that Holly should spend the next $2 on a third orange because marginal utility per dollar for the third orange is nine compared with eight for the second apple. Now, with one apple and three oranges, she is again indifferent between a second apple and a fourth orange because both provide eight utils per dollar. So Holly purchases one more of each. Now the last dollar spent on each product provides the same marginal utility per dollar (eight utils), and Holly's money income of $10 is exhausted.

The utility-maximizing combination of goods Holly can attain is two apples and four oranges. By summing marginal utility information from columns 2a and 3a, we find that Holly is getting 18 (= 10 + 8) utils of satisfaction from the two apples and 78 (= 24 + 20 + 18 + 16) utils of satisfaction from the four oranges. Her $10, optimally spent, yields 96 (= 18 + 78) utils of satisfaction.

Table 5-2 summarizes our step-by-step process for maximizing Holly's utility. Note that we have assumed Holly spends her entire income—she neither borrows nor saves. However, saving can be regarded as a "commodity" that yields utility and be incorporated into our analysis. In fact, we treat it that way in study question 3 at the end of this chapter. *(Key Question 3)*

INFERIOR OPTIONS

Holly can obtain other combinations of apples and oranges with $10, but none will yield as great a total utility as do two apples and four oranges. As an example, she can obtain four apples and three oranges for $10. But this combination yields only 93 utils, clearly inferior to the 96 utils she gets from two apples and four oranges. True, other combinations of apples and oranges exist (such as four apples and five oranges, or one apple and two oranges) in which the marginal utility of the last dollar

| TABLE 5-2 | **Sequence of Purchases to Achieve Consumer Equilibrium, Given the Data in Table 5-1** | | | |

Choice number	Potential choices	Marginal utility per dollar	Purchase decision	Income remaining
1	First apple First orange	10 12	First orange for $2	$8 = $10 – $2
2	First apple Second orange	10 10	First apple for $1 and second orange for $2	$5 = $8 – $3
3	Second apple Third orange	8 9	Third orange for $2	$3 = $5 – $2
4	Second apple Fourth orange	8 8	Second apple for $1 and fourth orange for $2	$0 = $3 – $3

WORKED PROBLEM 5.1
Consumer Choice

spent is the same for both apples and oranges. All such combinations are either unobtainable with Holly's limited money income (as four apples and five oranges) or do not exhaust her money income (as one apple and two oranges) and, therefore, do not yield the maximum utility attainable.

Algebraic Restatement

Economists generalize the utility-maximization rule by saying that a consumer will maximize satisfaction by allocating money income so that the last dollar spent on product A, the last on product B, and so forth, yield equal amounts of marginal utility. The marginal utility per dollar spent on A is indicated by MU of product A divided by the price of A (column 2b in Table 5-1), and the marginal utility per dollar spent on B by MU of product B divided by the price of B (column 3b in Table 5-1). Our utility-maximizing rule merely requires that these ratios be equal. Algebraically,

$$\frac{\text{MU of product A}}{\text{Price of A}} = \frac{\text{MU of product B}}{\text{Price of B}}$$

Of course, the consumer must exhaust her available income. Table 5-1 shows us that the combination of two units of A (apples) and four of B (oranges) fulfills these conditions in that

$$\frac{8 \text{ utils}}{\$1} = \frac{16 \text{ utils}}{\$2}$$

and the consumer's $10 income is spent.

If the equation is not fulfilled, then some reallocation of the consumer's expenditures between A and B (from the low to the high marginal-utility-per-dollar product) will increase the consumer's total utility. For example, if the consumer spent $10 on four units of A (apples) and three of B (oranges), we would find that

$$\frac{\text{MU of A: 6 utils}}{\text{Price of A: \$1}} < \frac{\text{MU of B: 18 utils}}{\text{Price of B: \$2}}$$

Here the last dollar spent on A provides only six utils of satisfaction, and the last dollar spent on B provides nine (= 18 ÷ $2). So, the consumer can increase total satisfaction by purchasing more of B and less of A. As dollars are reallocated from A to B, the marginal utility per dollar of A will increase while the marginal utility per dollar of B will decrease. At some new combination of A and B the two will be equal, and consumer equilibrium will be achieved. Here, that combination is two units of A (apples) and four of B (oranges).

5.3 | Utility Maximization and the Demand Curve

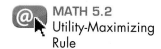

MATH 5.2
Utility-Maximizing
Rule

Once you understand the utility-maximizing rule, you can easily see why product price and quantity demanded are inversely related. Recall that the basic determinants of an individual's demand for a specific product are (1) preferences or tastes, (2) money income, and (3) the prices of other goods. The utility data in Table 5-1 reflect our consumer's preferences. We continue to suppose that her money income is $10. Concentrating on the construction of a simple demand curve for oranges, we assume that the price of apples, now representing all "other goods," is still $1.

Deriving the Demand Schedule and Curve

We can derive a single consumer's demand schedule for oranges by considering alternative prices at which oranges might be sold and then determining the quantity the consumer will purchase. We already know one such price–quantity combination in the utility-maximizing example: given tastes, income, and prices of other goods, Holly will purchase four oranges at $2.

Now let's assume the price of oranges falls to $1. The marginal-utility-per-dollar data of column 3b in Table 5-1 will double because the price of oranges has been halved; the new data for column 3b are identical to those in column 3a, but the purchase of two apples and four oranges is no longer an equilibrium combination. By applying the same reasoning we used previously, we now find that Holly's utility-maximizing combination is four apples and six oranges. As summarized in the table in Figure 5-2, Holly will purchase six oranges when the price of oranges is $1. Using the data in this table, we can sketch the downward-sloping demand curve D_B shown in Figure 5-2. This exercise, then, clearly links the utility-maximizing behaviour of a consumer and that person's demand curve for a particular product.

Income and Substitution Effects

income effect
A change in the price of a product changes a consumer's real income (purchasing power) and thus the quantity of the product purchased.

substitution effect
A change in the price of a product changes the relative expensiveness of that product and hence changes the consumer's willingness to buy it rather than other goods.

Recall from Chapter 3 that the **income effect** is the impact that a change in the price of a product has on a consumer's real income and consequently on the quantity demanded of that good. In contrast, the **substitution effect** is the impact that a change in a product's price has on its relative expensiveness and consequently on the quantity demanded. Both effects help explain why a demand curve such as that in Figure 5-2 is downsloping.

Let's first look at the substitution effect. Recall that before the price of oranges declined, Holly was in equilibrium when purchasing two apples and four oranges because

$$\frac{\text{MU of apples of 8}}{\text{Price of apples of \$1}} = \frac{\text{MU of oranges of 16}}{\text{Price of oranges of \$2}}$$

But after the price of oranges declines from $2 to $1,

$$\frac{\text{MU of apples of 8}}{\text{Price of apples of \$1}} < \frac{\text{MU of oranges of 16}}{\text{Price of oranges of \$1}}$$

More simply, the last dollar spent on oranges now yields more utility (16 utils) than does the last dollar spent on apples (8 utils). This will lead Holly to switch, or substitute, purchases away from apples and toward oranges so as to restore consumer equilibrium. This substitution effect contributes to the inverse relationship between price and quantity that is found along her demand curve for oranges: when the price of oranges declines, the substitution effect causes Holly to buy more oranges.

What about the income effect? The decline in the price of oranges from $2 to $1 increases Holly's real income. Before the price decline, she was two apples and four oranges. But at the lower $1 price for oranges, Holly would have to spend only $6 rather than $10 on the same combination of goods. That means the lower price of oranges has freed up $4 Holly can spend on buying more apples, more oranges, or more of both. How many more will be determined by applying the utility-maximizing rule to the new situation. But it is quite likely that the increase in real income caused by the reduction in the price of oranges will cause Holly to end up buying more oranges than before the price reduction.

FIGURE 5-2   Deriving an Individual Demand Curve

At a price of $2 the consumer represented by the data in the table maximizes utility by purchasing four oranges. The decline in the price of oranges to $1 upsets the consumer's initial utility-maximizing equilibrium. The consumer restores equilibrium by purchasing six rather than four oranges. Thus, a simple price–quantity schedule emerges, which locates two points on a downsloping demand curve.

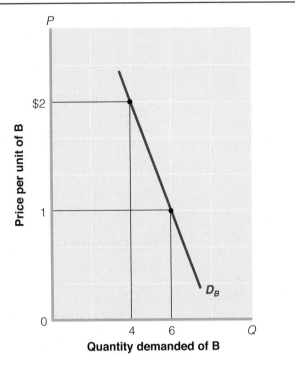

Price per unit of B	Quantity demanded
$2	4
1	6

ORIGIN 5.2
Income and
Substitution Effects

Any such increase in orange purchases is referred to as the income effect of the reduction in the price of oranges and it, too, helps to explain why demand curves are downward-sloping: when the price of oranges falls, the income effect causes Holly to buy more oranges. *(Key Question 4)*

QUICK REVIEW

▶ The theory of consumer choice assumes that, with limited income and a set of product prices, consumers make rational choices on the basis of well-defined preferences.

▶ A consumer maximizes utility by allocating income so that the marginal utility per dollar spent is the same for every good purchased.

▶ A downward-sloping demand curve can be derived by changing the price of one product in the consumer-choice model and noting the change in the utility-maximizing quantity of that product demanded.

▶ By providing insights on the income effect and substitution effect of a price decline, the utility-maximization model helps explain why demand curves are downsloping.

5.4 | Applications and Extensions

Many real-world phenomena can be explained by applying the theory of consumer choice.

iPods

Every so often a new product totally captures consumers' imaginations. One such product is Apple's iPod, which debuted in November 2001. Less than six years later, Apple sold its 100 millionth unit—units that in turn enabled Apple to sell more than 2.5 billion songs through its online iTunes store.

The swift ascendancy of the iPod resulted mainly from a leap in technology. The iPod is much more compact than the portable CD player it replaced, and it can store and play back several thousand songs—whereas a single CD only has a 74-minute recording capacity. The improved portability and storage—the enhanced consumer satisfaction—caused a major shift in consumer demand away from the portable CD player and toward the iPod.

In the language of our analysis, Apple's introduction of the iPod severely disrupted consumer equilibrium. Consumers concluded en masse that iPods had a higher marginal-utility-to-price ratio (= MU/P) than the ratios for alternative products. They therefore shifted spending away from those other products and toward iPods as a way to increase total utility. Of course, for most people the marginal utility of a second or third iPod relative to price is quite low, so most consumers purchased only a single unit. But Apple continued to enhance the iPod, enticing some of the buyers of older models to buy new models.

This example demonstrates a simple but important point: New products succeed by enhancing consumers' total utility. This "delivery of value" generates a revenue stream that, if greater than the costs of production, produces a profit.

The Diamond–Water Paradox

Early economists such as Adam Smith were puzzled that some essential goods had much lower prices than some unimportant goods. Why would water, essential to life, be priced below diamonds, which have much less usefulness? The paradox is resolved when we consider that water is in great supply relative to demand and thus has a very low price per litre. Diamonds, in contrast, are rare and are costly to mine, cut, and polish. Because their supply is small relative to demand, their price is very high per carat.

Moreover, the marginal utility of the last unit of water consumed is very low. The reason follows from our utility-maximizing rule. Consumers (and producers) respond to the very low price of water by using a great deal of it for generating electricity, irrigating crops, heating buildings, watering lawns, quenching thirst, and so on. Consumption is expanded until marginal utility, which declines as more water is consumed, equals its low price. Conversely, relatively few diamonds are purchased because of their prohibitively high price, meaning that their marginal utility remains high. In equilibrium,

$$\frac{\text{MU of water (low)}}{\text{Price of water (low)}} = \frac{\text{MU of diamonds (high)}}{\text{Price of diamonds (high)}}$$

Although the marginal utility of the last unit of water consumed is low and the marginal utility of the last diamond purchased is high, the total utility of water is very high and the total utility of diamonds is quite low. The total utility derived from the consumption of water is large because of the enormous amounts of water consumed. Total utility is the sum of the marginal utilities of all the litres of water consumed, including the trillions of litres that have far higher marginal utilities than the last unit consumed. In contrast, the total utility derived from diamonds is low since their high price means relatively few are bought. Thus the diamond–water paradox is solved: water has much more total utility (roughly, usefulness) than diamonds even though the price of diamonds greatly exceeds the price of water. These relative prices relate to marginal utility, not total utility.

ORIGIN 5.3
Diamond–Water
Paradox

The Value of Time

The theory of consumer choice can be generalized to account for the economic value of *time*. Both consumption and production take time. Time is a valuable economic commodity; by using an hour in productive work, a person can earn $6, $10, $50, or more, depending on education and skills. By using that hour for leisure or in consumption activities, the individual incurs the opportunity cost of forgone income and sacrifices the $6, $10, or $50 that could have been earned by working.

Imagine a self-employed consumer in Victoria named Linden who is considering buying a round of golf and a concert ticket. The market price of the golf game is $30 and that of the ticket is $40, but the golf game takes more time than the concert. Suppose Linden spends four hours on the golf course but only two hours at the concert. If Linden's time is worth $10 per hour as evidenced by the $10 wage obtained by working, then the full price of the golf game is $70 (the $30 market price plus $40 worth of time), while the full price of the concert is $60 (the $40 market price plus $20 worth of time). We find that, contrary to what market prices alone indicate, the full price of the concert is really less than the full price of the golf game.

If we now assume that the marginal utilities derived from successive golf games and concerts are identical, traditional theory would indicate that Linden should consume more golf games than concerts because the market price of the former ($30) is lower than that of the latter ($40). But when time is taken into account, the situation is reversed and golf games ($70) are more expensive than concerts ($60). So it is rational for Linden to consume more concerts than golf games.

Another example is the consumption of health care services. In Canada, government-sponsored insurance pays the full amount of a doctor's visit. The price the consumer pays is zero. But if we consider the time and cost of travelling to the doctor's office, and the waiting time in the office, the full price is considerably more than zero.

By accounting for time, we can see that it may be rational for the unskilled worker or retiree whose time has little market value to ride a bus from Edmonton to Saskatoon, but the corporate executive, whose time is very valuable, will find it cheaper to fly, even though bus fare is only a fraction of plane fare. It is sensible for the retiree, living on a modest income and having ample time, to spend many hours shopping for bargains at the mall or taking long trips in a motor home. It is equally rational for the highly paid physician, working 55 hours per week, to buy a new personal computer over the Internet and take short vacations at expensive resorts.

People in poor nations often conclude that affluent Canadians are wasteful of food and other material goods but overly economical in their use of time. Canadians who visit developing countries may think that time is used casually or squandered, while material goods are very highly prized and carefully used. These differences are not a paradox or a case of radically different temperaments; the differences are primarily a rational reflection that the high productivity of labour in an industrially advanced society gives time a high market value, whereas the opposite is true in a low-income, developing country.

Cash and Noncash Gifts

Marginal utility analysis also helps us understand why people generally prefer cash gifts to noncash gifts costing the same amount. The reason is simply that the noncash gifts may not match the recipient's preferences and thus may not add as much as cash to total utility. Thought of differently, consumers know their own preferences better than the gift giver does, and the $100 cash gift provides more choices.

Look back at Table 5-1. Suppose Holly has zero earned income but is given the choice of a $2 cash gift or a noncash gift of two apples. Because two apples can be bought with $2, these two gifts are of equal monetary value, but by spending the $2 cash gift on the first orange Holly could obtain 24 utils. The noncash gift of the first two apples would yield only 18 (= 10 + 8) units of utility. Conclusion: The noncash gift yields less utility to the beneficiary than the cash gift.

Since giving of noncash gifts is common, considerable value of those gifts is potentially lost because they do not match their recipients' tastes. For example, Aunt Flo may have paid $15 for the Avril Lavigne CD she gave you for your birthday, but you would pay only $7.50 for it. Thus, a $7.50, or 50 percent, value loss is involved. Multiplied by billions spent on gifts each year, the potential loss of value is large.

But some of that loss is avoided by the creative ways individuals handle the problem. For example, newlyweds set up gift registries for their weddings to help match their wants to the noncash gifts received. Also, people obtain cash refunds or exchanges for gifts, so they can buy goods that provide more utility. And people have even been known to recycle gifts by giving them to someone else at a later time. All three actions support the proposition that individuals take actions to maximize their total utility.

The **LAST WORD**

M&M's, Final Exams, and Retirement Savings: Insights from Behavioural Economics

Over the past 20 years, researchers called behavioural economists have noted behaviours that differ from the predictions of standard theory and have offered interesting explanations for why they occur.

We have just discussed how diminishing marginal utility underlies demand. The key insight is that even when we like a particular good or service, we like successive units of it less and less. Basically, we get fed up with it.

But consider this. Researchers offered moviegoers a mix of M&M's chocolate candies that contained only seven colours of M&M's and then counted how many of the candies they ate. Then, with a different group of moviegoers, they offered a mix of M&M's that had 10 different colours. In both cases, the candy was free and people could take as much or as little as they desired. The result? The moviegoers who were offered more colours ate 43 percent more candy even though every colour tastes exactly the same.

So does this mean that people do not actually experience diminishing marginal utility, as economists assume? Not really. It just means that how quickly utility diminishes varies depending on context. And part of that context is *variety*. To our ancient ancestors who were constantly struggling to have enough to eat, suddenly finding a rare type of food was such an unexpected blessing that it made sense to eat it immediately, regardless of whether they had just stuffed themselves with more ordinary foods. The vitamins and minerals of the rare and different food were simply too important to pass up. Hence, the modern human's instinct for

variety—and for the fact that diminishing marginal utility sets in more slowly when people are offered a variety of products rather than just one or two.

The pressing needs of the present rather than the elusive possibilities of the future also appear to have produced human brains that have trouble making decisions involving events that will take place more than a few days or weeks in the future. For instance, suppose that at the beginning of a semester researchers ask each student in a particular class if they would be willing to pay $20 to have the final exam delayed by one day. Typically only a handful of students are willing to pay the $20 fee for the one-day postponement. However, if you ask them the day before the exam, a large majority are suddenly willing to pay the $20 fee. Behavioural economists refer to this as "time inconsistency." Although people can correctly predict how they will feel in the future—panicked a day before the upcoming exam!—

those predicted feelings do not carry much weight when compared with their desire to spend the $20 today on current consumption.

This sort of behaviour has important implications for retirement savings. If you ask 55-year-olds if it is important to save for retirement, they will not only say yes but will back it up by saving a lot. But if you ask 25-year-olds if it is important to save for retirement, they will also say yes, but usually will hardly save at all. Most will spend nearly all their income, and the vast majority will continue to behave this way until they are near retirement. Then, they will boost their saving considerably because they begin to realize that an impoverished retirement is a near-term possibility rather than a distant concern.

Recognizing the fact that young people do not take saving for retirement very seriously, governments have instituted public policies designed to counter this reality. For example, the federal government requires nearly all workers to make Old Age pension contributions (which are used to pay benefits to currently eligible retirees). No "opt out" from the payroll taxes allowed! Because retirement benefits also will become available to workers when they age and retire, the system partially makes up for the fact that the human brain fails to put enough weight on distant possibilities, even very bad ones such as living in poverty in old age.

Question

People at buffets put more on their plates and eat more the greater the variety of items they have to select from. How does this relate to the idea that diminishing marginal utility must be understood in context? Many people buy too much on their credit cards, even though they know they will be sorry when they get their credit card bill. Relate this fact to the idea of time inconsistency.

CHAPTER SUMMARY

5.1 ▶ THE LAW OF DIMINISHING MARGINAL UTILITY

- The law of diminishing marginal utility states that, beyond a certain quantity, additional units of a specific good will yield declining amounts of extra satisfaction to a consumer.

5.2 ▶ THE THEORY OF CONSUMER CHOICE

- The utility-maximizing model assumes that the typical consumer is rational and acts based on well-defined preferences. Because income is limited and goods have prices, consumers cannot purchase all the goods and services they might want. Consumers therefore select the attainable combination of goods that maximizes their utility or satisfaction.

- A consumer's utility is maximized when income is allocated so that the last dollar spent on each product purchased yields the same amount of extra satisfaction. Algebraically, the utility-maximizing rule is fulfilled when

$$\frac{\text{MU of product A}}{\text{Price of A}} = \frac{\text{MU of product B}}{\text{Price of B}}$$

and the consumer's total income is spent.

5.3 ▶ UTILITY MAXIMIZATION AND THE DEMAND CURVE

- The utility-maximizing rule and the demand curve are logically consistent. Because marginal utility declines, a lower price is needed to induce the consumer to buy more of a particular product.

- The utility-maximization model illuminates the income and substitution effects of a price change. The income effect implies that a decline in the price of a product increases the consumer's real income and enables the consumer to buy more of that product with a fixed money income. The substitution effect implies that a lower price makes a product relatively more attractive and therefore increases the consumer's willingness to substitute it for other products.

5.4 ▶ APPLICATIONS AND EXTENSIONS

- The theory of consumer choice can be used to explain real-world phenomena. For example, consumers have switched from CD players to iPods because the new product succeeded in enhancing consumers' total utility. And the price of diamonds is high compared to the price of water because it is the marginal utility (MU) of diamonds that is high, and it is MU, not total utility, that determines what people are prepared to pay for an item.

TERMS AND CONCEPTS

law of diminishing marginal utility, p. 112
utility, p 112
total utility, p. 112
marginal utility, p. 112

rational behaviour, p. 114
budget constraint, p. 114
utility-maximizing rule, p. 115

income effect, p. 118
substitution effect, p. 118

STUDY QUESTIONS

5.1 1. **KEY QUESTION** Complete the following table and answer the questions that follow.

   a. At which rate is total utility increasing: a constant rate, a decreasing rate, or an increasing rate? How do you know?

   b. "A rational consumer will purchase only one unit of the product represented by these data, since that amount maximizes marginal utility." Do you agree? Explain why or why not.

   c. "It is possible that a rational consumer will not purchase any units of the product represented by these data." Do you agree? Explain why or why not.

Units consumed	Total utility	Marginal utility
0	0	
1	10	10
2	—	8
3	25	—
4	30	—
5	—	3
6	34	—

LO 5.2

2. Mrs. Simpson buys loaves of bread and litres of milk each week at prices of $1 and $0.80, respectively. At present she is buying these two products in amounts such that the marginal utilities from the last units purchased of the two products are 80 and 70 utils, respectively. Is she buying the utility-maximizing combination of bread and milk? If not, how should she reallocate her expenditures between the two goods?

Units of X	MUx	Units of Y	MUy
1	10	1	8
2	8	2	7
3	6	3	6
4	4	4	5
5	3	5	4
6	2	6	3

LO 5.2

3. **KEY QUESTION** Columns 1 through 4 in the table below show the marginal utility, measured in utils, that Ricardo would get by purchasing various amounts of products A, B, C, and D. Column 5 shows the marginal utility Ricardo gets from saving. Assume that the prices of A, B, C, and D are $18, $6, $4, and $24, respectively, and that Ricardo has an income of $106.

   a. What quantities of A, B, C, and D will Ricardo purchase in maximizing his utility?

   b. How many dollars will Ricardo choose to save?

   c. Check your answers by substituting them into the algebraic statement of the utility-maximizing rule.

4. **KEY QUESTION**   You are choosing between two goods, **LO**
   X and Y, and your marginal utility from each is as shown below. If your income is $9 and the prices of X and Y are $2 and $1, respectively, what quantities of each will you purchase to maximize utility? What total utility will you realize? Assume that, other things remaining unchanged, the price of X falls to $1. What quantities of X and Y will you now purchase? Using the two prices and quantities for X, derive a demand schedule (price–quantity demanded table) for X.

5. How can time be incorporated into the theory of consumer **LO**
   behaviour? Explain the following comment: "Want to make millions of dollars? Devise a product that saves Canadians lots of time."

6. Explain: **LO**
   a. "Before economic growth, there were too few goods; after growth, there is too little time."
   b. "It is irrational for an individual to take the time to be completely rational in economic decision making."
   c. "Telling Santa what you want for Christmas makes sense in terms of utility maximization."

7. In the last decade or so there has been a dramatic expan- **LO**
   sion of small retail convenience stores (such as Mac's, 7-Eleven, Becker's), although their prices are generally much higher than prices in large supermarkets. What explains the success of the convenience stores?

8. Many apartment-complex owners are installing water **LO**
   meters for each apartment and billing the occupants according to the amount of water they use, in contrast to the former procedure of having a central meter for the entire complex and dividing up the water expense as part of the rent. Where individual meters have been installed, water usage has declined 10 to 40 percent. Explain that drop, referring to price and marginal utility.

Column 1		Column 2		Column 3		Column 4		Column 5	
Units of A	MU	Units of B	MU	Units of C	MU	Units of D	MU	Number of dollars saved	MU
1	72	1	24	1	15	1	36	1	5
2	54	2	15	2	12	2	30	2	4
3	45	3	12	3	8	3	24	3	3
4	36	4	9	4	7	4	18	4	2
5	27	5	7	5	5	5	13	5	1
6	18	6	5	6	4	6	7	6	½
7	15	7	2	7	3½	7	4	7	¼
8	12	8	1	8	3	8	2	8	⅛

5.3 9. Using the utility-maximization rule as your point of reference, explain the income and substitution effects of an increase in the price of product B with no change in the price of product A.

5.3 10. A vice president argues that the president of the company should raise workers' wages if she wants less absenteeism. The president says that wages probably should be cut so that workers could not afford to miss so much work. Evaluate the two views using the income and substitution effects in your analysis.

5.4 11. Use marginal utility analysis to explain the growing popularity of iPods over portable CD players.

12. **ADVANCED ANALYSIS**   A mathematically "fair bet" is one in which a gambler bets, say, $100 for a 10 percent chance to win $1000 ($100 = 0.10 × 1000). Assuming diminishing marginal utility of dollars, explain why this is *not* a fair bet in terms of utility. Why is it an even less fair bet when the house takes a cut of each dollar bet? So is gambling irrational?   **LO 5.3**

13. **ADVANCED ANALYSIS**   Let $MU_A = z = 10 - x$ and $MU_B = z = 21 - 2y$, where z is marginal utility per dollar measured in utils, x is the amount spent on product A, and y is the amount spent on product B. Assume that the consumer has $10 to spend on A and B—that is, $x + y = 10$. How is the $10 best allocated between A and B? How much utility will the marginal dollar yield?   **LO 5.3**

INTERNET APPLICATION QUESTIONS @

1. **Consumer Choice—Individual Choice and Attainable Combination.** Assume that you and several classmates each receive a $500 credit voucher (good for today only) from the Hudson's Bay Company. Go to the McConnell-Brue-Flynn-Barbiero Web site (Chapter 5) to access The Bay's home page and select $500 worth of merchandise. Use "Add to Basket" to keep a running total. Compare your list with your classmates' lists. What explains the differences? Would you have purchased your items if you had received $500 in cash to be spent whenever and wherever you pleased?

2. **The ESP Sportzone—To Fee or Not to Fee.** The ESPN cable TV network runs a major sports information site at www.espn.com. Access its site by going to the McConnell-Brue-Flynn-Barbiero Web site (Chapter 5). Most of the content is free, but ESPN has a premium membership (see its "Insider") available for a monthly or an annual fee. Similar, but fee-free, sports content can be found at the Web sites of CNN/Sports Illustrated, and CBS Sports Line. Since ESPN has put a price tag on some of its sports content, it implies that the utility of a premium membership cannot be found at a no-fee site and is therefore worth the price. Is this the case? Use the utility-maximization rule to justify your subscribing or not subscribing to the premium membership.

Appendix to Chapter 5

The utility-maximization rule requires individuals to measure and compare utility, much as a business would measure and compare costs or revenues. Such *cardinal utility* is measured in units such as 1, 2, 3, 4, and can be added, subtracted, multiplied, and divided, just like the cardinal numbers in mathematics. More importantly, cardinal utility allows us to precisely quantify the marginal utilities upon which the utility-maximizing rule depends. In fact, the marginal-utility theory of consumer demand that we explained in the body of this chapter rests squarely on the assumption that economists are able to measure cardinal utility. However, measuring cardinal utility in real people is nearly impossible. (Can you, for instance, state exactly how many utils you are getting from reading this book right now, or how many utils you would get from watching a sunset?) As a result, economists have developed an alternative explanation of consumer choice and equilibrium in which such measurement is not required. In this more advanced analysis, the consumer must simply *rank* various combinations of goods in terms of preference. For instance, Sally can simply report that she *prefers* four units of A to six units of B without having to put number values on how much she likes either option. The model of consumer choice that is based on such *ordinal utility* rankings is called indifference curve analysis. It has two main elements: budget lines and indifference curves.

The Budget Line: What Is Attainable

We know from Chapter 1 that a **budget line** (or, more technically, a *budget constraint*) is a schedule or curve showing various combinations of two products a consumer can purchase with a specific money income. If the price of product A is $1.50 and the price of product B is $1.00, a consumer could purchase all the combinations of A and B shown in the table of Figure A5-1 with $12 of money income. At one extreme, the consumer might spend all the income on eight units of A and have nothing left to spend on B. Or, by giving up two units of A and thereby freeing $3, the consumer could have six units of A and three of B. At the other extreme, the consumer could buy 12 units of B at $1.00 each, spending his or her entire money income on B with nothing left to spend on A.

Figure A5-1 also shows the budget line graphically. Note that the graph is not restricted to whole units of A and B as is the table. Every point on the graph represents a possible combination of A and B, including fractional quantities. The slope of the graphed budget line measures the ratio of the price of B to the price of A; more precisely, the absolute value of the slope is $P_B/P_A = \$1.00/\$1.50 = 2/3$. This is the mathematical way of saying that the consumer must forgo two units of A (measured on the vertical axis) to buy three units of B (measured on the horizontal

---

A Consumer's Budget Line

The budget line shows all the combinations of any two products that can be purchased given the prices of the products and the consumer's money income.

Units of A (price = $1.50)	Units of B (price = $1.00)	Total expenditure
8	0	$12 (= $12 + $0)
6	3	$12 (= $9 + $3)
4	6	$12 (= $6 + $6)
2	9	$12 (= $3 + $9)
0	12	$12 (= $0 + $12)

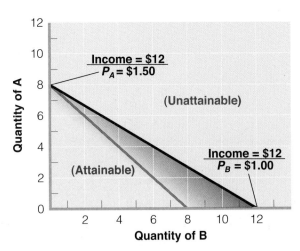

axis). In moving down the budget or price line, two units of A (at $1.50 each) must be given up to obtain three more units of B (at $1.00 each). This yields a slope of 2/3.

The budget line has two other significant characteristics:

1. ***Income Changes***   The location of the budget line varies with money income. An increase in money income shifts the budget line to the right; a decrease in money income shifts it to the left. To verify this, recalculate the table in Figure A5-1, assuming that money income is (a) $24 and (b) $6, and plot the new budget lines.

2. ***Price Changes***   A change in product prices also shifts the budget line. A decline in the prices of both products—the equivalent of an increase in real income—shifts the curve to the right. (You can verify this by recalculating the table in Figure A5-1 and replotting the graph, assuming that $P_A = \$0.75$ and $P_B = \$0.50$.) Conversely, an increase in the prices of A and B shifts the curve to the left. (Assume $P_A = \$3$ and $P_B = \$2$ and rework the table and the graph to substantiate this statement.)

Note what happens if P_B changes while P_A and money income remain constant. In particular, if P_B drops, say from $1.00 to $0.50, the lower end of the budget line fans outward to the right. Conversely, if P_B increases, say from $1.00 to $1.50, the lower end of the line fans inward to the left as illustrated in Figure A5-1. In both instances the line remains anchored at eight units on the vertical axis because P_A has not changed.

Indifference Curves: What Is Preferred

ORIGIN A5.1
Indifference Curves

Budget lines reflect objective market data, specifically income and prices. They reveal combinations of products A and B that can be purchased given current money income and prices.

Indifference curves, on the other hand, reflect subjective information about consumer preferences for A and B. An **indifference curve** shows all the combinations of two products A and B that will yield the same total satisfaction or total utility to a consumer. Figure A5-2 presents a hypothetical indifference curve for products A and B. The consumer's subjective preferences are such that he or she will realize the same total utility from each combination of A and B shown in the table or on the curve. The consumer will be indifferent (will not care) as to which combination is actually obtained.

Indifference curves have several important characteristics.

INDIFFERENCE CURVES SLOPE DOWNWARD

An indifference curve slopes downward because more of one product means less of the other if total utility is to remain unchanged. Suppose the consumer moves from one combination of A and B to another, say from *j* to *k* in Figure A5-2. In so doing, the consumer obtains more of product B, increasing total utility. But because total utility is the same everywhere on the curve, the consumer must give up some of the other product, A, to reduce total utility by a precisely offsetting amount.

FIGURE A5-2   **A Consumer's Indifference Curve**

Every point on indifference curve I represents some combination of products A and B, and all those combinations are equally satisfactory to the consumer. That is, each combination of A and B on the curve yields the same total utility.

Combination	Units of A	Units of B
j	12	2
k	6	4
l	4	6
m	3	8

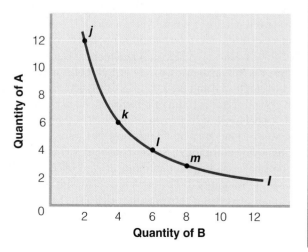

Thus more of B necessitates less of A, and the quantities of A and B are inversely related. A curve that reflects inversely related variables is downward sloping.

INDIFFERENCE CURVES ARE CONVEX TO THE ORIGIN

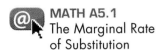

MATH A5.1
The Marginal Rate of Substitution

Recall from the appendix to Chapter 1 that the slope of a curve at a particular point is measured by drawing a straight line that is tangent to that point and then measuring the "rise over run" of the straight line. If you drew such straight lines for several points on the curve in Figure A5-2, you would find that their slopes decline (in absolute terms) as you move down the curve. Technically, the slope of the indifference curve at each point measures the **marginal rate of substitution (MRS)** of the combination represented by that point. The slope or MRS shows the rate at which the consumer who possesses that combination must substitute one good for the other (say, B for A) to remain equally satisfied. The diminishing slope of the indifference curve means that the willingness to substitute B for A diminishes as more of B is obtained.

The rationale for this convexity—that is, for a diminishing MRS—is that consumers' subjective willingness to substitute B for A (or A for B) will depend on the amounts of B and A they have to begin with. Consider Figure A5-2 again, beginning at point *j*. Here, in relative terms, the consumer has a substantial amount of A and very little of B. Within this combination, a unit of B is very valuable (that is, its marginal utility is high), while a unit of A is less valuable (its marginal utility is low). The consumer will then be willing to give up a substantial amount of A to get, say, two more units of B. In this case, the consumer is willing to forgo 6 units of A to get 2 more units of B; the MRS is 6/2, or 3, for the *j* segment of the curve.

But at point *k* the consumer has less A and more B. Here A is somewhat more valuable and B less valuable at the margin. In a move from point *k* to point *l*, the consumer is willing to give up only two units of A to get two more units of B, so the MRS is only 2/2, or 1. Having still less of A and more of B at point *l*, the consumer is willing to give up only one unit of A in return for two more units of B and the MRS falls to 1/2 between *l* and *m*.[1]

In general, as the amount of B *increases,* the marginal utility of additional units of B *decreases.* Similarly, as the quantity of A *decreases,* its marginal utility *increases.* In Figure A5-2 we see that in moving down the curve, the consumer will be willing to give up smaller and smaller amounts of A to offset acquiring each additional unit of B. The result is a curve with a diminishing slope, a curve that is convex to the origin. The MRS declines as one moves southeast along the indifference curve.

The Indifference Map

The single indifference curve of Figure A5-2 reflects some constant (but unspecified) level of total utility or satisfaction. It is possible and useful to sketch a whole series of indifference curves or an **indifference map,** as shown in Figure A5-3. Each curve reflects a different level of total utility and therefore never crosses another indifference curve. Specifically, each curve to the right of our original curve (labelled I_3 in Figure A5-3) reflects combinations of A and B that yield more utility than I_3. Each curve to the left of I_3 reflects less total utility than I_3. As we move out from the origin, each successive indifference curve represents a higher level of total utility. To demonstrate this fact, draw a line in a northeasterly direction from the origin; note that its points of intersection with successive curves entail larger amounts of both A and B and, therefore, higher levels of total utility.

Equilibrium at Tangency

Since the axes in Figures A5-1 and A5-3 are identical, we can superimpose a budget line on the consumer's indifference map, as shown in Figure A5-4. By definition, the budget line indicates all the combinations of A and B that the consumer can attain

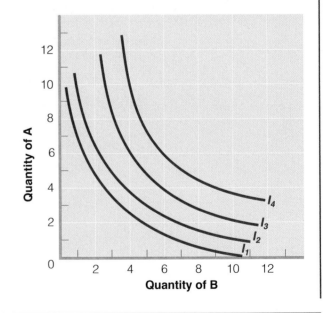

FIGURE A5-3   An Indifference Map

An indifference map is a set of indifference curves. Curves farther from the origin indicate higher levels of total utility. Thus, any combination of products A and B represented by a point on I_4 has greater total utility than any combination of A and B represented by a point on I_3, I_2, and I_1.

---

[1] MRS declines continuously between *j* and *k*, *k* and *l*, and *l* and *m*. Our numerical values for MRS relate to the curve segments between points and are not the actual values of the MRS at each point. For example, the MRS *at* point *l* is 2/3.

FIGURE A5-4	The Consumer's Equilibrium Position

The consumer's equilibrium position is represented by point X, where the black budget line is tangent to indifference curve I_3. The consumer buys four units of A at $1.50 per unit and six of B at $1.00 per unit with a $12 money income. Points Z and Y represent attainable combinations of A and B that yield less total utility, as is evidenced by the fact that they are on lower indifference curves. Point W would entail more utility than X, but it requires a greater income than the $12 represented by the budget line.

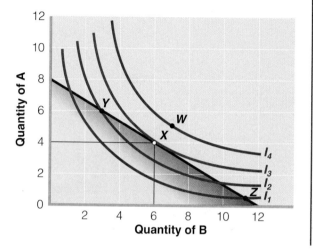

with his or her money income given the prices of A and B. Of these attainable combinations, the consumer will prefer that combination that yields the greatest satisfaction or utility. Specifically, the utility-maximizing combination will be the combination lying on the highest attainable indifference curve. It is called the consumer's **equilibrium position.**

In Figure A5-4 the consumer's equilibrium position is at point X, where the budget line is *tangent* to I_3. Why not point Y? Because Y is on a lower indifference curve, I_2. By moving down the budget line—by shifting dollars from purchases of A to purchases of B—the consumer can attain an indifference curve farther from the origin and thereby increase the total utility from the same income. Why not point Z? For the same reason as for Y: point Z is on a lower indifference curve, I_1. By moving up the budget line—by reallocating dollars from B to A—the consumer can get on the higher indifference curve I_3 and increase total utility.

How about point W on indifference curve I_4? While it is true that W would yield a greater total utility than X, point W is beyond (outside) the budget line and, hence, is *not* attainable by the consumer. Point X represents the optimal *attainable*

combination of products A and B. Note that, according to the definition of tangency, the slope of the highest attainable indifference curve equals the slope of the budget line. Because the slope of the indifference curve reflects the MRS (marginal rate of substitution) and the slope of the budget line is P_B/P_A, the consumer's optimal or equilibrium position is the point where

$$\text{MRS} = \frac{P_B}{P_A}$$

(You may benefit by trying to answer *Key Appendix Question 3* at this time.)

Equivalency at Equilibrium

As indicated at the beginning of this appendix, there is an important difference between the marginal utility theory of consumer demand and the indifference curve theory. The marginal utility theory assumes that utility is *numerically* measurable; that is, that the consumer can say how much extra utility he or she derives from each extra unit of A or B. The consumer needs that information to realize the utility-maximizing (equilibrium) position, as indicated by

$$\frac{\text{Marginal utility of A}}{\text{Price of A}} = \frac{\text{Marginal utility of B}}{\text{Price of B}}$$

The indifference curve approach imposes a less stringent requirement on the consumer, who need only specify whether a particular combination of A and B will yield more, less, or the same amount of utility than some other combination of A and B. The consumer need only say, for example, that six units of A and seven of B will yield more (or less) satisfaction than four of A and nine of B. Indifference curve theory does not require that the consumer specify *how much* more (or less) satisfaction will be realized.

That being said, it is a remarkable mathematical fact that both models of consumer behaviour will, in any given situation, point to exactly the same consumer equilibrium and, consequently, exactly the same demand behaviour. This fact allows us to combine the separate pieces of information that each theory gives us about equilibrium in order to deduce an interesting property about marginal utilities that must also hold true in equilibrium. To see this, note that when we compare the equilibrium situations in the two theories, we find that in the indifference curve analysis, the MRS equals P_B/P_A at equilibrium; however, in the marginal utility approach, the ratio of marginal utilities equals P_B/P_A. We therefore deduce that at equilibrium, the MRS is equivalent in the marginal utility approach to the ratio of the marginal utilities of the last purchased units of the two products.[2]

---

[2] If we begin with the utility-maximizing rule, $MU_A/P_A = MU_B/P_B$, and then multiply through by P_B and divide through by MU_A, we obtain $P_B/P_A = MU_B/MU_A$. In indifference curve analysis we know that at the equilibrium position MRS = P_B/P_A. Hence, at equilibrium, MRS also equals MU_B/MU_A.

The Derivation of the Demand Curve

We noted earlier that with a fixed price for A, an increase in the price of B will cause the bottom of the budget line to fan inward to the left. We can use that fact to derive a demand curve for product B. In Figure A5-5a we reproduce the part of Figure A5-4 that shows our initial consumer equilibrium at point X. The budget line determining this equilibrium position assumes that money income is $12 and that $P_A = \$1.50$ and $P_B = \$1.00$. Let's see what happens to the equilibrium position when we increase P_B to $1.50 and hold constant both money income and the price of A.

The result is shown in Figure A5-5a. The budget line fans to the left, yielding a new equilibrium point X' where it is tangent to lower indifference curve I_2. At X' the consumer buys three units of B and five of A compared with four of A and six of B at X. Our interest is in B, and we now have sufficient information to locate two points on the demand curve for product B. We know that at equilibrium point X, the price of B is $1.00 and six units are purchased; at equilibrium point X', the price of B is $1.50 and three units are purchased.

These data are shown graphically in Figure A5-5b as points on the consumer's demand curve for B. Note that the horizontal axes of Figure A5-5a and A5-5b are identical; both measure the quantity demanded of B. We can therefore drop vertical reference lines from Figure A5-5a down to the horizontal axis of Figure A5-5b. On the vertical axis of Figure A5-5b we locate the two chosen prices of B. Knowing that these prices yield the relevant quantities demanded, we locate two points on the demand curve for B. By simple manipulation of the price of B in an indifference curve–budget line context, we have obtained a downward-sloping demand curve for B. We have thus again derived the law of demand assuming other things are equal, since only the price of B was changed (the price of A and the consumer's money income and tastes remained constant). In this case, we have derived the demand curve without resorting to the questionable assumption that consumers can measure utility in units called utils. In this indifference-curve approach, consumers simply compare combinations of products A and B and determine which combination they prefer given their incomes and the prices of the two products.

Income and Substitution Effects

In the body of this chapter we noted that a change in price is composed of two effects. The *income effect* is the impact that a change in the price of a product has on a consumer's real income and the consequent effect on the quantity demanded of that good. In contrast, the *substitution effect* is the impact that a change in a product's price has on its relative expensiveness and consequently on the quantity demanded.

We can measure the magnitude of the income and substitution effects with the help of indifference curve analysis. Let's assume we have consumer Pam with a budget of $20 and that she consumes two normal goods, A and B. Good A is priced at

FIGURE A5-5 — Deriving the Demand Curve

Panel (a): When the price of product B is increased from $1.00 to $1.50, the equilibrium position moves from X to X', decreasing the quantity of product B demanded from six to three units. Panel (b): The demand curve for product B is determined by plotting the $1.00–six-unit and $1.50–three-unit price–quantity combinations for product B.

(a) Two equilibrium positions

(b) The demand curve for product B

$2 and good B at $1. In Figure A5-6a we can see that Pam can purchase a maximum of 20 units of good A and a maximum of 10 units of good B. Given Pam's indifference curve and the relative prices of goods A and B, she is at equilibrium at point X on indifference curve I_3, consuming 4 units of good B.

FIGURE A5-6   Income and Substitution Effects of a Fall in Price

When the price of product B falls, Pam demands more of product B and less of product A. In panel (a) the fall in price of product B leads Pam to move to point Z on a higher indifference curve. The move from X to Z in panel (a) represents the increased quantity demanded of product B due to both the substitution effect and income effect. In panel (b), if Pam's income is held constant (dashed line) the now lower price of B leads her to demand more of it and she moves to point Y on indifference curve I_3. This rise in quantity demanded is the substitution effect due to the lower price of product B. The move from Y on indifference curve I_3 to Z on indifference curve I_4 represents the increased demand of product B due to the income effect as a result of the lower price of good B. At point Y the MRS is equal to the new price ratio.

(a) Total effect of a price drop on quality demanded

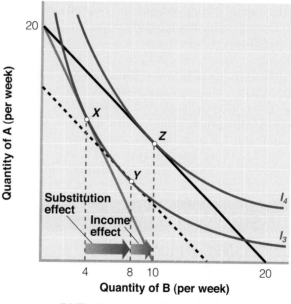

(b) The income and substitution effects

Now let's assume that the price of good B drops to $1. In Figure A5-6a you can see that when the price of good B drops from $2 to $1 Pam will be at a new equilibrium, at point Z, and on the higher indifference curve I_4. Pam now consumes more of good B (10 units, compared to 4 units previously) and less of good A.

The analysis so far has been similar to what we saw in Figure A5-5. But now we want to discover what part of Pam's increased purchase of good B from 4 units to 10 units was due to the sub-stitution effect and what part was due to the income effect. To determine the substitution effect in Figure A5-6b we have added a dashed line parallel to the new budget constraint to see the extra amount Pam would consume of product B solely due to lower price. In reality the dashed line keeps Pam's real income constant. The slope of the dashed line is the same as the new budget constraint, meaning that the price ratio between product A and product B is 1 (10/10 = 1). The initial price ratio between products A and B

CONSIDER THIS | Indifference Maps and Topographical Maps

Maps a la carte, Inc.

The familiar topographical map may help you understand the idea of indifference curves and indifference maps. Each line on a topographical map represents a particular elevation above sea level, say, 1200 metres. Similarly, an indifference curve represents a particular level of total utility. When you move from one point on a specific elevation line to another, the elevation remains the same. So it is with an indifference curve. A move from one position to another on the curve leaves total utility unchanged. Neither elevation lines nor indifference curves can intersect. If they did, the meaning of each line or curve would

be violated. An elevation line is an "equal-elevation line"; an indifference curve is an "equal-total-utility curve."

Like the topographical map, an indifference map contains not just one line but a series of lines. That is, the topographical map may have elevation lines representing successively higher elevations of 500, 1000, 1500, 2000, and 2500 metres. Similarly, the indifference curves on the indifference map represent successively higher levels of total utility. The climber whose goal is to maximize elevation wants to get to the highest possible elevation line; the consumer desiring to maximize total utility wants to get to the highest possible indifference curve.

Finally, both topographical maps and indifference maps show only a few of the many such lines that could be drawn. The topographical map, for example, leaves out the elevation lines for 501 metres, 502 metres, 503 metres, and so on. The indifference map leaves out all the indifference curves that could be drawn between those illustrated.

was 2 (20/10 = 2). Thus, we are holding Pam's income constant and keeping her on the original indifference curve to see how much of product B she will want at the lower price.

Holding Pam's income constant we find in Figure A5-6b that the drop in price of product B from $2 to $1 leads her to increase the purchase of product B by 4 units, moving her to point Y on indifference curve I_3. This is the substitution effect. Note that at point Y the MRS is equal to the new price ratio, which is 1.

The movement from point Y to point Z on indifference curve I_4 represents Pam's additional purchase of product B, in

this case two additional units, due to the income effect brought about by the drop in the price of product B. So now we can see in Figure A5-6b that a price drop for product B will increase Pam's demand for product B by a total of 6 units. Of the 6 unit increase in demand of product B, 4 units are attributable to the substitution effect and 2 units to the income effect.

If product B were an inferior good, the foregoing analysis would change somewhat. Recall from Chapter 4 that the consumption of an inferior good falls as income rises. Thus, the income effect would be negative for an inferior good.

APPENDIX | SUMMARY

A5.1 INDIFFERENCE CURVE ANALYSIS

- The indifference curve approach to consumer behaviour is based on the consumer's budget line and indifference curves.
- The budget line shows all combinations of two products that the consumer can purchase given product prices and money income.
- A change in either product prices or money income moves the budget line.
- An indifference curve shows all combinations of two products that will yield the same total utility to a consumer. Indifference curves are downward sloping and convex from the origin.
- An indifference map consists of a number of indifference curves; the farther from the origin, the higher the total utility associated with a curve.

- The consumer is in equilibrium (utility is maximized) at the point on the budget line that lies on the highest attainable indifference curve. At that point the budget line and indifference curve are tangent.
- Changing the price of one product shifts the budget line and determines a new equilibrium point. A downsloping demand curve can be determined by plotting the price–quantity combinations associated with two or more equilibrium points.
- A price change causes a change in the quantity demanded. The change in the quantity demanded is due to the substitution and income effects.

APPENDIX | TERMS AND CONCEPTS

budget line   A schedule or curve that shows various combinations of two products a consumer can purchase with a specific money income. (p. 126)

indifference curve   A curve showing the different combinations of two products that yield the same satisfaction or utility to a consumer. (p. 127)

marginal rate of substitution (MRS)   The rate at which a consumer is prepared to substitute one good for another (from

a given combination of goods) and remain equally satisfied (have the same total utility). (p. 128)

indifference map   A series of indifference curves, each of which represents a different level of total utility and together show the preferences of the consumer. (p. 128)

equilibrium position   The combination of products that yields the greatest satisfaction or utility. (p. 129)

APPENDIX | STUDY QUESTIONS

A5.1 1. What information is embodied in a budget line? What shifts occur in the budget line when money income (a) increases and (b) decreases? What shifts occur in the budget line when the price of the product shown on the vertical axis (a) increases and (b) decreases?

A5.1 2. What information is contained in an indifference curve? Why are such curves (a) downward sloping and (b) convex from the origin? Why does total utility increase as the consumer moves to indifference curves farther from the origin? Why can't indifference curves intersect?

A5.1 3. **KEY APPENDIX QUESTION**   Using Figure A5-4, explain why the point of tangency of the budget line with an indifference curve is the consumer's equilibrium position. Explain why any point where the budget line intersects an indifference curve is not equilibrium. Explain: "The consumer is in equilibrium where $MRS = P_B/P_A$."

A5.1 4. Assume that the data in the accompanying table give an indifference curve for Mr. Chen. Graph this curve, putting A on the vertical axis and B on the horizontal axis. Assuming that the prices of A and B are $1.50 and $1.00, respectively, and that Mr. Chen has $24 to spend, add his budget line to your graph. What combination of A and B will Mr. Chen purchase? Does your answer meet the $MRS = P_B/P_A$ rule for equilibrium?

Units of A	Units of B
16	6
12	8
8	2
4	24

5. Explain graphically how indifference analysis can be used to derive a demand curve. **LO A5.1**

6. Show the substitution and income effects of a decrease in the price of gasoline. Assume gasoline is a normal good. How would your result change if gasoline were an inferior good? **LO A5.1**

7. A consumer has a daily income of $120 and purchases two products, X (price = $3) and Y (price = $4). The following six pairs of points for X and Y define an indifference schedule: (7,40), (10,30), (15,20), (20,15), (30,10), and (40,8). In the graph below, draw the budget line and the indifference curve. What amounts of X and Y will allow the consumer to achieve equilibrium? **LO A5.1**

8. **ADVANCED ANALYSIS**   Demonstrate mathematically that the equilibrium condition $MRS = P_B/P_A$ is the equivalent of the utility-maximizing rule $MU_A/P_A = MU_B/P_B$. **LO A5.1**

9. **ADVANCED ANALYSIS**   First, graphically illustrate a doubling of income without price changes in the indifference curve model. Next, on the same graph, show a situation in which the person whose indifference curves you are drawing buys considerably more of good B than A after the income increase. What can you conclude about the relative coefficients of income elasticity of demand for goods A and B (Chapter 4)? **LO A5.1**

CHAPTER 6

The Organization and Costs of Production

Our attention now turns from the behaviour of consumers to the behaviour of producers. In market economies, a wide variety of firms, from family-owned businesses to large corporations, produce an even wider variety of goods and services. Each business requires inputs to produce its products. To acquire the needed inputs, a firm makes monetary payments to factor owners (for example, workers) and incurs opportunity costs when using resources it already owns (for example, entrepreneurial talent). Those payments and opportunity costs together make up the firm's *costs of production,* which we discuss in this chapter. Then in the next several chapters we bring product demand, product prices, and revenue back into the analysis and explain how firms compare revenues and costs to determine how much to produce. Our ultimate purpose is to show how those comparisons relate to economic efficiency.

6.1 | The Firm and the Business Sector

Businesses constitute the second major part of the private sector. Like households, they are a major element in the circular flow diagram that we discussed in Chapter 2. A firm can be organized in several ways. It will be useful to distinguish among a plant, a firm, and an industry.

- A **plant** is a physical establishment—a factory, farm, mine, store, or warehouse—that performs one or more functions in producing, fabricating, and distributing goods and services.

- A **firm** is an organization that employs resources to produce goods and services for profit and operates one or more plants.

- An **industry** is a group of firms that produce the same, or similar, products or services.

The organizational structures of firms are often complex and varied. *Multiplant firms* may be organized horizontally, with several plants performing much the same function. Examples are the multiple bottling plants of Coca-Cola and the many individual Canadian Tire stores. Firms may be *vertically integrated,* meaning they own plants that perform different

plant
A physical establishment that performs one or more functions in producing, fabricating, and distributing goods and services.

firm
An organization that employs resources to produce goods or services for profit and operates one or more plants.

industry
A group of firms that produce the same or similar products or services.

sole proprietorship
An unincorporated firm owned and operated by one person.

partnership
An unincorporated firm owned and operated by two or more people.

corporation
A legal entity chartered by the federal or provincial government that operates as a distinct and separate body from the individuals who own it.

stock (corporate)
A share in the ownership of a corporation.

bond
A financial device through which a borrower (a firm or government) is obligated to pay the principal and interest on a loan at a specific date in the future.

limited liability
Restriction of maximum loss to a predetermined amount for the owners (shareholders) of a corporation; the maximum loss is the amount they paid for their shares.

functions in the various stages of the production process. For example, oil companies such as Petro-Canada own oil fields, refineries, and retail gasoline stations. Some firms are *conglomerates,* so named because they have plants that produce products in several industries. For example, Power Corp. of Montreal operates in such diverse fields as communications and industrial, financial, and energy services.

Legal Forms of Business

The business population is diverse, ranging from giant corporations to neighbourhood specialty shops and mom-and-pop groceries. There are three major legal forms of business:

1. A **sole proprietorship** is a business owned and operated by one person. Usually, the proprietor (the owner) personally supervises its operation.

2. A **partnership** is a natural outgrowth of the sole proprietorship. In a partnership, two or more individuals (the partners) agree to own and operate a business together. Usually they pool their financial resources and business skills. Consequently, they share the risks and the profits or losses.

3. A **corporation** is a legal creation that can acquire resources, own assets, produce and sell products, incur debts, extend credit, sue and be sued, and perform the functions of any other type of enterprise. A corporation is distinct and separate from the individual shareholders who own it. Hired managers run most corporations.

Advantages of Corporations

Certain advantages of the corporate form of business enterprise have catapulted it into a dominant sales and profit position in Canada. The corporation is by far the most effective form of business organization for raising money to finance the expansion of its facilities and capabilities. The corporation employs unique methods of finance—selling stocks and bonds—that enable it to pool the financial resources of large numbers of people.

A common **stock** represents a share in the ownership of a corporation. The purchaser of a stock certificate has the right to vote for corporate officers and to share in dividends. If you buy 1000 of the 100,000 shares issued by OutTell Inc., then you own 1 percent of the company, are entitled to 1 percent of any dividends declared by the board of directors, and control 1 percent of the votes in the annual election of corporate officials.

In contrast, a corporate **bond** does not bestow any corporate ownership on the purchaser. A bond purchaser is simply lending money to a corporation. A bond is an IOU, in acknowledgment of a loan, whereby the corporation promises to pay the holder a fixed amount set forth on the bond at some specified future date and other fixed amounts (interest payments) every year up to the bond's maturity date. For example, you might purchase a 10-year OutTell bond with a face value of $1000 and a 5 percent rate of interest. This means that, in exchange for your $1000, OutTell promises you a $50 interest payment for each of the next 10 years and then repays your $1000 principal at the end of that period.

Financing by selling stocks and bonds also provides other advantages to those who purchase these *corporate securities.* An individual investor can spread risks by buying the securities of several corporations. And it is usually easy for holders of corporate securities to sell their holdings. Organized stock exchanges and bond markets simplify the transfer of securities from sellers to buyers. This "ease of sale" increases the willingness of savers to make financial investments in corporate securities. Besides, corporations have easier access to bank credit than do other types of business organizations. Corporations are better risks and are more likely to become profitable clients of banks.

Corporations provide **limited liability** to owners (shareholders), who risk only what they paid for their stock; their personal assets are not at stake if the corporation defaults on its debts. Creditors can sue the corporation as a legal entity but cannot sue the owners of the corporation as individuals.

Because of their ability to attract financial capital, successful corporations can easily expand the scope of their operations and realize the benefits of expansion. For example, they can take advantage of mass-production technologies and division of labour. A corporation can hire specialists in production, accounting, and marketing functions and thus improve efficiency.

The Principal–Agent Problem

Many of the world's corporations are extremely large. In 2007, 351 of the world's largest corporations had annual sales of more than $20 billion, and 121 firms had sales of more than $20 billion. U.S.-based Wal-Mart, the world's largest corporation, alone sold $351 billion ($US) of goods in 2007. In Canada, George Weston Corporation, a food conglomerate, had sales of almost $26 billion in 2008.

ORIGIN 6.1
Principal–Agent
Problem

principal–agent problem
A conflict of interest that occurs when agents (workers or managers) pursue their own objectives to the detriment of the principals' (shareholders') goals.

But large size creates a potential problem. In sole proprietorships and partnerships, the owners of the real and financial assets of the firm enjoy direct control of those assets. But ownership of large corporations is spread over tens or hundreds of thousands of shareholders. The owners of a corporation usually do not manage it—they hire others to do so.

That practice can create a **principal–agent problem.** The *principals* are the shareholders who own the corporation and who hire executives as their *agents* to run the business on their behalf. But the interests of these managers (the agents) and the wishes of the owners (the principals) do not always coincide. The owners typically want maximum company profit and stock price. However, the agent may want the power, prestige, and pay that often accompany control over a large enterprise, independent of its profitability and stock price.

So a conflict of interest may develop. For example, executives may build expensive office buildings, enjoy excessive perks such as corporate jets, and pay too much to acquire other corporations. Consequently, the firm's costs will be excessive, and the executives will fail to maximize profit and the stock price for the owners. *(Key Question 2)*

CONSIDER THIS | Unprincipled Agents

In the 1990s many corporations addressed the principal–agent problem by providing a substantial part of executive pay either as shares of the firm's stock or as stock options. Stock options are contracts that allow executives or other key employees to buy shares of their employers' stock at fixed, lower prices when the stock prices rise. The idea was to align the interests of the executives and other key employees more closely with those of the broader corporate owners. By pursuing high profits and share prices, the executives would enhance their own wealth as well as that of all the shareholders.

This "solution" to the principal–agent problem had an unexpected negative side effect: It prompted a few unscrupulous executives to inflate their firm's share prices by hiding costs, overstating revenues, engaging in deceptive transactions, and, in general, exaggerating profits. These executives then sold large quantities of their inflated stock, making quick personal fortunes. In some cases, "independent" outside auditing firms turned out to be not so independent because they held valuable consulting contracts with the firms being audited.

When the stock-market bubble of the late 1990s burst, many instances of business manipulations and fraudulent accounting were exposed. Several executives of large U.S. firms were indicted and a few large firms collapsed, among them Enron (energy trading), WorldCom (communications), and Andersen Consulting (business consulting; renamed Accenture after the debacle). In Canada, the stock price of Bre-X Minerals Limited skyrocketed in 1996 and 1997 after the onetime penny-stock company announced the discovery of the world's largest gold deposits in Indonesia, later revealed to have been a cruel hoax. General shareholders of many of these firms were left holding severely depressed or even worthless stock.

QUICK REVIEW

▶ A plant is a physical establishment that contributes to the production of goods and services; a firm is a business organization that owns and operates plants. Plants may be arranged horizontally, be vertically integrated, or take on a conglomerate form.

▶ The three basic legal forms of business are the sole proprietorship, the partnership, and the corporation.

▶ The major advantages of corporations are their ability to raise financial capital, the limited liability they bestow on owners, and their continuing life beyond the life of their owners and managers.

▶ The principal–agent problem is the conflict of interest that can occur when agents (executives) pursue their own objectives to the detriment of the principals' (shareholders') goals.

6.2 | Economic Costs

OPPORTUNITY COSTS

economic (opportunity) cost
A value equal to the quantity of other products that cannot be produced when resources are instead used to make a particular product.

Costs exist because resources are scarce and have alternative uses. When society uses a combination of resources to produce a particular product, it forgoes all alternative opportunities to use those resources for any other purpose. The measure of the **economic cost** or **opportunity cost** of any resource used to produce a good is the value or worth it would have in its best alternative use.

We stressed this point in our analysis of production possibilities in Chapter 1, where we found that the opportunity cost of producing more pizzas is the industrial robots that must be forgone. Similarly, the opportunity cost of the steel used in constructing office buildings is the value it would have in manufacturing automobiles or refrigerators. The paper used for printing economics textbooks is not available for printing encyclopedias or romance novels. And if an assembly-line worker is capable of assembling either personal computers or washing machines, then the cost to society of employing that worker in a computer plant is the contribution that worker would otherwise have made in producing washing machines.

Explicit and Implicit Costs

Now let's consider costs from the firm's viewpoint. Keeping opportunity costs in mind, we can say that economic costs are the payments a firm must make, or the incomes it must provide, to attract the factors of production it needs away from alternative production opportunities. Those payments to suppliers of factors are explicit (revealed and expressed) or implicit (present but not obvious). So, in producing products firms incur explicit costs and implicit costs:

explicit costs
The monetary payments a firm must make to an outsider to obtain a resource.

implicit costs
The monetary income a firm sacrifices when it uses a resource it owns rather than supplying the resource in the market; equals what the resource could have earned in the best-paying alternative employment (including a normal profit).

- A firm's **explicit costs** are the monetary payments it makes to those who supply labour services, materials, fuel, transportation services, and the like. Such money payments are for the use of resources owned by others.

- A firm's **implicit costs** are the opportunity costs of using its self-owned, self-employed resources. To the firm, implicit costs are the money payments that self-employed inputs could have earned in their best alternative use.

For example, suppose you are earning $22,000 a year as a sales representative for a T-shirt manufacturer in Saskatoon. At some point, you decide to open a retail store of your own in the centre of the city to sell T-shirts. You invest $20,000 of savings that has been earning you $1000 per year in interest. You decide that your new firm will occupy a small store that you own and have been renting out for $5000 per year. You hire one clerk to help you in the store, paying her $18,000.

A year after you open the store, you total up your accounts and find the following:

Total sales revenue		$120,000
Cost of T-shirts	$40,000	
Clerk's salary	18,000	
Utilities	5,000	
Total (explicit) costs		63,000
Accounting profit		57,000

Costs of production exist because resources are scarce and have alternative uses.

Looks good. You have an accounting profit of $57,000. A firm's accounting profit is what remains after it has paid individuals and other firms for the materials, capital, and labour they have supplied. But unfortunately your accounting profit of $57,000 ignores your implicit costs and thus overstates the economic success of your venture. By providing your own financial capital, building, and labour, you incur implicit costs (forgone incomes) of $1000 of interest, $5000 of rent, and $22,000 of wages. And, if your entrepreneurial talent is worth, say, $5000 annually in other business endeavours of similar scope, you have also ignored that implicit cost. So:

Accounting profit	$57,000
Forgone interest.................. $ 1,000	
Forgone rent 5,000	
Forgone wages 22,000	
Forgone entrepreneurial income 5,000	
Total implicit costs	33,000
Economic profit	24,000

Normal Profit as a Cost

normal profit
The payment made by a firm to obtain and retain entrepreneurial ability.

The $5000 implicit cost of your entrepreneurial talent in the above example is a **normal profit.** As is true of the forgone rent and forgone wages, the payment you could otherwise receive for performing entrepreneurial functions is indeed an implicit cost. If you did not realize at least this minimum, or normal, payment for your effort, you could withdraw from this line of business and shift to a more attractive endeavour. So a normal profit is a cost of doing business.

The economist includes as costs of production all costs—explicit and implicit, including a normal profit—required to attract and retain factors of production in a specific line of production. For economists, a firm's economic costs are the opportunity costs of the inputs used, whether those inputs are owned by others or by the firm. In our example, economic costs are $96,000 (= $63,000 of explicit costs + $33,000 of implicit costs).

Economic Profit (or Pure Profit)

economic profit
A firm's total revenue less its economic costs (both explicit costs and implicit costs).

Obviously, then, economists use the term *profit* differently from the way accountants use it. To the accountant, profit is the firm's total revenue less its explicit costs (or accounting costs). To the economist, **economic profit** is total revenue less economic costs (explicit and implicit costs, the latter including a normal profit to the entrepreneur). So, when an economist says a certain firm is earning only enough revenue to cover its costs, this means it is meeting all explicit and implicit costs and the entrepreneur is receiving a payment just large enough to retain his or her talents in the present line of production.

If a firm's total revenue exceeds all its economic costs (explicit + implicit), any residual goes to the entrepreneur. That residual is called an economic, or pure, profit. In short:

     Economic profit = Total revenue – Economic cost (the sum of all explicit and implicit costs)

In our example, economic profit is $24,000, found by subtracting the $96,000 of economic cost from the $120,000 of revenue. An *economic* profit is not a cost, because it is a return in excess of the normal profit that is required to retain the entrepreneur in this particular line of production. Even if the economic profit is zero, the entrepreneur is still covering all explicit and implicit costs, including a normal profit. In our example, as long as accounting profit is $33,000 or more (so that economic profit is zero or more), you will be earning a $5000 normal profit and will, therefore, continue to operate your T-shirt store.

WORKED PROBLEM 6.1
Economic Profit

Figure 6-1 shows the relationship among the various cost and profit concepts that we have just discussed. To test yourself, enter the cost data from our example in the appropriate blocks. *(Key Question 6)*

Short Run and Long Run

When the demand for a firm's product changes, the firm's profitability may depend on how quickly it can adjust the amounts of the various factors it employs. It can easily and quickly adjust the quantities employed of many resources such as hourly labour, raw materials, fuel, and power. It needs much more time, however, to adjust its *plant capacity*—the size of the factory building, the amount

| FIGURE 6·1 | **Economic Profit versus Accounting Profit** |

Economic profit is equal to total revenue less economic costs. Economic costs are the sum of explicit and implicit costs and include a normal profit to the entrepreneur. Accounting profit is equal to total revenue less accounting (explicit) costs.

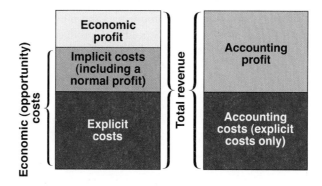

of machinery and equipment, and other capital resources. In some heavy industries, such as aircraft manufacturing, a firm such as Bombardier may need several years to alter plant capacity. Because of these differences in adjustment time, economists find it useful to distinguish between two conceptual periods: the short run and the long run. We will discover that costs differ in these two periods.

short run
A period of time in which producers are able to change the quantities of some but not all of the resources they employ.

- *Short Run: Fixed Plant*   As discussed in Chapter 4, the **short run** is a period too brief for a firm to alter its plant capacity, yet long enough to permit a change in the degree to which the fixed plant is used. The firm's plant capacity is fixed in the short run. However, the firm can vary its output by applying larger or smaller amounts of labour, materials, and other inputs to that plant, using its existing plant capacity more or less intensively in the short run.

long run
A period of time long enough to enable producers to change the quantities of all the resources they employ.

- *Long Run: Variable Plant*   For an existing firm, the **long run** is a period long enough for it to adjust the quantities of all the factors that it employs, including plant capacity. For the industry, the long run also includes enough time for existing firms to dissolve and leave the industry or for new firms to be created and enter the industry. While the short run is a "fixed-plant" period, the long run is a "variable-plant" period.

ILLUSTRATIONS

If Bombardier hires 100 extra workers for one of its aircraft plants or adds an entire shift of workers, we are speaking of the *short run*. If it adds a new production facility and installs more equipment, we are referring to the long run. The first situation is a *short-run adjustment;* the second is a *long-run adjustment.*

The short run and the long run are conceptual periods rather than calendar periods. In light-manufacturing industries, changes in plant capacity may be accomplished almost overnight. A small T-shirt manufacturer can increase its plant capacity in a matter of days by ordering and installing two or three new cutting tables and several extra sewing machines. But for heavy industry the long run is a different matter. Petro-Canada may require several years to construct a new oil refinery.

- ▸ Explicit costs are money payments a firm makes to outside suppliers of factors of production; implicit costs are the opportunity costs associated with a firm's use of inputs it owns.

- ▸ Normal profit is the implicit cost of entrepreneurship. Economic profit is total revenue less all explicit and implicit costs, including normal profit.

- ▸ In the short run, a firm's plant capacity is fixed; in the long run, a firm can vary its plant size and firms can enter or leave the industry.

6.3 | Short-Run Production Relationships

A firm's costs of producing a specific output depend on the prices of the needed inputs and the quantities of inputs needed to produce that output. Factor supply and demand determine input prices. The technological aspects of production, specifically the relationships between inputs and output, determine the quantities of factors of production needed. Our focus will be on the *labour*-output relationship, given a fixed-plant capacity. But before examining that relationship, we need to define three terms:

total product (TP)
The total output of a particular good or service produced by a firm.

1. **Total product (TP)** is the total quantity, or total output, of a particular good or service produced.

2. **Marginal product (MP)** is the extra output associated with adding a unit of variable input, in this case labour, to the production process. Thus,

marginal product (MP)
The extra output associated with adding a unit of a variable factor to the production process.

$$\text{Marginal product} = \frac{\text{change in total product}}{\text{change in labour input}}$$

3. **Average product (AP)**, also called labour productivity, is output per unit of labour input:

average product (AP)
The total output divided by the quantity of that employed resource.

$$\text{Average product} = \frac{\text{total product}}{\text{units of labour}}$$

Law of Diminishing Returns

 ORIGIN 6.2
Law of Diminishing Returns

law of diminishing returns
As successive increments of a variable factor are added to a fixed factor, the marginal product of the variable factor will eventually decrease.

In the short run, a firm can for a time increase its output by adding units of labour to its fixed plant. But by how much will output rise when a firm adds more labour? Why do we say "for a time"? The answers are provided in general terms by the **law of diminishing returns,** also called the *law of diminishing marginal product.* This law assumes that technology is fixed, so that the techniques of production do not change. It states that as successive units of a variable factor (say, labour) are added to a fixed factor (say, capital or land), beyond some point the extra, or marginal, product that can be attributed to each additional unit of the variable factor will decline. For example, if additional workers are hired to work with a constant amount of capital equipment, output will eventually rise by smaller and smaller amounts as more workers are hired. (See the Consider This box for a non-economic example of diminishing returns.)

RATIONALE

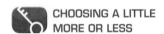 **CHOOSING A LITTLE MORE OR LESS**

Suppose a farmer in Ontario has a fixed supply of 80 hectares planted in corn. If the farmer does not cultivate the cornfields, the yield will be 40 bushels per hectare. If he cultivates the land once, output may rise to 50 bushels per hectare. A second cultivation may increase output to 57 bushels per hectare, a third to 61, and a fourth to 63. Succeeding cultivations would add less and less to the land's yield. If this were not so, the world's need for corn could be fulfilled by extremely intense cultivation of this single 80-hectare plot of land. Indeed, if diminishing returns did not occur, the world could be fed out of a flowerpot. Why not? Just keep adding more seed, fertilizer, and harvesters!

The law of diminishing returns also holds true in non-agricultural industries. Assume a wood shop is manufacturing chairs. It has a specific amount of equipment such as lathes, planers, saws, and sanders. If this shop hired just one or two workers, total output and productivity (output per worker) would be low. (Note that we assume all units of labour are of equal quality.) The workers would have to perform many different jobs, and the advantages of specialization would not be realized. Time would be lost switching from one job to another, and machines would stand idle much of the time. In short, the plant would be understaffed, and production would be inefficient because there would be too much capital relative to the amount of labour.

The shop could eliminate those difficulties by hiring more workers. Then the equipment would be more fully used, and workers could specialize in doing a single job. Time would no longer be lost switching from job to job. As more workers were added, production would become more efficient and the marginal product of each succeeding worker would rise.

CONSIDER THIS | Diminishing Returns from Study

A noneconomic example of the relationship between "inputs" and "output" may help you better understand the idea of diminishing returns. Suppose for an individual that total course learning = *f* (intelligence, quality of course materials, instructor effectiveness, class time, and study time) where *f* means "function of" or "depends on." So this relationship supposes that total course learning depends on intelligence (however defined), quality of course materials such as the textbook, the effectiveness of the instructor, the amount of class time, and the amount of personal study time outside the class.

Let's assume that one's intelligence, the quality of course materials, the effectiveness of the instructor, and the amount of class time are *fixed*—meaning they do not change over the length of the course. Now let's add units of study time per

day over the length of the course to "produce" greater course learning. The first hour of study time per day increases total course learning. Will the second hour enhance course learning by as much as the first? By how much will the third, fourth, fifth, . . . fifteenth hour of study per day contribute to total course learning relative to the *immediate previous hour*?

We think you will agree that diminishing returns to course learning eventually will set in as successive hours of study are added each day. At some point the marginal product of an extra hour of study time will decline and, at some further point, become zero.

This is also true of production relationships within firms. As successive units of a variable input (say, labour) are added to a fixed input (say, capital), the marginal product of the variable input eventually declines. In short, diminishing returns will occur sooner or later. Total product eventually will rise at a diminishing rate, reach a maximum, and then decline.

But the rise could not go on indefinitely. If still more workers were added, beyond a certain point overcrowding would set in. Since workers would then have to wait in line to use the machinery, it would be underused. Total output would increase at a diminishing rate, because, given the fixed size of the plant, each worker would have less capital equipment to work with as more and more labour was hired. The marginal product of additional workers would decline because there would be more labour in proportion to the fixed amount of capital. Eventually, adding still more workers would cause so much congestion that marginal product would become negative and total product would decline. At the extreme, the addition of more and more labour would exhaust all the standing room, and total product would fall to zero.

 WORKED PROBLEM 6.2
Total, Marginal, and Average Product

TABULAR EXAMPLE

Table 6-1 is a numerical hypothetical illustration of the law of diminishing returns in a wood shop manufacturing chairs. Column 2 shows the total product, or total output, resulting from combining each level of a variable input (labour) in column 1 with a fixed amount of capital.

Column 3 shows the marginal product (MP), the change in total product associated with each additional unit of labour. Note that with no labour input, total product is zero; a plant with no workers will produce no output. The first three units of labour reflect increasing marginal returns, with marginal products of 10, 15, and 20 units, respectively. But beginning with the fourth unit of labour, marginal product diminishes continually, becoming zero with the seventh unit of labour and negative with the eighth.

Average product, or output per labour unit, is shown in column 4. It is calculated by dividing total product (column 2) by the number of labour units needed to produce it (column 1). At five units of labour, for example, AP is 14 (= 70/5).

GRAPHICAL PORTRAYAL

Figure 6-2 (Key Graph) shows the diminishing returns data in Table 6-1 graphically and further clarifies the relationships between total, marginal, and average products. (Marginal product in Figure 6-2b is plotted halfway between the units of labour, since it applies to the addition of each labour unit.)

TABLE 6-1   Total, Marginal, and Average Product: The Law of Diminishing Returns

(1) Units of the variable factor (workers per day)	(2) Total product (TP) (chairs per day)	(3) Marginal product (MP) (chairs per additional worker) change in (2)/change in (1)	(4) Average product (AP) (chairs per worker) (2)/(1)
0	0		—
1	10	10 } Increasing marginal returns	10.00
2	25	15 } Increasing marginal returns	12.50
3	45	20 }	15.00
4	60	15 } Diminishing marginal returns	15.00
5	70	10 }	14.00
6	75	5 } Negative marginal returns	12.50
7	75	0 }	10.71
8	70	−5 }	8.75

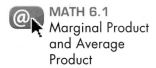

MATH 6.1
Marginal Product
and Average
Product

ORIGIN 6.3
Production
Relationships

Note first in Figure 6-2a that total product, TP, goes through three phases: it rises initially at an increasing rate; then it increases, but at a diminishing rate; finally, after reaching a maximum, it declines.

Geometrically, marginal product—shown by the MP curve in Figure 6-2b—is the slope of the total product curve. Marginal product measures the change in total output of chairs associated with each succeeding unit of labour. Thus, the three phases of total product are also reflected in marginal product. Where total product is increasing at an increasing rate, marginal product is rising. Here, extra units of labour are adding larger and larger amounts to total product. Similarly, where total product is increasing but at a decreasing rate, marginal product is positive but falling. Each additional unit of labour adds fewer chairs than did the previous unit. When total product is at a maximum, marginal product is zero. When total product declines, marginal product becomes negative.

Average product, AP in Figure 6-2b, displays the same tendencies as marginal product. It increases, reaches a maximum, and then decreases as more units of labour are added to the fixed plant. But note the relationship between marginal product and average product: Where marginal product exceeds average product, average product rises. And where marginal product is less than average product, average product declines. It follows that marginal product intersects average product where average product is at a maximum.

This relationship is a mathematical necessity. If you add a larger number to a total than the current average of that total, the average must rise; if you add a smaller number to a total than the current average of that total, the average must fall. You raise your average examination grade only when your score on an additional (marginal) examination is greater than the average of all your past scores. You lower your average when your grade on an additional exam is below your current average. In our production example, when the amount an extra worker adds to total product exceeds the average product of all workers currently employed, average product will rise. Conversely, when an extra worker adds to total product an amount that is less than the current average product, then average product will decrease.

The law of diminishing returns is reflected in the shapes of all three curves. But, as our definition of the law of diminishing returns indicates, we are most concerned with its effects on marginal product. The regions of increasing, diminishing, and negative marginal product (returns) are shown in Figure 6-2b. *(Key Question 8)*

KEY GRAPH

FIGURE 6-2 The Law of Diminishing Returns

Panel (a): As a variable resource (labour) is added to fixed amounts of other resources (land or capital), the total product that results will eventually increase by diminishing amounts, reach a maximum, and then decline. Panel (b): Marginal product is the change in total product associated with each new unit of labour. Average product is simply output per labour unit. Note that marginal product intersects average product at the maximum average product.

(a) Total product

(b) Marginal and average product

Quick Quiz

1. **Which of the following is an assumption underlying these figures?**
   a. Firms first hire highly skilled workers and then hire less skilled workers.
   b. Capital and labour are both variable, but labour increases more rapidly than capital.
   c. Consumers will buy all the output (total product) produced.
   d. Workers are of equal quality.

2. **Marginal product is**
   a. the change in total product divided by the change in the quantity of labour.
   b. total product divided by the quantity of labour.
   c. always positive.
   d. unrelated to total product.

3. **Marginal product in panel (b) is zero when**
   a. average product in panel (b) stops rising.
   b. the slope of the marginal-product curve in panel (b) is zero.
   c. total product in panel (a) begins to rise at a diminishing rate.
   d. the slope of the total-product curve in panel (a) is zero.

4. **Average product in panel (b)**
   a. rises when it is less than marginal product.
   b. is the change in total product divided by the change in the quantity of labour.
   c. can never exceed marginal product.
   d. falls whenever total product in panel (a) rises at a diminishing rate.

Answers: 1. d; 2. a; 3. d; 4. a

6.4 | Short-Run Production Costs

Production information such as that provided in Table 6-1 and Figure 6-2a and 6-2b must be coupled with prices of factors of production to determine the total and per-unit costs of producing various levels of output. We know that in the short run some factors, those associated with the firm's plant, are fixed. Other factors of production, however, are variable. So short-run costs are either fixed or variable.

Fixed, Variable, and Total Costs

Let's see what distinguishes fixed costs, variable costs, and total costs from one another.

FIXED COSTS

fixed costs
Costs that in total do not change when the firm changes its output.

Fixed costs are those costs that in total do not vary with changes in output. Fixed costs are associated with the very existence of a firm's plant and, therefore, must be paid even if its output is zero. Such costs as rental payments, interest on a firm's debts, and insurance premiums are generally fixed costs; they do not increase even if a firm produces more. In column 2 in Table 6-2 we assume that the firm's total fixed cost is $100. By definition, this fixed cost is incurred at all levels of output, including zero. The firm cannot avoid paying these costs in the short run.

TABLE 6-2   Total-Cost, Average-Cost, and Marginal-Cost Schedules for an Individual Firm in the Short Run

	TOTAL-COST DATA			AVERAGE-COST DATA			MARGINAL COST
(1) Total product (Q)	(2) Total fixed cost (TFC)	(3) Total variable cost (TVC)	(4) Total cost (TC)	(5) Average fixed cost (AFC)	(6) Average variable cost (AVC)	(7) Average total cost (ATC)	(8) Marginal cost (MC)
(chairs per day)	(dollars per day)			(dollars per chair)			(dollars per additional chair)
0	$100	$ 0	$ 100				
							$ 90
1	100	90	190	$100.00	$90.00	$190.00	
							80
2	100	170	270	50.00	85.00	135.00	
							70
3	100	240	340	33.33	80.00	113.33	
							60
4	100	300	400	25.00	75.00	100.00	
							70
5	100	370	470	20.00	74.00	94.00	
							80
6	100	450	550	16.67	75.00	91.67	
							90
7	100	540	640	14.29	77.14	91.43	
							110
8	100	650	750	12.50	81.25	93.75	
							130
9	100	780	880	11.11	86.67	97.78	
							150
10	100	930	1,030	10.00	93.00	103.00	

VARIABLE COSTS

variable costs
Costs that increase or decrease with a firm's output.

Variable costs are those costs that change with the level of output—payments for materials, fuel, power, transportation services, most labour, and similar variable resources. In column 3 of Table 6-2 we find that the total of variable costs changes directly with output, but note that the increases in variable cost associated with succeeding one-unit increases in output are not equal. As production begins, variable cost will for a time increase by a decreasing amount; this is true through the fourth unit of output in Table 6-2. Beyond the fourth unit, however, variable cost rises by increasing amounts for succeeding units of output.

The reason lies in the shape of the marginal product curve. At first, as in Figure 6-2b, marginal product is increasing, so smaller and smaller increases in the amounts of variable inputs are needed to produce successive units of output. Thus, the variable cost of successive units of output decreases. But when, as diminishing returns are encountered, marginal product begins to decline, larger and larger additional amounts of variable inputs are needed to produce successive units of output. Total variable cost, therefore, increases by increasing amounts.

TOTAL COST

total cost
The sum of fixed cost and variable cost.

Total cost is the sum of fixed cost and variable cost at each level of output:

$$TC = TFC + TVC$$

It is shown in column 4 in Table 6-2. At zero units of output, total cost is equal to the firm's fixed cost. Then for each unit of the 10 units of production, total cost increases by the same amount as variable cost.

Figure 6-3 shows graphically the fixed-cost, variable-cost, and total-cost data given in Table 6-2. Observe that total variable cost, TVC, is measured vertically from the horizontal axis at each level of output. The amount of fixed cost, shown as TFC, is added vertically to the total variable cost curve to obtain the points on the total-cost curve, TC.

The distinction between fixed and variable costs is significant to the business manager. Variable costs can be controlled or altered in the short run by changing production levels. Fixed costs are beyond the business manager's current control; they are incurred in the short run and must be paid regardless of output level.

FIGURE 6-3   **Total Cost Is the Sum of Fixed Cost and Variable Cost**

Total variable cost (TVC) changes with output. Total fixed cost (TFC) is independent of the level of output. The total cost (TC) at any output is the vertical sum of the fixed cost and variable cost at that output.

Per-Unit, or Average Costs

Producers are certainly interested in their total costs, but they are equally concerned with per-unit, or average costs. In particular, average-cost data are more meaningful for making comparisons with product price, which is always stated on a per-unit basis. Average fixed cost, average variable cost, and average total cost are shown in columns 5 to 7, Table 6-2.

AFC

average fixed cost (AFC)
A firm's total fixed cost divided by output.

Average fixed cost (AFC) for any output level is found by dividing total fixed cost (TFC) by that output (Q). That is,

$$AFC = \frac{TFC}{Q}$$

Because the total fixed cost is, by definition, the same regardless of output, AFC must decline as output increases. As output rises, the total fixed cost is spread over a larger and larger output. When output is just one unit in Table 6-2, TFC and AFC are the same at $100. But at two units of output, the total fixed cost of $100 becomes $50 of AFC or fixed cost per unit; then it becomes $33.33 per unit as $100 is spread over three units, and $25 per unit when spread over four units. This process is sometimes referred to as "spreading the overhead." Figure 6-4 shows that AFC graphs as a continuously declining curve as total output is increased.

AVC

average variable cost (AVC)
A firm's total variable cost divided by output.

Average variable cost (AVC) for any output level is calculated by dividing total variable cost (TVC) by that output (Q):

$$AVC = \frac{TVC}{Q}$$

As added variable inputs increase output, AVC declines initially, reaches a minimum, and then increases again. A graph of AVC is a U-shaped curve, as shown in Figure 6-4.

Because total variable cost reflects the law of diminishing returns, so must AVC, which is derived from total variable cost. Marginal returns increase initially because it takes fewer and fewer additional variable inputs to produce each of the first four units of output. As a result, variable cost per unit declines. AVC hits a minimum with the fifth unit of output, and beyond that point AVC rises as diminishing returns require more variable inputs to produce each additional unit of output.

FIGURE 6-4   **The Average-Cost Curves**

AFC falls as a given amount of fixed costs is apportioned over a larger and larger output. AVC initially falls because of increasing marginal returns but then rises because of diminishing marginal returns. Average total cost (ATC) is the vertical sum of average variable cost (AVC) and average fixed cost (AFC).

You can verify the U shape of the AVC curve by returning to Table 6-1. Assume the price of labour is $10 per unit. By dividing average product (output per labour unit) into $10 (price per labour unit), we determine the labour cost per unit of output. Because we have assumed labour to be the only variable input, the labour cost per unit of output is the variable cost per unit of output or AVC. When average product is initially low, AVC is high. As workers are added, average product rises and AVC falls. When average product is at its maximum, AVC is at its minimum. Then, as still more workers are added and average product declines, AVC rises. The hump of the average product curve is reflected in the U shape of the AVC curve. As you will soon see, the two are mirror images.

ATC

average total cost (ATC)
A firm's total cost divided by output.

Average total cost (ATC) for any output level is found by dividing total cost (TC) by that output (Q) or by adding AFC and AVC at that output:

$$ATC = \frac{TC}{Q} = \frac{TFC}{Q} + \frac{TVC}{Q}$$

$$= AFC + AVC$$

Graphically, ATC can be found by adding vertically the AFC and AVC curves, as in Figure 6-4. Thus, the vertical distance between the ATC and AVC curves measures AFC at any level of output.

Marginal Cost

marginal cost (MC)
The additional cost of producing one more unit of output.

One final and very crucial cost concept remains: **Marginal cost (MC)** is the extra, or additional, cost of producing one more unit of output. MC can be determined for each added unit of output by noting the change in total cost that that unit's production entails:

$$MC = \frac{\text{change in TC}}{\text{change in } Q}$$

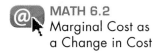
MATH 6.2
Marginal Cost as a Change in Cost

CALCULATIONS

In column 4, Table 6-2, production of the first unit of output increases total cost from $100 to $190. Therefore, the additional, or marginal, cost of that first unit is $90 (column 8). The marginal cost of the second unit is $80 (= $270 – $190); the MC of the third is $70 (= $340 – $270); and so forth. The MC for each of the 10 units of output is shown in column 8. MC can also be calculated from the total-variable-cost column, because the only difference between total cost and total variable cost is the constant amount of fixed costs ($100). Thus, the change in total cost and the change in total variable cost associated with each additional unit of output are always the same.

MARGINAL DECISIONS

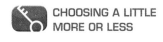
CHOOSING A LITTLE MORE OR LESS

Marginal costs are costs the firm can control directly and immediately. Specifically, MC designates all the additional cost incurred in producing the last unit of output. Thus, it also designates the cost that can be saved by not producing that last unit. Average-cost figures do not provide this information. For example, suppose the firm is undecided whether to produce three or four units of output. At four units Table 6-2 indicates that ATC is $100. But the firm does not increase its total costs by $100 by producing the fourth unit, nor does it save $100 by not producing that unit. Rather, the change in costs is only $60, as the MC column in Table 6-2 reveals.

WORKED PROBLEM 6.3
Per Unit Cost

A firm's decisions as to what output level to produce are typically decisions to produce a few more or a few less units. Marginal cost is the change in costs when one more or one less unit of output is produced. When coupled with marginal revenue, marginal cost allows a firm to determine whether it is profitable to expand or contract its production. The analysis in the next three chapters focuses on those marginal calculations.

GRAPHICAL PORTRAYAL

Marginal cost is shown graphically in **Figure 6-5 (Key Graph)**. Marginal cost at first declines sharply, reaches a minimum, and then rises rather abruptly. This pattern reflects the fact that the variable costs, and therefore total cost, increase at first by decreasing amounts and then by increasing amounts (see columns 3 and 4, Table 6-2).

FIGURE 6-5 The Relationship of the Marginal-Cost Curve to the Average-Total-Cost and Average-Variable-Cost Curves

The marginal-cost (MC) curve cuts through the average-total-cost (ATC) curve and the average-variable-cost (AVC) curve at their minimum points. When MC is below average total cost, ATC falls; when MC is above average total cost, ATC rises. Similarly, when MC is below average variable cost, AVC falls; when MC is above average variable cost, AVC rises.

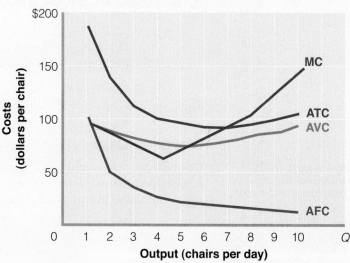

Quick Quiz

1. **The marginal-cost curve first declines and then increases because of**
   a. increasing, then diminishing, marginal utility.
   b. the decline in the gap between ATC and AVC as output expands.
   c. increasing, then diminishing, marginal returns.
   d. constant marginal revenue.

2. **The vertical distance between ATC and AVC measures**
   a. marginal cost.
   b. total fixed cost.
   c. average fixed cost.
   d. economic profit per unit.

3. **ATC is**
   a. AVC – AFC.
   b. MC + AVC.
   c. AFC + AVC.
   d. (AFC + AVC) × Q.

4. **When the marginal-cost curve lies**
   a. above the ATC curve, ATC rises.
   b. above the AVC curve, ATC rises.
   c. below the AVC curve, total fixed cost increases.
   d. below the ATC curve, total fixed cost falls.

MARGINAL COST AND MARGINAL PRODUCT

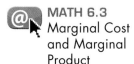

MATH 6.3
Marginal Cost and Marginal Product

The shape of the marginal-cost curve is a consequence of the law of diminishing returns. Looking back at Table 6-1, we can see the relationship between marginal product and marginal cost. If all units of a variable factor (here labour) are hired at the same price, the marginal cost of each extra unit of output will fall as long as the marginal product of each additional worker is rising, because marginal cost is the (constant) cost of an extra worker divided by his or her marginal product. Therefore, in Table 6-1, suppose that each worker can be hired for $10. Because the first worker's marginal product is 10 units of output, and hiring this worker increases the firm's costs by $10, the marginal cost of each of these 10 extra units of output is $1 (= $10 ÷ 10 units). The second worker also increases costs by $10, but the marginal product is 15, so the marginal cost of each of these 15 extra units of output is $0.67 (= $10 ÷ 15 units). Similarly, the MC of each of the 20 extra units of output contributed by the third worker is $0.50 (= $10 ÷ 20 units). To generalize, as long as marginal product is rising, marginal cost will fall.

But with the fourth worker, diminishing returns set in and marginal cost begins to rise. For the fourth worker, marginal cost is $0.67 (= $10 ÷ 15 units); for the fifth worker, MC is $1.00 ($10 ÷ 10 units); for the sixth, MC is $2.00 (= $10 ÷ 5 units), and so on. If the price (cost) of the variable resource remains constant, increasing marginal returns will be reflected in a declining marginal cost, and diminishing marginal returns in a rising marginal cost. The MC curve is a mirror reflection of the marginal-product curve. As you can see in Figure 6-6, when marginal product is rising, marginal cost is necessarily falling. When marginal product is at its maximum, marginal cost is at its minimum; when marginal product is falling, marginal cost is rising.

FIGURE 6-6   # The Relationship between Productivity Curves and Cost Curves

The marginal-cost (MC) curve and the average variable-cost (AVC) curve in panel (b) are mirror images of the marginal-product (MP) and average-product (AP) curves in panel (a). Assuming that labour is the only variable input and that its price (the wage rate) is constant, then when MP is rising, MC is falling, and when MP is falling, MC is rising. Under the same assumptions, when AP is rising, AVC is falling, and when AP is falling, AVC is rising.

(a) Production curves

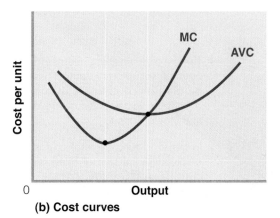

(b) Cost curves

RELATION OF MC TO AVC AND ATC

Figure 6-5 shows that the marginal-cost curve MC intersects both the AVC and ATC curves at their minimum points. As noted earlier, this marginal-average relationship is a mathematical necessity, which a simple illustration will reveal. Suppose a Toronto Raptors basketball player scored an average of 20 points a game in the first three games he has played. Now, whether his average rises or falls as a result of playing a fourth (marginal) game will depend on whether the additional points he scores in that game are fewer or more than his current 20-point average. If in the fourth game he scores fewer than 20 points, for example 16, his total points will rise from 60 to 76 and his average will fall from 20 to 19 (= 76/4). Conversely, if in the fourth (marginal) game he scores more than 20 points, say 24, his total will increase from 60 to 84 and his average will rise from 20 to 21 (= 84/4).

So it is with costs. When the amount (the marginal cost) added to total cost is less than the current average total cost, ATC will fall. Conversely, when the marginal cost exceeds ATC, ATC will rise, which means that in Figure 6-5, as long as MC lies below ATC, ATC will fall, and whenever MC lies above ATC, ATC will rise. At the point of intersection, where MC equals ATC, ATC has just stopped falling but has not yet begun rising. This point, by definition, is the minimum point on the ATC curve. The marginal-cost curve intersects the average-total-cost curve at the ATC curve's minimum point.

Marginal cost can be defined as the addition either to total cost or to total variable cost resulting from one more unit of output; thus, this same rationale explains why the MC curve also crosses the AVC curve at the AVC curve's minimum point. No such relationship exists between the MC curve and the average-fixed-cost curve, because the two are not related; marginal cost includes only those costs that change with output, and fixed costs by definition are those that are independent of output. *(Key Question 11)*

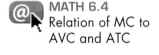

MATH 6.4
Relation of MC to AVC and ATC

Shifts of Cost Curves

Changes in either factors of production prices or technology will change costs, and therefore the cost curves will shift. If fixed costs were to double from $100 to $200, the AFC curve in Figure 6-5 would shift upward. At each level of output, fixed costs would be higher. The ATC curve would also move upward, because AFC is a component of ATC. The positions of the AVC and MC curves would be unchanged, because their locations are based on the prices of variable rather than fixed factors of production. However, if the price (wage) of labour or some other variable input rose, AVC, ATC, and MC would rise, and those cost curves would all shift upward. The AFC curve would remain in place because fixed costs have not changed.

The discovery of a more efficient technology would increase the productivity of all inputs, and the AVC, ATC, and MC cost figures in Table 6-2 would all be lower. To illustrate, if labour is the only variable input, if wages are $10 per hour, and if the average product is 10 units, then AVC would be $1. But if a technological improvement increases the average product of labour to 20 units, then AVC will decline to $0.50. More generally, an upward shift in the productivity curves shown in Figure 6-6a means a downward shift in the cost curves portrayed in Figure 6-6b.

QUICK REVIEW

▶ The law of diminishing returns indicates that, beyond some point, output will increase by diminishing amounts as more units of a variable factor (labour) are added to a fixed factor (capital).

▶ In the short run, the total cost of any level of output is the sum of fixed and variable costs (TC = TFC + TVC).

▶ Average fixed, average variable, and average total costs are fixed, variable, and total costs per unit of output; marginal cost is the extra cost of producing one more unit of output.

▶ Average fixed cost declines continuously as output increases; average-variable-cost and average-total-cost curves are U-shaped, reflecting increasing and then diminishing returns; the marginal-cost curve falls but then rises, intersecting both the average-variable-cost curve and the average-total-cost curve at their minimum points.

6.5 | Long-Run Production Costs

In the long run firms can undertake all desired input adjustments. The firm can alter its plant capacity; it can build a larger plant or revert to a smaller plant than that assumed in Table 6-2. The industry also can change its plant size; the long run allows sufficient time for new firms to enter or for existing firms to leave an industry. We will discuss the impact of the entry and exit of firms to and from an industry in the next chapter; here we are concerned only with changes in plant capacity made by a single firm. Let's express our analysis in terms of average total cost (ATC), making no distinction between fixed and variable costs because all inputs, and therefore all costs, are variable in the long run.

Firm Size and Costs

Suppose a single-plant manufacturer begins on a small scale and, as the result of successful operations, expands to successively larger plant sizes with larger output capacities. What happens to average total cost as this occurs? For a time, successively larger plants will lower average total cost. However, eventually the building of a still larger plant may cause ATC to rise.

Figure 6-7 illustrates this situation for five possible plant sizes. ATC-1 is the short-run average-total-cost curve for the smallest of the five plants, and ATC-5 is the curve for the largest. Constructing larger plants will lower the minimum average total costs through plant size 3, but then larger plants will mean higher minimum average total costs.

The Long-Run Cost Curve

The vertical lines perpendicular to the output axis in Figure 6-7 indicate those outputs at which the firm should change plant size to realize the lowest attainable average total costs of production. These are the outputs at which the per-unit costs for a larger plant drop below those for the current, smaller plant. For all outputs up to 20 units, the lowest average total costs are attainable with plant size 1. However, if the firm's volume of sales expands to between 20 and 30 units, it can achieve lower per-unit costs by constructing larger plant size 2. Although total cost will be higher at the expanded levels of production, the cost per unit of output will be less. For any output between 30 and 50 units, plant size 3 will yield the lowest average total costs. From 50 to 60 units of output, the firm must build plant size 4 to achieve the lowest unit costs. Lowest average total costs for any output over 60 units require construction of the still larger plant size 5.

FIGURE 6-7   **The Long-Run Average-Total-Cost Curve: Five Possible Plant Sizes**

The long-run average-total-cost curve is made up of segments of the short-run cost curves (ATC-1, ATC-2, etc.) of the various-size plants from which the firm might choose. Each point on the planning curve shows the least unit cost attainable for any output when the firm has had time to make all desired changes in its plant size.

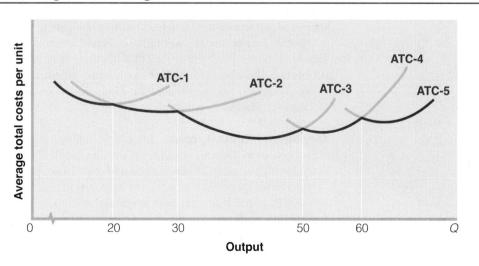

Tracing these adjustments, we find that the long-run ATC curve for the enterprise is made up of segments of the short-run ATC curves for the various plant sizes that can be constructed. The long-run ATC curve shows the lowest average total cost at which *any output level* can be produced after the firm has had time to make all appropriate adjustments in its plant size. In Figure 6-7 the dark blue, uneven curve is the firm's long-run ATC curve or, as it is often called, the firm's *planning curve*.

In most lines of production, the choice of plant size is much wider than in our illustration. In many industries the number of possible plant sizes is virtually unlimited, and in time quite small changes in the volume of output will lead to changes in plant size. Graphically, this implies an unlimited number of short-run ATC curves, one for each output level, as suggested by **Figure 6-8 (Key Graph)**. Then, rather than consisting of segments of short-run ATC curves as in Figure 6-7, the long-run ATC curve is made up of all the points of tangency of the unlimited number of short-run ATC curves from which the long-run ATC curve is derived. Therefore, the planning curve is smooth rather than bumpy. Each point on it tells us the minimum ATC of producing the corresponding level of output.

Economies and Diseconomies of Scale

We have assumed that for a time increasing plant sizes will lead to lower unit costs but that beyond some point successively larger plants will mean higher average total costs. That is, we have assumed that the long-run ATC curve is U-shaped. But why should this be? It turns out that the U shape is caused by economies and diseconomies of large-scale production, as we explain in a moment. But before we do, please understand that the U shape of the long-run average-total-cost curve *cannot* be the result of rising factor prices or the law of diminishing returns. First, our discussion assumes that factor prices are constant. Second, the law of diminishing returns does not apply to production in the long run. This is true because the law of diminishing returns deals only with situations in which a productive input is held constant. Under our definition of "long run," all resources and inputs are variable.

ECONOMIES OF SCALE

economies of scale
Reductions in the average total cost of producing a product as the firm increases plant size (output) in the long run.

Economies of scale, or economies of mass production, explain the downsloping part of the long-run ATC curve. As plant size increases, a number of factors will for a time lead to lower average costs of production.

Labour Specialization   Increased specialization in the use of labour becomes more achievable as a plant increases in size. Hiring more workers means jobs can be divided and subdivided. Each worker may now have just one task to perform instead of five or six. Workers can work full time on those tasks for which they have special skills. In a small plant, skilled machinists may spend half their time performing unskilled tasks, leading to higher production costs.

Further, by working at fewer tasks, workers become even more proficient at those tasks. The jack-of-all-trades doing five or six jobs is not likely to be efficient in any of them. By concentrating on one task, the same worker may become highly efficient.

Finally, greater labour specialization eliminates the loss of time that accompanies each shift of a worker from one task to another.

Managerial Specialization   Large-scale production also means better use of, and greater specialization in, management. A supervisor who can handle 20 workers is underused in a small plant that employs only 10 people. The production staff could be doubled with no increase in supervisory costs.

Small firms cannot use management specialists to best advantage. For example, a sales specialist working in a small plant may have to spend some time on functions outside her area of expertise, for example, marketing, personnel, and finance. A larger scale of operations means that the marketing expert can supervise marketing full time, while specialists perform other managerial functions. Greater efficiency and lower unit costs are the net result.

KEY GRAPH

FIGURE 6-8
The Long-Run Average-Total-Cost Curve: Unlimited Number of Plant Sizes

If the number of possible plant sizes is very large, the long-run average-total-cost curve approximates a smooth curve. Economies of scale, followed by diseconomies of scale, cause the curve to be U-shaped.

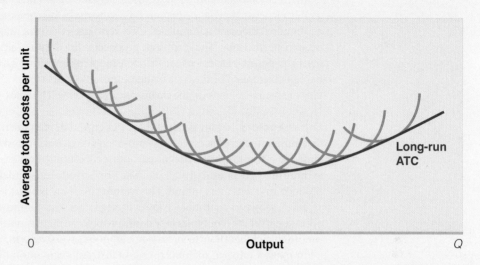

Quick Quiz

1. The unlabelled light blue curves in this figure illustrate the
   a. long-run average-total-cost curves of various firms constituting the industry.
   b. short-run average-total-cost curves of various firms constituting the industry.
   c. short-run average-total-cost curves of various plant sizes available to a particular firm.
   d. short-run marginal-cost curves of various plant sizes available to a particular firm.

2. The unlabelled light blue curves in this figure derive their shapes from
   a. decreasing, then increasing, short-run returns.
   b. increasing, then decreasing, short-run returns.
   c. economies, then diseconomies, of scale.
   d. diseconomies, then economies, of scale.

3. The long-run ATC curve in this figure derives its shape from
   a. decreasing, then increasing, short-run returns.
   b. increasing, then decreasing, short-run returns.
   c. economies, then diseconomies, of scale.
   d. diseconomies, then economies, of scale.

4. The long-run ATC curve is often called the firm's
   a. planning curve.
   b. capital-expansion path.
   c. total-product curve.
   d. production possibilities curve.

Efficient Capital Small firms often cannot afford the most efficient equipment. In many lines of production such machinery is available only in very large and extremely expensive units. Effective use of such equipment demands a high volume of production, and that again requires large-scale producers.

In the automobile industry the most efficient fabrication method in North America employs robotics and elaborate assembly-line equipment. Effective use of this equipment demands an annual output of several hundred thousand automobiles. Only very large-scale producers can afford to purchase and use this equipment efficiently. The small-scale producer is faced with a dilemma. Fabricating automobiles using other equipment is inefficient and therefore more costly per unit. But so, too, is buying and underutilizing the equipment used by the large manufacturers. Because it cannot spread the high equipment cost over very many units of output, the small-scale producer will be stuck with high costs per unit of output.

Other Factors Many products have design and development costs, as well as other startup costs, that must be incurred irrespective of projected sales. These costs decline per unit as output is increased. Similarly, advertising costs decline per auto, per computer, per stereo system, and per box of detergent as more units are produced and sold. The firm's production and marketing expertise usually rises as it produces and sells more output. This learning by doing is a further source of economies of scale.

All these factors contribute to lower average total costs for the firm that is able to expand its scale of operations. Where economies of scale are possible, an increase in all inputs of, say, 10 percent will cause a more-than-proportionate increase in output of, say, 20 percent. The result will be a decline in ATC.

In many Canadian manufacturing industries, from automobile to aircraft production, economies of scale have been of great significance. Firms that have expanded their scale of operations to obtain economies of mass production have survived and flourished. Those unable to expand have become relatively high-cost producers, doomed to struggle to survive.

DISECONOMIES OF SCALE

diseconomies of scale
Increases in the average total cost of producing a product as the firm increases plant size (output) in the long run.

In time the expansion of a firm may lead to diseconomies and, therefore, higher average total costs. The main factor causing **diseconomies of scale** is the difficulty of efficiently controlling and coordinating a firm's operations as it becomes a large-scale producer. In a small plant a single key executive may make all the basic decisions for the plant's operation. Because of the firm's small size, the executive is close to the production line, understands the firm's operations, and can make efficient decisions because the small plant size requires only a relatively small amount of information to be examined and understood in optimizing production. This neat picture changes as a firm grows. One person cannot assemble, digest, and understand all the information essential to decision making on a large scale. Authority must be delegated to many vice presidents, second vice presidents, and so forth. This expansion of the management hierarchy leads to problems of communication and cooperation, bureaucratic red tape, and the possibility that decisions will not be coordinated. Decision making may be slowed down to the point that decisions fail to reflect changes in consumer tastes or technology quickly enough. The result is impaired efficiency and rising average total costs.

Also, in massive production facilities workers may feel alienated from their employers and care little about working efficiently. Opportunities to shirk responsibilities, by avoiding work in favour of on-the-job leisure, may be greater in large plants than in small ones. Countering worker alienation and shirking may require additional supervision, which increases costs.

Where diseconomies of scale are operative, an increase in all inputs of, say, 10 percent will cause a less-than-proportionate increase in output of, say, 5 percent. As a consequence, ATC will increase. The rising portion of the long-run cost curves in Figure 6-9a illustrates diseconomies of scale.

CONSTANT RETURNS TO SCALE

constant returns to scale
The range of output between the points where economies of scale end and diseconomies of scale begin.

In some industries a rather wide range of output may exist between the output at which economies of scale end and the output at which diseconomies of scale begin. That is, a range of **constant returns to scale** may exist over which long-run average cost does not change. The q_1q_2 output range of Figure 6-9a is an example. Here a given percentage increase in all inputs of, say, 10 percent will cause a proportionate 10 percent increase in output. Thus, in this range ATC is constant.

FIGURE 6.9

FIGURE 6.9 — Various Possible Long-Run Average-Total-Cost Curves

In panel (a), economies of scale are rather rapidly obtained as plant size rises, and diseconomies of scale are not encountered until a considerably large scale of output has been achieved. Thus, long-run average total cost is constant over a wide range of output. In panel (b), economies of scale are extensive, and diseconomies of scale occur only at very large outputs. Average total cost, therefore, declines over a broad range of output. In panel (c), economies of scale are exhausted quickly, followed immediately by diseconomies of scale. Minimum ATC thus occurs at a relatively low output.

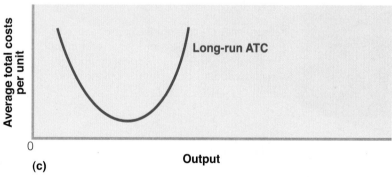

Minimum Efficient Scale and Industry Structure

minimum efficient scale (MES)
The lowest level of output at which a firm can minimize long-run average costs.

Economies and diseconomies of scale are an important determinant of an industry's structure. We now introduce the concept of **minimum efficient scale (MES)**, which is the lowest level of output at which a firm can minimize long-run average costs. In Figure 6-9a that level occurs at q_1 units of output. Because of the extended range of constant returns to scale, firms within the q_1 to q_2 range would be equally efficient, so we would not be surprised to find an industry with such cost conditions to be populated by firms of quite different sizes. The apparel, food processing, furniture, wood products, snowboard, and small-appliance industries are examples. With an extended range of constant returns to scale, relatively large and relatively small firms can coexist in an industry and be equally successful.

Compare this with Figure 6-9b, where economies of scale prevail over a wide range of output and diseconomies of scale appear only at very high levels of output. This pattern of declining long-run average total cost may occur over an extended range of output, as in the automobile, aluminum, steel, and other heavy industries. The same pattern holds in several of the new industries related to information technology, for example, computer microchips, operating system software, and Internet service provision.

Given consumer demand, efficient production will be achieved with a few large-scale producers. Small firms cannot realize the minimum efficient scale and will not be able to compete. In the extreme, economies of scale might extend beyond the market's size, resulting in what is termed **natural monopoly,** a relatively rare market situation in which average total cost is minimized when only one firm produces the particular good or service.

Where economies of scale are few and diseconomies come into play quickly, the minimum efficient size occurs at a low level of output, as shown in Figure 6-9c. In such industries a particular level of consumer demand will support a large number of relatively small producers. Many retail trades and some types of farming fall into this category. So do certain kinds of light manufacturing, such as the baking, clothing, and shoe industries. Fairly small firms are as efficient as, or more efficient than, large-scale producers in such industries.

Our point here is that the shape of the long-run average-total-cost curve is determined by technology and the economies and diseconomies of scale that result. The shape of the long-run ATC curve, in turn, can be significant in determining whether an industry has a relatively large number of small firms or is dominated by a few large producers—or lies somewhere in between.

But we must be cautious in our assessment, because industry structure does not depend on cost conditions alone. Government policies, the geographic size of markets, managerial strategy and skill, and other factors must be considered in explaining the structure of a particular industry. *(Key Question 14)*

natural monopoly
An industry in which economies of scale are so great that a single firm can produce the product at a lower average total cost than if more than one firm produced the product.

ORIGIN 6.4
Minimum Efficient Scale and Natural Monopoly

QUICK REVIEW

▸ Most firms have U-shaped long-run average-total-cost curves, reflecting economies and then diseconomies of scale.

▸ Economies of scale are the consequence of greater specialization of labour and management, more efficient capital equipment, and spreading startup costs among more units of output.

▸ Diseconomies of scale are caused by the problems of coordination and communication that arise in large firms.

▸ Minimum efficient scale is the lowest level of output at which a firm's long-run average total cost is at a minimum.

Applications and Illustrations

The business world offers many examples relating to short-run costs, economies of scale, and minimum efficient scale (MES). Here are just a few.

THE DOUBLING PRICE OF CORN

In the appendix to Chapter 3, we explained that the price of corn has more than doubled in recent years due to a sharp increase in the production of ethanol, an alcohol-like substance that is refined from corn and can be used as a partial substitute for gasoline. The increased production of ethanol has been the result of two factors. First, gasoline prices increased rapidly in 2007 and the first part of 2008, so that there is a much larger demand for ethanol as a gasoline substitute. Second, the government offered a subsidy to ethanol producers, thereby encouraging them to convert more corn into gasoline.

The large increase in the price of corn has had a wide impact because corn is used as an important resource for a variety of products: for example, it is heavily used as livestock feed for cattle, a sweetener (high-fructose corn syrup) for soft drinks, and the main ingredient in popular breakfast cereals. Corn is also used in tacos, tortillas, adhesives, candles, cardboard, and chewing gum.

Because of the higher price of corn, the firms producing these corn-based products experienced various degrees of increases in their short-run average variable costs, marginal costs, and average total costs. In terms of our analysis, their AVC, MC, and ATC curves all shifted upward. The extent of the upward shift depended upon the relative importance of corn as an input and thus the importance of the higher variable cost of corn in the production process.

Starting in September 2008, the price of oil, and consequently gasoline, fell precipitously as the world economy entered a recession. The price of oil fell from around $130 per barrel in the summer of 2008 to below $40 by February 2009. This sudden drop in the price of gasoline reduced the demand for ethanol, and thus the demand for corn. As we would expect, the price of corn also fell.

SUCCESSFUL STARTUP FIRMS

The Canadian economy has greatly benefited over the past few decades by explosive growth of startup firms. Where economies of scale are significant, firms can enjoy years or even decades of growth accompanied by lower average total costs—examples include Second Cup (coffee), Research In Motion (wireless communication), Celestica (computer components), and JDS Uniphase (fibre optics).

A major source of these economies of scale is the ability to spread huge product development and advertising costs over an increasing number of units of output. These firms also achieve economies of scale from learning by doing, through increased specialization of labour, management, and equipment. After starting up, such firms experience declining average total costs over the years or even decades it takes them to eventually reach their respective MES.

THE DAILY NEWSPAPER

The daily newspaper is undoubtedly one of the economy's great bargains. Think of all the resources that combine to produce it: reporters, photographers, editors, management, printing presses, delivery people, pulp mills, pulp mill workers, ink makers, loggers, logging truck drivers, and so on. Yet for under $1 you can buy a high-quality newspaper in major cities.

The main reason for such low prices is the low average total costs that result from the spreading of fixed costs and the achievement of economies of scale. If only 100 or 200 people bought the paper each day, the average cost of each paper would be exceedingly high because the overhead costs would be spread over so few buyers. But when publishers sell tens or hundreds of thousands of newspapers each day, they spread the overhead costs very widely. The large volume of sales also enables them to use specialized labour and large, highly efficient printing presses. Given sufficient scale and volume, the average total cost of a paper sinks to a few dimes. Moreover, the greater the number of readers, the greater the amount of money that advertisers are willing to pay for advertising space. That added revenue helps keep the price of the newspaper low.

THE VERSON STAMPING MACHINE

In 1996 Verson (a U.S. firm located in Chicago) introduced a 15-metre-tall metal-stamping machine that is the size of a house and weighs as much as 12 locomotives. This $30 million ($US) machine, which cuts and sculpts raw sheets of steel into automobile hoods and fenders, enables automakers to make new parts in just 5 minutes compared with 8 hours for older stamping presses. A single machine is designed to make 5 million auto parts per year. So, to achieve the cost saving from the machine, an auto manufacturer must have sufficient auto production to use all these parts. By allowing the use of this cost-saving piece of equipment, large firm size achieves economies of scale.

AIRCRAFT AND CONCRETE PLANTS

Economies and diseconomies of scale are important determinants of an industry's market structure.

Why are there only two plants in Canada (in Toronto and Montreal, both operated by Bombardier) that produce business and regional aircraft, but hundreds of plants that produce ready-mixed concrete? The simple answer is that MES is radically different in the two industries. Why is that? First, economies of scale are extensive in assembling business and regional aircraft and very modest in mixing concrete. Manufacturing airplanes is a complex process that requires huge facilities, thousands of workers, and very expensive, specialized machinery. Economies of scale extend to huge plant sizes. But mixing cement, sand, gravel, and water efficiently to produce concrete requires only a handful of workers and relatively inexpensive equipment. Economies of scale are exhausted at a relatively small size.

The differing MESs also derive from the vastly different sizes of the geographic markets. The market for business and regional airplanes is global, and aircraft manufacturers can deliver new airplanes anywhere in the world by flying them there. In contrast, the geographic market for a concrete plant is roughly the 75-kilometre radius that enables the concrete to be delivered before it "sets up." So hundreds of small concrete plants locate close to their customers in small and large cities in Canada, or even temporarily, such as next to a highway under construction.

The **LAST WORD**   Don't Cry Over Sunk Costs

Sunk costs are irrelevant in decision making.

There is an old saying: Don't cry over spilt milk. The message is that once you have spilled a glass of milk, there is nothing you can do to recover it, so you should forget about it and move on from there. This saying has great relevance to what economists call sunk costs. Such costs are like sunken ships on the ocean floor: once these costs are incurred, they cannot be recovered.

Let's gain an understanding of this idea by applying it first to consumers and then to businesses. Suppose you buy an expensive ticket to an upcoming Grey Cup football game between the Calgary Stampeders and the Hamilton Tiger Cats. But the morning of the game you wake up with a bad case of the flu. Feeling miserable, you step outside to find that the wind chill is about –20°C. You absolutely do not want to go to the game, but you remind yourself that you paid a steep price for the ticket. You call several people to try to sell the ticket, but you soon discover that no one is interested in it, even at a discounted price. You conclude that everyone who wants a ticket has one.

Should you go to the game? Economic analysis says that you should not take actions for which marginal cost exceeds marginal benefit. In this situa-

tion, the price you paid for the ticket is irrelevant to the decision; both marginal or additional costs and marginal or additional benefit are forward-looking. If the marginal cost of going to the game is greater than the marginal benefit, the best decision is to go back to bed. This decision should be the same whether you paid $2, $20, or $200 for the game ticket, because the price that you pay for something does not affect its marginal benefit. Once the ticket has been purchased and cannot be resold, its cost is irrelevant to the decision to attend the game. Since you absolutely do not want to go, clearly the marginal cost exceeds the marginal benefit of the game.

Here is a second consumer example. Suppose a family is on vacation in B.C.'s Okanagan Valley and stops at a roadside stand to buy some apples. The kids get back into the car and bite into their

apples, immediately pronouncing them "totally mushy" and unworthy of another bite. Both parents agree that the apples are terrible, but the father continues to eat his, because, as he says, "We paid a premium price for them." One of the older children replies, "Dad, that's irrelevant." Although not stated very diplomatically, the child is exactly right. In making a new decision, you should ignore all costs that are not affected by the decision. The prior bad decision (in retrospect) to buy the apples should not dictate a second decision for which marginal benefit is less than marginal cost.

Now let's apply the idea of sunk costs to firms. Some of a firm's costs not only are fixed (recurring, but unrelated to the level of output), but also are sunk (unrecoverable). For example, a nonrefundable annual lease payment for the use of a store cannot be recouped once it has been paid. A firm's decision about whether to move from the store to a more profitable location does not depend on the amount of time remaining on the lease. If moving means greater profit, it makes sense to move whether there are 300 days, 30 days, or 3 days left on the lease.

Or, as another example, suppose a firm spends $1 million on R&D to bring out a new product, only to discover that the product sells very poorly. Should the firm continue to produce the product at a loss even when there is no realistic hope for future success? Obviously, it should not. In making this decision, the firm realizes that the amount it has spent in developing the product is irrelevant; it should stop production of the product and cut its losses. In fact, many firms have dropped products after spending millions of dollars on their development. A recent example is Pfizer's decision in 2007 to shelve its novel insulin inhaler because of poor sales and concerns about long-term side effects. The product withdrawal forced Pfizer to take a $2.8 billion pre-tax loss on this highly touted product.

Consider a final real-world example. Nortel Networks is one of the best-known Canadian telecommunications compa-

nies. It started business in 1895, when it began making equipment for traditional phone companies. It was originally part of Bell Telephone, before it became known as Northern Telecom, later shortened to Nortel. In the 1990s, especially under the leadership of John Roth beginning in 1997, Nortel experienced explosive growth as it transformed itself from a telephone equipment manufacturer to providing network gear and optical transmission lines for the Internet. By the late 1990s it was also heavily into wireless transmission gear. As the Internet quickly grew, Nortel could not keep up with the large number of orders flowing in. At its peak in early 2000, Nortel employed over 90,000 employees worldwide and the company's stock rose to over $100. The frenzied expansion came to an abrupt end as overextended telephone companies

sharply reduced capital expenditures, especially on fibre optics equipment. By the end of 2008, Nortel had only 32,000 employees and was shedding part of its unprofitable lines. During this downsizing, in October 2002, Nortel sold its optical transmitter and receiver business and its pump laser and amplifiers business, which it had acquired during the heady days of rapid expansion, to a British company for a small fraction of the original purchase price. But at that point, the original acquisition cost was irrelevant because the telecommunication business had changed.

In short, if a cost has been incurred and cannot be partly or fully recouped by some other choice, a rational consumer or firm should ignore it. Sunk costs are irrelevant. Don't cry over sunk costs.

Question

What is sunk cost? Provide an example of a sunk cost other than the one in the text. Why are such costs irrelevant in making decisions about future actions?

CHAPTER SUMMARY

6.1 ▸ THE FIRM AND THE BUSINESS SECTOR

- The firm is the most efficient form of organizing production and distribution. The main goal of a firm is to maximize profit.

- Sole proprietorships, partnerships, and corporations are the major legal forms that business enterprises may assume.

- Corporations have grown to their position of dominance in the business sector primarily because they are characterized by limited liability and can acquire money capital for expansion more easily than other firms can.

6.2 ▸ ECONOMIC COSTS

- Economic costs include all payments that must be received by resource owners of factors of production to ensure a continued supply of needed inputs to a particular line of production.

- Explicit costs flow to factors of production owned and supplied by others; implicit costs are payments for the use of self-owned and self-employed factors of production. One implicit cost is a normal profit to the entrepreneur.

- Economic profit occurs when total revenue exceeds total cost (= explicit costs + implicit costs, including a normal profit).

6.3 ▸ SHORT-RUN PRODUCTION RELATIONSHIPS

- In the short run a firm's plant capacity is fixed. The firm can use its plant more or less intensively by adding or subtracting units of various factors of production, but it does not have sufficient time in the short run to alter plant size.

- The law of diminishing returns describes what happens to output as a fixed plant is used more intensively; as successive units of a variable factor such as labour are added to a fixed plant, beyond some point the marginal product associated with each additional worker declines.

6.4 ▶ SHORT-RUN PRODUCTION COSTS

- Because some factors of production are fixed and others are variable, costs can be classified as fixed or variable in the short run. Fixed costs are independent of the level of output; variable costs vary with output. The total cost of any output is the sum of fixed and variable costs at that output.

- Average fixed costs, average variable costs, and average total costs are fixed, variable, and total costs per unit of output. Average fixed cost declines continuously as output increases because a fixed sum is being spread over an increasing number of units of production. A graph of average variable cost is U-shaped, reflecting the law of diminishing returns. Average total cost is the sum of average fixed and average variable costs; its graph is also U-shaped.

- Marginal cost is the extra cost of producing one more unit of output. It is the amount by which total cost and total variable cost change when one more or one fewer unit of output is produced. Graphically, the marginal cost curve intersects the ATC and AVC curves at their minimum points.

- Lower input prices shift cost curves downward, as does technological progress. Higher input prices shift cost curves upward.

6.5 ▶ LONG-RUN PRODUCTION COSTS

- The long run is a period of time sufficiently long for a firm to vary the amounts of all inputs used, including plant size. In the long run all costs are variable. The long-run ATC, or planning, curve is composed of segments of the short-run ATC curves, and it represents the various plant sizes a firm can construct in the long run.

- The long-run ATC curve is generally U-shaped. Economies of scale are first encountered as a small firm expands. Greater specialization in the use of labour and management, the ability to use the most efficient equipment, and spreading startup costs among more units of output all contribute to economies of scale. As the firm continues to grow, it will encounter diseconomies of scale stemming from the managerial complexities that accompany large-scale production. The output ranges over which economies and diseconomies of scale occur in an industry are often an important determinant of the structure of that industry.

- A firm's minimum efficient scale (MES) is the lowest level of output at which it can minimize its long-run average cost. In some industries, MES occurs at such low levels of output that numerous firms can populate the industry. In other industries, MES occurs at such high output levels that only a few firms can exist in the long run.

TERMS AND CONCEPTS

plant, p. 135
firm, p. 135
industry, p. 135
sole proprietorship, p. 135
partnership, p. 135
corporation, p. 135
stock, p. 135
bond, p. 135
limited liability, p. 135
principal–agent problem, p. 136
economic (opportunity) cost, p. 137

explicit costs, p. 137
implicit costs, p. 137
normal profit, p. 138
economic profit, p. 138
short run, p. 139
long run, p. 139
total product (TP), p. 140
marginal product (MP), p. 140
average product (AP), p. 140
law of diminishing returns, p. 140
fixed costs, p. 144

variable costs, p. 145
total cost, p. 145
average fixed cost (AFC), p. 146
average variable cost (AVC), p. 146
average total cost (ATC), p. 147
marginal cost (MC), p. 147
economies of scale, p. 152
diseconomies of scale, p. 154
constant returns to scale, p. 154
minimum efficient scale (MES), p. 155
natural monopoly, p. 156

STUDY QUESTIONS

LO 6.1 1. Distinguish among a plant, a firm, and an industry. Why is an industry often difficult to define?

LO 6.1 2. **KEY QUESTION** What are the major legal forms of business organization? Briefly state the advantages and disadvantages of each. How do you account for the dominant role of corporations in the Canadian economy?

3. "The legal form an enterprise takes is dictated primarily by the financial requirements of its particular line of production." Do you agree? Why or why not? **LO**

4. Distinguish between explicit and implicit costs, giving examples of each. What are some explicit and implicit costs of attending college or university? Why does the economist classify normal profit as a cost? Is economic profit a cost of production? **LO**

6.2 5. Jane quits her job at Research In Motion, where she earned $50,000 a year, to set up a commuter service between Waterloo and Toronto. To buy a minibus, she cashes in $50,000 in corporate bonds that earned 10 percent interest annually. One thousand people will pay $400 a year each for the commuter service; $280 from each person goes for gas, maintenance, insurance, depreciation, and so on.

(a) Complete the following questions: (1) What are Jane's total revenues? (2) What are Jane's explicit costs? (3) What is her accounting profit?

(b) List two important implicit costs that Jane has not included.

(c) What is Jane's pure economic profit (loss)?

6.2 6. **KEY QUESTION** Gomez runs a small pottery firm. He hires one helper at $12,000 per year, pays annual rent of $5000 for his shop, and spends $20,000 per year on materials. He has $40,000 of his own funds invested in equipment (pottery wheels, kilns, and so forth) that could earn him $4000 per year if alternatively invested. He has been offered $15,000 per year to work as a potter for a competitor. He estimates his entrepreneurial talents are worth $3000 per year. Total annual revenue from pottery sales is $72,000. Calculate the accounting profit and the economic profit for Gomez's pottery firm.

6.3 7. Which of the following are short-run and which are long-run adjustments? (a) Wendy's builds a new restaurant. (b) Acme Steel Corporation hires 200 more workers. (c) A farmer increases the amount of fertilizer used on his corn crop. (d) An Alcan aluminum plant adds a third shift of workers.

6.3 8. **KEY QUESTION** Complete the following table by calculating marginal product and average product from the data given.

Inputs of labour	Total product	Marginal product	Average product
0	0	___	___
1	15	15	15
2	34	19	17
3	51	17	17
4	65	14	16.25
5	74	9	14.8
6	80	6	13.33
7	83	3	11.86
8	82	-1	10.25

Plot the total, marginal, and average products and explain in detail the relationship between each pair of curves.

Explain why marginal product first rises, then declines, and ultimately becomes negative. What bearing does the law of diminishing returns have on short-run costs? Be specific. "When marginal product is rising, marginal cost is falling. When marginal product is diminishing, marginal cost is rising." Explain and illustrate graphically.

LO 6.4 9. Why can the distinction between fixed costs and variable costs be made in the short run? Classify the following as fixed or variable costs: advertising expenditures, fuel, interest on company-issued bonds, shipping charges, payments for raw materials, real estate taxes, executive salaries, insurance premiums, wage payments, depreciation and obsolescence charges, sales taxes, and rental payments on leased office machinery. "There are no fixed costs in the long run; all costs are variable." Explain.

LO 6.4 10. List several fixed and variable costs associated with owning and operating an automobile. Suppose you are considering whether to drive your car or fly 2000 kilometres for spring break. Which costs—fixed, variable, or both—would you take into account in making your decision? Would any implicit costs be relevant? Explain.

LO 6.4 11. **KEY QUESTION** A firm has $60 in fixed costs and variable costs as indicated in the table below. Complete the table on the next page; check your calculations by referring to study question 4 at the end of Chapter 7.

a. Graph total fixed cost, total variable cost, and total cost. Explain how the law of diminishing returns influences the shapes of the variable-cost and total-cost curves.

b. Graph AFC, AVC, ATC, and MC. Explain the derivation and shape of each of these four curves and their relationships to one another. Specifically, explain in non-technical terms why the MC curve intersects both the AVC and ATC curves at their minimum points.

c. Explain how the location of each curve graphed in question 11(b) would be altered if (1) total fixed cost had been $100 rather than $60, and (2) total variable cost had been $10 less at each level of output.

LO 6.4 12. Indicate how each of the following would shift the (1) marginal-cost curve, (2) average-variable-cost curve, (3) average-fixed-cost curve, and (4) average-total-cost curve of a manufacturing firm. In each case specify the direction of the shift.

a. A reduction in business property taxes

b. An increase in the nominal wages of production workers

c. A decrease in the price of electricity

d. An increase in insurance rates on plant and equipment

e. An increase in transportation costs

LO 6.5

13. Suppose a firm has only three possible plant-size options, represented by the ATC curves shown in the accompanying figure. What plant size will the firm choose in producing (a) 50, (b) 130, (c) 160, and (d) 250 units of output? Draw the firm's long-run average-cost curve on the diagram and describe this curve.

14. **KEY QUESTION**   Use the concepts of economies and diseconomies of scale to explain the shape of a firm's long-run ATC curve. What is the concept of minimum efficient scale? What bearing can the shape of the long-run ATC curve have on the structure of an industry?

LO

Total product	Total fixed cost	Total variable cost	Total cost	Average fixed cost	Average variable cost	Average total cost	Marginal cost
0	$ 60	$ 0	$ 60	$ /	$ /	$ /	$ /
1	60	45	105	60	45	105	45
2	60	85	145	30	42.5	72.5	40
3	60	120	180	20	40	60	35
4	60	150	210	15	37.5	52.5	30
5	60	185	245	12	37	49	35
6	60	225	285	10	37.5	47.5	40
7	60	270	330	8.57	38.57	47.14	45
8	60	325	385	7.5	40.625	48.125	55
9	60	390	450	6.67	43.33	50	65
10	60	465	515	6	46.5	52.5	75

INTERNET APPLICATION QUESTIONS @

1. **Economics of Scale—Differences among Industries.** Access the Forbes 2000 list on the McConnell-Brue-Flynn-Barbiero Web site (Chapter 6). From the top 10 list, select three firms from three different industries and discuss the likely sources of economies of scale that underlie their large size.

2. **Economic Costs and Profit.** Use the McConnell-Brue-Flynn-Barbiero Web site (Chapter 6) to access the Google search engine and locate the home page of a company of your choice. Find and review the company's income statement in its annual report and classify the non-revenue items as either fixed or variable costs. Are all costs clearly identifiable as either fixed or variable? What item would be considered as accounting profit? Would economic profit be higher or lower than this accounting profit?

CHAPTER 7

Perfect Competition

In Chapter 5 we examined the relationship between product demand and total revenue, and in Chapter 6 we discussed costs of production. Now we want to connect revenues and costs to see how a business decides what price to charge and how much output to produce. But a firm's decisions concerning price and production depend greatly on the market structure of the industry in which it operates. No "average" or "typical" industry exists. At one extreme is a single producer that dominates the market; at the other extreme are industries in which thousands of firms each produce a minute fraction of market supply. Between these extremes are many other industries.

Since we cannot examine each industry individually, we will focus on four basic models of market structure. Together, these models will help you to understand how price and output are determined in the many product markets in the economy, and *to evaluate the efficiency or inefficiency of those markets.* These four models also provide a crucial background for assessing public policies (such as anticombines policy) relating to certain firms and industries, which we will explore in later chapters.

7.1 | Four Market Structures

Economists group industries into four distinct market structures: perfect competition, monopoly, monopolistic competition, and oligopoly. These four market models differ in several respects: the number of firms in the industry, whether those firms produce a standardized product or try to differentiate their products from those of other firms, and how easy or how difficult it is for firms to enter the industry.

Very briefly, the four models are as follows:

- **Perfect competition** is a market structure characterized by a very large number of firms producing a standardized product (that is, a product identical to that of other producers, such as corn or cucumbers). New firms can enter the industry very easily.

- **Monopoly** is a market structure in which one firm is the sole seller of a product or service (for example, a regional electrical power supplier). Since the entry of additional firms is blocked, one firm constitutes the entire industry. The monopolist produces a unique product, so product differentiation is not an issue.

| TABLE 7-1 | Characteristics of the Four Basic Market Models |

Characteristics of the Four Basic Market Models

MARKET MODEL

Characteristic	Perfect competition	Monopolistic competition	Oligopoly	Monopoly
Number of firms	A very large number	Many	Few	One
Type of product	Standardized	Differentiated	Standardized or differentiated	Unique; no close substitutes
Control over price	None	Some, but within rather narrow limits	Limited by mutual interdependence; considerable with collusion	Considerable
Conditions of entry	Very easy, no obstacles	Relatively easy	Significant obstacles	Blocked
Nonprice competition	None	Considerable emphasis on advertising, brand names, trademarks	Typically a great deal, particularly with product differentiation	Mostly public relations advertising
Examples	Agriculture	Retail trade, dresses, shoes	Steel, automobiles, farm implements, many household appliances	Local utilities

perfect competition
A market structure in which a very large number of firms produce a standardized product.

monopoly
A market structure in which one firm is the sole seller of a product or service.

monopolistic competition
A market structure in which a relatively large number of sellers produce differentiated products.

oligopoly
A market structure in which a few large firms produce homogeneous or differentiated products.

imperfect competition
The market models of monopoly, monopolistic competition, and oligopoly considered as a group.

- **Monopolistic competition** is characterized by a relatively large number of sellers producing differentiated products (clothing, furniture, books). Present in this model is widespread *nonprice competition*, a selling strategy in which one firm tries to distinguish its product or service from all competing products based on attributes like design and quality (an approach called *product differentiation*). Entry to monopolistically competitive industries is quite easy.

- **Oligopoly** involves only a few sellers of a homogeneous or differentiated product; consequently each firm is affected by the decisions of its rivals and must take those decisions into account when determining its own price and output.

Table 7-1 summarizes the characteristics of the four models for easy comparison and later reference. In discussing these four market models, we occasionally distinguish the characteristics of *perfect competition* from those of the three other basic market structures, which together we designate as **imperfect competition.**

7.2 | Characteristics of Perfect Competition and the Firm's Demand Curve

Although perfect competition is relatively rare in the real world, this market model is highly relevant. A few industries more closely approximate perfect competition than any other market structure. In particular, we can learn much about markets for agricultural goods, fish products, foreign exchange, basic metals, and stock shares by studying the perfect competition model. Also, perfect competition is a meaningful starting point for any discussion of price and output determination. The operation of a competitive economy provides a standard, or norm, for evaluating the efficiency of the real-world economy. Let's take a fuller look at perfect competition, the focus of the remainder of this chapter.

Firms in a perfectly competitive industry produce a standardized product.

Royalty-Free/CORBIS

price-taker
A firm in a purely competitive market that cannot change market price, only adjust to it.

Although perfect competition is rare in the real world, by studying it we can learn much about markets such as the market for agricultural products.

average revenue
Total revenue from the sale of a product divided by the quantity of the product sold.

total revenue
The total number of dollars received by a firm from the sale of a product.

✔• **Very Large Numbers** A basic feature of a perfectly competitive market is the presence of a large number of independently acting sellers offering their products in large national or international markets. Examples: the farm commodities market, the stock market, and the foreign exchange market.

✔• **Standardized Product** Firms in perfect competition produce a standardized (identical or homogeneous) product. As long as the price is the same, consumers will be indifferent about which seller to buy the product from. Buyers view the products of firms B, C, D, and E as perfect substitutes for the product of firm A. Because firms in a perfectly competitive industry sell standardized products, they make no attempt to differentiate their products and do not engage in other forms of nonprice competition.

✔• **Price-Takers** Individual firms in perfectly competitive markets do not exert control over product price. Each firm produces such a small fraction of total output that increasing or decreasing its output will not noticeably influence total supply or, therefore, product price. In short, the competitive firm is a **price-taker:** it cannot change market price, it can only adjust to it. Asking a price higher than the market price would be futile; consumers will not buy from firm A at $2.05 per unit when its 9999 competitors are selling an identical product at $2 per unit. Conversely, because firm A can sell as much as it chooses at $2 per unit, it has no reason to charge a lower price, say, $1.95. Doing that would lower its profit.

• **Easy Entry and Exit** New firms can easily enter, and existing firms can easily leave perfectly competitive industries in the long run. No significant legal, technological, financial, or other obstacles prohibit new firms from selling their output in any competitive market.

Demand for a Firm in Perfect Competition

We begin by examining demand from a competitive seller's viewpoint to see how it affects revenue. This seller might be a wheat farmer, a strawberry grower, or a sheep rancher. Each firm in a perfectly competitive industry offers only a negligible fraction of total market supply, so it must accept the price determined by the market; it is a price-taker, not a price-maker.

PERFECTLY ELASTIC DEMAND

The demand schedule faced by the *individual firm* in a purely competitive industry is perfectly elastic at the market price, as demonstrated in Figure 7-1. As shown in column 1 of the table in Figure 7-1, the market price is $131. The firm cannot obtain a higher price by restricting its output, nor does it need to lower its price to increase its sales volume. Columns 1 and 2 show that the firm can produce as little or as much as it wants and sell all the units at $131 each.

We are *not* saying that *market* demand is perfectly elastic in a competitive market. Rather, market demand graphs as a downsloping curve. An entire industry (all firms producing a particular product) can affect price by changing industry output. For example, all firms, acting independently but simultaneously, can increase price by reducing output. But the individual competitive firm cannot do that. Its demand curve will plot as a straight, horizontal line such as *D* in Figure 7-1.

Average, Total, and Marginal Revenue

The firm's demand schedule is also its average-revenue schedule. Price per unit to the purchaser is also revenue per unit, or average revenue, to the seller. To say that all buyers must pay $131 per unit is to say that the revenue per unit, or **average revenue** received by the seller, is $131. Price and average revenue are the same thing from different viewpoints.

The **total revenue** for each sales level is found by multiplying price by the corresponding quantity the firm can sell (column 1 multiplied by column 2 in the table in Figure 7-1 yields column 3). In this case, total revenue increases by a constant amount, $131, for each additional unit of sales. Each unit sold adds exactly its constant price—no more or no less—to total revenue.

FIGURE 7-1   The Demand and Revenue Curves for a Firm in Perfect Competition

FIRM'S DEMAND SCHEDULE		FIRM'S REVENUE DATA	
(1) **Product price (P)** **(average revenue)**	**(2)** **Quantity demanded** **(Q)**	**(3)** **Total revenue (TR)** **(1) × (2)**	**(4)** **Marginal revenue** **(MR)**
$131	0	$ 0	
			$131
131	1	131	
			131
131	2	262	
			131
131	3	393	
			131
131	4	524	
			131
131	5	655	
			131
131	6	786	
			131
131	7	917	
			131
131	8	1048	
			131
131	9	1179	
			131
131	10	1310	

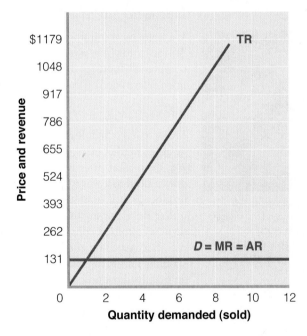

The demand curve (D) of a firm in a perfectly competitive industry is a horizontal line (perfectly elastic) because the firm can sell as much output as it wants at the market price (here, $131). Because each additional unit sold increases total revenue by the amount of the price, the firm's total-revenue curve (TR) is a straight upward-sloping line and its marginal-revenue curve (MR) coincides with the firm's demand curve. The average-revenue curve (AR) also coincides with the demand curve.

marginal revenue
The change in total revenue that results from selling one more unit of a firm's product.

When a firm is pondering a change in its output, it considers how its total revenue will change as a result. **Marginal revenue** is the change in total revenue (or the extra revenue) that results from selling one more unit of output. In column 3 of the table in Figure 7-1, total revenue is zero when zero units are sold. The first unit of output sold increases total revenue from zero to $131, so marginal revenue for that unit is $131. The second unit sold increases total revenue from $131 to $262, and marginal revenue is again $131. Note in column 4 that marginal revenue is a constant $131, as is price. *In perfect competition, marginal revenue and price are equal. (Key Question 3)*

Figure 7-1 shows the perfectly competitive firm's total-revenue, demand, marginal-revenue, and average-revenue curves. Total revenue (TR) is a straight line that slopes upward to the right. Its slope is constant because each extra unit of sales increases TR by $131. The demand curve (D) is horizontal, indicating perfect price elasticity. The marginal-revenue curve (MR) coincides with the demand curve because the product price (and hence MR) is constant. The average revenue equals price and therefore also coincides with the demand curve.

<table>
<tr><td>QUICK
R E V I E W</td><td>

▶ In a perfectly competitive industry a large number of firms produce a standardized product and no significant barriers to entry exist.

▶ The demand of a competitive firm is perfectly elastic—horizontal on a graph—at the market price.

</td><td>

▶ Marginal revenue and average revenue for a competitive firm coincide with the firm's demand curve; total revenue rises by the product price for each additional unit sold.

</td></tr>
</table>

7.3 | Profit Maximization in the Short Run

Since the firm in a perfectly competitive industry is a price-taker, it can maximize its economic profit (or minimize its loss) only by adjusting its *output*. And in the short run, the firm has a fixed plant. Thus, it can adjust its output only through changes in the amount of variable inputs (materials, labour) it uses. It adjusts its variable inputs to achieve the output level that maximizes its profit.

Two methods exist to determine the level of output at which a competitive firm will obtain maximum profit or minimum loss. One method is to compare total revenue and total cost; the other is to compare marginal revenue and marginal cost. Both approaches apply to all firms, whether they are perfectly competitive, monopolists, monopolistic competitors, or oligopolists.[1]

Total-Revenue–Total-Cost Approach

WORKED
PROBLEM 7.1
Profit
Maximization:
TR–TC Approach

We begin by examining profit maximization using the total-revenue–total-cost approach. Confronted with the market price of its product, the competitive producer will ask: (1) Should we produce this product? (2) If so, in what amount? (3) What economic profit (or loss) will we realize?

Let's demonstrate how a firm in perfect competition answers these questions, given certain cost data and a specific market price. Our cost data are familiar to you because they are the total fixed-cost, total variable-cost, and total-cost data from Table 6-2, repeated in columns 1 to 4 in the table in Figure 7-2. (Recall that these data reflect explicit and implicit costs, including a normal profit.) Assuming that the market price is $131, the total revenue for each output level is found by multiplying output (total product) by price. Total revenue data are in column 5. Then in column 6 we find the profit or loss at each output level by subtracting total cost, TC (column 4), from total revenue, TR (column 5).

Should the firm produce? Definitely. It can make a profit by doing so. How much should it produce? Nine units. Column 6 tells us that this is the output at which total economic profit is at a maximum. What economic profit (or loss) will the firm realize? A $299 economic profit—the difference between total revenue ($1179) and total cost ($880).

---

[1] To make sure you understand these two approaches, we will apply them both to output determination under perfect competition, but since we want to emphasize the marginal approach, we will limit our graphical application of the total-revenue approach to a situation where the firm maximizes profits. We will then use the marginal approach to examine three cases: profit maximization, loss minimization, and shutdown.

Figure 7-2a compares total revenue and total cost graphically for this profit-maximizing case. Observe again that the total-revenue curve for a firm in a perfectly competitive industry is a straight line. Total cost increases with output because more production requires more factors of production, but the rate of increase in total cost varies with the relative efficiency of the firm. Specifically, the cost data reflect Chapter 6's law of diminishing marginal returns. From zero to four units of output, total cost increases at a decreasing rate as the firm uses its fixed factors more efficiently. With additional output, total cost begins to rise by ever-increasing amounts because of the diminishing returns accompanying more intensive use of the plant.

Total revenue and total cost are equal where the two curves in Figure 7-2a intersect (at roughly two units of output). Total revenue covers all costs (including a normal profit, which is included in the cost curve) but there is no economic profit. For this reason economists call this output a **break-even point:** an output at which a firm makes a *normal profit* but not an economic profit. If we extended the data beyond 10 units of output, another break-even point would occur where total cost would catch up with total revenue somewhere between 13 and 14 units of output in Figure 7-2a. Any output between the two break-even points identified in the figure will yield an economic profit. The firm achieves maximum profit, however, where the vertical distance between the total-revenue and total-cost curves is greatest. For our particular data, this is at nine units of output, where maximum profit is $299.

The profit-maximizing output is easier to see in Figure 7-2b, where total economic profit is graphed for each level of output. Where the total-revenue and total-cost curves intersect in Figure 7-2a, economic profit is zero, as shown by the total-profit line in Figure 7-2b. Where the vertical distance between TR and TC is greatest in the upper graph, economic profit is at its peak ($299), as shown in the lower graph. This firm will choose to produce nine units, since that output maximizes its profit.

Marginal-Revenue–Marginal-Cost Approach

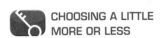
CHOOSING A LITTLE MORE OR LESS

In the second approach, the firm compares the amounts that each *additional* unit of output would add to total revenue and to total cost. In other words, the firm compares the *marginal revenue* (MR) and the *marginal cost* (MC) of each successive unit of output. Assuming that producing is preferable to shutting down, the firm will produce any unit of output whose marginal revenue exceeds its marginal cost because the firm would gain more in revenue from selling that unit than it would add to its costs by producing it. Conversely, if the marginal cost of a unit of output exceeds its marginal revenue, the firm will not produce that unit. Producing it would add more to costs than to revenue, and profit would decline or loss would increase.

In the initial stages of production, where output is relatively low, marginal revenue will usually (but not always) exceed marginal cost. So it is profitable to produce through this range of output. But at later stages of production, where output is relatively high, rising marginal costs will exceed marginal revenue. Obviously, a profit-maximizing firm will want to avoid output levels in that range. Separating these two production ranges is a unique point at which marginal revenue equals marginal cost. This point is the key to the output-determining rule: *In the short run, the firm will maximize profit or minimize loss by producing the output at which marginal revenue equals marginal cost (as long as producing is preferable to shutting down).* This profit-maximizing guide is known as the **MR = MC rule.**

Keep in mind these features of the MR = MC rule:

- For most sets of MR and MC data, MR and MC will be precisely equal at a fractional level of output. In such instances the firm should produce the last complete unit of output for which MR exceeds MC.

- The rule applies only if producing is preferable to shutting down. We will show shortly that if marginal revenue does not equal or exceed average variable cost, the firm will shut down rather than produce the MR = MC output.

---

break-even point
An output at which a firm makes a normal profit but not an economic profit.

MR = MC rule
A method of determining the total output at which economic profit is at a maximum (or losses are at a minimum).

FIGURE 7-2

Total-Revenue–Total-Cost Approach to Profit Maximization for a Firm in a Perfectly Competitive Industry

PRICE: $131

(1) Total product (output), Q	(2) Total fixed cost, TFC	(3) Total variable cost, TVC	(4) Total cost, TC	(5) Total revenue, TR	(6) Profit (+) or loss (−)
0	$100	$ 0	$ 100	$ 0	$− 100
1	100	90	190	131	− 59
2	100	170	270	262	− 8
3	100	240	340	393	+ 53
4	100	300	400	524	+124
5	100	370	470	655	+185
6	100	450	550	786	+236
7	100	540	640	917	+277
8	100	650	750	1048	+298
9	100	780	*880*	*1179*	*+299*
10	100	930	1030	1310	+280

Panel (a): The firm's profit is maximized at that output (nine units) where total revenue, TR, exceeds total cost, TC, by the maximum amount. Panel (b): The vertical distance between TR and TC in panel (a) is plotted as a total-economic-profit curve. Maximum economic profit is $299 at nine units of output.

(a) Profit-maximizing case

(b) Total economic profit

- The rule is an accurate guide to profit maximization for all firms, whether they are perfectly competitive, monopolistic, monopolistically competitive, or oligopolistic.

- The rule can be restated as $P = MC$ when applied to a firm in a perfectly competitive industry. Because the demand schedule faced by a competitive seller is perfectly elastic at the going market price, product price and marginal revenue are equal. So under perfect competition (and only under perfect competition) we may substitute P for MR in the rule: When producing is preferable to shutting down, the competitive firm should produce at that point where price equals marginal cost ($P = MC$).

MATH 7.1
MR = MC

Now let's apply the MR = MC rule, first using the same price as in our total-revenue–total-cost approach to profit maximization. Then, by considering other prices, we will demonstrate two additional cases: loss minimization and shutdown. It is crucial that you understand the MR = MC analysis that follows, since it reappears in Chapters 8 and 9.

PROFIT-MAXIMIZING CASE

The first five columns in the table of **Figure 7-3 (Key Graph)** reproduce the AFC, AVC, ATC, and MC data in Table 6-2. It is the marginal-cost data of column 6 that we will compare with price (equals marginal revenue) for each unit of output. Suppose first that the market price, and therefore marginal revenue, is $131, as shown in column 7.

What is the profit-maximizing output? Each of the first nine units adds to the firm's profit and will be produced. The tenth unit, however, will not be produced. It would add more to cost ($150) than to revenue ($131). So, nine units is the profit-maximizing output.

The economic profit realized by producing nine units can be calculated by subtracting total cost from total revenue. Multiplying price ($131) by output (9), we find that total revenue is $1179. From the average-total-cost data in Figure 7-3, we see that ATC is $97.78 at nine units of output. Multiplying $97.78 by 9 gives us total cost of $880.[2] The difference of $299 (= $1179 − $880) is the economic profit. Clearly, this firm will prefer to operate rather than shut down.

WORKED PROBLEM 7.2
Profit Maximization: MR = MC Approach

Perhaps an easier way to calculate the economic profit is to use this simple equation, in which A is average total cost:

$$\text{Profit} = (P - A) \times Q$$

So by subtracting the average total cost ($97.78) from the product price ($131), we obtain a per-unit profit of $33.22. Multiplying that amount by nine units of output, we determine that the profit is $299. Take some time now to verify the numbers in column 7. You will find that any output other than that which adheres to the MR = MC rule will mean either profits below $299 or losses.

Figure 7-3 shows price (= MR) and marginal cost graphically. Price equals marginal cost at the profit-maximizing output of nine units. There the per-unit economic profit is $P - A$, where P is the market price and A is the average total cost for an output of nine units. The total economic profit is $9 \times (P - A)$, shown by the grey rectangular area.

Note that the firm wants to maximize its total profit, not its per-unit profit. Per-unit profit is greatest at seven units of output, where price exceeds average total cost by $39.57 (= $131 − $91.43). But by producing only seven units, the firm would not produce two additional units of output that would clearly contribute to total profit. The firm is happy to accept lower per-unit profits for additional units of output because they nonetheless add to total profit.

LOSS-MINIMIZING CASE

Now let's assume that the market price is $81 rather than $131. Should the firm still produce? If so, how much? What will be the resulting profit or loss? The answers, respectively, are "yes," "six units," and "a loss of $64."

---

[2] Most of the unit-cost data are rounded figures. Therefore, economic profits calculated from them will typically vary by a few cents from the profits determined in the total-revenue–total-cost approach. Here we simply ignore the few-cents differentials to make our answers consistent with the results of the total-revenue–total-cost approach.

KEY GRAPH

FIGURE 7-3 Short-Run Profit-Maximizing for a Firm in a Perfectly Competitive Industry

The MR = MC output enables the firm in a perfectly competitive industry to maximize profits or to minimize losses. In this case MR (= P in pure competition) and MC are equal at an output Q of nine units. There, P exceeds the average total cost A = $97.78, so the firm realizes an economic profit of P – A per unit. The total economic profit is represented by the grey rectangle and is 9 × (P – A).

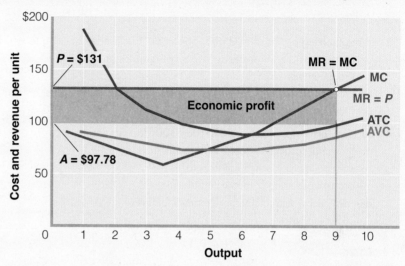

(1) Total product (output)	(2) Average fixed cost, AFC	(3) Average variable cost, AVC	(4) Average total cost, ATC	(5) Total cost, TC	(6) Marginal cost, MC	(7) Price = marginal revenue, MR	(8) Total economic profit (+) or loss (−)
0				$100			$ – 100
					$ 90		
1	$100.00	$ 90.00	$190.00	190		$ 131	– 59
					80		
2	50.00	85.00	135.00	270		131	– 8
					70		
3	33.33	80.00	113.33	340		131	+ 53
					60		
4	25.00	75.00	100.00	400		131	+ 124
					70		
5	20.00	74.00	94.00	470		131	+ 185
					80		
6	16.67	75.00	91.67	550		131	+ 236
					90		
7	14.29	77.14	91.43	640		131	+ 277
					110		
8	12.50	81.25	93.75	750		131	+ 298
					130		
9	11.11	86.67	97.78	880		131	+ 299
					150		
10	10.00	93.00	103.00	1030		131	+ 280

Quick Quiz

1. Curve MR is horizontal because
   a. product price falls as output increases.
   b. the law of diminishing marginal utility is at work.
   c. the market demand for this product is perfectly elastic.
   d. the firm is a price-taker.

2. **At a price of $131 and seven units of output**
   a. MR exceeds MC, and the firm should expand its output.
   b. total revenue is less than total cost.
   c. AVC exceeds ATC.
   d. the firm would earn only a normal profit.

3. **In maximizing profits at nine units of output, this firm is adhering to which of the following decision rules?**
   a. Produce where MR exceeds MC by the greatest amount.
   b. Produce where P exceeds ATC by the greatest amount.
   c. Produce where total revenue exceeds total cost by the greatest amount.
   d. Produce where average fixed costs are zero.

4. **Suppose price declined from $131 to $100. This firm's**
   a. marginal-cost curve would shift downward.
   b. economic profit would fall to zero.
   c. profit-maximizing output would decline.
   d. total cost would fall by more than its total revenue.

The first five columns in the table of Figure 7-4 are the same as those in the table of Figure 7-3. Column 6 shows the new price (equal to MR), $81. Comparing columns 5 and 6, we find that the first unit of output adds $90 to total cost but only $81 to total revenue. One might conclude: "Don't produce—close down!" But that would be hasty. For units two through six, price exceeds marginal cost. Each of these five units adds more to revenue than to cost and, as shown in column 7, they decrease the total loss. Together they more than compensate for the loss taken on the first unit. Beyond six units, however, MC exceeds MR (= P). The firm should therefore produce six units.

Will production be profitable? No, because at six units of output the average total cost of $91.67 exceeds the price of $81 by $10.67 per unit. If we multiply that by the six units of output, we find the firm's total loss is $64.

Then why produce? Because this loss is less than the firm's $100 of fixed costs, which is the $100 loss the firm would incur in the short run by closing down. The firm receives enough revenue per unit ($81) to cover its average variable costs of $75 and also provide $6 per unit, or a total of $36, to apply against fixed costs. Therefore, the firm's loss is only $64 (= $100 − $36), not $100.

This loss-minimizing case is also shown graphically in Figure 7-4. Wherever price P exceeds average variable cost, AVC, the firm can pay part, but not all, of its fixed costs by producing. The loss is minimized by producing the output at which MC = MR (here, six units). At that output, each unit contributes $P − V$ to covering fixed cost, where V is the AVC at six units of output. The per-unit loss is $A − P = \$10.67$, and the total loss is $6 \times (A − P)$, or $64, as shown by the grey area.

SHUTDOWN CASE

Suppose now that the market price is only $71. Should the firm produce? No, because at every output the firm's average variable cost is greater than the price (compare columns 3 and 8 in the table of Figure 7-4). The smallest loss the firm can incur by producing is greater than the $100 fixed cost it will lose by shutting down (as shown by column 9). The best action is to shut down.

You can see this shutdown situation in Figure 7-5. Price comes closest to covering average variable costs at the MR (= P) = MC output of five units. But even here, price or revenue per unit would fall short of average variable cost by $3 (= $74 − $71). By producing at the MR (= P) = MC output, the firm would lose its $100 worth of fixed cost plus $15 ($3 of variable cost on each of the

The Short-Run Loss-Minimizing Position of a Firm in a Perfectly Competitive Industry

FIGURE 7·4

(1) Total product (output)	(2) Average fixed cost, AFC	(3) Average variable cost, AVC	(4) Average total cost, ATC	(5) Marginal cost, MC	(6) $81 price = marginal revenue, MR	(7) Profit (+) or loss (−), $81 price	(8) $71 price = marginal revenue, MR	(9) Profit (+) or loss (−), $71 price
0						$−100		$−100
1	$100.00	$90.00	$190.00	$ 90	$81	−109	$71	−119
2	50.00	85.00	135.00	80	81	−108	71	−128
3	33.33	80.00	113.33	70	81	− 97	71	−127
4	25.00	75.00	100.00	60	81	− 76	71	−116
5	20.00	74.00	94.00	70	81	− 65	71	−115
6	16.67	75.00	91.67	80	81	− 64	71	−124
7	14.29	77.14	91.43	90	81	− 73	71	−143
8	12.50	81.25	93.75	110	81	−102	71	−182
9	11.11	86.67	97.78	130	81	−151	71	−241
10	10.00	93.00	103.00	150	81	−220	71	−320

If price *P* exceeds the minimum AVC (here $74 at Q = 5) but is less than ATC, the MR = MC output (here six units) will permit the firm to minimize its losses. In this instance the loss is *A* − *P* per unit, where *A* is the average total cost at six units of output. The total loss is shown by the grey area and is equal to 6 × (*A* − *P*).

five units), for a total loss of $115. This compares unfavourably with the $100 fixed-cost loss the firm would incur by shutting down and producing no output. So, it will make sense for the firm to shut down rather than produce at a $71 price—or at any price less than the minimum average variable cost of $74.

The shutdown case reminds us of the qualifier to our MR (= *P*) = MC rule. A competitive firm will maximize profit or minimize loss in the short run by producing that output at which MR (= *P*) = MC, provided that market price exceeds minimum average variable cost.

CONSIDER THIS | The Still There Motel

Have you ever driven by a poorly maintained business facility and wondered why the owner doesn't either fix up the property or go out of business? The somewhat surprising answer is that it may be unprofitable to improve the facility, yet profitable to continue to operate it as it deteriorates. Seeing why will aid your understanding of fixed cost, variable cost, profit-maximization, and shutdown points.

Consider the story of the Still There Motel, a one-story motel on Old Highway North, Any Town, Canada. The owner of Still There built the motel on the basis of traffic patterns and competition that existed several decades ago. As more highways were built, Still There found itself located on a relatively vacant stretch of road. Also, it faced greatly heightened competition from new "chain" motels located closer to the main highway that crossed the province.

As demand and revenue fell, Still There moved from profitability to loss. But at first its room rates and annual revenue were sufficient to cover its total variable costs and contribute some to the payment of fixed costs such as

insurance and property taxes (or $P > \text{AVC}$; $P < \text{ATC}$). By staying open, Still There lost less than it would have if it shut down. But since its total revenue did not cover its total costs (or $P < \text{ATC}$), the owner realized that something must be done in the long run. The owner decided to lower costs by reducing annual maintenance. In effect, the owner opted to allow the motel to deteriorate as a way of regaining temporary profitability.

This renewed profitability of Still There cannot last because in time no further reduction of maintenance costs will be possible. The deterioration of the motel structure will produce even lower room rates, and therefore even less total revenue. The owner of Still There knows that sooner or later total revenue will again fall below total cost (or P will again fall below ATC), even with an annual maintenance expense of zero. When that occurs, the owner will close down the business, tear down the structure, and sell the vacant property. But, in the meantime, the motel is still there—open, deteriorating, and profitable.

FIGURE 7-5   The Short-Run Shutdown Position of a Firm in Perfect Competition

If price P falls below the minimum AVC (here $74 at $Q = 5$), the competitive firm will minimize its losses in the short run by shutting down. There is no level of output at which the firm can produce and incur a loss smaller than its total fixed cost

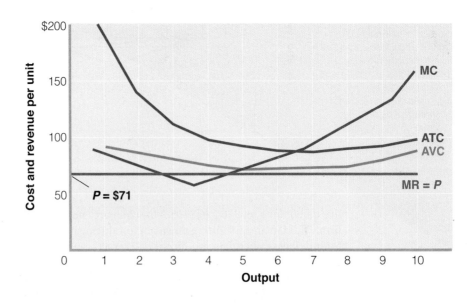

7.4 | Marginal Cost and Short-Run Supply

In the preceding section we simply selected three different prices and asked what quantity the profit-seeking competitive firm, faced with certain costs, would choose to offer in the market at each price. This set of product prices and corresponding quantities supplied constitutes part of the supply schedule for the competitive firm.

TABLE 7-2

The Supply Schedule of a Competitive Firm with the Cost Data in Figure 7-3

Price	Quantity supplied	Maximum profit (+) or minimum loss (−)
$151	10	$+480
131	9	+299
111	8	+138
91	7	− 3
81	6	− 64
71	0	−100
61	0	−100

Table 7-2 summarizes the supply schedule data for those three prices ($131, $81, and $71) and four others. This table confirms the direct relationship between product price and quantity supplied that we identified in Chapter 3. Note first that the firm will not produce at price $61 or $71, because both are less than the $74 minimum AVC. Then note that quantity supplied increases as price increases. Observe finally that economic profit is higher at higher prices.

Generalized Depiction

Figure 7-6 (Key Graph) generalizes the MR = MC rule and the relationship between short-run production costs and the firm's supply behaviour. The ATC, AVC, and MC curves are shown, along with several marginal-revenue lines drawn at possible market prices. Let's observe quantity supplied at each of these prices.

- Price P_1 is below the firm's minimum average variable cost, so at this price the firm won't operate at all. Quantity supplied will be zero, as it will be at all other prices below P_2.
- Price P_2 is just equal to the minimum average variable cost. The firm will supply Q_2 units of output (where $MR_2 = MC$) and just cover its total variable cost. Its loss will equal its total fixed cost. (Actually, the firm would be indifferent as to shutting down or supplying Q_2 units of output, but we assume it produces.)
- At price P_3 the firm will supply Q_3 units of output to minimize its short-run losses. At any other price between P_2 and P_4 the firm will minimize its losses by producing and supplying the quantity at which MR (= P) = MC.
- The firm will just break even at price P_4, where it will supply Q_4 units of output (where $MR_4 = MC$), earning a normal profit but not an economic profit. Total revenue will just cover total cost, including a normal profit, because the revenue per unit ($MR_4 = P_4$) and the total cost per unit (ATC) are the same.
- At price P_5 the firm will earn an economic profit by producing and supplying Q_5 units of output. In fact, at any price above P_4 the firm will earn an economic profit by producing to the point where MR (= P) = MC.

Note that each of the MR (= P) = MC intersection points labelled *b, c, d,* and *e* in Figure 7-6 indicates a possible product price (on the vertical axis) and the corresponding quantity that the firm would supply at that price (on the horizontal axis). Thus, points such as these are on the upsloping supply curve of the competitive firm. Note, too, that quantity supplied would be zero at any price below the minimum average variable cost (AVC). *We can conclude that the portion of the firm's*

KEY GRAPH

FIGURE 7-6 The *P* = MC Rule and the Competitive Firm's Short-Run Supply Curve

Application of the *P* = MC rule, as modified by the shutdown case, reveals that the (solid) segment of the firm's MC curve that lies above AVC is the firm's short-run supply curve. More specifically, at price P_1, $P = $ MC at point *a*, but the firm will produce no output because P_1 is less than minimum AVC. At price P_2 the firm will operate at point *b*, where it produces Q_2 units and incurs a loss equal to its total fixed cost. At P_3 it operates at point *c*, where output is Q_3 and the loss is less than the total fixed cost. With the price of P_4, the firm operates at point *d*; in this case the firm earns a normal profit because at output Q_4 price equals ATC. At price P_5 the firm operates at point *e* and maximizes its economic profit by producing Q_5 units.

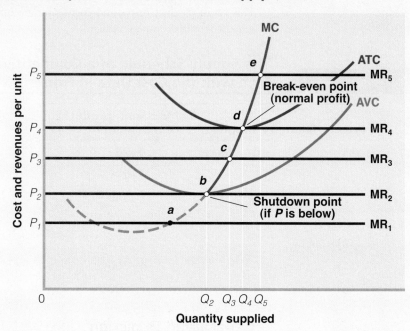

Quick Quiz

1. **Which of the following might increase product price from P_3 to P_5?**
   a. An improvement in production technology
   b. A decline in the price of a substitute good
   c. An increase in the price of a complementary good
   d. Rising incomes if the product is a normal good

2. **An increase in price from P_3 to P_5 would**
   a. shift this firm's MC curve to the right.
   b. mean that MR_5 exceeds MC at Q_3 units, inducing the firm to expand output to Q_5.
   c. decrease this firm's average variable costs.
   d. enable this firm to obtain a normal, but not an economic, profit.

3. **At P_4**
   a. this firm has no economic profit.
   b. this firm will earn only a normal profit and thus will shut down.
   c. MR_4 will be less than MC at the profit-maximizing output.
   d. the profit-maximizing output will be Q_5.

4. **Suppose P_4 is $10, P_5 is $15, Q_4 is 8 units, and Q_5 is 10 units. This firm's**
   a. supply curve is elastic over the Q_4–Q_5 range of output.
   b. supply curve is inelastic over the Q_4–Q_5 range of output.
   c. total revenue will decline if price rises from P_4 to P_5.
   d. marginal-cost curve will shift downward if price falls from P_5 to P_4.

Answers: 1. d; 2. b; 3. a; 4. b

marginal-cost curve lying above its average-variable-cost curve is its short-run supply curve. In Figure 7-6, the solid segment of the marginal-cost curve MC is this firm's **short-run supply curve.** It tells us the amount of output the firm will supply at each price in a series of prices.

Diminishing Returns, Production Costs, and Product Supply

We have now identified the links between the law of diminishing returns (Chapter 6), production costs, and product supply in the short run. Because of the law of diminishing returns, marginal cost eventually rises as more units of output are produced. And because marginal cost rises with output, a firm in a perfectly competitive industry must get successively higher prices to motivate it to produce additional units of output.

Supply Curve Shifts

In Chapter 6 we saw that changes in such factors as the prices of variable inputs or in technology will shift the marginal-cost or short-run supply curve to a new location. All else equal, a wage increase, for example, would shift the supply curve in Figure 7-6 upward and to the left, which means a decrease in supply. Similarly, technological progress that increases the productivity of labour would shift the marginal-cost or supply curve downward to the right, representing an increase in supply.

Firm and Industry: Equilibrium Price

In the preceding section we established the competitive firm's short-run supply curve by applying the MR (= P) = MC rule. But which of the various possible prices will actually be the market equilibrium price? From Chapter 3 we know that the market equilibrium price is the price at which the total quantity supplied of the product equals the total quantity demanded. So to determine equilibrium price, we first need to obtain a total supply schedule and a total demand schedule. We find the total supply schedule by assuming a particular number of firms in the industry and supposing that each firm has the same individual supply schedule as the firm represented in Figure 7-6. Then we sum the quantities supplied at each price level to obtain the total (or market) supply schedule. Columns 1 and 3 in Table 7-3 repeat the supply schedule for the individual competitive firm, as derived in Table 7-2. Suppose 1000 firms compete in this industry, all having the same total and unit costs as the single firm we discussed. This assumption allows us to calculate the market supply schedule (columns 2 and 3) by multiplying the quantity-supplied figures of the single firm (column 1) by 1000.

short-run supply curve
A curve that shows the quantities of the product a firm in a purely competitive industry will offer to sell at various prices in the short run.

TABLE 7-3 — Firm and Market Supply and Market Demand

(1) Quantity supplied, single firm	(2) Total quantity supplied, 1000 firms	(3) Product price	(4) Total quantity demanded
10	10,000	$151	4,000
9	9,000	131	6,000
8	*8,000*	*111*	*8,000*
7	7,000	91	9,000
6	6,000	81	11,000
0	0	71	13,000
0	0	61	16,000

MARKET PRICE AND PROFITS

To determine the equilibrium price and output, these total-supply data must be compared with total-demand data. Let's assume that total demand is as shown in columns 3 and 4 in Table 7-3. By comparing the total quantity supplied and the total quantity demanded at the seven possible prices, we determine that the equilibrium price is $111 and the equilibrium quantity is 8000 units for the industry—eight units for each of the 1000 identical firms.

Will these conditions of market supply and demand make this a profitable industry? Multiplying product price ($111) by output (8 units), we find that the total revenue of each firm is $888.

The total cost is $750, found by looking at column 4 in the table of Figure 7-2. The $138 difference is the economic profit of each firm. For the industry, total economic profit is $138,000. This, then, is a profitable industry.

Another way of calculating economic profit is to determine per-unit profit by subtracting average total cost ($93.75) from product price ($111) and multiplying the difference (per-unit profit of $17.25) by the firm's equilibrium level of output (8). Again we obtain an economic profit of $138 per firm and $138,000 for the industry.

Figure 7-7 shows this analysis graphically. The individual supply curves of each of the 1000 identical firms—one of which is shown as $s = MC$ in Figure 7-7a—are summed horizontally to get the total-supply curve $S = \Sigma MC$ of Figure 7-7b. Together with total-demand curve D, it determines the equilibrium price $111 and equilibrium quantity (for the industry) 8000 units. This equilibrium price is given and unalterable to the individual firm; that is, each firm's demand curve is perfectly elastic at the equilibrium price, as indicated by d in Figure 7-7a. Because the individual firm is a price-taker, the marginal-revenue curve coincides with the firm's demand curve d. This $111 price exceeds the average total cost at the firm's equilibrium $MR = MC$ output of eight units, so the firm earns an economic profit represented by the grey area in Figure 7-7a.

Assuming costs and market demand do not change, these diagrams reveal a genuine equilibrium in the short run. No shortages or surpluses occur in the market to cause price or total quantity to change. Nor can any one firm in the industry increase its profit by changing its output. Note, too, that higher unit and marginal costs on the one hand, or weaker market demand on the other, could change the situation so that Figure 7-7a resembles Figure 7-4 or Figure 7-5.

Table 7-4 summarizes the $MR = MC$ approach to determining the competitive firm's profit-maximizing output. It also shows the equivalent analysis in terms of total revenue and total cost.

FIGURE 7-7

Short-Run Competitive Equilibrium for a Firm (Panel A) and the Industry (Panel B)

The horizontal sum of the 1000 firms' individual supply curves (s) determines the industry supply curve (S). Given industry demand (D), the short-run equilibrium price and output for the industry are $111 and 8000 units. Taking the equilibrium price as given, the individual firm establishes its profit-maximizing output at eight units and, in this case, realizes the economic profit represented by the grey area.

(a) Single firm

(b) Industry

TABLE 7-4	Output Determination in Perfect Competition in the Short Run

Question	Answer
Should this firm produce?	Yes, if price is equal to, or greater than, minimum average variable cost. This means that the firm is profitable or that its losses are less than its fixed cost.
What quantity should this firm produce?	Produce where MR (= *P*) = MC; there, profit is maximized (TR exceeds TC by a maximum amount) or loss is minimized.
Will production result in economic profit?	Yes, if price exceeds average total cost (TR will exceed TC). No, if average total cost exceeds price (TC will exceed TR).

WORKED PROBLEM 7.3
Short-Run Competitive Equilibrium

FIRM VERSUS INDUSTRY

Figure 7-7 underscores a point made earlier: Product price is a given fact to the *individual* competitive firm, but the supply plans of all competitive producers *as a group* are a basic determinant of product price. If we recall the fallacy of composition (The Last Word, Chapter 1), we find there is no inconsistency here. Although one firm, supplying a negligible fraction of total supply, cannot affect price, the industry supply curve does have an important bearing on price. *(Key Question 4)*

QUICK REVIEW

▶ Profit is maximized, or loss minimized, at the output at which marginal revenue (or price in pure competition) equals marginal cost.

▶ If the market price is below the minimum average variable cost, the firm will minimize its losses by shutting down.

▶ The segment of the firm's marginal-cost curve that lies above the average-variable-cost curve is its short-run supply curve.

▶ Table 7-4 summarizes the MR = MC approach to determining the competitive firm's profit-maximizing output. It also shows the equivalent analysis in terms of total revenue and total cost.

▶ Under perfect competition, equilibrium price is a given to the individual firm and simultaneously is the result of the production (supply) decisions of all firms as a group.

7.5 | Profit Maximization in the Long Run

In the short run the industry is composed of a specific number of firms, each with a fixed, unalterable plant. Firms may shut down in the sense that they can produce zero units of output in the short run, but they do not have enough time to liquidate their assets and go out of business. By contrast, in the long run firms already in an industry have sufficient time either to expand or to contract their plant capacities. More important, the number of firms in the industry may either increase or decrease as new firms enter or existing firms leave. You need to know how these long-run adjustments affect price, quantity, and profits.

Assumptions

We make three simplifying assumptions, none of which alters our conclusions:

1. **Entry and Exit Only**   The only long-run adjustment is the entry or exit of firms. Moreover, we ignore all short-run adjustments to concentrate on the effects of the long-run adjustments.

✓ 2. **Identical Costs**   All firms in the industry have identical cost curves. This assumption allows us to discuss a representative firm, knowing that all other firms in the industry are similarly affected by any long-run adjustments that occur.

✓ 3. **Constant-Cost Industry**   The industry is a constant-cost industry, which means that the entry or exit of firms does not affect resource prices or, consequently, shift the average-total-cost or marginal curves of individual firms.

The Goal of Our Analysis

The basic conclusion we want to explain is this: After all long-run adjustments are completed, product price will be exactly equal to, and production will occur at, each firm's minimum average total cost.

This conclusion follows from two basic facts: (1) firms seek profits and avoid losses, and (2) under perfect competition, firms are free to enter and leave an industry. If market price in the short run exceeds average total costs, the resulting economic profits will attract new firms to the industry, but this industry expansion will increase supply until price is brought back down to equality with minimum average total cost in the long run. Conversely, if price in the short run is less than average total cost, resulting losses will cause firms to leave the industry in the long run. As they leave, total supply will decline, bringing the price back up to equality with minimum average total cost.

Long-Run Equilibrium

Consider the average firm in a perfectly competitive industry that is initially in long-run equilibrium. This firm is represented in Figure 7-8a, where MR = MC and price and minimum average total cost are equal at $50. Economic profit here is zero; the industry is in equilibrium and there is no tendency for firms to enter or to leave. The $50 market price is determined in Figure 7-8b by market demand D_1 and supply S_1. (S_1 is a short-run supply curve; we will develop the long-run industry supply curve in our discussion.)

As shown on the quantity axes of the two graphs, equilibrium output in the industry is 100,000, while equilibrium output for the single firm is 100. If all firms in the industry are identical, there must be 1000 firms (= 100,000/100).

FIGURE 7-8

Temporary Profits and the Re-establishment of Long-Run Equilibrium in a Representative Firm (Panel A) and the Industry (Panel B)

A favourable shift in demand (D_1 to D_2) will upset the original industry equilibrium and produce economic profits. But those profits will entice new firms to enter the industry, increasing supply (S_1 to S_2) and lowering product price until economic profits are once again zero.

(a) Single firm

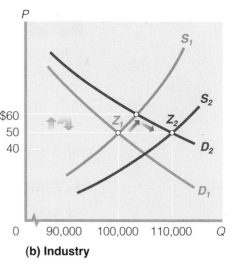

(b) Industry

ENTRY ELIMINATES ECONOMIC PROFITS

Let's upset the long-run equilibrium in Figure 7-8 and see what happens. Suppose a change in consumer tastes increases product demand from D_1 to D_2. Price will rise to $60, as determined at the intersection of D_2 and S_1, and the firm's marginal-revenue curve will shift upward to $60. This $60 price exceeds the firm's average total cost of $50 at output 100, creating an economic profit of $10 per unit. This economic profit will lure new firms into the industry. Some entrants will be newly created firms; others will shift from less prosperous industries.

As firms enter, the market supply of the product increases, pushing the product price below $60. Economic profits persist, and entry continues until short-run supply increases to S_2. Market price falls to $50, as does marginal revenue for the firm. Price and minimum average total cost are again equal at $50. The economic profits caused by the boost in demand have been eliminated, and, as a result, the previous incentive for more firms to enter the industry has disappeared. Long-run equilibrium has been restored.

Observe in Figure 7-8a and 7-8b that total quantity supplied is now 110,000 units and each firm is producing 100 units. Now 1100 firms rather than the original 1000 populate the industry. Economic profits have attracted 100 more firms.

EXIT ELIMINATES LOSSES

Now let's consider a shift in the opposite direction. We begin in Figure 7-9b with curves S_1 and D_1 setting the same initial long-run equilibrium situation as in our previous analysis, including the $50 price.

Suppose consumer demand declines from D_1 to D_3. This decline forces the market price and marginal revenue down to $40, making production unprofitable at the minimum ATC of $50. In time the resulting losses will induce firms to leave the industry. Their owners will seek a normal profit elsewhere rather than accept the below-normal profits (loss) now confronting them. Other firms will simply go out of business. As this exodus of firms proceeds, however, industry supply in the long run decreases, pushing the price up from $40 toward $50. Losses continue and more firms leave the industry until the supply curve shifts to S_3. Once this happens, price is again $50, just equal to the minimum average total cost. Losses have been eliminated and long-run equilibrium is restored.

In Figure 7-9b, total quantity supplied is now 90,000 units and each firm is producing 100 units. Only 900 firms, not the original 1000, populate the industry. Losses have forced 100 firms out.

FIGURE 7-9

Temporary Losses and the Re-establishment of Long-Run Equilibrium in a Representative Firm (Panel A) and the Industry (Panel B)

An unfavourable shift in demand (D_1 to D_3) will upset the original industry equilibrium and produce losses, but those losses will cause firms to leave the industry, decreasing supply (S_1 to S_3) and increasing product price until all losses have disappeared.

(a) Single firm

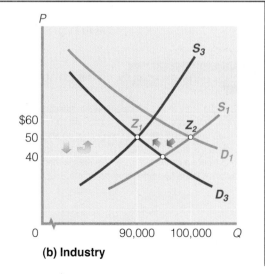

(b) Industry

We have now reached an intermediate goal: Our analysis verifies that competition, reflected in the entry and exit of firms, eliminates economic profits or losses by adjusting price to equal minimum long-run average total cost. In addition, this competition forces firms to select output levels at which average total cost is minimized.

Long-Run Supply for a Constant-Cost Industry

long-run supply curve
A curve that shows the prices at which a purely competitive industry will make various quantities of the product available in the long run.

constant-cost industry
An industry in which the entry of new firms has no effect on resource prices and thus no effect on production costs.

Although our analysis has dealt with the long run, we have noted that the market supply curves in Figures 7-8b and 7-9b are short-run curves. What then is the character of the **long-run supply curve** of a competitive industry? The analysis points us toward an answer. The crucial factor here is the effect, if any, that changes in the number of firms in the industry will have on costs of the individual firms in the industry.

In our analysis of long-run competitive equilibrium we assumed that the industry under discussion was a **constant-cost industry,** which means that industry expansion or contraction will not affect resource prices or production costs. Graphically, it means that the entry or exit of firms does not shift the long-run ATC curves of individual firms. This is the case when the industry's demand for factors of production is small in relation to the total demand for those resources; the industry can expand or contract without significantly affecting factor prices and costs.

What does the long-run supply curve of a constant-cost industry look like? The answer is contained in our previous analysis. There we saw that the entry and exit of firms changes industry output but always brings the product price back to its original level, where it is just equal to the constant minimum ATC. Specifically, we discovered that the industry would supply 90,000, 100,000, or 110,000 units of output, all at a price of $50 per unit. In other words, the long-run supply of a constant-cost industry is perfectly elastic.

This is demonstrated graphically in Figure 7-10, which uses data from Figures 7-8 and 7-9. Suppose industry demand is originally D_1, industry output is Q_1 (100,000 units), and product price is P_1 ($50). This situation, from Figure 7-8, is one of long-run equilibrium. We saw that when demand increases to D_2, upsetting this equilibrium, the resulting economic profits attract new firms. Because this is a constant-cost industry, entry continues and industry output expands until the price is driven back down to the level of the unchanged minimum ATC, which is at price P_2 ($50) and output Q_2 (110,000).

From Figure 7-9, we saw that a decline in market demand from D_1 to D_3 causes an exit of firms and ultimately restores equilibrium at price P_3 ($50) and output Q_3 (90,000 units). The points Z_1, Z_2, and Z_3 in Figure 7-10 represent these three price–quantity combinations. A line or curve connecting all such points shows the various price–quantity combinations that firms would produce if they had enough time to make all desired adjustments to changes in demand. This line or curve is the industry's long-run supply curve. In a constant-cost industry this curve (straight line) is horizontal, as in Figure 7-10, thus representing perfectly elastic supply.

FIGURE 7-10   The Long-Run Supply Curve for a Constant-Cost Industry Is Horizontal

Because the entry or exit of firms does not affect resource prices or, therefore, unit costs, an increase in demand (D_1 to D_2) causes an expansion in industry output (Q_1 to Q_2) but no alteration in price ($50). Similarly, a decrease in demand (D_1 to D_3) causes a contraction of output (Q_1 to Q_3) but no change in price. This means that the long-run industry supply curve (S) is horizontal through points Z_1, Z_2, and Z_3.

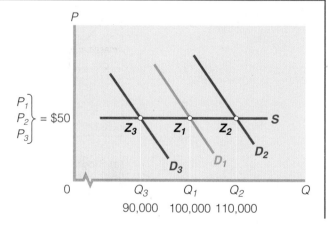

Long-Run Supply for an Increasing-Cost Industry

increasing-cost industry
An industry in which the entry of new firms raises resource prices and thus increases production costs.

Constant-cost industries are a special case. Most industries are **increasing-cost industries,** in which firms' ATC curves shift upward as the industry expands and downward as the industry contracts. Usually, the entry of new firms will increase factor prices, particularly so in industries using specialized inputs whose long-run supplies do not readily increase in response to increases in factor demand. Higher input prices result in higher long-run average total costs for all firms in the industry. These higher costs cause upward shifts in each firm's long-run ATC curve.

Thus, when an increase in product demand results in economic profits and attracts new firms to an increasing-cost industry, a two-way squeeze works to eliminate those profits. As before, the entry of new firms increases market supply and lowers the market price, but now the entire ATC curve shifts upward. The overall result is a higher-than-original equilibrium price. The industry produces a larger output at a higher product price because the industry expansion has increased factor prices and the minimum average total cost. Since greater output will be supplied at a higher price, the long-run industry supply curve is upsloping. Instead of supplying 90,000, 100,000, or 110,000 units at the same price of $50, an increasing-cost industry might supply 90,000 units at $45; 100,000 units at $50; and 110,000 units at $55. A higher price is required to induce more production, because costs per unit of output increase as production rises.

Figure 7-11 nicely illustrates the situation. Original market demand is D_1 and industry price and output are P_1 ($50) and Q_1 (100,000 units), respectively, at equilibrium point Y_1. An increase in demand to D_2 upsets this equilibrium and leads to economic profits. New firms enter the industry, increasing both market supply and production costs of individual firms. A new price is established at point Y_2, where P_2 is $55 and Q_2 is 110,000 units.

Conversely, a decline in demand from D_1 to D_3 makes production unprofitable and causes firms to leave the industry. The resulting decline in factor prices reduces the minimum average total cost of production for firms that stay. A new equilibrium price is established at some level below the original price, say at point Y_3, where P_3 is $45 and Q_3 is 90,000 units. Connecting these three equilibrium positions, we derive the upsloping long-run supply curve S in Figure 7-11.

Long-Run Supply for a Decreasing-Cost Industry

decreasing-cost industry
An industry in which the entry of firms lowers resource prices and thus decreases production costs.

In a **decreasing-cost industry,** a firm experiences lower costs as the industry expands. For example, as demand for personal computers increased, new manufacturers entered the personal computer industry and greatly increased the input demand for the components used to build them (memory chips, hard drives, monitors, and operating software). The expanded production of those components enabled the producers of those items to achieve substantial economies of scale. The decreased production costs of the components reduced their prices, which greatly lowered

FIGURE 7-11

The Long-Run Supply Curve for an Increasing-Cost Industry Is Upsloping

In an increasing-cost industry the entry of new firms in response to an increase in demand (D_3 to D_1 to D_2) will bid up resource prices and thereby increase unit costs. As a result, an increased industry output (Q_3 to Q_1 to Q_2) will be forthcoming only at higher prices ($55 > $50 > $45). The long-run industry supply curve (S) therefore slopes upward through points Y_3, Y_1, and, Y_2.

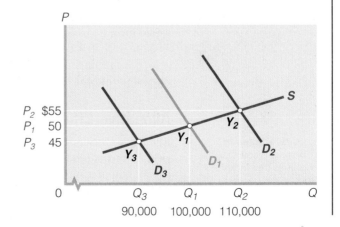

the computer manufacturers' average costs of production. The supply of personal computers increased by more than demand, and the price of personal computers declined.

You should rework the analysis underlying Figure 7-11 to show that the long-run supply curve of a decreasing-cost industry is downsloping. *(Key Question 7)*

7.6 | Perfect Competition and Efficiency

Figure 7-12 (Key Graph) demonstrates the efficiency characteristics of the individual firms (Figure 7-12a) and the market (Figure 7-12b) after long-run adjustments in perfect competition. Whether a perfectly competitive industry is a constant-cost industry or an increasing-cost industry, the final long-run equilibrium positions of all firms have the same basic efficiency characteristics. As shown in Figure 7-12a, price (and marginal revenue) will settle where it is equal to minimum average total cost: P (and MR) = minimum ATC. Moreover, since the marginal-cost curve intersects the average-total-cost curve at its minimum point, marginal cost and average total cost are equal: MC = minimum ATC. So in long-run equilibrium a triple equality occurs: P (and MR) = MC = minimum ATC. Output for each firm is Q_f.

This triple equality tells us that although a competitive firm may realize economic profit or loss in the short run, it will earn only a normal profit by producing in accordance with the MR (= P) = MC rule in the long run. Also, this triple equality suggests certain conclusions of great social significance concerning the efficiency of a purely competitive economy.

Economists agree that, subject to qualifications relating to public goods and externalities, an idealized perfectly competitive economy leads to an efficient use of society's scarce resources. This is true because a competitive market economy uses the limited amounts of resources available to society in a way that maximizes the satisfaction of consumers. In particular, competitive market economies generate both productive efficiency and allocative efficiency.

Productive Efficiency: *P* = Minimum ATC

productive efficiency
Producing a good in the least costly way.

Productive efficiency requires that goods be produced in the least costly way. In the long run, perfect competition forces firms to produce at the minimum average total cost of production and to charge a price that is just consistent with that cost. That is a highly favourable situation from the consumer's point of view. It means that unless firms use the best-available (least-cost) production methods and combinations of inputs, they will not survive. Stated differently, it means that the minimum amount of resources will be used to produce any particular output. Let's suppose that output in Figure 7-12a is cucumbers.

In the final equilibrium position shown in Figure 7-12a, suppose each firm in the cucumber industry is producing 120 units (say, pickup truckloads) of output by using $5000 (equal to average total cost of $50 × 120 units) worth of resources. If one firm produced that same output at a total cost of, say, $7000, its resources would be used inefficiently. Society would be faced with a net loss of $2000 worth of alternative products. But this cannot happen in perfect competition; this firm would incur a loss of $2000, requiring it either to reduce its costs or go out of business.

Note, too, that consumers benefit from productive efficiency by paying the lowest product price possible under the prevailing technology and cost conditions. And the firm receives only a normal profit, which is part of its economic costs and thus incorporated in its ATC curve.

Allocative Efficiency: *P* = MC

allocative efficiency
Apportioning resources among firms and industries to produce the goods most wanted by society.

Allocative efficiency requires that resources be apportioned among firms and industries so as to yield the mix of products and services that is most wanted by society (least-cost production at each level of output assumed). Allocative efficiency has been realized when it is impossible to alter the combination of goods produced and achieve a net gain for society. Productive efficiency alone does

FIGURE 7-12 Long-Run Equilibrium: A Competitive Firm and Market

Panel (a): The equality of price (P), marginal cost (MC), and minimum average total cost (ATC) at output Q_f indicates that the firm is achieving productive efficiency and allocative efficiency. It is using the most efficient technology, charging the lowest price, and producing the greatest output consistent with its costs. It is receiving only a normal profit, which is incorporated into the ATC curve. The equality of price and marginal cost indicates that society is allocating its scarce resources in accordance with consumer preferences. Panel (b): In the perfectly competitive market, allocative efficiency occurs at the market equilibrium output Q_e. The sum of consumer surplus (green area) and producer surplus (blue area) is maximized.

(a) Single firm

(b) Market

Quick Quiz

1. **We know the firm is a price-taker because**
   a. its MC curve slopes upward.
   b. its ATC curve is U-shaped.
   c. its MR curve is horizontal.
   d. MC and ATC are equal at the profit-maximizing output.

2. **At this firm's profit-maximizing output,**
   a. total revenue equals total cost.
   b. it is earning an economic profit.
   c. allocative, but not necessarily productive, efficiency is achieved.
   d. productive, but not necessarily allocative, efficiency is achieved.

3. **The equality of P, MC, and minimum ATC**
   a. occurs only in constant-cost industries.
   b. encourages entry of new firms.
   c. means that the "right goods" are being produced in the "right ways."
   d. results in a zero accounting profit.

4. **When P = MC = lowest ATC for individual firms, in the market**
   a. consumer surplus necessarily exceeds producer surplus.
   b. consumer surplus plus producer surplus is at a maximum.
   c. producer surplus necessarily exceeds consumer surplus.
   d. supply and demand are identical.

Answers: 1. d; 2. a; 3. c; 4. b

not ensure the efficient allocation of resources. Least-cost production must be used to provide society with the "right goods"—the goods that consumers want most. Before we can show that the competitive market system does just that, we must discuss the social meaning of product prices. Two elements here are critical:

- The money price of any product is society's measure of the relative worth of an additional unit of that product—for example, cucumbers. So the price of a unit of cucumbers is the marginal benefit derived from that unit of the product.

- Similarly, recalling the idea of opportunity cost, we see that the marginal cost of an additional unit of a product measures the value, or relative worth, of the other goods sacrificed to obtain it. In producing cucumbers, resources are drawn away from producing other goods. The marginal cost of producing a unit of cucumbers measures society's sacrifice of those other products.

ORIGIN 7.1
Allocative
Efficiency

MATH 7.2
Allocative
Efficiency

In perfect competition, when profit-motivated firms produce each good or service to the point where price (marginal benefit) and marginal cost are equal, society's resources are being allocated efficiently. Each item is being produced to the point at which the value of the last unit is equal to the value of the alternative goods sacrificed by its production. Altering the production of cucumbers would reduce consumer satisfaction. Producing cucumbers beyond the $P = MC$ point in Figure 7-12a would sacrifice alternative goods whose value to society exceeds that of the extra cucumbers. Producing cucumbers short of the $P = MC$ point would sacrifice cucumbers that society values more than the alternative goods its resources could produce. *(Key Question 8)*

Maximum Consumer and Producer Surplus

consumer surplus
The difference between the maximum price consumers are willing to pay and the actual price.

producer surplus
The difference between the actual price producers are willing to accept and the minimum acceptable price.

We confirm the existence of allocative efficiency in Figure 7-12b, where we see that perfect competition maximizes the sum of the "benefit surpluses" to consumers and producers. Recall from Chapter 4 that **consumer surplus** is the difference between the maximum prices that consumers are willing to pay for a product (as shown by the demand curve) and the market price of that product. In Figure 7-12b, consumer surplus is the green triangle, which is the sum of the vertical distances between the demand curve and equilibrium price. In contrast, **producer surplus** is the difference between the minimum prices that producers are willing to accept for a product (as shown by the supply curve) and the market price of the product. Producer surplus is the sum of the vertical distances between the equilibrium price and supply curve. Here producer surplus is the blue area.

At the equilibrium quantity Q_e, the combined amount of consumer surplus and producer surplus is maximized. Allocative efficiency occurs because, at Q_e, marginal benefit, reflected by points on the demand curve, equals marginal cost, reflected by the points on the supply curve. Alternatively, the maximum willingness of consumers to pay for unit Q_e equals the minimum acceptable price of that unit to producers. At any output less than Q_e, the sum of consumer and producer surplus—the combined size of the green and blue areas—would be less than that shown. At any output greater than Q_e, an efficiency loss would subtract from the combined consumer and producer surplus shown by the green and blue areas.

After long-run adjustments, perfect competition produces allocative efficiency: A level of output at which $P = MC$ = lowest ATC; marginal benefit = marginal cost, maximum willingness to pay for the last unit = minimum acceptable price for that unit, and combined consumer and producer surplus are maximized.

Dynamic Adjustments

A further attribute of perfectly competitive markets is their ability to restore the efficiency just described when disrupted by changes in the economy. A change in consumer tastes, resource supplies, or technology will automatically set in motion the appropriate realignments of resources. For example, suppose that cucumbers and pickles become dramatically more popular. First, the demand for cucumbers will increase in the market, increasing the price of cucumbers. So, at current output, the price of cucumbers will exceed their marginal cost. At this point efficiency will be lost, but the higher price will create economic profits in the cucumber industry and stimulate its expansion. The profitability of cucumbers will permit the industry to bid resources away from now less pressing uses, say, watermelons. Expansion of the industry will end only when the supply of cucumbers has expanded such that the price of cucumbers and their marginal cost are equal—that is, when allocative efficiency has been restored.

Similarly, a change in the supply of a particular resource—for example, the field labourers who pick cucumbers—or in a production technique will upset an existing price–marginal cost equality by either raising or lowering marginal cost. The resulting inequality of MC and P will cause producers, in either pursuing profit or avoiding loss, to reallocate resources until product supply is such that price once again equals marginal cost. In so doing, they will correct any inefficiency in the allocation of resources that the original change may have temporarily imposed on the economy.

"Invisible Hand" Revisited

Finally, the highly efficient allocation of resources that a perfectly competitive economy promotes comes about because businesses and resource suppliers seek to further their self-interest. For private goods with no externalities, the invisible hand is at work (Chapter 2). The competitive system not only maximizes profits for individual producers but at the same time creates a pattern of resource allocation that maximizes consumer satisfaction. The invisible hand thus organizes the private interests of producers in a way that is fully in sync with society's interest in using scarce resources efficiently. Striving for profit (and avoiding losses) produces highly desirable economic outcomes.

QUICK REVIEW

▸ In the long run, the entry of firms into an industry will compete away any economic profits, and the exit of firms will eliminate losses so that price and minimum average total cost are equal.

▸ The long-run supply curves of constant-cost, increasing-cost, and decreasing-cost industries are horizontal, upsloping, and downsloping, respectively.

▸ In perfectly competitive markets both productive efficiency (price equals minimum average total cost) and allocative efficiency (price equals marginal cost) are achieved in the long run.

▸ After long-run adjustments, purely competitive markets maximize the combined amounts of consumer surplus and producer surplus.

The LAST WORD   Efficiency Gains from Entry: The Case of Generic Drugs

When a generic drug becomes available, the price of the drug falls, consumer surplus rises, and society experiences an efficiency gain.

The competitive model predicts that entry will lower price, expand output, and increase efficiency. A good actual-economy test of this prediction occurs where entry of new producers occurs in a formerly monopolized market. Such a situation occurs when prescription drugs lose their patent protection. A patent on a prescription drug gives the pharmaceutical company that developed it an exclusive right to produce and sell the medication for 20 years from the time of patent application. The purpose of drug patents is to encourage research and development (R&D),

leading to new medications and the increased well-being they enable. With patent protection a firm can charge prices that exceed marginal cost and average total cost and earn economic profits on its popular brand-name medicines. Those economic profits provide a return on past development costs and help fund more R&D.

Although competitors can and often do develop similar drugs, they cannot copy and sell the patented medication. Such drugs as Lipitor (for high cholesterol), Zoloft (for depression), and Nexium (for gastrointestinal disorders) are examples of best-selling, brand-name, patented drugs.

When a patent expires, a pharmaceutical company can produce and sell the drug under the generic name for the medication if it gets approval from Health Canada and if it can demonstrate that the production of a specific drug will not infringe any existing patents. Because such generic drugs have the same chemical composition as the branded drug, they directly compete against it. The generic price is lower than the branded price, so the price of the drug (at least on average) drops as "generics" claim a share of the market. Studies indicate that price drop is typically 30–40 percent. Medical insurance plans either mandate that patients buy generics or provide financial incentives to encourage them do

so when generics become available. Today, generics make up about 65 percent of all prescriptions dispensed in Canada.

It is useful to see how patent expiration and the competition from generic drugs relate to consumer surplus and efficiency gains. Consider the accom-

panying figure, which is similar to Figure 7-12b. The patent gives the firm monopoly power that allows it to charge a higher-than-competitive price. Suppose that the sole seller's profit-maximizing price is P_1. (We will examine how a monopolist would choose this price in the following chapter.)

The expiration of the patent creates competition from generics, which reduces the price of the medication from P_1 to, say, P_2. If you compare the consumer surplus triangles above the price lines, you can see that consumer surplus rises from *bac* to *daf* when the price falls. As the price of the medication drops from P_1 to P_2, output increases from Q_1 to Q_2. In this case, the efficiency gain from competition is shown by the addition of the grey triangle. At price P_2 and quantity Q_2, the combined amounts of consumer surplus and producer surplus are at a maximum. (In reality, the price might not drop all the way to P_2 because of continued loyalty to the branded drug by prescribing physicians.)

Patents aid consumers and society by encouraging the development of new medicines that might otherwise not be available. Entry of the generics at the time of patent expiration further helps consumers by lowering prices, increasing consumer surplus, and enhancing efficiency—just like the competitive model predicts.

Question

How does a generic drug differ from its brand-name, previously patented equivalent? Explain why the price of a brand-name drug typically declines when an equivalent generic drug becomes available. Explain how that drop in price affects allocative efficiency.

CHAPTER SUMMARY

7.1 ▶ FOUR MARKET STRUCTURES

- Economists group industries into four models based on their market structures: (a) perfect competition, (b) monopoly, (c) monopolistic competition, and (d) oligopoly.

7.2 ▶ CHARACTERISTICS OF PERFECT COMPETITION AND THE FIRM'S DEMAND CURVE

- A perfectly competitive industry consists of a large number of independent firms producing a standardized product. Perfect competition assumes that firms and factors of production are mobile among different industries.

- In a competitive industry, no single firm can influence market price, which means that the firm's demand curve is perfectly elastic and price equals marginal revenue.

7.3 ▶ PROFIT MAXIMIZATION IN THE SHORT RUN

- We can analyze short-run profit maximization by a competitive firm by comparing total revenue and total cost or by applying marginal analysis. A firm maximizes its short-run profit by producing the output at which total revenue exceeds total cost by the greatest amount.

- Provided price exceeds minimum average variable cost, a competitive firm maximizes profit or minimizes loss in the short run by producing the output at which price or marginal revenue equals marginal cost. If price is less than average variable cost, the firm minimizes its loss by shutting down. If price is greater than average variable cost but is less than average total cost, the firm minimizes its loss by producing the $P = MC$ output. If price also exceeds average total cost, the firm maximizes its economic profit at the $P = MC$ output.

7.4 ▶ MARGINAL COST AND SHORT-RUN SUPPLY

- Applying the MR (= P) = MC rule at various possible market prices leads to the conclusion that the segment of the firm's short-run marginal-cost curve that lies above the firm's average-variable-cost curve is its short-run supply curve.

7.5 ▶ PROFIT MAXIMIZATION IN THE LONG RUN

- In the long run, the market price of a product will equal the minimum average total cost of production. At a higher price, economic profits would cause firms to enter the industry until those profits had been competed away. At a lower price, losses would force the exit of some firms from the industry until the product price rose to equal average total cost.

- The long-run supply curve is horizontal for a constant-cost industry, upsloping for an increasing-cost industry, and downsloping for a decreasing-cost industry.

7.6 ▶ PERFECT COMPETITION AND EFFICIENCY

- The long-run equality of price and minimum average total cost means that competitive firms will use the most efficient technology and charge the lowest price consistent with their production costs. That is, the firms will achieve productive efficiency.

- The long-run equality of price and marginal cost implies that resources will be allocated in accordance with consumer tastes. Allocative efficiency will occur. In the market, the combined amount of consumer surplus and producer surplus will be at a maximum.

- The competitive price system will reallocate resources in response to a change in consumer tastes, in technology, or in factor supplies and will thereby maintain allocative efficiency over time.

TERMS AND CONCEPTS

perfect competition, p. 164
monopoly, p. 164
monopolistic competition, p. 164
oligopoly, p. 164
imperfect competition, p. 164
price-taker, p. 165
average revenue, p. 165

total revenue, p. 165
marginal revenue, p. 166
break-even point, p. 168
MR = MC rule, p. 168
short-run supply curve, p. 177
long-run supply curve, p. 182
constant-cost industry, p. 182

increasing-cost industry, p. 183
decreasing-cost industry, p. 183
productive efficiency, p.184
allocative efficiency, p.184
consumer surplus, p.186
producer surplus, p.186

STUDY QUESTIONS

LO 7.1 1. Briefly state the basic characteristics of perfect competition, monopoly, monopolistic competition, and oligopoly. Under which of these market classifications does each of the following most accurately fit? (a) a supermarket in your home town; (b) the steel industry; (c) a Saskatchewan wheat farm; (d) the chartered bank in which you or your family has an account; (e) the automobile industry. In each case justify your classification.

LO 7.2 2. Strictly speaking, perfect competition has never existed and probably never will. Then why study it?

LO 7.3 3. **KEY QUESTION** Use the following demand schedule to determine total revenue and marginal revenue for each possible level of sales:

Product price	Quantity demanded	Total revenue	Marginal revenue
$2	0	$____	$____
2	1	____	____
2	2	____	____
2	3	____	____
2	4	____	____
2	5	____	____

a. What can you conclude about the structure of the industry in which this firm is operating? Explain.

b. Graph the demand, total-revenue, and marginal-revenue curves for this firm.

c. Do the demand and marginal-revenue curves coincide? If so, why? If not, why not?

d. "Marginal revenue is the change in total revenue associated with additional units of output." Explain in words and graphically, using the data in the table.

LO 7.3 4. **KEY QUESTION** Assume the following cost data are for a perfectly competitive producer:

Total product	Average fixed cost	Average variable cost	Average total cost	Marginal cost
0				
1	$60.00	$45.00	$105.00	$45
2	30.00	42.50	72.50	40
3	20.00	40.00	60.00	35
4	15.00	37.50	52.50	30
5	12.00	37.00	49.00	35
6	10.00	37.50	47.50	40
7	8.57	38.57	47.14	45
8	7.50	40.63	48.13	55
9	6.67	43.33	50.00	65
10	6.00	46.50	52.50	75

a. At a product price of $56, will this firm produce in the short run? Why or why not? If it does produce, what will be the profit-maximizing or loss-minimizing output? Explain. What economic profit or loss will the firm realize per unit of output?

b. Answer the questions in 4(a) assuming product price is $41.

c. Answer the questions in 4(a) assuming product price is $32.

d. In the table below, complete the short-run supply schedule for the firm (columns 1 and 2) and indicate the profit or loss incurred at each output (column 3).

(1) Price	(2) Quantity supplied, single firm	(3) Profit (+) or loss (−)	(4) Quantity supplied, 1500 firms
$26	0	$−60	0
32	0	−60	0
38	5	−55	7500
41	6	−39	9000
46	7	−8	10500
56	8	63	12000
66	9	144	13500

e. Explain: "That segment of a competitive firm's marginal-cost curve that lies above its average-variable-cost curve constitutes the short-run supply curve for the firm." Illustrate graphically.

f. Now assume that there are 1500 identical firms in this competitive industry; that is, there are 1500 firms, each of which has the cost data shown in the table. Complete the industry supply schedule (column 4).

g. Suppose the market demand data for the product are as follows:

Price	Total quantity demanded
$26	17,000
32	15,000
38	13,500
41	12,000
46	10,500
56	9,500
66	8,000

What will be the equilibrium price? What will be the equilibrium output for the industry? For each firm? What will profit or loss be per unit? Per firm? Will this industry expand or contract in the long run?

7.4 5. Assume a single firm in a perfectly competitive industry has variable costs as indicated in the following table in column 2. Complete the table and answer the questions.

(1) Total product	(2) Total vari- able cost	(3) Total cost	(4) AFC	(5) AVC	(6) ATC	(7) MC
0	$ 0	$ 40	$__	$__	$__	
1	55	__	__	__	__	$__
2	75	__	__	__	__	__
3	90	__	__	__	__	__
4	110	__	__	__	__	__
5	135	__	__	__	__	__
6	170	__	__	__	__	__
7	220	__	__	__	__	__
8	290	__	__	__	__	__

(a) At a product price of $52, will this firm produce in the short run? Explain. What will its profit or loss be?

(b) At a product price of $28, will this firm produce in the short run? Explain. What will its profit or loss be?

(c) At a product price of $22, will this firm produce in the short run? Explain. What will its profit or loss be?

(d) Complete the following short-run supply schedule for this firm.

Product price	Quantity supplied	Profit (+) or loss (−)
$72	___	$___
52	___	___
45	___	___
28	___	___
22	___	___
15	___	___

Assume there are 500 identical firms in this industry, that they have identical cost data to the firm above, and that the industry demand schedule is as follows:

Price	Quantity demanded
$72	2500
52	3500
45	4000
28	5200
22	5900
15	6700

(e) What will be the equilibrium price?

(f) What will be the equilibrium output for each firm?

(g) What will be profit or loss per unit?

(h) What will be profit or loss per firm?

6. Why is the equality of marginal revenue and marginal cost **LO ▸ 7.4** essential for profit maximization in all market structures? Explain why price can be substituted for marginal revenue in the MR = MC rule when an industry is perfectly competitive.

7. **KEY QUESTION** Using diagrams for both the industry **LO ▸ 7.5** and a representative firm, illustrate competitive long-run equilibrium. Assuming constant costs, employ these diagrams to show how (a) an increase and (b) a decrease in market demand will upset that long-run equilibrium. Trace graphically and describe in words the adjustment processes by which long-run equilibrium is restored. Now rework your analysis for increasing-cost and decreasing-cost industries and compare the three long-run supply curves.

8. **KEY QUESTION** In long-run equilibrium, P = minimum **LO ▸ 7.6** ATC = MC. Of what significance for economic efficiency is the equality of P and minimum ATC? The equality of P and MC? Distinguish between productive efficiency and allocative efficiency in your answer.

9. Suppose that firms in a perfectly competitive industry pro- **LO ▸ 7.6** ducing cashews discover that P exceeds MC. Will their combined output of cashews be too little, too much, or just right to achieve allocative efficiency? In the long run, what will happen to the supply of cashews and the price of cashews? Use a supply and demand diagram to show how that response will change the combined amount of consumer surplus and producer surplus in the market for cashews.

INTERNET APPLICATION QUESTIONS @

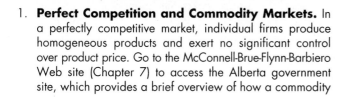

1. **Perfect Competition and Commodity Markets.** In a perfectly competitive market, individual firms produce homogeneous products and exert no significant control over product price. Go to the McConnell-Brue-Flynn-Barbiero Web site (Chapter 7) to access the Alberta government site, which provides a brief overview of how a commodity exchange functions and has links to the main commodity exchanges in North America. Also, visit the Winnipeg Commodity Exchange and select "Daily Market Summary." Which of the main crops has had the largest price movement and why?

CHAPTER 8

Monopoly

We turn now from perfect competition to monopoly, which is at the opposite end of the spectrum of market structures listed in Table 7-1. You deal with monopolies more often than you might think. When you see the logo for Microsoft's Windows on your computer, you are dealing with a monopoly (or at least near-monopoly). When you purchase certain prescription drugs, you may be buying monopolized products. When you make a local telephone call, turn on your lights, or subscribe to cable TV, you may be patronizing a monopoly, depending on your location.

What precisely do we mean by monopoly and what conditions allow it to arise and survive? How does a monopolist determine its profit-maximizing price and output quantity? Does a monopolist achieve the efficiencies associated with perfect competition? If not, what should the government do about it? A simplified model of monopoly will help us answer these questions. This is the first of three models of imperfect competition; the other two are discussed in Chapter 9.

8.1 | Characteristics of Monopoly

Monopoly exists when a single firm is the sole producer of a product or service for which no close substitutes exist. Here are the main characteristics of monopoly.

- *Single Seller*   A monopoly is an industry in which a single firm is the sole producer or seller of a specific good or the sole supplier of a service.

- *No Close Substitutes*   A monopoly's product is unique in that there are no close substitutes.

- *Price-Maker*   The monopolist controls the total quantity supplied and thus has considerable control over price; it is a *price-maker*. The monopolist confronts the usual downward-sloping product demand curve. It can change its product price by changing the quantity of the product it produces. The monopolist will use this power whenever it is advantageous to do so.

ORIGIN 8.1
Monopoly

monopoly
An industry in which one firm is the sole producer or seller of a product or service for which no close substitutes exist.

A monopoly exists when a single firm is the sole producer of a product or service for which no close substitutes exist.

- **Blocked Entry**   A monopolist has no competitors because certain barriers keep potential competitors from entering the industry. Those barriers may be economic, technological, legal, or of some other type, but entry is totally blocked in monopoly.

- **Nonprice Competition**   The product produced by a monopolist may be either standardized (as with natural gas and electricity) or differentiated (as with Windows or Frisbees). Monopolists that have standardized products engage mainly in public relations advertising, whereas those with differentiated products sometimes advertise their products' attributes.

Examples of Monopoly

Examples of a single-price monopoly are relatively rare in Canada, but many examples of less pure forms exist. In many cities, government-owned or government-regulated public utilities—natural gas and electric companies, the water company, the cable TV company, and the local telephone company—may be monopolies or virtually so. In some Canadian markets, competition has been introduced for some of these traditional monopolies. Many urban areas now have more than one gas supplier to choose from. Rapid technological change has dramatically altered the delivery of communications services, effectively eliminating what was a virtual monopoly by Bell Canada. In some urban markets, such as Toronto and Montreal, Rogers Cable Communications now competes with Bell Canada in the local telephone market. Wireless telephone services by relative newcomers Telus and Rogers have further eroded Bell's monopoly position in local markets. Ontario and Alberta have moved toward deregulating their electricity markets, although the public furor that this has caused has delayed full deregulation.

Many "near-monopolies" also exist in which a single firm has the bulk of sales in a specific market. Intel, for example, provides 80 percent of the central microprocessors used in personal computers. Microsoft's Windows operating system is on some 95 percent of home and business computers; Wham-O, through its Frisbee brand, sells 90 percent of plastic throwing disks. The De Beers diamond syndicate effectively controls 55 percent of the world's supply of rough-cut diamonds (see this chapter's The Last Word).

Professional sports teams are, in a sense, monopolies because they are the sole suppliers of specific services in large geographic areas. With a few exceptions, a single major-league team in each sport serves each large Canadian city. If you want to see a live major-league baseball game in Toronto, you must patronize the Blue Jays. Other geographic monopolies exist. For example, a small town may be served by only one airline or railroad. In a small, isolated community, the local barber shop, dry cleaner, or grocery store may approximate a monopoly.

Of course, some competition almost always exists. Satellite television is a substitute for cable, and amateur softball is a substitute for professional baseball. The Linux operating system can substitute for Windows, and so on. But such substitutes are typically either more costly or in some way less appealing.

Dual Objectives of the Study of Monopoly

Monopoly is worth studying both for its own sake and because it provides insights about the more common market structures of monopolistic competition and oligopoly (see Chapter 9). These two market structures combine, in differing degrees, characteristics of perfect competition and monopoly.

∨ Barriers to Entry

barriers to entry
Anything that artificially prevents the entry of firms into an industry.

The factors that prohibit firms from entering an industry are called **barriers to entry.** In monopoly, strong barriers to entry effectively block all potential competition. Somewhat weaker barriers may permit oligopoly, a market structure dominated by a few firms. Still weaker barriers may permit the entry of a fairly large number of competing firms, giving rise to monopolistic competition.

The absence of any effective entry barriers permits the entry of a very large number of firms, which provides the basis of perfect competition. So, barriers to entry are pertinent not only to the extreme case of monopoly but also to other market structures in which there is some degree of monopolistic conditions and behaviour.

ECONOMIES OF SCALE

Modern technology in some industries is such that economies of scale—declining average total cost with added firm size—are extensive. So, a firm's long-run average-cost schedule will decline over a wide range of output. Given market demand, only a few large firms or, in the extreme, only a single large firm can achieve low average total costs.

Figure 8-1 indicates economies of scale over a wide range of outputs. If total consumer demand is within that output range, then only a single producer can satisfy demand at least cost. Note, for example, that a monopolist can produce 200 units at a per-unit cost of $10 and a total cost of $2000. If there are two firms in the industry and each produces 100 units, the unit cost is $15 and total cost rises to $3000 (= 200 units × $15). A still more competitive situation with four firms each producing 50 units would boost unit and total cost to $20 and $4000, respectively. Conclusion: When long-run average total cost (ATC) is declining, only a single producer, a monopolist, can produce any particular output at minimum total cost.

If a monopoly exists in such an industry, economies of scale will serve as an entry barrier and will protect the monopolist from competition. New firms that try to enter the industry as small-scale producers cannot realize the cost economies of the monopolist and therefore cannot obtain the normal profits necessary for survival or growth. A new firm might try to enter the industry as a large-scale producer so as to achieve the necessary economies of scale, but the massive plant facilities needed would require huge amounts of financing, which a new and untried enterprise would find difficult to secure. In most cases the financial obstacles and risks to starting big are prohibitive, which explains why efforts to enter such industries as automobiles, computer operating software, commercial aircraft, and basic steel are rare.

ORIGIN 8.2
Minimum Efficient Scale

In the extreme circumstance in which the market demand curve cuts the long-run ATC curve where average total costs are still declining, the single firm is called a *natural monopoly*. It might seem that a natural monopolist's lower unit cost would enable it to charge a lower price than if the industry were more competitive. But that won't necessarily happen. A monopolist may, instead, set its price far above ATC and obtain substantial economic profit. In that event, the cost advantage of a natural monopolist would accrue to the monopolist as profit and not as lower prices to consumers. That is why the government regulates some natural monopolies, specifying the price they may charge. We will say more about that later.

FIGURE 8-1   **Economies of Scale: The Natural Monopoly Case**

A declining long-run average-total-cost curve over a wide range of output quantities indicates extensive economies of scale. A single monopoly firm can produce, say, 200 units of output at lower cost ($10 each) than could two or more firms that had a combined output of 200 units.

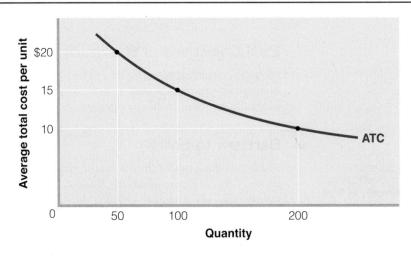

LEGAL BARRIERS TO ENTRY: PATENTS AND LICENCES

Government also creates legal barriers to entry by awarding patents and licences.

- **Patents**   A *patent* is the exclusive right of an inventor to use, or to allow another to use, her or his invention. Patent laws protect the inventor from rivals who would use the invention without having shared in the effort and expense of developing it. Patents thus provide the inventor with a monopoly position for the life of the patent. The world's nations have agreed on a uniform patent length of 20 years from the time of application. Patents have figured prominently in the growth of modern-day giants such as IBM, Microsoft, Pfizer, Xerox, Bombardier, General Electric, and Research In Motion.

  Research and development (R&D) is what leads to most patentable inventions and products. Firms that gain monopoly power through their own research or by purchasing the patents of others can use patents to strengthen their market position. The profit from one patent can finance the research required to develop new patentable products. In the pharmaceutical industry, patents on prescription drugs have produced large monopoly profits that have helped finance the discovery of new patentable medicines. So, monopoly power achieved through patents may well be self-sustaining, even though patents eventually expire and generic drugs then compete with the original brand.

- **Licences**   Government may also limit entry into an industry or occupation through *licensing*. At the national level, the Canadian Radio-television and Telecommunications Commission (CRTC) licenses a limited number of radio and television stations in each geographic area. In many large cities one of a limited number of municipal licences is required to drive a taxicab. The restriction of the supply of cabs creates economic profit for cab owners and drivers. New cabs cannot enter the industry to force prices and profit lower. In a few instances the government might license itself to provide some product and thereby create a public monopoly. For example, in some provinces only province-owned retail outlets can sell liquor. Similarly, many provinces have licensed themselves to run lotteries.

OWNERSHIP OR CONTROL OF ESSENTIAL RESOURCES

A monopolist can use private property as an obstacle to potential rivals. For example, a firm that owns or controls a resource essential to the production process can prohibit the entry of rival firms. At one time the International Nickel Company of Canada (now called Vale Inco) controlled 90 percent of the world's known nickel reserves. A municipal sand and gravel firm may own all the nearby deposits of sand and gravel. And it is very difficult for new professional sports leagues to be created because existing leagues have contracts with the best players and long-term leases on the major stadiums and arenas.

✓ PRICING AND OTHER STRATEGIC BARRIERS TO ENTRY

Even if a firm is not protected from entry by, say, extensive economies of scale or ownership of essential resources, entry may effectively be blocked by the way the monopolist responds to attempts by rivals to enter the industry. Confronted with a new entrant, the monopolist may create an entry barrier by slashing prices, stepping up advertising, or taking other strategic action to make it difficult for the entrant to succeed.

A prominent example of entry deterrence is the case of Microsoft, the software giant. In 2001 a U.S. court of appeals upheld a lower court's finding that Microsoft used a series of illegal actions to maintain its monopoly in Intel-compatible PC operating systems (95 percent market share). One such action was charging higher prices for its Windows operating system to computer manufacturers that featured Netscape's Navigator rather than Microsoft's Internet Explorer.

Monopoly Demand

Now that we have explained the sources of monopoly, we will build a model of monopoly so that we can analyze its price and output decisions. Let's start by making three assumptions:

1. Economies of scale, patents, or resource ownership secure the monopolist's status.

2. Government does not regulate the firm.

3. The firm is a single-price monopolist; it charges the same price for all units of output.

The crucial difference between a monopolist and seller in perfect competition lies on the demand side of the market. The seller in a competitive market faces a perfectly elastic demand at the price determined by market supply and demand. It is a *price-taker* that can sell as much or as little as it wants at the going market price.

The demand curve for the monopolist (and for any imperfectly competitive seller) is quite different from that of a firm in perfect competition. Because the monopolist *is* the industry, its demand curve is *the market demand curve,* which is downward-sloping. Columns 1 and 2 in Table 8-1 illustrate this; note that quantity demanded increases as price decreases.

In Chapter 7 we drew separate demand curves for the perfectly competitive industry and for a single firm in such an industry; only a single demand curve is needed in monopoly because the firm and the industry are one and the same. We have graphed part of the demand data in Table 8-1 as demand curve *D* in Figure 8-2. This is the monopolist's demand curve *and* the market demand curve. The downward-sloping demand curve has three implications that are essential to understanding the monopoly model.

1. MARGINAL REVENUE IS LESS THAN PRICE

With a fixed downsloping demand curve, the monopolist can increase sales only by charging a lower price. Consequently, marginal revenue is less than price (average revenue) for every level of output

TABLE 8-1   Revenue and Cost Data of a Monopolist

	REVENUE DATA				COST DATA		
(1) Quantity of output (Q)	(2) Price (average revenue) (P)	(3) Total revenue (TR = P × Q)	(4) Marginal revenue $MR = \frac{\Delta TR}{\Delta Q}$	(5) Average total cost (ATC)	(6) Total cost Q × ATC (TC)	(7) Marginal cost (MC)	(8) Profit (+) or loss (−)
0	$172	$ 0			$ 100		$−100
			$162			$ 90	
1	162	162		$190.00	190		− 28
			142			80	
2	152	304		135.00	270		+ 34
			122			70	
3	142	426		113.33	340		+ 86
			102			60	
4	132	528		100.00	400		+128
			82			70	
5	122	610		94.00	470		+140
			62			80	
6	112	672		91.67	550		+122
			42			90	
7	102	714		91.43	640		+ 74
			22			110	
8	92	736		93.75	750		− 14
			2			130	
9	82	738		97.78	880		−142
			−18			150	
10	72	720		103.00	1030		−310

FIGURE 8-2   Price and Marginal Revenue in Monopoly

A monopolist with a downsloping demand curve such as *D* must set a lower price to sell more output. Here, by charging $132 rather than $142, the monopolist sells an extra unit (the fourth unit) and gains $132 from that sale. But from this gain must be subtracted $30, which reflects the $10 less the monopolist charged for each of the first 3 units. Thus, the marginal revenue of the fourth unit is $102 (= $132 – $30), considerably less than its $132 price.

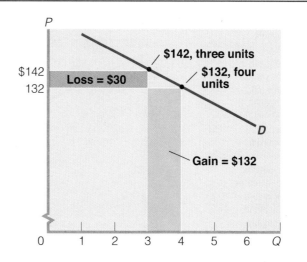

except the first. Why? The reason is that the lower price of the extra unit of output also applies to all prior units of output. Each additional unit of output sold increases total revenue by an amount equal to its own price less the sum of the price cuts that apply to all prior units of output.

Figure 8-2 confirms this point. There, we have highlighted two price–quantity combinations from the monopolist's demand curve. The monopolist can sell one more unit at $132 than it can at $142 and that way get an additional $132 of revenue (the light blue area). But to sell that fourth unit for $132, the monopolist must also sell the first three units at $132 rather than $142. This $10 reduction in revenue on three units results in a $30 revenue loss (the pink area). The net difference in total revenue from selling a fourth unit is $102: the $132 gain from the fourth unit minus the $30 forgone on the first three units ($10 per unit × 3 units = $30). This net gain of $102—the marginal revenue of the fourth unit—is clearly less than the $132 price of the fourth unit.

Column 4 in Table 8-1 shows that marginal revenue is always less than the corresponding product price in column 2, except for the first unit of output. Because marginal revenue is the change in total revenue associated with each *additional* unit of output, the declining amounts of marginal revenue in column 4 mean that total revenue increases at a diminishing rate (as shown in column 3).

We show the relationship between the monopolist's marginal-revenue curve and total-revenue curve in Figure 8-3. For this figure, we extended the demand and revenue data of columns 1 through 4 in Table 8-1, assuming that successive $10 price cuts each increase sales by one unit. For example, the monopolist can sell 11 units at $62, 12 units at $52, and so on.

Note that the monopolist's MR curve lies below the demand curve, indicating that marginal revenue is less than price at every output quantity but the very first unit. Observe also the special relationship between total revenue (shown in the lower graph) and marginal revenue (shown in the top graph). Because marginal revenue is the change in total revenue, marginal revenue is positive while total revenue is increasing. When total revenue reaches its maximum, marginal revenue is zero. When total revenue is diminishing, marginal revenue is negative.

2. THE MONOPOLIST IS A PRICE-MAKER

All firms in imperfectly competitive market structures, whether monopoly, oligopoly, or monopolistic competition, face downward-sloping demand curves. So, firms in those industries can to some degree influence total supply through their own output decisions. In changing market supply, they can also influence product price. Firms with downward-sloping demand curves are *price-makers*.

FIGURE 8-3 ✓   Demand, Marginal Revenue, and Total Revenue for a Monopolist

Panel (a): Because an imperfectly competitive firm must lower its price on all units sold in order to increase its sales, the marginal-revenue curve (MR) lies below its downsloping demand curve (D). The elastic and inelastic regions of demand are highlighted. Panel (b): Total revenue (TR) increases at a decreasing rate, reaches maximum, and then declines. Note that in the elastic region, TR is increasing and hence MR is positive. When TR reaches its maximum, MR is zero. In the inelastic region of demand, TR is declining, so MR is negative.

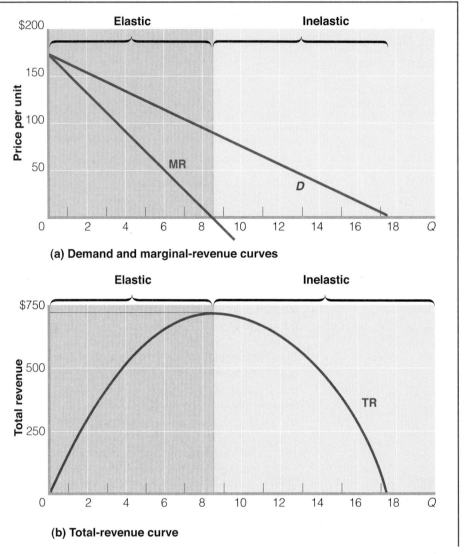

(a) Demand and marginal-revenue curves

(b) Total-revenue curve

This is most evident in monopoly, where one firm controls total output. The monopolist faces a downsloping demand curve in which each amount of output is associated with some unique price. Thus, in deciding on the quantity of output to produce, the monopolist is also indirectly determining the price it will charge. Through control of output, it can make the price. From columns 1 and 2 in Table 8-1 we find that the monopolist can charge a price of $72 if it produces 10 units, a price of $82 if it produces 9 units, and so forth.

3. THE MONOPOLIST SETS PRICES IN THE ELASTIC REGION OF DEMAND

@ **MATH 8.1**
Monopoly and the Elasticity of Demand

The total-revenue test for price elasticity of demand is the basis for our third implication. Recall from Chapter 4 that the total-revenue test reveals that when demand is elastic, a decline in price will increase total revenue. Similarly, when demand is inelastic, a decline in price will *reduce* total revenue. Beginning at the top of demand curve D in Figure 8-3a, observe that as the price declines from $172 to approximately $82, total revenue increases (and marginal revenue, therefore, is positive), which means that demand is elastic in this price range. Conversely, for price declines below $82, total revenue decreases (marginal revenue is negative), which indicates that demand is inelastic there.

The implication is that a profit-maximizing monopolist will always want to avoid the inelastic segment of its demand curve in favour of some price–quantity combination in the elastic region. Here's why: To get into the inelastic region, the monopolist must lower price and increase output. In the inelastic region a lower price means less total revenue. And increased output always means increased total cost. Less total revenue and higher total cost yield lower profit. *(Key Question 4)*

▶ A monopolist is the sole supplier of a product or service for which no close substitutes exist.

▶ A monopoly survives because of entry barriers such as economies of scale, patents and licences, the ownership of essential resources, and strategic actions to exclude rivals.

▶ The monopolist's demand curve is downsloping, and its marginal-revenue curve lies below its demand curve.

▶ The downsloping demand curve means that the monopolist is a price-maker.

▶ The monopolist will operate in the elastic region of demand since it can increase total revenue and reduce total cost by reducing output.

8.2 | Output and Price Determination

At what specific price–quantity combination will a profit-maximizing monopolist choose to operate? To answer this question, we must add production costs to our analysis.

Cost Data

On the cost side, we will assume that, although the firm is a monopolist in the product market, it hires factors of production in competitive markets and employs the same technology as Chapter 7's competitive firm. This assumption lets us use the cost data we developed in Chapter 6 and applied in Chapter 7, so we can compare the price–output decisions of a monopoly with those of a firm in perfect competition. Columns 5 through 7 in Table 8-1 reproduce the relevant cost data from Table 6-2.

MR = MC Rule

A monopolist seeking to maximize total profit will employ the same rationale as a profit-seeking firm in a competitive industry. It will produce another unit of output as long as that unit adds more to total revenue than it adds to total cost. The firm will increase output up to the output at which marginal revenue equals marginal cost (MR = MC).

A comparison of columns 4 and 7 in Table 8-1 indicates that the profit-maximizing output is five units, because the fifth unit is the last unit of output whose marginal revenue exceeds its marginal cost. What price will the monopolist charge? The demand schedule shown as columns 1 and 2 in Table 8-1 indicates there is only one price at which five units can be sold: $122.

This analysis is shown in **Figure 8-4 (Key Graph)**, where we have graphed the demand, marginal-revenue, average-total-cost, and marginal-cost data of Table 8-1. The profit-maximizing output occurs at five units of output (Q_m) where the marginal-revenue (MR) and marginal-cost (MC) curves intersect (MR = MC).

To find the price the monopolist will charge, we extend a vertical line from Q_m up to the demand curve D. The price P_m at which Q_m units can be sold is $122, which is in this case the profit-maximizing price. The monopolist sets the quantity at Q_m to charge its profit-maximizing price of $122.

KEY GRAPH

FIGURE 8-4 ✓

Profit Maximization by a Monopolist

The monopolist maximizes profit by producing the MR = MC output, here Q_m = 5 units. Then, as shown by the demand curve, it will charge price P_m = $122. Average total cost will be A = $94, meaning that per-unit profit is $P_m - A$ and total profit is $5 \times (P_m - A)$. Total economic profit is thus represented by the grey rectangle.

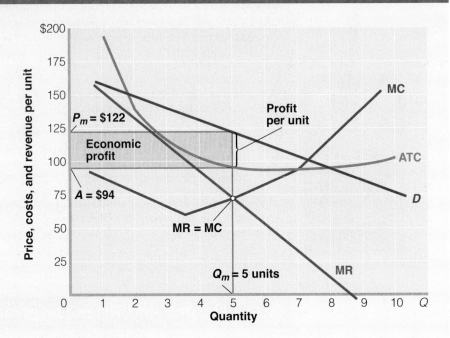

Quick Quiz

1. **The MR curve lies below the demand curve in this figure because**
   a. the demand curve is linear (a straight line).
   b. the demand curve is highly inelastic throughout its full length.
   c. the demand curve is highly elastic throughout its full length.
   d. the gain in revenue from an extra unit of output is less than the price charged for that unit of output.

2. **The area labelled "Economic profit" can be found by multiplying the difference between *P* and ATC by quantity. It also can be found by**
   a. dividing profit per unit by quantity.
   b. subtracting total cost from total revenue.
   c. multiplying the coefficient of demand elasticity by quantity.
   d. multiplying the difference between *P* and MC by quantity.

3. **This monopolist**
   a. charges the highest price it can get.
   b. earns only a normal profit in the long run.
   c. restricts output to create an insurmountable entry barrier.
   d. restricts output to increase its price and total economic profit.

4. **At this monopolist's profit-maximizing output**
   a. price equals marginal revenue.
   b. price equals marginal cost.
   c. price exceeds marginal cost.
   d. profit per unit is maximized.

Answers: 1. d; 2. b; 3. d; 4. c

WORKED
PROBLEM 8.1
Monopoly Price
and Output

Columns 2 and 5 in Table 8-1 show that, at five units of output, the product price ($122) exceeds the average total cost ($94). The monopolist thus earns an economic profit of $28 per unit and the total economic profit is $140 (= 5 units × $28). In Figure 8-4, per-unit profit is $P_m - A$, where A is the average total cost of producing Q_m units. Total economic profit is found by multiplying this per-unit profit by the profit-maximizing output Q_m.

Another way we can determine the profit-maximizing output is by comparing total revenue and total cost at each level of production and choosing the output with the greatest positive difference. Use columns 3 and 6 in Table 8-1 to verify our conclusion that five units is the profit-maximizing output. Graphing total revenue and total cost also shows the greatest difference (the maximum profit) at five units of output. Table 8-2 is a step-by-step summary of the process for determining the profit-maximizing output, the profit-maximizing price, and economic profit in monopoly. *(Key Question 5)*

No Monopoly Supply Curve

Recall that for firms in perfect competition MR equals P and the supply curve of a firm is determined by applying the MR (= P) = MC profit-maximizing rule. The supply curve for each firm is the portion of the firm's MC curve that lies above the average-variable-cost curve (see Figure 7-6).

At first glance we would suspect that the monopolist's marginal-cost curve would also be its supply curve, but that is *not* the case. *The monopolist has no supply curve.* Like the competitive firm, the monopolist equates marginal revenue and marginal cost to determine output, but for the monopolist marginal revenue is less than price. Because the monopolist does not equate marginal cost to price, it is possible for different demand conditions to bring about different prices for the same output. To understand this point, refer to Figure 8-4 and pencil in a new, steeper marginal-revenue curve that intersects the marginal-cost curve at the same point as does the present marginal-revenue curve. Then draw in a new demand curve that is roughly consistent with your new marginal-revenue curve. With the new curves, the same MR = MC output of five units now means a higher profit-maximizing price. Conclusion: There is no supply curve for the monopolist.

TABLE 8-2

Steps for Graphically Determining the Profit-Maximizing Price and Economic Profit (if any) in Monopoly

Step 1	Determine the profit-maximizing output by finding where MR = MC.
Step 2	Determine the profit-maximizing price by extending a vertical line upward from the output determined in step 1 to the monopolist's demand curve.
Step 3	Determine the monopolist's economic profit using one of two methods.

	Method 1	Find profit per unit by subtracting the average total cost of the profit-maximizing output from the profit-maximizing price. Then multiply the difference by the profit-maximizing output to determine economic profit (if any).
	Method 2	Find total cost by multiplying the average total cost of the profit-maximizing output by that output. Find total revenue by multiplying the profit-maximizing output by the profit-maximizing price. Then subtract total cost from total revenue to determine economic profit (if any).

Misconceptions about Monopoly Pricing

Our analysis exposes two fallacies about the behaviour of a monopolist.

- **Not the Highest Price** Because a monopolist can manipulate output and price, people often believe it will charge the highest price it can get. That is incorrect. Prices above P_m in Figure 8-4 yield less than maximum total profit. The monopolist seeks maximum total profit, not maximum price. Prices above P_m would reduce sales and total revenue by more than a decrease in total cost.

- **Total, Not Unit, Profit** The monopolist seeks maximum total profit, not maximum unit profit. In Figure 8-4 a comparison of the vertical distance between average total cost and price at various possible outputs indicates that per-unit profit is greater at a point slightly to the left of the profit-maximizing output Q_m. This is shown in Table 8-1 where unit profit at four units of output is $32 (= $132 − $100) compared with $28 (= $122 − $94) at the profit-maximizing output of five units. Here the monopolist accepts a lower-than-maximum per-unit profit because additional sales more than compensate for the lower unit profit. A profit-maximizing monopolist prefers to sell five units at a profit of $28 per unit (for a total profit of $140) than four units at a profit of $32 per unit (for a total profit of only $128).

Possibility of Losses by Monopolist

The likelihood of economic profit is greater for a monopolist than for a firm in perfect competition; in the long run only a normal profit is possible in a perfectly competitive industry, whereas barriers to entry mean that for the monopolist economic profits can persist. In monopoly there are no new entrants to increase supply, drive down price, and eliminate economic profit.

But monopoly does not *guarantee* profit. The monopolist is not immune to changes in tastes that reduce the demand for its product. Nor is it immune to upward-shifting cost curves caused by escalating prices of factors of production. If the demand and cost situation faced by the monopolist is far less favourable than that in Figure 8-4, the monopolist will incur losses in the short run. Despite its dominance in the market, the monopoly enterprise in Figure 8-5 suffers a loss, as shown, because of weak demand and relatively high costs. Yet it will continue to operate because its total loss is less than its fixed cost. More precisely, at output Q_m the monopolist's price P_m exceeds its average variable cost V. Its loss per unit is $A − P_m$, and the total loss is shown by the pink rectangle.

Like a firm in perfect competition, the monopolist will not operate at a loss in the long run. Faced with continuing losses, in the long run the firm's owners will move their resources to other industries that offer better profit opportunities. A monopolist such as the one depicted in Figure 8-5 must obtain a minimum of a normal profit in the long run or it will go out of business.

FIGURE 8·5   The Loss-Minimizing Position of a Monopolist

If demand *D* is weak and costs are high, the monopolist may be unable to make a profit. Because P_m exceeds *V*, the average variable cost at the MR = MC output Q_m, the monopolist will minimize losses in the short run by producing at that output. The loss per unit is $A − P_m$, and the total loss is indicated by the pink rectangle.

8.3 | Economic Effects of Monopoly

Let's now evaluate monopoly from the standpoint of society as a whole. The standard reference for this evaluation is the long-run efficiency in a perfectly competitive market, identified by the triple equality $P = \text{MC} = \text{minimum ATC}$.

Price, Output, and Efficiency

Figure 8-6 graphically contrasts the price, output, and efficiency outcomes of monopoly and a perfectly competitive *industry*. Recall that in perfect competition at the equilibrium price–output combination both productive efficiency and allocative efficiency are achieved. *Productive efficiency* is achieved because competitive pressures force firms to operate where average total cost is at a minimum, Q_c. Product price is at the lowest level consistent with minimum average total cost. Also, *allocative efficiency* is achieved because production occurs up to that output at which price (the measure of a product's value or marginal benefit to society) equals marginal cost (the worth of the alternative products forgone by society in producing any given commodity). In short: $P = \text{MC} = \text{minimum ATC}$.

Now let's suppose that this industry becomes a monopoly (Figure 8-6b) as a result of one firm acquiring all its competitors. We also assume that no changes in costs or market demand result from this dramatic change in the industry structure. What were formerly thousands of competing firms is now a single monopolist.

The competitive market supply curve S has become the marginal-cost curve (MC) of the monopolist. (Since the monopolist does not have a supply curve as such, we have removed the S label.) The important change, however, is on the demand side. From the viewpoint of each individual competitive firm, demand was perfectly elastic, and marginal revenue was therefore equal to price.

FIGURE 8-6

Inefficiency of Monopoly Relative to a Perfectly Competitive Industry

Panel (a): In a perfectly competitive industry, entry and exit of firms ensures that price (P_c) equals marginal cost (MC) and that the minimum average-total-cost output (Q_c) is produced. Both productive efficiency ($P = $ minimum ATC) and allocative efficiency ($P = \text{MC}$) are obtained. Panel (b): In monopoly, the MR curve lies below the demand curve. The monopolist maximizes profit at output Q_m, where MR = MC, and charges price P_m. Thus, output is lower (Q_m rather than Q_c) and price is higher (P_m rather than P_c) than they would be in a perfectly competitive industry. Monopoly is inefficient, since output is less than that required for achieving minimum ATC (here at Q_c) and because the monopolist's price exceeds MC.

(a) Perfectly competitive industry

(b) Monopoly

Each firm equated MR (= price) and MC in maximizing profits. But market demand and individual demand are the same to the monopolist. The firm *is* the industry, and thus the monopolist sees the downsloping demand curve D shown in Figure 8-6b.

This means that marginal revenue is less than price, and that graphically the MR curve lies below demand curve D. In using the MR = MC rule, the monopolist selects output Q_m and price P_m. A comparison of both graphs in Figure 8-6 reveals that the monopolist finds it profitable to sell a smaller output at a higher price than would prevail in a competitive industry.

Monopoly yields neither productive nor allocative efficiency. The monopolist's output is less than Q_c, the output at which average total cost is lowest. And price is higher than the competitive price P_c, which in the long-run equilibrium of competitive firms equals minimum average total cost. Thus, the monopoly price *exceeds* minimum average total cost. Also, at the monopolist's Q_m output, product price is considerably higher than marginal cost, which means that society values additional units of the monopolist's output more highly than it values the alternative products the resources could otherwise produce. So the monopolist's profit-maximizing output results in an underallocation of resources. The monopolist finds it profitable to restrict output and therefore employ fewer resources than are justified from society's standpoint. So the monopolist does not achieve allocative efficiency.

As confirmed by the blue triangle labelled *abc* in Figure 8-6, monopoly creates an efficiency loss (or deadweight loss) for society. The sum of consumer surplus and producer surplus is not maximized. In monopoly, then,

- *P* exceeds MC
- *P* exceeds lowest ATC
- an efficiency loss occurs (the sum of consumer surplus + producer surplus is less than maximum).

Section 8.6 presents a more detailed discussion of the efficiency loss brought about by monopoly.

Income Transfer

In general, a monopoly transfers income from consumers to shareholders who own the monopoly. Because of its market power, a monopolist charges a higher price than would a perfectly competitive firm with the same costs; in effect, it levies a "private tax" on consumers and often obtains substantial economic profits. Monopoly profit is not equally distributed, because corporate stock is largely owned by high-income groups. The owners of a monopoly are enriched at the expense of the rest of consumers who "overpay" for the product. Because, on average, these owners have more income than the buyers, monopoly increases income inequality.

Cost Complications

Our evaluation of monopoly has led us to conclude that, given identical costs, a monopolist will charge a higher price, produce a smaller output, and allocate economic resources less efficiently than a perfectly competitive industry. These inferior results are rooted in the entry barriers characterizing monopoly.

But costs may not be the same for a firm in a perfectly competitive industry and a monopolist. The unit cost incurred by a monopolist may be either larger or smaller than that incurred by a firm in a competitive industry. There are four reasons why costs may differ: (1) economies of scale, (2) a phenomenon called *X-inefficiency*, (3) the need for monopoly-preserving expenditures, and (4) the very long-run perspective, which allows for technological advance.

ECONOMIES OF SCALE ONCE AGAIN

Where economies of scale are extensive, market demand may not be sufficient to support a large number of competing firms, each producing at minimum efficient scale. In such cases, an industry of one or two firms will have a lower average total cost than the same industry made up of numerous competitive firms. At the extreme, only a single firm—a natural monopoly—might be able to achieve the lowest long-run average total cost.

Some firms whose business is in new information technologies—computer software, Internet service, wireless communications—have displayed extensive economies of scale. As these firms have grown, their long-run average total costs have declined. Greater use of specialized inputs, the spreading of product development costs, and learning by doing all have produced economies of scale. Also, *simultaneous consumption* and *network effects* have reduced costs.

simultaneous consumption
A product's ability to satisfy a large number of consumers at the same time.

A product's ability to satisfy a large number of consumers at the same time is called **simultaneous consumption** (or *nonrivalrous consumption*). Dell Computers needs to produce a personal computer for each customer, but Microsoft needs to produce its Windows program only once. Then, at very low marginal cost, Microsoft delivers its program by disc to millions of consumers. Similar low cost of delivering product to additional customers is true for Internet service providers, such as Rogers and Bell Canada, music producers, and wireless communication firms such as Research In Motion and Telus. Because marginal costs are so low, the average total cost of output declines as more customers are added.

network effects
Increases in the value of a product to each user, including existing users, as the total number of users rises.

Network effects are increases in the value of a product to each user, including existing users, as the total number of users rises. Good examples are computer software, cell phones, social networking software, palm computers, and other products related to the Internet. When others have Internet service and devices to access it, you can conveniently send email messages to them. When they have similar software, you can easily pass around attachments like spreadsheets and photos. The more people connected to the product, the more its benefits to each person are magnified.

Such network effects may drive a market toward monopoly, because consumers tend to choose standard products that everyone else is using. The focused demand for these products permits their producers to grow rapidly and thus achieve economies of scale. Smaller firms, which either have higher-cost "right" products or "wrong" products, get acquired or go out of business.

Economists generally agree that some new information firms have not yet exhausted their economies of scale, but it is questionable whether such firms are truly natural monopolies. Most firms eventually achieve their minimum efficient scale at less than the full size of the market. That means competition among firms is possible.

But even if natural monopoly develops, it's unlikely the monopolist will pass cost reductions along to consumers. So, with perhaps a handful of exceptions, economies of scale do not change the general conclusion that monopolies are inefficient relative to more competitive industries.

ORIGIN 8.3
X-Inefficiency

X-inefficiency
The production of output, whatever its level, at higher average (and total) cost than is necessary.

X-INEFFICIENCY

In constructing all the average-total-cost curves used in this book, we have assumed that the firm uses the most efficient technology. In other words, it uses the technology that permits it to achieve the lowest average total cost of whatever level of output it chooses to produce. **X-inefficiency** occurs when a firm's actual cost of producing any output is greater than the lowest possible cost of producing it. In Figure 8-7, X-inefficiency is represented by operation at points X and X′ above the lowest-cost ATC curve. At these points, per-unit costs are ATC_x (as opposed to ATC_1) for output Q_1 and $ATC_{x'}$ (as opposed to ATC_2) for output Q_2. Producing at any point above the average-total-cost curve in Figure 8-7 reflects inefficiency or bad management by the firm.

Why does X-inefficiency occur if it reduces profits? The answer is that managers of a firm may have goals such as expanding power, an easier work life, avoiding business risk, or giving jobs to incompetent relatives, all which conflict with cost minimization. Or X-inefficiency may arise because a firm's workers are poorly motivated or ineffectively supervised. Or a firm may simply become lethargic and inert, relying on rules of thumb in decision making as opposed to relevant calculations of costs and revenues.

FIGURE 8-7   X-Inefficiency

The average-total-cost curve (ATC) is assumed to reflect the minimum cost of producing each particular unit of output. Any point above this lowest-cost ATC curve, such as X or X', implies X-inefficiency: operation at greater than lowest cost for a particular level of output.

For our purposes the relevant question is whether a monopolist suffers more X-inefficiency than competitive firms do. There is evidence that it does. Firms in competitive industries are continually under pressure from rivals, forcing them to be internally efficient to survive. But monopolists are sheltered from such competitive forces by entry barriers, and that lack of pressure may lead to X-inefficiency.

RENT-SEEKING EXPENDITURES

rent-seeking behaviour
The actions by persons, firms, or unions to gain special benefits from government at taxpayers' or someone else's expense.

Rent-seeking behaviour is an activity designed to transfer income or wealth to a particular firm or resource supplier at someone else's, or even society's, expense. We have seen that a monopolist can obtain an economic profit even in the long run. Therefore, it is no surprise that a firm may go to great expense to acquire or maintain a monopoly granted by government through legislation or an exclusive licence. Such rent-seeking expenditures add nothing to the firm's output, but they clearly increase its costs. Taken alone, rent seeking implies that monopoly has even higher costs and less efficiency than suggested in Figure 8-6b.

TECHNOLOGICAL ADVANCE

In the very long run, firms can reduce their costs through the discovery and implementation of new technology. If monopolists are more likely than competitive firms to develop more efficient production techniques over time, then the inefficiency of monopoly might be overstated.

The general view of economists is that a monopolist will not be technologically progressive. Although its economic profit provides ample means to finance research and development, it has little incentive to implement new techniques (or products). Because of its sheltered market position, the monopolist can afford to be inefficient and lethargic; there simply is no penalty for being so.

One caveat: Research and technological advance can be a barrier to entry. Thus, the monopolist may continuously seek technological advance to avoid falling prey to new rivals. In this case, technological advance is essential to maintaining monopoly. But it is potential competition—not the monopoly market structure—that drives this technological advance. By assumption, no such competition exists in the monopoly model; entry is completely blocked.

Assessment and Policy Options

Monopoly is a legitimate concern because the monopolist can charge higher-than-competitive prices that result in an underallocation of resources. Monopolists can stifle innovation, foster X-inefficiency, and engage in rent-seeking behaviour. Even when their costs are low because of economies of scale, monopolists are unlikely to charge a price that reflects those low costs. The cost savings may simply accrue to the monopoly as greater economic profit.

Fortunately, however, monopoly is not widespread in the Canadian economy. Barriers to entry are seldom completely successful. Although research and technological advance may strengthen the market position of a monopoly, technology may also undermine monopoly power. Over time, the creation of new technologies may work to destroy monopoly positions. For example, the development of courier delivery, fax machines, and email has eroded the monopoly power of Canada Post Corporation. Cable television monopolies are now challenged by satellite TV and by new technologies that permit the transmission of audio and visual signals over the Internet.

Similarly, patents eventually expire—and even before they do, the development of new and distinct products can undermine existing patent advantages. New sources of monopolized resources can be found, and competition from foreign firms may emerge (see Global Perspective 8.1). Finally, if a monopoly is sufficiently fearful of future competition from new products, it may keep its prices relatively low to discourage rivals from developing such products. If so, consumers may pay nearly competitive prices even though present competition is lacking.

So what should government do about monopoly when it arises in the real world? Government needs to look carefully at monopoly on a case-by-case basis. Three general policy options are available:

1. If the monopoly is achieved and sustained through anticompetitive actions, creates substantial economic inefficiency, and appears to be long lasting, the government can file charges against the monopoly under Canada's anticombines laws. If found guilty of monopoly abuse, the firm can either be prohibited from engaging in certain business activities or broken into two or more competing firms.

2. If the monopoly is a natural monopoly, it may be allowed to continue expanding. If no competition emerges from new products, government may then decide to regulate its prices and operations.

3. If the monopoly appears to be unsustainable over a long period, say because of emerging new technology, government can simply choose to ignore it.

8.1 | GLOBAL PERSPECTIVE

Competition from foreign multinational corporations

Competition from foreign multinational corporations diminishes the market power of firms in Canada. Here are just a few of the hundreds of foreign multinational corporations that compete strongly with Canadian firms in certain Canadian markets.

Source: Compiled from the Fortune 500 listing of the world's largest firms, www.fortune.com.

Company (country)	Main products
Bayer (Germany)	chemicals
BP Amoco (United Kingdom)	gasoline
Michelin (France)	tires
NEC (Japan)	computers
Nestlé (Switzerland)	food products
Nokia (Finland)	wireless phones
Royal Dutch/Shell (Netherlands)	gasoline
Royal Philips (Netherlands)	electronics
Sony (Japan)	electronics
Toyota (Japan)	automobiles
Unilever (Netherlands)	food products

8.4 | Price Discrimination

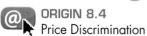

@ ORIGIN 8.4
Price Discrimination

price discrimination
Selling a product to different buyers at different prices when the price differences are not justified by differences in cost.

We have assumed in this chapter that the monopolist charges a single price to all buyers. But under certain conditions the monopolist can increase its profit by charging different prices to different buyers. In so doing, the monopolist is engaging in **price discrimination,** the practice of selling a product or service at more than one price when the price differences are not justified by cost differences. Price discrimination can take three forms:

- Charging each customer in a single market the maximum price she or he is willing to pay.
- Charging each customer one price for the first set of units purchased and a lower price for subsequent units purchased.
- Charging some customers one price and other customers another price.

Conditions

The opportunity to engage in price discrimination is not readily available to all sellers. Price discrimination is possible when the following conditions are met:

- *Monopoly Power*   The seller must be a monopolist with some ability to control output and price.
- *Market Segregation*   The seller must be able to segregate buyers into distinct classes, each of which has a different willingness or ability to pay for the product. This separation of buyers is usually based on different price elasticities of demand, as the examples that follow will make clear.
- *No Resale*   The original purchaser cannot resell the product or service. If buyers in the low-price segment of the market could easily resell in the high-price segment, the monopolist's price-discrimination strategy would create competition in the high-price segment. This competition would reduce the price in the high-price segment and undermine the monopolist's price-discrimination policy. This suggests that service industries such as transportation or legal and medical services, where resale is impossible, are good candidates for price discrimination.

Examples of Price Discrimination

Price discrimination is widely practised in the Canadian economy. For example, we noted in Chapter 4's The Last Word that airlines, such as Air Canada, charge high fares to travelling executives, whose demand for travel is inelastic, and offer lower highly restricted, nonrefundable fares to attract vacationers and others whose demands are more elastic.

Movie theatres and golf courses vary their charges on the basis of time (higher rates in the evening and on weekends when demand is strong) and age (ability to pay). Railways vary the rate charged per tonne-kilometre of freight according to the market value of the product being shipped; the shipper of 10 tonnes of television sets or costume jewellery is charged more than the shipper of 10 tonnes of gravel or coal.

Issuing discount coupons redeemable at purchase is a form of price discrimination. It enables firms to give price discounts to their most price-sensitive customers who have elastic demand. Less price-sensitive consumers who have less elastic demand are not as likely to take the time to clip and redeem coupons. The firm thus makes a larger profit than if it had used a single-price, no-coupon strategy.

Price discrimination can often occur in international trade. A Russian aluminum producer, for example, might sell aluminum for less in Canada than in Russia. In Canada, this seller faces an elastic demand because several substitute suppliers are available. But in Russia, where the manufacturer dominates the market and trade barriers impede imports, consumers have fewer choices and thus demand is less elastic. (See the Consider This box for another example of price discrimination.)

Graphical Analysis

Figure 8-8 demonstrates graphically the most common form of price discrimination—charging different prices to different classes of buyers. The two side-to-side graphs are for a monopolist selling its product, say, software, in two segregated parts of the market. Figure 8-8a illustrates demand for software by small-business customers; Figure 8-8b illustrates demand for software by students. Student versions of the software are identical to the versions sold to businesses but are available (one per person) only to customers with a student ID. Presumably, students have lower ability to pay for the software and are charged a discounted price.

The demand curve D_b, in the graph to the left, indicates a relatively inelastic demand for the product on the part of business customers. The demand curve D_s, located in the right-hand graph, reflects the more elastic demand of students. The marginal revenue curves (MR_b and MR_s) lie below their respective demand curves, reflecting the demand–marginal revenue relationship previously described.

For visual clarity we have assumed that average total cost (ATC) is constant. Therefore, marginal cost (MC) equals ATC at all quantities of output. These costs are the same for both versions of the software and therefore appear as the identical straight lines labelled "MC = ATC."

What price will the monopolist charge to each set of customers? Using the MR = MC rule for profit maximization, the firm will offer Q_b units of the software for sale to small businesses. It can sell that profit-maximizing output by charging price P_b. Again using the MR = MC rule, the monopolist will offer Q_s units of software to students. To sell those Q_s units, the firm will charge students the lower price P_s.

CONSIDER THIS | Price Discrimination at the Ballpark

Professional baseball teams such as the Montreal Expos and the Toronto Blue Jays earn substantial revenues through ticket sales. To maximize profit they offer significantly lower ticket prices for youths (whose demand is elastic) than for adults (whose demand is inelastic). This discount may be as much as 50 percent.

If this type of price discrimination increases revenue and profit, why don't teams also price discriminate at the concession stands? Why don't they offer half-price hot dogs, soft drinks, and peanuts to children?

The answer involves the three requirements for successful price discrimination. All three requirements are met for game tickets: (1) the team has monopoly power; (2) it can segregate ticket buyers by age group, each group having a different elasticity of demand; and (3) youths cannot resell their discounted tickets to adults.

It's a different situation at the concession stands. Specifically, the third condition is *not* met. If the team had dual prices, it could not prevent the exchange or "resale" of the concession goods from youths to adults. Many adults would send youths to buy food and soft drinks for them: "Here's some money, Billy. Go buy *six* hot dogs." In this case, price discrimination would reduce, not increase, team profit. Thus, youths and adults are charged the same high prices at the concession stands. (These prices are high relative to those for the same goods at the local convenience store because the stadium sellers have a captive audience and thus considerable monopoly power.)

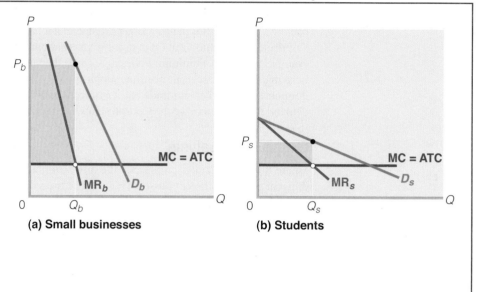

FIGURE 8-8   **Price Discrimination to Different Groups of Buyers**

The price-discriminating monopolist represented here maximizes its total profit by dividing the market into two segments based on differences in elasticity of demand. It then produces and sells the MR = MC output in each market segment. (For visual clarity, average total cost (ATC) is assumed to be constant. Therefore MC equals ATC at all output levels.) Panel (a): The firm charges a higher price (here, P_b) to customers who have a less elastic demand curve and in panel (b) a lower price (here, P_s) to customers with a more elastic demand. The price discriminator's total profit is larger than it would be with no discrimination and therefore a single price.

(a) Small businesses

(b) Students

Firms engage in price discrimination because it enhances their profit. The numbers (not shown) behind the curves in Figure 8-8 would clearly reveal that the sum of the two profit rectangles shown in colour exceeds the single profit rectangle the firm would obtain from a single monopoly price. How do consumers fare? In this case, students clearly benefit by paying a lower price than they would if the firm charged a single monopoly price; in contrast, the price discrimination results in a higher price for business customers. Therefore, compared to the single-price situation, students buy more of the software and small businesses buy less.

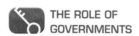

**WORKED
PROBLEM 8.2**
Price Discrimination

Such price discrimination is widespread in the economy and is illegal only when it is part of a firm's strategy to lessen or eliminate competition. We will discuss illegal price discrimination in Chapter 10 where we discuss anticombines policy. *(Key Question 6)*

8.5 | Regulated Monopoly

**THE ROLE OF
GOVERNMENTS**

Natural monopolies traditionally have been subject to *rate regulation* (price regulation), although the recent trend has been to deregulate those parts of the industries where competition seems possible. For example, long-distance phone service, natural gas distribution, wireless communication, cable television, and long-distance electricity transmission have been, to one degree or another, deregulated over the past several decades. And regulators in some provinces are beginning to allow new entrants to compete with local telephone and electricity providers. Nevertheless, provincial and local regulatory commissions still regulate the prices that most local natural gas distributors, regional telephone companies, and local electricity suppliers can charge. These locally regulated monopolies are commonly called "public utilities."

Let's consider the regulation of a local natural monopoly, for example a firm selling natural gas. Figure 8-9 shows the demand and long-run cost curves facing our firm. Because of extensive economies of scale, the demand curve cuts the natural monopolist's long-run average-total-cost curve at a point where that curve is still falling. It would be inefficient to have several firms in this industry because each firm's lowest average total cost would be substantially higher than that of a single firm. So, this circumstance requires a single seller.

We know by application of the MR = MC rule that Q_m and P_m are the profit-maximizing output and price that an unregulated monopolist would choose. Because price exceeds average total cost at output Q_m, the monopolist enjoys a substantial economic profit. Furthermore, price exceeds marginal cost, indicating an underallocation of resources to this product or service. Can government regulation bring about better results from society's point of view?

Socially Optimal Price: P = MC

If the objective of a regulatory commission is to achieve allocative efficiency, it should establish a legal (ceiling) price for the monopolist equal to marginal cost. We see that P_r is the only price on the demand curve equal to marginal cost. The ceiling price effectively causes the monopolist's demand curve to become horizontal (indicating perfectly elastic demand) from zero out to point r, where the regulated price ceases to be effective. Also, out to point r we have MR = P_r.

Confronted with the ceiling price P_r, the monopolist will maximize profit or minimize loss by producing Q_r units of output, because at this output MR $(= P_r)$ = MC. By making it illegal to charge more than P_r per unit, the regulatory agency has removed the monopolist's incentive to restrict output to Q_m to obtain a higher price and greater profit.

In short, the regulatory commission can simulate the allocative forces of pure competition by imposing the legal price P_r and letting the monopolist choose its profit-maximizing or loss-minimizing output. Production takes place where P_r = MC, and this equality indicates an efficient allocation of resources to this product or service. The price that achieves allocative efficiency is called the **socially optimal price.**

socially optimal price
The price of a product that results in the most efficient allocation of an economy's resources.

Fair-Return Price: P = ATC

But the socially optimal price, P_r, that equals marginal cost may be so low that average total costs are not covered, as is the case in Figure 8-9. The result is a loss for the firm. The reason is that our firm is required to meet the heaviest peak demands (both daily and seasonally) for natural gas, and thus must maintain substantial excess production capacity when demand is relatively "normal." Its high level of investment in production facilities and economies of scale mean that its average total cost is likely to be greater than its marginal cost over a very wide range of outputs. In particular, as in Figure 8-9, average total cost is likely to be greater than the price P_r at the intersection of the demand curve and marginal-cost curve. Therefore, forcing the socially optimal price P_r on the regulated monopolist would result in short-run losses and long-run bankruptcy for the utility.

FIGURE 8-9   **Regulated Monopoly**

The socially optimal price P_r, found where D and MC intersect, will result in an efficient allocation of resources but may entail losses to the monopoly. The fair-return price P_f will allow the monopolist to break even but will not fully correct the underallocation of resources.

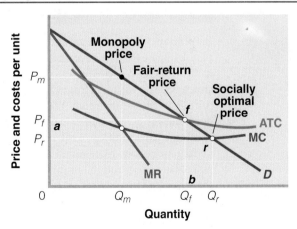

What to do? One option is to provide a public subsidy to cover the loss that marginal-cost pricing would entail. Another possibility is to condone price discrimination and hope that the additional revenue gained will permit the firm to cover costs.

In practice, regulatory commissions have often pursued a third option: They modify the objective of allocative efficiency and $P = \text{MC}$ pricing. Most regulatory agencies in Canada establish a **fair-return price.**

fair-return price
The price of a product that enables its producer to obtain a normal profit and that is equal to the average cost of producing it.

Since total cost includes a normal or "fair" profit, we see in Figure 8-9 that a fair-return price is on the average-total-cost curve. Because the demand curve cuts average total cost only at point f, clearly P_f is the only price on the demand curve that permits a fair return. The corresponding output at regulated price P_f will be Q_f. Total revenue of $0afb$ will equal the utility's total cost of the same amount, and the firm will realize a normal profit.

Dilemma of Regulation

Comparing results of the socially optimal price ($P = \text{MC}$) and the fair-return price ($P = \text{ATC}$) suggests a policy dilemma, sometimes termed the *dilemma of regulation*. When its price is set to achieve the most efficient allocation of resources ($P = \text{MC}$), the regulated monopoly is likely to suffer losses. Survival of the firm would depend on permanent public subsidies from tax revenues. Conversely, although a fair-return price ($P = \text{ATC}$) allows the monopolist to cover costs, it only partially resolves the underallocation of resources that the unregulated monopoly price would foster. That is, the fair-return price would increase output only from Q_m to Q_f in Figure 8-9, while the socially optimal output is Q_r. Despite this dilemma, regulation can improve on the results of monopoly from the social point of view. Price regulation (even at the fair-return price) can simultaneously reduce price, increase output, and reduce the economic profits of monopolies. *(Key Question 13)*

That said, we need to provide an important caution: "Fair-price" regulation of monopoly looks rather simple in theory but is amazingly complex in reality. In the actual economy, rate regulation is accompanied by large, expensive rate-setting bureaucracies and maze-like sets of procedures. Also, rate decisions require extensive public input via letters and through public hearings. Rate decisions are subject to lengthy legal challenges. Further, because regulatory commissions must set prices sufficiently above costs to create fair returns, regulated monopolists have little incentive to minimize average total costs. When these costs creep up, the regulatory commissions must set higher prices.

Regulated firms therefore are noted for higher-than-competitive wages, more managers and staff than necessary, nicer-than-typical office buildings, and other forms of X-inefficiency. These inefficiencies help explain the trend of federal, provincial, and municipal governments to abandon price regulation where the possibility of competition looks promising.

8.6 | Monopoly and Deadweight Loss

In Section 8.3 we briefly restated the efficiency of monopoly using consumer surplus and producer surplus. In Figure 8-10 we have once again put a perfectly competitive industry alongside a monopoly to compare them. We have indicated the extent of consumer and producer surplus in each of the market structures. You will recall from Chapter 7 that in a perfectly competitive market structure, equilibrium price P_c ($= \text{MC} = $ minimum ATC) will create the maximum amount of consumer surplus and producer surplus, as indicated in Figure 8-10a. We also noted that in perfect competition marginal benefit equals marginal cost (MB = MC) at the equilibrium price and quantity, ensuring allocative efficiency.

deadweight loss
The loss of consumer surplus and producer surplus when output is either above or below its efficient level.

In a monopoly, represented in Figure 8-10b, the output is lower than in a perfect competitive market structure, and the profit-maximizing price P_m is above P_c, so consumers pay a price above the firm's (and the industry's) MC. At the lower output Q_m, the sum of consumer surplus and producer surplus has been reduced, compared to the perfect-competition scenario. The net loss of consumer surplus and producer surplus is referred to as **deadweight loss** of monopoly, and is indicated by the

| FIGURE 8-10 | Monopoly and Deadweight Loss |

Panel (a): In perfect competition the long-run equilibrium price (P_c) and quantity (Q_c) maximize the sum of consumer surplus and producer surplus. Panel (b): A monopolist restricts output to Q_m and increases price to P_m. Although the monopolist gains, a deadweight loss is created as a result of the lower consumer surplus brought about by the fall in output and rise in price.

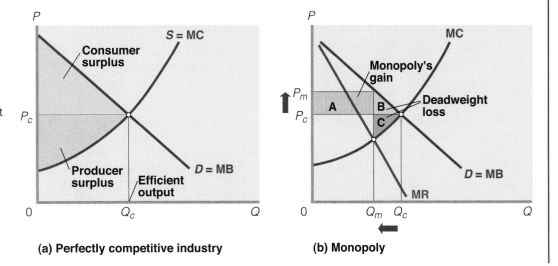

(a) Perfectly competitive industry   (b) Monopoly

area covered by triangles B and C. At output Q_m, marginal benefit is greater than marginal cost (MB > MC), indicating that the monopolist is not producing as much output as consumers would like. Thus, allocative efficiency is not achieved.

Figure 8-10b shows that there has been a redistribution of resources from the consumer to the monopolist. The higher price results in a gain for the monopolist, represented by the grey area A. Consumers lose the consumer surplus represented by areas A and B, while the monopolist loses the producer surplus represented by area C, but gains area A. The monopolist will enjoy a net gain if its gain (area A) is larger than its loss of producer surplus (area C). The monopolist's gain is the difference between the monopoly price (P_m) and the equilibrium price in perfect competition (P_c) multiplied by the quantity sold (Q_m).

QUICK REVIEW

▶ Price discrimination occurs when a firm sells a product at different prices that are not based on cost differences.

▶ The conditions necessary for price discrimination are (1) monopoly power, (2) the ability to segregate buyers based on demand elasticities, and (3) the inability of buyers to resell the product.

▶ Compared with single pricing by a monopolist, perfect price discrimination results in greater profit and greater output. Many consumers pay higher prices, but other buyers pay prices below the single price.

▶ Monopoly price can be reduced and output increased through government regulation.

▶ The socially optimal price (P = MC) achieves allocative efficiency but may result in losses; the fair-return price (P = ATC) yields a normal profit but falls short of allocative efficiency.

▶ The inefficiency brought about by monopoly is referred to as deadweight loss.

The **LAST WORD**   De Beers Diamonds: Are Monopolies Forever?

De Beers was one of the world's strongest and most enduring monopolies.
But in mid-2000 it announced that it could no longer control the supply of diamonds
and thus would abandon its 66-year policy of monopolizing the diamond trade.

De Beers, a Swiss-based cartel controlled by a South African corporation, produces about 45 percent of the world's rough-cut diamonds and purchases for resale a sizable number of the rough-cut diamonds produced by other mines worldwide. As a result, De Beers markets 55 percent of the world's diamonds to a select group of diamond cutters and dealers—but that percentage has declined from 80 percent in the mid-1980s and continues to shrink. Therein lies De Beers' problem.

Classic Monopoly Behaviour De Beers' past monopoly behaviour and results are a classic example of the unregulated monopoly model illustrated in Figure 8-4. No matter how many diamonds it mined or purchased, De Beers sold only that quantity of diamonds that would yield an appropriate (monopoly) price. That price was well above production costs, and De Beers and its partners earned monopoly profits.

When demand fell, De Beers reduced its sales to maintain price. The excess of production over sales was then reflected in growing diamond stockpiles held by De Beers. It also attempted to bolster demand through advertising ("Diamonds are forever"). When demand was strong, it increased sales by reducing its diamond inventories.

De Beers used several methods to control the production of many mines it did not own. First, it convinced a number of independent producers that *single-channel* or monopoly marketing through De Beers would maximize their profit. Second, mines that circumvented

De Beers often found their market suddenly flooded with similar diamonds from De Beers' vast stockpiles. The resulting price decline and loss of profit often would encourage the "rogue" mine into the De Beers fold. Finally, De Beers simply purchased and stockpiled diamonds produced by independent mines so their added supplies would not undercut the market.

The End of an Era? Several factors have come together to unravel the monopoly. New diamond discoveries resulted in a growing leakage of diamonds into world markets outside De Beers' control. For example, significant prospecting and trading in Angola occurred. Recent Canadian diamond discoveries, in the Northwest Territories, pose another threat. Although De Beers is a participant in Canada, a large uncontrolled supply of diamonds is expected to emerge. Similarly, Russia's diamond monopoly, Alrosa, has recently agreed with European antitrust authorities to sell progressively larger quantities of diamonds directly

to the international diamond market rather than continuing to market them through De Beers.

If that were not enough, Australian diamond producer Argyle opted to withdraw from the De Beers monopoly. Its annual production of mostly low-grade industrial diamonds accounts for about 6 percent of the global $8 billion diamond market. The international media has begun to focus heavily on the role that diamonds play in financing the bloody civil wars in Africa. Fearing a consumer boycott of diamonds, De Beers has pledged not to buy these conflict diamonds or do business with any firm that does. These diamonds, however, continue to find their way into the marketplace, eluding De Beers' control.

In mid-2000 De Beers abandoned its attempt to control the supply of diamonds. It announced that it planned to transform itself from a diamond cartel to a modern firm selling premium diamonds and other luxury goods under the De Beers label. It therefore would gradually reduce its $4 billion stockpile of diamonds and turn its efforts to increasing the overall demand for diamonds through advertising. De Beers proclaimed that it was changing its strategy to being "the diamond supplier of choice."

Diamonds may be forever, but not necessarily the De Beers monopoly. Nevertheless, with high market share and ability to control its own production levels, De Beers will continue to wield considerable influence over the price of rough-cut diamonds.

Question

How was De Beers able to control the world price of diamonds over the past several decades even though it produced only 50 percent of the diamonds? What factors ended its monopoly? What is De Beers' new strategy for earning economic profit, rather than just normal profit?

CHAPTER SUMMARY

8.1 ▶ CHARACTERISTICS OF MONOPOLY

- A monopolist is the sole producer of a commodity for which there are no close substitutes.

- The existence of monopoly and other imperfectly competitive market structures is explained by barriers to entry, in the form of (a) economies of scale, (b) patents and licences, (c) ownership or control of essential factors of production, and (d) pricing and other strategic behaviour.

- The monopolist's market situation differs from that of a competitive firm in that the monopolist's demand curve is downsloping, causing the marginal-revenue curve to lie below the demand curve. Like the competitive seller, the monopolist will maximize profit by equating marginal revenue and marginal cost. Barriers to entry may permit a monopolist to acquire economic profit even in the long run. However, (a) the monopolist does not charge the highest price it can get; (b) the price that yields maximum total profit to the monopolist rarely coincides with the price that yields maximum unit profit; (c) high costs and a weak demand may prevent the monopolist from realizing any profit at all; and (d) the monopolist avoids the inelastic region of its demand curve.

8.2 ▶ OUTPUT AND PRICE DETERMINATION IN MONOPOLY

- With the same costs, the monopolist will find it profitable to restrict output and charge a higher price than would sellers in a purely competitive industry. This restriction of output causes resources to be misallocated, as is shown by the fact that price exceeds marginal cost in monopolized markets.

8.3 ▶ ECONOMIC EFFECTS OF MONOPOLY

- In general, monopoly increases income inequality by transferring income from consumers to the owners of the monopoly. Monopoly creates an efficiency loss for society.

- The costs monopolists and competitive producers face may not be the same. On the one hand, economies of scale may make lower unit costs available to monopolists but not to competitors, and monopoly may be more likely than perfect competition to reduce costs via technological advance because of the monopolist's ability to realize economic profit, which can be used to finance research. On the other hand, X-inefficiency is more common among monopolists than among competitive firms. Also, monopolists may make costly expenditures to maintain monopoly privileges that are conferred by government. Finally, the blocked entry of rival firms weakens the monopolist's incentive to be technologically progressive.

8.4 ▶ PRICE DISCRIMINATION

- A monopolist can increase its profit by practising price discrimination, provided (a) it can segregate buyers on the basis of elasticities of demand, and (b) its product or service cannot be readily transferred between the segregated markets.

8.5 ▶ REGULATED MONOPOLY

- Price regulation can be invoked to wholly or partially eliminate the tendency of monopolists to underallocate resources and to earn economic profits. The socially optimal price is determined where the demand and marginal-cost curves intersect; the fair-return price is determined where the demand and average-total-cost curves intersect.

8.6 ▶ MONOPOLY AND DEADWEIGHT LOSS

- The inefficiency of monopoly can be measured using the concepts of consumer surplus and producer surplus. The efficiency loss associated with monopoly is called deadweight loss.

TERMS AND CONCEPTS

monopoly, p. 193
barriers to entry, p. 193
simultaneous consumption, p. 205
network effects, p. 205

X-inefficiency, p. 205
rent-seeking behaviour, p. 206
price discrimination, p. 208
socially optimal price, p. 211

fair-return price, p. 212
deadweight loss, p. 212

STUDY QUESTIONS

LO 8.1 1. "No firm is completely sheltered from rivals; all firms compete for consumer dollars. If that is so, then pure monopoly does not exist." Do you agree? Explain. How might you use Chapter 4's concept of cross elasticity of demand to judge whether monopoly exists?

LO 8.1 2. Discuss the major barriers to entry into an industry. Explain how each barrier can foster either monopoly or oligopoly. Which barriers, if any, do you believe give rise to monopoly that is socially justifiable?

LO 8.1 3. How does the demand curve faced by a monopolistic seller differ from that confronting a perfectly competitive firm? Why does it differ? Of what significance is the difference? Why is the monopolist's demand curve not perfectly inelastic?

LO 8.2 4. **KEY QUESTION** Use the demand schedule that follows to calculate total revenue and marginal revenue at each quantity. Plot the demand, total-revenue, and marginal-revenue curves, and explain the relationships among them. Explain why the marginal revenue of the fourth unit of output is $3.50, even though its price is $5.00. Use Chapter 4's total-revenue test for price elasticity to designate the elastic and inelastic segments of your graphed demand curve. What generalization can you make about the relationship between marginal revenue and elasticity of demand? Suppose the marginal cost of successive units of output were zero. What output would the profit-seeking firm produce? Finally, use your analysis to explain why a monopolist would never produce in the inelastic region of demand.

Price (*P*)	Quantity demanded (*Q*)	Price (*P*)	Quantity demanded (*Q*)
$7.00	0	$4.50	5
6.50	1	4.00	6
6.00	2	3.50	7
5.50	3	3.00	8
5.00	4	2.50	9

5. **KEY QUESTION** Suppose a monopolist is faced with the demand schedule shown below and the same cost data as the competitive producer discussed in question 4 at the end of Chapter 7. Calculate the missing total-revenue and marginal-revenue amounts, and determine the profit-maximizing price and profit-earning output for this monopolist. What is the monopolist's profit? Verify your answer graphically and by comparing total revenue and total cost.

Price	Quantity demanded	Total revenue	Marginal revenue
$115	0	$ 0	
100	1	100	$ 100
83	2	166	66
71	3	213	47
63	4	252	39
55	5	275	23
48 -13 ×	6	288	13
42 =210	7	294	6
37	8	296	2
33	9	297	1
29	10	290	-7

6. **KEY QUESTION** Suppose that a price-discriminating monopolist has segregated its market into two groups of buyers, the first group described by the demand and revenue data that you developed for question 5. The demand and revenue data for the second group of buyers is shown in the accompanying table. Assume that MC is $13 in both markets and MC = ATC at all output levels. What price will the firm charge in each market? Based solely on these two prices, what can you conclude about the relative elasticities of demand in the two markets? What will be this monopolist's total economic profit?

Price	Quantity demanded	Total revenue	Marginal revenue
$71	0	$ 0	
			$63
63	1	63	
			47
55	2	110	
			34
48	3	144	
			24
42	4	168	
			17
37	5	185	
			13
33	6	198	
			5
29	7	203	

(handwritten: (33 –15)× 6 →720 ; 7 +240 ; 330)

8.3

7. Assume that a monopolist and a perfectly competitive firm have the same unit costs. Contrast the two with respect to (a) price, (b) output, (c) profits, (d) allocation of resources, and (e) impact on the distribution of income. Since both monopolists and competitive firms follow the MC = MR rule in maximizing profits, how do you account for the different results? Why might the costs of a perfectly competitive firm and a monopolist be different? What are the implications of such a cost difference?

8.3

8. Critically evaluate and explain:

a. "Because they can control product price, monopolists are always assured of profitable production by simply charging the highest price consumers will pay."

b. "The monopolist seeks the output that will yield the greatest per-unit profit."

c. "An excess of price over marginal cost is the market's way of signalling the need for more production of a good."

d. "The more profitable a firm, the greater its monopoly power."

e. "The monopolist has a pricing policy; the competitive producer does not."

f. "With respect to resource allocation, the interests of the seller and of society coincide in a perfectly competitive market but conflict in a monopolized market."

g. "In a sense the monopolist makes a profit for not producing; the monopolist produces profit more than it does goods."

8.3

9. Assume a monopolistic publisher has agreed to pay an author 15 percent of the total revenue from the sales of a text. Will the author and the publisher want to charge the same price for the text? Explain.

8.4

10. U.S. pharmaceutical companies charge different prices for prescription drugs to buyers in different nations, including Canada, depending on elasticity of demand and government-imposed price ceilings. Explain why these companies oppose laws allowing the re-importation of drugs to the United States.

11. Explain verbally and graphically how price (rate) regulation may improve the performance of monopolies. In your answer distinguish between (a) socially optimal (marginal-cost) pricing and (b) fair-return (average-total-cost) pricing. What is the "dilemma of regulation"? **LO 8.2**

12. In the table below are cost and demand data for a monopolist. **LO 8.4**

Quantity demanded	Price	Marginal revenue	Average cost	Marginal cost
0	$35.00			
		$ 32.00		$48.00
1	32.00		$48.00	
		26.00		12.00
2	29.00		30.00	
		20.00		10.00
3	26.00		23.34	
		14.00		14.00
4	23.00		21.00	
		8.00		16.00
5	20.00		20.00	
		2.00		17.00
6	17.00		19.50	
		– 4.00		18.00
7	14.00		19.28	
		–10.00		18.50
8	11.00		18.68	
		–16.00		19.00
9	8.00		18.72	

a. What is the level of price, output, and amount of profit for an unregulated monopolist? *(handwritten: 4×(23–21)=8)*

b. Using the data in the table, what are the price, output, and profit for a regulated monopolist that sets price equal to marginal cost compared with an unregulated monopolist? *(handwritten: 6×(17-19.5) = –15)*

c. Using the data in the table, what are the price, output, and profit for a regulated monopolist that charges a "fair-return" price compared with an unregulated monopolist? *(handwritten: 5×7 = 100 , 0)*

d. Analyze the effect of regulation on the allocation of resources. Which situation is most efficient? Which situation is most likely to be chosen by government? Why?

13. KEY QUESTION It has been proposed that natural monopolists should be allowed to determine their profit-maximizing outputs and prices and then government should tax their profits away and distribute them to consumers in proportion to their purchases from the monopoly. Is this proposal as socially desirable as requiring monopolists to equate price with marginal cost or average total cost? **LO 8.3**

14. Use Figure 8-10 to explain why monopoly generates deadweight loss. **LO 8.6**

INTERNET APPLICATION QUESTIONS @

1. **Is Microsoft a Monopoly?** In 2002 a U.S. Court of Appeals imposed remedies relating to a lower court's findings that Microsoft had a monopoly in personal computer (PC) operating systems and had maintained its monopoly through illegal actions. Go to the McConnell-Brue-Flynn-Barbiero Web site (Chapter 8) to access the details of the case. On what basis did the court conclude that Microsoft was a monopoly (see Market Share)? What was Microsoft's market share of Intel-compatible PC operating systems? of all operating systems, including Apple computers? What evidence did the court cite in claiming that Microsoft charged above-competitive prices (see Microsoft's Pricing Behaviour)?

CHAPTER 9

Monopolistic Competition and Oligopoly

Most markets in the Canadian economy fall between the two poles of perfect competition and monopoly. Real-world industries usually have fewer than the hundreds of producers required for perfect competition and more than a single producer that defines monopoly. Most firms have distinguishable rather than standardized products and have some discretion over the prices they charge. Competition often occurs on the basis of price, quality, location, service, and advertising. Entry to most real-world industries ranges from easy to very difficult but rarely is completely blocked.

This chapter examines two models that more closely approximate these widespread markets. You will discover that *monopolistic competition* mixes a small amount of monopoly power with a large amount of competition. *Oligopoly,* in contrast, blends a large amount of monopoly power, a small amount of competition to entry, and considerable rivalry among industry firms. (You should quickly review Table 7-1 at this point.)

9.1 | Characteristics of Monopolistic Competition

Let's begin by examining **monopolistic competition,** which is characterized by (1) a relatively large number of sellers, (2) differentiated products (often promoted by heavy advertising), and (3) easy entry to, and exit from, the industry. The first and third characteristics provide the "competitive" aspect of monopolistic competition; the second characteristic provides the "monopolistic" aspect. In general, however, monopolistically competitive industries are more competitive than they are monopolistic.

Relatively Large Number of Sellers

Monopolistic competition is characterized by a fairly large number of firms, say, 25, 35, 60, or 70, not by the hundreds or thousands of firms in perfect competition. Consequently, monopolistic competition involves:

- **Small Market Shares** Each firm has a comparatively small percentage of the total market and consequently has limited control over market price.

ORIGIN 9.1
Monopolistic
Competition

monopolistic competition
A market structure in which
a relatively large number of
sellers produce differentiated
products.

- *No Collusion* The presence of a relatively large number of firms makes collusion by a group of firms to restrict output and set prices unlikely.

- *Independent Action* With many firms in an industry, there is little interdependence among them; each firm can determine its own pricing policy without considering the possible reactions of rival firms. A single firm may realize a modest increase in sales by cutting its price, but the effect of that action on competitors' sales will be nearly imperceptible and will probably not trigger a response.

Differentiated Products

product differentiation
A strategy in which one firm's
product is distinguished from
competing products by means
of its design, related services,
quality, location, or other
attribute (except price).

In contrast to perfect competition, in which there is a standardized product, monopolistic competition is distinguished by **product differentiation.** Firms in monopolistic competition turn out variations of a particular product. They produce products with slightly different physical characteristics; offer varying degrees of customer service; provide varying amounts of location convenience; or proclaim special qualities, real or imagined, for their products.

Let's examine these aspects of product differentiation in more detail.

PRODUCT ATTRIBUTES

Product differentiation may take the form of physical or qualitative differences in the products themselves. Real differences in functional features, materials, design, and quality of work are vital aspects of product differentiation. Personal computers, for example, differ in terms of storage capacity, speed, graphic displays, and included software. There are dozens of competing principles of economics textbooks that differ in content, organization, presentation and readability, pedagogical aids, and graphics and design. Most cities have a variety of retail stores selling men's and women's clothing that differ greatly in styling, materials, and quality of work.

SERVICE

Service and the conditions surrounding the sale of a product are also forms of product differentiation. One grocery store may stress the helpfulness of its clerks who bag your groceries and carry them to your car. A warehouse supermarket may leave bagging and carrying to its customers but feature lower prices. Customers may prefer one-day over three-day dry cleaning of equal quality. The prestige appeal of a store, the courteousness and helpfulness of clerks, the firm's reputation for servicing or exchanging its products, and the credit it makes available are all service aspects of product differentiation.

LOCATION

Product differentiation may also be created through the use of brand names and trademarks, packaging, and celebrity connections.

Products may also be differentiated through the location and accessibility of the stores that sell them. Small convenience stores manage to compete with large supermarkets, even though these minimarts have a more limited range of products and charge higher prices. They compete mainly on the basis of location—being close to customers and situated on busy streets. A motel's proximity to a main highway gives it a locational advantage that may allow it to charge a higher room rate than nearby motels in less convenient locations.

BRAND NAMES AND PACKAGING

Product differentiation may also be created through the use of brand names and trademarks, packaging, and celebrity connections. Most aspirin tablets are very much alike, but many headache sufferers believe that one brand—for example, Bayer, Anacin, or Bufferin—is superior and worth a higher price than a generic substitute. A celebrity's name associated with watches, perfume, or athletic shoes may enhance the appeal of those products for some buyers. Many customers prefer one style of ballpoint pen to another. Packaging that touts "natural spring" bottled water may attract additional customers.

SOME CONTROL OVER PRICE

Despite the relatively large number of firms, monopolistic competitors do have some control over their product prices because of product differentiation. If consumers prefer the products of specific sellers, then within limits they will pay more to satisfy their preferences. But the control a firm in monopolistic competition has over price is quite limited, since there are numerous potential substitutes for its product.

Easy Entry and Exit

Entry into industries characterized by a monopolistic competition market structure is relatively easy compared to oligopoly or monopoly. Because firms are typically small, both absolutely and relatively, economies of scale are few and capital requirements are low. However, compared with perfect competition, financial barriers may result from the need to develop and advertise a different product from one's rivals. Some firms may have trade secrets relating to their products or hold trademarks on their brand names, making it difficult and costly for other firms to imitate them.

Exit from industries in monopolistic competition is easier still. Nothing prevents an unprofitable firm from holding a going-out-of-business sale and shutting down.

Advertising

nonprice competition
A selling strategy in which one firm tries to distinguish its product or service from all competing ones based on attributes other than price.

The expense and effort involved in product differentiation would be wasted if consumers were not made aware of product differences. Thus, firms in monopolistic competition advertise their products, often heavily. The goal of product differentiation and advertising—so-called **nonprice competition**—is to make price less of a factor in consumer purchases and make product differences a greater factor. If successful, the firm's demand curve will shift to the right and will become less elastic.

FIGURE 9-1

Percentage of Output Produced by the Four Largest Firms in Selected Low-Concentration Sectors, 1997*

Several Canadian manufacturing industries approximate monopolistic competition, with a relatively large number of sellers, producing differentiated products. There is easy entry into the industry and firms often differentiate their products through advertising.

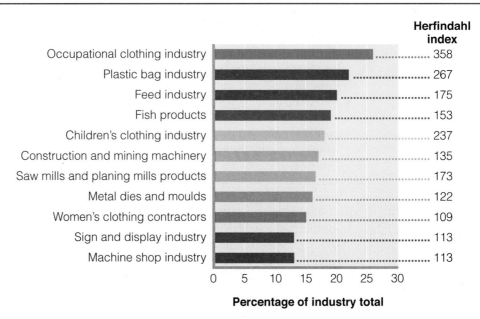

Industry	Herfindahl index
Occupational clothing industry	358
Plastic bag industry	267
Feed industry	175
Fish products	153
Children's clothing industry	237
Construction and mining machinery	135
Saw mills and planing mills products	173
Metal dies and moulds	122
Women's clothing contractors	109
Sign and display industry	113
Machine shop industry	113

Percentage of industry total

Source: Statistics Canada, *Industrial Organization and Concentration in Manufacturing, Mining and Logging Industries*, Catalogue No. 31C0024, April 1, 2005.
*As measured by dollar value of shipments.

Monopolistically Competitive Industries

Figure 9-1 lists several manufacturing industries that approximate monopolistic competition. Economists measure the degree of industry concentration—the extent to which the largest firms account for the bulk of the industry's output—to identify monopolistic competitive (versus oligopolistic) industries. Two such measures are the four-firm concentration ratio and the Herfindahl index.

four-firm concentration ratio
The percentage of total industry sales accounted for by the top four firms in the industry.

A **four-firm concentration ratio,** expressed as a percentage, is the ratio of the output (sales) of the four largest firms in an industry relative to total industry sales.

$$\text{Four-firm concentration ratio} = \frac{\text{Output of four largest firms}}{\text{Total output in the industry}}$$

Four-firm concentration ratios are very low in perfectly competitive industries in which there are hundreds or even thousands of firms each with a tiny market share. In contrast, four-firm ratios are high in oligopoly and monopoly. Industries in which the largest four firms account for 40 percent or more of the market are generally considered to be oligopolies. If the largest four firms account for less than 40 percent, they are likely to be monopolistically competitive. Observe that the concentration ratios in Figure 9-1 range from 13 percent to 27 percent.

Published concentration ratios such as those in Figure 9-1 are helpful in categorizing industries, but must be used cautiously because the market shares (percentage of total sales) are national in scope. Some markets with low national concentration ratios are highly localized. For example, the four-firm concentration ratio for ready-mix concrete (not shown) is usually low, suggesting a monopolistically competitive industry. But the sheer bulk of ready-mix concrete and the fact that it sets up as it dries limits the relevant market to a specific town, city, or metropolitan area. In such localized markets only two or three ready-mix producers may compete, not the numerous firms present in monopolistic competition.

Herfindahl index
The sum of the squared percentage market shares of all firms in the industry.

Figure 9-1 lists a second measure of concentration: the **Herfindahl index.** This index is the sum of the squared percentage market shares of all firms in the industry. In equation form:

$$\text{Herfindahl index} = (\%S_1)^2 + (\%S_2)^2 + (\%S_3)^2 + \ldots + (\%S_n)^2$$

where $\%S_1$ is the percentage market share of firm 1, $\%S_2$ is the percentage market share of firm 2, and so on for each firm in the industry. By squaring the percentage market shares of all firms in the industry, the Herfindahl index purposely gives much greater weight to larger, and thus more powerful, firms than to smaller ones. For a perfectly competitive industry, the index would approach zero, since each firm's market share—$\%S$ in the equation—is extremely small. In the case of the single-firm industry, the index would be at its maximum of 10,000 ($= 100^2$), indicating an industry with complete monopoly power.

We will discover later in this chapter that the Herfindahl index is important for assessing oligopolistic industries. For purposes here, the relevant generalization is that the lower the Herfindahl index, the greater the likelihood an industry is monopolistic competitive rather than oligopolistic. Note that in Figure 9-1 the Herfindahl index values (computed for the top four firms, not all the industry firms) are decidedly closer to the bottom limit of the Herfindahl index—0—than to its top limit—10,000.

The numbers in Figure 9-1 are for manufacturing industries. In addition, many retail establishments in metropolitan areas fall into the category of monopolistic competition, including grocery stores, gas stations, hair salons, dry cleaners, clothing stores, and restaurants. Also, many providers of professional services such as legal assistance, real estate sales, and basic bookkeeping are monopolistic competitors.

9.2 | Price and Output in Monopolistic Competition

How does a firm in monopolistic competition decide on its price and output? To explain, we initially assume that each firm in the industry is producing a specific differentiated product and engaging in a particular amount of advertising. Later we'll see how changes in the product and in the amount of advertising modify our conclusions.

The Firm's Demand Curve

Our explanation is based on **Figure 9-2 (Key Graph)**. The basic feature of that diagram is the elasticity of demand, as shown by the individual firm's demand curve. The demand curve of each firm is highly, but not perfectly, elastic. It is precisely this feature that distinguishes monopolistic competition from monopoly and perfect competition. The demand is more elastic than the demand faced by a monopolist because the firm in monopolistic competition has many competitors producing close substitutes. The monopolist has no rivals at all. Yet, there are two reasons why the demand curve of a firm in monopolistic competition is not perfectly elastic, as is the case in perfect competition. First, it has fewer rivals; second, its products are differentiated, so they are not perfect substitutes.

The price elasticity of demand faced by the firm in monopolistic competition depends on the number of rivals and the degree of product differentiation. The larger the number of rivals and the weaker the product differentiation, the greater the price elasticity of each firm's demand; that is, the closer monopolistic competition will be to perfect competition.

The Short Run: Profit or Loss

The firm in monopolistic competition maximizes its profit or minimizes its loss in the short run just as firms in the other market structures we have discussed do: by producing the output at which marginal revenue equals marginal cost (MR = MC). In Figure 9-2a the firm produces output Q_1, where MR = MC. As shown by demand curve D_1, the firm then can charge price P_1. It realizes an economic profit, shown by the grey area $[= (P_1 - A_1) \times Q_1]$.

But with less favourable demand or costs, the firm may incur a loss in the short run. This possibility is shown in Figure 9-2b, where the firm's best strategy is to minimize its loss. It does so by producing output Q_2 (where MR = MC) and, as determined by demand curve D_2, by charging price P_2. Because price P_2 is less than average total cost A_2, the firm incurs a per unit loss of $A_2 - P_2$ and a total loss represented as the pink area $[= (A_2 - P_2) \times Q_2]$.

The Long Run: Only a Normal Profit

In the long run, firms will enter a profitable monopolistically competitive industry and exit an unprofitable one. So, a firm in monopolistic competition will earn only a normal profit in the long run. (Remember that the cost curves include both explicit and implicit costs, including a normal profit.)

PROFITS: FIRMS ENTER

In the case of short-run profit in Figure 9-2a, economic profits attract new rivals because entry to the industry is relatively easy. As new firms enter, the demand curve faced by the typical firm shifts to the left (falls) because each firm has a smaller share of total demand. This decline in the firm's demand reduces its economic profit. When entry of new firms has reduced demand to the extent that the demand curve is tangent to the average-total-cost curve at the profit-maximizing output, the firm is just making a normal profit. This situation is shown in Figure 9-2c, where demand is D_3 and the firm's long-run equilibrium output is Q_3. As Figure 9-2c indicates, any greater or lesser output will entail an average total cost that exceeds product price P_3, meaning a loss for the firm. At the tangency point between the demand curve and ATC, total revenue equals total costs. With the economic profit gone, no further incentive exists for additional firms to enter.

GRAPH

-2 A Monopolistically Competitive
Run and Long Run

The firm in monopolistic competition maximizes profit or mini-mizes loss by producing the output at which MR = MC. The economic profit shown in panel (a) will induce new firms to enter, eventually eliminating economic profit. The loss shown in panel (b) will cause an exit of firms until normal profit is restored. After such entry and exit, the price will settle in panel (c) to where it just equals average total cost at the MR = MC output. At this price P_3 and output Q_3, the firm in monopolistic competition earns only a normal profit, and the industry is in long-run equilibrium.

(a) Short-run profits

(b) Short-run losses

Quick Quiz

1. **Price exceeds MC in**
   a. graph (a) only.
   b. graph (b) only.
   c. graphs (a) and (b) only.
   d. graphs (a), (b), and (c).

2. **Price exceeds ATC in**
   a. graph (a) only.
   b. graph (b) only.
   c. graphs (a) and (b) only.
   d. graphs (a), (b), and (c).

3. **The firm represented by Figure 9-2c is**
   a. making a normal profit.
   b. incurring a loss, once opportunity costs are considered.
   c. producing at the same level of output as a perfectly competitive firm.
   d. producing a standardized product.

4. **Which of the following pairs are both competition-like elements in monopolistic competition?**
   a. Price exceeds MR; standardized product.
   b. Entry is relatively easy; only a normal profit in the long run.
   c. Price equals MC at the profit-maximizing output; economic profits are likely in the long run.
   d. The firm's demand curve is downsloping; differentiated products.

(c) Long-run equilibrium

Answers: 1. d; 2. a; 3. a; 4. b

LOSSES: FIRMS LEAVE

When the industry suffers short-run losses, as in Figure 9-2b, some firms will exit in the long run. Faced with fewer substitute products and with an expanded share of total demand, the surviving firms will see their demand curves shift to the right (rise), as to D_3. Their losses will disappear and give way to normal profits, shown in Figure 9-2b. (For simplicity we have assumed constant costs; shifts in the cost curves as firms enter or leave would complicate our discussion slightly but would not alter our conclusions.)

COMPLICATIONS

The representative firm in the monopolistic competition model earns only a normal profit in the long run. That outcome may not always occur for the following reasons:

- Some firms may achieve sufficient product differentiation that other firms cannot duplicate them, even over time. For example, one hotel in a major city may have the best location for business and tourist activities. Or a firm may have developed a well-known brand name that gives it a slight but very long-lasting advantage over imitators. Such firms may have sufficient monopoly power to realize modest economic profits even in the long run.

- Entry to some monopolistically competitive industries may not be easy. Because of product differentiation, greater financial barriers to entry are likely to exist than if the product were standardized. This suggests some monopoly power, with small economic profits continuing even in the long run.

With all things considered, however, the outcome that yields only a normal profit—the long-run equilibrium—shown in Figure 9-2c is a reasonable approximation of reality.

Monopolistic Competition and Efficiency

We know from Chapter 7 that economic efficiency requires the triple equality $P = \text{MC} = $ minimum ATC. The equality of price and minimum average total cost yields *productive efficiency*. The good is being produced in the least costly way, and the price is just sufficient to cover average total cost, including a normal profit. The equality of price and marginal cost also yields *allocative efficiency*. The right amount of output is being produced, and thus the right amount of society's scarce resources is being devoted to this specific use. How efficient is monopolistic competition, as measured against this triple equality?

NEITHER PRODUCTIVE NOR ALLOCATIVE EFFICIENCY

In monopolistic competition, neither productive nor allocative efficiency is achieved in long-run equilibrium. Figure 9-3, which includes an enlargement of part of Figure 9-2c, clearly shows this. First note that the profit-maximizing price P_3 slightly exceeds the lowest average total cost, A_4. In producing the profit-maximizing output Q_3, the firm's average total cost therefore is slightly higher than optimal from society's perspective—productive efficiency is not achieved. Also note that the profit-maximizing price P_3 exceeds marginal cost (here M_3), meaning that monopolistic competition causes an underallocation of resources. Society values each unit of output between Q_3 and Q_4 more highly than the goods it would have to forgo to produce those units. Thus, to a modest extent, monopolistic competition also fails the allocative-efficiency test. Consumers pay a higher-than-competitive price and obtain a less-than-optimal output. Indeed, firms in monopolistic competition must charge a higher-than-competitive price in the long run to achieve a normal profit. The price–marginal cost gap experienced by each monopolistic competitive firm creates an industry-wide efficiency loss (or deadweight loss).

FIGURE 9-3 **The Inefficiency of Monopolistic Competition**

In long-run equilibrium a firm in monopolistic competition achieves neither productive nor allocative efficiency. Productive efficiency is not realized because production occurs where the average total cost A_3 exceeds the minimum average total cost A_4. Allocative efficiency is not achieved because the product price P_3 exceeds the marginal cost M_3. The result is an underallocation of resources and excess productive capacity of $Q_4 - Q_3$.

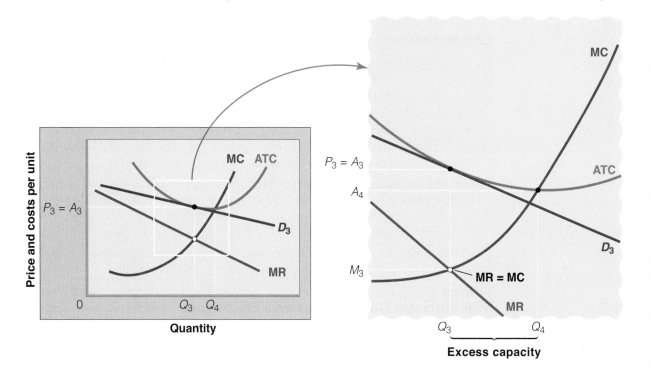

EXCESS CAPACITY

excess capacity
Plant or equipment that is underused because the firm is producing less than the minimum-ATC output.

In monopolistic competition, the gap between the minimum-ATC output and the profit-maximizing output identifies **excess capacity:** plant or equipment that is underused because firms are producing less than the minimum-ATC output. This gap is shown as the distance between Q_4 and Q_3 in Figure 9-3. If each firm could profitably produce at the minimum-ATC output, fewer firms could produce the same total output, and the product could be sold at a lower price. Industries that have a monopolistic-competition market structure are thus overcrowded with firms, each operating below its optimal capacity. This situation is typified by many kinds of retail establishments. For example, most cities have an abundance of small motels and restaurants that operate well below half capacity. *(Key Question 2)*

PRODUCT VARIETY

The situation portrayed in Figures 9-2c and 9-3 is not very satisfying to firms in monopolistic competition, since it allows only a normal profit. But the profit-realizing firm of Figure 9-2a need not stand by and watch new competitors eliminate its profit by imitating its product, matching its customer service, and copying its advertising. Each firm has a product that is distinguishable in some way from those of the other producers. So, the firm can attempt to stay ahead of competitors and sustain its profit through further product differentiation and more effective advertising. By developing or improving its product, it may be able to postpone, at least for a while, the outcome of Figure 9-2c.

Although product differentiation and advertising add to the firm's costs, they can also increase the demand for its product. If demand increases by more than enough to compensate for the added costs, the firm will have improved its profit position. As Figure 9-3 suggests, the firm has little or no prospect of increasing profit by price cutting. So why not engage in nonprice competition?

Benefits of Product Variety

The product variety and product improvement that accompany the drive to maintain above-normal profit in monopolistic competition are a benefit for society—they may offset the cost of the inefficiency associated with monopolistic competition. Consumers have a wide diversity of tastes: Some like hip-hop bands, others like punk bands; some like contemporary furniture, others like traditional furniture. If a product is differentiated, then at any time the consumer will be offered a wide range of types, styles, brands, and quality gradations of that product. Compared with perfect competition, this provides an advantage to the consumer. The range of choice is widened, and producers more fully meet the wide variation in consumer tastes.

In fact, product differentiation creates a tradeoff between consumer choice and productive efficiency. The stronger the product differentiation, the greater is the excess capacity and, therefore, the greater is the productive inefficiency. But the greater the product differentiation, the more likely the firms will satisfy the great diversity of consumer tastes. The greater the excess capacity problem, the wider the range of consumer choice.

Further Complexity

Finally, the ability to engage in nonprice competition makes the firm's situation in monopolistic competition more complex than Figure 9-3 indicates. That figure assumes a given (unchanging) product and a given level of advertising expenditures. But we know that, in practice, product attributes and advertising are not fixed. The firm in monopolistic competition juggles three factors—price, product, and advertising—in seeking maximum profit. It must determine what variety of product, selling at what price, and supplemented by what level of advertising will result in the greatest profit. This complex situation is not easily expressed in a simple economic model. At best, we can say that each possible combination of price, product, and advertising poses a different demand and cost (production cost plus advertising cost) situation for the firm, and that only one combination yields the maximum profit. In practice, this optimal combination cannot be readily forecast but must be found by trial and error.

QUICK REVIEW

▶ Monopolistic competition involves a relatively large number of firms operating in a noncollusive way and producing differentiated products, with easy industry entry and exit.

▶ In the short run, a firm in monopolistic competition will maximize profit or minimize loss by producing that output at which marginal revenue equals marginal cost.

▶ In the long run, the easy entry and exit of firms in monopolistic competition means they earn only a normal profit.

▶ The long-run equilibrium output for a firm in monopolistic competition is such that price exceeds the minimum average total cost (implying that consumers do not get the product at the lowest price attainable) and price exceeds marginal cost (indicating that resources are underallocated to the product).

▶ The efficiency loss associated with monopolistic competition is greatly muted by the benefits consumers receive from product variety.

9.3 | Oligopoly

In terms of competitiveness, the spectrum of market structures reaches from perfect competition to monopolistic competition, to oligopoly, to monopoly (review Table 7-1). We now direct our attention to **oligopoly,** a market structure dominated by a few large producers of a homogeneous or differentiated product. Because of their small number, oligopolists have considerable control over their prices, but each must consider the possible reaction of rivals to its own pricing, output, and advertising decisions.

A Few Large Producers

The phrase "a few large producers" is necessarily vague because the market model of oligopoly covers much ground, ranging between monopoly and monopolistic competition. Oligopoly encompasses the Canadian steel industry, in which two firms dominate an entire national market, and the situation in which four or five much smaller auto parts stores enjoy roughly equal shares of the market in a medium-sized town. Generally, however, when you hear a term such as Big Three, Big Four, or Big Six, you can be sure it refers to an oligopolistic industry.

Homogeneous or Differentiated Products

An oligopoly may be either a **homogeneous oligopoly** or a **differentiated oligopoly,** depending on whether the firms in the oligopoly produce standardized or differentiated products. Many industrial products (steel, zinc, copper, aluminum, lead, cement, industrial alcohol) are virtually standardized products that are produced in oligopolies. Many consumer goods industries (automobiles, tires, household appliances, electronics equipment, breakfast cereals, cigarettes, sporting goods) are differentiated oligopolies. An example of a differentiated oligopoly in Canada is the media and telecommunications sector. It is dominated by Canwest Global Communications, which owns a daily newspaper in almost every big city in Canada and a variety of television stations, and BCE, which controls Bell Canada and owns satellite broadcaster Bell ExpressVu, television stations, and *The Globe and Mail.* These differentiated oligopolies typically engage in considerable nonprice competition supported by heavy advertising.

Control over Price, but Mutual Interdependence

Because firms are few in oligopolistic industries, each firm is a price-maker; like the monopolist, it can set its price and output levels to maximize its profit. But unlike the monopolist, which has no rivals, the oligopolist must consider how its rivals will react to any change in its price, output, product characteristics, or advertising. Oligopoly is thus characterized by *strategic behaviour* and *mutual interdependence.* By **strategic behaviour** we simply mean self-interested behaviour that takes into account the reactions of others. Firms develop and implement price, quality, location, service, and advertising strategies to grow their business and expand their profits. But because rivals are few, there is **mutual interdependence:** a situation in which each firm's profit depends on its own price and sales strategies as well as those of its rivals. For example, in deciding whether to increase the price of its cosmetics, L'Oréal will try to predict the response of other major cosmetics producers, such as Estée Lauder. In deciding on its advertising strategy, Burger King will take into consideration how McDonald's might react.

Entry Barriers

The same barriers to entry that create monopoly also contribute to the creation of oligopoly. Economies of scale are important entry barriers in a number of oligopolistic industries, such as the aircraft, rubber, and cement industries. In those industries, three or four firms might each have sufficient

---

oligopoly ⑤
A market structure in which a few large firms produce homogeneous or differentiated products.

homogeneous oligopoly
An oligopoly in which the firms produce a standardized product.

differentiated oligopoly
An oligopoly in which the firms produce a differentiated product.

strategic behaviour
Self-interested behaviour that takes into account the reactions of others.

mutual interdependence
A situation in which a change in strategy (usually price) by one firm will affect the sales and profits of other firms.

sales to achieve economies of scale, but new firms would have such a small market share that they could not do so. They would then be high-cost producers, and as such they could not survive. A closely related barrier is the large expenditure for capital—the cost of obtaining necessary plant and equipment—required for entering certain industries. The automobile, commercial aircraft, and petroleum-refining industries, for example, are all characterized by very high capital requirements. In Canada, the domestic automobile industry is dominated by Ford, General Motors, and Chrysler, whose plants are concentrated in Ontario and Quebec; Quebec's Bombardier is one of the world's largest manufacturers of small short-haul passenger planes, such as the Dash 8; and Suncor Energy is Canada's largest oil refiner, as well as a major international player in the oil and gas sector.

Ownership and control of raw materials helps explain why oligopoly exists in many mining industries, including gold, silver, and copper. In the computer, chemicals, consumer electronics, and pharmaceutical industries, patents have served as entry barriers. Oligopolists can also preclude the entry of new competitors through preemptive and retaliatory pricing and advertising strategies.

Mergers

Some oligopolies have emerged mainly through the growth of the dominant firms in a given industry (breakfast cereals, chewing gum, candy bars). But for other industries the route to oligopoly has been through mergers (examples: steel, in its early history; and, more recently, airlines, banking, and entertainment). The merging, or combining, of two or more competing firms may substantially increase their market share, which in turn may allow the new firm to achieve greater economies of scale.

Oligopolistic Industries

Figure 9-4 lists the four-firm concentration ratio—the percentage of total industry sales accounted for by the four largest firms—for a number of oligopolistic industries. For example, the four largest Canadian producers of tobacco products manufacture more than 90 percent of all cigarettes produced in Canada. (In fact, the domestic tobacco market is largely controlled by the *three* largest Canadian companies: Imperial Tobacco Ltd., owned by Imasco Ltd.; Rothmans, Benson & Hedges Inc.; and JTI-MacDonald Ltd.)

When the largest four firms in an industry control 40 percent or more of the market (as in Figure 9-4), that industry is considered oligopolistic. Using this benchmark, about one-half of all Canadian manufacturing industries are oligopolies. Although concentration ratios help identify oligopoly, they have four shortcomings.

Localized Markets We have already noted that concentration ratios relate to the nation as a whole, whereas the markets for some products are highly localized because of high transportation costs. Local oligopolies can exist even though national concentration ratios are low.

Interindustry Competition Concentration ratios are based on somewhat arbitrary definitions of industries. In some cases, they disguise significant **interindustry competition**—competition between two products associated with different industries. The high concentration ratio for the steel pipe and tube industry shown in Figure 9-4 understates the competition in that industry, because copper and plastic tubing compete with steel tubing in many applications.

World Trade The data in Figure 9-4 are for Canadian production only, and may overstate concentration because they do not account for the **import competition** of foreign suppliers. The automobile industry is a good example. Although Figure 9-4 shows that three firms produce almost 90 percent of the domestic output of those goods, it ignores the fact that a large portion of the automobiles and auto tires bought in Canada are imports. Many of the world's largest corporations are foreign, and many of them do business in Canada.

interindustry competition
The competition between the products of one industry and the products of another industry.

import competition
The competition domestic firms encounter from the products and services of foreign producers.

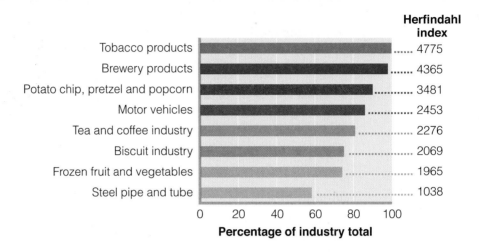

FIGURE 9-4

Percentage of Output Produced by the Four Largest Firms in Selected High-Concentration Industries, 1997*

A concentration ratio reveals the percentage of total output produced and sold by an industry's four largest firms. The Herfindahl index is the sum of the squared percentage market share of all the firms in the industry. The higher the Herfindahl index, the greater the market power within an industry. The tobacco industry is the most concentrated sector in Canada.

	Herfindahl index
Tobacco products	4775
Brewery products	4365
Potato chip, pretzel and popcorn	3481
Motor vehicles	2453
Tea and coffee industry	2276
Biscuit industry	2069
Frozen fruit and vegetables	1965
Steel pipe and tube	1038

Percentage of industry total

Source: Statistics Canada, *Industrial Organization and Concentration in Manufacturing, Mining and Logging Industries*, Catalogue No. 31C0024, April 1, 2005.
*As measured by dollar value of shipments

WORKED PROBLEM 9.1
Measures of Industry Competition

Dominant Firms   The four-firm concentration ratio does not reveal the extent to which one or two firms dominate an industry. Suppose that in industry X one firm produces the entire industry output. In a second industry, Y, four firms compete, each with 25 percent of the market. The concentration ratio is 100 percent for both these industries. But industry X is a pure monopoly, while industry Y is an oligopoly that may be experiencing significant economic rivalry. Most economists would agree that monopoly power (or market power) is substantially greater in industry X than in industry Y, a fact disguised by their identical 100 percent concentration ratios.

The Herfindahl index addresses this problem. Recall from section 9.1 that this index is the sum of the squared percentage market shares of all firms in the industry. Again, in equation form:

$$\text{Herfindahl index} = (\%S_1)^2 + (\%S_2)^2 + (\%S_3)^2 + \dots + (\%S_n)^2$$

where $\%S_1$ is the percentage market share of firm 1, $\%S_2$ is the percentage market share of firm 2, and so on for each firm in the industry. Also remember that by squaring the percentage market shares of all firms in the industry, the Herfindahl index gives much greater weight to larger, and thus more powerful, firms than to smaller ones. In the case of the single-firm industry X, the index would be at its maximum of 100^2 or 10,000, indicating an industry with complete monopoly power. For our supposed four-firm industry Y, the index would be $25^2 + 25^2 + 25^2 + 25^2$, or 2500, indicating much less market power.

The larger the Herfindahl index, the greater the market power within an industry. Note in Figure 9-4 that the four-firm concentration ratios for the tobacco products industry and the brewery products industry are similar. But the Herfindahl index of 4775 for the tobacco products industry suggests greater market power than the 4365 index for the brewery products industry. Also, contrast the much larger Herfindahl indexes in Figure 9-4 with those for the low-concentration industries in Figure 9-1. *(Key Question 7)*

9.4 | Oligopoly Pricing Behaviour: A Game Theory Overview

ORIGIN 9.2
Game Theory

game theory model
A means of analyzing the pricing behaviour of oligopolists using the theory of strategy associated with games such as chess and bridge.

Oligopoly pricing behaviour has the characteristics of certain games of strategy, such as poker, chess, and bridge. The best way to play such a game depends on the way one's opponent plays. Players (and oligopolists) must plan their actions according to the actions and expected reactions of rivals. The study of how people behave in strategic situations is called *game theory*. We will use a simple **game theory model** to analyze the pricing behaviour of oligopolists. Game theory was first developed in the 1920s, and expanded rapidly during World War II in response to the military need of developing formal ways of thinking about strategy.

Basic Concepts

Any interaction in which individuals or firms must make choices and in which the final outcome depends on what each individual or firm chooses to do is termed a *game*. Games have four basic components: (1) the players, (2) the rules, (3) the possible strategies, and (4) the payoffs. Games may be *cooperative,* meaning players in the game make specific agreements that are binding on the parties, or *noncooperative,* where agreements among the players are not possible.

- *Players*   Each participant is referred to as a player. The players may be individuals, as in a chess game; firms, usually in imperfectly competitive markets; or countries, involved for example in a regional conflict. Game theory assumes players can choose among a set of possible actions. The players (decision makers) are rational in that they pursue well-defined objectives. For individuals, the primary objective is utility maximization; for firms, it is profit maximization. Players are assumed to reason strategically, meaning they take into account other players' knowledge and expectations. Games can have any number of players, but for simplicity we will focus on two-player games. We assume that each player chooses a course of action that will yield the greatest benefit for himself or herself.

- *Rules*   Games generally have clearly defined rules that players must follow in pursuing their strategies and goals, for example the rules chess players follow as they choose their moves. The rules of a game may also be viewed as *constraints* that players face as they make choices.

- *Strategies*   A possible course of action for a player in a game is called a strategy. Usually players can choose among a number of strategies, while considering the likely response from other players in the game. We will focus on possible strategies in cooperative (collusive) and noncooperative (noncollusive) games in a two-firm oligopoly.

- *Payoffs*   Players in a game seek the best possible outcomes for themselves. The final returns to each player are called *payoffs*. Payoffs may be large, small, or even negative. In some instances, referred to as *zero-sum games*, one player may gain exactly what the other player loses. *Positive-sum games* offer positive payoffs to all players.

EQUILIBRIUM

Recall from Chapter 3 that competitive markets bring about equilibrium price and quantity for specific products or services. There is no unique equilibrium outcome in game theory. This is because outcomes depend not only on what one player may do, but also on how the other players in the game decide to react to any given initial move by the player making the first move.

Prisoner's Dilemma

prisoner's dilemma
A type of game between two players that shows the difficulty of cooperating when the two cannot communicate with each other, even when it is in their best interest to cooperate.

To illustrate game theory in action, we'll look at the **prisoner's dilemma,** first introduced in the 1940s by Canadian economist A. W. Tucke. The prisoner's dilemma is a type of game between two prisoners that shows the difficulty of cooperating when the two cannot communicate with each other, even when it is in their best interests to cooperate. Let's take a look at an example.

Two individuals, Al and Bruno, are caught by police in the act of breaking into a warehouse containing valuable carpets. On the way to headquarters, the police investigators run a check on other crimes in the area and discover that two men closely matching Al's and Bruno's physical profiles stole $2 million worth of diamonds just six months earlier, in a robbery for which the police have no leads or witnesses. (Al and Bruno had indeed carried out the diamond robbery.) In the hope of getting a confession, the police investigators decide to interrogate Al and Bruno in different rooms so they can't communicate with each other. The game has been set in motion.

The police investigators inform Al and Bruno that they are now suspects in the diamond robbery. Since they were caught red-handed trying to break into the carpet warehouse, Al and Bruno know they each will get the mandatory two-year jail sentence for that crime alone. If both confess to the diamond robbery each will get four years for both crimes. But if one confesses and the other does not, the one who confesses will still receive 1 year, while the one who does not confess will get 12 years.

What are the options for Al and Bruno given the "rules" for this game? Figure 9-5 sets out the *payoff matrix* for Al and Bruno. Four combinations are possible, and each of the four combinations is represented by a lettered cell. If both confess, they each will get four years in jail (Cell A). If neither confesses to the diamond robbery, each will get only two years in jail (Cell D). If Bruno confesses, but Al does not, he gets 1 year and Al gets 12 years (Cell B). Alternatively, if Al confesses, but Bruno does not, Al gets 1 year and Bruno goes to the slammer for 12 years (Cell C).

Recall that a player in a game will choose a strategy on the basis of what he or she expects the other players will do. If both Al and Bruno expect the other to deny they participated in the diamond robbery, then each will not confess. Both Al and Bruno know this, but each cannot be sure the other will deny participating in the diamond robbery. If they were allowed to communicate with each other they could cooperate (collude) to minimize their jail sentence. But they can't communicate, which means that they are in a noncooperative game. The dilemma is that Al and Bruno should cooperate to minimize jail time, but if one confesses and the other does not, the one who does not confess will face a heavier penalty.

FIGURE 9-5 ⏵ **Prisoner's Dilemma Payoff Matrix**

Al and Bruno each have two possible strategies. Each lettered cell of this four-cell payoff matrix represents the jail terms, in years, that both Al and Bruno would receive under various conditions.

Given the uncertainty of what the other will do, confessing is the best strategy for both Al and Bruno in this game. The risk of a much higher jail term is too great for either Al or Bruno to consider denying involvement in the diamond robbery. By not confessing, the best that either Al or Bruno can hope for is a 1-year jail term, but the possibility exists for a 12-year term. If either Al or Bruno confesses, his worst-case scenario is a four-year jail sentence. You should be able to see that the *dominant strategy* for both Al and Bruno is to confess.

Strategies in a Two-Firm Oligopoly

Let's now apply the game theory model to a two-firm oligopoly, also known as a *duopoly*. We assume a two-firm oligopoly producing athletic shoes. Each firm—let's call them RareAir and Uptown—has a choice of two pricing strategies: price high or price low. The profit each firm earns will depend on the strategy it chooses and the strategy its rival chooses.

Four possible combinations of strategies are possible for the two firms, and a lettered cell in Figure 9-6 represents each combination, also called the payoff matrix. For example, cell C represents a low-price strategy for Uptown along with a high-price strategy for RareAir. Cell C shows that if Uptown adopts a low-price strategy and RareAir a high-price strategy, then Uptown will earn $15 million (green portion) and RareAir will earn $6 million (orange portion).

Mutual Interdependence Revisited

The data in Figure 9-6 are hypothetical, but their relationships are typical of real situations. Recall that oligopolistic firms can increase their profits, and influence their rivals' profits, by changing their pricing strategies. Each firm's profit depends on its own pricing strategy and that of its rivals. This mutual interdependence of oligopolists is the most obvious point demonstrated by Figure 9-6. If Uptown adopts a high-price strategy, its profit will be $12 million, provided that RareAir also employs a high-price strategy (cell A). But if RareAir uses a low-price strategy against Uptown's high-price strategy (cell B), RareAir will increase its market share and boost its profit from $12 million to $15 million. RareAir's higher profit will come at the expense of Uptown, whose profit will fall from $12 million to $6 million. Uptown's high-price strategy is a good strategy only if RareAir also employs a high-price strategy.

 KEY GRAPH

FIGURE 9-6   Profit Payoff (in millions) for a Two-Firm Oligopoly

Each firm has two possible pricing strategies. RareAir's strategies are shown in the top margin, and Uptown's in the left margin. Each lettered cell of this four-cell payoff matrix represents one combination of a RareAir strategy and an Uptown strategy and shows the profit, in millions of dollars, that combination would earn for each firm.

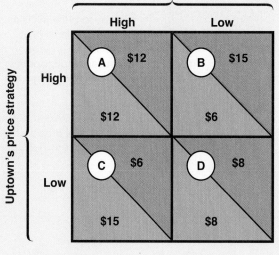

Collusion

collusion
A situation in which firms act together and in agreement to fix prices, divide a market, or otherwise restrict competition.

Figure 9-6 also suggests that oligopolists often can benefit from **collusion**—that is, cooperation with rivals. To see the benefits of collusion, first suppose that both firms in Figure 9-6 are acting independently and following high-price strategies. Each realizes a $12 million profit (cell A).

Note that either RareAir or Uptown could increase its profit by switching to a low-price strategy (cell B or C). The low-price firm would increase its profit to $15 million, and the high-price firm's profit would fall to $6 million. The high-price firm would be better off if it, too, adopted a low-price policy. Doing so would increase its profit from $6 million to $8 million (cell D). The effect of all this independent strategy shifting would be to reduce both firms' profits from $12 million (cell A) to $8 million (cell D).

In real situations, too, independent action by oligopolists may lead to mutual competitive low-price strategies: Independent oligopolists compete with respect to price, which leads to lower prices and lower profits. This is clearly beneficial to consumers but not to the oligopolists' profits.

How could oligopolists avoid the low-profit outcome of cell D? The answer is that they could collude, rather than establish prices competitively or independently. In our example, the two firms could agree to establish and maintain a high-price policy. Each firm will increase its profit from $8 million (cell D) to $12 million (cell A).

Incentive to Cheat

The payoff matrix also explains why an oligopolist might be strongly tempted to cheat on a collusive agreement. Suppose Uptown and RareAir agree to maintain high-price policies, with each earning $12 million in profit (cell A). Both are tempted to cheat on this collusive pricing agreement, because either firm can increase its profit to $15 million by lowering its price. If Uptown secretly cheats on the agreement by charging low prices, the payoff moves from cell A to cell C. Uptown's profit rises to $15 million, and RareAir's falls to $6 million. If RareAir cheats, the payoff moves from cell A to cell B, and RareAir gets the $15 million. Each fearful that the other will cheat, both firms will probably cheat and the game will settle back to cell D, with each firm using its low-price strategy. (The appendix to this chapter provides several additional applications of game theory.) *(Key Question 9)*

QUICK REVIEW

▸ An oligopoly is made up of relatively few firms producing either homogeneous or differentiated products; these firms are mutually interdependent.

▸ Barriers to entry such as scale economies, control of patents or strategic resources, or the ability to engage in retaliatory pricing characterize oligopolies. Oligopolies may result from internal growth of firms, mergers, or both.

▸ The four-firm concentration ratio shows the percentage of an industry's sales accounted for by its four largest firms; the Herfindahl index measures the degree of market power in an industry by summing the squares of the percentage market shares held by the individual firms in the industry.

▸ The prisoner's dilemma is a type of game that shows the difficulty of cooperating when the participants cannot communicate with each other.

▸ Game theory reveals that (1) oligopolies are mutually interdependent in their pricing policies, (2) collusion enhances oligopoly profits, and (3) there is a temptation for oligopolists to cheat on a collusive agreement.

9.5 | The Incentives and Obstacles to Collusion: Two Oligopoly Strategies

To gain further insight into oligopolistic pricing and output behaviour, we will examine two distinct pricing strategies: (1) collusive pricing, and (2) price leadership. Why not a simple single model as in our discussions of the other market structures? There are two reasons:

1. **Diversity of Oligopolies** Oligopoly has a greater range and diversity of market situations than other market structures, including the *tight* oligopoly, in which two or three firms dominate an entire market, and the *loose* oligopoly, in which six or seven firms share, say, 70 or 80 percent of a market while a competitive fringe of firms shares the remainder. Oligopoly includes both differentiated and standardized products. It includes cases in which firms act in collusion and those in which they act independently. The diversity of oligopoly makes it impossible to explain all oligopolistic behaviours with a single market model.

2. **Complications of Interdependence** The mutual interdependence of oligopolistic firms is what complicates matters. Because firms cannot predict the reactions of their rivals with certainty, they cannot estimate their own demand and marginal-revenue data. Without such data, firms cannot determine their profit-maximizing price and output.

Despite these analytical difficulties, two interrelated characteristics of oligopolistic pricing have been observed. First, prices change less frequently under oligopoly than under perfect competition, monopolistic competition, and, in some instances, monopoly. Second, when oligopolists do change prices, firms are likely to change their prices together, suggesting a tendency to act in concert, or collusively, in setting and changing prices (as we mentioned in the preceding section). The diversity of oligopolies and the presence of mutual interdependence are reflected in the models that follow.

Cartels and Other Collusion: Cooperative Strategies

Our game theory model demonstrates that one possible outcome of an oligopoly market structure is collusion. Collusion occurs whenever firms in an industry reach an agreement to fix prices, divide up the market, or otherwise restrict competition among themselves. The danger of noncollusive oligopolies is that a price war may break out, especially during a general business recession. Then

 CONSIDER THIS | Creative Strategic Behaviour

The following story, offered with tongue in cheek, illustrates a localized market that exhibits some characteristics of oligopoly, including strategic behaviour.

Tracy Proudfoot's Native Canadian Arts and Crafts store is located in the centre of a small tourist town that borders on a national park. In the business's early days, Tracy had a mini-monopoly. Business was brisk and prices and profits were high.

But to Tracy's chagrin, two copycat shops opened up right next door, one on either side of her store. Worse yet, the competitors named their shops to take advantage of Tracy's advertising. One was "Native Arts and Crafts," the other "Indian Arts and Crafts." These new sellers drew business away from Tracy's store, forcing her to lower her prices. The

three adjacent stores in the small, isolated town constituted a localized oligopoly for Native Canadian arts and crafts.

Tracy began to think strategically about ways to boost profit. She decided to distinguish her shop from those on either side by offering a greater mix of high-quality, expensive products and fewer inexpensive "souvenir" items. The tactic worked for a while, but the other stores eventually imitated her product mix.

Then, one of the competitors next door escalated the rivalry by hanging up a large sign proclaiming "We Sell for Less!" Shortly thereafter, the other shop put up a large sign stating, "We Won't Be Undersold!"

Not to be outdone, Tracy painted a colourful sign of her own and hung it above her door. It read, "Main Entrance."

each firm finds that, because of unsold goods and excess capacity, it can reduce per-unit costs by increasing market share. The possibility also exists that a new firm may surmount entry barriers and initiate aggressive price cutting to gain a foothold in the market. In addition, the oligopoly's tendency toward rigid prices may adversely affect profits if general inflationary pressures increase costs. But by controlling price through collusion, oligopolists may be able to reduce uncertainty, increase profits, and perhaps even prohibit the entry of new rivals.

PRICE AND OUTPUT

Assume that three oligopolistic firms (Gypsum, Sheetrock, and GSR) produce homogeneous products. All three firms have identical cost curves. Each firm's demand curve is indeterminate unless we know how its rivals will react to any price change. Therefore, we suppose each firm assumes that its two rivals will match either a price cut or a price increase. And, since they have identical cost data, and the same demand and thus marginal-revenue data, we can say that Figure 9-7 represents the position of each of our three oligopolistic firms.

What price and output combination should, say, Gypsum select? If Gypsum were a monopolist, the answer would be clear: Establish output at Q_0, where marginal revenue equals marginal cost, charge the corresponding price P_0, and enjoy the maximum profit attainable. However, Gypsum does have two rivals selling identical products, and if Gypsum's assumption that its rivals will match its price of P_0 proves to be incorrect, the consequences could be disastrous for Gypsum. Specifically, if Sheetrock and GSR actually charge prices below P_0 then Gypsum's demand curve D will shift sharply to the left as its potential customers turn to its rivals, which are now selling the same product at a lower price. Of course, Gypsum can retaliate by cutting its price too, but this will move all three firms down their demand curves, lowering their profits. It may even drive them to a point where average total cost exceeds price and losses are incurred.

So the question becomes, will Sheetrock and GSR want to charge a price below P_0? Under our assumptions, and recognizing that Gypsum has little choice except to match any price they may set below P_0, the answer is no. Faced with the same demand and cost circumstances, Sheetrock and GSR will find it in their interest to produce Q_0 and charge P_0. This is a curious situation; each firm finds it most profitable to charge the same price, P_0, but only if its rivals actually do so! How can the three firms ensure the price P_0 and quantity Q_0 solution in which each is keenly interested? How can they avoid the less profitable outcomes associated with either higher or lower prices?

The answer is evident: They could collude. They could get together, talk it over, and agree to charge the same price, P_0. In addition to reducing the possibility of price wars, this will give each

---

FIGURE 9-7 **Collusion and Joint-Profit Maximization**

If oligopolistic firms face identical or highly similar demand and cost conditions, they may collude to limit their joint output and to set a single, common price. Thus each firm acts as if it were a pure monopolist, setting output at Q_0 and charging price P_0. This price and output combination maximizes each oligopolist's profit (grey area) and thus their combined or joint profit.

9.1 | GLOBAL PERSPECTIVE

The 12 OPEC nations, daily oil production agreement as of February 2009

The OPEC nations produce about 40 percent of the world's oil and 60 percent of the oil sold in world markets.

OPEC country	Barrels of oil
Saudi Arabia	7,885,000
Iran	3,613,000
Kuwait	2,231,000
Venezuela	2,144,000
Iraq	2,315,000
UAE	2,251,000
Nigeria	1,820,000
Angola	1,725,000
Libya	1,544,000
Algeria	1,286,000
Qatar	740,000
Ecuador	476,000

Source: OPEC Secretariat, www.opec.org.

firm the maximum profit. (But it will also subject them to anticombines prosecution if they are caught!) For society, the result will be the same as would occur if the industry were a monopoly composed of three identical plants.

OVERT COLLUSION: THE OPEC CARTEL

cartel
A formal agreement among firms in an industry to set the price of a product and establish the outputs of the individual firms or to divide the market among them.

Collusion may assume a variety of forms. The most comprehensive form of collusion is the **cartel,** a group of producers that typically creates a formal written agreement specifying how much each member will produce and charge. Output must be controlled to maintain the agreed-on price. The collusion is overt, or open to view.

Undoubtedly the most significant international cartel is the Organization of the Petroleum Exporting Countries (OPEC), comprising 12 oil-producing nations (see Global Perspective 9.1). OPEC produces 40 percent of the world's oil and supplies 60 percent of all oil traded internationally. In the late 1990s OPEC reacted vigorously to very low oil prices by greatly restricting supply. Some non-OPEC producers supported the cutback in production and within a 15-month period the price of oil shot up from $11 a barrel to $34 a barrel. Gasoline prices in Canada rose by as much as 50 percent in some markets. Fearing a global political and economic backlash from the major industrial nations, OPEC upped the production quotas for its members in mid-2000. The increases in oil supply that resulted reduced the price of oil to about $25, where it remained through 2002.

OPEC supply restrictions were less of a factor in the rising oil prices in the 2005–09 period, when rapidly rising demand for oil in China and supply uncertainties related to armed conflict in the Middle East drove the price of oil to more than $140 a barrel in 2008—before the price came crashing down with the deepening of the financial crisis in September of that year. In early 2009 the price of oil dropped below $40. The global financial crisis of 2008–09 showed that production cuts by OPEC could not prevent the price from dropping precipitously. Still, OPEC has the market power to hold the price of oil substantially above its marginal cost of production.

COVERT COLLUSION: EXAMPLES

Cartels are illegal in Canada, and hence any collusion that exists is covert, or secret. Yet there are examples, found in evidence from anticombines (antimonopoly) cases. One example of covert collusion is the case of four cement firms in the Quebec City Region. In 1996, St. Lawrence Cement Inc., Lafarge Canada Inc., Cement Quebec Inc., and Beton Orleans Inc. were fined a total of $5.8 million for price fixing. The conspiracy was discovered by a Quebec City newspaper that reported that the cost of the city's new convention centre was higher than anticipated. The first three of these firms had previously been fined in 1983 for a similar violation of the Competition Act. More recently, in 2008 LG Display, Sharp, and Chunghwa Picture Tubes were fined a total of US$585 million by the U.S. Justice Department for conspiring to drive up the price of liquid-crystal display monitors (LCDs), used on most notebook computers, cell phones, and new televisions.

tacit understanding
Any method by competing oligopolists to set prices and outputs that does not involve outright collusion.

In many other instances collusion is even more subtle. **Tacit understandings** (historically called "gentlemen's agreements") are frequently made at cocktail parties, on golf courses, through phone calls, or at trade association meetings. In such agreements, competing firms reach a verbal understanding on product price, leaving market shares to be decided by nonprice competition. Although these agreements, too, violate anticombines laws—and can result in severe personal and corporate penalties—the elusive character of tacit understandings makes them difficult to detect.

OBSTACLES TO COLLUSION

Normally, cartels and similar collusive arrangements are difficult to establish and maintain, for several reasons:

- *Demand and Cost Differences*   When oligopolists face different costs and demand curves, it is difficult for them to agree on a price. Even with highly standardized products, firms usually have somewhat different market shares and operate with differing degrees of productive efficiency. Thus, it is unlikely that even homogeneous oligopolists would have the same demand and cost curves.

  In either case, differences in costs and demand mean that the profit-maximizing price will differ among firms; no single price will be readily acceptable to all, as we assumed was true in Figure 9-7. So, price collusion depends on compromises and concessions that are not always easy to obtain, and hence they act as obstacles to collusion.

- *Number of Firms*   Other things equal, the larger the number of firms, the more difficult it is to create a cartel or other form of price collusion. Agreement on price by three or four producers that control an entire market may be relatively easy to accomplish, but such agreement is more difficult to achieve where there are, say, 10 firms, each with roughly 10 percent of the market, or where the Big Three have 70 percent of the market while a competitive fringe of 8 or 10 smaller firms battle for the remainder.

- *Cheating*   As the game theory model makes clear, there is a temptation for collusive oligopolists to engage in secret price cutting to increase sales and profit. The difficulty with such cheating is that buyers who are paying a high price for a product may become aware of the lower-priced sales and demand similar treatment. Or buyers receiving a price concession from one producer may use the concession as a wedge to get even larger price concessions from a rival producer. Buyers' attempts to play producers against one another may precipitate price wars among the producers. Although secret price concessions are potentially profitable, they threaten collusive oligopolies over time. Collusion is more likely to succeed when cheating is easy to detect and punish.

- *Recession*   Long-lasting recession usually serves as an enemy of collusion, because slumping markets increase average total cost. In technical terms, as the oligopolists' demand and marginal revenue curves shift to the left in Figure 9-7 in response to a recession, each firm moves leftward and upward to a higher operating point on its average-total-cost curve. Firms find they have substantial excess production capacity, sales are down, unit costs are up, and profits are being squeezed. Under such conditions, businesses may feel they can avoid serious profit reductions (or even losses) by cutting price and thus gaining sales at the expense of rivals.

- *Potential Entry*   The greater prices and profits that result from collusion may attract new entrants, including foreign firms. Since that would increase market supply and reduce prices and profits, successful collusion requires that colluding oligopolists block the entry of new producers.

- *Legal Obstacles: Competition Policy*   Canadian anticombines laws prohibit cartels and price-fixing collusion, so less obvious means of price control have evolved in Canada.

Price Leadership Model: Another Cooperative Strategy

price leadership
An implicit understanding oligopolists use that has the dominant firm initiate price changes and all other firms follow.

Price leadership is a type of implicit understanding by which oligopolists can coordinate prices. A practice evolves whereby the "dominant firm" initiates price changes and all other firms more or less automatically follow the leader. Many industries, including cement, newsprint, glass containers, steel, beer, fertilizer, cigarettes, and tin, practise or have recently practised price leadership.

LEADERSHIP STRATEGY

An examination of price leadership in a variety of industries suggests that the price leader is likely to use the following strategies.

- *Infrequent Price Changes*   Because price changes always carry the risk that rivals will not follow the lead, price adjustments are made only infrequently, when cost and demand conditions have been altered significantly.

- *Communications*   The price leader often communicates impending price adjustments to the industry through speeches by major executives, trade publication interviews, or press releases. By publicizing the need to raise prices, the price leader seeks agreement among its competitors regarding the actual increase.

- *Limit Pricing*   The price leader does not always choose the price that maximizes short-run profits for the industry because the industry may want to discourage new firms from entering. To discourage new competitors and to maintain the current oligopolistic structure of the industry, the price leader may keep price below the short-run profit-maximizing level. The strategy of establishing a price that blocks the entry of new firms is called limit pricing.

- *Breakdowns in Price Leadership: Price Wars*   Price leadership in oligopoly occasionally breaks down, and sometimes results in a price war. An example of disruption of price leadership occurred in the breakfast cereal industry, in which Kellogg traditionally had been the price leader. General Mills countered Kellogg's leadership in 1995 by reducing the prices of its cereals by 11 percent. In 1996 Post responded with a 20 percent price cut, which Kellogg then followed. Not to be outdone, Post reduced its prices by another 11 percent.

As another example, in late 2002 Burger King set off a price war in the United States by offering its bacon cheeseburger for 99¢. McDonald's countered by placing a price tag of $1 on its Big N' Tasty burger, which competed directly against Burger King's popular Whopper. Burger King then offered a "limited-time special" of 99¢ for Whoppers.

Most price wars eventually run their course. When all firms recognize that low prices are severely reducing their profits, they again cede price leadership to one of the industry's leading firms. That firm then begins to raise prices, and the other firms willingly follow suit.

QUICK REVIEW

▶ Cartels agree on production limits and set a common price to maximize the joint profit of their members as if each were a unit of a single pure monopoly.

▶ Collusion among oligopolists is difficult because of (1) demand and cost differences among sellers, (2) the complexity of output coordination among producers, (3) the potential for cheating, (4) a tendency for agreements to break down during recessions, (5) the potential entry of new firms, and (6) competition laws.

▶ Price leadership involves an informal understanding among oligopolists to match any price change initiated by a designated firm (often the industry's dominant firm).

9.6 | Oligopoly and Advertising

We have noted that oligopolists would rather not compete on the basis of price and may become involved in price collusion. Nonetheless, each firm's share of the total market is typically determined through product development and advertising, for two reasons:

1. Product improvements and successful advertising can produce more permanent gains in market share because they cannot be duplicated as quickly and completely as price reductions.

2. Oligopolists have sufficient financial resources to engage in product development and advertising.

In recent years, Canadian advertising has exceeded $6 billion annually, and worldwide advertising, $630 billion. Advertising is prevalent in both monopolistic competition and oligopoly.

Advertising may affect prices, competition, and efficiency both positively and negatively, depending on the circumstances. While our focus here is on advertising by oligopolists, the analysis is equally applicable to advertising by firms in monopolistic competition.

Positive Effects of Advertising

To make rational (efficient) decisions, consumers need information about product characteristics and prices. Media advertising may be a low-cost means for consumers to obtain that information. Suppose you are in the market for a high-quality camera and there is no advertising for such a product in newspapers or magazines or on the Internet. To make a rational choice, you may have to spend several days visiting stores to determine the prices and features of various brands. This search has both direct costs (gasoline, parking fees) and indirect costs (the value of your time). By providing information about the available options, advertising reduces your search time and minimizes these costs.

By providing information about the various competing goods that are available, advertising diminishes monopoly power. In fact, advertising is frequently associated with the introduction of new products designed to compete with existing brands. Could Toyota and Honda have so strongly challenged North American auto producers without advertising? Could Federal Express have sliced market share away from UPS and Canada Post without advertising?

Viewed this way, advertising is an efficiency-enhancing activity. It is a relatively inexpensive means of providing useful information to consumers and thus lowering their search costs. By enhancing competition, advertising results in greater economic efficiency. By facilitating the introduction of new products, advertising speeds up technological progress. And by increasing output, advertising can reduce long-run average total cost by enabling firms to obtain economies of scale.

Potential Negative Effects of Advertising

Not all the effects of advertising are positive. Much advertising is designed simply to persuade consumers in favour of the advertiser's product. A television commercial that indicates a popular personality drinks a particular brand of soft drink conveys little or no information to consumers about price or quality. Indeed, in some cases advertising may well persuade consumers to pay high prices for much-acclaimed but inferior products, forgoing better but unadvertised products selling at lower prices. For example, *Consumer Reports* recently found that heavily advertised premium motor oils and fancy additives provide no better engine performance and longevity than do cheaper brands.

9.2 | GLOBAL PERSPECTIVE

The world's top 10 brand names, 2007

Here are the world's top 10 brands, based on four criteria: the brand's market share within its category, the brand's world appeal across age groups and nationalities, the loyalty of customers to the brand, and the ability of the brand to stretch to products beyond the original product.

Coca-Cola
IBM
Microsoft
General Electric
Nokia
Toyota
Intel
McDonald's
Disney
Google

Source: Interbrand, www.interbrand.com.

Firms often establish substantial brand-name loyalty and thus achieve monopoly power via their advertising (see Global Perspective 9.2). As a consequence, they are able to increase their sales, expand their market share, and enjoy greater profits. Larger profit permits still more advertising and further enlargement of the firm's market share and profit. In time, consumers may lose the advantages of competitive markets and face the disadvantages of monopolized markets. Moreover, new entrants to the industry need to incur large advertising costs to establish their products in the marketplace; thus, advertising costs may be a barrier to entry. *(Key Question 12)*

Advertising may also be self-cancelling. The advertising campaign of one fast-food hamburger chain may be offset by equally costly campaigns waged by rivals, so each firm's demand actually remains unchanged. Few, if any, extra burgers will be purchased, and each firm's market share will stay the same. But because of the advertising, the cost and hence the price of hamburgers will be higher.

When advertising either leads to increased monopoly power or is self-cancelling, economic inefficiency results.

Oligopoly and Efficiency

Is oligopoly, then, an efficient market structure from society's standpoint? How do the price and output decisions of the oligopolist measure up to the triple equality $P = MC = $ minimum ATC that occurs in perfect competition?

PRODUCTIVE AND ALLOCATIVE EFFICIENCY

Many economists believe that the outcome of some oligopolistic markets is approximately as shown in Figure 9-7. This view is bolstered by evidence that many oligopolists sustain sizable economic profits year after year. In that case, the oligopolist's production occurs where price exceeds marginal cost and average total cost. Moreover, production is below the output at which average total cost is minimized. In this view, neither productive efficiency ($P = $ minimum ATC) nor allocative efficiency ($P = MC$) is likely to occur under oligopoly.

QUALIFICATIONS

A few observers assert that oligopoly is actually less desirable than pure monopoly, because government usually regulates monopoly to guard against abuses of monopoly power. Informal collusion among oligopolists may yield price and output results similar to those under monopoly yet give the outward appearance of competition involving independent firms. We should note, however, three qualifications to this view:

- **Increased Foreign Competition**   In recent decades foreign competition has increased rivalry in a number of oligopolistic industries—steel, automobiles, photographic film, electric shavers, outboard motors, and copy machines, for example. This has helped to break down such cozy arrangements as price leadership and to stimulate much more competitive pricing.

- **Limit Pricing**   Recall that some oligopolists may purposely keep prices below the short-run profit-maximizing level in order to bolster entry barriers. In essence, consumers and society may get some of the benefits of competition—prices closer to marginal cost and minimum average total cost—even without the competition that free entry would provide.

- **Technological Advance**   Over time, oligopolistic industries may foster more rapid product development and greater improvement of production techniques than would be possible if they were perfectly competitive. Oligopolists have large economic profits from which they can fund expensive research and development (R&D). Moreover, the existence of barriers to entry may give the oligopolist some assurance that it will reap the rewards of successful R&D. Thus, the short-run economic inefficiencies of oligopolists may be partly or wholly offset by the oligopolists' contributions to better products, lower prices, and lower costs over time.

The LAST WORD   Oligopoly in the Beer Industry

The beer industry was once populated by dozens of firms and an even larger number of brands. It is now an oligopoly dominated by a handful of producers.

The brewing industry has undergone profound changes since World War II that have increased the degree of concentration in the industry. In 1945 more than 60 independent brewing companies operated in Canada. By 1967 there were 18, and by 1984 only 11. While the three largest brewers sold only 19 percent of the nation's beer in 1947, the big three brewers (Labatt, Molson, and Carling O'Keefe) sold 97 percent of the nation's domestically produced beer in 1989, the same year Molson and Carling O'Keefe merged. In 1995, Belgium-based Interbrew SA (which later merged with AmBev to become InBev) bought Labatt Canada. In 2005, Molson joined forces with

U.S.-based Coors, creating Molson-Coors, the fifth largest brewer in the world. Currently, the big two—Labatt (InBev) and Molson-Coors (each pro-

ducing 40 percent)—brew most of the beer in Canada. The industry is clearly an oligopoly.

Changes on the demand side of the market have contributed to the shakeout of small brewers from the industry. First, consumer tastes have generally shifted from the stronger-flavoured beers of the small brewers to the light products of the larger brewers. Second, there has been a shift from the consumption of beer in taverns to consumption in the home. The significance of this change is that taverns were usually supplied with kegs from local brewers to avoid the relatively high cost of shipping kegs. But the acceptance of aluminum cans for home consumption made it possible for large, distant brewers to compete with the local brewers, because the former could now ship their products by truck or rail without breakage.

Developments on the supply side of the market have been even more profound. Technological advances have increased the speed of the bottling and canning lines. Today, large brewers can fill and close 2000 cans per line per minute. Large plants are also able to reduce labour costs through automating brewing and warehousing. Furthermore, plant construction costs per barrel are about one-third less for a 4.0-million-hectolitres plant than for a 1.5-million-barrel plant. As a consequence of these and other factors, the minimum efficient scale in brewing is a plant size of about 4.0 million hectolitres, with multiple plants. Because the construction cost of a modern brewery that size is $330 million, economies of scale may now constitute a significant barrier to entry.

Blind taste tests confirm that most mass-produced Canadian beers taste alike, so brewers greatly emphasize advertising. Here, Labatt and Molson-Coors, who sell national brands, enjoy major cost advantages over producers that have regional brands (for example, Creemore Springs, Upper Canada, and Okanagan Spring). The reason is because national television advertising is less costly *per viewer* than local spot TV advertising.

Mergers in the brewing industry have been a fundamental cause of the rising concentration. Dominant firms have expanded by heavily advertising their main brands—such as Labatt Blue and Blue Light, and Molson Canadian and Coors Light—sustaining significant product differentiation despite the declining number of major brewers.

But there are problems brewing for Canada's large beer producers. Imported beers such as Beck's, Corona, Foster's, and Guinness constitute about 13 percent of the Canadian market, with individual brands seeming to wax and wane in popularity. Some local or regional microbreweries such as Upper Canada (purchased by Sleeman), which brew specialty beers, and low cost producers such as Lakeport in Ontario have whittled into the sales of the major brewers. For example, according to the Brewers Association, Canadian microbrewery sales rose slightly in 2007, while mass-produced beer actually declined. Overall, both imports and microbreweries are becoming a threat to the two major brewers in Canada.

Sources: Based on Kenneth G. Elzinga, "Beer," in Walter Adams and James Brock (eds.), *The Structure of American Industry*, 9th ed. (Englewood Cliffs, NJ: Prentice-Hall, 1995), pp. 119–151; Douglas F. Greer, "Beer: Causes of Structural Change," in Larry Duetsch (ed.), *Industry Studies*, 2nd ed. (New York: M. E. Sharpe, 1998), pp. 28–64; authors' updates; the Conference Board of Canada, *The Canadian Brewing Industry: Historical Evolution and Competitive Structure* (Toronto: International Studies and Development Group, 1989).

Question

What firm(s) dominate the beer industry? What demand and supply factors have contributed to the small number of firms in this industry?

CHAPTER SUMMARY

9.1 ▶ CHARACTERISTICS OF MONOPOLISTIC COMPETITION

- The distinguishing features of monopolistic competition are (a) enough firms are in the industry to ensure each firm has only limited control over price, mutual interdependence is absent, and collusion is nearly impossible; (b) products are characterized by real or perceived differences so that economic rivalry entails both price and nonprice competition; and (c) entry to the industry is relatively easy. Many aspects of retailing, and some manufacturing industries in which economies of scale are few, approximate monopolistic competition.

- The four-firm concentration ratio measures the percentage of total industry output accounted for by the largest four firms. The Herfindahl index sums the squares of the market shares of all firms in the industry.

9.2 ▶ PRICE AND OUTPUT IN MONOPOLISTIC COMPETITION

- Monopolistically competitive firms may earn economic profits or incur losses in the short run. The easy entry and exit of firms result in only normal profits in the long run.

- The long-run equilibrium position of the monopolistically competitive producer is less socially desirable than that of the pure competitor. Under monopolistic competition, price exceeds marginal cost, suggesting an underallocation of resources to the product, and price exceeds minimum average total cost, indicating that consumers do not get the product at the lowest price that cost conditions might allow.

- Nonprice competition provides a means by which monopolistically competitive firms can offset the long-run tendency for economic profit to fall to zero. Through product differentiation, product development, and advertising, a firm may strive to increase the demand for its product more than enough to cover the added cost of such nonprice competition. Consumers benefit from the wide diversity of product choice that monopolistic competition provides.

- In practice, the monopolistic competitor seeks the specific combination of price, product, and advertising that will maximize profit.

9.3 ▶ OLIGOPOLY

- Oligopolistic industries are characterized by the presence of few firms, each having a significant fraction of the market. Firms thus situated are mutually interdependent: the behaviour of any one firm directly affects, and is affected by, the actions of rivals. Products may be either virtually uniform or significantly differentiated. Various barriers to entry, including economies of scale, underlie and maintain oligopoly.

- High concentration ratios are an indication of oligopoly (monopoly) power. By giving more weight to larger firms, the Herfindahl index is designed to measure market dominance in an industry.

9.4 ▶ OLIGOPOLY PRICING BEHAVIOUR: A GAME THEORY OVERVIEW

- The prisoner's dilemma is a type of game that shows the difficulty of cooperating when the participants cannot communicate with one another.

- Game theory (a) shows the interdependence of oligopolists' pricing policies; (b) reveals the tendency of oligopolists to collude; and (c) explains the temptation of oligopolists to cheat on collusive arrangements.

9.5 ▶ THE INCENTIVES AND OBSTACLES TO COLLUSION: TWO OLIGOPOLY STRATEGIES

- The uncertainties inherent in oligopoly promote collusion. Collusive oligopolists such as cartels maximize joint profits—that is, they behave like pure monopolists. Demand and cost differences, a large number of firms, cheating through secret price concessions, recessions, and the anti-combines laws are all obstacles to collusive oligopoly.

- Price leadership is an informal means of collusion whereby one firm, usually the largest or most efficient, initiates price changes and the other firms in the industry follow the leader.

- Market shares in oligopolistic industries are usually determined based on product development and advertising. Oligopolists emphasize nonprice competition because (a) advertising and product variations are harder for rivals to match and (b) oligopolists frequently have ample resources to finance nonprice competition.

9.6 ▶ OLIGOPOLY AND ADVERTISING

- Advertising may affect prices, competition, and efficiency either positively or negatively. Positive: It can provide consumers with low-cost information about competing products, help introduce new competing products into concentrated industries, and generally reduce monopoly power and its attendant inefficiencies. Negative: It can promote monopoly power via persuasion and the creation of entry barriers. Moreover, when engaged in by rivals it can be self-cancelling by boosting costs and increasing economic inefficiency while accomplishing little else.

- Neither productive nor allocative efficiency is realized in oligopolistic markets, but oligopoly may be superior to pure competition in promoting research and development and technological progress.

TERMS AND CONCEPTS

monopolistic competition, p. 220
product differentiation, p. 220
nonprice competition, p. 221
four-firm concentration ratio, p. 222
Herfindahl index, p. 222
excess capacity, p. 226
oligopoly, p. 228

homogeneous oligopoly, p. 228
differentiated oligopoly, p. 228
strategic behaviour, p. 228
mutual interdependence, p. 228
interindustry competition, p. 229
import competition, p. 229

game theory model, p. 231
prisoner's dilemma, p. 232
collusion, p. 234
cartel, p. 237
tacit understanding, p. 238
price leadership, p. 239

STUDY QUESTIONS

9.1 1. How does monopolistic competition differ from perfect competition in its basic characteristics? From monopoly? Explain fully what product differentiation may involve. Explain how the entry of firms into its industry affects the demand curve facing a monopolistic competitor and how that, in turn, affects its economic profit.

9.2 2. **KEY QUESTION** Compare the elasticity of the monopolistic competitor's demand with that of a perfectly competitive firm and a monopolist. Assuming identical long-run costs, compare graphically the prices and outputs that would result in the long run under perfect competition and under monopolistic competition. Contrast the two market structures in terms of productive and allocative efficiency. Explain: "Monopolistically competitive industries are characterized by too many firms, each of which produces too little."

9.2 3. "Monopolistic competition is monopolistic up to the point at which consumers become willing to buy close substitute products and competitive beyond that point." Explain.

9.2 4. "Competition in quality and service may be just as effective as price competition in giving buyers more for their money." Do you agree? Why? Explain why monopolistically competitive firms frequently prefer nonprice competition to price competition.

9.2 5. Critically evaluate and explain:

a. "In monopolistically competitive industries, economic profits are competed away in the long run; hence, there is no valid reason to criticize the performance and efficiency of such industries."

b. "In the long run, monopolistic competition leads to a monopolistic price but not to monopolistic profits."

9.3 6. Why do oligopolies exist? List five or six oligopolists whose products you own or regularly purchase. What distinguishes oligopoly from monopolistic competition?

9.3 7. **KEY QUESTION** Answer the following questions, which relate to measures of concentration:

a. What is the meaning of a four-firm concentration ratio of 60 percent? 90 percent? What are the shortcomings of concentration ratios as measures of monopoly power?

b. Suppose that the five firms in industry A have annual sales of 30, 30, 20, 10, and 10 percent of total industry sales. For the five firms in industry B the figures are 60, 25, 5, 5, and 5 percent. Calculate the Herfindahl index for each industry and compare their likely competitiveness.

9.4 8. The following questions relate to the "prisoner's dilemma."

a. Invent a prisoner's dilemma in which two students writing a multiple choice exam at opposite ends of a classroom are caught using hand signals to communicate. The professor in the room suspects they are cheating but has

no definitive proof. Design a payoff matrix that gives each of the students an incentive to confess. Is there an equilibrium point in this game?

b. Repeat the game assuming the two students are a brother and sister who care deeply about, and trust, each other.

9. **KEY QUESTION** Explain the general meaning of the following payoff matrix for oligopolists C and D. All profit figures are in thousands.   **LO ▸ 9.5**

C's possible prices

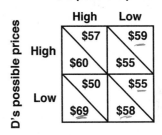

a. Use the payoff matrix to explain the mutual interdependence that characterizes oligopolistic industries.

b. Assuming no collusion between C and D, what is the likely pricing outcome?

c. In view of your answer to 9b, explain why price collusion is mutually profitable. Why might a temptation to cheat on the collusive agreement exist?

10. Consider the following payoff matrix in which the numbers indicate the profit in millions of dollars for a duopoly based either on a high-price or a low-price strategy.   **LO ▸ 9.5**

Firm A

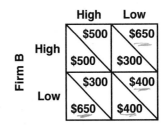

a. What will be the result when each firm chooses a high-price strategy?

b. What will be the result when Firm A chooses a low-price strategy while Firm B maintains a high-price strategy?

c. What will be the result when Firm B chooses a low-price strategy while Firm A maintains a high-price strategy?

d. What will be the result when each firm chooses a low-price strategy?

e. What two conclusions can you draw about collusion?

LO 9.5 11. Why might price collusion occur in oligopolistic industries? Assess the economic desirability of collusive pricing. What are the main obstacles to collusion? Speculate why price leadership is legal in Canada, whereas price fixing is not.

LO 9.6 12. **KEY QUESTION** Why is there so much advertising in monopolistic competition and oligopoly? How does such advertising help consumers and promote efficiency? Why might it be excessive at times?

13. **(Advanced Analysis)** Construct a game theory matrix involving two firms and their decisions on high versus low advertising budgets and the effects of each decision on profits. Show a circumstance in which both firms select high advertising budgets even though both would be more profitable with low advertising budgets. Why won't they unilaterally cut their advertising budget? **LO**

INTERNET APPLICATION QUESTIONS

1. **Nonprice Competition in Book Sales.** Use a search engine to find the current *Globe and Mail* bestseller lists. Choose one book of fiction and one book of non-fiction from the top-five lists. Next, access Indigo and Amazon through the McConnell-Brue-Flynn-Barbiero Web site (Chapter 9) and find the price, including shipping to your address, of your two books. Is one company less expensive? Identify the nonprice competition that might lead you to order from one company rather than the other.

Appendix to Chapter 9

ADDITIONAL GAME THEORY APPLICATIONS

We have seen that game theory is helpful in explaining mutual interdependence and strategic behaviour by oligopolists. This appendix provides additional oligopoly-based applications of game theory.

A9.1 | A ONE-TIME GAME: STRATEGIES AND EQUILIBRIUM

Consider Figure A9-1, which lists strategies and outcomes for two fictitious producers of the computer memory chips referred to as DRAMs (Dynamic Random Access Memory circuits). Chipco is the single producer of these chips in Canada and Dramco is the only producer in China. Each firm has two alternative strategies: an international strategy in which it competes directly against the other firm in both countries; and a national strategy in which it confines its sales to its home country.

The game and payoff matrix shown in Figure A9-1 is a **one-time game** because the firms select their optimal strategy in a single time period without regard to possible interactions in subsequent time periods. The game is also a **simultaneous game,** because the firms choose their strategies at the same time, and a **positive-sum game,** a game in which the sum of the two firms' outcomes (here, profits) is positive. (In contrast, the net gain in a **zero-sum game** is zero because one firm's gain must equal the other firm's loss, and the net gain in a **negative-sum game** is negative.) In some positive-sum games, both firms may have positive outcomes; that is the case in Figure A9-1.

To determine optimal strategies, Chipco looks across the two rows in the payoff matrix (blue portion of cells in millions of dollars) and Dramco looks down the two columns (green portion of cells). These payoffs indicate that both firms have a **dominant strategy**—an option that is better than any alternative option *regardless of what the other firm does.* To see this, notice that Chipco's international strategy will give it a higher profit than its national strategy—regardless of whether Dramco chooses to utilize an international or a national strategy. An international strategy will produce an $11 million profit for Chipco (tan portion of cell A) if Dramco also uses an international strategy, while a national strategy will result in a $20 million profit for Chipco (tan portion of cell B) if Dramco uses a national strategy. Chipco's possible $11 million and $20 million outcomes are clearly better than the $5 million (cell C) and $17 million (cell D) outcomes it

FIGURE A9-1   One-Time Game

In this single-period, positive-sum game, Chipco's international strategy is its dominant strategy—the alternative that is superior to any other strategy regardless of whatever Dramco does. Similarly, Dramco's international strategy is also its dominant strategy. With both firms choosing international strategies, the outcome of the game is cell A, where each firm receives an $11 million profit. cell A is a Nash equilibrium because neither firm will independently want to move away from it given the other firm's strategy.

could receive if it chose to pursue a national strategy. Chipco's international strategy is, consequently, its dominant strategy. Using similar logic, Dramco also concludes that its international strategy is its dominant strategy.

In this particular case, the outcome (cell A) of the two dominant strategies is the game's **Nash equilibrium**—an outcome from which neither rival wants to deviate.[1] At the Nash equilibrium, both rivals see their current strategy as optimal *given the other firm's strategic choice*. The Nash equilibrium is the only outcome in the payoff matrix in Figure A9-1 that, once achieved, is stable and therefore will persist.[2]

Credible and Empty Threats

In looking for optimal strategies, Chipco and Dramco both note that they could increase their profit from $11 million to $17 million if they could agree to jointly pursue national strategies (cell D) instead of independently pursuing international strategies (cell A). Presumably the national strategies would leave the firms as pure monopolists in their domestic economies, with each able to set higher prices and obtain greater profits as a result. But if this territorial agreement were put in place, both firms would have an incentive to cheat on the agreement by secretly selling DRAMs in each other's countries. That would temporarily move the game to either cell B or cell C. Once discovered, however, such cheating would undermine the territorial agreement and return the game to the Nash equilibrium (cell A).

Now let's add a new twist—a credible threat—to the game shown in Figure A9-1. A **credible threat** is a statement of coercion (a threat!) that is believable by the other firm. Suppose that Chipco is the low-cost producer of DRAMs because of its superior technology. Also, suppose that Chipco approaches Dramco saying that Chipco intends to use its national strategy and expects Dramco to do the same. If Dramco decides against the national strategy or agrees to the strategy and then later cheats on the agreement, Chipco will immediately drop its price to an ultra-low level equal to its average total cost (ATC). Both firms know that Chipco's ATC price is below Dramco's ATC. Although Chipco will see its economic profit fall to zero, Dramco will suffer an economic loss and possibly go out of business.

If Chipco's threat is credible, the two firms represented in Figure A9-1 will abandon the Nash equilibrium (cell A) to deploy their national strategies and achieve highly profitable cell D. In game theory, credible threats such as this can help establish and maintain collusive agreements. A strong "enforcer"

can help prevent cheating and maintain the group discipline needed for cartels, price-fixing conspiracies, and territorial understandings to successfully generate high profits.

But credible threats are difficult to achieve in the actual economy. For example, Dramco might rightly wonder why Chipco had not previously driven it out of business through an ultra-low price strategy. Is Chipco fearful of the Canadian Competition Bureau?

If Dramco does not wish to participate in the proposed scheme, it might counter Chipco's threat with its own: Forget that you ever talked to us and we will not take this illegal "offer" to the Competition Bureau. Dramco can make this threat because strict laws are in place against attempts to restrain trade through price fixing and territorial agreements.

So Dramco may view Chipco's threat as simply an **empty threat**—a statement of coercion that is not believable by the threatened firm. If so, the Nash equilibrium will prevail, with both firms pursuing an international strategy.

Repeated Games and Reciprocity Strategies

The Chipco–Dramco game was a one-time game, but many strategic situations are repeated by the same oligopolists over and over. For example, Coca-Cola and Pepsi face mutual interdependency on pricing, advertising, and product development year after year, decade after decade. The same is true for Boeing and Airbus, Wal-Mart and Zellers, Toyota and General Motors, Labatt and Molson, Nike and Adidas, and numerous other dominant pairs.

In a **repeated game**—a game that recurs more than once—the optimal strategy may be to cooperate and restrain oneself from competing as hard as possible so long as the other firm reciprocates by also not competing as hard as possible.[3] To see how this works, consider two hypothetical producers of soft drinks: 2Cool and ThirstQ. If 2Cool competes hard with ThirstQ in today's situation, in which ThirstQ would like 2Cool to take things easy, ThirstQ will most likely retaliate against 2Cool in any subsequent situation where the circumstances are reversed. In contrast, if ThirstQ cooperates with 2Cool in game 1, ThirstQ can expect 2Cool to reciprocate in game 2 of their repeated interaction. Both firms know full well the negative long-run consequences of ever refusing to cooperate. So the cooperation continues, not only in game 2, but in games 3, 4, 5, and beyond.

Figure A9-2 shows side-by-side payoff matrixes for the two games. In Figure A9-2a, 2Cool and ThirstQ face a situation in which 2Cool is introducing a new cola called Cool Cola and

---

[1] The Nash equilibrium is named for its discoverer, John F. Nash. Nash's life and Nobel Prize are the subject of the motion picture *A Beautiful Mind*, produced by Ron Howard and starring Russell Crowe.

[2] Dominant strategies in games are not required for Nash equilibriums to exist.

[3] We are assuming either an infinitely repeated game or a game of unknown time-horizon. Games with a known ending date undermine reciprocity strategies.

has two advertising options: a high promotional budget to introduce the new product and a normal advertising budget. ThirstQ has the same two options: a high promotional budget to try to counter 2Cool's product introduction and a normal advertising budget.

The analysis is now familiar to you, so we will speed the pace. The dominant strategies for both firms are their large promotional advertising budgets, and the Nash equilibrium is cell A. Both firms could do better at cell D if each agreed to use normal advertising budgets. But 2Cool could do better still. It could achieve the $16 million of profit in cell B, but only if ThirstQ holds its advertising budget to its normal level during the introduction of Cool Cola.

ThirstQ might voluntarily do just that! It knows that game 2 (Figure A9-2b) is forthcoming, in which it will be introducing its new product, Quench It. By leaving its advertising budget at its normal level during Cool2's introduction of Cool Cola, and thereby sacrificing profit of $2 million (= $10 million in cell A − $8 million in cell B), it can expect ThirstQ to reciprocate in the subsequent game in which it introduces Quench It. Without formally colluding—and risking antitrust penalties—

game 1 ends at cell B and repeated game 2 ends at cell C. Using reciprocity, 2Cool's total profit of $26 million (= $16 million in game 1 + $10 million in game 2) exceeds the $21 million (= $10 million + $11 million) it would have earned without the reciprocity. ThirstQ similarly benefits. To check your understanding, confirm this fact using the numbers in the two matrixes.

First-Mover Advantages and Preemption of Entry

In the games we have highlighted thus far the two firms simultaneously select their optimal strategies. But in some actual economic circumstances, firms apply strategies sequentially: One firm moves first and commits to a strategy to which a rival firm must subsequently respond. In such a **sequential game,** the final outcome may depend critically upon which firm moves first since the first mover may have the opportunity to establish a Nash equilibrium that works in its favour.

Consider Figure A9-3, which identifies a zero-sum game in which two large retailers—let's call them Big Box and Huge Box—are each considering building a large retail store in a small

---

FIGURE A9·2   **A Repeated Game with Reciprocity**

(a) In the payoff matrix to the left, 2Cool introduces its new Cool Cola with a large promotional advertising budget, but its rival ThirstQ maintains its normal advertising budget even though it could counter 2Cool with a large advertising budget of its own and drive the outcome from cell B to cell A. ThirstQ forgoes this $2 million of extra profit because it knows that it will soon be introducing its own new product (Quench It). (b) In the payoff matrix to the right, ThirstQ introduces Quench It with a large promotional advertising budget. Cool2 reciprocates ThirstQ's earlier accommodation by not matching ThirstQ's promotional advertising budget and instead allowing the outcome of the repeated game to be cell C. The profit of both 2Cool and ThirstQ therefore is larger over the two periods than if each firm had aggressively countered the other's single-period strategy.

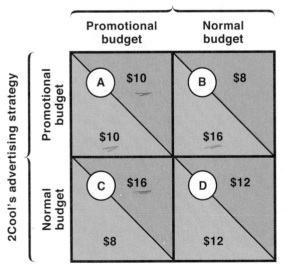

(a) 2Cool introduces Cool Cola

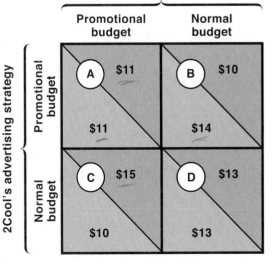

(b) ThirstQ's introduces Quench It

FIGURE A9-3   A First-Mover Advantage and the Preemption of Entry

In this game in which strategies are pursued sequentially, the firm that moves first can take advantage of the particular situation represented in which only a single firm can exist profitably in some geographical market. Here, we suppose that Big Box moves first with its "Build" strategy to achieve the $12 million profit outcome in cell C. Huge Box then will find that it will lose money if it also builds in this market because that will result in a $5 million loss, as shown in cell A.

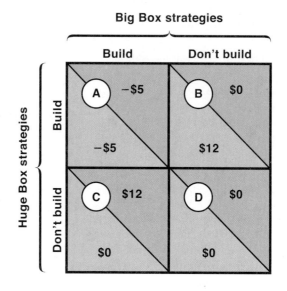

rural city. As indicated in the figure, each firm has two strategies: Build or Do Not Build. The payoff matrix reflects that the city is not large enough to support two big box retailers profitably. If both retailers simultaneously build, the outcome will be cell A and each firm will lose $5 million. If neither firm builds the outcome will be cell D with both firms securing zero profit. If only Big Box builds, the outcome will be cell B and Big Box will profit handsomely at $12 million. If Huge Box builds but Big Box stays out, the outcome will be cell C and Huge Box will secure the $12 million profit. Either cell B or cell C is the possible Nash equilibrium. At either cell, both firms will have selected their best option in view of the strategy taken by the other firm.

The payoff matrix in Figure A9-3 clearly reveals that whoever builds first will preempt the other retailer from entering the market. An extremely large **first-mover advantage** exists in this particular game. Suppose that a well-thought-out strategy and adequate financing leave Big Box better prepared than Huge Box to move quickly to build a large retail store in this city. By exploiting its first-mover advantage, Big Box preempts Huge Box's entry to this market.

Many actual firms have used variations of this first-mover strategy to a greater or lesser extent to preempt major rivals, or at least greatly slow their entry. Examples are Canadian Tire, The Bay, Wal-Mart, Home Depot, Costco, Starbucks, and many more. The strategy, however, is highly risky because it requires the commitment of huge amounts of investment funds to saturate the market and preclude entry by other firms. Also, to be the first mover in places that are being transformed from rural land into urban areas, firms may need to build their stores many months prior to the time when the area in question becomes developed enough to provide significant business. That may mean losses until the market grows sufficiently for profitability. Some firms like Wal-Mart have become huge, profitable international enterprises by using a first-mover strategy. Other firms, such as Krispy Kreme Donuts, have lost millions of dollars because their extremely rapid expansion turned out to be unprofitable in many of their outlets when the expected customers never materialized.

APPENDIX | SUMMARY

- Positive-sum games are games in which the payoffs to the firms sum to a positive number; zero-sum games are games in which the payoffs sum to zero; and negative-sum games are games in which the payoffs sum to less than zero. Positive-sum games allow for "win-win" opportunities, whereas zero-sum games always feature "I win/You lose" outcomes. Games can be either one-time games or repeated games. Decisions in games may be made either simultaneously or sequentially.

- When two firms are playing strategic game, a firm is said to have a dominant strategy if there is an option that leads to better outcomes than all other options regardless of what the other firm does. Not all games have dominant strategies. The Nash equilibrium is an outcome from which neither firm wants to deviate because both firms see their current strategy as optimal given the other firm's chosen strategy. The Nash equilibrium is stable and persistent. Attempts by the firms to rig games to some other outcome

are difficult to accomplish and maintain, although credible threats can sometimes work. In contrast, empty threats accomplish nothing and leave the outcome at the Nash equilibrium.

- Reciprocity can improve outcomes for firms participating in repeated games. In such games, one firm avoids taking advantage of the other firm because it knows that the other firm can take advantage of it in subsequent games. Therefore, the profits of the firms are higher over time than they would be without reciprocity.

- Two possible Nash equilibriums can exist in sequential games with first-mover advantages; which one occurs depends on which firm moves first, since that firm can preempt the other firm making it unprofitable for the other to match the move. Several real-world firms have successfully used first-mover advantages to saturate markets and preempt entry by rivals.

APPENDIX | TERMS AND CONCEPTS

one-time game A game in which firms select their optimal strategy in a single time period without regard to possible interactions in subsequent time periods. (p. 247)

simultaneous game A game in which both parties choose their strategies and execute them at the same time. (p. 247)

positive-sum game A game in which the gains (+) and losses (–) add up to more than zero. (p. 247)

zero-sum game A game in which the gains (+) and losses (–) add up to zero. (p. 247)

negative-sum game A game in which the gains (+) and losses (–) add up to some amount less than zero. (p. 247)

dominant strategy In game theory, an option that is better than any alternative option regardless of what the other firm does. (p. 247)

Nash equilibrium In game theory, an outcome from which neither firm wants to deviate; the outcome that once achieved is stable and therefore lasting. (p. 248)

credible threat A statement of harmful intent by one party that the other party views as believable. (p. 248)

empty threat A statement of harmful intent that is easily dismissed by the second party because the threat is not viewed as believable. (p. 248)

repeated game A game that is played again sometime after the previous game ends. (p. 248)

sequential game A game in which the parties make their moves in turn, with one party making the first move, followed by the other party making the next move, and so on. (p. 249)

first-mover advantage In game theory, the benefit obtained by the party that moves first in a sequential game. (p. 250)

APPENDIX | STUDY QUESTIONS

LO ▸ A9.1 1. Is the game shown in Figure 9-5 a zero-sum game or a positive-sum game? How can you tell? Are there dominant strategies in this game? If so, what are they? What cell represents a Nash equilibrium and why? Explain why it is so difficult for Uptown and RareAir to achieve and maintain a more favourable cell than the Nash equilibrium in this single-period pricing game.

LO ▸ A9.1 2. Refer to the payoff matrix in study question 9 at the end of the chapter. First, assume this is a one-time game. Explain how the $60/$57 outcome might be achieved through a credible threat. Next, assume this is a repeated game, not a one-time game, such that the interaction between the two firms occurs indefinitely. Why might collusion with a credible threat not be necessary to achieve the $60/$57 outcome?

LO ▸ A9.1 3. Refer to the payoff matrix below.

Firm A

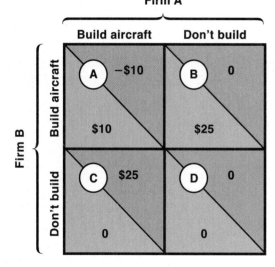

Assuming this is a sequential game with no collusion, what is the outcome if Firm A moves first to build a new type of commercial aircraft? Explain why first-mover strategies in the real world are only as good as the profit projections on which they are based. How could a supposed win from moving first turn out to be a big loss, whereas the loss of being preempted turns out to be a blessing in disguise?

4. **(Advanced Analysis)** Suppose you are playing a game in which you and one other person each pick a number between 1 and 100, with the person closest to some randomly selected number between 1 and 100 winning the jackpot. (Ask your instructor to fund the jackpot.) Your opponent picks first. What number do you expect her to choose? Why? What number would you then pick? Why are the two numbers so close? How might this example relate to why PharmaPlus and Shoppers Drug Mart, McDonald's and Burger King, and other major pairs of rivals locate so close to each other in many well-defined geographical markets that are large enough for both firms to be profitable?

LO ▸

CHAPTER 10

Competition Policy and Regulation

In Chapter 7 we extolled the virtues of competitive markets in bringing about allocative and productive efficiency in an economy. But competition does not always arise spontaneously in private markets and sometimes requires government action to promote and enhance competitive forces in an economy. To what extent should government intervene in markets to promote competition? And are there instances where intense competition may create incentives for firms to produce shoddy and potentially dangerous products for consumers, or intolerable working conditions for employees? To what extent should governments intervene to regulate quality and the conditions under which goods and services are produced?

In this chapter we look at three sets of government policies toward business: competition policy, industrial regulation, and social regulation. Competition policy consists of the laws and government actions designed to prevent monopoly and promote competition. Industrial regulation consists of government regulation of firms' prices (or rates) within selected industries. Social regulation is government regulation of the conditions under which goods are produced, the physical characteristics of goods, and the impact of the production and consumption of goods on society.

IN THIS CHAPTER YOU WILL LEARN:

10.1 What industrial concentration is and how governments combat it

10.2 About industrial regulation and how governments deal with it

10.3 The definition of social regulation and what its goals are

10.1 | Industrial Concentration

In Chapter 8 we developed and applied a strict definition of monopoly. A *monopoly,* we said, is a one-firm industry—a situation whereby a unique product is being produced entirely by a single firm and entry to the industry is totally blocked.

In this chapter we will use the term *industrial concentration* to include monopoly and markets in which much potential monopoly power exists. Industrial concentration occurs whenever a single firm or a small number of firms control the major portion of an industry's output. One, two, or three firms dominate, potentially resulting in higher-than-competitive prices and profits. This definition, which is closer to how the general public understands the monopoly problem, includes many industries we have previously designated as oligopolies.

Industrial concentration in this chapter thus refers to industries in which firms are large in absolute terms and in relation to the total market. Examples are the wireless mobile communications industry, in which Research In Motion dominates the market; the automobile industry, where General Motors of Canada and Ford of Canada are still dominant, although in recent years Honda and Toyota, both Japanese firms with manufacturing facilities in Ontario, have been catching up; the petro-chemical industry, dominated by Suncor, Imperial Oil (Exxon), and Shell Canada; the aluminum industry, where industrial giant Rio Tinto Alcan reigns supreme; and the steel industry, where the two large producers, Dofasco and U.S. Steel Canada, command the lion's share of the market.

Competition Policy

The underlying purpose of **competition policy** is to prevent industrial concentration or monopolization, to promote competition, and to achieve allocative efficiency. Although all economists would agree that these are praiseworthy goals, conflicting opinion exists about the effectiveness of Canadian competition law.

The main economic case against monopoly is familiar to you from Chapter 8. Monopolists produce less output and charge higher prices than if their industries were competitive. With perfect competition, production occurs where $P = MC$. This equality represents an efficient allocation of resources because P measures the marginal benefit to society of an extra unit of output, while marginal cost MC reflects the cost of an extra unit. When $P = MC$, society cannot gain by producing one more or one fewer unit of the product. In contrast, a monopolist maximizes profit by equating marginal revenue (not price) with marginal cost. At this $MR = MC$ point, price exceeds marginal cost, meaning that society would obtain more benefit than it would incur cost by producing extra units. There is an underallocation of resources to the monopolized product, and so the economic well-being of society is less than it would be with greater competition.

Government long ago concluded that market forces in monopolized industries did not provide sufficient control to protect consumers, achieve competition, and achieve allocative efficiency. So it instituted two alternative means of control as substitutes for, or supplements to, market forces:

- *Regulatory Agencies*   In the few markets where the nature of the product or technology creates a *natural monopoly,* the government established public regulatory agencies to control such firms.

- *Competition Law*   In most other markets, government control took the form of laws designed to inhibit or prevent the growth of monopoly.

We will shortly review the anticombines legislation that constitutes the basic law of the land with respect to corporate size and concentration. Before we do, let's examine merger types.

Merger Types

Mergers of firms are one of the main causes of industrial concentration. There are three basic types of mergers. A **horizontal merger** is a merger between two competitors selling similar products in the same market. Examples of horizontal mergers would be the buyout of Eaton's by Sears, Air Canada's merger with Canadian Airlines, and Best Buy's merger with Future Shop. A **vertical merger** is a merger between firms at different stages of the production process. Vertical mergers involve firms having buyer–seller relationships. Examples of mergers of this type are PepsiCo's mergers with Pizza Hut, Taco Bell, and Kentucky Fried Chicken; PepsiCo supplies soft drinks to each of these fast-food outlets. A **conglomerate merger** is officially defined as any merger that is not horizontal or vertical; in general, it is the combination of firms in different industries or firms operating in different geographical areas. Conglomerate mergers can extend the line of products sold, or combine totally unrelated companies. A real-world example of a conglomerate is Power Corporation of Canada, headquartered in Montreal. Among its holdings are Great-West Life Co. Inc., a life insurance subsidiary, and Power Broadcast Inc., a subsidiary that owns newspapers and radio stations. In Europe, Power Corporation has investments in major communications, industrial, energy, utility, financial services, and food companies.

THE ROLE OF GOVERNMENTS

competition policy
The laws and government actions designed to prevent monopoly and promote competition.

horizontal merger
A merger between two competitors selling similar products in the same market.

vertical merger
The merger of firms engaged in different stages of the production process of a final product.

conglomerate merger
The merger of a firm in one industry with a firm in another industry or region.

Competition Law

The basis of competition policy in Canada is the Competition Act, passed in 1986. It replaced the Combines Investigation Act, which had been in force in different forms since 1910. The Competition Act is administered and enforced by the federal Competition Bureau, which promotes and maintains fair competition in Canada. One of the main innovations of the Competition Act was that uncompetitive market structures (monopoly and oligopoly) and mergers, previously adjudicated under criminal law, came under the jurisdiction of civil law, making it easier to prosecute mergers and monopolies not deemed to be in the public interest. Price fixing, however, is still handled by the regular courts, where the standard of evidence is "beyond a reasonable doubt." Those sections of the Competition Act now under the jurisdiction of civil law are adjudicated by the federal **Competition Tribunal.** The tribunal is made up of judges of the Federal Court and laypersons, with a judge as chairperson. It must be emphasized that the Competition Act does not directly prohibit monopoly: a firm can legally have 100 percent of the market as long as it does not abuse its monopoly position.

Competition Tribunal
A government body adjudicating under a civil law framework that permits the issuing of remedial orders to restore and maintain competition in the market.

Merger Guidelines

The federal government has established merger guidelines based on the concentration ratio. Recall from Chapter 9 that the concentration ratio reveals the percentage of total output produced and sold by an industry's four largest firms (sometimes referred to as the CR4). The Competition Bureau's main concern in the case of a *horizontal merger* is unilateral market power of the new merged entity as well as the combined market power of the four largest firms in the sector. In its assessment of the degree of market power in an industry in which there has been a merger, the Competition Bureau considers such factors as economies of scale created by the new merged firm, the degree of foreign competition, and ease of entry of new firms. Furthermore, horizontal mergers are usually allowed if one of the merging firms is suffering major continuing losses (this is one reason why Air Canada was allowed to acquire Canadian Airlines in 1999). Most *vertical mergers* escape anticombines prosecution because they do not substantially lessen competition in either of the two markets. However, a vertical merger between large firms in a highly concentrated industry may be challenged. *Conglomerate mergers* are generally permitted. If an auto manufacturer acquires a blue jean producer no anticombines action is likely, since neither firm has increased its own market share as a result.

PRICE FIXING

Price fixing among firms is treated strictly. Evidence of price fixing, even by small firms, will bring the action of the Competition Tribunal, as will other collusive activities such as scheming to rig bids on government contracts or dividing up sales in a market. To gain a conviction, the government or other party making the charge need show only that there was a conspiracy to fix prices, rig bids, or divide up markets, not that the conspiracy succeeded or caused serious damage to other parties.

PRICE DISCRIMINATION

Price discrimination is a common business practice that rarely reduces competition and therefore is rarely challenged by the Competition Tribunal. The exception occurs when a firm engages in price discrimination as part of a strategy to block entry or drive out competitors.

TYING CONTRACTS

The Competition Tribunal strictly enforces the prohibition of tying contracts, particularly when practised by dominant firms. A **tying contract** is a requirement imposed by a seller that a buyer purchase another (or other) of its products as a condition for buying a desired product.

tying contract
A requirement imposed by a seller that a buyer purchase another (or other) of its products as a condition for buying a desired product.

RECENT CASES

The Competition Act is designed to achieve economic efficiency and to be adaptable to changing market conditions and international trade. Only those mergers resulting in an unacceptable lessening of competition can be prohibited or modified by the competition tribunal. Mergers that result in efficiency gains through capturing economies of scale have generally been allowed. For example, in April 2003, the Competition Bureau reported it would not challenge the merger of certain assets of the coal businesses of Fording Inc., Teck Cominco Ltd., Luscar Ltd., and Consol Energy Inc., in the thermal coal, metallurgical coal, and coal terminal port businesses in Canada.

The Competition Bureau recommended against chartered bank mergers in 1998, when the Royal Bank of Canada and the Bank of Montreal announced their intention to merge. Soon after, the Canadian Imperial Bank of Commerce and the Toronto Dominion Bank also decided to merge. The banks argued that they needed to merge to capture economies of scale and be able to compete internationally. The Competition Bureau was not convinced by the banks' argument, citing fears that competition would be greatly curtailed in smaller centres for both consumers and small- and medium-sized firms. The Bureau noted that even if more foreign banks were allowed to compete in the Canadian market, the large established network of branches of the Canadian banks provided a large barrier to entry for any new competitor. The Royal Bank of Canada and the Bank of Montreal were, however, successful in merging their credit card operations.

In December 2002, the standing Senate Committee on Banking, Trade, and Commerce came out with an endorsement of mergers among Canada's chartered banks, with the proviso that the Competition Bureau ensure competition in the financial services sector to protect consumers. It remains to be seen whether the government will accept these recommendations and pass legislation to make it possible for the chartered banks to merge, if they so wish.

In May 2005 the Competition Bureau announced that Mitsubishi Corporation, Japan's largest trading company, pleaded guilty to charges of attempting to maintain the international price of graphite electrodes, used mainly in electric arc furnace steel production. Mitsubishi Corporation was fined $1,000,000 by the Federal Court of Canada under the price maintenance provision of the Act. Earlier in 2005 Robert J. Hart and Company, with headquarters in the United Kingdom, was fined $50,000 in the same graphite electrodes price maintenance scheme.

ISSUES OF ENFORCEMENT: TRADEOFFS AMONG GOALS

Promoting competition is only one of society's goals, and strict enforcement of competition laws may sometimes conflict with some other goal.

Occasionally, new technologies combine to create new products and services. A current example is the meshing of computer and communications technologies relating to the Internet. This interactive network has improved the communications capabilities of households, businesses, and governments across the globe.

CONSIDER THIS | Bio-Insecticide and Insect Control and Market Power in Canada

The Competition Bureau began an investigation of two companies, GDG Environnement Ltée and La Société générale de foresterie Sylvico Inc., in 2007 to determine if these two companies had arranged with competitors to maintain their market share in the supply of bio-insecticides and insect control services by colluding on bids or tenders. The investigation concluded that these two Quebec-based companies lessened competition and frustrated the competitive tendering process. In 2008 the Superior Court of Quebec used the result of the Bureau's investigation as evidence in an order asking the two companies and their CEOs to comply with the conspiracy and bid-rigging provisions of the Competition Act. Both firms were made to notify all their employees to comply with the court order to stop efforts to reduce competition in the bidding process, otherwise the employees could be disciplined or even dismissed.

Vigilance by the Competition Bureau and prosecution of lawbreakers prompts firms to think carefully before engaging in anti-competitive activities that lead to higher prices for Canadian consumers.

Competition Bureau Canada
http://www.competitionbureau.gc.ca/eic/site/cb-bc.nsf/eng/02645.html

ORIGIN 10.1
Creative and
Destruction

Should the government strictly enforce competition laws to block some of those mergers, specifically ones that produce dominant firms and threaten to reduce competition? Or should the government temporarily suspend competition rules to encourage the restructuring of industries and speed the expansion of this new technology? Hastening the advance of Internet-related technologies might also increase Canadian exports of electronic services.

Each of these enforcement tradeoffs, by itself, triggers controversy. Some argue that the gains from competition policy must be weighed against the effects of the policy on conflicting objectives. Others contend that selective enforcement of competition laws dangerously interferes with the market process. Obviously, different policymakers and different administrations may view such considerations and tradeoffs differently. *(Key Questions 2 and 3)*

QUICK REVIEW

▸ Industrial concentration exists where a single firm or a small number of firms control the major portion of an industry's output.

▸ Three types of mergers can occur: horizontal, vertical, and conglomerate.

▸ The Competition Act, passed in 1986, allows mergers that bring about significant efficiency gains.

10.2 | Industrial Regulation

THE ROLE OF GOVERNMENTS

Competition policy assumes that society will benefit if monopoly is prevented from evolving or if it is dissolved where it already exists. We now return to the special situation, first introduced in Chapter 6, in which an economic reason exists for an industry to be a monopoly.

Natural Monopoly

A *natural monopoly* exists when economies of scale are so extensive that a single firm can supply the entire market at a lower unit cost than could a number of competing firms. Clear-cut circumstances of natural monopoly are relatively rare, but such conditions exist for many public utilities, such as local electricity and water. As we discussed in Chapter 8, large-scale operations are necessary in some cases to obtain low unit costs and a low product price. Where natural monopoly exists, competition does not enhance efficiency. If the market were divided among many producers, economies of scale would not be achieved and unit costs and prices would increase.

Two possible alternatives exist for promoting better economic outcomes where natural monopoly occurs. One is public ownership, and the other is public regulation. *Public ownership* or some approximation of it has been established in a few instances, such as Canada Post, water supply systems, and garbage collection at the local level. But *public regulation,* or what economists call industrial regulation, has been the preferred option in Canada. In this type of regulation, government commissions regulate the prices (usually called rates) charged by natural monopolists. Table 10-1 lists the major federal regulatory commissions.

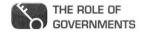

TABLE 10-1 | **The Main Federal Regulatory Agencies**

Atomic Energy Control Board

Canadian Dairy Commission

Canadian Grain Commission

Canadian Radio-television and Telecommunications Commission

Canadian Wheat Board

National Energy Board

National Farm Products Marketing Council

Canada Ports Corporation

National Transport Agency of Canada

public interest theory of regulation
The theory that industrial regulation is necessary to keep a natural monopoly from charging monopoly prices and thus harming consumers and society.

The economic objective of industrial regulation is reflected in the **public interest theory of regulation,** where industrial regulation is necessary to keep a natural monopoly from charging monopoly prices and thus harming consumers and society. The goal of such regulation is to garner for society at least part of the cost reductions associated with natural monopoly while avoiding the restrictions of output and high prices that come with unregulated monopoly. If competition is impractical, society should allow or even encourage a monopoly but regulate its prices. Regulation should then be structured so that ratepayers benefit from the economies of scale—the lower per-unit costs—that natural monopolists are able to achieve.

In practice, regulators seek to establish rates that will cover production costs and yield a fair return to the enterprise. The goal is to set price equal to average total cost so that the regulated firm receives a normal profit, as described in the "Regulated Monopoly" section of Chapter 8. In particular, you should carefully review Figure 8-9.

Problems with Industrial Regulation

There is considerable disagreement on the effectiveness of industrial regulation. Let's examine two criticisms.

COSTS AND INEFFICIENCY

An unregulated firm has a strong incentive to reduce its costs at each level of output, because that will increase its profit. The regulatory commission, however, confines the regulated firm to a normal profit or a fair return on the value of its assets. If a regulated firm lowers its operating costs, the rising profit eventually will lead the regulatory commission to require the firm to lower its rates and return its profits to normal. The regulated firm, therefore, has no incentive to reduce its operating costs.

Worse yet, higher costs do not result in lower profit. Because the regulatory commissions must allow the public utility a fair return, the regulated monopolist can simply pass higher production costs to consumers by charging higher rates. A regulated firm may reason that it might as well have high salaries for its workers, luxurious working conditions for management, and the like, since the return is the same in percentage terms whether costs are minimized or not. So, although a natural monopoly reduces costs through economies of scale, industrial regulation fosters considerable X-inefficiency (refer to Figure 8-7). Because of the absence of competition, the potential cost savings from natural monopoly may never actually materialize.

PERPETUATING MONOPOLY

A second general problem with industrial regulation is that it sometimes perpetuates monopoly long after the conditions of natural monopoly have ended.

Technological change often creates the potential for competition in at least some or all portions of the regulated industry, such as when trucks began competing with railroads; transmission of voice and data by microwave and satellites began competing with transmission over telephone wires; satellite television began competing with cable television, and cell phones began competing with regular phones. But, spurred by the firms they regulate and believing that the regulated firms are natural monopolies, commissions often protect the regulated firms from new competition by either blocking entry or extending regulation to competitors. The rationale usually is that the competitors simply want to "skim the cream" from selected highly profitable portions of the regulated industry but do not want to offer the universal service required of the regulated firm. By losing the highly profitable portion of their business, the regulated firms would have to increase rates for services that do not pay their own way to continue to receive a fair rate of return on their assets.

But where regulators block entry or extend regulation to competitive firms, industrial regulation may perpetuate a monopoly that is no longer a natural monopoly and that would otherwise erode.

Ordinary monopoly, protected by government, may then supplant natural monopoly. If so, then the regulated prices may be higher than they would be with competition. The beneficiaries of outdated regulations are the regulated firms, their employees, and perhaps consumers of some services. The losers are all other consumers and the potential entrants. *(Key Question 8)*

Legal Cartel Theory

The regulation of potentially competitive industries has produced the **legal cartel theory of regulation.** In place of socially minded officials forcing regulation on natural monopolies to protect consumers, holders of this view see practical politicians as supplying regulation to local, regional, and national firms that fear the impact of competition on their profits or even on their long-term survival. These firms desire regulation because it yields a legal monopoly that can guarantee a profit. Specifically, the regulatory commission performs such functions as blocking entry, or, where there are several firms, the commission divides up the market much like an illegal cartel (for example, before airline deregulation, the federal government assigned routes to specific airlines). The commission may also restrict potential competition by enlarging the "cartel."

Private cartels are illegal, unstable, and often break down, and the special attraction of a government-sponsored cartel under the guise of regulation is that it endures. The legal cartel theory of regulation suggests that regulation results from the rent-seeking activities of private firms and the desire of politicians to be responsive.

Occupational licensing is a labour-market application of the legal cartel theory. Certain occupational groups—dentists, barbers, hairstylists, dietitians, lawyers—demand stringent licensing on the grounds that it protects the public from charlatans and quacks, but skeptics say the real reason may be to limit entry into the occupational group so that practitioners can receive monopoly incomes.

Deregulation

Beginning in the 1970s, the legal cartel theory, evidence of inefficiency in regulated industries, and the contention that the government was regulating potentially competitive industries all contributed to a wave of deregulation. Since then, Parliament and most provincial legislatures have passed legislation that has deregulated in varying degrees the airline, trucking, banking, railroad, natural gas, electricity, and television broadcasting industries. Deregulation has also occurred in the telecommunications industry. Bell Canada now competes with other carriers, such as Rogers Home Phone, in the local and long-distance markets. Bell Canada also competes with cellular companies, such as Telus. Deregulation in the 1970s and 1980s was one of the most extensive experiments in economic policy to take place during the past 50 years.

The overwhelming consensus among economists is that deregulation has produced large net benefits for consumers and society. Most of the gains from deregulation have occurred in three industries: airlines, railroads, and trucking. Airfares (adjusted for inflation) have declined by about one-third, and airline safety has improved. Railroad and trucking freight rates (again, adjusted for inflation) have dropped by about one-half. Significant efficiency gains have occurred in long-distance telecommunications, and slight efficiency gains have been made in cable television, stock brokerage services, and the natural gas industry. Deregulation has unleashed a wave of technological advances that have resulted in such new and improved products and services as fax machines, cellular phones, fibre-optic cable, microwave systems in communications, and the Internet.

The success of past deregulation has led to further calls for deregulation. The latest industry to begin the deregulation process is electricity, led by Alberta and Ontario. Deregulation is now occurring at the wholesale level, where firms are free to build generating facilities and sell electricity at market prices.

QUICK REVIEW

▶ Natural monopoly occurs where economies of scale are so extensive that only a single firm can produce the product at minimum average total cost.

▶ The public interest theory of regulation says that government must regulate natural monopolies to prevent abuses arising from monopoly power. Regulated firms, however, have less incentive than competitive firms to reduce costs; that is, regulated firms tend to be X-inefficient.

▶ The legal cartel theory of regulation suggests that some firms seek government regulation to reduce price competition and ensure stable profits.

▶ Deregulation initiated by government in the past three decades has yielded large annual efficiency gains for society.

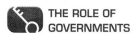

THE ROLE OF GOVERNMENTS

social regulation
Government regulation of the conditions under which goods are produced, the physical characteristics of goods, and the impact of the production on society.

10.3 | Social Regulation

The industrial regulation discussed in the preceding section has focused on the regulation of prices (or rates) in natural monopolies. But in the early 1960s, a new type of regulation began to emerge. **Social regulation** is concerned with the conditions under which goods and services are produced, the impact of production on society, and the physical qualities of the goods themselves.

Distinguishing Features

Social regulation differs from industrial regulation in several ways. First, social regulation is often applied across the board to all industries and directly affects more producers than does industrial regulation. For instance, while the industrial regulation by the Air Transport Committee of the National Transport Agency of Canada controls only the air transport industry, the rules and regulations of the Canada Labour (Safety) Code and its provincial counterparts apply to every employer.

Second, social regulation intrudes into the day-to-day production process to a greater extent than industrial regulation. While industrial regulation focuses on rates, costs, and profits, social regulation often dictates the design of products, the conditions of employment, and the nature of the production process. For example, rather than specifying safety standards for vehicles, the Motor Vehicle Safety Act includes six standards limiting motor vehicle exhaust and noise emission.

Finally, social regulation has expanded rapidly during the same period in which industrial regulation has waned. Under this social regulation, firms must provide reasonable accommodations for qualified workers and job applicants with disabilities. Also, sellers must provide reasonable access for customers with disabilities. As much of our society had achieved a fairly affluent standard of living by the 1960s, attention shifted to improvement in the nonmaterial quality of life. That focus called for safer products, less pollution, improved working conditions, and greater equality of economic opportunity.

The Optimal Level of Social Regulation

While economists agree on the need for social regulation, they disagree on whether the current level of such regulation is optimal. Recall that an activity should be expanded so long as its marginal benefit (MB) exceeds its marginal cost (MC). If the MB of social regulation exceeds its MC, there is too little social regulation; if MC exceeds MB, there is too much social regulation. Unfortunately, the marginal costs and benefits of social regulation are not always easy to measure and therefore may be illusory. So, ideology about the proper size and role of government often drives the debate over social regulation as much as, or perhaps more than, economic cost–benefit analysis.

IN SUPPORT OF SOCIAL REGULATION

Defenders of social regulation say that it has achieved notable successes and, overall, has greatly enhanced society's well-being. They point out that the problems social regulation confronts are serious and substantial. Hundreds of workers die annually in job-related accidents and many thousands of workers suffer injuries that force them to miss a day or more of work. Air pollution continues to cloud major Canadian cities, imposing large costs in terms of reduced property values and increased health care expense. Numerous children and adults die each year because of poorly designed or manufactured products (for example, car tires) or tainted food (for example, *E.coli* in beef). Discrimination against some ethnic minorities, persons with disabilities, and older workers reduces their earnings and imposes heavy costs on society.

Proponents of social regulation acknowledge that social regulation is costly, but they correctly point out that a high price for something does not necessarily mean that it should not be purchased. They say that the appropriate economic test should be not whether the costs of social regulation are high or low but whether the benefits of social regulation exceed the costs. After decades of neglect, they further assert, society cannot expect to cleanse the environment, enhance the safety of the workplace, and promote economic opportunity for all without incurring substantial costs. So statements about the huge costs of social regulation are irrelevant, say defenders, since the benefits are even greater. The public often underestimates those benefits, since they are more difficult to measure than costs and often become apparent only after some time has passed (for example, the benefits of reducing global warming).

Proponents of social regulation point to its many specific benefits. It is estimated that highway fatalities would be 40 percent greater annually in the absence of auto safety features mandated through regulation. Compliance with child safety-seat and seatbelt laws has significantly reduced the auto fatality rate for small children. The national air quality standards set by law have been reached in nearly all parts of the nation for sulphur dioxide, nitrogen dioxide, and lead. Recent studies clearly link cleaner air, other things equal, with increases in the values of homes. Employment equity regulations have increased the labour demand for ethnic minorities and females. The use of childproof lids has resulted in a 90 percent decline in child deaths caused by accidental swallowing of poisonous substances.

Some defenders of social regulation say many areas remain in which greater regulation would generate net benefits to society. For example, some call for greater regulation of the meat, poultry, and seafood industries to improve food safety. Others say that more regulation is needed to ensure that violent movies, CDs, and video games are not marketed to children.

Advocates of social regulation claim that the benefits of such regulation are well worth the considerable costs. The costs are simply the price we must pay to create a hospitable, sustainable, and just society. *(Key Question 11)*

CRITICISMS OF SOCIAL REGULATION

Critics of social regulation contend that, in many instances, it has been expanded to the point where the marginal costs exceed the marginal benefits. In this view, society would achieve net benefits by cutting back on meddlesome social regulation. Critics say that many social regulation laws are poorly written, making regulatory objectives and standards difficult to understand. As a result, regulators pursue goals well beyond the original intent of the legislation. Businesses complain that regulators often press for additional increments of improvement, unmindful of costs.

Also, opponents of social regulation say that the regulatory agencies may attract overzealous workers who are hostile toward the market system and believe too fervently in regulation. For example, some staff members of government agencies may view large corporations as "bad guys" who regularly cause pollution, provide inadequate safety for workers, deceive their customers, and generally abuse their power in the community. Such biases can lead to seemingly never-ending calls for more regulation, rather than objective assessments of the costs and benefits of added regulation.

CONSIDER THIS | Canada and the Kyoto Accord

Scientists widely believe that greenhouse gases, primarily from the burning of fossil fuels, are significant contributors to global climate change. In 1997 in Kyoto, Japan, 38 industrialized countries agreed to cut greenhouse gas emissions by 5.2 percent compared to emissions in 1990. Developing nations were excluded from the quotas to avoid hindering the economic growth necessary to alleviate severe and widespread poverty.

At the end of 2002, the Canadian federal government ratified the Kyoto Accord on climate change and committed to reduce emissions by the required amount by the year 2012. In essence, the federal government passed social regulations that would reduce harmful pollutants to the environment. A federal government study revealed that the likely impact of the Kyoto Accord on the Canadian economy would be minimal. Moreover, the majority of Canadians approved of reducing greenhouse gases.

Not everyone in Canada agrees that reducing greenhouse gases will cost little, or even that it is necessary. Some scientists maintain the global climate change is a normal ecological occurrence not created by the burning of fossil fuels. And the business lobby worries that the opting out of the Kyoto Accord by the U.S.—our largest trading partner—will put our exports at a competitive disadvantage in its market. The premier of Alberta complained that the passage of the Kyoto Accord would cause his province's energy sector to bear a disproportionately large percentage of the implementation costs.

Given the many variables involved, it is difficult, if not impossible, to estimate the expected costs and benefits for each province. For example, if rapid technological progress were to occur in the development of hydrogen fuel cells to power machines and vehicles currently using natural gas and oil, the expected costs of the Kyoto Accord would be negligible since consumers would shift to the new power source if the price were comparable.

The Kyoto Accord is a classic example of social regulations with potential economic consequences. These regulations can be costly, but its proponents point out that continuing to pollute the earth's environment could be even more costly in the long run if extreme climate change makes the globe uninhabitable for humans.

Two Reminders

The debate over the proper amount of social regulation will surely continue. By helping determine costs and benefits, economic analysis can lead to more informed discussion and to better decisions. In this regard, we leave both ardent supporters and opponents of social regulation with pertinent reminders.

THERE IS NO FREE LUNCH

Fervent supporters of social regulation need to remember that there is no free lunch. Social regulation can produce higher prices, stifle innovation, and reduce competition.

Social regulation raises product prices in two ways. It does so directly because compliance costs normally get passed on to consumers, and it does so indirectly by reducing labour productivity. Resources invested in making workplaces accessible to workers with disabilities, for example, are not available for investment in new machinery designed to increase output per worker. Where the wage rate is fixed, a drop in labour productivity increases the marginal and average total costs of production. In effect, the supply curve for the product shifts leftward, causing the price of the product to rise.

Social regulation may have a negative impact on the rate of innovation. Technological advance may be stifled by, say, the fear that a new plant will not meet Environment Canada's guidelines or that a new medicine will require years of testing before being approved by the federal government.

Social regulation may weaken competition, since it usually places a relatively greater burden on small firms than on large ones. The costs of complying with social regulation are, in effect, fixed costs. Because smaller firms produce less output over which to distribute those costs, their compliance costs per unit of output put them at a competitive disadvantage with their larger rivals. Social regulation is more likely to force smaller firms out of business, thus contributing to the increased concentration of industry.

Less Government Is Not Always Better Than More

On the opposite side of the issue, passionate opponents of social regulation need to remember that less government is not always better than more government. Although the market system is a powerful engine for producing goods and services and generating income, it has its flaws. Through appropriate amounts of social regulation government can clearly increase economic efficiency and thus society's well-being. Ironically, by taking the rough edges off capitalism, social regulation may be a strong pro-capitalist force. Properly conceived and executed, social regulation helps maintain political support for the market system. Such support could quickly wane if there were a steady stream of reports of unsafe workplaces, unsafe products, discriminatory hiring, choking pollution, deceived loan customers, and the like. Social regulation helps the market system deliver not only goods and services but also a "good society."

QUICK REVIEW

▶ Social regulation is concerned with the conditions under which goods and services are produced, the effects of production on society, and the physical characteristics of the goods themselves.

▶ Defenders of social regulation point to the benefits arising from policies that keep dangerous products from the marketplace, reduce workplace injuries and deaths,

contribute to clean air and water, and reduce employment discrimination.

▶ Critics of social regulation say uneconomical policy goals, inadequate information, unintended side effects, and overzealous personnel create excessive regulation, for which regulatory costs exceed regulatory benefits.

The LAST WORD   The United States versus Microsoft

The recent Microsoft antitrust case in the United States is the most significant monopoly case since the break-up of AT&T in the early 1980s, and will have repercussions in Canada.

The Charges In May 1998, the U.S. Justice Department (under President Clinton), 19 individual states, and the District of Columbia (hereafter, "the government") filed antitrust charges against Microsoft under the Sherman Antitrust Act (a U.S. anticombines law). The government charged that Microsoft had violated Section 2 of the Act through a series of unlawful actions designed to maintain its Windows monopoly. It also charged that some of that conduct violated Section 1 of the Act.

Microsoft denied the charges, arguing it had achieved its success through product innovation and lawful business practices. Microsoft contended that it should not be penalized for its superior foresight, business acumen, and technological prowess. It also pointed out that its monopoly was highly transitory because of rapid technological advances.

The District Court Findings In June 2000, the District Court ruled that the relevant market was software used to operate Intel-compatible personal

computers (PCs). Microsoft's 95 percent share of that market clearly gave it monopoly power. The Court pointed out, however, that being a monopoly is not illegal. The violation of the Sherman Act occurred because Microsoft used anticompetitive means to maintain its monopoly power.

According to the Court, Microsoft feared that the success of Netscape's Navigator, which allowed people to browse the Internet, might allow Netscape to expand its software to include a competitive PC operating system—software that would threaten

Microsoft's Windows monopoly. It also feared that the Internet applications of Sun's Java programming language might eventually threaten the Windows monopoly.

To counter these and similar threats, Microsoft illegally signed contracts with PC makers that required them to feature Internet Explorer on the PC desktop and penalized companies that promoted software products that competed with Microsoft products. Moreover, it gave friendly companies coding that linked Windows to software applications and withheld it from companies featuring Netscape. Finally, under license from Sun, Microsoft developed Windows-related Java software that made Sun's own software incompatible with Windows.

The District Court Remedy The District Court ordered Microsoft split into two competing companies, one initially selling the Windows operating system and the other initially selling Microsoft applications and services (such as Word, Hotmail, MSN, PowerPoint, and Internet Explorer). Both companies would be free to develop new products that competed with each other, and both could derive those products from the intellectual property embodied in the common products existing at the time the company was split.

The Appeals Court's Ruling In late 2000 Microsoft appealed the District Court decision to a U.S. Court of Appeals. In 2001 the higher court

affirmed that Microsoft illegally maintained its monopoly, but tossed out the District's Court decision to break up Microsoft. It agreed with Microsoft that it was denied due process during the penalty phase of the trial and concluded that the District Court judge had displayed an appearance of bias by holding extensive interviews with the press. The Appeals Court sent the remedial phase of the case to a new District Court judge to determine appropriate remedies. The Appeals Court also raised issues relating to the wisdom of a remedy that involved changing the structure of Microsoft.

The Final Settlement At the urging of the new District Court judge, the federal government (then under President Bush) and Microsoft negotiated a proposed settlement. With minor modification, the settlement became the final court order in 2002. The break-up was overturned and replaced with a remedy that places limits on the company's behaviour. It:

1. prevents Microsoft from retaliating against any firm that develops, sells, or uses software that competes with Microsoft Windows or Internet Explorer or that ships a personal computer that includes both Windows and a non-Microsoft operating system;

2. requires Microsoft to establish uniform royalty and licensing terms for computer manufacturers that want to include Windows on their PCs;

3. requires that manufacturers be allowed to remove Microsoft icons and replace them with other icons on the Windows desktop; and

4. calls for Microsoft to provide technical information to other companies so they can develop programs that work as well with Windows as Microsoft's own products do.

The Microsoft actions and conviction have indirectly resulted in billions of dollars of fines and payouts by Microsoft. Main examples: To AOL Time Warner (Netscape) $750 million; to Sun Microsystems, $1.6 billion; to Novell, $536 million; to Burst.com, $60 million; to Gateway, $150 million; to InterTrust, $440 million; to RealNetworks, $761 million; and to IBM, $850 million. The European Commission of the European Union also brought a case against Microsoft for abuse of its dominant position and eventually levied a $600 million fine against Microsoft.

Sources: United States v. Microsoft (District Court Conclusions of Law), April 2000; United States v. Microsoft (Court of Appeals), June 2001; U.S. v. Microsoft (Final Judgment), November 2002; and Reuters and Associated Press News Services.

Question

Under what law and on what basis did the U.S. federal government find Microsoft guilty of violating U.S. antitrust laws? What was the initial District Court's remedy? How did Microsoft fare with its appeal to the Court of Appeals? Was the final remedy in the case a structural or behavioural remedy?

CHAPTER SUMMARY

10.1 ▶ INDUSTRIAL CONCENTRATION

- Mergers can be of three types: horizontal, vertical, and conglomerate.

- The Competition Act was passed in 1986, supplanting the Combines Investigation Act.

10.2 ▶ INDUSTRIAL REGULATION

- The objective of industrial regulation is to protect the public from the market power of natural monopolies by regulating prices and quality of service.

- Critics of industrial regulation contend that it can lead to inefficiency and rising costs and that in many instances it constitutes a legal cartel for the regulated firms. Legislation passed in the late 1970s and the 1980s has brought about varying degrees of deregulation in the airline, trucking, banking, railroad, and television broadcasting industries. Studies indicate that deregulation is producing sizable annual gains to society through lower prices, lower costs, and increased output. The latest Canadian industries to begin the deregulation process are telecommunications, electricity, and natural gas.

10.3 ▶ SOCIAL REGULATION

- Social regulation is concerned with product safety, working conditions, and the effects of production on society. While industrial regulation is on the wane, social regulation continues to expand. The optimal amount of social regulation occurs where MB = MC.

- People who support social regulation point to its numerous specific successes and assert that it has greatly enhanced society's well-being. Critics of social regulation contend that businesses are excessively regulated to the point where marginal costs exceed marginal benefits. They also say that social regulation often produces unintended and costly side effects.

TERMS AND CONCEPTS

competition policy, p. 254
horizontal merger, p. 254
vertical merger, p. 254

conglomerate merger, p. 254
Competition Tribunal, p. 255
tying contract, p. 255

public interest theory of regulation, p. 258
legal cartel theory of regulation, p. 259
social regulation, p. 260

STUDY QUESTIONS

10.1 1. Both competition policy and industrial policy deal with monopoly. What distinguishes their approaches? How does government decide to use one form of remedy rather than the other?

10.1 2. **KEY QUESTION** Explain how strict enforcement of competition laws might conflict with (a) promoting exports to achieve a balance of trade, and (b) encouraging new technologies. Do you see any dangers in using selective competition enforcement as part of a broader policy to increase exports?

10.1 3. **KEY QUESTION** How would you expect competition authorities to react to (a) a proposed merger of Ford and General Motors; (b) evidence of secret meetings by contractors to rig bids for highway construction projects;

(c) a proposed merger of a large shoe manufacturer and a chain of retail shoe stores; and (d) a proposed merger of a small life-insurance company and a regional candy manufacturer.

4. Suppose a proposed merger of firms would simultaneously **LO 10.2** lessen competition and reduce unit costs through economies of scale. Do you think such a merger should be allowed?

5. In the 1980s, PepsiCo Inc., which then had 28 percent of **LO 10.2** the soft-drink market, proposed to acquire the 7-Up Company. Shortly thereafter the Coca-Cola Company, with 39 percent of the market, indicated it wanted to acquire the Dr. Pepper Company. Seven-Up and Dr. Pepper each controlled about 7 percent of the market. In your judgment, was the government's decision to block these mergers appropriate?

LO ▸ 10.2 6. "The competition laws tend to penalize efficiently managed firms." Do you agree? Why or why not?

LO ▸ 10.2 7. "The social desirability of any particular firm should be judged not on the basis of its market share but on the basis of its conduct and performance." Make a counterargument, referring to the monopoly model in your statement.

LO ▸ 10.2 8. **KEY QUESTION** What types of industry, if any, should be subjected to industrial regulation? What specific problems does industrial regulation entail?

LO ▸ 10.2 9. In view of the problems involved in regulating natural monopolies, compare socially optimal (marginal-cost) pricing and fair-return pricing by referring again to Figure 8-9.

Assuming that a government subsidy might be used to cover any loss resulting from marginal-cost pricing, which pricing policy would you favour? Why? What problems might such a subsidy entail?

10. Use economic analysis to explain why the optimal amount of product safety may be less than the amount that would totally eliminate risks of accidents and deaths. Use automobiles as an example. **LO**

11. **KEY QUESTION** How does social regulation differ from industrial regulation? What types of benefits and costs are associated with social regulation? **LO**

INTERNET APPLICATION QUESTIONS @

1. **Recent Competition Bureau Cases.** Connect to Canada's Competition Bureau site through the McConnell-Brue-Flynn-Barbiero Web site (Chapter 10). Review the current filings. What companies does the latest filing include? On what basis did the Competition Bureau make its decision on the Fording Coal Merger in April 2003?

Microeconomics of Factor Markets

PART 3

CHAPTER 11

The Demand for Factors of Production

When you finish your education, you will probably be looking for a new job. But why would someone want to hire you? The answer, of course, is that you have much to offer. Employers have a demand for educated, productive workers like you.

We need to learn more about the demand for labour and other factors. So, we now turn from the pricing and production of *goods and services* to the pricing and employment of *resources,* or *factors of production.* Although firms come in various sizes and operate under highly different market conditions, they each have a demand for factors of production. They obtain those resources from households—the owners of land, labour, capital, and entrepreneurial resources. So, referring to the circular flow model (Figure 2-2), we shift our attention from the bottom loop of the diagram (which shows that firms supply products and services that households want) to the top loop (which shows the demand for factors of production that households supply).

This chapter looks at the *demand* for factors of production. Although the discussion concentrates on labour, the principles we develop also apply to land, capital, and entrepreneurial ability. In Chapter 12 we will combine factor (labour) demand with labour *supply* to analyze wage rates. Then in Chapter 13 we will use factor demand and factor supply to examine the prices of, and returns to, other productive factors.

IN THIS CHAPTER YOU WILL LEARN:

11.1 How factor prices are determined

11.2 What determines the demand for a factor

11.3 What determines the elasticity of factor demand

11.4 How a firm arrives at the optimal combination of factors to use in the production process

11.1 | Factor Pricing and Demand

Studying factor pricing is important for several reasons:

- ***Money-Income Determination*** Factor prices are a major determinant of household income. The expenditures that firms make in acquiring factors of production flow as wage, rent, interest, and profit incomes to households.

- ***Cost Minimization*** To the firm, factor prices are costs, and to realize maximum profit the firm must produce the profit-maximizing output with the most efficient (least costly) combination of resources. Factor prices determine the quantities of land, labour, capital, and entrepreneurial ability that will be combined in producing each good or service.

- ***Resource Allocation*** Just as product prices allocate finished goods and services to consumers, factor prices allocate inputs among industries and firms. In a dynamic economy, where technology and tastes often change, the efficient allocation of resources over time means a continuous shift of factors of production from one use to another. Changes in factor prices are a major determinant of those shifts.

- ***Policy Issues*** There are many policy issues surrounding the factor market: To what extent should government redistribute income through taxes and transfers? Should government do anything to discourage "excess" pay to corporate executives? Should it increase the legal minimum wage? Does it make sense to provide subsidies to farmers? Should it encourage or restrict labour unions? The facts and debates relating to these policy questions are based on factor pricing.

Marginal Productivity Theory of Factor Demand

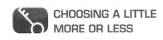
CHOOSING A LITTLE MORE OR LESS

In discussing factor demand, we will first assume that a firm sells its output in a perfectly competitive product market and hires a certain factor in a perfectly competitive factor market. This assumption keeps things simple and is consistent with the model of a competitive factor market that we will develop in Chapter 12. In a competitive *product market* the firm is a price-taker and can dispose of as much output as it chooses at the market price. The firm sells such a negligible fraction of total output that it exerts no influence on product price. Similarly, in the competitive *factor market,* the firm is a wage-taker. It hires such a negligible fraction of the total supply of the factor that it cannot influence its price.

FACTOR DEMAND AS A DERIVED DEMAND

derived demand
The demand for a factor that depends on the products it can be used to produce.

Factor demand is the starting point for any discussion of factor prices. The demand for a factor is an inverse relationship between the price of the factor and the quantity of the factor demanded, other things equal. The demand for factors is a **derived demand**: it is derived from the products or services that those factors of production help produce. Factors usually do not directly satisfy customer wants but do so indirectly through their use in producing goods and services. No one wants to consume a hectare of land, a tractor, or the labour services of a farmer, but households do want to consume the food products that these factors help produce.

MARGINAL REVENUE PRODUCT (MRP)

Because resource demand is derived from product demand, the strength of the demand for any factor of production will depend on (a) the productivity of the factor, and (b) the price of the good it helps to produce.

A factor that is highly productive in turning out a highly valued commodity will be in great demand, while a relatively unproductive factor that is capable of producing only a slightly valued commodity will be in little demand. And no demand whatsoever will exist for a factor of production that is phenomenally efficient in producing something that no one wants to buy.

TABLE 11-1   The Demand for Labour: Perfect Competition in the Sale of the Product

(1) Units of a factor	(2) Total product (output)	(3) Marginal product, MP	(4) Product price	(5) Total revenue, or (2) × (4)	(6) Marginal revenue product, MRP
0	0		$2	$ 0	
		7			$14
1	7		2	14	
		6			12
2	13		2	26	
		5			10
3	18		2	36	
		4			8
4	22		2	44	
		3			6
5	25		2	50	
		2			4
6	27		2	54	
		1			2
7	28		2	56	

- *Productivity* Table 11-1 shows the roles of productivity and product price in determining demand for factors of production. Here, we assume that a firm adds one variable factor, labour, to its fixed plant. Columns 1 and 2 give the number of units of the factor employed and the resulting total product (output). Column 3 shows the **marginal product (MP)**, or additional output, from each additional factor unit. Columns 1 through 3 remind us that the law of diminishing returns applies here, causing the marginal product of labour to fall beyond some point. For simplicity, we assume that diminishing marginal returns begin after the first worker hired.

marginal product (MP)
The extra output produced with one additional unit of a factor.

- *Product Price* The derived demand for a factor depends also on the price of the product it produces. Column 4 in Table 11-1 adds this price information. Product price is constant, in this case at $2, because the product market is competitive. The firm is a price-taker and will sell units of output only at this market price. Multiplying column 2 by column 4 gives us the total-revenue data of column 5. From these total-revenue data we can compute **marginal revenue product (MRP)**, the change in total revenue resulting from the use of each additional unit of a factor (labour, in this case). In equation form,

marginal revenue product (MRP)
The change in total revenue from employing one additional unit of a factor.

$$\text{Marginal revenue product} = \frac{\text{change in total revenue}}{\text{unit change in factor quantity}}$$

The MRPs are listed in column 6 in Table 11-1.

RULE FOR EMPLOYING FACTORS: MRP = MFC

The MRP schedule, shown as columns 1 and 6, is the firm's demand schedule for labour. To understand why, you must first know the rule that guides a profit-seeking firm in hiring any factor of production: To maximize profit, a firm will hire additional units of a specific factor as long as each successive unit adds more to the firm's total revenue than it adds to total cost.

We have seen that MRP measures how much each successive unit of a factor adds to total revenue. The amount that each additional unit of a factor adds to the firm's total (factor) cost is called its **marginal factor cost (MFC).**

In equation form,

$$\text{Marginal factor cost} = \frac{\text{change in total (factor) cost}}{\text{unit change in factor quantity}}$$

The demand for factors is derived from the products or services that those factors help produce.

marginal factor cost (MFC)
The amount that each additional unit of a factor adds to the firm's total (factor) cost.

MATH 11.1
MRP = MFC

MRP = MFC rule
To maximize economic profit (or minimize losses) a firm should use the quantity of a factor at which its marginal revenue product is equal to its marginal factor cost.

So, we can restate our rule for hiring factors as follows: It will be profitable for a firm to hire additional units of a factor up to the point at which that factor's MRP is equal to its MFC. For example, as the rule applies to labour, if the number of workers a firm is currently hiring is such that the MRP of the last worker exceeds his or her MFC, the firm can increase profit by hiring more workers. But if the number being hired is such that the MFC of the last worker exceeds his or her MRP, the firm is hiring workers who are not paying their way, and it can increase its profit by laying off some workers. You may have recognized that this **MRP = MFC rule** is similar to the MR = MC profit-maximizing rule employed throughout our discussion of price and output determination. The rationale of the two rules is the same, but the point of reference is now *inputs* of a factor of production, not *outputs* of a product.

MRP AS A FACTOR DEMAND SCHEDULE

Let's continue with our focus on labour, knowing that the analysis also applies to other factors. In a perfectly competitive labour market, supply and demand establish the wage rate. Because each firm hires such a small fraction of market supply, it cannot influence the market wage rate; it is a wage-taker, not a wage-maker. This means that for each additional unit of labour hired, total factor cost increases by exactly the amount of the constant market wage rate. The MFC of labour exactly equals the market wage rate. Thus, factor "price" (the market wage rate) and factor "cost" (marginal factor cost) are equal for a firm that hires labour in a competitive labour market. Then the MRP = MFC rule tells us that, in perfect competition, the firm will hire workers up to the point at which the market *wage rate* (its MFC) is equal to its MRP.

In terms of the data in columns 1 and 6 in Table 11-1, if the market wage rate is, say, $13.95, the firm will hire only one worker, because the first worker adds $14 to total revenue and slightly less—$13.95—to total cost. In other words, because MRP exceeds MFC for the first worker, it is profitable to hire that worker. For each successive worker, however, MFC (= $13.95) exceeds MRP (= $12 or less), indicating that it will not be profitable to hire any of those workers. If the wage rate is $11.95, by the same reasoning we discover that it will pay the firm to hire both the first and second workers. Similarly, if the wage rate is $9.95, three workers will be hired; if $7.95, four; if $5.95, five, and so forth. So here is the key generalization: The MRP schedule constitutes the firm's demand for labour, because each point on this schedule (or curve) indicates the number of workers the firm would hire at each possible wage rate.

In Figure 11-1, we show the D = MRP curve based on the data in Table 11-1. The perfectly competitive firm's factor demand curve identifies an inverse relationship between the wage rate and the quantity of labour demanded, other things equal. The curve slopes downward because of diminishing marginal returns.[1]

FACTOR DEMAND UNDER IMPERFECT PRODUCT MARKET COMPETITION

Our analysis of factor demand (here labour demand) becomes more complex when the firm is selling its product in an imperfectly competitive market, one in which the firm is a price-maker. Monopoly, oligopoly, and monopolistic competition in the product market all mean that the firm's product demand curve is downsloping; when the curve is fixed in place, the firm can increase its sales only by setting a lower price.

The productivity data in Table 11-1 are retained in columns 1 to 3 in Table 11-2. But here in Table 11-2 we show in column 4 that product price must be lowered to sell the marginal product of each successive worker. The MRP of the perfectly competitive seller of Table 11-1 falls for one reason: marginal product diminishes. The MRP of the imperfectly competitive seller of Table 11-2 falls for two reasons: marginal product diminishes *and* product price falls as output increases.

---

[1] Note that we plot the points in Figures 11-1 and 11-2 halfway between succeeding numbers of factor units, because MRP is associated with the addition of one more unit. Thus, in Figure 11-2, for example, we plot the MRP of the second unit ($13.00) not at 1 or 2, but rather at 1.5. This smoothing enables us to sketch a continuously downsloping curve rather than one that moves downward in discrete steps as each new unit of labour is hired.

FIGURE 11-1   The Perfectly Competitive Seller's Demand for a Factor

The MRP curve is the factor demand curve; each of its points relates a particular factor price (= MRP when profit is maximized) with a corresponding quantity of the factor demanded. Under perfect competition, product price is constant; therefore, the downward slope of the D = MRP curve is due solely to the decline in the factor's marginal product (law of diminishing marginal returns).

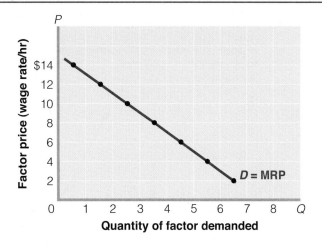

We emphasize that the lower price accompanying each increase in output (total product) applies not only to the marginal product of each successive worker but also to *all prior output*. Note that the second worker's marginal product is six units. These six units can be sold for $2.40 each, or, as a group, for $14.40. But $14.40 is not the MRP of the second worker. To sell these six units, the firm must take a 20-cent price cut on the seven units produced by the first worker—units that otherwise could have been sold for $2.60 each. Thus, the MRP of the second worker is only $13.00 [= $14.40 − (7 × 20 cents)], as shown.

Similarly, the third worker adds five units to total product, and these units are worth $2.20 each, or $11.00 total. But to sell these five units the firm must take a 20-cent price cut on the 13 units produced by the first two workers. So the third worker's MRP is only $8.40 [= $11.00 − (13 × 20 cents)]. The other figures in column 6 are derived in the same way.

In Figure 11-2 we graph the MRP data from Table 11-2 and label it "D = MRP (imperfect competition)." The broken-line factor demand curve, in contrast, is that of the perfectly competitive seller represented in Figure 11-1. A comparison of the two curves demonstrates that, other things

TABLE 11-2   The Demand for Labour: Imperfect Competition in the Sale of the Product

(1) Units of a factor	(2) Total product (output)	(3) Marginal product, MP	(4) Product price	(5) Total revenue, or (2) × (4)	(6) Marginal revenue product, MRP
0	0		$2.80	$ 0	
		7			$18.20
1	7		2.60	18.20	
		6			13.00
2	13		2.40	31.20	
		5			8.40
3	18		2.20	39.60	
		4			4.40
4	22		2.00	44.00	
		3			2.25
5	25		1.85	46.25	
		2			1.00
6	27		1.75	47.25	
		1			1.05
7	28		1.65	46.20	

The Imperfectly Competitive Seller's Demand Curve for a Factor

An imperfectly competitive seller's factor demand curve *D* (solid) slopes downward because both marginal product and product price fall as factor employment and output rise. This downward slope is greater than that for a perfectly competitive seller (dashed factor demand curve) because the perfect competitor can sell the added output at a constant price.

Quantity of a factor demanded

equal, the factor demand curve of an imperfectly competitive seller is less elastic than that of a perfectly competitive seller. Consider the effects of an identical percentage decline in the wage rate (factor price) from $11 to $6. Comparison of the two curves and a quick mental calculation reveals that the firm in imperfect competition does not expand the quantity of labour by as large a percentage as does the firm in perfect competition.

The result is that the MRP curve—the factor demand curve—of the imperfectly competitive producer is less elastic than that of the perfectly competitive producer. At a wage rate or MRC of $11.95, both the perfectly competitive and the imperfectly competitive seller will hire two workers. But at $9.95 the competitive firm will hire three, and the imperfectly competitive firm only two. You can see this difference in factor demand elasticity when we graph the MRP data in Table 11-2 and compare the graph with Figure 11-1, as we do in Figure 11-2.

It is not surprising that the imperfectly competitive producer is less responsive to factor price cuts than the perfectly competitive producer. The imperfect competitor's relative reluctance to employ more factors of production, and produce more output, when factor prices fall reflects its tendency to restrict output in the product market. Other things equal, the imperfectly competitive seller produces less of a product than a perfectly competitive seller. In producing that smaller output, it demands fewer factors of production. *(Key Question 2)*

WORKED PROBLEM 11.1
Factor Demand

MARKET DEMAND FOR A FACTOR

Recall that the total, or market, demand curve for a *product* is found by summing horizontally the demand curves of all individual buyers in the market. The market demand curve for a particular *factor* is derived the same way—by summing horizontally the individual demand or MRP curves for all firms employing that factor (see the Consider This box for a story about the marginal revenue product of superstars).

CONSIDER THIS | Superstars

In what economist Robert Frank calls "winner-take-all markets," a few highly talented performers have huge earnings relative to the average performers in the market. Because consumers and firms seek out the best performers, small differences in talent or popularity get magnified into huge differences in pay.

In winner-take-all markets, consumer spending gets channelled toward a few performers. The media then hypes these new stars, which further increases the public's awareness of their talents. More consumers then buy the stars' products, and superstars emerge. The high earnings of superstars result from the high revenues they generate from their work. Consider Beyoncé Knowles. If she sold only a few thousand CDs and attracted only a few hundred fans to each concert, the revenue she would produce—her

marginal revenue product—would be quite modest. So, too, would be her earnings. But consumers have anointed Beyoncé as queen of the R&B and hip-hop portion of pop culture. The demand for her CDs and concerts are extraordinarily high. She sells millions of CDs, not thousands, and draws thousands to her concerts, not hundreds. Her extraordinarily high net earnings derive from her extraordinarily high marginal revenue product.

So it is for the other superstars in winner-take-all markets. Influenced by media hype but coerced by no one, consumers direct their spending toward a select few. The high marginal revenue product that results means strong demand for these stars' services. And because top talent (by definition) is very limited, superstars receive amazingly high earnings.

QUICK REVIEW

▶ To maximize profit a firm will purchase or hire a factor of production in an amount at which the factor's marginal revenue product equals its marginal factor cost (MRP = MFC).

▶ Application of the MRP = MFC rule to a firm's MRP curve demonstrates that the MRP curve is the firm's factor demand curve. In a perfectly competitive factor market, factor price (the wage rate) equals MFC.

▶ The factor demand curve of a firm in perfect competition is downsloping solely because the marginal product of the factor diminishes; the factor demand curve of a firm in imperfect competition is downsloping because marginal product diminishes and product price falls as output is increased.

11.2 | Determinants of Factor Demand

What will shift the factor demand curve? The fact that factor demand is derived from *product demand* and depends on *factor productivity* suggests two things that can shift factor demand. Also, our analysis of how changes in the prices of other products can shift a product's demand curve (Chapter 3) suggests another reason: changes in the prices of other *factors of production*.

Changes in Product Demand

Other things equal, an increase in the demand for a product that uses a particular factor will increase the demand for that factor of production, whereas a decrease in product demand will decrease the resource demand.

Let's see how this works. The first thing to recall is that a change in the demand for a product will change its price. In Table 11-1, let's assume that an increase in product demand boosts the product price from $2 to $3. You should calculate the new factor demand schedule (columns 1 and 6), and plot it in Figure 11-1 to verify that the new factor demand curve lies to the right of the old demand curve. Similarly, a decline in the product demand (and price) will shift the factor demand curve to the left.

Example: Assuming no offsetting change in supply, an increase in the demand for new houses will drive up house prices. Those higher prices will increase the MRP of construction workers, and therefore the demand for construction workers will rise. The factor demand curve such as in Figure 11-1 or Figure 11-2 will shift to the right.

Changes in Productivity

Other things equal, an increase in the productivity of a factor of production will increase the demand for that factor. If we doubled the MP data of column 3 in Table 11-1, the MRP data of column 6 would also double, indicating an increase (rightward shift) in the factor demand curve.

The productivity of any factor may be altered over the long run in several ways:

- *Quantities of Other Factors* The marginal productivity of any factor will vary with the quantities of the other factors used with it. The greater the amount of capital and land resources used with, say, labour, the greater will be labour's marginal productivity and, thus, labour demand.

- *Technological Advance* Technological improvements that increase the quality of other factors, such as capital, have the same effect. The better the quality of capital, the greater the productivity of labour used with it. Office workers employed with a specific amount of real capital in the form of desktop computers are more productive than office workers with the same amount of real capital embodied in typewriters and filing cabinets.

- *Quality of the Variable Factor* Improvements in the quality of the variable factor, such as labour, will increase its marginal productivity and therefore its demand.

All these considerations help explain why the average level of (real) wages is higher in industrially advanced nations (for example, Canada, the United States, Germany, Japan, and France) than in developing nations (for example, Nicaragua, Ethiopia, Angola, and Cambodia). Workers in industrially advanced nations are generally healthier, better educated, and better trained than are workers in developing countries. Also, in most industries, workers in industrially advanced nations work with a larger and more efficient stock of capital goods and more abundant natural resources. This creates a strong demand for labour. On the supply side of the market, labour is *relatively* scarce compared with that in most developing nations. A strong demand and a relatively scarce supply of labour result in high wage rates in the industrially advanced nations.

Changes in the Prices of Other Factors

Just as changes in the prices of other products will change the demand for a specific product, changes in the prices of other factors of production will change the demand for a specific factor. Also recall that the effect of a change in the price of product X on the demand for product Y depends on whether X and Y are substitute goods or complementary goods *in consumption.* Similarly, the effect of a change in the price of factor A on the demand for factor B depends on their complementarity in production.

SUBSTITUTE FACTORS OF PRODUCTION

Suppose the technology in a certain production process is such that labour and capital can be substituted. A firm can produce a specific amount of output using a relatively small amount of labour and a relatively large amount of capital, or vice versa. Now assume that the price of machinery (capital) falls. The effect on the demand for labour will be the net result of two opposed effects: the substitution effect and the output effect.

substitution effect
A firm will purchase more of an input whose relative price has declined and use less of an input whose relative price has increased.

- *Substitution Effect* The decline in the price of machinery prompts the firm to substitute machinery for labour. This substitution allows the firm to produce its output at a lower cost. So, at the fixed wage rate, smaller quantities of labour are now employed. This **substitution effect** decreases the demand for labour. More generally, the substitution effect indicates that a firm will purchase more of an input whose relative price has declined and, conversely, use less of an output whose relative price has increased.

output effect
An increase in the price of one input will increase a firm's production costs and reduce its level of output, thus reducing the demand for other inputs (and vice versa).

- **Output Effect**   Because the price of machinery has fallen, the costs of producing various outputs must also decline. With lower costs, the firm finds it profitable to produce and sell a greater output. The greater output increases the demand for all factors of production, including labour. So, this **output effect** increases the demand for labour. More generally, the output effect means that the firm will purchase more of one particular input when the price of the other input falls and less of that particular input when the price of the other input rises.

- **Net Effect**   The substitution and output effects are both present when the price of an input changes. The net change in factor demand depends on the relative sizes of the two effects. For example, if the substitution effect outweighs the output effect, a decrease in the price of capital decreases the demand for labour. If the output effect exceeds the substitution effect, a decrease in the price of capital increases the demand for labour.

COMPLEMENTARY FACTORS OF PRODUCTION

Recall from Chapter 3 that certain products, such as computers and software, are complementary goods; they go together and are jointly demanded. Factors of production can also be complementary; an increase in the quantity of one of them used in the production process requires an increase in the amount used of the other as well, and vice versa. Suppose a small design firm does computer-assisted design (CAD) with relatively expensive personal computers as its basic piece of capital equipment. Each computer requires a single design engineer to operate it.

Now assume that a technological advance in the production of these computers substantially reduces their price. No substitution effect can occur, because labour and capital must be used in *fixed proportions,* one person for one machine. Capital cannot be substituted for labour. But there is an output effect. Other things equal, the reduction in the price of capital goods means lower production costs. It will, therefore, be profitable to produce a larger output. In doing so, the firm will use both more capital and more labour. When labour and capital are complementary, a decline in the price of capital increases the demand for labour through the output effect.

We have cast our analysis of substitute factors and complementary factors mainly in terms of a decline in the price of capital. In Table 11-3 we summarize the effects of an *increase* in the price of capital on the demand for labour; study it carefully.

Now that we have discussed the full list of the determinants of labour demand, let's again review their effects. Stated in terms of the labour resource, the demand for labour will increase (the labour demand curve will shift rightward) when

- The demand for the product produced by that labour *increases.*

- The productivity (MP) of labour *increases.*

TABLE 11·3

The Effect of an Increase in the Price of Capital on the Demand for Labour, D_L

(1) Relationship of inputs	(2) Increase in the price of capital		
	(a) Substitution effect	(b) Output effect	(c) Combined effect
Substitutes in production	Labour substituted for capital	Production costs up, output down, and less of both capital and labour used	D_L increases if the substitution effect exceeds the output effect; D_L decreases if the output effect exceeds the substitution effect
Complements in production	No substitution of labour for capital	Production costs up, output down, and less of both capital and labour used	D_L decreases

| TABLE 11-4 | Determinants of Labour Demand: Factors that Shift the Labour Demand Curve |

Determinant	Examples
Changes in product demand	Gambling increases in popularity, increasing the demand for workers at casinos.
	Consumers decrease their demand for leather coats, decreasing the demand for tanners.
	The federal government reduces spending on the military, reducing the demand for military personnel.
Changes in productivity	An increase in the skill levels of physicians increases the demand for their services.
	Computer-assisted graphic design increases the productivity of, and demand for, graphic artists.
Changes in the price of another factor	An increase in the price of electricity increases the cost of producing aluminum and reduces the demand for aluminum workers.
	The price of security equipment used by businesses to protect against illegal entry falls, decreasing the demand for night guards.
	The price of cell phone equipment decreases, reducing the cost of cell phone service, which in turn increases the demand for cell phone assemblers.

- The price of a substitute input *decreases,* provided the output effect exceeds the substitution effect.
- The price of a substitute input *increases,* provided the substitution effect exceeds the output effect.
- The price of a complementary input *decreases.*

Be sure that you can reverse these effects to explain a *decrease* in labour demand.

Table 11-4 provides several illustrations of the determinants of labour demand, listed by the categories of determinants we have discussed. You will benefit from giving them a close look.

11.3 | Elasticity of Factor Demand

The employment changes we have just discussed result from shifts of factor demand curves. Such changes in demand must be distinguished from changes in the quantity demanded of a factor of production caused by a change in the price of the specific factor. Such a change is not caused by a shift of the demand curve but rather by a movement from one point to another on a fixed factor demand curve. For example, in Figure 11-1 we note that an increase in the wage rate from $5 to $7 will reduce the quantity of labour demanded from five to four units. This is a change in the *quantity of labour demanded* as distinct from a *change in demand*.

elasticity of factor demand
The percentage change in factor quantity divided by the percentage change in factor price.

The sensitivity of factor quantity to changes in factor prices is measured by the **elasticity of factor demand.** In coefficient form,

$$E_{fd} = \frac{\text{percentage change in factor quantity}}{\text{percentage change in factor price}}$$

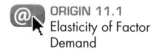

ORIGIN 11.1
Elasticity of Factor Demand

When E_{fd} is greater than one, factor demand is elastic; when E_{fd} is less than one, factor demand is inelastic; and when E_{fd} equals one, factor demand is unit-elastic. (Recall from Chapter 4 that demand elasticity has a negative sign, but we use the absolute value.) What determines the elasticity of factor demand? Several determinants are at work.

Ease of Factor Substitutability

The greater the substitutability of other factors, the more elastic is the demand for a particular factor. Because automated voice-mail systems are highly substitutable for telephone receptionists, the demand for receptionists is quite elastic. In contrast, there are few good substitutes for physicians, so demand for them is less elastic or even inelastic. If a furniture manufacturer finds that several types of wood are equally satisfactory in making coffee tables, a rise in the price of any one type of wood may cause a sharp drop in the amount demanded as the producer substitutes one of the other woods. At the other extreme, no reasonable substitutes may exist; bauxite is absolutely essential in the production of aluminum ingots. Thus the demand for bauxite by aluminum producers is inelastic.

Time can play a role in the ease of input substitution. For example, a firm's truck drivers may obtain a substantial wage increase with little or no immediate decline in employment. But over time, as the firm's trucks wear out and are replaced, that wage increase may motivate the company to purchase larger trucks and in that way deliver the same total output with fewer drivers.

Elasticity of Product Demand

The elasticity of demand for any factor depends on the elasticity of demand for the product that it helps produce. Other things equal, the greater the elasticity of product demand, the greater the elasticity of factor demand. The derived nature of factor demand leads us to expect this relationship. A small rise in the price of a product with great elasticity of demand will sharply reduce output, bringing about relatively large declines in the amounts of various factors of production demanded; the demand for the factor is elastic.

Ratio of Factor Cost to Total Cost

The larger the proportion of total production costs accounted for by a factor of production, the greater the elasticity of demand for that factor. For example, if labour cost is the only production cost, then a 20 percent increase in wage rates will shift all the firm's cost curves upward by the full 20 percent. If product demand is elastic, this substantial increase in wage costs will cause a relatively large decline in sales and a sharp decline in the amount of labour demanded. So labour demand is highly elastic. Conversely, if labour cost is a small percentage of the same firm's cost, labour demand would be relatively inelastic. *(Key Question 5)*

QUICK REVIEW

▸ A factor demand curve will shift because of changes in product demand, changes in the productivity of the factor, and changes in the prices of other inputs.

▸ If factors A and B are substitutable, a decline in the price of A will decrease the demand for B provided the substitution effect exceeds the output effect. If the output effect exceeds the substitution effect, the demand for B will increase.

▸ If factors C and D are complements, a decline in the price of C will increase the demand for D.

▸ Elasticity of factor demand measures the extent to which producers change the quantity of a factor they hire when its price changes.

▸ The elasticity of factor demand will be less the smaller the number of substitutes, the smaller the elasticity of product demand, and the smaller the proportion of total cost accounted for by the factor.

11.4 | Optimal Combination of Factors*

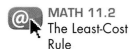

CHOOSING A LITTLE MORE OR LESS

So far our main focus has been on one variable input, labour. But in the long run, firms can vary the amounts of all the factors of production they use. That's why we need to consider what combination of factors a firm will choose when *all* its inputs are variable. While our analysis is based on two factors, it can be extended to any number of inputs.

We will consider two interrelated questions: (1) What combination of factors will minimize costs at a specific level of output? and (2) What combination of factors will maximize profit?

The Least-Cost Rule

least-cost combination of factors
The quantity of each factor a firm must employ to produce a particular output at the lowest total cost.

A firm is producing a specific output with the **least-cost combination of factors** when the last dollar spent on each factor yields the same marginal product. In competitive factor markets marginal factor cost is the market factor price; the firm can hire as many or as few units of the factors as it wants at that price. Then, with just two factors, labour and capital, a competitive firm minimizes its total cost of a specific output when

$$\frac{\text{Marginal Product of Labour (MP}_L)}{\text{Price of Labour } (P_L)} = \frac{\text{Marginal Product of Capital (MP}_C)}{\text{Price of Capital } (P_C)} \qquad (1)$$

MATH 11.2
The Least-Cost Rule

Throughout, we will refer to the marginal products of labour and capital as MP_L and MP_C, respectively, and symbolize the price of labour by P_L and the price of capital by P_C.

A concrete example shows why fulfilling the condition in equation (1) leads to least-cost production. Assume that the price of both capital and labour is $1 per unit, but that they are currently employed in such amounts that the marginal product of labour is 10 and the marginal product of capital is 5. Our equation immediately tells us that this is not the least costly combination of resources:

$$\frac{\text{MP}_L = 10}{P_L = \$1} > \frac{\text{MP}_C = 5}{P_C = \$1}$$

Suppose the firm spends $1 less on capital and shifts that dollar to labour. It loses five units of output produced by the last dollar's worth of capital, but it gains 10 units of output from the extra dollar's worth of labour. Net output increases by 5 (= 10 − 5) units for the same total cost. More such shifting of dollars from capital to labour will push the firm *down* along its MP curve for labour and *up* along its MP curve for capital, increasing output and moving the firm toward a position of equilibrium where equation (1) is fulfilled. At that equilibrium position, the MP per dollar for the last unit of both labour and capital might be, for example, seven. The firm will be producing a greater output for the same (original) cost.

Whenever the same total resource cost can result in a greater total output, the cost per unit—and therefore the total cost of any specific level of output—can be reduced. The cost of producing any specific output can be reduced as long as equation (1) does not hold. But when dollars have been shifted between capital and labour to the point where equation (1) holds, no additional changes in the use of capital and labour will reduce costs further. The firm is now producing that output using the least-cost combination of capital and labour.

All the long-run cost curves developed in Chapter 6 and used thereafter assume that the least-cost combination of inputs has been realized at each level of output. Any firm that combines factors of production in violation of the least-cost rule will have a higher-than-necessary average total cost at each level of output; that is, it will incur *X-inefficiency,* as shown in Figure 8-7.

---

* *Note to Instructors:* We consider this section optional; it can be skipped without loss of continuity, or deferred until after the discussion of wage determination in Chapter 12.

The Profit-Maximizing Rule

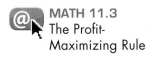

MATH 11.3
The Profit-
Maximizing Rule

Minimizing cost is not sufficient for maximizing profit. A firm can produce any level of output in the least costly way by applying equation (1), but only one unique level of output can maximize profit. Our earlier analysis of product markets showed that this profit-maximizing output occurs where marginal revenue equals marginal cost (MR = MC). Near the beginning of this chapter, we determined that we could write this profit-maximizing condition as MRP = MFC as it relates to factor inputs.

In a perfectly competitive factor market, the marginal factor cost (MFC) is exactly equal to the factor price, P. Thus, for any competitive factor market, we have as our profit-maximizing equation

MRP (factor) = P (factor)

profit-maximizing combination of factors
The quantity of each factor a firm must employ to maximize its profits or minimize its losses.

This condition must hold for every variable factor—and in the long run all factors are variable. In competitive markets, a firm will, therefore, achieve its **profit-maximizing combination of factors** when each factor is employed to the point at which its marginal revenue product equals its price. For two factors, labour and capital, we need both $P_L = MRP_L$ and $P_C = MRP_C$.

We can combine these conditions by dividing both sides of each equation by their respective prices and equating the results, to get

$$\frac{MRP_L}{P_L} = \frac{MRP_C}{P_C} = 1 \tag{2}$$

Note in equation (2) that it is not sufficient that the MRPs of the two factors be *proportionate* to their prices; the MRPs must be *equal* to their prices and the ratios, therefore, equal to one. For example, if $MRP_L = \$15$, $P_L = \$5$, $MRP_C = \$9$, and $P_C = \$3$, the firm is underemploying both capital and labour even though the ratios of MRP to resource price are identical for both factors. The firm can expand its profit by hiring additional amounts of both capital and labour until it moves down their downsloping MRP curves to the points at which $MRP_L = \$5$ and $MRP_C = \$3$. The ratios will then be 5/5 and 3/3 and equal to one.

The profit-maximizing position in equation (2) includes the cost-minimizing condition of equation (1). That is, if a firm is maximizing profit according to equation (2), then it must be using the least-cost combination of inputs to do so. However, the converse is not true: a firm operating at least cost according to equation (1) may not be operating at the output that maximizes its profit.

WORKED PROBLEM 11.2
Optimal Combination of Factors

Numerical Illustration

A numerical illustration will help you understand the least-cost and profit-maximizing rules. In columns 2, 3, 2′, and 3′ in Table 11-5, we show the total products and marginal products for various amounts of labour and capital that are assumed to be the only inputs needed in producing some product, say key chains. Both inputs are subject to diminishing returns.

We also assume that labour and capital are supplied in competitive factor markets at $8 and $12, respectively, and that key chains sell competitively at $2 per unit. For both labour and capital, we can determine the total revenue associated with each input level by multiplying total product by the $2 product price. These data are shown in columns 4 and 4′. They enable us to calculate the marginal revenue product of each successive input of labour and capital as shown in columns 5 and 5′, respectively.

PRODUCING AT LEAST COST

What is the least-cost combination of labour and capital to use in producing, say, 50 units of output? The answer, which we can obtain by trial and error, is three units of labour and two units of capital. Columns 2 and 2′ indicate that this combination of labour and capital does, indeed, result in the required 50 (= 28 + 22) units of output. Now, note from columns 3 and 3′ that hiring three units of labour gives us $MP_L/P_L = {}^6/_8 = {}^3/_4$, and hiring two units of capital gives us $MP_C/P_C = {}^9/_{12} = {}^3/_4$. So, equation (1) is fulfilled. How can we verify that costs are actually minimized? First, we see that the total cost of employing three units of labour and two of capital is $48 [= (3 × \$8) + (2 × \$12)]$.

TABLE 11-5	Data for Finding the Least-Cost and Profit-Maximizing Combination of Labour and Capital*

	LABOUR (PRICE = $8)					CAPITAL (PRICE = $12)				
(1) Quantity	(2) Total product (output)	(3) Marginal product	(4) Total revenue	(5) Marginal revenue product	(1') Quantity	(2') Total product (output)	(3') Marginal product	(4') Total revenue	(5') Marginal revenue product
0	0		$ 0		0	0		$ 0	
		12		$24			13		$26
1	12		24		1	13		26	
		10		20			9		18
2	22		44		2	22		44	
		6		12			6		*12*
3	28		56		**3**	28		56	
		5		10			4		8
4	33		66		4	32		64	
		4		**8**			3		6
5	37		74		5	35		70	
		3		6			2		4
6	40		80		6	37		74	
		2		4			1		2
7	42		84		7	38		76	

* To simplify, it is assumed in this table that the productivity of each factor is independent of the quantity of the other. For example, the total and marginal product of labour is assumed not to vary with the quantity of capital employed.

Other combinations of labour and capital will also yield 50 units of output but at a higher cost than $48. For example, five units of labour and one unit of capital will produce 50 (= 37 + 13) units, but total cost is higher at $52 [= (5 × $8) + (1 × $12)]. This result comes as no surprise, because five units of labour and one unit of capital violate the least-cost rule—$MP_L/P_L = {}^4/_8$, $MP_C/P_C = {}^{13}/_{12}$. Only the combination (three units of labour and two units of capital) that minimizes total cost will satisfy equation (1).

MAXIMIZING PROFIT

Will 50 units of output maximize the firm's profit? No, because the profit-maximizing terms of equation (2) are not satisfied when the firm employs three units of labour and two of capital. To maximize profit, each input should be employed until its price equals its marginal revenue product. But for three units of labour, labour's MRP in column 5 is $12 while its price is only $8; the firm could increase its profit by hiring more labour. Similarly, for two units of capital, we see in column 5' that capital's MRP is $18 and its price is only $12. This result indicates that more capital should also be employed. By producing only 50 units of output (even though they are produced at least cost), labour and capital are being used in less-than-profit-maximizing amounts. The firm needs to expand its employment of labour and capital, thereby increasing its output.

Table 11-5 shows that the MRPs of labour and capital are equal to their prices, so that equation (2) is fulfilled when the firm is employing five units of labour and three units of capital. This is the profit-maximizing combination of inputs.[2] The firm's total cost will be $76, made up of $40 (= 5 × $8) of labour and $36 (= 3 × $12) of capital. Total revenue will be $130, found either by multiplying

---

[2] Because we are dealing with discrete (non-fractional) units of the two outputs here, the use of four units of labour and two units of capital is equally profitable. The fifth unit of labour's MRP and its price (cost) are equal at $8, so that the fifth labour unit neither adds to nor subtracts from the firm's profit; similarly, the third unit of capital has no effect on profit.

the total output of 65 (= 37 + 28) by the $2 product price or by summing the total revenues attributable to labour ($74) and to capital ($56). The difference between total revenue and total cost in this instance is $54 (= $130 – $76). Experiment with other combinations of labour and capital to demonstrate that they yield an economic profit of less than $54.

Note that the profit-maximizing combination of five units of labour and three units of capital is also a least-cost combination for this particular level of output. Using these factor amounts satisfies the least-cost requirement of equation (1) in that $MP_L/P_L = {}^4/_8 = 1/2$ and $MP_C/P_C = {}^6/_{12} = {}^1/_2$. (**Key Questions 6 and 7**)

Marginal Productivity Theory of Income Distribution

ORIGIN 11.2
Marginal
Productivity
Theory of Income
Distribution

marginal productivity theory of income distribution
The contention that the distribution of income is fair when each unit of each factor receives a money payment equal to its marginal contribution to the firm's revenue (its marginal revenue product).

Our discussion of factor pricing is the cornerstone of the controversial view that fairness and economic justice are two of the outcomes of a competitive market economy. Table 11-5 demonstrates, in effect, that workers receive income payments (wages) equal to the marginal contributions they make to their employers' outputs and revenues. In other words, workers are paid according to the value of the labour services that they contribute to production. Similarly, owners of the other factors of production receive income based on the value of the factors they supply in the production process.

In this **marginal productivity theory of income distribution,** income is distributed according to the contribution to society's output. So, if you are willing to accept the proposition "To each according to the values of what he or she creates," income payments based on marginal revenue product provide a fair and equitable distribution of society's income.

This sounds reasonable, but you need to be aware of serious criticisms of this theory of income distribution:

- *Inequality* Critics argue that the distribution of income resulting from payment according to marginal productivity may be highly unequal because productive factors are very unequally distributed in the first place. Aside from their differences in mental and physical attributes, individuals encounter substantially different opportunities to enhance their productivity through education and training. Some people may not be able to participate in production at all because of mental or physical disabilities, and they would obtain no income under a system of distribution based solely on marginal productivity. Ownership of property resources is also highly unequal. Many owners of land and capital resources obtain their property by inheritance rather than through their own productive effort. Hence, income from inherited property resources conflicts with the "To each according to the values of what he or she creates" idea. This reasoning, say critics, calls for progressive taxation and government spending programs that modify the income distributions made strictly according to marginal productivity.

- *Market Imperfections* The marginal productivity theory of income distribution rests on the assumptions of competitive markets. But, as we will see in Chapter 12, not all labour markets are highly competitive. Employers in some labour markets exert their wage-setting power to pay less-than-competitive wages. And some workers, through labour unions, professional associations, and occupational licensing laws, wield wage-setting power to increase their wages in selling their services. In addition, discrimination in the labour market can distort earnings patterns. In short, because of real-world market imperfections, wage rates and other factor prices are not always based solely on contributions to output.

The LAST WORD   Input Substitution: the Case of ABMs

Banks are using more automated banking machines (ABMs) and employing fewer human tellers.

As you have learned from this chapter, a firm achieves its least-cost combination of inputs when the last dollar it spends on each input makes the same contribution to total output. This raises an interesting real-world question: What happens when technological advance makes available a new, highly productive capital good for which MP/P is greater than it is for other inputs, say a particular type of labour? The answer is that the least-cost mix of factors abruptly changes and the firm responds accordingly. If the new capital is a substitute for labour (rather than a complement), the firm replaces the particular type of labour with the new capital. That is exactly what is happening in the banking industry, in which ABMs are replacing human bank tellers.

ABMs made their debut about 38 years ago when Diebold, a U.S. firm, introduced the product. Today, Diebold and NCR (also a U.S. firm) dominate global sales, with the Japanese firm Fujitsu a distant third. The number of ABMs has exploded, and currently more than 50,000 ABMs are in use in Canada. We rank number one in the world in the number of ABMs per inhabitant: 1631 ABMs per million inhabitants, compared to 1335 for second place U.S. and 1289 for third ranking Belgium.

ABMs are highly productive: A single machine can handle hundreds of transactions daily, thousands weekly, and millions over the course of several years. ABMs not only can handle cash withdrawals, but also can accept deposits and facilitate switches of funds between various accounts. Although ABMs are expensive for banks to buy and install, they are available 24 hours a day, and their cost per transaction is one-fourth the cost for human tellers. They rarely get held up, and they do not quit their jobs (turnover among human tellers is nearly 50 percent per year). ABMs are highly convenient; unlike human tellers, they are located not only at banks but also at busy street corners, workplaces, colleges and universities, and shopping malls.

The same bank card that enables you to withdraw cash from your local ABM also enables you to withdraw pounds from an ABM in London, yen from an ABM in Tokyo, and even rubles from an ABM in Moscow (assuming, of course, you have money in your account).

In the terminology of this chapter, the more productive, lower-priced ABMs have reduced the demand for a substitute in production—human tellers. Between 1990 and 2000, 8000 human teller positions were eliminated, and more positions will disappear by 2010. Where will the people holding these jobs go? Some will eventually move to other occupations. Others will be retrained and move to the chartered banks' extensive customer service departments to become investment advisers and wealth-management representatives. Although the lives of some individual tellers are disrupted, society clearly wins. Society gets cheaper, more convenient banking services and more of the other goods that these freed-up labour resources help to produce.

Source: Based partly on Ben Craig, "Where Have All the Tellers Gone?" *Economic Commentary* (Federal Reserve Bank of Cleveland), April. 15, 1997; and statistics compiled by the Canadian Bankers Association. These statistics can be found at www.cba.ca/

Question

Explain the economics of the substitution of ABMs for human tellers. Some banks assess transaction fees when customers use human tellers rather than ABMs. What are these banks trying to accomplish?

CHAPTER SUMMARY

11.1 ▶ FACTOR PRICING AND DEMAND

- Factor prices help determine money incomes, and they simultaneously ration factors of production to various industries and firms.

- The demand for any factor is derived from the product it helps produce. That means the demand for a factor will depend on its productivity and on the market value (price) of the good it is producing.

- Marginal revenue product is the extra revenue a firm obtains when it employs one more unit of a factor. The MRP curve for any factor is the demand curve for that factor, because the firm equates factor price and MRP in determining its profit-maximizing level of factor employment. Thus, each point on the MRP curve indicates how many factor units the firm will hire at a specific factor price.

- The firm's demand curve for a factor slopes downward, because the marginal product of additional units declines in accordance with the law of diminishing returns. When a firm is selling in an imperfectly competitive market, the factor demand curve falls for a second reason: Product price must be reduced for the firm to sell a larger output. We can derive the market demand curve for a factor by summing horizontally the demand curves of all the firms hiring that factor.

11.2 ▶ DETERMINANTS OF FACTOR DEMAND

- The demand curve for a factor will shift as the result of (a) a change in the demand for, and therefore the price of, the product the factor is producing; (b) changes in the productivity of the factor; and (c) changes in the prices of other factors.

- If factors A and B are substitutable for each other, a decline in the price of A will decrease the demand for B provided the substitution effect is greater than the output effect. But if the output effect *exceeds* the substitution effect, a decline in the price of A will increase the demand for B.

- If factors C and D are complementary or jointly demanded, there is only an output effect; a change in the price of C will change the demand for D in the opposite direction.

11.3 ▶ ELASTICITY OF FACTOR DEMAND

- The elasticity of demand for a factor measures the responsiveness of producers to a change in the factor's price. The coefficient of the elasticity of factor demand is

$$E_{fd} = \frac{\text{percentage change in factor quantity}}{\text{percentage change in factor price}}$$

When E_{fd} is greater than one, factor demand is elastic; when E_{fd} is less than one, factor demand is inelastic; and when E_{fd} equals one, factor demand is unit elastic.

- The elasticity of demand for a factor will be greater (a) the greater the ease of substituting other resources for labour, (b) the greater the elasticity of demand for the product, and (c) the larger the proportion of total production costs attributable to the factor.

11.4 ▶ OPTIMAL COMBINATION OF FACTORS

- Any specific level of output will be produced with the least costly combination of variable factors when the marginal product per dollar's worth of each input is the same—that is, when

$$\frac{\text{MP of labour}}{\text{price of labour}} = \frac{\text{MP of capital}}{\text{price of capital}}$$

- A firm is employing the profit-maximizing combination of factors when each factor is used to the point where its marginal revenue product equals its price. In terms of labour and capital, that occurs when the MRP of labour equals the price of labour and the MRP of capital equals the price of capital—that is, when

$$\frac{\text{MRP of labour}}{\text{price of labour}} = \frac{\text{MRP of capital}}{\text{price of capital}} = 1$$

- The marginal productivity theory of income distribution holds that all factors are paid what they are economically worth: their marginal contribution to output. Critics assert that such an income distribution is too unequal and the real-world market imperfections result in pay above and below marginal contributions to output.

TERMS AND CONCEPTS

derived demand, p. 268
marginal product (MP), p. 269
marginal revenue product (MRP), p. 269
marginal factor cost (MFC), p. 269
MRP = MFC rule, p. 270

substitution effect, p. 274
output effect, p. 275
elasticity of factor demand, p. 276
least-cost combination of factors, p. 278

profit-maximizing combination
    of factors, p. 279
marginal productivity theory of income
    distribution, p. 281

STUDY QUESTIONS

LO ▶ 11.1 1. What is the significance of factor pricing? Explain how the determinants of factor demand differ from those underlying product demand. Explain the meaning and significance of the fact that the demand for a factor is a derived demand. Why do factors demand curves slope downward?

LO ▶ 11.2 2. **KEY QUESTION** Complete the following labour demand table for a firm that is hiring labour competitively and selling its product in a competitive market.

    a. How many workers will the firm hire if the market wage rate is $27.95? $19.95? Explain why the firm will not hire a larger or smaller number of units of labour at each of these wage rates.

    b. Show in schedule form and graphically the labour demand curve of this firm.

    c. Now redetermine the firm's demand curve for labour, assuming that it is selling in an imperfectly competitive market and that, although it can sell 17 units at $2.20 per unit, it must lower product price by 5 cents to sell the marginal product of each successive labour unit. Compare this demand curve with that derived in question 2(b). Which curve is more elastic? Explain.

Units of labour	Total product	Marginal product	Product price	Total revenue	Marginal revenue product
0	0		$2	$ ___	
1	17	___	2	___	$ ___
2	31	___	2	___	___
3	43	___	2	___	___
4	53	___	2	___	___
5	60	___	2	___	___
6	65	___	2	___	___

LO ▶ 11.2 3. Suppose that marginal product tripled while product price fell by one-half in Table 11-1. What would be the new MRP values in Table 11-1? What would be the net impact on the location of the factor demand curve in Figure 11-1?

LO ▶ 11.2 4. In 2005 General Motors (GM) announced that it would reduce employment by 30,000 workers. What does this decision reveal about how it viewed its marginal revenue product (MRP) and marginal factor cost (MFC)? Why didn't GM reduce employment by more than 30,000 workers? By fewer than 30,000 workers?

5. **KEY QUESTION** What are the determinants of the elasticity of factor demand? What effect will each of the following have on the elasticity or the location of the demand for factor C, which is being used to produce commodity X? Where there is any uncertainty as to the outcome, specify the causes of that uncertainty.

    a. An increase in the demand for product X

    b. An increase in the price of substitute factor D

    c. An increase in the number of factors substitutable for C in producing X

    d. A technological improvement in the capital equipment with which factor C is combined

    e. A decline in the price of complementary factor E

    f. A decline in the elasticity of demand for product X due to a decline in the competitiveness of product market X

6. **KEY QUESTION** Suppose the productivity of capital and labour are as shown in the accompanying table. The output of these factors sells in a perfectly competitive market for $1 per unit. Both capital and labour are hired under perfectly competitive conditions at $3 and $1, respectively.

Units of capital	MP of capital	Units of labour	MP of labour
0		0	
1	24	1	11
2	21	2	9
3	18	3	8
4	15	4	7
5	9	5	6
6	6	6	4
7	3	7	1
8	1	8	½

    a. What is the least-cost combination of labour and capital the firm should employ in producing 80 units of output? Explain.

    b. What is the profit-maximizing combination of labour and capital the firm should use? Explain. What is the resulting level of output? What is the economic profit? Is this the least costly way of producing the profit-maximizing output?

11.4 7. **KEY QUESTION** In each of the following four cases, MRP_L and MRP_C refer to the marginal revenue products of labour and capital, respectively, and P_L and P_C refer to their prices. Indicate in each case whether the conditions are consistent with maximum profits for the firm. If not, state which factor(s) should be used in larger amounts and which factor(s) should be used in smaller amounts.

a. $MRP_L = \$8$; $P_L = \$4$; $MRP_C = \$8$; $P_C = \$4$

b. $MRP_L = \$10$; $P_L = \$12$; $MRP_C = \$14$; $P_C = \$9$

c. $MRP_L = \$6$; $P_L = \$6$; $MRP_C = \$12$; $P_C = \$12$

d. $MRP_L = \$22$; $P_L = \$26$; $MRP_C = \$16$; $P_C = \$19$

8. Florida citrus growers say that the recent crackdown on illegal immigration is increasing the market wage rates necessary to get their oranges picked. Some are turning to $100,000-to-$300,000 mechanical harvesters known as "trunk, shake, and catch" pickers, which vigorously shake oranges from the trees. If widely adopted, what will be the effect on the demand for human orange pickers? What does that imply about the relative strengths of the substitution and output effects? **LO 11.4**

INTERNET APPLICATION QUESTIONS @

1. **Selected Occupations—What Are Their Economic Outlooks?** Visit Human Resources and Skills Development Canada through the McConnell-Brue-Flynn-Barbiero Web site (Chapter 11) to determine the specific employment outlooks for several occupations. For which jobs are prospects good up until 2012?

2. **The Overall Demand for Labour—In Which Countries Has It Increased the Most?** Increases in employment reflect increases in labour demand, accompanied by increases in labour supply. Go to the McConnell-Brue-Flynn-Barbiero Web site (Chapter 11) and select International Labour Statistics (at the bottom). Find the percentage increases in employment for Canada, the United States, Japan, Germany, France, Great Britain, and Italy for the most recent 10-year period. Which three countries have had the fastest growth of labour demand, as measured by the employment outcome? Which three have been slowest?

CHAPTER 12

Wage Determination

Over 16 million Canadians go to work each day. We work at an amazing variety of jobs for thousands of different firms for considerable differences in pay. What determines our hourly wage or annual salary? Why is the salary for, say, a top major league baseball player $18 million a year, whereas the pay for a first-rate schoolteacher is $80,000? Why are starting salaries for university graduates who major in engineering and accounting so much higher than for graduates majoring in journalism and sociology?

Having explored the major factors that underlie labour demand, we now bring *labour supply* into our analysis to help answer these questions. Generally, labour supply and labour demand interact to determine the hourly wage rate or annual salary in each occupation. Collectively, those wages and salaries make up about 75 percent of the national income in Canada.

12.1 | Productivity and the General Level of Wages

Economists use the term "labour" broadly to apply to (1) blue-collar and white-collar workers of all varieties; (2) professionals such as lawyers, physicians, dentists, and teachers; and (3) owners of small businesses, including barbers, plumbers, and a host of retailers who provide labour as they carry on their own business.

Wages are the price that employers pay for labour. Wages take the form not only of direct money payments such as hourly pay, annual salaries, bonuses, royalties, and commissions, but also fringe benefits, such as paid vacations and dental insurance. We will use the term "wages" to mean all such payments and benefits converted to an hourly basis. That will remind us that the **wage rate** is a price paid per unit of labour services, in this case an hour of work. It will also let us distinguish between the wage rate and labour earnings, the latter being determined by multiplying the number of hours worked per week, per month, or per year by the hourly wage or wage rate.

We must also distinguish between nominal wages and real wages. A **nominal wage** is the amount of money received per hour, per day, and so on. A **real wage** is the quantity

wage rate
A price paid per unit of labour services.

nominal wage
The amount of money received by a worker per unit of time (hour, day, etc.).

real wage
The amount of goods and services a worker can purchase with a nominal wage.

Wages are the price that employers pay for labour.

of goods and services a worker can obtain with nominal wages; real wages reveal the purchasing power of nominal wages.

Your real wage depends on your nominal wage and the prices of the goods and services you purchase. Suppose you receive a 5 percent increase in your nominal wage during a certain year, but in that same year the price level increases by 3 percent. Then your real wage has increased by 2 percent (= 5 percent *minus* 3 percent). Unless otherwise indicated, we will discuss only *real* wages.

Wages differ among nations, regions, occupations, and individuals. Wage rates are much higher in Canada than in China or India. Wages are slightly higher in central Canada and the west than in the east. Plumbers are paid less than NHL hockey players, and lawyer Adam may earn twice as much as lawyer Bharti for the same number of hours of work. Wage rates also differ by gender, race, and ethnic background.

The general level of wages includes a wide range of different wage rates. It includes the wages of bakers, barbers, brick masons, and brain surgeons. By averaging such wages, we can more easily compare wages among regions and among nations.

As Global Perspective 12.1 suggests, the general level of real wages in Canada, especially in the skilled trades, is relatively high—although not the highest in the world. The explanation for the high real wages in Canada and other industrially advanced economies (referred to hereafter as advanced economies) is that the demand for labour in these nations is relatively large compared to the supply of labour.

The Role of Productivity

We know from the previous chapter that the demand for labour, or for any other factor, depends on its productivity. Generally, the greater the productivity of labour, the greater the demand for it. If the total supply of labour is fixed, then the stronger the demand for labour, and the higher

12.1 | GLOBAL PERSPECTIVE

Hourly wages of production workers, selected nations

Worldwide wage differences are pronounced. The data shown here indicate that hourly compensation in Canada is not as high as in some European nations. It is important to note, however, that the prices of goods and services vary greatly among nations, and the process of converting foreign wages into dollars may not accurately reflect such variations.

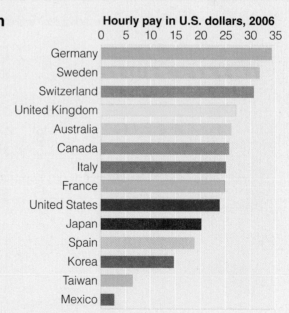

Hourly pay in U.S. dollars, 2006

Germany, Sweden, Switzerland, United Kingdom, Australia, Canada, Italy, France, United States, Japan, Spain, Korea, Taiwan, Mexico

Source: U.S. Bureau of Labor Statistics <www.bls.gov>

the average level of real wages. The demand for labour in Canada and the other major advanced economies is large because labour in these countries is highly productive. There are several reasons for that high productivity:

- *Plentiful Capital*   Workers in the advanced economies have access to large amounts of physical capital equipment (machinery and buildings). The total physical capital per worker in Canada is one of the highest in the world.

- *Access to Abundant Natural Resources*   In advanced economies, natural resources are abundant in relation to the size of the labour force. Some of those resources are available domestically and others are imported from abroad. Canada, for example, is richly endowed with arable land, mineral resources, and sources of energy for industry.

- *Advanced Technology*   The level of technological progress is generally high in advanced economies. Not only do workers in these economies have more capital equipment to work with but that equipment is also technologically superior to the equipment available to the vast majority of workers worldwide. Work methods in the advanced economies are also steadily being improved through scientific study and research.

- *Labour Quality*   The health, education, and training of workers in advanced economies are generally superior to those of workers in developing nations. Thus, even with the same quantity and quality of natural and capital resources, workers in advanced economies tend to be more productive than many of their counterparts.

- *Other Factors*   Less obvious factors also underlie the high productivity in some of the advanced economies. In Canada, for example, such factors include (1) the efficiency and flexibility of management; (2) business, social, and political environments that emphasize production and productivity; (3) access to a large market, which enables firms to engage in mass production; and (4) increased specialization of production made possible by free trade agreements with other nations.

FIGURE 12-1   Output per Hour and Real Hourly Compensation in Canada

Over the years a close relationship exists between output per hour of work and real hourly earnings.

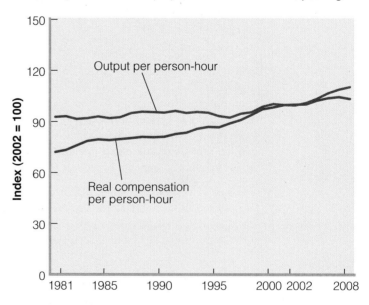

SOURCE: Adapted from Statistics Canada CANSIM database, http://cansim2.statcan.ca, Table 383-0008, June 2009.

FIGURE 12-2   **The Long-Run Trend of Real Wages in Canada**

The productivity of Canadian labour has increased substantially over the long run, causing the demand for labour, D, to shift rightward more rapidly than increases in the supply of labour, S. The result has been increases in real wages.

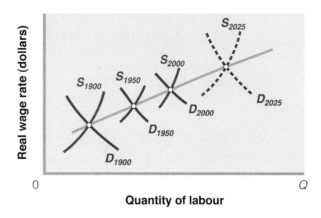

Real Wages and Productivity

Figure 12-1 shows the close long-run relationship between output per hour of work and real hourly earnings in Canada. Because real income and real output are two ways of viewing the same thing, real income (earnings) per worker can increase only at about the same rate as output per worker. When workers produce more real output per hour, more real income is available to distribute to them for each hour worked.

However, suppliers of land, capital, and entrepreneurial talent also share in the income from production. Real wages, therefore, do not always rise in lockstep with gains in productivity over short spans of time. But over long periods, productivity and real wages tend to rise together.

Long-Run Trend of Real Wages

Basic supply and demand analysis helps explain the long-term trend of real-wage growth in Canada. The nation's labour force has grown significantly over the decades. But, as a result of the productivity-increasing factors we have mentioned, increases in labour demand have outstripped increases in labour supply. Figure 12-2 shows several such increases in labour supply and labour demand. The result has been a long-run increase in wage rates and employment. For example, real hourly compensation in Canada has roughly doubled since 1960. Over that same period, employment has increased by about 11 million workers.

12.2 | Wages in a Perfectly Competitive Labour Market

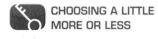

CHOOSING A LITTLE MORE OR LESS

perfectly competitive labour market
A factor market in which a large number of firms demand a particular type of labour supplied by a large number of nonunion workers.

Average levels of wages, however, disguise the great variation of wage rates among occupations and within occupations. What determines the wage rate paid for a specific type of labour? Demand and supply analysis is again revealing. Let's begin by examining labour demand and labour supply in a **perfectly competitive labour market.** In this type of market:

- Numerous firms compete with one another in hiring a specific type of labour.

- Many qualified workers with identical skills supply that type of labour.

- Individual firms and individual workers are wage-takers, since neither can exert any control over the market wage rate.

Market Demand for Labour

Suppose 200 firms demand a particular type of labour, say, carpenters. These firms need not be in the same industry. Thus, firms producing wood-framed furniture, wood windows and doors, houses and apartment buildings, and wood cabinets will demand carpenters. To find the total, or market, labour demand curve for a particular labour service, we sum horizontally the labour demand curves (the marginal revenue product curves) of the individual firms, as indicated in **Figure 12-3 (Key Graph)**. The horizontal summing of the 200 labour demand curves like *d* in Figure 12-3b yields the market labour demand curve *D* in Figure 12-3a.

Market Supply of Labour

On the supply side of a perfectly competitive labour market, we assume that no union is present and that workers individually compete for available jobs. The supply curve for each type of labour slopes upward, indicating that employers as a group must pay higher wage rates to obtain more workers. They must do this to bid workers away from other industries, occupations, and localities. Within limits, workers have alternative job opportunities. For example, they may work in other industries in the same locality, they may work in their present occupations in different cities or provinces, or they may work in other occupations.

Firms that want to hire these workers (here, carpenters) must pay higher wage rates to attract them away from the alternative job opportunities available to them. They must also pay higher wages to induce people who are not currently in the labour force—perhaps doing household activities or enjoying leisure—to seek employment. In short, assuming that wages are constant in other labour markets, higher wages in a particular labour market entice more workers to offer their labour services in that market—a fact confirmed by the upward-sloping market supply of labour curve *S* in Figure 12-3a.

Labour Market Equilibrium

The intersection of the market labour demand curve and the market supply curve determines the equilibrium wage rate and level of employment in purely competitive labour markets. In Figure 12-3a the equilibrium wage rate is W_c ($10), and the number of workers hired is Q_c (1000). To the individual firm the market wage rate W_c is given. Each of the many firms employs such a small fraction of the total available supply of this type of labour that no single firm can influence the wage rate. As shown by the horizontal line *s* in Figure 12-3b, the supply of this labour is perfectly elastic to the individual firm.

Each individual firm will find it profitable to hire this type of labour up to the point at which marginal revenue product is equal to marginal factor cost. This is merely an application of the MRP = MFC rule we developed in Chapter 11.

As Table 12-1 indicates, when the price of a factor is given to the individual competitive firm, the marginal cost of that factor (MFC) is constant and is equal to the factor price. Note that MFC is constant at $10 and matches the $10 wage rate. Each additional worker hired adds precisely his or her own wage rate ($10 in this case) to the firm's total resource cost. So the firm in a perfectly competitive labour market maximizes its profit by hiring workers to the point at which its wage rate equals MRP. In Figure 12-3b this firm will hire Q_c (five) workers, paying each worker the market wage rate, W_c ($10). The other 199 firms (not shown) that are hiring workers in this labour market will also each employ 5 workers and pay $10 per hour.

To determine a firm's total revenue from employing a particular number of labour units, we sum the MRPs of those units. For example, if a firm employs three labour units with marginal revenue products of $14, $13, and $12, respectively, then the firm's total revenue is $39 (= $14 + $13 + $12). In Figure 12-3b, where we are not restricted to whole units of labour, total revenue is represented by area 0*abc* under the MRP curve to the left of Q_c. What area represents the firm's total cost, including a normal profit? For Q_c units, the same area—0*abc*. The green rectangle represents the firm's

KEY GRAPH

FIGURE 12-3 Labour Supply and Labour Demand in (Panel a) a Perfectly Competitive Labour Market and (Panel b) a Single Competitive Firm

In a perfectly competitive labour market (panel a), the equilibrium wage rate, W_c, and the number of workers, Q_c, are determined by labour supply S and labour demand D. Because this market wage rate is given to the individual firm (panel b) hiring in this market, its labour supply curve $S = MFC$ is perfectly elastic. Its labour demand curve is its MRP curve (here labelled mrp). The firm maximizes its profit by hiring workers up to where MRP = MFC. Area $0abc$ represents both the firm's total revenue and its total cost. The green area is its total wage cost; the blue area is its nonlabour costs, including a normal profit—that is, the firm's payments to the suppliers of land, capital, and entrepreneurship.

(a) Labour market

(b) Individual firm

Quick Quiz

1. The supply of labour curve S slopes upward in graph (a) because
   a. the law of diminishing marginal utility applies.
   b. the law of diminishing returns applies.
   c. workers can afford to buy more leisure when their wage rates rise.
   d. higher wages are needed to attract workers away from other labour markets, household activities, and leisure.

2. This firm's labour demand curve d in graph (b) slopes downward because
   a. the law of diminishing marginal utility applies.
   b. the law of diminishing returns applies.
   c. the firm must lower its price to sell additional units of its product.
   d. the firm is a competitive employer, not a monopsonist.

3. In employing five workers, the firm represented in graph (b)
   a. has a total wage cost of $6000.
   b. is adhering to the general principle of undertaking all actions for which the marginal benefit exceeds the marginal cost.
   c. uses less labour than would be ideal from society's perspective.
   d. experiences increasing marginal returns.

4. A rightward shift of the labour supply curve in graph (a) would shift curve
   a. $d = mrp$ leftward in graph (b).
   b. $d = mrp$ rightward in graph (b).
   c. $s = MFC$ upward in graph (b).
   d. $s = MFC$ downward in graph (b).

Answers: 1. d; 2. b; 3. b; 4. d

| TABLE 12-1 | The Supply of Labour: Perfect Competition in the Hire of Labour | | |

(1) Units of labour	(2) Wage rate	(3) Total labour cost (wage bill)	(4) Marginal factor (labour) cost
0	$10	$ 0	
			$10
1	10	10	
			10
2	10	20	
			10
3	10	30	
			10
4	10	40	
			10
5	10	50	
			10
6	10	60	

total wage cost $(0Q_c \times 0W_c)$. The blue triangle (total revenue minus total wage cost) represents the firm's nonlabour costs—its explicit and implicit payments to land, capital, and entrepreneurship. Thus, in this case, total cost (wages plus other income payments) equals total revenue. This firm and others like it are earning only a normal profit. Figure 12-3b represents a long-run equilibrium for a firm that is selling its product in a perfectly competitive product market and hiring its labour in a perfectly competitive labour market. *(Key Questions 3 and 4)*

12.3 | Monopsony Model

monopsony
A market structure in which there is only a single buyer.

In the perfectly competitive labour market described in the preceding section, each employer hires too small an amount of labour to influence the wage rate. The situation is quite different in **monopsony,** a market in which a single employer of labour has substantial buying (hiring) power. Labour market monopsony has the following characteristics:

- There is only a single buyer of a particular type of labour.

- This type of labour is relatively immobile, either geographically or because workers would have to acquire new skills.

- The firm is a wage-maker, because the wage rate it must pay varies directly with the number of workers it employs.

As is true of monopoly power, there are various degrees of monopsony power. In a perfect monopsony such power is at its maximum, because only a single employer exists in the labour market. The best real-world examples are probably the labour markets in some towns that depend almost entirely on one major firm. For example, a copper-mining concern may be almost the only source of employment in a remote British Columbia town, and a textile mill in Quebec's Eastern Townships, a paper mill in Gatineau, or a fish processor in Newfoundland may provide most of the employment in its locale.

In other cases three or four firms may each hire a large portion of the supply of labour in a certain market and, therefore, have some monopsony power. If they tacitly or openly act in concert in hiring labour, they greatly enhance their monopsony power.

ORIGIN 12.1
Monopsony

When a firm hires most of the available supply of a particular type of labour, its decision to hire more or fewer workers affects the wage rate it pays to those workers.

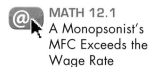

MATH 12.1
A Monopsonist's
MFC Exceeds the
Wage Rate

Upward-Sloping Labour Supply to a Firm

When a firm hires most of the available supply of a certain type of labour, its decision to employ more or fewer workers affects the wage rate it pays to those workers. If a firm is large in relation to the size of the labour market, it will have to pay a higher wage rate to obtain more labour. Suppose that only one employer of a particular type of labour exists in a certain geographic area. In this monopsony situation, the labour supply curve for the *firm* and the total labour supply curve for the *labour market* are identical. The monopsonist's supply curve—represented by curve S in Figure 12-4—is upsloping because the firm must pay higher wage rates if it wants to attract and hire additional workers. This same curve is also the monopsonist's average-cost-of-labour curve. Each point on curve S indicates the wage rate (cost) per worker that must be paid to attract the corresponding number of workers.

MFC Higher than the Wage Rate

When a monopsonist pays a higher wage to attract an additional worker, it must pay that higher wage to all the workers it is currently employing at a lower wage. If not, labour morale will deteriorate, and the employer will be plagued with labour unrest because of wage-rate differences for the same job. Paying a uniform wage to all workers means that the cost of an extra worker—the marginal factor (labour) cost (MFC)—is the sum of that worker's wage rate and the amount necessary to bring the wage rate of all current workers up to the new wage level.

Table 12-2 illustrates this point. One worker can be hired at a wage rate of $6, but hiring a second worker forces the firm to pay a higher wage rate of $7. The marginal factor (labour) cost of the second worker is $8—the $7 paid to the second worker plus a $1 raise for the first worker. From another viewpoint, total labour cost is now $14 (= 2 × $7), up from $6. So the MFC of the second worker is $8 (= $14 − $6), not just the $7 wage rate paid to that worker. Similarly, the marginal labour cost of the third worker is $10—the $8 that must be paid to attract this worker from alternative employment, plus $1 raises, from $7 to $8, for the first two workers.

Here is the key point: Because the monopsonist is the only employer in the labour market, its marginal resource (labour) cost exceeds the wage rate. Graphically, the monopsonist's MFC curve lies above the average-cost-of-labour curve, or labour supply curve S, as is clearly shown in Figure 12-4.

The Wage Rate and Level of Employment in a Monopsonistic Labour Market

FIGURE 12-4

In a monopsonistic labour market, the employer's marginal factor (labour) cost curve (MFC) lies above the labour supply curve, S. Equating MFC with MRP at point b, the monopsonist hires Q_m workers (compared with Q_c under competition). As indicated by point c on S, it pays only wage rate W_m (compared with the competitive wage W_c).

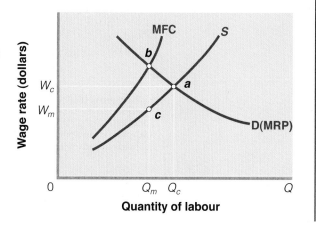

TABLE 12-2   The Supply of Labour: Monopsony in Hiring Labour

(1) Units of labour	(2) Wage rate	(3) Total labour cost (wage bill)	(4) Marginal factor (labour) cost
0	$ 5	$ 0	
			$ 6
1	6	6	
			8
2	7	14	
			10
3	8	24	
			12
4	9	36	
			14
5	10	50	
			16
6	11	66	

Equilibrium Wage and Employment

How many units of labour will the monopsonist hire and what wage rate will it pay? To maximize profit, the monopsonist will employ the quantity of labour Q_m in Figure 12-4, because at that quantity MFC and MRP are equal (point b).[1] The monopsonist next determines how much it must pay to attract these Q_m workers. From the supply curve S, specifically point c, it sees that it must pay wage rate W_m. Clearly, it need not pay a wage equal to MRP; it can attract and hire exactly the number of workers it wants (Q_m) with wage rate W_m. And that is the wage rate it will pay.

Contrast these results with those that would prevail in a competitive labour market. With competition in the hiring of labour, the level of employment would be greater (at Q_c) and the wage rate would be higher (at W_c). Other things equal, the monopsonist maximizes its profit by hiring a smaller number of workers and thereby paying a less-than-competitive wage rate. Society obtains a smaller output, and workers receive a wage rate that is less by bc than their marginal revenue product. Just as a monopolist finds it profitable to restrict product output to realize an above-competitive price for its goods, the monopsonist finds it profitable to restrict employment to reduce wage rates below those that would occur under competitive conditions.

WORKED PROBLEM 12.1
Labour Markets: Competition and Monopsony

Examples of Monopsony Power

Fortunately, monopsonistic labour markets are uncommon in the Canadian economy. In most labour markets, several employers compete for workers, particularly for workers who are occupationally and geographically mobile. Also, in a potential monopsony in a local labour market,

---

[1] The fact that MFC exceeds factor price when factors are hired or purchased under imperfectly competitive (monopsonistic) conditions calls for adjustments in Chapter 11's least-cost and profit-maximizing rules for hiring factors. (See equations (1) and (2) in the "Optimal Combination of Factors" section of Chapter 11.) Specifically, we must substitute MFC for resource price in the denominators of our two equations. That is, with imperfect competition in the hiring of both labour and capital, equation (1) becomes

$$\frac{MP_L}{MFC_L} = \frac{MP_C}{MFC_C} \qquad (1')$$

and equation (2) is restated as

$$\frac{MRP_L}{MFC_L} = \frac{MRP_C}{MFC_C} = 1 \qquad (2')$$

In fact, equations (1) and (2) can be regarded as special cases of (1') and (2') in which firms happen to be hiring under perfectly competitive conditions and factor price is, therefore, equal to, and can be substituted for, marginal factor cost.

unions spring up to counteract that power by forcing firms to negotiate wages. Nevertheless, there is evidence of monopsony power in such diverse labour markets as the markets for nurses, professional athletes, public-school teachers, newspaper employees, and some building trades workers. *(Key Question 7)*

QUICK REVIEW

▶ Real wages have increased over time in Canada because labour demand has increased relative to labour supply.

▶ Over the long term, real wages per worker have increased at approximately the same rate as worker productivity.

▶ The competitive employer is a wage-taker and employs workers at the point where the wage rate (= MFC) equals MRP.

▶ The labour supply curve for a monopsonist is upward-sloping, causing MFC to exceed the wage rate for each worker. Other things equal, the monopsonist, hiring where MFC = MRP, will employ fewer workers and pay a lower wage rate than would a perfectly competitive employer.

12.4 | Unions and the Labour Market: Three Models

Our assumption thus far has been that workers compete with one another in selling their labour services. But in some labour markets, workers unionize and sell their labour services collectively. When a union is formed in an otherwise competitive labour market, it usually bargains with a relatively large number of employers. It has many goals, the most important of which is to raise wage rates. It can pursue that objective in several ways.

Demand-Enhancement Model

Unions recognize that their ability to influence the demand for labour is limited. But, from the union's viewpoint, increasing the demand for union labour is highly desirable. As Figure 12-5 shows, an increase in labour demand will create a higher union wage along with more jobs. Unions can increase the demand for their labour by increasing the demand for the goods or services they help produce. Political lobby is the main tool for increasing the demand for union-produced goods or services. For example, construction unions lobby for new highways, mass-transit systems, and stadium projects. Teachers' unions and associations have pushed for increased public spending on education. Unions in the steel sector and forest-products workers have lobbied for tariffs and quotas on imports of steel and lumber, respectively. Such trade restrictions shift the demand for labour away from foreign countries and toward unionized Canadian labour.

Unions can also increase the demand for union labour by altering the price of other inputs. For example, although union members are generally paid significantly more than the minimum wage, unions have strongly supported increases in the minimum wage. The purpose may be to raise the price of low-wage, nonunion labour, which in some cases is substitutable for union labour. A higher minimum wage for nonunion workers will discourage employers from substituting such workers for union workers and thereby increase the demand for union members.

Similarly, unions have sometimes sought to increase the demand for their labour by supporting policy that reduces or holds down the price of complementary factors of production. For example, unions that represent workers who transport fruit and vegetables may support legislation that allows low-wage foreign agricultural workers to temporarily work in Canada. Where union labour and other resources are complementary, a price decrease for the other factors will increase the demand for union labour through Chapter 11's output effect.

FIGURE 12-5 Unions and Demand Enhancement

When unions can increase the demand for labour (say, from D_1 to D_2), they can realize higher wage rates (W_c to W_u) and more jobs (Q_c to Q_u).

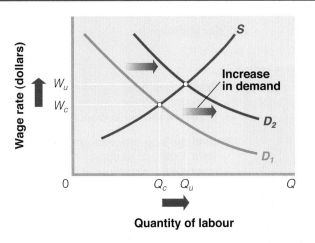

Exclusive or Craft Union Model

Unions can also boost wage rates by reducing the supply of labour, and over the years organized labour has favoured policies to do just that. The Canadian Labour Congress, an umbrella organization representing 2.3 million workers, has supported legislation that has (1) restricted permanent immigration, (2) reduced child labour, (3) encouraged compulsory retirement, and (4) enforced a shorter workweek.

Moreover, certain types of workers have adopted techniques designed to restrict the number of workers who can join their union. This is especially true of *craft unions,* whose members possess a particular skill, such as carpenters or brick masons or plumbers. Craft unions have frequently forced employers to agree to hire only union members, thereby gaining virtually complete control of the labour supply. Then, by following restrictive membership policies—for example, long apprenticeships, very high initiation fees, and limits on the number of new members admitted—they artificially restrict labour supply. As indicated in Figure 12-6, such practices result in higher wage rates and constitute what is called **exclusive unionism.** By excluding workers from unions and therefore from the labour supply, craft unions succeed in elevating wage rates.

exclusive unionism
The practice of a labour union of restricting the supply of skilled union labour to increase the wages received by union members.

FIGURE 12-6 Exclusive or Craft Unionism

By reducing the supply of labour (say, from S_1 to S_2) through the use of restrictive membership policies, exclusive unions achieve higher wage rates (W_c to W_u). However, restriction of the labour supply also reduces the number of workers employed (Q_c to Q_u).

occupational licensing
The laws of provincial or municipal governments that require a worker to satisfy certain specified requirements and obtain a licence from a licensing board before engaging in a particular occupation.

Occupational licensing is another means of restricting the supply of specific kinds of labour. Here a group of workers in a given occupation pressure provincial or municipal governments to pass a law that says that some occupational group (for example, barbers, physicians, plumbers, car mechanics, or pest controllers) can practise their trade only if they meet certain requirements. Those requirements might include level of education, amount of work experience, the passing of an examination, and personal characteristics ("the practitioner must be of good moral character"). Members of the licensed occupation typically dominate the licensing board that administers such laws. The result is self-regulation, which often leads to policies that serve only to restrict entry to the occupation and reduce the labour supply.

The expressed purpose of licensing is to protect consumers from incompetent practitioners—surely a worthy goal. But such licensing also results in above-competitive wages and earnings for those in the licensed occupation (Figure 12-6). Moreover, licensing often includes a residency requirement, which inhibits the interprovincial movement of qualified workers. Some 300 occupations are now licensed in Canada.

Inclusive or Industrial Union Model

Instead of trying to limit their membership, however, most unions seek to organize all available workers. This is especially true of the *industrial unions,* such as the Canadian Auto Workers and the United Steelworkers. Such unions seek as members all available unskilled, semiskilled, and skilled workers in an industry. A union can afford to be exclusive when its members are skilled craftspersons for whom there are few substitutes. But for a union composed of unskilled and semiskilled workers, a policy of limited membership would make available to the employers numerous nonunion workers who can easily be substituted for the union workers.

An industrial union that includes virtually all available workers in its membership can put firms under great pressure to agree to its wage demands. Because of its legal right to strike, such a union can threaten to deprive firms of their entire labour supply; an actual strike can do just that.

inclusive unionism
The practice of a labour union of including as members all workers employed in an industry.

We illustrate such **inclusive unionism** in Figure 12-7. Initially, the competitive equilibrium wage rate is W_c and the level of employment is Q_c. Now suppose an industrial union is formed that demands a higher, above-equilibrium wage rate of, say, W_u. That wage rate W_u would create a perfectly elastic labour supply over the range ae in Figure 12-7. If firms wanted to hire any workers in this range, they would have to pay the union-imposed wage rate. If they decide against meeting this wage demand, the union will supply no labour at all, and the firms will be faced with a strike. If firms decide it is better to pay the higher wage rate than to suffer a strike, they will cut back on employment from Q_c to Q_u.

FIGURE 12-7   Inclusive or Industrial Unionism

By organizing virtually all available workers to control the supply of labour, inclusive industrial unions may impose a wage rate, such as W_u, which is above the competitive wage rate W_c. The effect is to change the labour supply curve from S to aeS. At wage rate W_u, employers will cut employment from Q_c to Q_u.

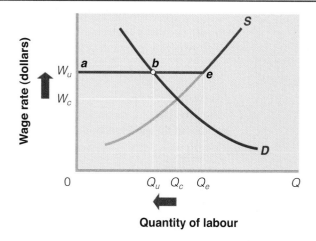

By agreeing to the union's W_u wage demand, individual employers become wage-takers. Because labour supply is perfectly elastic over range ae, the marginal resource (labour) cost is equal to the wage rate W_u over this range. The Q_u level of employment is the result of employers equating this MFC (now equal to the wage rate) with MRP, according to our profit-maximizing rule.

Note from point e on labour supply curve S that Q_e workers desire employment at wage W_u. But, as indicated by point b on labour demand curve D, only Q_u workers are employed. The result is a surplus of labour of $Q_e - Q_u$ (also shown by distance eb). In a perfectly competitive labour market without the union, the effect of a surplus of unemployed workers would be lower wages. Specifically, the wage rate would fall to the equilibrium level, W_c, where the quantity of labour supplied equals the quantity of labour demanded (each Q_c).

Wage Increases and Unemployment

Have Canadian unions been successful in raising the wages of their members? Evidence suggests that union members on average achieve a 15 percent wage advantage over nonunion workers.

As Figures 12-6 and 12-7 show, the effect of wage-raising actions by both exclusive and inclusive unionism is to reduce employment in unionized firms. A union's success in achieving above-equilibrium wage rates thus tends to be accompanied by a decline in the number of workers employed. That result acts as a restraining influence on union wage demands. A union cannot expect to maintain solidarity within its ranks if it demands a wage rate so high that joblessness will result for, say, 20 or 30 percent of its members.

Bilateral Monopoly Model

bilateral monopoly
A market in which there is a single seller (monopoly) and a single buyer (monopsony).

Suppose a strong industrial union is formed in a monopsonist labour market rather than a competitive market, creating a combination of the monopsony model and the inclusive unionism model. Economists call the result **bilateral monopoly** because there is a single seller and a single buyer. The union is a monopolistic "seller" of labour that controls labour supply and can influence wage rates, but it faces a monopsonistic "buyer" of labour that can also affect wages by altering its employment. This is not an uncommon case, particularly in less-pure forms in which a single union confronts two, three, or four large employers, such as steel, automobiles, construction equipment, and professional sports.

INDETERMINATE OUTCOME OF BILATERAL MONOPOLY

We show this situation in Figure 12-8, where Figure 12-7 is superimposed onto Figure 12-4. The monopsonistic employer will seek the below-competitive-equilibrium wage rate W_m, and the union will press for some above-competitive-equilibrium wage rate such as W_u. Which will be the outcome? We cannot say with certainty because the bilateral monopoly model does not explain what will happen at the collective bargaining table. We can expect the wage outcome to lie somewhere between W_m and W_u. Beyond that, about all we can say is that the party with the greater bargaining power and the more effective negotiating strategy will probably get a wage closer to the one it seeks.

DESIRABILITY OF BILATERAL MONOPOLY

The wage and employment outcomes in this situation might be more economically desirable than the term "bilateral monopoly" implies. The monopoly on one side of the market might in effect cancel out the monopoly on the other side, yielding competitive or near-competitive results. *(Key Question 8)*

FIGURE 12-8

FIGURE 12-8   **Bilateral Monopoly in the Labour Market**

A monopsonist seeks to hire Q_m workers (where MFC = MRP) and pay wage rate W_m corresponding to Q_m labour on labour supply curve S. The inclusive union it faces seeks the above-equilibrium wage rate W_u. The actual outcome cannot be predicted.

QUICK REVIEW

▸ In the demand-enhancement union model, a union increases the wage rate by increasing labour demand through actions that increase product demand, or alter the prices of related inputs.

▸ In the exclusive (craft) union model, a union increases wage rates by artificially restricting labour supply, through, say, long apprenticeships or occupational licensing.

▸ In the inclusive (industrial) union model, a union raises the wage rate by gaining control over a firm's labour supply and threatening to withhold labour via a strike unless a negotiated wage is obtained.

▸ Bilateral monopoly occurs in a labour market where a monopsonist bargains with an inclusive, or industrial, union. Wage and employment outcomes are determined by collective bargaining in this situation.

12.5 | The Minimum Wage Controversy

minimum wage
The lowest wage employers may legally pay for an hour of work.

In Canada both the federal and provincial governments have enacted **minimum wage** legislation, but it is the provincial laws that cover most workers. The provincial minimum wage ranges from $8.00 per hour in New Brunswick to $9.50 per hour in Ontario. The purpose of the minimum wage is to provide a living wage for less-skilled workers to keep them and their families from poverty.

Case against the Minimum Wage

Critics, reasoning in terms of Figure 12-7, contend that an above-equilibrium minimum wage (say, W_u) will cause employers to hire fewer workers. Downsloping labour demand curves are a reality. The higher labour costs may even force some firms out of business. Then, some of the poor, low-wage workers whom the minimum wage was designed to help will find themselves out of work. Critics point out that a worker who is *unemployed* at a minimum wage of $6.00 per hour is clearly worse off than if *employed* at a market wage rate of, say, $5.50 per hour.

A second criticism of the minimum wage is that it is "poorly targeted" to reduce household poverty. Critics point out that much of the benefit of the minimum wage accrues to workers, including many teenagers, who do not live in poverty households.

Case for the Minimum Wage

Advocates of the minimum wage say that critics analyze its impact in an unrealistic context. Figure 12-7, advocates claim, assumes a competitive, static market. But in a less competitive, low-pay labour market where employers possess some monopsony power (Figure 12-8), the minimum wage can increase wage rates without causing significant unemployment. Indeed, a higher minimum wage may even produce more jobs by eliminating the motive that monopsonistic firms have for restricting employment. For example, a minimum wage floor of W_c in Figure 12-8 would change the firm's labour supply curve to $W_c aS$ and prompt the firm to increase its employment from Q_m workers to Q_c workers.

Moreover, even if the labour market is competitive, the higher wage rate might prompt firms to find more productive tasks for low-paid workers, thereby raising their productivity. Alternatively, the minimum wage may reduce *labour turnover* (the rate at which workers voluntarily quit). With fewer low-productive trainees, the *average* productivity of the firm's workers would rise. In either case, the alleged negative employment effects of the minimum wage might not occur.

Evidence and Conclusions

Which view is correct? Unfortunately, there is no clear answer. All economists agree that firms will not hire workers who cost more per hour than the value of their hourly output. So some minimum wage is sufficiently high—say, $20 an hour—that it would severely reduce employment. But no current consensus exists on the employment effects of the present level of the minimum wage. Evidence in the 1980s suggested that minimum wage hikes reduced employment of minimum wage workers, particularly teenagers (16- to 19-year-olds). The consensus then was that a 10 percent increase in the minimum wage would reduce teenage employment by about 1 to 3 percent. But recent evidence suggests that the minimum wage hikes in the 1990s produced even smaller employment declines among teenagers. It is possible that the more recent minimum wage increases merely matched the sort of wage increases that would have occurred in any event in competitive low-wage labour markets. Negative employment effects of minimum wages occur only when such minimums are above equilibrium wages.

The overall effect of the minimum wage is thus uncertain. On the one hand, the employment and unemployment effects of the minimum wage do not appear to be as great as many critics fear. On the other hand, because a large part of its effect is dissipated on non-poverty families, the minimum wage is not as strong an anti-poverty tool as many supporters contend.

12.6 | Wage Differentials

wage differentials
The difference between the wage received by one worker or group of workers and that received by another worker or group of workers.

Hourly wage rates and annual salaries differ greatly among occupations. In Table 12-3 we list average weekly wages for several industries to illustrate such occupational **wage differentials.** For example, observe that construction workers on average earn one-third more than those workers in the health and social service industry. Large wage differentials also exist within some of the occupations listed (not shown). For example, although average wages for retail salespersons are relatively low, some top salespersons selling on commission make several times the average wages for their occupation.

What explains wage differentials such as these? Once again, the forces of demand and supply are revealing. As we demonstrate in Figure 12-9, wage differentials can arise on either the supply or demand side of labour markets. Figures 12-9a and 12-9b represent labour markets for two occupational groups that have identical *labour supply curves*. The labour market in panel (a) has a relatively high equilibrium wage (W_a) because labour demand is very strong. The labour market in panel (b) has an equilibrium wage that is relatively low (W_b) since labour demand is weak. Clearly, the wage differential between occupations (a) and (b) results solely from differences in the magnitude of labour demand.

FIGURE 12·9   **Labour Demand, Labour Supply, and Wage Differentials**

The wage differential between labour markets (a) and (b) results solely from differences in labour demand.
In labour markets (c) and (d), differences in labour supply cause the wage differential.

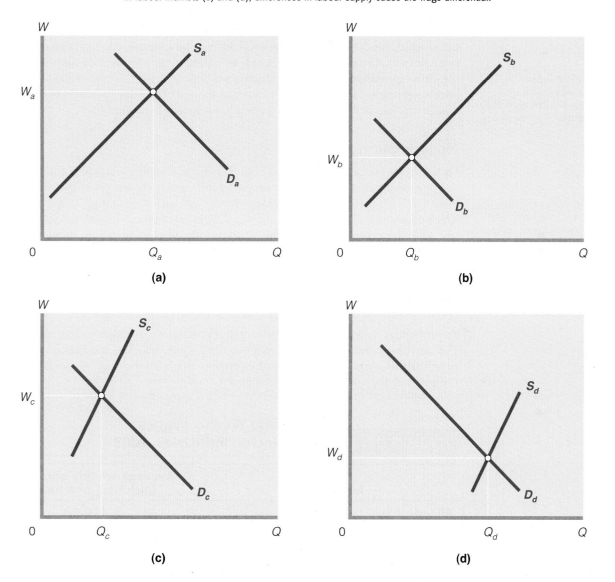

Contrast that situation with Figure 12-9c and 12-9d, where the *labour demand curves* are identical. In the labour market in panel (c), the equilibrium wage is relatively high (W_c) because labour supply is highly restricted. In the labour market in panel (d) labour supply is highly abundant, so the equilibrium wage (W_d) is relatively low. The wage differential between (c) and (d) results solely from the differences in the magnitude of the labour supply.

Although Figure 12-9 provides a good starting point for understanding wage differentials, we need to know *why* demand and supply conditions differ in various labour markets.

Marginal Revenue Productivity

marginal revenue productivity
How much workers contribute to their employers' revenue.

The strength of labour demand—how far rightward the labour demand curve is located—differs greatly among occupations because of differences in how much various occupational groups contribute to their employers' revenue. This revenue contribution, in turn, depends on the workers' productivity and the strength of the demand for the products they are helping to produce. Where labour is highly productive and product demand is strong, labour demand also is strong and, other things equal, pay is high. Top professional athletes, for example, are highly productive at sports entertainment, for which millions of people are willing to pay billions of dollars over the course of a season. So the **marginal revenue productivity** of these top players is exceptionally high, as are their salaries, represented in Figure 12-9a. In contrast, in most occupations workers generate much more modest revenue for their employers, so their pay is lower, as in Figure 12-9b.

Noncompeting Groups

noncompeting groups
Collections of workers in the economy who do not compete with each other for employment because the skills and training of the workers in one group are substantially different from those in other groups.

On the supply side of the labour market, workers are not homogeneous; they differ in their mental and physical capabilities and in their education and training. At any given time the labour force is made up of many **noncompeting groups** of workers, each representing several occupations for which the members of a particular group qualify. In some groups qualified workers are relatively few, whereas in others they are highly abundant. Workers in one group do not qualify for the occupations of other groups.

ABILITY

Only a few workers have the ability or physical attributes to be brain surgeons, concert violinists, top fashion models, research scientists, or professional athletes. Because the supply of these particular types of labour is very small in relation to labour demand, their wages are high, as in Figure 12-9c. The members of these and similar groups do not compete with one another or with other skilled or semiskilled workers. The violinist does not compete with the surgeon, nor does the surgeon compete with the violinist or the fashion model.

TABLE 12-3

Average Weekly Wages in Selected Industries, 2008

Industry	Average weekly earnings (including overtime)
All industries	**$ 810.45**
Mining, and oil and gas extraction	1527.98
Construction	1014.51
Finance, insurance, and real estate	1000.76
Manufacturing	949.54
Logging and forestry	935.84
Transportation and warehousing	883.28
Educational and related services	862.64
Real estate services	772.87
Health and social services	743.94

Source: Adapted from Statistics Canada CANSIM database, http://cansim2.statcan.ca, Table 281-0027, June 2008.

The concept of noncompeting groups can be applied to various subgroups and even to specific individuals in a particular group. An especially skilled violinist can command a higher salary than colleagues who play the same instrument. A handful of top corporate executives earn 10 to 20 times as much as the average chief executive officer. In each of these cases, the supply of top talent is highly limited, since less talented colleagues are only imperfect substitutes.

EDUCATION AND TRAINING

human capital
Any expenditure to improve the education, skills, health, or mobility of workers, with an expectation of greater productivity and thus a positive return on the investment.

Another source of wage differentials is differing amounts of **human capital,** which is the personal stock of knowledge, know-how, and skills that enables a person to be productive and thus to earn income. Such stocks result from investments in human capital. Like expenditures on machinery and equipment, productivity-enhancing expenditures on education or training are investments. In both cases, people incur *present costs* with the intention that those expenditures will lead to a greater flow of *future earnings*.

ORIGIN 12.2
Human Capital

Although education yields higher incomes, it carries substantial costs. A college or university education involves not only direct costs (tuition, fees, books) but also indirect or opportunity costs (forgone earnings). Does the higher pay received by better-educated workers compensate for these costs? The answer is yes. Rates of return are estimated to be 10 to 13 percent for investments in secondary education and 8 to 12 percent for investments in college and university education. One generally accepted estimate is that each year of schooling raises a worker's wage by about 8 percent.

Compensating Differences

If the workers in a particular noncompeting group are equally capable of performing several different jobs, you might expect the wage rates to be identical for all these jobs. Not so. A group of high-school graduates may be equally capable of becoming sales clerks or construction workers, but these jobs pay different wages. In virtually all locales, construction labourers receive much higher wages than sales clerks. These wage differentials are called **compensating differences,** because they must be paid to compensate for nonmonetary differences in various jobs.

compensating differences
Differences in the wages received by workers in different jobs to compensate for nonmonetary differences in the jobs.

The construction job involves dirty working conditions, the hazard of accidents, and irregular employment. The retail sales job means clean clothing, pleasant air-conditioned surroundings, and less fear of injury or layoff. Other things equal, it is easy to see why some workers would rather pick up a credit card than a shovel. So labour supply is less for construction firms, as in Figure 12-9c, than for retail shops, as in Figure 12-9d. Construction firms must pay higher wages than retailers to compensate for the unattractive aspects of construction jobs.

 CONSIDER THIS | My Entire Life

Human capital is the accumulation of outcomes of prior investments in education, training, and other factors that increase productivity and earnings. It is the stock of knowledge, know-how, and skills that enables individuals to be productive and thus earn income. A valuable stock of human capital, together with a strong demand for one's services, can add up to a large capacity to earn income. For some people, high earnings have little to do with actual hours of work and much to do

with their tremendous skill, which reflects their accumulated stock of human capital.

The point is demonstrated in the following story: It is said that a tourist once spotted the famous Spanish artist Pablo Picasso (1881–1973) in a Paris café. The tourist asked Picasso if he would do a sketch of his wife for pay. Picasso sketched the wife in a matter of minutes and said, "That will be 10,000 francs [roughly $2000]." Hearing the high price, the tourist became irritated, saying, "But that took you only a few minutes."

"No," replied Picasso, "it took me my entire life!"

Reunion des Musées Nationaux/Art Resource, NY © Estate of Pablo Picasso/Artisits Right Society (ARS), New York.

Compensating differences play an important role in allocating society's scarce labour resources. If very few workers want to be garbage collectors, then society must pay high wages to attract garbage collectors. If many more people want to be sales clerks than are needed, then society need not pay them as much as garbage collectors to get those services performed.

Market Imperfections

Differences in marginal revenue productivity, amounts of human capital, and nonmonetary aspects of jobs explain most of the wage differentials in the economy. But other persistent differentials result from various market imperfections that impede workers moving from lower-paying jobs to higher-paying jobs.

- *Lack of Job Information* Workers may simply be unaware of job opportunities and wage rates in other geographic areas and in other jobs for which they qualify. Consequently, the flow of qualified labour from lower-paying to higher-paying jobs may not be sufficient to equalize wages within occupations.

- *Geographic Immobility* Many workers are reluctant to move to new places, to leave friends, relatives, and associates, to force their children to change schools, to sell their houses, or to incur the costs and inconveniences of adjusting to a new job and a new community. As Adam Smith noted more than two centuries ago, "A [person] is of all sorts of luggage the most difficult to be transported." The reluctance of workers to move creates persistent geographic wage differentials within the same occupation. Some economists point out that Canada's employment insurance program contributes to labour immobility.

- *Unions and Government Restraints* Wage differentials may be reinforced by artificial restrictions on mobility imposed by unions and government. We have noted that craft unions keep their wages high by restricting membership. Thus, the low-paid nonunion carpenter of Edmonton, Alberta, may be willing to move to Vancouver in the pursuit of higher wages, but her chances of succeeding are slim. She may be unable to get a union card, and no card means no job. Similarly, an optometrist or lawyer qualified to practise in one province may not meet licensing requirements of other provinces, so his ability to move is limited. Other artificial barriers involve pension plans and seniority rights that might be jeopardized by moving from one job to another.

- *Discrimination* Despite legislation to the contrary, discrimination results in lower wages being paid to women and visible-minority workers than to white males doing virtually identical work. Also, women and minorities may be crowded into certain low-paying occupations, driving down wages there and raising them elsewhere. If discrimination keeps qualified women and minorities from taking the higher-paying jobs, then differences in pay will persist.

All four considerations—differences in marginal revenue productivity, noncompeting groups, compensating differences, and market imperfections—come into play in explaining actual wage differentials. For example, the differential between the wages of a physician and those of a construction worker can be explained based on marginal revenue productivity and noncompeting groups. Physicians generate considerable revenue because of their high productivity and the strong willingness of consumers (via provincial governments) to pay for health care. Physicians also fall into a noncompeting group where, because of stringent training requirements, only a relatively few persons qualify. So the supply of labour is small in relation to demand.

12.7 | Pay for Performance and the Principal–Agent Problem

The models of wage determination we have described in this chapter assume that worker pay is always a standard amount for each hour's work, for example $15 per hour. But pay schemes are often more complex than that in both composition and purpose. For instance, many workers receive annual salaries rather than hourly pay. Many workers also receive fringe benefits: dental insurance, life insurance, paid vacations, paid sick-leave days, pension contributions, and so on. Finally, some pay plans are designed to elicit a desired level of performance from workers. This last aspect of pay plans requires further elaboration.

The Principal–Agent Problem Revisited

In Chapter 6 we first identified the *principal–agent problem* as it relates to possible differences in the interests of corporate shareholders (principals) and the executives (agents) they hire. This problem extends to all paid employees. Firms hire workers to help produce the goods and services the firms sell for a profit. Workers are the firms' agents; they are hired to advance the interest (profit) of the firms. The principals are the firms; they hire agents to advance their goals. Firms and workers have one interest in common: they both want the firm to survive and thrive. That will ensure profit for the firm and continued employment and wages for the workers.

But the interests of the firm and of the workers are not identical. A principal–agent problem arises when those interests diverge. Workers may seek to increase their utility by shirking on the job, that is, by providing less than the agreed-on effort or by taking unauthorized breaks. The night security guard in a warehouse may leave work early or spend time reading a novel rather than making the assigned rounds. A salaried manager may spend time away from the office visiting friends rather than attending to company business.

Firms (principals) have a profit incentive to reduce or eliminate shirking. One option is to monitor workers, but monitoring is difficult and costly. Hiring another worker to supervise or monitor the security guard might double the cost of maintaining a secure warehouse. Another way of resolving the principal–agent problem is through some sort of **incentive pay plan** that ties worker compensation more closely to output or performance. Such incentive pay schemes include piece rates, commissions and royalties, bonuses and profit sharing, and efficiency wages.

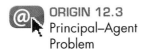

ORIGIN 12.3
Principal–Agent Problem

incentive pay plan
A compensation structure, such as piece rates, commissions, royalties, bonuses, stock options, and profit sharing that ties worker pay directly to performance.

PIECE RATES

Piece rates are compensation paid according to the number of units of output a worker produces. If a principal pays fruit pickers by the bushel or typists by the page, it need not be concerned with shirking or with monitoring costs.

COMMISSIONS OR ROYALTIES

Unlike piece rates, commissions and royalties tie compensation to the value of sales. Employees who sell products or services—including real estate agents, insurance agents, stockbrokers, and retail salespersons—commonly receive *commissions* that are computed as a percentage of the monetary value of their sales. Recording artists and authors are paid *royalties,* computed as a certain percentage of sales revenues from their works. These types of compensation link the financial interests of the salespeople or artists and authors to the profit interest of the firms.

BONUSES, STOCK OPTIONS, AND PROFIT SHARING

Bonuses are payments in addition to one's annual salary that are based on some factor such as the performance of the individual worker, or of a group of workers, or of the firm itself. A professional baseball player may receive a bonus based on a high batting average, the number of home runs hit, or the number of runs batted in. A business manager may receive a bonus based on the profitability of her or his unit. *Stock options* allow workers to buy shares of their employer's stock at a fixed price. If the firm does well and its stock prices rise, the workers' stock holdings rise in value. Such options are part of the compensation packages of top corporate officials, as well as many workers in relatively new high-technology firms. *Profit-sharing plans* allocate a percentage of a firm's profit to its employees. Such plans have in recent years resulted in large annual payments to many Canadian workers.

Addendum: the Negative Side Effects of Pay for Performance

Although pay for performance may help to overcome the principal–agent problem and enhance worker productivity, such plans may have negative side effects and so require careful design. Here are a few examples:

- The rapid production pace that piece rates encourage may result in poor product quality and may compromise the safety of workers. Such outcomes can be costly to the firm over the long run.

- Commissions may cause some salespeople to engage in questionable or even fraudulent sales practices, such as making exaggerated claims about products or recommending unneeded repairs. Such practices may lead to private lawsuits or government legal action.

- Bonuses based on personal performance may disrupt the close cooperation needed for maximum team production. A professional hockey player who receives a bonus for goals scored may be reluctant to pass the puck to teammates.

- Since profit sharing is usually tied to the performance of the entire firm, less energetic workers can free-ride by obtaining their profit share based on the hard work of others.

QUICK REVIEW

▶ Proponents of the minimum wage argue that it is needed to assist the working poor and to counter monopsony where it might exist; critics say that it is poorly targeted to reduce poverty and that it reduces employment.

▶ Wage differentials are generally attributable to the forces of supply and demand, influenced by differences in workers' marginal revenue productivity, workers' education and skills, and nonmonetary differences in jobs. Several labour market imperfections also play a role.

▶ As it applies to labour, the principal–agent problem is one of workers pursuing their own interests to the detriment of the employer's profit objective.

▶ Pay-for-performance plans (piece rates, commissions, royalties, bonuses, stock options, and profit sharing) are designed to improve worker productivity by overcoming the principal–agent problem.

The LAST WORD   Are Top Executives in Canada Overpaid?

The multimillion-dollar pay of major corporate CEOs has drawn considerable criticism.

Top executives of Canadian corporations typically receive total annual pay (salary, bonuses, and stock options) in the millions of dollars. As shown in the table below, each of the five highest-paid Canadian executives earned more than $40 million in 2008. The highest paid CEO earned over $320 million!

The Five Highest-Paid Canadian CEOs, 2007*

Name	Company	Total Pay (in millions)
1. William Doyle	Potash Corporation	$320.4
2. J. Balsillie and M. Lazaridis	Research In Motion	178.5
3. Gerald Schwartz	Onex Corporation	61.7
4. Andre and Paul Desmarais	Power Corporation	43.1
5. Edward Sampson	Niko Resources	42.9

CEO pay in Canada is not only exceptionally high relative to the average pay of Canadian managers and workers, but is also the second highest CEO pay among industrialized countries. The U.S. has the highest CEO pay among industrialized countries. Among the highest paid CEOs in the U.S. in 2007, Lawrence J. Ellison of Oracle was paid U.S.$192 million, while Howard D. Schultz of Starbucks took home U.S.$99 million.

Is high CEO pay simply the outcome of labour supply and labour demand, as is the pay for star athletes and entertainers? Does it reflect marginal revenue productivity—that is, the contributions by CEOs to their company's output and revenue?

Observers who answer affirmatively point out that decisions made by the CEOs of large corporations affect the productivity of every employee in the organization. Good decisions enhance productivity throughout the organization and increase revenue; bad decisions reduce productivity and revenue. Only executives who have consistently made good business decisions attain the top positions in large corporations. Because the supply of these people is highly limited and their marginal revenue productivity is

enormous, top CEOs command huge salaries and performance bonuses.

Also, some economists note that CEO pay in Canada may be like the prizes professional golfers and tennis players receive for winning tournaments. These valuable prizes are designed to promote the productivity of all those who aspire to achieve them. In corporations the top prizes go to the winners of the "contests" among managers to attain, at least eventually, the CEO positions. Thus high CEO pay does not derive solely from the CEO's direct productivity. Instead, it may exist because the high pay creates incentives that raise

the productivity of scores of other corporate executives who seek to achieve the top position. In this view, high CEO pay is still based on high productivity.

Critics of existing CEO pay acknowledge that CEOs deserve substantially higher salaries than ordinary workers or typical managers, but they question pay packages that run into the millions of dollars. They reject the "tournament pay" idea on the grounds that corporations require cooperative team effort by managers and executives, not the type of high-stakes competition promoted by "winner-take-most" pay. They believe that corporations, although owned by their shareholders, are controlled by corporate boards and professional executives. Because many board members are present or past CEOs of other corporations, they often exaggerate CEO importance and, consequently, overpay their own CEOs. These overpayments are at the expense of the firm's shareholders.

In summary, defenders of CEO pay say that high pay is justified by the direct or indirect marginal revenue contribution of CEOs. Like it or not, CEO pay is market-determined pay. In contrast, critics say that multimillion-dollar CEO pay bears little relationship to marginal revenue productivity and is unfair to ordinary shareholders. It is clear from our discussion that these issues remain unsettled.

---

* Source for salary data: "Canada's Highest-Paid CEO Spotlighted in Home Province," by Brian Banks. *Financial Post Daily Magazine*, November 18, 2008. Material reprinted with the express permission of "The National Post Company," a Canwest Partnership.

Question

Do you think exceptionally high pay to CEOs is economically justified? Why or why not?

CHAPTER SUMMARY

12.1 ▶ PRODUCTIVITY AND THE GENERAL LEVEL OF WAGES

- The term "labour" encompasses all people who work for pay. The wage rate is the price paid per unit of time for labour. Labour earnings comprise total pay and are found by multiplying the number of hours worked by the hourly wage rate. The nominal wage rate is the amount of money received per unit of time; the real wage rate is the purchasing power of the nominal wage.

- The long-run growth of real hourly earnings—the average real wage—roughly matches that of productivity, with both increasing over the long run.

- Global comparisons suggest that real wages in Canada are relatively high, but not the highest internationally. High real wages in the advanced industrial countries stem largely from high labour productivity.

12.2 ▶ WAGES IN A PERFECTLY COMPETITIVE LABOUR MARKET

- Specific wage rates depend on the structure of the particular labour market. In a competitive labour market, the equilibrium wage rate and level of employment are determined at the intersection of the labour supply curve and labour demand curve. For the individual firm, the market wage rate establishes a horizontal labour supply curve, meaning that the wage rate equals the firm's constant marginal resource cost. The firm hires workers to the point where its MRP equals this MFC.

12.3 ▶ MONOPSONY MODEL

- Under monopsony the MFC curve lies above the factor supply curve because the monopsonist must bid up the wage rate to hire extra workers and must pay that higher wage rate to all workers. The monopsonist hires fewer workers than are hired under competitive conditions, pays less-than-competitive wage rates (has lower labour costs), and thus obtains greater profit.

12.4 ▶ UNIONS AND THE LABOUR MARKET: THREE MODELS

- A union may raise competitive wage rates by (a) increasing the derived demand for labour, (b) restricting the supply of labour through exclusive unionism, or (c) directly enforcing an above-equilibrium wage rate through inclusive unionism.

- In many industries the labour market takes the form of bilateral monopoly, in which a strong union sells labour to a monopsonistic employer. The wage-rate outcome of this labour market model depends on union and employer bargaining power.

- On average, unionized workers realize wage rates 15 percent higher than those of comparable nonunion workers.

12.5 ▶ THE MINIMUM WAGE

- Economists disagree about the desirability of the minimum wage as an antipoverty mechanism. While it causes unemployment for some low-income workers, it raises the incomes of those who retain their jobs.

12.6 ▶ WAGE DIFFERENTIALS

- Wage differentials are largely explainable in terms of (a) marginal revenue productivity of various groups of workers; (b) noncompeting groups arising from differences in the capacities and education of different groups of workers; (c) compensating differences, that is, wage differences that must be paid to offset nonmonetary differences in jobs; and (d) market imperfections in the form of lack of job information, geographical immobility, union and government restraints, and discrimination.

12.7 ▶ PAY FOR PERFORMANCE AND THE PRINCIPAL–AGENT PROBLEM

- The principal–agent problem arises when workers provide less-than-expected effort. Firms may combat this by monitoring workers or by creating incentive pay schemes that link worker compensation to performance.

TERMS AND CONCEPTS

wage rate, p. 287
nominal wage, p. 287
real wage, p. 287
perfectly competitive labour market, p. 289
monopsony, p. 292

exclusive unionism, p. 296
occupational licensing, p. 297
inclusive unionism, p. 297
bilateral monopoly, p. 298
minimum wage, p. 299
wage differentials, p. 300

marginal revenue productivity, p. 302
noncompeting groups, p. 302
human capital, p. 303
compensating differences, p. 303
incentive pay plan, p. 305

STUDY QUESTIONS

12.1 1. Explain why the general level of wages is high in Canada and other industrially advanced countries. What is the single most important factor underlying the long-run increase in average real-wage rates in Canada?

12.2 2. Why is a firm in a perfectly competitive labour market a *wage-taker*? What would happen if that firm decided to pay less than the going market wage rate?

12.2 3. **KEY QUESTION** Describe wage determination in a labour market in which workers are unorganized and many firms actively compete for the services of labour. Show this situation graphically, using W_1 to indicate the equilibrium wage rate and Q_1 to show the number of workers hired by the firms as a group. Show the labour supply curve of the individual firm and compare it with that of the total market. Why are there differences? In the diagram representing the firm, identify total revenue, total wage cost, and revenue available for the payment of nonlabour resources.

12.2 4. **KEY QUESTION** Complete the following labour supply table for a firm hiring labour competitively:

Units of labour	Wage rate	Total labour cost (wage bill)	Marginal factor (labour) cost
0	$14	$ ——	
1	14	——	$ ——
2	14	——	——
3	14	——	——
4	14	——	——
5	14	——	——
6	14	——	——

a. Show graphically the labour supply and marginal factor (labour) cost curves for this firm. Explain the relationship of these curves to one another.

b. Plot the labour demand data of question 2 in Chapter 11 on the graph used in a above. What are the equilibrium wage rate and level of employment? Explain.

5. Suppose a single firm has the marginal revenue product schedule for a particular type of labour given in the following table. **LO ▶ 12.3**

Number of units of labour	MRP of labour
1	$12
2	11
3	10
4	9
5	8
6	7
7	6
8	5

a. Assume there are 150 firms with the same marginal-revenue-product schedules for this particular type of labour. Compute the total or market demand for this labour by completing column 1 in the table below.

(1) Quantity of labour demanded	(2) Wage rate	(3) Quantity of labour supplied
——	$12	1350
——	11	1200
——	10	1050
——	9	900
——	8	750
——	7	600
——	6	450
——	5	300

b. What will be the equilibrium wage rate and how many workers will be hired?

c. What will be the marginal labour cost and wage rate for the individual firm? How many workers will the firm employ?

d. How would the imposition of a $9 minimum wage rate change the total amount of labour hired in this market?

www.mcgrawhillconnect.ca

LO 12.3 6. Suppose the formerly competing firms in question 3 form an employers' association that hires labour as a monopsonist would. Describe verbally the effect on wage rates and employment. Adjust the graph you drew for question 3, showing the monopsonistic wage rate and employment level as W_2 and Q_2, respectively. Using this monopsony model, explain why hospital administrators sometimes complain about a shortage of nurses. How might such a shortage be corrected?

LO 12.3 7. **KEY QUESTION** Assume a firm is a monopsonist that can hire its first worker for $6 but must increase the wage rate by $3 to attract each successive worker. Draw the firm's labour supply and marginal labour cost curves and explain their relationships to one another. On the same graph, plot the labour demand data of question 2 in Chapter 11. What are the equilibrium wage rate and level of employment? Why do these differ from your answer to question 4?

LO 12.4 8. **KEY QUESTION** Assume a monopsonistic employer is paying a wage rate of W_m and hiring Q_m workers, as indicated in Figure 12-8. Now suppose an industrial union is formed that forces the employer to accept a wage rate of W_c. Explain verbally and graphically why in this instance the higher wage rate will be accompanied by an increase in the number of workers hired.

9. Have you ever worked for the minimum wage? If so, for how long? Would you favour increasing the minimum wage by a dollar? By two dollars? By five dollars? Explain your reasoning.

10. "Many of the lowest-paid people in society—for example, short-order cooks—also have relatively poor working conditions. Hence, the notion of compensating wage differentials is disproved." Do you agree? Explain.

11. What is meant by investment in human capital? Use this concept to explain (a) wage differentials, and (b) the long-run rise of real wage rates in Canada.

12. What is the principal–agent problem? Have you ever worked in a setting where this problem arose? If so, do you think increased monitoring would have eliminated the problem? Why don't firms simply hire more supervisors to eliminate shirking?

INTERNET APPLICATION QUESTIONS

1. **Men's and Women's Earnings in Professional Golf—Why the Difference?** Go to the McConnell-Brue-Flynn-Barbiero Web site (Chapter 12) to access earnings of professional golfers. What are the annual earnings to date of the top 10 male golfers on the PGA tour? What are the earnings of the top 10 female golfers on the LPGA tour? What are the general differences in earnings between the male and female golfers? Can you explain them?

CHAPTER 13

Rent, Interest, and Profit

How do land prices (and land rents) get established and why do they differ? For example, a hectare of land in the middle of Toronto or Vancouver can sell for more than $100 million, while a hectare in northern Manitoba may fetch no more than $500.

What determines interest rates and causes them to change? For instance, why were interest rates on a one-year guaranteed investment certificate (GIC) 5.08 percent in Canada in March 2000, 3.94 percent in March 2006, and 1.8 percent in September 2009? How does interest compound over time, and how does that compounding relate to the so-called *present value* and *future value* of a particular sum of money?

What are the sources of profits and losses? Why do profits change over time? For example, why did the Royal Bank turn a profit in 2005, whereas Rogers Communications incurred a loss in the same year?

In Chapter 12 we focused on wages and salaries, which account for about 75 percent of all income paid to Canadian factor suppliers. In this chapter we examine the other factor payments—rent, interest, and profit—that make up the remaining 25 percent of national income. We begin by looking at rent.

13.1 | Economic Rent

To most people, "rent" means the money they must pay for the use of an apartment or a room. To the business executive, "rent" is a payment made for the use of a factory building, machine, or warehouse facility owned by others. Such definitions of rent can be confusing and ambiguous, however. On-campus residence rent, for example, may include other payments as well: interest on money the university borrowed to finance the residence, wages for maintenance services, utility payments, and so on.

Economists use rent in a much narrower sense. **Economic rent** is the price paid for the use of land and other natural resources that are completely fixed in total supply. As you will see, this fixed overall supply distinguishes rental payments from wage, interest, and profit payments.

economic rent
The price paid for the use of land and other natural resources, the supply of which is fixed (perfectly inelastic).

Let's examine this idea and some of its implications through supply and demand analysis. We first assume that all land is of the same quality, meaning that each arable (tillable) hectare of land is as productive as every other hectare. We assume, too, that all land has a single use, for example producing wheat. And we suppose that land is leased in a competitive market in which many producers are demanding land and many landowners are offering land in the market.

In Figure 13-1, curve S represents the supply of arable land available in the economy as a whole, and curve D_2 represents the demand of producers for use of that land. As with all economic resources, this demand is derived from the demand for the product being produced. Demand curves such as D_2 reflect the marginal revenue product (MRP = MP × P) of land. The curve slopes downward because of diminishing returns (MP declines) and because, for producers as a group, additional units of land result in greater output and lower output prices (P is less).

Perfectly Inelastic Supply

The unique feature of our analysis is on the supply side. For all practical purposes the supply of land is perfectly inelastic (in both the short run and long run), as reflected in supply curve S. Land has no production cost; it is a "free and non-reproducible gift of nature." The economy has only so much land, and that's that. Of course, within limits any parcel of land can be made more usable by clearing, drainage, and irrigation, but these are capital improvements and not changes in the amount of land itself.

Equilibrium Rent and Changes in Demand

Since the supply of land is fixed, demand is the only determinant of land rent. In this case, supply is passive. And what determines the demand for land? The factors we discussed in Chapter 11 do: the price of the product produced on the land, the productivity of land (which depends in part on the quantity and quality of the factors of production with which land is combined), and the prices of the other factors that are combined with land.

If demand is D_2, as we have suggested, the equilibrium rent will be R_2. The quantity of land L_0 that producers wish to rent will equal the quantity of land available (also L_0). But if the demand for land in Figure 13-1 increased from D_2 to D_1, land rent would rise from R_2 to R_1. If the demand for land declined from D_2 to D_3, land rent would fall from R_2 to R_3. In either case, the amount of land supplied would remain the same at quantity L_0. Changes in economic rent have no effect on the amount of land available since the supply of land cannot be augmented. If the demand for land were only D_4, land rent would be zero. Land would be a *free good*—a good for which demand is so low

---

FIGURE 13·1   The Determination of Land Rent

Because the supply S of land (and other natural resources) is perfectly inelastic, demand is the sole active determinant of land rent. An increase in demand from D_2 to D_1 or a decrease in demand from D_2 to D_3 will cause a considerable change in rent: from R_2 to R_1 in the first instance and from R_2 to R_3 in the second. But the amount of land supplied will remain at L_0. If demand is very low (D_4) relative to supply, land will be a free good, commanding no rent.

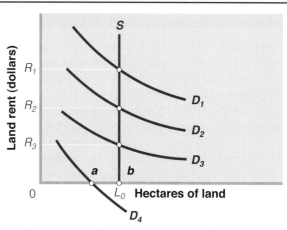

relative to supply that there is an excess supply of it even if the market price is zero. In Figure 13-1, we show this excess supply as distance $b - a$ at rent of zero. This essentially was the situation in the free-land era of Canadian history.

The ideas underlying Figure 13-1 help answer one of our chapter-opening questions. Land prices and rents are so high in central Toronto and Vancouver because the demand for that land is tremendous; it is capable of producing exceptionally high revenue from offices, hotel lodging, and entertainment. In contrast, the demand for isolated land in northern Manitoba is highly limited because very little revenue can be generated from its use. (It is an entirely different matter, of course, if gold can be mined from the land!)

Land Rent: a Surplus Payment

The perfectly inelastic supply of land must be contrasted with the relatively elastic supply of capital, such as apartment buildings, machinery, and warehouses. In the long run, capital is *not* fixed in total supply. A higher price gives entrepreneurs the incentive to construct and offer larger quantities of property resources. Conversely, a decline in price induces suppliers to allow existing facilities to depreciate and not be replaced. The supply curves of these non-land factors of production are upward-sloping, meaning that the prices paid to such factors have an **incentive function.** A high price provides an incentive to offer more of the factor, whereas a low price prompts factor suppliers to offer less.

incentive function of price
The inducement that an increase in the price of a commodity gives to sellers to make more of it available.

Not so with unimproved land. Whether rent is $10,000, $500, $1, or $0 per hectare, the same amount of land is available to society for use in production, which is why economists consider rent a *surplus payment* not necessary to ensure that land is available to the economy as a whole.

Productivity Differences and Rent Differences

So far we have assumed that all units of land are of the same grade. That is plainly not so. Different pieces of land vary greatly in productivity, depending on soil fertility and on such climatic factors as rainfall and temperature. Such factors explain, for example, why southern Ontario soil is excellently suited to corn production, why the Prairies are less well suited, and why Yukon is nearly incapable of corn production. Such productivity differences are reflected in factor demand and prices. Competitive bidding by producers will establish a high rent for highly productive southern Ontario land; less productive prairie land will command a much lower rent; and Yukon land may command no rent at all.

Location itself may be just as important in explaining differences in land rent. Other things equal, renters will pay more for a unit of land that is strategically located with respect to materials, labour, and customers than they will for a unit of land whose location is remote from these things. For example, enormously high land prices are paid for major ski resorts in such places as Whistler, B.C., and for land in Alberta that has oil under it.

Figure 13-1, viewed from a slightly different perspective, reveals the rent differentials from quality differences in land. Assume, again, that only wheat can be produced on four grades of land, each of which is available in the fixed amount L_0. When combined with identical amounts of labour, capital, and entrepreneurial talent, the productivity—or, more specifically, the marginal revenue product—of each of the four grades of land is reflected in demand curves D_1, D_2, D_3, and D_4. Grade 1 land is the most productive, as shown by D_1, while grade 4 is the least productive, as shown by D_4. The resulting economic rents for grade 1, 2, and 3 land will be R_1, R_2, and R_3, respectively; the rent differential will mirror the differences in productivity of the three grades of land. Grade 4 land is so poor in quality that, given its supply S, farmers won't pay anything to use it. It will be a free good because it is not sufficiently scarce in relation to the demand for it to command a price or a rent.

Alternative Uses of Land

We have assumed that land has only one use. Actually, we know that land normally has alternative uses. A hectare of Ontario farmland may be useful not only for raising corn but also for raising oats, barley, and cattle, or it may be useful for building a house, or a highway, or as a factory site.

In other words, any particular use of land involves an opportunity cost—the forgone production from the next best use of the resource. Where there are alternative uses, individual firms must pay rent to cover those opportunity costs to secure the use of land for their particular purpose. To the individual firm, rent is a cost of production, just as wages and interest are.

Recall that, as viewed by society, economic rent is not a cost. Society would have the same amount of land with or without the payment of economic rent. From society's perspective, economic rent is a surplus payment above that needed to gain the use of a resource. But individual firms do need to pay rent to attract land resources away from alternative uses. For firms, rental payments are a *cost*. *(Key Question 2)*

QUICK REVIEW

▶ Economic rent is the price paid for factors such as land whose supply is perfectly inelastic.

▶ Land rent is a surplus payment because land would be available to society even if this rent were not paid.

▶ Differential rents allocate land among alternative uses.

13.2 | Interest: the Price of Money

Interest is the price paid for the use of money. It is the price that borrowers need to pay lenders for transferring purchasing power from the present to the future (see the Consider This box). It can be thought of as the amount of money that must be paid for the use of $1 for one year. Two points are important to this discussion.

1. ***Interest Is Stated as a Percentage*** Interest is paid in kind, meaning that the borrower pays for the loan of money with money (interest). For that reason, interest is stated as a percentage of the amount of money borrowed rather than as a dollar amount. By expressing interest as a percentage, we can immediately compare an interest payment of, say, $432 per year per $2880 with one of $1800 per year per $12,000. Both interest payments are 15 percent per year, which is not obvious from the actual dollar figures. This interest of 15 percent per year is referred to as a 15 percent interest rate.

2. ***Money Is Not a Resource*** Money is *not* a factor of production. Money is not productive; it cannot produce goods and services. However, businesses buy the use of money because it can be used to acquire capital goods such as factories, machinery, warehouses, and so on. Such facilities clearly do contribute to production. Thus, in hiring the use of money capital, business executives are often indirectly buying the use of real capital goods.

Loanable Funds Theory of Interest

loanable funds theory of interest
The concept that the supply of and demand for loanable funds determines the equilibrium rate of interest.

In macroeconomics the interest rate is viewed through the lens of the economy's total supply of and demand for money. But since our present focus is on microeconomics, it will be useful to consider a more micro-based theory of interest here. Specifically, the **loanable funds theory of interest** explains the interest rate not in terms of the total supply of and demand for *money* but rather in terms of supply of and demand for *funds available for lending (and borrowing)*. As Figure 13-2 shows, the equilibrium interest rate (here, 8 percent) is the rate at which the quantities of loanable funds supplied and demanded are equal.

Let's first consider the loanable funds theory in simplified form. Specifically, assume households or consumers are the sole suppliers of loanable funds and businesses are the sole demanders. Also assume that lending occurs directly between households and businesses; there are no intermediate financial institutions.

CONSIDER THIS | That Is Interest

The following story told by economist Irving Fisher (1867–1947) helps illustrate the time value of money.*

In the process of a massage, a masseur informed Fisher that he was a Socialist who believed that "interest is the basis of capitalism, and is robbery." Following the massage, Fisher asked, "How much do I owe you?"

The masseur replied, "Thirty dollars."

"Very well," said Fisher, "I will give you a note payable a hundred years hence. I suppose you have no objections to taking this note without any interest. At the end of that time, you, or perhaps your grandchildren, can redeem it."

"But I cannot afford to wait that long," said the masseur.

"I thought you said that interest was robbery. If interest is robbery, you ought to be willing to wait indefinitely for the money. If you are willing to wait ten years, how much would you require?"

"Well, I would have to get more than thirty dollars."

His point now made, Fisher replied, "That is interest."

---

*Irving Fisher, as quoted in Irving Norton Fisher, *My Father Irving Fisher* (New York: Comet, 1956), p. 77.

SUPPLY OF LOANABLE FUNDS

The supply of loanable funds is represented by curve S in Figure 13-2. Its upward slope indicates that households will make available a larger quantity of funds at high interest rates than at low interest rates. Most people prefer to use their income to purchase pleasurable goods and services *today*, rather than to delay purchases to sometime in the *future*. For people to delay consumption and increase their saving, they must be compensated by an interest payment. The larger the amount of that payment, the greater the deferral of household consumption and thus the greater the amount of money made available for loans.

Disagreement exists among economists as to how much the quantity of loanable funds made available by suppliers changes in response to changes in the interest rate. Most economists view saving as being relatively insensitive to changes in the interest rate. The supply curve of loanable funds may, therefore, be more inelastic—displaying less quantity response to changes in i—than S in Figure 13-2 implies.

KEY GRAPH

FIGURE 13-2 The Market for Loanable Funds

The upsloping supply curve S for loanable funds reflects the idea that at higher interest rates, households will defer more of their present consumption (save more), making more funds available for lending. The downsloping demand curve D for loanable funds indicates that businesses will borrow more at lower interest rates than at higher interest rates. At the equilibrium interest rate (here, 8 percent), the quantities of loanable funds lent and borrowed are equal (here, F_0 each).

DEMAND FOR LOANABLE FUNDS

Businesses borrow loanable funds primarily to add to their stocks of capital goods, such as new plants or warehouses, machinery, and equipment. Assume that a firm wants to buy a machine that will increase output and sales such that the firm's total revenue will rise by $110 for the year. Also assume that the machine costs $100 and has a useful life of just one year. Comparing the $10 earned with the $100 cost of the machine, we find that the expected rate of return on this investment is 10 percent (= $10/$100) for one year.

To determine whether the investment would be profitable and whether it should be made, the firm must compare the interest rate—the price of loanable funds—with the 10 percent expected rate of return. If funds can be borrowed at some rate less than the rate of return, say, at 8 percent, as in Figure 13-2, then the investment is profitable and should be made. But if funds can be borrowed only at an interest rate above the 10 percent rate of return, say, at 14 percent, the investment is unprofitable and should not be made.

Why is the demand for loanable funds downsloping, as in Figure 13-2? At higher interest rates fewer investment projects will be profitable and therefore a smaller quantity of loanable funds will be demanded. At lower interest rates, more investment projects will be profitable and, therefore, more loanable funds will be demanded. Indeed, as we have just seen, it is profitable to purchase the $100 machine if funds can be borrowed at 8 percent but not if the firm must borrow at 14 percent.

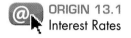

ORIGIN 13.1
Interest Rates

Extending the Model

We now make this simple model more realistic in several ways.

FINANCIAL INSTITUTIONS

Households rarely directly lend their savings to the businesses that are borrowing funds for investment. Instead, they place their savings in chartered banks (and other financial institutions). The banks pay interest to savers to attract loanable funds and in turn lend those funds to businesses. Businesses borrow the funds from the banks, paying them interest for the use of the money. Financial institutions profit by charging borrowers higher interest rates than the interest rates they pay savers. Both interest rates, however, are based on the supply of and demand for loanable funds.

Changes in Supply   Anything that causes households to be thriftier will prompt them to save more at each interest rate, shifting the supply curve rightward. For example, if interest earned on savings were to be suddenly exempted from taxation, we would expect the supply of loanable funds to increase and the equilibrium interest rate to decrease. In 2009 the federal government introduced the Tax Free Savings Account (TFSA), which exempts up to $5000 a year in a saving account from taxation. This new policy will undoubtedly give many Canadians an incentive to save more of their income.

Conversely, a decline in thriftiness would shift the supply-of-loanable-funds curve leftward and increase the equilibrium interest rate. For example, if the government expanded social insurance to cover more fully the costs of hospitalization, prescription drugs, and retirement living, the incentive of households to save might diminish.

Changes in Demand   On the demand side, anything that increases the rate of return on potential investments will increase the demand for loanable funds. Let's return to our earlier example, where a firm would receive additional revenue of $110 by purchasing a $100 machine and, therefore, would realize a 10 percent return on investment. What factors might increase or decrease the rate of return? Suppose a technological advance raised the productivity of the machine so that the firm's total revenue increased by $120 rather than $110. The rate of return would then be 20 percent, not 10 percent. Before the technological advance, the firm would have demanded zero loanable funds at, say, an interest rate of 14 percent, but now it will demand $100 of loanable funds at that interest rate, meaning that the demand curve for loanable funds has shifted to the right.

Similarly, an increase in consumer demand for the firm's product will increase the price of its product. So even though the productivity of the machine is unchanged, its potential revenue will rise from $110 to perhaps $120, increasing the firm's rate of return from 10 to 20 percent. Again, the firm will be willing to borrow more than previously at our presumed 8 or 14 percent interest rate, implying that the demand curve for loanable funds has shifted rightward. This shift in demand increases the equilibrium interest rate.

Conversely, a decline in the productivity or in the price of the firm's product would shift the demand curve for loanable funds leftward, reducing the equilibrium interest rate.

Other Participants   We must recognize that participation in the loanable funds market goes well beyond our simplification of households as suppliers of funds and businesses as demanders of funds. For example, while households are suppliers of loanable funds, many are also demanders of such funds. Households borrow to finance expensive purchases such as housing, automobiles, furniture, and household appliances. Governments also are on the demand side of the loanable funds market when they borrow to finance budgetary deficits. And businesses that have revenues in excess of their current expenditures may offer some of those revenues in the market for loanable funds. Thus, like households, businesses operate on both the supply and the demand sides of the market.

Finally, in addition to gathering and making available the savings of households, banks and other financial institutions also increase funds through the lending process and decrease funds when loans are paid back and not lent out again. The Bank of Canada (the nation's central bank) controls the amount of this bank activity and thus influences interest rates.

This fact helps answer one of our chapter-opening questions: Why did the interest rate on a one-year GIC drop from 5.08 percent in March 2000 to 1.8 percent in September 2009? There are two reasons: (1) the demand for loanable funds decreased because businesses did not need to purchase more capital goods; and (2) the Bank of Canada, in an effort to stimulate aggregate expenditures, took monetary actions that increased the supply of loanable funds. *(Key Question 5)*

Time Value of Money

time value of money
The idea that a specific amount of money is more valuable to a person the sooner it is received because the money can be placed in a financial account or investment and earn compound interest over time.

Interest is central to understanding the **time value of money**—the idea that a specific amount of money is more valuable to a person the sooner it is obtained. A sum of money received today is equivalent to a larger amount in the future, because today's sum can be placed in an interest-bearing account. The interest rate determines how fast the amount in the account will grow over time. It also determines a way in which a given amount of money today can be thought of as being equivalent to a larger amount in the future, and how a future amount of money can be thought of as being equivalent to a smaller amount today.

COMPOUND INTEREST

Compound interest is the total interest that cumulates over time on money placed into an interest-bearing account. Table 13-1 helps explain compound interest, as well as the related ideas of future value and present value. Suppose that Max places $1000 into an interest-bearing account at 10 percent interest with the intent to let the principal (the initial deposit) and interest compound for three years. The first row of each column shows the beginning period sum; the second column shows the yearly computation as to how that sum grows, given a particular interest rate. That growth is found by multiplying the dollar amount by $1 + i$, where i is the interest rate expressed as a decimal.

In year 1 the 10 percent interest rate increases the money in the account from $1000 to $1100 (= $1000 × 1.10). So, as shown in column 3, total interest is $100. Column 4 simply again lists the $1100, but reinforces that it consists of the original principal plus total interest. Similarly, in year 2, the $1100 now in the account grows to $1210 (= $1100 × 1.10) because $110 of new interest accrues on the $1100. At the end of year 2, the principal remains $1000, but the total interest is $210, and the total amount in the account is $1210. Interest in year 3 is $121 and total interest rises to $331. After this $331 of total interest is added to the $1000 principal, the accumulation is $1331. As shown in Column 3, compound interest builds and builds over time.

FUTURE VALUE AND PRESENT VALUE

Now note from Table 13-1 that we can look at the time value of money in two distinct ways. **Future value** is the amount to which some current amount of money will grow as interest compounds over time. In our table, the future value (FV) of $1000 today at 10 percent interest is $1331 three years from now. Future value is always forward looking.

But we can just as easily look backward from the end value of $1331 and ask how much that amount is worth today, given the 10 percent interest rate. **Present value** is today's value of some amount of money to be received in the future. In terms of the table, the present value (PV) of $1331 is $1000. Here, FV is "discounted" by three years at 10 percent to remove all interest compounding and that way obtain PV. (We will defer explaining the discounting procedure to our chapter on financial economics in *Macroeconomics,* but for readers interested in the mathematics, see the footnote below).˙

With any positive real interest rate, a person would prefer to receive $1000 today rather than $1000 at some time in the future. The higher the interest rate, the greater is the *future value* of a specific amount of money today. To confirm, substitute a 20 percent interest rate for the 10 percent rate in Table 13-1 and rework the analysis. Finally, you should know that the analysis presented through the table is extendable to any number of years.

The time value of money is an important concept. For example, we will use it in the chapter on natural resource economics that follows. Also, we will discuss present discounted value in much more detail in our chapter on financial economics in *Macroeconomics.* Our simple goal in this chapter is to stress that *money has time value because of the potential for compound interest. (Key Question 6)*

Range of Interest Rates

Although economists often speak in terms of a single interest rate, a number of interest rates exist. Table 13-2 lists several interest rates often referred to in the media. These rates range from 0.4 to 19.50 percent. Why are there differences?

- **Risk** Loans to different borrowers for different purposes carry varying degrees of risk. The greater the chance that the borrower will not repay the loan, the higher the interest rate the lender will charge to compensate for that risk.

- **Maturity** The time length of a loan or its *maturity* (when it needs to be paid back) also affects the interest rate. Other things equal, longer-term loans usually command higher interest rates

future value
The amount to which some current amount of money will grow if the interest earned on the amount is left to compound over time.

present value
Today's value of some amount of money that is to be received sometime in the future.

Compound Interest, Future Value, and Present Value, 10 Percent Interest Rate

TABLE 13-1

(1) Beginning Period Value	(2) Computation	(3) Total Interest	(4) End Period Value
$1000 (Year 1)	$1000 × 1.10 = $1100	$100	$1100 (= $1000 + $100)
$1100 (Year 2)	$1100 × 1.10 = $1210	$210 (= $100 + $110)	$1210 (= $1000 + $210)
$1210 (Year 2)	$1210 × 1.10 = $1331	$331 (= $110 + $121)	$1331 (= $1000 + $331)

* The mathematics is as follows
FV
$FV = PV (1 + i)^t$ and $PV = FV/(1 + i)^t$
where i is the interest rate and t is time, here the number of years of compounding

TABLE 13-2	Selected Interest Rates, April 2009

Type of interest rate	Annual percentage
10-year Government of Canada bond	3.00
5-year Government of Canada bond	1.90
3-year Government of Canada bond	1.45
91-day Treasury Bill (Government of Canada)	0.40
5-year closed mortgage	5.75
Prime rate (rate charged by banks to their best corporate customers)	3.00
Overnight lending rate	0.50
Visa interest rate	19.50

Source: Bank of Canada.

than shorter-term loans. The long-term lender suffers the inconvenience and possible financial sacrifice of forgoing alternative uses for the money for a greater period.

- *Loan Size*   If there are two loans of equal maturity and risk, the interest rate on the smaller of the two loans usually will be higher. The costs of issuing a large loan and a small loan are about the same in dollars, but the cost is greater *as a percentage* of the smaller loan.

- *Market Imperfections*   Market imperfections also explain some interest rate differentials. The small-town bank that monopolizes local lending may charge high interest rates on consumer loans because households find it inconvenient and costly to shop around at banks in distant cities. The large corporation, however, can survey rival lenders to float a new bond issue and secure the lowest obtainable rate.

Pure Rate of Interest

pure rate of interest
An essentially risk-free, long-term interest rate not influenced by market imperfections.

Economists and financial specialists talk of "the" interest rate to simplify the cluster of rates (Table 13-2). When they do so, they usually have in mind the **pure rate of interest.** The pure rate is best approximated by the interest paid on long-term, virtually riskless securities such as 30-year long-term bonds of the Canadian government. This interest payment can be thought of as being made solely for the use of money over an extended time, because risk and administrative costs are negligible and the interest rate on these bonds is not distorted by market imperfections. In early 2009 the pure rate of interest in Canada was 3.7 percent.

Role of the Interest Rate

The interest rate is a critical price that affects the *level* and *composition* of investment goods production, as well as the *amount* of R&D spending.

INTEREST AND TOTAL OUTPUT

A lower equilibrium interest rate encourages businesses to borrow more for investment. As a result, total spending in the economy rises and, if the economy has unused resources, so does total output.

Conversely, a higher equilibrium interest rate discourages business from borrowing for investment, reducing investment and total spending. Such a decrease in spending may be desirable if any economy is experiencing inflation.

Central banks often manage the interest rate to try to expand investment and output on the one hand, or to reduce investment and inflation on the other. Central banks affect the interest rate by changing the supply of money. Increases in the money supply increase the supply of loanable funds, causing the equilibrium interest rate to fall. This boosts investment spending and expands the economy. In contrast, decreases in the money supply decrease the supply of loanable funds, boosting the equilibrium interest rate. As a result, investment is constrained and so is the economy.

INTEREST AND THE ALLOCATION OF CAPITAL

Prices are rationing devices. The price of money—the interest rate—is certainly no exception. The interest rate rations the available supply of loanable funds to investment projects that have expected rates of return at or above the interest rate cost of the borrowed funds.

If, say, the computer industry expects to earn a return of 12 percent on the money it invests in physical capital and it can secure the required funds at an interest rate of 8 percent, it can borrow and expand its physical capital. If the expected rate of return on additional capital in the steel industry is only 6 percent, that industry will find it unprofitable to expand its capital stock at 8 percent interest. The interest rate allocates money, and ultimately physical capital, to those industries in which it will be most productive and, therefore, most profitable. Such an allocation of capital goods benefits society.

INTEREST AND THE LEVEL AND COMPOSITION OF R&D SPENDING

The decision on how much to spend on R&D depends on the cost of borrowing funds in relationship to the expected rate of return. Other things equal, the lower the interest rate, and thus the lower the cost of borrowing funds for R&D, the greater the amount of R&D spending that is profitable. The higher the interest rate, the less the amount of R&D spending.

Also, the interest rate allocates R&D funds to those firms and industries for which the expected rate of return on R&D is the greatest. Ace Microcircuits may have an expected rate of return of 16 percent on an R&D project, while Glow Paints has only a 2 percent expected rate of return on its R&D project. With the interest rate at 8 percent, loanable funds will flow to Ace, not to Glow. Society will benefit by having R&D spending allocated to projects that have sufficiently high expected rates of return to justify using scarce resources for R&D rather than for other purposes.

NOMINAL AND REAL INTEREST RATES

nominal interest rate
The interest rate expressed in terms of annual amounts currently charged for interest and not adjusted for inflation.

real interest rate
The interest rate expressed in dollars of constant value (adjusted for inflation); equal to the nominal interest rate less the expected rate of inflation.

This discussion of the role of interest in investment decisions and in R&D decisions assumes that there is no inflation. If inflation exists, we must distinguish between nominal and real interest rates, just as we needed to distinguish between nominal and real wages in Chapter 12. The **nominal interest rate** is the rate of interest expressed in dollars of current value. The **real interest rate** is the rate of interest expressed in purchasing power—dollars of inflation-adjusted value. (For a comparison of nominal interest rates on bank loans in selected countries, see Global Perspective 13.1.)

For example, suppose the nominal interest rate and the rate of inflation are both 10 percent. If you borrow $100, you must pay back $110 a year from now. However, because of 10 percent inflation, each of these 110 dollars will be worth 10 percent less. Thus, the real value or purchasing power of your $110 at the end of the year is only $100. In inflation-adjusted dollars you are borrowing $100 and at year's end you are paying back $100. While the nominal interest rate is 10 percent, the real interest rate is zero. We determine this by subtracting the 10 percent inflation rate from the 10 percent nominal interest rate. It is the real interest rate, not the nominal rate, that affects investment and R&D decisions. *(Key Question 9)*

13.1 | GLOBAL PERSPECTIVE

Short-term nominal interest rates, selected nations

These data show the short-term nominal interest rates (those on three-month loans) in various countries in 2007. Because these are nominal rates, much of the variation reflects differences in rates of inflation, but differences in central bank monetary policies and in risk of default also explain the variations.

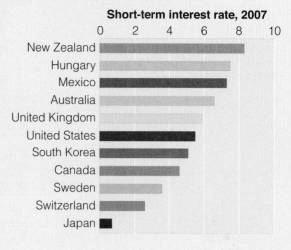

Short-term interest rate, 2007

Source: Organisation for Economic Co-operation and Development, www.oecd.org

QUICK REVIEW

▶ Interest is the price paid for the use of money.

▶ In the loanable funds model, the equilibrium interest rate is determined by the demand for and supply of loanable funds.

▶ The time value of money is the idea that $1 can be converted into more than $1 of future value through compound interest, therefore $1 to be received sometime in the future has less than $1 of present value.

▶ The range of interest rates is influenced by risk, maturity, loan size, taxability, and market imperfections.

▶ The equilibrium interest rate affects the total level of investment and, therefore, the levels of total spending and total output; it also allocates money and real capital to specific industries and firms. Similarly, the interest rate affects the level and composition of R&D spending.

explicit costs
The monetary payments a firm must make to an outsider to obtain a resource.

implicit costs
The monetary incomes a firm sacrifices when it uses a resource it owns rather than supplying the resource to the market.

economic (pure) profit
The total revenue of a firm less its economic costs (which includes both explicit costs and implicit costs); also called *above normal profit*.

13.3 | Economic Profit

Recall from previous chapters that economists define profit narrowly. To accountants, profit is what remains of a firm's total revenue after it has paid individuals and other firms for the materials, capital, and labour they have supplied to the firm. To the economist, this definition overstates profit. The reason is that the accountant's view of profit considers only **explicit costs:** payments made by the firm to outsiders. It ignores **implicit costs:** the monetary income the firm sacrifices when it uses resources that it owns, rather than supplying those resources to the market. The economist considers implicit costs to be opportunity costs and hence to be real costs that must be accounted for in determining profit. **Economic** or **pure profit** is what remains after all costs—both explicit and implicit, the latter including a normal profit—have been subtracted from a firm's total revenue. Economic profit may be either positive or negative (a loss).

Role of the Entrepreneur

The economist views profit as the return on a particular type of human resource: entrepreneurial ability. We know from earlier chapters that the entrepreneur (1) combines factors of production to produce a good or service, (2) makes basic, nonroutine policy decisions for the firm, (3) introduces innovations in the form of new products or new production processes, and (4) bears the economic risks associated with all those functions.

Part of the entrepreneur's return is a **normal profit,** which is the minimum payment necessary to retain the entrepreneur in the current line of production. We saw in Chapter 6 that normal profit is a cost—the cost of using entrepreneurial ability for a particular purpose. We saw also that a firm's total revenue may exceed its total cost; the excess revenue above all costs is its economic profit. This *residual profit* also goes to the entrepreneur. The entrepreneur is the *residual claimant*: the factor that receives what is left after all costs are paid.

Why should there be residual profit? We next examine three possible reasons, two relating to the risks involved in business and one based on monopoly power.

normal profit
The payment made by a firm to obtain and retain entrepreneurial ability.

Sources of Economic Profit

Let's first construct an artificial economic environment in which economic profit would be zero. Then, by noting how the real world differs from such an environment, we will see where economic profit arises.

We begin with a perfectly competitive, static economy. A **static economy** is one in which the basic forces such as factor supplies, technological knowledge, and consumer tastes are constant and unchanging. As a result, all cost and supply data, and all demand and revenue data, are constant.

Given the nature of these data, the economic future is perfectly certain. The outcome of any price or production policy can be accurately predicted. Furthermore, no product or production process is ever improved. Under perfect competition any economic profit or loss that might have existed in an industry will disappear with the entry or exit of firms in the long run. All costs, explicit and implicit, are just covered in the long run, so no economic profit exists in our static economy.

The idea of zero economic profit in a static competitive economy suggests that profit is linked to the dynamic nature of real-world market economy and its accompanying uncertainty. Moreover, it indicates that economic profit may arise from a source other than the directing, innovating, and risk-bearing functions of the entrepreneur. That source is the presence of some amount of monopoly power.

static economy
An economy in which factor supplies, technological knowledge, and consumer tastes are constant and unchanging.

RISK AND PROFIT

In a real, dynamic economy the future is not predictable; there is uncertainty. This means that the entrepreneur must assume risks. Some or all economic profit may be a reward for assuming risks.

In linking economic profit with uncertainty and risk-bearing, we must distinguish between risks that are insurable and risks that are not. Some types of risk—fire, floods, theft, and accidents to employees—are measurable; that is, their frequency of occurrence can be estimated accurately. Firms can avoid losses due to **insurable risks** by paying an annual fee (an insurance premium) to an insurance company. The entrepreneur need not bear such risks.

However, the entrepreneur must bear the uninsurable risks of business, and those risks are a potential source of economic profit. **Uninsurable risks** are mainly the uncontrollable and unpredictable changes in the demand and supply conditions facing the firm (and hence its revenues and costs). Uninsurable risks stem from three general sources:

insurable risk
An event that would result in a loss but whose frequency of occurrence can be estimated with considerable accuracy.

uninsurable risk
An event that would result in a loss and whose occurrence is uncontrollable and unpredictable.

1. *Changes in the General Economic Environment* A downturn in business (a recession), for example, can lead to greatly reduced demand, sales, and revenues, and thus to business losses. A prosperous firm may experience such losses through no fault of its own.

2. *Changes in the Structure of the Economy* Consumer tastes, technology, factor availability, and prices change constantly in the real world, bringing changes in production costs and revenues. For example, an airline earning economic profit one year may find its profit plunging the next year as the result of a significant increase in the price of jet fuel.

3. **Changes in Government Policy**   A newly instituted regulation, the removal of a tariff, or a change in a national policy may significantly alter the cost and revenue data of the affected industry and firms.

Regardless of how such revenue and cost changes come about, they are risks that the firm and entrepreneur must take to stay in business. Some or all the economic profit in a real, dynamic economy may be compensation for taking risks.

INNOVATIONS AND PROFIT

Such uninsurable risks are beyond the control of the individual firm or industry and thus are external to it. One dynamic feature of a market economy, however—innovation—occurs at the initiative of the entrepreneur. Business firms deliberately introduce new products and new methods of production to affect their costs and revenues favourably. The entrepreneur intentionally undertakes to upset existing cost and revenue data in a way that promises to be profitable.

But again uncertainty enters the picture. Despite exhaustive market surveys, new products or modifications of existing products may be economic failures. Similarly, of the many new novels, textbooks, movies, and video games that appear every year, only a handful garner large profits. Nor is it certain whether new production machinery will actually yield projected cost economies. Thus, innovations undertaken by entrepreneurs entail uncertainty and the possibility of losses, not just the potential for increased profit. Some of the economic profit in an innovative economy may be compensation for dealing with the uncertainty of innovation.

MONOPOLY AND PROFIT

So far, we have linked economic profit with the uncertainties surrounding (1) the dynamic environment to which enterprises are exposed, and (2) the dynamic business processes they initiate themselves. *The existence of monopoly power is a final source of economic profit.* Because a monopolist can restrict output and deter entry, it may persistently enjoy above-competitive prices and economic profit if demand is strong relative to cost. *(Key Question 10)*

Functions of Profit

Economic profit is the main energizer of the market economy. It influences both the level of economic output and the allocation of resources among alternative uses.

- **Profit and Total Output**   The expectation of economic profit motivates firms to innovate. Innovation stimulates new investment, increasing total output and employment.

- **Profit and Resource Allocation**   Profit also helps to allocate resources among alternative lines of production. Entrepreneurs seek profit and avoid losses. Economic profit in an industry is a signal that society wants that particular industry to expand. It attracts factors of production from industries that are not profitable. But the rewards of profit are more than an inducement for an industry to expand; they also attract the financing needed for expansion. In contrast, continuing losses penalize firms or industries that fail to adjust their productive efforts to match wants. Such losses signal society's desire for the afflicted industries to contract.

One dynamic feature of a market economy, innovation, occurs at the initiative of the entrepreneur.

QUICK REVIEW

▶ Pure or economic profit is what remains after all explicit and implicit costs (including a normal profit) are subtracted from a firm's total revenue.

▶ Economic profit has three sources: the bearing of uninsurable risk, the uncertainty of innovation, and monopoly power.

▶ Profit and profit expectations affect the levels of investment, total spending, and domestic output; profit and loss also allocate resources among alternative uses.

The LAST WORD   Determining the Price of Credit

A variety of lending practices may cause the effective interest rate
to be quite different from what it appears to be.

Borrowing and lending—receiving and granting credit—are a way of life. Individuals receive credit when they negotiate a mortgage loan and when they use their credit cards. Individuals make loans when they open a savings account in a chartered bank or buy a bond.

It is sometimes difficult to determine exactly how much interest we pay and receive when we borrow and lend. Let's suppose that you borrow $10,000, which you agree to repay with $1000 of interest at the end of one year. In this instance, the interest rate is 10 percent per year. To determine the interest rate i, we compare the interest paid with the amount borrowed:

$$i = \frac{\$1,000}{\$10,000} = 10\%$$

But in some cases a lender—say, a bank—will discount the interest payment at the time the loan is made. Thus, instead of giving the borrower $10,000, the bank discounts the $1000 interest payment in advance, giving the borrower only $9000. This increases the interest rate:

$$i = \frac{\$1,000}{\$9,000} = 11\%$$

While the absolute amount of interest paid is the same, in this second case the borrower has only $9000 available for the year.

An even more subtle point is that, to simplify their calculations, some finan-cial institutions assume a 360-day year (twelve 30-day months), which means the borrower has the use of the lend-er's funds for five fewer days than the normal year. This use of a short year also increases the actual interest rate paid by the borrower.

The interest rate paid may change dramatically if a loan is repaid in installments. Suppose a bank lends you $10,000 and charges interest in the amount of $1000 to be paid at the end of the year. But the loan contract requires that you repay the $10,000 loan in 12 equal monthly installments. In effect, then, the average amount of the loan outstanding during the year is only $5000. Therefore:

$$i = \frac{\$1,000}{\$5,000} = 20\%$$

Here interest is paid on the total amount of the loan ($10,000) rather than on the outstanding balance (which averages $5000 for the year), making for a much higher interest rate.

Another factor that influences the effective interest rate is whether inter-est is compounded. Suppose you deposit $10,000 in a savings account that pays a 10 percent interest rate compounded semiannually. In other words, interest is paid on your loan to the bank twice a year. At the end of the first six months, $500 of inter-est (10 percent of $10,000 for half a year) is added to your account. At the end of the year, interest is calculated on $10,500 so that the second inter-est payment is $525 (10 percent of $10,500 for half a year). Thus:

$$i = \frac{\$1,025}{\$10,000} = 10.25\%$$

This means that a chartered bank advertising a 10 percent interest rate compounded semiannually is actually paying more interest to its customers than a competitor paying a simple (noncompounded) interest rate of 10.20 percent.

Similarly, late-payment fees on credit card accounts can boost the actual interest rate paid on credit card balances to extremely high levels. Fur-thermore, low "teaser" rates designed to attract new customers often contain fine print that raises the interest rate to 16 percent, or even 28 percent, if there is a late payment on the account.

"Let the borrower (or depositor) beware" remains a fitting motto in the world of credit.

Question

Assume that you borrow $5000 and pay back the $5000 plus $250 in interest at the end of the year. Assuming no inflation, what is the real interest rate? What would the interest rate be if the $250 of interest had been discounted at the time the loan was made? What would the interest rate be if you were required to repay the loan in 12 equal monthly installments?

CHAPTER SUMMARY

13.1 ▸ ECONOMIC RENT

- Economic rent is the price paid for the use of land and other natural resources whose total supplies are fixed.

- Rent is a surplus payment that is socially unnecessary since land would be available to the economy even without rental payments.

- Differences in land rent result from differences in the fertility and climatic features of the land and difference in location.

- Although land rent is a surplus payment rather than a cost to the economy as a whole, to individual firms and industries rental payments are correctly regarded as costs. These payments must be made to gain the use of land, which has alternative uses.

13.2 ▸ INTEREST: THE PRICE OF MONEY

- Interest is the price paid for the use of money. In the loanable funds theory, the equilibrium interest rate is determined by the demand for and supply of loanable funds. Other things equal, an increase in the supply of loanable funds reduces the equilibrium interest rate, whereas a decrease in supply increases it; increases in the demand for loanable funds raise the equilibrium interest rate, whereas decreases in demand reduce it.

- The time value of money is the idea that $1 today has more value than $1 sometime in the future because the $1 today can be placed in an interest-bearing account and earn compound interest over time. Future value is the amount to which a current amount of money will grow through interest compounding. Present value is the current value of some money payment to be received in the future.

- Interest rates vary in size because loans differ as to risk, maturity, amount, and taxability; market imperfections cause additional variations. The pure rate of interest is the interest rate on virtually riskless long-term Government of Canada bonds.

- The equilibrium interest rate influences the level of investment and helps ration financial and physical capital to specific firms and industries. Similarly, this rate influences the size and composition of R&D spending. The real interest rate, not the nominal rate, is critical to investment and R&D decisions.

13.3 ▸ ECONOMIC PROFIT

- Economic, or pure, profit is the difference between a firm's total revenue and the sum of its explicit and implicit costs, the latter including a normal profit. Profit accrues to entrepreneurs for assuming the uninsurable risks associated with organizing and directing economic resources and for innovating. Profit also results from monopoly power.

- Profit expectations influence innovation and investment activities and, therefore, the economy's levels of employment and economic growth. The basic function of profits and losses, however, is to allocate resources in accord with consumers' preferences.

TERMS AND CONCEPTS

economic rent, p. 312
incentive function of price, p. 313
loanable funds theory of interest, p. 314
time value of money, p. 317
future value, p. 318
present value, p. 318

pure rate of interest, p. 319
nominal interest rate, p. 320
real interest rate, p. 320
explicit costs, p. 321
implicit costs, p. 321

economic (pure) profit, p. 321
normal profit, p. 322
static economy, p. 322
insurable risks, p. 322
uninsurable risks, p. 322

STUDY QUESTIONS

13.1 1. How does the economist's use of the term "rent" differ from everyday usage? Explain: "Though rent need not be paid by society to make land available, rental payments are very useful in guiding land into the most productive uses."

13.1 2. **KEY QUESTION** Explain why economic rent is a surplus payment when viewed by the economy as a whole but as a cost of production from the standpoint of individual firms

and industries. Explain: "Rent performs no 'incentive function' in the economy."

3. In the 1980s land prices in Japan surged upward in a "speculative bubble." Land prices then fell for 11 straight years between 1990 and 2001. What can we safely assume happened to land *rent* in Japan over those 11 years? Use graphical analysis to illustrate your answer. **LO ▸ 13.1**

LO 13.2 4. If money is not an economic resource, why is interest paid and received for its use? What considerations account for the fact that interest rates differ greatly on various types of loans? Use those considerations to explain the relative sizes of the interest rates on the following:

    a. A 10-year $1000 government bond

    b. A $20 pawnshop loan

    c. A 30-year mortgage loan on a $145,000 house

    d. A 24-month $12,000 bank loan to finance the purchase of an automobile

    e. A 60-day $100 loan from a personal finance company

LO 13.2 5. **KEY QUESTION**   Why is the supply of loanable funds upsloping? Why is the demand for loanable funds downsloping? Explain the equilibrium interest rate. List some factors that might cause it to change.

LO 13.2 6. **KEY QUESTION**   Suppose that the interest rate is 4 percent. What is the future value of $100 four years from now? How much of the future value is total interest? By how much would total interest be greater at 6 percent interest than at 4 percent interest?

LO 13.2 7. Suppose the total demand and supply of loanable funds (in billions) are as follows:

Quantity demanded of loanable funds	Interest rate (percent)	Quantity supplied of loanable funds	Surplus (+) or shortage (−)
85	4	72	_____
80	6	73	_____
75	8	75	_____
70	10	77	_____
65	12	79	_____
60	14	81	_____

    a. What will be the market or equilibrium interest rate? What is the equilibrium quantity of loanable funds? Complete the surplus-shortage column.

    b. Why will 4 percent not be the equilibrium interest rate in this market? Why not 14 percent?

8. What are the major economic functions of the interest rate? **LO** How might the fact that many businesses finance their investment activities internally affect the efficiency with which the interest rate performs its functions?

9. **KEY QUESTION**   Distinguish between nominal and real **LO** interest rates. Which is more relevant in making investment and R&D decisions? If the nominal interest rate is 12 percent and the inflation rate is 8 percent, what is the real rate of interest?

10. **KEY QUESTION**   How do the concepts of accounting **LO** profit and economic profit differ? Why is economic profit smaller than accounting profit? What are the three basic sources of economic profit? Classify each of the following according to those sources:

    a. A firm's profit from developing and patenting a new medication that greatly reduces cholesterol and thus diminishes the likelihood of heart disease and stroke

    b. A restaurant's profit that results from construction of a new highway past its door

    c. The profit received by a firm due to an unanticipated change in consumer tastes

11. Why is the distinction between insurable and uninsurable **LO** risks significant for the theory of profit? Carefully evaluate: "All economic profit can be traced to either uncertainty or the desire to avoid it." What are the major functions of economic profit?

12. Explain the absence of economic profit in a perfectly com- **LO** petitive, static economy. Realizing that the major function of profit is to allocate resources according to consumer preferences, describe the allocation of resources in such an economy.

INTERNET APPLICATION QUESTIONS

1. **What Are the Current Nominal and Real Interest Rates?** The real interest rate is the nominal rate less the rate of inflation. Assume the Consumer Price Index (CPI) is a proxy for the inflation rate and one-year Treasury Bill rates represent the nominal interest rate. Find the current CPI at the McConnell-Brue-Flynn-Barbiero Web site (Chapter 13), and then subtract it from the current one-year Treasury Bill rate. Repeat the process for the one-month Treasury Bills and the CPI rate of change for the past month. Is there a difference between the 1-month and the 12-month real interest rates? If so, why is there a difference?

CHAPTER 14

Natural Resource and Energy Economics

People like to consume goods and services. But to produce those goods and services, natural resources must be used up. Some natural resources—solar energy, forests, fisheries—are renewable and can potentially be exploited indefinitely. Other resources—oil, iron ore, coal—are in fixed supply and can be used only once. This chapter explores two issues in relation to our supplies of resources and energy. The first is whether we are likely to run out of resources in the near or even distant future and thereby face the possibility of either a drastic reduction in living standards or even, perhaps, the collapse of civilization as we know it. The second is how to best utilize and manage our resources so that we can maximize the benefits we receive from them both now and in the future. We begin the chapter by addressing the issue of whether we are about to run out of resources. We then turn to energy economics and natural resource economics, focusing on the incentive structures that help to promote conservation and sustainability.

14.1 | Resource Supplies: Doom or Boom?

Since the beginning of the Industrial Revolution in the late 18th century, a historically unprecedented increase has occurred in both population and living standards. The world's population has increased from 1 billion people in 1800 to about 6.6 billion today, and the average person living in Canada enjoys a standard of living at least 12 times higher than that of the average Canadian living in 1800. Stated slightly differently, there are both many more people alive today as well as much higher levels of consumption per person. These two factors mean that human beings are now consuming vastly more resources than before the Industrial Revolution both in absolute terms and in per capita terms. This fact has led many observers to wonder whether our current economic system and its high living standards are sustainable. In particular, will the availability of natural resources be sufficient to meet the growing demand for them?

A sensible response clearly involves looking at *both* resource demand and resource supply. We begin by examining human population growth, because larger populations mean greater demand for resources.

Population Growth

We can trace the debate over the sustainability of resources back to 1798, when an Anglican minister in England named Thomas Malthus published *An Essay on the Principle of Population.* In that essay, Malthus argued that human living standards could rise above subsistence levels only temporarily. Any temporary increase in living standards would cause people to have more children and thereby increase the population. With so many more people to feed, per capita living standards would be driven back down to subsistence levels.

Unfortunately for Malthus's theory—but fortunately for society—higher living standards have *not* produced higher birth rates. In fact, just the opposite has happened. Higher standards of living are associated with *lower* birth rates. Such rates are falling rapidly throughout the world, and the majority of the world's population is now living in countries that have birth rates lower than the **replacement rate** necessary to keep their respective populations from falling over time.

Table 14-1 lists the total fertility rates for 12 selected nations including Canada. The **total fertility rate** is the average number of children a woman is expected to have during her lifetime. Taking into account infant and child mortality, a total fertility rate of about 2.1 births per woman per lifetime is necessary to keep the population constant—1 child to replace the mother, 1 child to replace the father, and 0.1 extra children that can be expected to die before they are old enough to reproduce.

As you can see from Table 14-1, total fertility rates in many nations are well below the 2.1 rate necessary to keep the population stable over time. As a result, populations are expected to fall rapidly in many countries over the next few decades, with, for instance, the population of Russia expected to fall by about one-third from its current level of 143 million people to fewer than 100 million in 2050. And Russia is not alone. Thirty countries are expected to see their populations fall by at least 10 percent by 2050, and of these 13 are expected to experience a decline of at least 20 percent.

Worldwide, the precipitous fall of birth rates means that many **demographers** (scientists who study human populations) now expect the world's population to reach a peak of 9 billion people or fewer sometime around the middle of this century before beginning to fall, perhaps quite rapidly. For instance, if the worldwide total fertility rate declines to 1 birth per woman per lifetime (which is higher than Hong Kong's current rate of 0.95 per woman per lifetime) then each generation will be only half as large as the previous one because there will be only one child on average for every two parents. And even a rate of 1.3 births per woman per lifetime will reduce a country's population by half in just under 45 years.

The world's population increased so rapidly from 1800 to the present day because the higher living standards that arrive when a country begins to modernize bring with them much lower death rates. Before modernization happens, death rates are typically so high that women have to give birth to over six children per lifetime just to ensure that, on average, two will survive to adulthood. But once living standards begin to rise and modern medical care becomes available, death rates plummet so that nearly all children survive to adulthood. This causes a temporary population explosion because parents—initially unaware that such a revolutionary change in death rates has taken place—for a while keep having six or more children. The impression persists that they must have several children to ensure that at least two or more will survive to adulthood. The result is one or two generations of very rapid population growth until parents adjust to the new situation and reduce the number of children that they choose to have.

replacement rate
The birthrate necessary to keep the size of a population constant without relying on immigration.

total fertility rate
The average total number of children that a woman is expected to have during her lifetime.

demographers
Scientists who study trends in human populations.

TABLE 14·1	Total Fertility Rates for Selected Countries, 2007

Country	Total fertility rate
Australia	1.76
Canada	1.61
China	1.75
France	1.98
Germany	1.40
Hong Kong	0.98
Italy	1.29
Japan	1.23
Russia	1.39
South Korea	1.28
Sweden	1.66
United States	2.09

Source: *The World Factbook,* www.cia.gov. Data are 2007 estimates.

The overall world population is still increasing because many countries such as India and Indonesia began modernizing only relatively recently and are still in the transition phase where death rates have fallen but birth rates are still relatively high. Nevertheless, birth rates are falling rapidly nearly everywhere, which means the end of rapid population growth is at hand. Furthermore, because fertility rates tend to fall below the replacement rate as countries modernize, we can also expect total world population to begin to decline during the 21st century. This is a critical fact to keep in mind when considering whether we are likely to ever face a resource crisis: fewer people means fewer demands placed on society's scarce resources.

Demographers have been surprised, however, at just how low fertility rates have fallen and why they have fallen so far below the replacement rate in so many countries. The decline of fertility rates to such low levels is especially surprising given the fact that couples typically tell demographers they would like to have *at least* two children. Because this implies that most couples would prefer higher total fertility rates than we actually observe, it seems probable that there are social or economic factors constraining couples to have fewer children than they desire and causing total fertility rates to fall so low. Demographers have not yet reached agreement on which factors are most important, but possible candidates include changing attitudes toward religion, the much wider career opportunities available to women in modern economies, and the fact that having children has become very costly in modern societies. Indeed, children have been transformed from economic assets that could be put to work at an early age in agricultural societies into economic liabilities that are very costly to raise in modern societies where child labour is illegal and where children must attend school until adulthood. The Consider This box discusses current government efforts to raise birth rates by offering financial incentives to parents.

Resource Consumption per Person

Thomas Malthus's tradition of predicting a collapse in living standards has been carried on to this day by various individuals and groups. One well-reported prediction was made by Stanford University butterfly expert Paul Erlich. In his 1968 book *The Population Bomb*, he made the Malthusian prediction that the population would soon outstrip resources so that, "In the 1970s and 1980s hundreds of millions of people will starve to death in spite of any crash programs embarked upon now." Contrary to this prediction, no famines approaching these magnitudes materialized then and none appear likely today.

CONSIDER THIS | Can Governments Raise Birth Rates?

Low birth rates pose major problems for governments. Few children being born today means few workers will be available in coming decades to pay the taxes necessary for governments to keep their current promises regarding old-age pension programs. Too few young workers will be supporting too many elderly retirees.

Another potential problem is a lack of soldiers. With Russia's population expected to fall by one-third by mid-century, it will be much harder for the country to defend its borders. As a response, Russian President Vladimir Putin announced a new policy in 2006 that would pay any Russian woman who chooses to have a second child a bounty worth 250,000 rubles ($9280). In addition, the Russian government promised to double monthly child benefits in an effort to make having children less financially burdensome for parents.

Many other countries have experimented with similar policies. In 2004, France began offering its mothers a payment of 800 euros ($1200) for each child born, and Italy began offering a 1000 euro ($1500) payment for second children.

As far as demographers can tell, however, these and other policies aimed at raising birth rates (offering maternity leave, free day care, or other subsidies to mothers or their children) have not been able to generate any sustained increases in fertility levels in any country in which they have been attempted. Unless more effective policies are developed, it seems very likely that fertility rates will remain low and that, as a result, the total demand placed on our limited supplies of natural resources may never again face the problem of a rapidly expanding population.

One reason why Erlich's pessimism was not borne out was that the population growth rate slowed dramatically as living standards around the world rose. Another reason is that the long-run evidence indicates the supply of productive resources available to be made into goods and services has been increasing faster than the demand for those resources for at least 150 years. This is best seen by looking at Figure 14-1, which tracks *The Economist* magazine's commodity price index for the years 1850 to 2007. The index currently contains 25 important commodities including aluminum, copper, corn, rice, wheat, coffee, rubber, sugar, and soybeans. In earlier days, it included commodities such as candle wax, silk, and indigo, which were important at the time. The index also adjusts for inflation so that one can see how the real cost of commodities has evolved over time, and it is standardized so that the real price of commodities during the years 1845 to 1850 is given a value of 100.

As Figure 14-1 demonstrates, a dramatic long-run decline in real commodity prices has occurred. With the current value of the index at about 30, the real cost of buying commodities today is roughly 70 percent lower than it was in the initial 1845–1850 period. This means that commodity supplies have increased faster than commodity demands, since the only way that commodity prices could have fallen so much in the face of increasing demand is if the supply curve for commodities shifted outward and to the right faster than the demand curve.

A key point is that the long-run fall of commodity prices implies that commodity supplies have grown faster than the sum total of the two pressures that have acted over this time to increase

FIGURE 14-1   *The Economist* **Magazine's Commodity Price Index, 1850–2007**

The Economist magazine's commodity price index attempts to keep track of the prices of the commodities most common in international trade. It is adjusted for inflation and scaled so that commodity prices in the years 1845-1850 are set to an index value of 100. The figure shows that real commodity prices are volatile (vary considerably from year to year) but are now 70 percent lower than they were in the mid-19th century. This implies that commodity supplies have increased faster than commodity demands.

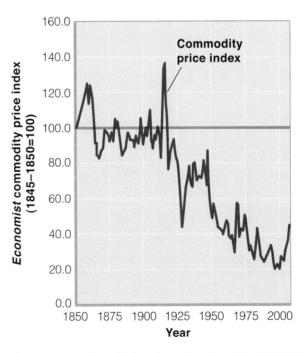

Source: *The Economist* magazine, www.economist.com. Inflation adjustments made using the GDP deflator for the United States calculated by the Bureau of Economic Analysis, www.bea.gov.

commodity demands. The first is the huge rise in the total number of people alive and therefore consuming resources (since 1850, the world's population has risen from 1.25 billion to 6.6 billion). The second is the huge rise in the amount of consumption *per person*. That is, more people are alive today than in 1850, and each person alive today is on average consuming several times more than the average person alive in 1850. Still, the long-run fall in commodities prices confirms that supplies have managed to grow fast enough to overcome both these demand-increasing pressures.

But will supplies be able to overcome these two pressures in the future? Prospects are hopeful. First, the rapid and continuing decline in birth rates means that the huge population increases that occurred during the 19th and 20th centuries are not likely to recur in the future. Indeed, we have seen that population decline has begun in several countries and it now seems likely that overall world population will begin to decline within this century. This trend will moderate future increases in the total demand for goods and services. Second, it is also the case that resource consumption *per person* (as distinct from goods and services consumption per person) in the past decade or so has either levelled off or declined in the richest countries such as Canada and the United States, which together currently consume the largest fraction of the world's resources.

That being said, there will very likely be substantial increases in resource demand for the next few decades as large parts of the world modernize and begin to consume as much per capita as the citizens of rich countries do today. For instance, per capita energy use in Canada in 2008 was over 400 million BTUs per person. If every person in the world used that much energy, total annual energy demand would be about 2,500 quadrillion BTUs, or about 4.5 times the 2006 world production of 480 quadrillion BTUs. One of the world's great economic challenges over the coming decades will be to supply the resources that will be demanded as living standards in poorer countries rise to rich-country levels. But because population growth rates are slowing and because per capita resource uses in rich countries have levelled off, we can now foresee a maximum total demand for resources even if living standards all over the world rise to rich-country levels.

Significant challenges, however, are still likely to appear in those places where local supplies of certain resources are extremely limited. Water, for instance, is a rare and precious commodity in many places including the Middle East and the American Southwest. Governments will have to work hard to ensure that the limited supplies of water in such areas are used efficiently and that disputes over water rights are settled peacefully. Along the same lines, resources are often produced in certain areas but consumed in others—with, for instance, one-quarter of the world's oil being produced in the Middle East but most of the demand for oil coming from Europe, North America, and East Asia. In such cases, institutions must be developed that can move such resources from the areas in which they originate to the areas in which they are used.

QUICK REVIEW

▶ Thomas Malthus and others have worried that increases in our demand for resources will outrun the supply of resources, but commodity prices have been falling for more than a century, indicating that supply has increased faster than demand.

▶ Because total fertility rates are very low and falling, population growth for the world will soon turn negative and thereby reduce the demand for natural resources.

▶ Per capita consumption of resources such as water, energy, and solids has either fallen or remained constant. If per capita consumption continues to stay the same or decrease while populations fall, total resource demand will fall—meaning that there is little chance that the demand for resources will threaten to use up the available supply of resources.

14.2 | Energy Economics

Energy economics studies how people deal with energy scarcity. This involves both supply and demand. In terms of energy supply, people are interested in attempting to find and exploit low-cost energy sources. But since energy is only one input into a production process, it is paradoxically often the case that the best energy source to use in a given situation is actually rather expensive—but still the best choice when other costs are taken into account. The economy therefore develops and exploits many different energy sources, from fossil fuels to nuclear power.

In terms of energy demand, the most interesting fact is that per capita energy usage has levelled off in recent years in developed countries. This fact implies that our economy has become increasingly efficient at using energy to produce goods and services.

Efficient Energy Use

While Canada has grown increasingly efficient at using energy, the same is true for other developed countries. An interesting fact about energy efficiency, however, is that it often involves using a mix of energy inputs, some of which are much more expensive than others. The best way to see why this is true is to examine electric power generation.

A typical electric plant has to serve tens of thousands of homes and businesses and is expected to deliver an uninterrupted supply of electricity 24 hours a day, seven days a week. This task is not easy. The problem is that massive changes in energy demand occur over the course of a day. Demand is low at night when people are sleeping, begins to rise rapidly in the morning as people wake up and turn on their lights, rises even more when they are at work, falls a bit as they commute home, rises back up a bit in the evening when they turn on their lights to deal with the darkness and their televisions to deal with their boredom, and finally collapses as they turn out their lights and go to sleep.

The problem for electric companies as they try to minimize the costs of providing for such large variations in demand is that the power plants with the lowest operating costs also have the highest fixed costs in terms of construction. For instance, large coal-fired plants can produce energy at a cost of about 4 cents per kilowatt hour. But they can do this only if they are built large enough to exploit economies of scale and then operated at full capacity. To see why this can be a problem, imagine that such a plant has a maximum generating capacity of 20 megawatts per hour but that its customers' peak afternoon demand for electricity is 25 megawatts per hour. One solution would be to build two 20-megawatt coal-fired plants. But that would be very wasteful given that such plants cost hundreds of millions of dollars to build, since while one was operating at full capacity (and hence minimum cost) the other would be producing only 5 megawatts of its 20 megawatt capacity.

The solution that electric companies employ is to use a mix of different types of generation technology. This turns out to be optimal because even though some electricity generation plants are very expensive in terms of operating costs, they have low fixed costs (that is, they are very inexpensive to build). Thus, the power company in our example might build one large coal-fired plant to generate 20 of the required 25 megawatts of energy at 4 cents per kilowatt hour, but would then build a small 5-megawatt natural gas generator to supply the rest. Such plants produce electricity at the much higher cost of 15 cents per kilowatt hour, but they are relatively inexpensive to build. As a result, this solution would save the electric company from having to build a second very expensive coal-fired plant that would wastefully operate well below its full capacity.

Running Out of Energy?

Some observers worry that we may soon run out of the energy needed to power our economy. Their fears are based largely on the possibility that the world may run out of oil sometime in the next century. It is the case, however, that there is no likelihood of running out of energy. If anything, running out of oil would not mean running out of energy—just running out of *cheap* energy.

Consider Table 14-2, which compares oil prices with the prices at which other energy sources become economically viable. For instance, biodiesel, a type of diesel fuel made from decomposed plant wastes, is so expensive to produce that it becomes economically viable (that is, less costly to produce than oil) only if oil costs $80 or more per barrel. On the other hand, ethanol made from corn costs less to produce and would be an economically viable alternative to oil even if the price of oil were only $60 per barrel.

The key point to gather from this table, however, is that even if we were to run out of oil, alternatives would quickly become available. At a price of $40 per barrel, vast reserves of energy derived from tar sands in Alberta, the conversion of natural gas and coal to liquid petroleum, and even ethanol derived from cheap Brazilian sugar cane become economically viable alternatives. At $50 per barrel, shale oil becomes a viable alternative. At $60 per barrel, corn-based ethanol becomes viable, and at $80 per barrel, so does biodiesel.

In fact, these prices can be thought of as a giant supply curve for energy, with rising energy prices leading to increased energy production. The result is that even if the supply of oil begins to dry up and oil prices consequently rise, other energy supplies will quickly be brought on line to fill the energy gap created by the decline in the amount of oil available. Also, the alternative prices listed in Table 14-2 are *current* alternative prices. As technologies improve, the costs of producing these alternatives are likely to fall and, as a result, the potential costs of replacing oil if it runs out will be even lower than suggested by the figures in the table. As a result, economists do not worry about running out of oil or, more generally, running out of energy. There is plenty of energy—the only question is price, and the impact of potentially increasing energy prices on the standard of living.

Finally, we need to acknowledge that energy sources differ not only with regard to their prices but also with regard to the extent of negative externalities they may generate. Negative externalities are costs—such as those associated with air pollution—that are transferred to society during the production process and therefore not reflected in product price. Such externalities need to be accounted for. Some energy sources are relatively "clean," creating little pollution or other externalities. Other sources currently are more problematic. For example, burning coal generates substantial particulate

---

| TABLE 14-2 | Oil Prices at Which Alternative Energy Sources Become Economically Viable |

Our economy is not totally dependent on oil because alternative fuels do exist. They are, however, more costly to produce than oil, which costs only about $20 per barrel to produce profitably. This table lists the oil price per barrel at which various more costly alternatives become economically viable.

Oil price ($U.S.) per barrel at which alternative is economically viable	Alternative fuel
$80	Bio-diesel
60	Corn-based ethanol*
50	Shale oil
40	Tar sands; Brazilian sugar cane–based ethanol; gas-to-liquids**; coal-to-liquids***
20	Conventional oil

Sources: Cambridge Energy Research Associates, www.cera.com; *The Economist*, April 22, 2006, www.economist.com.

* Excludes tax credits.

**Gas-to-liquid is economically viable at $40 if natural gas price is $2.50 or less per million BTUs.

***Coal-to-liquid is economically viable at $40 if coal price is $15 per ton or less.

and carbon dioxide emissions that can contribute to health problems and global warming. But a caution is needed here: At sufficiently high prices of electricity, coal burning can be both economical and clean. This is true because at sufficiently high electricity prices, the companies that burn coal to generate electricity are able to afford extensive expenditures on pollution reduction. Scrubbers can reduce soot from emissions and new technologies can capture and sequester carbon dioxide in underground storage. At sufficiently high energy prices, clean methods of producing energy are not confined to wind, solar, and other so-called alternative energy sources. We will say much more about externalities and the policies designed to reduce them in Chapter 15. (*Key Question 5*)

CONSIDER THIS | Turning Entrails (and nearly anything else) into Oil

It takes Mother Nature millions of years to apply the heat and pressure necessary to convert organic matter like dead plants and animals into oil. A company called Changing World Technologies can do the job in just 2 hours at a factory it opened in 2005 outside a turkey slaughterhouse in Carthage, Missouri.

Each day, 270 tons of discarded turkey parts (entrails, heads, feet, lungs, etc.) get converted into 500 barrels of fuel oil by means of a reaction tank that heats the debris to 500ºF while simultaneously pressurizing it to 600 pounds per square inch. The process replicates geologic pressures that normally take place in the Earth's crust, which break down the long chains of hydrocarbons found in plants and animals into the short chains of hydrocarbons that make up fossil fuels like methane, gasoline, and diesel. Even more amazing, the

reaction tank can gulp down any sort of organic debris—used tires, Styrofoam cups, sewage water, plastic car parts—and turn it into a grade of fuel oil that can be immediately sold to utility companies for use in electric generators or further refined into gasoline, diesel, and even hydrogen.

The factory produces the oil at a cost of $80 per barrel, which is about double the cost of buying similar oil produced the old-fashioned way (that is, by pumping it out of the ground after Mother Nature does the dirty work). But with a federal biofuel subsidy of $42 per barrel, the firm is able to make a modest profit and hopes that expanding the process to a much larger scale will allow it to drive the cost of the process down to only $30 per barrel—less than the mid-2009 market price of similar grades of oil produced the old-fashioned way.

QUICK REVIEW

- ▶ Energy efficiency has consistently improved so that more output can be produced for every unit of energy used by the economy.

- ▶ After taking the very different fixed costs of different electricity generating plants into account, utility companies find it efficient to use a variety of energy sources (coal, natural gas, nuclear) to deal with the large daily variations in energy demand.

- ▶ Even if we run out of oil, we will not run out of energy because there are many alternative sources of energy available. These alternatives are, however, more costly than oil so that if we were to run out of oil energy costs in the economy would most likely increase.

14.3 | Natural Resource Economics

net benefits
The total benefits of some activity or policy less the total costs of that activity or policy.

The major focus of natural resource economics is to design policies for extracting or harvesting a natural resource that will maximize the **net benefits** from doing so. The net benefits are simply the total dollar value of all benefits minus the total dollar value of all costs, so that a project's net benefit is equal to the dollar value of the gains or losses to be made. A key feature of such policies is that they take into account the fact that present and future decisions about how fast to extract or harvest a resource typically cannot be made independently. Taking more today means having less in the future and having more in the future is possible only by taking less today.

In applying this general rule, however, there are large differences between renewable natural resources and nonrenewable natural resources. **Renewable natural resources** include forests and wildlife that are capable of growing back, or renewing themselves, if they are harvested at moderate rates. This leaves open the possibility of enjoying their benefits in perpetuity. Solar energy, the atmosphere, the oceans, and aquifers are also considered renewable natural resources either because they will continue providing us with their benefits no matter what we do (as is the case with solar energy), or because if we manage them well we can continue to enjoy their benefits in perpetuity (as is the case with the atmosphere, the oceans, and aquifers). **Nonrenewable natural resources** include oil, coal, and metals that are either in actual fixed supply (like the metals found in the Earth's crust) or which are renewed so slowly as to be in virtual fixed supply when viewed from a human time perspective (as is the case with fossil fuels like oil and coal, which take millions of years to form out of decaying plants and animals).

The key to optimally managing both renewable and nonrenewable resources is designing incentive structures that prompt decision makers to consider not only the net benefits from using the resources under their control in the present but also the net benefits from conserving the resources under their control in the present in order to be able to use more of them in the future. Once these incentive structures are in place, decision makers can weigh the costs and benefits of present use against the costs and benefits of future use to determine the optimal allocation of the resource. The key tool used in weighing these alternatives is **present value,** which allows decision makers to sensibly compare the net benefits of potential present uses with the net benefits of potential future uses.

Using Present Values to Evaluate Future Possibilities

Natural resource economics studies the optimal use of our limited supplies of resources. It is the case, however, that decisions about optimal resource use typically involve choosing how resources will be exploited inter-temporally, or over time. For instance, suppose a poor country has just discovered it possesses a small oil field. Should the country pump this oil today, when it can make a profit of $50 per barrel, or should it wait five years given that the profit is then expected to be $60 per barrel due to lower production costs?

Answering this question requires consideration of the time value of money, discussed in Chapter 13. We need to compare $60 worth of money in 5 years with $50 worth of money today. Economists make this comparison by converting the future quantity of money (in this case $60) into a present-day equivalent measured in present-day money. That way it is possible to compare both quantities of money using the same unit of measurement, present-day dollars.

The formula for calculating the present value for any future sum of money (in this case, $60 in 5 years) is described in detail in Chapter 14 of *Macroeconomics*, but the intuition is simple. Suppose the current market rate of interest is 5 percent per year. How much money would a person have to save and invest today at 5 percent interest in order to end up with exactly $60 in five years? The correct answer turns out to be $47.01: if $47.01 is invested at an interest rate of 5 percent per year, it will grow into precisely $60 in five years. Stated slightly differently, $47.01 today can be thought of as being equivalent to $60 in five years because it is possible to transform $47.01 today into $60 in five years by simply investing it at the market rate of interest.

This fact is very important because it allows for a direct comparison of the benefits from the country's two possible courses of action. If it pumps its oil today, it will get $50 per barrel's worth of present-day dollars. But if it pumps its oil in 5 years and gets $60 per barrel at that time, it will get only $47.01 per barrel's worth of present-day dollars since the present value of $60 in 5 years is precisely $47.01 today. By measuring both possibilities in present-day dollars, it becomes obvious that the better choice of action would be for the country to pump its oil today since $50 worth of present-day money is obviously greater than $47.01 worth of present-day money.

renewable natural resources
Resources that are capable of renewing themselves if they are harvested at moderate rates.

nonrenewable natural resources
Resources that either are in actual fixed supply or that renew so slowly as to be in virtual fixed supply when viewed from a human time perspective.

present value
Today's value of some amount of money that is to be received sometime in the future.

The ability to calculate present values also allows decision makers to use cost–benefit analysis in situations where the costs and benefits happen at different points in time. For instance, suppose a forestry company is considering spending $1000 per hectare to plant seedlings that it hopes will grow into trees it will be able to harvest in 100 years. It expects the wood from the trees will be worth $125,000 per hectare in 100 years. Should it undertake this investment? No—at the current market interest rate of 5 percent per year, the present value of $125,000 in 100 years is only $950.56, which is less than the $1000 per hectare the firm would have to invest today to plant the seedlings. When both the benefits and costs of the project are measured in the same units (present-day dollars), it is clear that the project is a money loser and should be avoided.

More generally, the ability of policymakers to calculate present values and put present-day dollar values on future possibilities is vitally important because it helps to ensure that resources are allocated to their best possible uses over time. By making it possible for a decision maker to compare the costs and benefits of present use with the costs and benefits of future use, present-value calculations help to ensure a resource will be used at whatever point in time it will be most valuable.

This is especially important when it comes to conservation, because there is always a temptation to use up a resource as fast as possible in the present rather than conserving some or all of it for future use. By putting a present-day dollar value on the net benefits to be gained by conservation and future use, present-value calculations provide a financial incentive to make sure resources will be conserved for future use whenever doing so will generate higher net benefits than using them in the present. Indeed, a large part of natural resource economics focuses on nothing more than ensuring the net benefits that can be gained from conservation and future use are accounted for by the governments, companies, and individuals in charge of deciding when and how to use our limited supply of resources. When these future net benefits are properly accounted for, resource use tends to be conservative and sustainable; when they are not properly accounted for environmental devastation tends to take place, including—as we will discuss in detail below—deforestation and fisheries collapse.

Nonrenewable Resources

Nonrenewable resources like oil, coal, and metals must be mined or pumped from the ground before they can be used. Oil companies and mining companies specialize in the extraction of nonrenewable resources and attempt to make a profit from extracting and then selling the resources they mine or pump out of the ground. But because extraction is costly and because the price they will get on the market for their products is uncertain, profits are not guaranteed and such companies must plan their operations carefully if they hope to realize a profit.

We must note, however, that because an oil field or a mineral deposit is typically very large and will take many years to fully extract, an extraction company's goal of "maximizing profits" actually involves attempting to choose an extraction strategy that will maximize a *stream* of profits—both potential profits today as well as potential profits in the future. There is, of course, a trade-off. If the company extracts more today, its revenues today will be larger since it will have more product to sell today. On the other hand, more extraction today means less of the resource left in the ground for future extraction and, consequently, smaller future revenues since future extraction will necessarily be reduced. Indeed, every bit of resource that is extracted and sold today comes at the cost of not being able to extract it and sell it in the future. Natural resource economists refer to this cost as the **user cost** of extraction because current extraction and use means lower future extraction and use.

user cost
The cost to the user of extracting a resource; current extraction and use means lower future extraction and use.

Present Use versus Future Use

The concept of user cost is very helpful in showing how a resource extraction firm interested in maximizing its flow of profits over time will choose to behave in terms of how much it will choose to extract in the present as opposed to the future. To give a simple example, consider the case of a coal-mining company called Black Rock, which will have to shut down in two years when the company's

FIGURE 14-2 Choosing the Optimal Extraction Level

A firm that takes account only of current extraction costs, *EC*, will produce Q_0 units of output in the current period—that is, all units for which the market price *P* exceeds extraction costs, *EC*. If it also takes account of user cost (*UC*) and the fact that current output reduces future output, it will produce only Q_1 units of output—that is, only those units for which price exceeds the sum of extraction costs and user cost.

First-year quantity extracted

mine lease expires. Because the mine will close in two years, the mine's production can be thought of as taking place either during the current year or next year. Black Rock's problem is to figure out how much to mine this year in order to maximize its stream of profits.

To see how Black Rock's managers might think about the problem look at Figure 14-2, which shows the situation facing the company during the first year. Begin by noticing *P*, the market price at which Black Rock can sell each and every ton of coal that it extracts. The firm's managers will obviously want to take this price into consideration when deciding how much output to produce.

extraction costs
All costs associated with extracting a natural resource and readying it for sale.

Next, consider the company's production costs, which we will refer to as **extraction costs,** or *EC*, since this is an extraction company. The extraction costs include all costs associated with running the mine, digging out the coal, and preparing the coal for sale. Notice that the *EC* curve that represents extraction costs in Figure 14-2 is upward sloping to reflect the fact that the company's marginal extraction costs increase the more the company extracts because faster extraction involves having to rent or buy more equipment and having to either hire more workers or pay overtime to existing workers. Rapid extraction is costly, and the *EC* curve slopes upward to reflect this fact.

Next, consider how much output the firm's managers will choose to produce if they fail to take user cost into account. If the firm's managers ignore user cost, then they will choose to extract and sell Q_0 tons of coal (given by where the horizontal *P* line crosses the upward sloping *EC* line at point *A*). They will do this because for each and every ton of coal that is extracted up to Q_0, the market price at which it can be sold exceeds its extraction cost—making each of those tons of coal profitable to produce.

But, this analysis considers only potential first-year profits. None of those tons of coal *has* to be mined this year. Each could be left in the ground and mined during the second year. The question that Black Rock's managers have to ask is whether the company's total stream of profits would be increased by leaving some or all of those tons of coal in the ground this year to be mined and sold next year.

This question can be answered by taking account of user cost. Specifically, the company's managers can put a dollar amount on how much future profits are reduced by current extraction and then take that dollar amount into account when determining the optimal amount to extract this year. This process is best understood by looking once again at Figure 14-2. There, each ton of coal extracted this year is assumed to have a user cost of UC dollars per ton that is set equal to the present value of the profits the firm would earn if the extraction and sale of each ton of coal were delayed until the second year. Taking this user cost into account results in a total cost curve, or TC, that is exactly UC dollars higher than the extraction cost curve at every extraction level. This parallel upward shift reflects the fact that once the company takes user cost into account, its total costs must be equal to the sum of extraction costs and user cost. That is, $TC = EC + UC$.

If the firm's managers take user cost into account in this fashion, then they will choose to produce less output. In fact, they will choose to extract only Q_1 units of coal (given by where the horizontal P line crosses the upward sloping TC line at point B). They will produce exactly this much coal because for each and every ton of coal that is extracted up to Q_1, the market price at which it can be sold exceeds its total cost—including not only the current extraction cost but also the cost of forgone future profits, UC.

Another way to understand why Black Rock will limit its production to only Q_1 tons of coal is to realize that for every ton of coal up to Q_1, it is more profitable to extract during the current year than during the second year. This is best seen by looking at a particular ton of coal like Q_2. The profit that the firm can get by extracting Q_2 this year is equal to the difference between Q_2's extraction cost and the market price that it can fetch when it is sold. In terms of the figure, this first-year profit is equal to the length of the vertical red line that runs between the point on the EC curve above output level Q_2 and the horizontal P line.

Notice that the red line is longer than the vertical distance between the EC curve and the TC curve. This means that the first-year profit is greater than the present value of the second-year profit because the vertical distance between the EC curve and the TC curve is equal to UC, which is by definition the present value of the amount of profit the company would get if it delayed producing Q_2 until the second year. It is therefore clear that if the firm wants to maximize its profit, it should produce Q_2 during the first year rather than during the second year since the profit to be made by current production exceeds the present value of the profit to be made by second-year production.

FIGURE 14·3 An Increase in Expected Future Profits Leads to Less Current Extraction

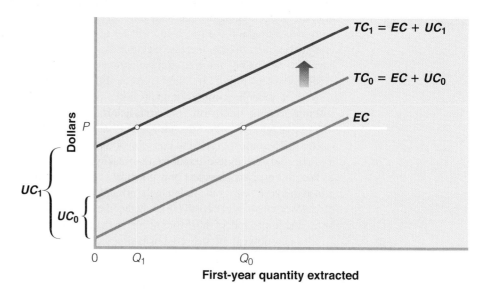

An increase in future profitability increases user cost from UC_0 to UC_1, thereby raising the total cost curve from TC_0 to TC_1. The firm responds by reducing current production from Q_0 to Q_1 in order to be able to extract more in the future and take advantage of the increase in future profitability.

This is not true for the tons of coal between output levels Q_1 and Q_0. For these tons of coal, the first-year profit—which is, as before, equal to the vertical distance between the EC curve and the horizontal P line—is less than UC, the present value of the second-year profit that can be obtained by delaying production until the second year. Consequently, the extraction of these units should be delayed until the second year.

The model presented in Figure 14-2 demonstrates that the goal of profit-maximizing extraction firms is not to simply mine coal or pump oil as fast as possible. Instead, they are interested in extracting resources at whatever rate will maximize their streams of profit over time. This incentive structure is very useful to society because it means that our limited supplies of nonrenewable resources will be conserved for future extraction and use if extraction firms expect that demand (and hence profits) in the future will be higher than they are today. This can be seen in Figure 14-3, where user cost has increased in the current period from UC_0 to UC_1 to reflect an increase in expected future profits. This increase in user cost causes Black Rock's total cost curve to shift up from $TC_0 = EC + UC_0$ to $TC_1 = EC + UC_1$. This shift, in turn, reduces the optimal amount of current extraction from Q_0 tons of coal to only Q_1 tons of coal.

More generally speaking, Black Rock's behaviour in this case demonstrates that under the right institutional structure profit-maximizing firms will extract resources efficiently over time, meaning that each unit of the resource will tend to be extracted when the gains from doing so are the greatest. *(Key Question 7)*

Incomplete Property Rights Lead to Excessive Present Use

We have just demonstrated that profit-maximizing extraction companies are very happy to decrease current extraction if they can benefit financially from doing so. In particular, they are willing to reduce current extraction if they have the ability to profit from the future extraction and sale of their product. Indeed, this type of financial situation gives them the incentive to conserve any and all resources that would be more profitably extracted in the future.

This pleasant result breaks down completely if there are market failures such as weak or uncertain property rights that do not allow extraction companies to profit from conserving resources for future use. For instance, look back at Figure 14-2 and consider how much Black Rock would produce if it were suddenly told that its lease would expire at the end of this year rather than at the end of next year. This would be the equivalent of having a user cost equal to zero because there would be no way for the company to profit in the future by reducing current extraction. As a result, the firm will ignore user cost and take into account only current extraction costs, EC. The result will be that it will extract and sell Q_0 tons of coal, more than the Q_1 tons that it would extract if it could profit from conservation.

QUICK REVIEW

▶ Because nonrenewable resources are finite, it is very important to allocate their limited supply efficiently between present and future uses.

▶ If resource extraction companies can benefit from both present and future extraction, they will limit current extraction to only those units that are more profitable to extract in the present rather than in the future. This conserves resources for future use.

▶ If resource users do not have any way of benefiting from the conservation of a resource, they will use too much of it in the present and not save enough of it for future use—even if future use would be more beneficial than present use.

14.4 | Renewable Resources

We just saw that under the right circumstances, extraction companies have a strong profit incentive to moderate their current extraction rates and conserve nonrenewable resources for future use. A similar incentive can also hold true for companies and individuals dealing with renewable resources like forests and wildlife. If property rights are structured properly, then decision makers will have an incentive to preserve resources and manage them on a sustainable basis, meaning they will harvest the resources slowly enough that the resources can always replenish themselves. This section discusses the economics of renewable resources as well as policies that promote the sustainable use of renewable resources. To keep things concrete, we focus on forests and then fisheries.

Forest Management

Forests provide many benefits including wildlife habitat, erosion prevention, oxygen production, recreation, and, of course, wood. In 2005, just under 4 billion hectares, or about 30 percent of the world's land area, was forested and about 225 million hectares, or about 20 percent of Canada's land area, was forested. The amount of land covered by forests is, however, growing in some places but declining in others. This fact is apparent in Global Perspective 14.1, which gives the average annual percentage change over the years 1990 to 2000 in the amount of forest-covered land in 12 selected countries as well as in the entire world.

14.1 | GLOBAL PERSPECTIVE

Average annual percentage change in the amount of land covered by forests, 1990–2000

Average annual percentage change in the amount of land covered by forests varies greatly by nation, as indicated below.

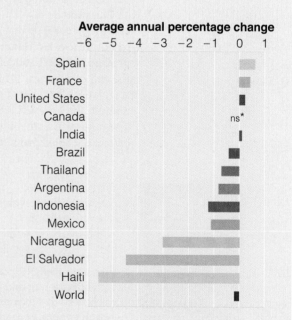

*No significant change

Source: *State of the World's Forests 2005*, United Nations Food and Agriculture Organization, www.fao.org

Economists believe that the large variation in growth rates seen in Global Perspective 14.1 is largely the result of differences in property rights. In certain areas including North America and Western Europe, forests are either private property or strictly regulated government property. In either case, individuals or institutions have an incentive to harvest their forests on a sustainable basis because they can benefit not just from cutting down the trees currently alive but also from keeping their forests going in order to reap the benefits they will give off in the future if they are managed on a sustainable basis.

By contrast, deforestation is proceeding rapidly in countries where property rights over forests are poorly enforced or nonexistent. Consider the situation facing competing loggers if nobody owns the property rights to a given forest: whoever chops down the forest first will be able to reap economic benefits. While nobody can have ownership or control over a living tree, anybody can establish a property right to it by chopping it down and bringing it to market. In such a situation, everybody has an incentive to chop down as many trees as fast as they can in order to get to them before anyone else. Sadly, nobody has an incentive to preserve trees for future use, because without enforceable property rights there is no way for person A to prevent person B from chopping down the trees that person A would like to preserve.

To reduce and hopefully eliminate nonsustainable logging, governments and international agencies have been taking increasingly strong steps to define and enforce property rights over forest areas. One major result is that in areas such as Canada, the United States, and Europe, where strong property rights over forests have been established, virtually all wood production is generated by commercially run forestry companies. These companies buy up large tracts of land on which they plant and harvest trees. Whenever a harvest takes place and the trees in a given area are chopped down, seedlings are planted to replace the felled trees, thereby replenishing the stock of trees. These companies are deeply concerned about the long-term sustainability of their operations and often plant trees in the expectation that it may be more than a century before they are harvested.

Optimal Forest Harvesting

In cases where the property rights to a forest are clear and enforceable (as they are in Canada), forest owners have a strong incentive to manage their forests on a sustainable basis because they can reap the long-term benefits that derive from current acts of conservation. A key part of their long-term planning is deciding how often to harvest and then replant their trees.

This is an interesting problem because a commercial forestry company that grows trees for lumber or paper production must take into consideration the fact that trees grow at different rates over the course of their lifetimes. Indeed, if the company plants an acre of land with seedlings and lets those seedlings grow into mature trees, the amount of wood contained in the trees at first grows rather slowly as the seedlings slowly grow into saplings, then grows quite quickly as the saplings mature into adult trees, and then tapers off as the trees reach their maximum adult sizes.

This growth pattern means that forestry companies have to think very carefully about when to harvest their trees. If they harvest and replant the acre of land when the trees are only 50 years old, they will miss out on the most rapid years of growth. On the other hand, there is not much point in letting the trees get much more than 100 years old before harvesting and replanting since at that age there is very little growth left in them. The result is that the forestry company will choose to harvest the trees and replant the land when the trees reach an age of somewhere between 50 and 100 years old. The precise age will be chosen to maximize firm profits and will be affected not only by the growth rate of trees but also by other factors including the cost of harvesting the trees and, of course, the market price of wood and how it is expected to vary over time.

The key point to keep in mind, however, is that forestry companies that have secure property rights over their trees do not harvest them as soon as possible. Instead, they shepherd their resource and harvest their trees only when it finally becomes more profitable to replace older, slow-growing trees with younger, fast-growing trees.

Optimal Fisheries Management

fishery
A stock of fish or other marine animal that is composed of a distinct group, for example Newfoundland cod, Pacific tuna, or Alaska crab.

A **fishery** is a stock of fish or other marine animal that can be thought of as a logically distinct group. A fishery is typically identified by location and species—for example, Newfoundland cod or Pacific salmon. The key difficulty with fishery management is that the only way to establish property rights over a fish swimming in the open ocean is to catch it and kill it. As long as the fish is alive and swimming in the open ocean, it belongs to nobody. But as soon as it is caught, it belongs to whoever catches it. This property rights system means that the only way to benefit economically from a fish is to catch it and thereby turn it into a private good, creating This creates an incentive for fishers to be very aggressive and try to out-fish each other since the only way for them to benefit from a particular fish is to catch it before someone else does. The natural result of this perverse incentive has been tremendous over-fishing that has caused many fisheries to collapse and which threatens many others with collapse as well. A **fishery collapse** happens when a fishery's population is sent into a rapid decline because fish are being harvested faster than they can reproduce. The speed of the decline depends on how much faster harvesting is than reproduction. In Atlantic Canada, for example, the landings of cod decreased by over 80 percent between 1992 and 2007 because the rapid declining cod population.

fishery collapse
A rapid decline in a fishery's population because the fish are being harvested faster than they can reproduce.

Overfishing and fishery collapse are now extremely common, so much so that worldwide stocks of large predatory fish like tuna, halibut, swordfish, and cod are believed to be 90 percent smaller than they were just 50 years ago. In addition, just 3 percent of world fisheries in 2003 were estimated to be underexploited while 76 percent were categorized as either fully exploited, overexploited, depleted, or (hopefully) recovering from depletion.

POLICIES TO LIMIT CATCH SIZES

Governments have tried several different polices to limit the amount of fish caught each year in order to try to prevent fisheries from collapsing and to lower annual catch sizes down to sustainable levels where the size of the catch does not exceed the fishery's ability to regenerate. Unfortunately, many of these policies not only fail to reduce catch sizes but also create perverse incentives that raise fishing costs because they do not stop the free-for-all nature of fishing whereby each fisher tries to catch as many fish as possible as fast as possible before anyone else can get to them.

total allowable catch (TAC)
A limit on the total number or tonnage of fish that fishers. collectively can harvest during a particular time period.

A policy that does work to reduce catch size goes by the acronym **TAC,** which stands for **total allowable catch.** Under this system, biologists determine the TAC for a given fishery, for instance 100,000 tons per year. Fishers can then fish until a total of 100,000 tons have been brought to shore. At that point, fishing is halted for the year.

This policy has the benefit of actually limiting the size of the catch to sustainable levels. But it still encourages an arms race between the fishers because each fisher wants to try to catch as many fish as possible before the TAC limit is reached. The result is that even under TACs, fishing costs rise because fishers buy bigger, faster boats as each one tires to fulfill as much of the overall TAC limit as possible.

individual transferable quota (ITQ)
A limit on the total number or tonnage of fish that individual fishers can harvest during a particular time period.

The catch-limiting system that economists prefer not only limits the total catch size but also eliminates the arms race between fishers that drives up costs. The system is based on the issuance of **individual transferable quotas (ITQ)**, which are individual catch size limits that specify that the holder of an ITQ has the right to harvest a given quantity of a given species during a given time period.

The individual catch sizes of all the ITQs that are issued for a given fishery during a given year add up to the fishery's overall TAC for the year so that they put a sustainable limit on the overall catch size. This preserves the fishery from overexploitation. But the fact that the ITQ quotas are *individual* also eliminates the need for an arms race. Because each fisher knows that he can take as long as he wants to catch his individual quota, he does not need a super-expensive, technologically sophisticated boat that is capable of hauling in massive amounts of fish in only a few days in order to beat his competitors to the punch.

This move toward smaller boats and more leisurely fishing greatly reduces fishing costs. But ITQs offer one more cost-saving benefit. They encourage all of the fishing to be done by the lowest-cost, most-efficient fishing vessels. This is true because ITQs are *tradable* fishing quotas, meaning that they can be sold and thereby traded to other fishers. As we will explain, market pressures will cause them to be sold to the fishers who can catch fish most efficiently, at the lowest possible cost.

To see how this works, imagine a situation in which the market price of tuna is $10 per ton but in which a fisherman named Sven can barely make a profit because his old, slow boat is so expensive it costs him $9 per ton to catch tuna. At that cost, if he does his own fishing and uses his ITQ quota of 1000 tons himself, he will make a profit of only $1000. At the same time, one of his neighbours, Tammy, has just bought a new, super-efficient ship that can harvest fish at the very low cost of $6 per ton. This difference in costs means that Sven and Tammy will both find it advantageous to negotiate the sale of Sven's ITQ to Tammy. Sven, for his part, would be happy to accept any price higher than $1000 since $1000 is the most that he can make if he does his own fishing. Suppose they agree on a price of $2 per ton or $2000 total. In such a case, both are better off. Sven is happy because he gets $2000 rather than the $1000 he would have earned if he had done his own fishing. Tammy is happy because she is about to make a tidy profit. The 1000 tons of tuna that she can now catch will bring $10,000 in revenues when sold at the market price of $10 per ton, while her costs of bringing in that catch will only be $8000 since it costs $6000 in fishing costs at $6 per ton to bring in the catch plus the $2000 she pays to Sven for the right to use his 1000-ton ITQ.

It remains to be seen, however, whether ITQs and other catch-reduction policies will be enough to save the world's fisheries. Since current international law allows countries to enforce ITQs and other conservation measures only within 200 miles of their shores, most of the world's oceans are a fishing free-for-all. Unless this changes and incentive structures are put in place to limit catch sizes in these areas, economic theory suggests that the fisheries in these areas will continue to decline as fishers compete to catch as many fish as possible as fast as possible before anyone else can get to them. *(Key Question 11)*

The **LAST WORD**   Is Economic Growth Bad for the Environment?

Measures of environmental quality are higher in richer countries.

Many people are deeply concerned that environmental degradation is an inevitable consequence of economic growth. Their concern is lent credence by sensational media events like oil and chemical spills and by the undisputable fact that modern chemistry and industry have created and released into the environment many toxic chemicals and substances that human beings did not even know how to make a couple of centuries ago.

Economists, however, tend to be rather positive about economic growth and its consequences for the environment. They feel this way because there is significant evidence that richer societies spend much more money on keeping their respective environments healthy than do poorer societies. Viewed from this perspective, economic growth and rising living standards are good for the environment because as societies get richer, they tend to spend more on things like reducing emissions from smokestacks, preventing the dumping of toxic chemicals, and insisting that sewage be purified before its water is returned to the environment. They also tend to institute better protections for sensitive ecosystems and engage in greater amounts of habitat preservation for endangered species.

But are these increasing expenditures on environmentally beneficial goods and services enough to overcome the massive increases in environmental harm that seem likely to accompany the enormous amounts of production and consumption in which rich societies engage? The empirical record suggests the answer is yes. The best evidence for this is given by the accompanying figure, in which each of 133 countries is represented by a point that indicates both its GDP per capita (measured on the horizontal axis using a logarithmic scale) and its year 2006 score on the Environmental Performance Index, or EPI.

This index is produced by researchers at Yale University and compares countries based on how well they are doing in terms of 16 environmental indicators, including atmospheric carbon emissions, measures of air and water quality, the degree of wilderness protection, energy efficiency, and measures of whether or not a country's fisheries and forests are being overexploited. Out of a maximum possible EPI score of 100, New Zealand and Sweden received the highest scores of, respectively, 88.0 and 87.8. Canada was ranked 8th with a score of 84.0, while the lowest ranked country, Niger, received a score of 25.7.

When EPI scores are combined with measures of GDP per person in the figure, an extremely strong pattern emerges: richer countries have higher EPI scores. In fact, the relationship between the two variables is so strong that 70 percent of the differences between countries in terms of EPI scores are explained by their differences in GDP per person. In addition, the logarithmic scale used on the horizontal axis allows us to look at the best-fit line drawn through the data and concluded that a tenfold increase in GDP per capita (from, for instance, $1000 to $10,000) is associated with a 20-point increase in EPI. The figure is therefore clear confirmation that economic growth and a healthy environment can not only go together, but that economic growth actually promotes a healthy environment by making people rich enough to pay for pollution-reduction

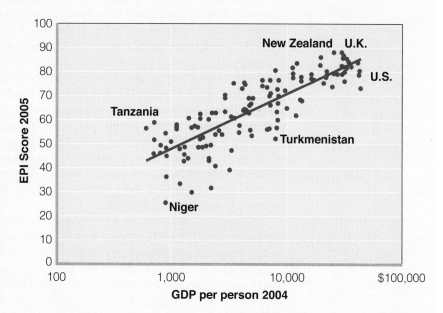

technologies that people living in poorer countries cannot afford.

Looking to the future, many economists are hopeful that economic growth and rising living standards will pay for the invention and implementation of new technologies that could make for an even cleaner environment. If the current pattern continues to hold, increased standards of living will lead to better environmental outcomes.

Note: The horizontal axis is measured using a logarithmic scale, so that each successive horizontal unit represents a tenfold increase in GDP per person. This is useful because it happens to be the case that the relationship between EPI and GDP per person is such that a tenfold increase in GDP per person is associated with a 20 point increase in EPI. Graphing the data using a logarithmic scale makes this relationship obvious.

Source: The EPI data are from the Yale Center for Environmental Law and Policy, www.yale.edu/epi/. The data on real GDP per person (at purchasing power parity) in 2004 are from *The World Factbook*, www.cia.gov.

Question

The figure in "The Last Word" section shows that a tenfold increase in a country's GDP per person is associated with about a 20-point increase in EPI. Do you think that this pattern can be extrapolated into the future? That is, could Canada (which currently has an EPI of 84.0) gain another 20 points if it increased its GDP per person by a factor of ten from its current level? (Hint: Consider diminishing returns.)

CHAPTER SUMMARY

14.1 ▸ RESOURCE SUPPLIES: DOOM OR BOOM?

- An increase in living standards has entailed using more resources to produce the larger amounts of goods and services currently consumed. This increase can be attributed to two factors: more resource use per person, and more people alive and consuming resources.

- The large increase in total resource use has led to a spirited debate about whether our high and rising living standards are sustainable. In particular, will our demand for resources soon outstrip the supply of resources? A proper answer to this question involves examining both the demand for resources as well as the supply of resources.

- A good way to examine the demand for resources is to think of total resource demand as being the product of the amount of resources used per person times the number of people alive; this makes it clear that we should be interested in both the total worldwide population as well as how much each person is consuming.

- World population growth is not only slowing but is actually turning negative in many countries, which may lead to less demand for resources in the future.

- In Canada and other rich countries resource use per person has either fallen or levelled off during the past several decades; the total demand for resources is likely to reach a peak in the relatively near future before falling over time as populations decline.

- Resource supplies are likely to grow faster than resource demands in the future.

14.2 ▸ ENERGY ECONOMICS

- Living standards can continue to rise without consuming more energy thanks to more efficient productive technologies that can produce more output using the same amount of energy input.

- Differences in fixed costs mean that a wide variety of energy sources are used in the economy despite the fact that some of these energy sources are much more costly than others.

14.3 ▸ NATURAL RESOURCE ECONOMICS

- Renewable natural resources like forests and fisheries as well as nonrenewable natural resources like oil and coal tend to be overused in the present unless institutions that provide resource users with a way to benefit from conservation are created and enforced.

14.4 ▸ RENEWABLE RESOURCES

- A lack of property rights leads to severe overfishing and an eventual collapse of the fishery. Governments can define property rights within their sovereign waters and impose limits on fishing. The best system involves combining total allowable catch (TAC) limits for a given fishery with individual transferable quota (ITQ) limits for individual fishers.

TERMS AND CONCEPTS

replacement rate, p. 328
total fertility rate, p. 328
demographers, p. 328
net benefits, p. 334
renewable natural resources, p. 335

nonrenewable natural resources, p. 335
present value, p. 335
user cost, p. 336
extraction costs, p. 337

fishery, p. 342
fishery collapse, p. 342
total allowable catch (TAC), p. 342
individual transferable quota (ITQ), p. 342

STUDY QUESTIONS

14.1 ▸ 1. Describe Thomas Malthus's theory of human reproduction. Does it make sense for some species—say bacteria or rabbits? What do you think makes humans different?

14.1 ▸ 2. Suppose the current (first) generation consists of 1 million people, half of whom are women. If the total fertility rate is 1.3 and the only way people die is of old age, how big will the fourth generation (the great-grandchildren) be? How much smaller (in percentage terms) is each generation than the previous generation? How much smaller (in percentage terms) is the fourth generation than the first generation? Are you surprised by how quickly the population declines?

LO▶14.1 3. Demographers have been very surprised that total fertility rates have fallen below 2.0, especially because most people in most countries tell pollsters they would like to have at least two children. Can you think of any possible economic factors that may be causing women in so many countries to average fewer than two children per lifetime? What about other social or political changes?

LO▶14.1 4. Resource consumption per person in Canada is either flat or falling, depending on the resource. Yet living standards are rising due to improvements in technology that allow more output to be produced for every unit of input used in production. What does this say about the likelihood of our running out of resources? Could we possibly maintain or improve our living standards even if the population were expected to rise in the future rather than fall?

LO▶14.2 5. **KEY QUESTION** Suppose you hear two people arguing about energy. One says we are running out of energy. The other counters that we are running out of *cheap* energy. Which person is correct, and why?

LO▶14.2 6. A community has a nighttime energy demand of 50 megawatts, but a peak daytime demand of 75 megawatts. It has the chance to build a 90 megawatt coal-fired plant that could easily supply all of its energy uses even at peak daytime demand. Should it proceed? Could there be lower-cost options? Explain.

LO▶14.3 7. **KEY QUESTION** Recall the model of nonrenewable resource extraction presented in Figure 14-2. Suppose a technological breakthrough means that extraction costs will fall in the future (but not in the present). What will this do to future profits and, therefore, to current user cost? Will current extraction increase or decrease? Compare this to a situation where future extraction costs remain unchanged but current extraction costs fall. In this situation, does current extraction increase or decrease? Does the firm's behaviour make sense in both situations? That is, does its response to the changes in production costs in each case maximize the firm's stream of profits over time?

LO▶14.3 8. If the current market price rises, does current extraction increase or decrease? What if the future market price rises? Do these changes in current extraction help to ensure the resource is extracted and used when it is most valuable?

9. **ADVANCED ANALYSIS** Suppose a government wants to reduce its economy's dependence on coal and decides as a result to tax coal-mining companies $1 per ton for every ton of coal they mine. Assuming that coal-mining companies treat this tax as an increase in extraction costs, what effect will the tax have on current extraction in the model used in Figure 14-2? Now, think one step ahead. Suppose that the tax will be in place forever, so that it will also affect extraction costs in the future. Will the tax increase or decrease user cost? Does this effect increase or decrease the change in current extraction caused by the shift of the *EC* curve? Given what you have found, should environmental taxes be temporary?

10. **ADVANCED ANALYSIS** User cost is equal to the present value of future profits in the model presented in Figure 14-2. Will the optimal quantity to mine in the present year increase or decrease if the market rate of interest rises? Does your result make any intuitive sense? (*Hint:* If interest rates are up, would you want to have more or less money right now to invest at the market rate of interest?)

11. **KEY QUESTION** Various cultures have come up with their own methods to limit catch size and prevent fishery collapse. In old Hawaii, certain fishing grounds near shore could be used only by certain individuals. And among lobster fishers in Maine, strict territorial rights are handed out so that only certain people can harvest lobsters in certain waters. Discuss specifically how these systems provide incentives for conservation. Then think about the enforcement of these property rights. Do you think similar systems could be successfully enforced for deep sea fishing, far off shore?

12. Aquaculture is the growing of fish, shrimp, and other seafood in enclosed cages or ponds. The cages and ponds not only keep the seafood from swimming away but also provide aquaculturalists with strong property rights over their animals. Does this provide a good incentive for low-cost production as compared with fishing in the open seas where there are few if any property rights?

INTERNET APPLICATION QUESTIONS @

1. **What Are Current Trends in Regulating the Consumption of Nonrenewable Resources?** Per capita consumption of water, energy, and solid objects like plastics and metals has been constant or falling in recent decades. The consumption of fossil fuels, however, is of special concern because of worries about global warming caused by the emission into the atmosphere of carbon dioxide and other so-called greenhouse gases. Go to the McConnell-Brue-Flynn-Barbiero Web site (Chapter 14) and scan the International Emissions Data links; click on the one that says Per Capita Emissions to open up an Excel spreadsheet that contains per capita carbon dioxide emissions for almost all countries for each of the previous 20 years or so. Have per capita carbon dioxide emissions in Canada, the United States, Japan, and France grown, stayed about the same, or fallen over the past couple of decades? Does it surprise you to learn that over this time period France has moved to generate more than 80 percent of its electricity from nuclear power, which emits no carbon dioxide?

2. **How Does Canada Compare with Other Countries in Its Birth Rate?** Go to the McConnell-Brue-Flynn-Barbiero Web site (Chapter 14) and link to the Index Mundi Web site, where you will find an interactive graph of fertility rates for all countries. Which countries have the lowest birth rates? the highest? Is Canada's birth rate lower or higher than the one reported for the United States?

PART 4 | Microeconomics of Government and International Economics

IN THIS CHAPTER YOU WILL LEARN:

15.1 How public goods are distinguished from private goods and the method for determining the optimal quantity of a public good

15.2 About externalities (spillover costs and benefits) and the methods to remedy them

15.3 How information failures can justify government interventions in some markets

15.4 About the peculiarities of the health care market

CHAPTER 15

Public Goods, Externalities, Information Asymmetries, and Market Failure

The economic activities of government affect your well-being every day. If you drive to work or to school, you are using publicly provided highways and streets. If you attend college or university, taxpayers subsidize your education. When you receive a cheque from your job, you see deductions for income taxes and social insurance taxes. Government antipollution laws affect the air you breathe. Laws requiring seat belts and motorcycle helmets and auto insurance are all government mandates.

This chapter examines *market failure*—a circumstance in which private markets do not bring about the allocation of resources that best satisfies society's wants. Where private markets fail, an economic role for government may arise. We want to examine that role as it relates to three types of market failure: public goods, externalities, and information asymmetries. Our discussion of externalities in turn facilitates a discussion of pollution, climate change, and health care.

Our discussion of the microeconomics of government continues in Chapter 16 with an analysis of potential government inefficiencies—called *government failure*—and then considers the economics of taxation.

15.1 | Public Goods

THE ROLE OF
GOVERNMENTS

To understand public goods, we first need to specify the characteristics of private goods.

Private Goods Characteristics

private good
A good or service that is individually consumed and that can be profitably provided by privately owned firms because they can exclude nonpayers from receiving the benefits.

We have seen that a full range of **private goods** are produced through the competitive market system. These are the goods offered for sale in stores, shops, and on the Internet. Examples include automobiles, clothing, personal computers, household appliances, and sporting goods. Private goods have two characteristics: rivalry and excludability.

- *Rivalry* (in consumption) means that when one person buys and consumes a product, it is not available for another person to buy and consume. When Adams purchases and drinks a bottle of mineral water, it is not available for Benson to purchase and consume.

- *Excludability* means that sellers can keep people who do not pay for a product from obtaining its benefits. Only people who are willing and able to pay the market price for bottles of mineral water can obtain these drinks and the benefits they confer.

Consumers fully express their personal demands for private goods in the market. If Adams likes bottled mineral water, that fact will be known by her desire to purchase the product. Other things equal, the higher the price of bottled water, the fewer bottles she will buy. So Adams's demand for bottled water will reflect an inverse relationship between the price of bottled water and the quantity of it demanded. This is simply *individual* demand, as described in Chapter 3.

The *market* demand for a private good is the horizontal summation of the individual demand schedules (review Figure 3-2). Suppose there are just two consumers in the market for bottled water and the price is $1 per bottle. If Adams will purchase 3 bottles and Benson will buy 2, the market demand will reflect that consumers demand 5 bottles at the $1 price. Similar summations of quantities demanded at other prices will generate the market demand schedule and curve.

Suppose the equilibrium price of bottled water is $1. Adams and Benson will buy a total of 5 bottles, and the sellers will obtain total revenue of $5 (= $1 × 5). If the sellers' cost per bottle is $0.80, their total cost will be $4 (= $0.80 × 5). So sellers charging $1 per bottle will obtain $5 of total revenue, incur $4 of total cost, and earn $1 of profits for the 5 bottles sold.

Because firms can profitably tap market demand for private goods, they will produce and offer them for sale. Consumers demand private goods, and profit-seeking suppliers produce goods that satisfy the demand. Consumers willing to pay the market price obtain the goods; nonpayers go without.

A competitive market not only makes private goods available to consumers but also allocates society's resources efficiently to the particular product. There is neither underproduction nor overproduction of the product.

Public Goods Characteristics

public good
A good or service that can be simultaneously consumed by everyone, and from which no one can be excluded, even if they don't pay for it.

Certain other goods and services—**public goods**—have the opposite characteristics of private goods. Public goods are distinguished by nonrivalry and non-excludability.

- *Nonrivalry* (in consumption) means that one person's consumption of a good does not preclude consumption of the good by others. Everyone can simultaneously obtain the benefit from a public good such as a global positioning system, national defence, street lighting, and environmental protection.

- *Non-excludability* means there is no effective way of excluding individuals from the benefit of the good once it comes into existence.

CONSIDER THIS | Art for Art's Sake

Suppose an enterprising sculptor creates a piece of art costing $600 and, with permission, places it in the town square. Also suppose that Jack gets $300 of enjoyment from the art and Diane gets $400. Sensing this enjoyment and hoping to make a profit, the sculptor approaches Jack for a donation equal to his satisfaction. Jack falsely says that, unfortunately, he does not particularly like the piece. The sculptor then tries

Diane, hoping to get $400 or so. Same deal: Diane professes not to like the piece either. Jack and Diane have become free riders. Although feeling a bit guilty, both reason that it makes no sense to pay for something when anyone can receive the benefits without paying for them. The artist is a quick learner; he vows never to try anything like that again.

free-rider problem
The inability of potential providers of an economically desirable but indivisible good or service to obtain payment from those who benefit, because the exclusion principle is not applicable.

These two characteristics create a **free-rider problem.** Once a producer has provided a public good, everyone, including nonpayers, can obtain the benefit. Most people do not voluntarily pay for something they can obtain for free!

With only free riders, the demand for a public good does not get expressed in the market. With no market demand, there is no potential for firms to tap the demand for revenues and profits. The free-rider problem makes it impossible for firms to gather resources and profitably provide the good. If society wants a public good, society will have to direct government to provide it. Government can finance the provision of such goods through taxation.

Optimal Quantity of a Public Good

@ MATH 15.1
The Optimal
Amount of
Public Good

If consumers need not reveal their true demand for a public good in the marketplace, how can society determine the optimal amount of that good? The answer is that the government has to try to estimate the demand for a public good through surveys or public votes. It can then compare the marginal benefit (MB) of an added unit of the good against the government's marginal cost (MC) of providing it. Adhering to the MB = MC rule, government can provide the "right"—meaning "efficient"—amount of the public good.

Demand for Public Goods

The demand for a public good is somewhat unusual. Suppose Adams and Benson are the only two people in the society, and their marginal willingness to pay for a public good, this time national defence, is as shown in columns 1, 2, and 3 in Table 15-1.

One person's consumption of a public good does not preclude consumption of the same good by others.

TABLE 15-1   Demand for a Public Good, Two Individuals

(1) Quantity of public good	(2) Adams's willingness to pay (price)		(3) Benson's willingness to pay (price)		(4) Collective willingness to pay (price)
1	$4	+	$5	=	$9
2	3	+	4	=	7
3	2	+	3	=	5
4	1	+	2	=	3
5	0	+	1	=	1

Notice that the schedules in Table 15-1 are demand schedules. Rather than depicting demand in the usual way—the quantity of a product someone is willing to buy at each possible price—these schedules show the price someone is willing to pay for the marginal unit of each possible quantity. That is, Adams is willing to pay $4 for the first unit of the public good, $3 for the second, $2 for the third, and so on.

Suppose the government produces one unit of this public good. Because of the non-excludability characteristic of a public good, Adams's consumption of the good does not preclude Benson from also consuming it, and vice versa. So both consume the good, and neither volunteers to pay for it. But from Table 15-1 we can find the amount these two people would be willing to pay, together. Columns 1 and 2 show that Adams would be willing to pay $4 for the first unit of the public good; columns 1 and 3 show that Benson would be willing to pay $5 for it. So the two people are jointly willing to pay $9 (= $4 + $5) for this unit.

For the second unit of the public good, the collective price they are willing to pay is $7 (= $3 from Adams plus $4 from Benson); for the third unit they will pay $5 (= $2 plus $3); and so on. By finding the collective willingness to pay for each additional unit (column 4), we can construct a collective demand schedule (a willingness-to-pay schedule) for the public good. Here, we are not adding the quantities demanded at each possible price as when we determine the market demand for a private good. Instead, we are adding *the prices that people are willing to pay for the last unit of the public good at each possible quantity demanded.*

Figure 15-1 shows the same adding procedure graphically, using the data from Table 15-1. Note that we sum Adams's and Benson's willingness-to-pay curves *vertically* to derive the collective willingness-to-pay curve (demand curve). The summing procedure is upward from the lower graph to the middle graph to the top (total) graph. For example, the height of the collective demand curve D_c at two units of output in the top graph is $7, the sum of the amounts that Adams and Benson are each willing to pay for the second unit (= $3 + $4). Likewise, the height of the collective demand curve at four units of the public good is $3 (= $1 + $2).

What does it mean in Figure 15-1a that, for example, Adams is willing to pay $3 for the second unit of the public good? It means that Adams expects to receive $3 of extra benefit or utility from that unit. And we know from the law of diminishing marginal utility that successive units of any good yield less and less added benefit. This is also true for public goods, explaining the downward slope of the willingness-to-pay curves of both Adams and Benson, and of the collective demand curve. These curves, in essence, are marginal benefit curves. *(Key Question 1)*

Comparing MB and MC

The supply curve for any good, private or public, is its marginal cost (MC) curve. Marginal cost rises as more of a good is produced. In the short run, government has fixed factors (public capital) with which to produce public goods such as national defence. As it adds more units of a variable factor (labour) to these fixed factors, total product eventually rises at a diminishing rate. That means that marginal product falls and marginal cost rises, explaining why curve S in Figure 15-1c slopes upward.

We can now determine the optimal quantity of the public good. The collective demand curve D_c in Figure 15-1c measures society's marginal benefit of each unit of this particular good. The supply curve S in that figure measures society's marginal cost of each unit. The optimal quantity of this public good occurs where marginal benefit equals marginal cost, or where the two curves intersect. In Figure 15-1c that point is three units of the public good, where the collective willingness to pay for the last (third) unit—the marginal benefit—just matches that unit's marginal cost ($5 = $5). As we saw in Chapter 1, equating marginal benefit and marginal cost efficiently allocates society's scarce resources. *(Key Question 2)*

WORKED PROBLEM 15.1
Optimal Amount of a Public Good

cost–benefit analysis
Comparing the marginal costs with the marginal benefits to decide whether to employ more or less resources in that project.

Cost–Benefit Analysis

The above example suggests a practical means, called **cost–benefit analysis,** for deciding whether to provide a particular public good and how much of it to provide. Like our example, cost–benefit analysis (or marginal benefit–marginal cost analysis) involves a comparison of marginal costs and marginal benefits.

FIGURE 15·1   The Optimal Amount of a Public Good

The collective demand curve for a public good, as shown by D_c in panel (c), is found by summing vertically the individual willingness-to-pay curves D_1 in panel (a) and D_2 in panel (b) of Adams and Benson, the only two people in the economy. The supply curve of the public good represented in panel (c) slopes upward and to the right, reflecting rising marginal costs. The optimal amount of the public good is three units, determined by the intersection of D_c and S. At that output, marginal benefit (reflected in the collective demand curve D_c) equals marginal cost (reflected in the supply curve S).

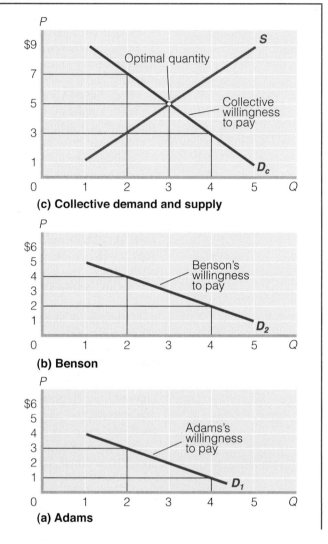

(c) Collective demand and supply

(b) Benson

(a) Adams

CONCEPT

Suppose the federal government is contemplating a highway construction plan. Because the economy's resources are limited, any decision to use more resources in the public sector will mean fewer resources for the private sector. There will be both a cost and a benefit. The cost is the loss of satisfaction resulting from the accompanying decline in the production of private goods; the benefit is the extra satisfaction resulting from the output of more public goods. Should the needed resources be shifted from the private to the public sector? The answer is yes if the benefit from the extra public goods exceeds the cost that results from having fewer private goods. The answer is no if the cost of the forgone private goods is greater than the benefit associated with the extra public goods.

ILLUSTRATION

Although a few private toll roads exist, highways clearly have public-good characteristics because the benefits are widely diffused and the exclusion principle is not easily applied. Should the federal government expand the national highway system? If so, what is the proper size or scope for the overall project?

Table 15-2 lists a series of increasingly costly highway projects: widening existing two-lane highways; building new two-lane highways; building new four-lane highways; building new six-lane

TABLE 15-2 — Cost–Benefit Analysis for a National Highway Construction Project, billions of dollars

(1) Plan	(2) Total cost of project	(3) Marginal cost	(4) Total benefit	(5) Marginal benefit	(6) Net benefit (4) – (2)
No new construction	$0		$0		$0
		$4		$5	
A: Widen existing highways	4		5		1
		6		8	
B: Two-lane highways	10		13		3
		8		10	
C: Four-lane highways	18		23		5
		10		3	
D: Six-lane highways	28		26		–2

highways. The extent to which government should undertake highway construction depends on the costs and benefits. The costs are largely the costs of constructing and maintaining the highways; the benefit is an improved flow of people and goods throughout the country.[1]

The table shows that total benefit (column 4) exceeds total cost (column 2) for plans A, B, and C, indicating that some highway construction is economically justifiable. We see this directly in column 6, where total costs (column 2) are subtracted from total annual benefits (column 4). Net benefits are positive for plans A, B, and C. Plan D is not justifiable because net benefits are negative.

But the question of optimal size or scope for this project remains. Comparing the marginal cost (the change in total cost) and the marginal benefit (the change in total benefit) relating to each plan determines the answer. In this case plan C (building new four-lane highways) is the best plan. For plans A and B, the marginal benefits exceed the marginal costs. Plan D's marginal cost ($10 billion) exceeds the marginal benefit ($3 billion) and therefore cannot be justified; it overallocates resources to the project. Plan C is closest to the optimum because its marginal benefit ($10 billion) still exceeds marginal cost ($8 billion) but approaches the MB = MC (or MC = MB) ideal.

MC = MB rule
For a government project, marginal benefit should equal marginal cost to produce maximum benefit to society.

This **marginal cost = marginal benefit rule** actually tells us which plan provides society with the maximum net benefit. You can confirm directly in column 6 that the maximum net benefit (= $5 billion) is associated with plan C.

Cost–benefit analysis shatters the myth that "economy in government" and "reduced government spending" are synonymous. "Economy" is concerned with using scarce resources efficiently. If the cost of a proposed government program exceeds its benefits, then the proposed public program should not be undertaken, but if the benefits exceed the cost, then it would be uneconomical or "wasteful" not to spend on that government program. Economy in government does not mean minimization of public spending; it means allocating resources between the private and public sectors to achieve maximum net benefit. *(Key Question 3)*

QUICK REVIEW

▸ Public goods are characterized by non-rivalry and non-excludability.

▸ The demand (marginal benefit) curve for a public good is found by vertically adding the prices all the members of society are willing to pay for the last unit of output at various output levels.

▸ The socially optimal amount of a public good is the amount at which the marginal cost and marginal benefit of the good are equal.

▸ Cost–benefit analysis is the method of evaluating alternative projects by comparing the marginal cost and marginal benefits and applying the MC = MB rule.

[1] Because the costs of public goods typically are immediate while the benefits often accrue over longer time periods, economists convert both costs and benefits to present values for comparison. Using present value properly accounts for the time value of money, discussed in Chapter 14.

15.2 | Externalities

externalities
Benefits or costs from
production or consumption
accruing without compensation
to nonbuyers and nonsellers
of the product.

Government not only produces public goods but also corrects for market failures called **externalities** or spillovers. An externality is a cost or a benefit accruing to an individual or group—a third party—that is *external* to a market transaction. An example of a spillover cost or a negative externality is the cost of breathing polluted air; an example of a spillover benefit or a positive externality is the benefit of having everyone else inoculated against some communicable disease. When there are negative externalities, there is an overproduction of the product and an overallocation of resources to this product. Conversely, underproduction and underallocation of resources result when positive externalities are present. We can demonstrate both graphically.

Negative Externalities

@ ORIGIN 15.1
Externalities

An example of a negative externality is the cost of breathing polluted air.

Figure 15-2a illustrates how negative externalities affect the allocation of resources. When producers shift some of their costs onto the community as externality costs, producers' marginal costs are lower than otherwise. So their supply curves do not include or capture all the costs associated with the production of their goods. A polluting producer's supply curve such as S in Figure 15-2a, therefore, understates the total cost of production. The firm's supply curve lies to the right of the full-cost supply curve, S_t, that would include the spillover cost. Through polluting and thus transferring cost to others in society, the firm enjoys lower production costs and has the supply curve S.

The outcome is shown in Figure 15-2a, where equilibrium output Q_e is larger than the optimal output Q_o. This means that resources are overallocated to the production of this commodity; too many units of it are produced.

Positive Externalities

Figure 15-2b shows the impact of positive externalities on resource allocation. When external benefits occur, the market demand curve D lies to the left of the full-benefits demand curve. That is, D does not include the external benefits of the product, whereas D_t does. Consider inoculations against a communicable disease. Watson and Weinberg benefit when they get vaccinated but so do their associates Singh and Anderson, who are less likely to contract the disease from them. The market demand curve reflects only the direct, private benefits to Watson and Weinberg; it does not reflect the external benefits—the positive externalities—to Singh and Anderson, which are included in D_t. The outcome is that the equilibrium output, Q_e, is less than the optimal output, Q_o. The market fails to produce enough vaccinations and resources are underallocated to this product.

FIGURE 15-2

Negative Externalities and Positive Externalities

Panel (a): With negative externalities borne by society, the producers' supply curve S is to the right of (below) the full-cost curve S_t. Consequently, the equilibrium output Q_e is greater than the optimal output Q_o. Panel (b): When positive externalities accrue to society, the market demand curve D is to the left of (below) the full-benefit demand curve D_t. As a result, the equilibrium output Q_e is less than the optimal output Q_o.

(a) Negative externalities

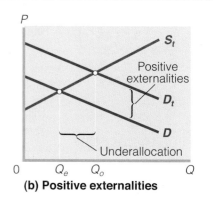

(b) Positive externalities

Economists have explored several approaches to the problems of negative externalities and positive externalities. Let's first look at situations where government intervention is not needed and then at some possible government solutions.

THE EFFECTIVENESS OF MARKETS

ORIGIN 15.2
Coase theorem

Coase theorem
The idea first stated by economist Ronald Coase that externalities may be resolved through private negotiations of the affected parties.

Individual Bargaining: Coase Theorem

In the **Coase theorem,** conceived by economist Ronald Coase at the University of Chicago, government is not needed to remedy external costs or benefits where (1) property ownership is clearly defined, (2) the number of people involved is small, and (3) bargaining costs are negligible. Under these circumstances the government should confine its role to encouraging bargaining between affected individuals or groups. Because the economic self-interests of the parties are at stake, bargaining will enable them to find a mutually acceptable solution to the externality problem.

EXAMPLE OF THE COASE THEOREM

Suppose the owner of a large parcel of forest land is considering a plan to clear-cut (totally level) hundreds of hectares of mature fir trees. The complication is that the forest surrounds a lake with a popular resort on its shore. The resort is on land it owns. The unspoiled beauty of the general area attracts vacationers from all over the nation to the resort, and the resort owner is against the clear-cutting. Should provincial or municipal government intervene to allow or prevent the tree cutting?

According to the Coase theorem, the forest owner and the resort owner can resolve this situation without government intervention. As long as one of the parties to the dispute has property rights to what is at issue, an incentive will exist for both parties to negotiate a solution acceptable to each. In our example, the owner of the timberland holds the property rights to the land to be logged and thus has the right to clear-cut it. The owner of the resort, therefore, has an economic incentive to negotiate with the forest owner to reduce the logging impact. Excessive logging of the forest surrounding the resort will reduce tourism and revenues to the resort owner.

What is the economic incentive to the forest owner to negotiate with the resort owner? The answer draws directly on the idea of opportunity cost. One cost incurred in logging the forest is the forgone payment that the forest owner could obtain from the resort owner for agreeing not to clear-cut the fir trees. The resort owner might be willing to make a lump-sum or annual payment to the owner of the forest to avoid or minimize the negative externality. Or perhaps the resort owner might be willing to buy the forested land to prevent the logging. As viewed by the forest owner, a payment for not clear-cutting or a purchase price above the market value of the land is an opportunity cost of logging the land.

It is likely that both parties would regard a negotiated agreement as better than clear-cutting the firs.

LIMITATIONS

Unfortunately, many externalities involve large numbers of affected parties, high bargaining costs, and community property such as air and water. In such situations private bargaining often does not work. As an example, the climate change problem affects billions of people in many nations. The vast number of affected parties could not individually negotiate an agreement to remedy this problem. Instead, they must rely on their governments to represent the billions of affected parties and find an acceptable solution. We discuss some of these potential solutions later in this chapter.

Liability Rules and Lawsuits

Although private negotiation may not be a realistic solution to many externality problems, clearly established property rights may help in another way. The government has erected a framework of laws that define private property and protect it from damage done by other parties. Those laws, and the damage recovery system to which they give rise, permit parties suffering negative externalities to sue for compensation.

Suppose the Ajax Degreaser Company regularly dumps leaky barrels containing solvents into a nearby canyon owned by Bar Q Ranch. Bar Q eventually discovers this dumpsite and, after tracing the drums to Ajax, immediately contacts its lawyer. Soon after, Bar Q sues Ajax. If Ajax loses the case, it will have to pay for the cleanup, but it may also have to pay Bar Q additional damages for ruining its property.

Clearly defined property rights and government liability laws thus help remedy some externality problems. They do so directly by forcing the perpetrator of the harmful externality to pay damages to those injured. They do so indirectly by discouraging firms and individuals from generating negative externalities for fear of being sued. It is not surprising, then, that many externalities do not involve private property but rather property held in common by society. It is the public bodies of water, the public lands, and the public air, where ownership is less clear, that often bear the brunt of negative externalities.

Government Intervention

Government intervention may be needed to achieve economic efficiency when externalities affect large numbers of people or when community interests are at stake. Government can use direct controls and taxes to counter negative externalities; government may provide subsidies or public goods to deal with positive externalities.

DIRECT CONTROLS

The direct way to reduce negative externalities from a certain activity is to pass legislation limiting that activity. Such direct controls force the offending firms to incur the actual costs of the offending activity. To date, this approach has dominated public policy in Canada. Historically, direct controls in the form of uniform emissions standards—limits on allowable pollution—have dominated Canadian air pollution policy. Clean air legislation forces factories, cars, and businesses to install "maximum achievable control technology" to reduce emissions. Clean-water legislation limits the amount of heavy metals, detergents, and other pollutants firms can discharge into rivers and bays. Toxic-waste laws dictate special procedures and dump sites for disposing of contaminated soil and solvents. Violating these laws means fines and, in some cases, imprisonment.

FIGURE 15-3   **Correcting for Negative Externalities**

Panel (a): Negative externalities result in an overallocation of resources. Panel (b): Government can correct this overallocation in two ways: (1) using direct controls, which would shift the supply curve from S to S_t and reduce output from Q_e to Q_o, or (2) imposing a specific tax T, which would also shift the supply curve from S to S_t, eliminating the overallocation of resources.

(a) Negative externalities

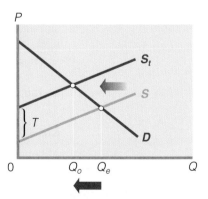

(b) Correcting the overallocation of resources via direct controls or via a tax

Direct controls raise the marginal cost of production because the firms must operate and maintain pollution-control equipment. The supply curve S in Figure 15-3b, which does not reflect the external costs, shifts leftward (upward) to the full-cost supply curve, S_t. Product price increases, equilibrium output falls from Q_e to Q_o, and the initial overallocation of resources shown in Figure 15-3a is corrected.

SPECIFIC TAXES

A second policy approach to negative externalities is for government to levy taxes or charges specifically on the related good. For example, the government has placed a manufacturing tax on CFCs, which deplete the stratospheric ozone layer protecting the Earth from excessive solar ultraviolet radiation. Facing such a tax, manufacturers must decide whether to pay the tax or expend additional funds to purchase or develop substitute products. In either case, the tax raises the marginal cost of producing CFCs, shifting the private supply curve for this product leftward.

In Figure 15-3b, a tax equal to T per unit increases the firm's marginal cost, shifting the supply curve from S to S_t. The equilibrium price rises and the equilibrium output declines from Q_e to the economically efficient level Q_o. The tax thus eliminates the initial overallocation of resources.

SUBSIDIES AND GOVERNMENT PROVISION

Where positive externalities are large and diffuse, as in our earlier example of inoculations, government has three options for correcting the underallocation of resources:

1. **Subsidies to Buyers** Figure 15-4a shows the supply–demand situation for positive externalities. Government could correct the underallocation of resources, for example to inoculations, by subsidizing consumers of the product; it could give each new mother a discount coupon to be used to obtain a series of inoculations for her child. The coupon would reduce the price to the mother by, say, 50 percent. As shown in Figure 15-4b, this program would shift the demand curve for inoculations from too-low D to the appropriate D_t. The number of inoculations would rise from Q_e to the optimal Q_o, eliminating the underallocation of resources shown in Figure 15-4a.

FIGURE 15·4 ## Correcting for Positive Externalities

Panel (a): Positive externalities result in an underallocation of resources. Panel (b): This underallocation can be corrected by a subsidy to consumers, which shifts market demand from D to D_t and increases output from Q_e to Q_o. Panel (c): Alternatively, the underallocation can be eliminated by providing producers with a subsidy of U, which shifts their supply curve from S_t to S'_t, increasing output from Q_e to Q_o.

(a) Positive externalities

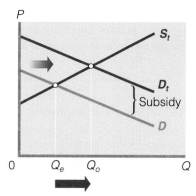

(b) Correcting the underallocation of resources via a subsidy to consumers

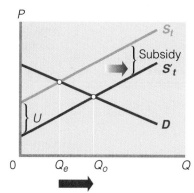

(c) Correcting the underallocation of resources via a subsidy to producers

2. **Subsidies to Producers**   A subsidy to producers is a specific tax in reverse. Taxes impose an extra cost on producers, while subsidies reduce producers' costs. As shown in Figure 15-4c, a subsidy of U per inoculation to physicians and medical clinics would reduce their marginal costs and shift their supply curve rightward from S_t to S'_t. The output of inoculations would increase from Q_e to the optimal level Q_o, correcting the underallocation of resources shown in Figure 15-4a.

3. **Government Provision**   Finally, where positive externalities are large, the government may decide to provide the product as a public good. The Canadian government largely eradicated the crippling disease polio by administering free vaccines to all children. India ended smallpox by paying people in rural areas to come to public clinics to have their children vaccinated. *(Key Question 4)*

A Market-Based Approach to Negative Externalities

Another approach to negative externalities involves the creation of a market for externality rights. But before describing that approach, we first need to understand the **tragedy of the commons.**

tragedy of the commons
Air, water, and public land rights are held in common by society and freely available, so no incentive exists to maintain or use them carefully; the result is overuse, degradation, and pollution.

THE TRAGEDY OF THE COMMONS

The air, rivers, lakes, oceans, and public lands, such as parks and streets, are prone to being polluted because the rights to use those resources are held in common by society. No private individual or institution has an incentive to maintain the purity or quality of such resources.

We maintain the property we own—we paint and repair our homes periodically, for example—in part because we will recoup the value of these improvements at the time of sale. But as long as rights to air, water, and certain land resources are commonly held and are freely available, no incentive exists to maintain them or use them carefully. As a result, these natural resources are overused or polluted. For example, a common pasture in which anyone can graze cattle will quickly be overgrazed, because each rancher has an incentive to graze as many cattle as possible. Similarly, manufacturers will choose to dump waste chemicals into rivers and lakes rather than pay for proper disposal.

The problem is mainly one of incentives. There is no incentive to incur internal costs associated with reducing or eliminating pollution when those costs can be transferred externally to society. Each person and company reasons that their individual contribution to pollution is so small that it has little or no overall consequence. But their actions, multiplied by hundreds, thousands, or millions, overwhelm the absorptive capacity of the common resources. Society ends up with a degradation or pollution problem.

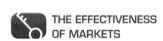
THE EFFECTIVENESS
OF MARKETS

market for externality rights
A market in which firms can buy rights to discharge pollutants.

A MARKET FOR EXTERNALITY RIGHTS

A novel policy approach to negative externalities—one that is market oriented—is the idea that the government can create a **market for externality rights.** We confine our discussion to pollution, although this same approach can be used with other externalities.

OPERATION OF THE MARKET

In this market-based approach—commonly called a *cap-and-trade* program—an appropriate pollution-control agency determines the amount of pollutants that firms can discharge into the water or air of a specific region annually while maintaining the water or air quality at some acceptable level. Suppose the agency decides that 500 tonnes of pollutants can be discharged into Metropolitan Lake and "recycled" by nature each year. Then 500 pollution rights, each entitling the owner to dump one tonne of pollutants into the lake in one year, are made available for sale to producers each year. The supply of these pollution rights is fixed and, therefore, perfectly inelastic, as shown in Figure 15-5.

The demand for pollution rights, represented by D_{2010} in the figure, is the same downsloping form as the demand for any other input. At higher prices there is less pollution, as polluters either stop polluting or pollute less by acquiring pollution-abatement equipment. An equilibrium market price

FIGURE 15-5 **FIGURE 15-5**   **A Market for Pollution Rights**

The supply of pollution rights, *S*, is set by the government, which determines that a specific body of water can safely recycle 500 tonnes of waste. In 2010, the demand for pollution rights is D_{2010} and the one-tonne price is $100. The quantity of pollution is 500 tonnes, not the 750 tonnes it would have been without the pollution rights. Over time, the demand for pollution rights increases to D_{2020} and the one-tonne price rises to $200. But the amount of pollution stays at 500 tonnes, rather than rising to 1000 tonnes.

for pollution rights, here $100, will be determined at which the environment-preserving quantity of pollution rights is rationed to polluters. Figure 15-5 shows that if the use of the lake as a dumpsite for pollutants were free, 750 tonnes of pollutants would be discharged into the lake; it would be overconsumed, or polluted, in the amount of 250 tonnes.

Over time, as human and business populations expand, demand will increase, as from D_{2010} to D_{2020}. Without a market for pollution rights, pollution in 2020 would be 1000 tonnes, 500 tonnes beyond what can be assimilated by nature. With the market for pollution rights, the price would rise from $100 to $200, and the amount of pollutants would remain at 500 tonnes—the amount the lake can recycle.

ADVANTAGES

This scheme has several advantages over direct controls, the most important of which is that it reduces society's costs by allowing pollution rights to be bought and sold. This trading of pollution rights is the "trade" portion of the "cap-and-trade" terminology given to this type of scheme. Let's see how this cost reduction works. Assume that the present equilibrium price of pollution rights is $100, as shown by the intersection of the supply curve and demand curve (2010) in Figure 15-5. Next, suppose the pollution in question is some specific noxious discharge into Metropolitan Lake. Suppose it costs Acme Pulp Mill $20 a year to reduce this pollution by one tonne, while it costs Zemo Chemicals $8000 a year to accomplish the same one-tonne reduction. Also assume that Zemo wants to expand production, but doing so will increase its pollution discharge by one tonne.

Without a market for pollution rights, Zemo would have to use $8000 of society's scarce resources to keep the one-tonne pollution discharge from occurring. But with a market for pollution rights, Zemo has a better option: it buys one tonne of pollution rights for the $100 price shown in Figure 15-5. Acme is willing to sell Zemo one tonne of pollution rights for $100 because that amount is more than Acme's $20 cost of reducing its pollution by one tonne. Zemo increases its discharge by one tonne; Acme reduces its discharge by one tonne. Zemo benefits (by $8000 – $100), Acme benefits (by $100 – $20), and society benefits (by $8000 – $20). Rather than using $8000 of its scarce resources to hold the discharge at the specified level, society uses only $20 of those resources. Cap-and-trade programs, with pollution rights, thus decrease the cost of reducing pollution.

Market-based plans have other advantages. Potential polluters have a monetary incentive not to pollute because they must pay for the rights to discharge effluent. Conservation groups can fight pollution by buying up and withholding pollution rights, thereby reducing pollution below

TABLE 15-3	Methods for Dealing with Externalities	
Problem	**Resource allocation outcome**	**Ways to correct externalities**
Negative externalities (spillover costs)	Overproduction of output therefore overallocation	1. Individual bargaining 2. Liability rules and lawsuits 3. Tax on producers 4. Direct controls 5. Market for externality rights
Positive externalities (spillover benefits)	Underproduction of output therefore underallocation	1. Individual bargaining 2. Subsidy to consumers 3. Subsidy to producers 4. Government provision

governmentally determined standards. As the demand for pollution rights increases over time, the growing revenue from the sale of a fixed quantity of pollution rights could be devoted to environmental improvement. At the same time, the rising price of pollution rights stimulates the search for improved pollution-control techniques.

Table 15-3 reviews the major methods for correcting externalities.

Society's Optimal Amount of Externality Reduction

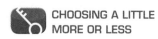 **CHOOSING A LITTLE MORE OR LESS**

Negative externalities such as pollution reduce the utility of those affected. These spillovers are not economic goods but economic "bads." If something is bad, shouldn't society eliminate it? Why should society allow firms or municipalities to discharge *any* impure waste into public waterways or to emit *any* pollution into the air?

Reducing a negative externality has a price. Society must decide how much of a reduction it wants to buy. Eliminating pollution entirely might not be desirable, even if it were technologically feasible. Because of the law of diminishing returns, cleaning up the last 10 percent of pollutants from an industrial smokestack is normally far more costly than cleaning up the prior 10 percent.

The marginal cost (MC) to the firm and hence to society—the opportunity cost of the extra resources used—rises as pollution is reduced further. At some point MC may rise so high that it exceeds society's marginal benefit (MB) of further pollution abatement (reduction). Additional actions to reduce pollution will therefore lower society's well-being; total cost will rise more than total benefit.

MC, MB, AND EQUILIBRIUM QUANTITY

Figure 15-6 shows both the rising marginal cost curve, MC, for pollution reduction and the downsloping marginal benefit curve, MB, for this outcome. MB slopes downward because of the law of diminishing marginal utility: the more pollution reduction society accomplishes, the lower the utility (and benefit) of the next unit of pollution reduction.

optimal reduction of an externality
The point at which society's marginal cost and marginal benefit of reducing that externality are equal.

The **optimal reduction of an externality** occurs when society's marginal cost and marginal benefit of reducing that externality are equal (MC = MB). In Figure 15-6 this optimal amount of pollution abatement is Q_1 units. When MB exceeds MC, additional abatement moves society toward economic efficiency; the added benefit of cleaner air or water exceeds the benefit of any alternative use of the required resources. When MC exceeds MB, additional abatement reduces

| FIGURE 15-6 | Money Facilitates Trade when Wants Do Not Coincide |

The optimal amount of externality reduction—in this case, pollution abatement—occurs at Q_1, where society's marginal cost MC and marginal benefit MB of reducing the spillover are equal.

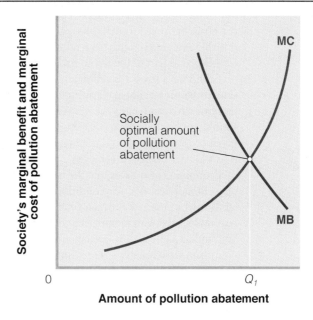

economic efficiency; there would be greater benefits from using resources in some other way than to further reduce pollution.

In reality, it is difficult to measure the marginal costs and benefits of pollution control. Nevertheless, Figure 15-6 demonstrates that some pollution may be economically efficient not because pollution is desirable but because beyond some level of control, further abatement may reduce our net well-being. *(Key Question 7)*

Climate Change

climate-change problem
The problem of rising world temperatures that most climate experts believe are caused in part by increased carbon dioxide and other greenhouse gases.

Canada has made significant progress in cleaning its air. But significant air pollution problems remain, including the controversial **climate-change problem.** The Earth's surface has warmed over the last century, with acceleration of warming during the last two decades. Some of this surface warming may simply reflect natural fluctuations of the Earth's warming and cooling, but the balance of scientific evidence suggests that human activity is a contributing factor. According to various international study groups, carbon dioxide and other gas emissions from factories, power plants, and automobiles are accumulating in the atmosphere and creating a greenhouse effect.

Because of the greenhouse effect, average temperatures are predicted to rise by 1 to 3 degrees Celsius over the next 50 years and 2 to 7 degrees by the year 3000. Although there is significant regional variation, scientist say many parts of the world will experience noticeable climatic changes. Rainfall will increase, rainfall patterns will change, and ocean level will rise. Snow accumulations will decline in some regions and rise in others. More violent storms, such as tornadoes, typhoons, and hurricanes, may occur in some regions. Global Perspective 15.1 lists carbon dioxide emissions on a per capita basis for selected nations.

The world's nations have responded to the climate-change threat collectively and individually. In the Kyoto Protocol of 1997, the industrially advanced nations agreed to cut their greenhouse gas emissions 6 to 8 percent below 1990 levels by 2012. Canada committed to a 6 percent reduction below 1990 levels by 2012. Since 1997, all signatory nations except the United States have ratified the Kyoto agreement, although few are likely to meet the 2012 goals. The Canadian government ratified the Kyoto Protocol in 2002. Many contentious issues remain to be resolved through further meetings and negotiations. For example, to what extent should developing nations such as China and India, currently exempt from the limits, participate in reducing emissions? China is currently one of the largest total emitters of carbon dioxide and other greenhouse gases. Should all industrial countries be forced to make, say, at least half their agreed reduction at home, rather than buying tradable emissions credits from other nations and making no reductions at home? Such credits were established as part of the Kyoto Protocol.

Economists stress that climate-change policies that reduce greenhouse gas emissions and thus slow or eliminate global warming create costs as well as benefits. It is imperative to consider the marginal costs and marginal benefits carefully when making policy decisions. Greenhouse gas limits should not be so stringent that they end up costing society more than the value of the benefits they produce. But limits should not be so lenient that society forgoes substantial potential benefits that it would have otherwise achieved.

Economists also stress that the market mechanism will make appropriate adjustments based on new climatic realities. Air conditioner sales will rise; snow shovel sales will fall. Some agricultural lands will be deserted; others farther north will be cultivated. Nevertheless, the *transition costs*—the costs associated with making economic adjustments—of global warming will undoubtedly be very high unless some actions are taken to reduce greenhouse gases. But industrial economies are built on carbon-based energy sources, so the costs of reducing such gases are also quite high. The relevant question from the economic perspective becomes: Will it be less costly for society to reduce greenhouse gas emissions or simply to try to mitigate their effects? No easy answer exists for this question. Some yet-unknown combination of reduction and mitigation may in fact turn out to be optimal.

If the federal government decides to aggressively reduce carbon emissions, what general policies are available to it? Our prior discussion of externalities revealed two clear options: (1) a carbon tax, and (2) a cap-and-trade program. The federal government could impose a carbon tax on each tonne of carbon emitted. This tax would increase the marginal cost of production to all firms that emit carbon into the air through their production processes. Because of the added marginal cost,

15.1 | GLOBAL PERSPECTIVE

Carbon dioxide emissions, tonnes per capita, selected nations

Carbon dioxide emissions, the major type of greenhouse gas emissions, vary per capita by nation primarily because of different degrees of industrialization and energy production from fossil fuels (coal, oil, and natural gas). The burning of such fuels is the major contributor to global warming.

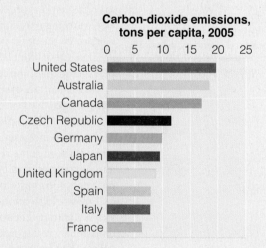

Source: OECD Environmental Data, www.oecd.org.

the supply curves within affected markets would shift to the left (as illustrated by the move from S to S_t in Figure 15-3). The reduced market supply would increase equilibrium price and reduce equilibrium quantity. With the lower output, carbon emissions in these industries would fall.

A carbon tax would require minimum government interference in the economy once the tax was in place. The federal government could direct the revenues from the tax to research on cleaner production technologies or simply use the new revenues to reduce other taxes. An alternative approach is a cap-and-trade program, based on the concepts embodied within Figure 15-5. The federal government could place a cap or lid on total carbon emissions and then either hand out emission rights or auction them off. In ways previously discussed, the cap-and-trade program would reduce society's overall cost of lowering carbon emissions. In that regard, it would more efficient than direct controls requiring each producer of greenhouse gas to reduce emissions by a fixed percentage amount. Existing cap-and-trade programs—including current European markets for carbon certificates—prove that this program can work. But such programs require considerable government oversight and enforcement of the rules.

QUICK REVIEW

▶ Policies for coping with the overallocation of resources caused by negative externalities are (1) private bargaining, (2) liability rules and lawsuits, (3) direct controls, (4) specific taxes, and (5) markets for externality rights.

▶ Policies for correcting the underallocation of resources associated with positive externalities are (1) private bargaining, (2) subsidies to producers, (3) subsidies to consumers, and (4) government provision.

▶ The optimal amount of negative-externality reduction occurs where society's marginal cost and marginal benefit of reducing the externality are equal.

▶ Society's pollution problem has largely resulted from increasing population, rising per capita consumption, certain changes in technology, and the so-called tragedy of the commons.

▶ The world's advanced industrial nations are struggling to reduce emissions of greenhouse gases, which most scientists conclude are contributing to global warming.

▶ Two alternative policies for reducing greenhouse gases are (1) a carbon tax, and (2) a cap-and-trade system.

15.3 | Information Failures

THE ROLE OF GOVERNMENTS

asymmetric information
A situation in which one party to a market transaction has much more information about a product or service than the other does.

ORIGIN 15.3
Information Failures

Thus far, we have looked at two types of market failure: public goods and externalities. Another market failure results when either buyers or sellers have incomplete or inaccurate information and their cost of obtaining better information is prohibitive. Technically stated, this market failure is the result of **asymmetric information**—unequal information available to buyers and sellers about price, quality, or some other aspect of the good or service.

Sufficient market information is normally available to ensure that goods and services are produced and purchased efficiently. But in some cases, inadequate information makes it difficult to distinguish trustworthy from untrustworthy sellers or buyers (see the Consider This box). In these markets, society's scarce resources may not be used efficiently, implying that the government should intervene by increasing the information available to the market participants. Under rare circumstances the government may itself supply a good for which information problems have prohibited efficient production.

Inadequate Buyer Information about Sellers

Inadequate information among buyers about sellers and their products can cause market failure in the form of underallocation of resources. Examining the market for the services of surgeons will show us how this comes about.

EXAMPLE: LICENSING OF SURGEONS

Suppose that anyone could hang out a shingle and claim to be a surgeon, much as anyone can become a house painter. The market would eventually sort out the true surgeons from those who were learning by doing or were fly-by-night operators. As people died from unsuccessful surgery, lawsuits for malpractice eventually would identify and eliminate most of the medical impostors. People needing surgery for themselves or their loved ones could obtain information from newspaper reports or from people who had undergone similar operations. But this process of obtaining information for those needing surgery would take considerable time and would impose unacceptably high human and economic costs. There is a fundamental difference between getting an amateurish paint job on one's house and being on the receiving end of heart surgery by a bogus physician! The marginal cost of obtaining information about surgeons would be excessively high. The risk of proceeding without good information would result in much less surgery than desirable—an underallocation of resources to surgery.

The government has remedied this market failure through a system of qualifying tests and licensing. The licensing provides consumers with inexpensive information about a service they buy infrequently. The government has taken a similar role in several other areas of the economy. For example, it approves new medicines, regulates the securities industry, and requires warnings on containers of potentially hazardous substances. It also requires warning labels on cigarette packages and disseminates information about communicable diseases. And it issues warnings about unsafe toys and inspects restaurants for health-related violations.

Inadequate Seller Information about Buyers

Just as inadequate information about sellers can keep markets from achieving economic efficiency, so can inadequate information about buyers. The buyers may be consumers who buy products, or firms that buy resources.

MORAL HAZARD PROBLEM

moral hazard problem
The possibility that individuals will change their behaviour as the result of a contract or agreement.

Private markets may underallocate resources to a particular good or service for which there is a severe **moral hazard problem.** The moral hazard problem is the tendency of one party to a contract to alter her or his behaviour after the contract is signed in ways that could be costly to the other party.

Suppose a firm offers an insurance policy that pays a set amount of money per month to couples that divorce. The attractiveness of such insurance is that it would pool the economic risk of divorce among thousands of people and, in particular, would protect spouses and children from the economic hardship that divorce often brings. Unfortunately, the moral hazard problem reduces the likelihood that insurance companies can profitably provide this type of insurance. After taking out such insurance, married couples would have less incentive to get along and to iron out marital difficulties. Some couples might be motivated to obtain a divorce, collect the insurance, and then continue to live together. Such insurance could even promote more divorces, the very outcome it is intended to protect against. The moral hazard problem would force the insurer to charge such high premiums for this insurance that few policies would be bought. If the insurer could identify in advance those people most prone to alter their behaviour, the firm could exclude them from buying it. But the firm's marginal cost of getting such information is too high compared with the marginal benefit. Thus, this market would fail. Although divorce insurance is not available in the marketplace, society recognizes the benefits of insuring against the hardships of divorce. It has corrected for this underallocation of hardship insurance through child-support laws that dictate payments to the spouse who retains the children, when the economic circumstances warrant such payments. Alimony laws also play a role.

The moral hazard problem is also illustrated in the following statements:

- Drivers may be less cautious because they have car insurance.
- Medical malpractice insurance may increase the amount of malpractice.
- Guaranteed contracts for professional athletes may reduce the quality of their performance.
- Employment compensation insurance may lead some workers to shirk.
- Government insurance on bank deposits may encourage banks to make risky loans.

ADVERSE SELECTION PROBLEM

adverse selection problem
A problem arising when information known to one party to a contract is not known to the other party, causing the latter to incur major costs.

Another problem resulting from inadequate information about buyers is the **adverse selection problem.** This problem arises when information known by the first party to a contract is not known by the second and, as a result, the second party incurs major costs. Unlike the moral hazard problem, which arises after a person signs a contract, the adverse selection problem arises at the time a person signs a contract.

In insurance, the adverse selection problem is that people who are most likely to need insurance payouts are those who buy insurance. For example, those in poorest health are more likely to buy the most generous health insurance policies. Or, at the extreme, a person planning to hire an arsonist to torch his failing business has an incentive to buy fire insurance.

The adverse selection problem thus tends to eliminate the pooling of low and high risks, which is the basis of profitable insurance. Insurance rates then must be so high that few people would want to (or be able to) buy such insurance.

Where private firms underprovide insurance because of information problems, the government often establishes some type of social insurance. It can require everyone in a particular group to take the insurance and thereby can overcome the adverse selection problem. For example, in Canada every citizen is covered by publicly funded health care insurance. The national health care program requires universal participation: People who are most likely to need the health care benefits are automatically participants in the program. So, too, are those not likely to need the benefits. Consequently, no adverse selection problem emerges.

Advocates of our publicly funded health care system point out that we need such a system because private markets would make it impossible for many Canadians who are seriously ill, or are at high risk of serious diseases, to get adequate health insurance. Private insurers would be unwilling to take

CONSIDER THIS | "Lemons"

A new car loses substantial market value when it is purchased, even though the same new car can sit on the dealer's lot for weeks, or even months, and retain its market value. One plausible explanation of this paradox is based on the idea of *asymmetric information* and adverse selection.[*]

Used-car owners (potential sellers) have much better information about the mechanical condition of their cars than do potential buyers. Because of this asymmetric information, an adverse selection problem occurs. Owners of defective cars—so-called "lemons"—have an incentive to sell them to unsuspecting buyers, whereas owners of perfectly operating cars have an incentive to retain their cars. Although both good and bad used cars are offered for sale, the *average* quality of the used cars offered on the market is poorer than the same makes and models that are *not* for sale. The typical consumer finds it difficult to identify the poorer quality used cars simply by looking at them or taking them for a test drive. Anticipating repair costs, the customer is willing to pay only a price that reflects the lower quality.[**]

So we have a solution to the paradox. When purchased, the market values of new cars drop quickly to the average market value established in the used-car market. This is true even though many used cars may be in perfect operating condition. Adverse selection, asymmetric information, and the resulting risk of "buying someone else's problem" drop the value of used cars relative to new cars still on the lot.

---

[*] This explanation is based on the work of economist George Akerlof.

[**] Transferable warranties reduce, but do not eliminate, the potential repair costs of used cars. Consumers lose time in arranging repairs and forgo the use of their cars when the repairs are being done.

on clients at high risk for developing serious diseases because of the very high costs that would entail for the insurer. Thus advocates of our present health care system claim that private markets would underallocate resources to health care. Such underallocation of resources in private markets is a powerful argument for a fully publicly funded health care system. *(Key Question 13)*

Qualification

Households and businesses have found ingenious ways to overcome information difficulties without government intervention. For example, many firms offer product warranties to overcome the lack of information about themselves and their products. Franchising also helps overcome this problem. When you visit a McDonald's or a Holiday Inn, you know precisely what you are going to get, unlike when you stop at Slim's Hamburger Shop or the Ghost Buster Motel.

Also, some private firms and organizations specialize in providing information to buyers and sellers. Credit reports provide information about credit histories and past bankruptcies to lending institutions and insurance companies. Brokers, bonding agencies, and intermediaries also provide information to clients.

Economists agree, however, that the private sector cannot remedy all information problems. In some situations, government intervention is desirable to promote an efficient allocation of society's scarce resources.

QUICK REVIEW

▶ Asymmetric information is a source of potential market failure, causing society's scarce resources to be allocated inefficiently.

▶ Inadequate information about sellers and their products may lead to an underallocation of resources to those products.

▶ The moral hazard problem is the tendency of one party to a contract to alter its behaviour in ways that are costly to the other party; for example, a person who buys insurance may willingly incur added risk.

▶ The adverse selection problem arises when one party to a contract has less information than the other party and incurs a cost because of that asymmetrical information. For example, an insurance company offering "no-medical-exam-required" life insurance policies may attract customers who have life-threatening diseases.

15.4 | The Economics of Health Care

There is a major debate over the funding, delivery, and cost of health care in Canada. The Canadian health care system provides universal access for covered services. There are no user fees across Canada for basic health services, including hospital and physician services. The Canadian health care system is in essence an insurance program funded by both provincial and federal governments, with zero deductibility. To the individual consumer, health services are "free," even if in reality these services are paid by Canadian taxpayers. The heated debate has arisen because some Canadians are concerned about declining standards and increasing waiting time to see specialists and have surgery.

We noted in Chapter 3 that competitive markets will eliminate surpluses or shortages of a particular product or service. If markets clear, why are there "shortages" in the current Canadian health care system as manifested through longer waiting times for needed health service?

Peculiarities of the Health Care Market

Competitive markets bring about both allocative and productive efficiency, two concepts you came across in Chapter 4. But the health care sector in Canada is not a competitive market industry. Indeed, a competitive market system in health care may not be desirable or attainable because of the unique properties of health care. Here, we discuss some of the unique properties of the health care market.

Ethical questions inevitably intervene in markets when decisions involve the quality of life or, literally, life or death. Although we might not consider it immoral if a person cannot buy a Mercedes or a personal computer, Canadians regard the denial of basic health care as unjust. Generally, Canadians look upon health care as an entitlement or a right and are reluctant to ration it on the basis of price and income.

Competitive markets may not be fully appropriate in health care delivery because of asymmetric information—unequal knowledge possessed by the parties to a market transaction. Health care buyers typically have little or no understanding of the complex diagnostic and treatment procedures, while the physicians who are the health care sellers of those procedures possess detailed information. This creates the unusual situation in which the doctor (supplier) as the agent of the patient (consumer) tells the patient what health care services he or she should consume. For example, if a physician tells a patient she needs a follow-up visit in a few weeks, few health care consumers would be informed enough to know whether such a visit was actually needed.

The moral hazard problem is the tendency of one party to an agreement to alter her or his behaviour in a way which is costly to the other party. Health care insurance can change behaviour in two ways. First, some insured people might be less careful about their health, taking fewer steps to prevent accident or illness. Second, insured individuals have greater incentives to use health care more intensively than they would if they did not have insurance.

Another information problem arising from inadequate information is the adverse selection problem. This problem arises when information known to the first party to a contract is not known by the second, and, as a result, the second party incurs major costs. In health insurance, the adverse selection problem is that people who are most likely to need insurance payouts are those who buy insurance. Those with the poorest health will seek to buy the most generous health insurance policies. Private insurers, knowing this, will try to attract those clients least likely to get sick. Thus, in a competitive health care industry, people either already sick or at a high risk of serious illness will find it difficult to get health insurance except at very high premiums. Those who cannot afford the high premiums will not be covered if they get sick. In the present Canadian system, government insurance covers every citizen, no matter what their state of health.

The medical care market generates positive externalities (spillover benefits), a concept you encountered earlier in this chapter. For example, an immunization against polio, smallpox, or measles benefits the immediate purchaser, but it also benefits society because it reduces the risk that other members of society will be infected with highly contagious diseases. Similarly, a healthy labour force is more productive, contributing to the general prosperity and well-being of society. Freely functioning markets underallocate resources to products and services that generate positive externalities. Thus, a competitive health care sector may not deliver as much output as society deems desirable.

Third-Party Payments: Insurance

In Canada, essential health care expenses are paid primarily through public insurance. Health care consumers do not pay out-of-pocket the prices they would otherwise. The zero prices are distortions that result in excess consumption of health care services.

GRAPHICAL PORTRAYAL

In Canada, most essential health care expenses are paid primarily through public insurance.

A simple demand and supply model illustrates the effect of health insurance on the health care market. Figure 15-7a depicts a competitive market for health care services; curve D shows the demand for health care services if all consumers are uninsured, and S represents the supply of health care services. At market price P_u the equilibrium quantity of health care is Q_u. The market clears, and there is no excess demand or supply.

FIGURE 15-7 — **Insurance and the Overallocation of Resources to Health Care**

Panel (a) Without health insurance, the optimal amount of health care consumed is Q_u, where the marginal benefit and marginal cost of health care are equal. Panel (b) The availability of private and public insurance reduces the direct price of health care from P_u to P_i, resulting in its overconsumption (Q_i rather than Q_u) and an overallocation of resources to the health care industry. The area abc represents the efficiency loss from that overallocation.

(a) Without health insurance

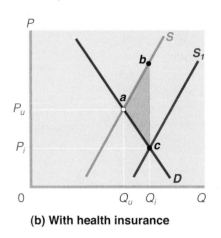

(b) With health insurance

What happens when we introduce private or government health insurance that covers, say, one half of all health care costs? In Figure 15-7b, with health insurance paying half the price, the consumer is confronted with price $P_i (= 1/2\, P_u)$. The health care consumer reacts by purchasing Q_i units rather than Q_u. An excess demand for health care services has been created. If the health care consumer does not pay any portion of health care costs, as is the case in Canada, the shortage would become more acute.

Possible Solutions to Excess Demand

Solutions to the existing excess demand for health care services in Canada come down to either increasing the supply by diverting more tax revenues to health care, or instituting user fees to reduce quantity demanded of health care services. An infusion of more resources is depicted by a rightward shift the supply curve to S_1 in Figure 15-7b. Although increased resources for health care services will resolve the excess demand, there is as yet no consensus as to whether this is the way Canadians want to move.

In Chapter 1 we discussed the necessary tradeoffs that face any society with limited resources. The federal and provincial governments must either divert tax revenues from other government programs or increase taxes to properly fund the health care needs of Canadians. Neither option is pleasant, but more importantly it is not clear which option the majority of Canadians prefer. Critics argue that even if more resources are made available to the Canadian health care system it will not solve the current shortage problem. They point out that the demand for health care rises with income and the age of its citizens. Both will rise in the future, particularly the number of older Canadians, who generally require more health care services. Critics also point out that there is little competition for the delivery of health care services in Canada, which has created what they see as "inefficiencies" that waste scarce resources.

Proponents of the national health care system in Canada emphasize that, compared to the system in the United States, our system is efficient. Administrative costs of health care delivery are lower in Canada, and the Canadian system costs less than the American system. Canada spends just under 10 percent of gross domestic product (GDP) on health care, while the U.S. health care system consumes almost 16 percent of GDP. The advocates of the existing national health care system in Canada say that even if we have to divert more resources to health care, knowing every Canadian will have the health care he or she needs is a comfort well worth paying for. *(Key Question 14)*

The LAST WORD   Lojack: A Case of Positive Externalities

Economists Ian Ayres and Steven Levitt find that an auto antitheft device
called Lojack produces large spillover benefits.

Private expenditures to reduce crime are estimated to be $30 billion annually and are growing at a faster rate than spending on public crime prevention. Unfortunately, some forms of private crime prevention simply redistribute crime rather than reduce it. For example, car alarm systems that have red blinking warning lights may simply divert professional auto thieves to vehicles that do not have such lights and alarms. The owner of a car with such an alarm system benefits through the reduced likelihood of theft but imposes a cost on other car owners who do not have such alarms. Their cars are more likely to be targeted by thieves because other cars have visible security systems.

Some private crime prevention measures, however, actually reduce crime, rather than simply redistributing it. One such measure is installation of a Lojack (or some similar) car retrieval system. Lojack is a tiny radio transmitter that is hidden in one of many possible places within the car. When an owner reports a stolen car, the police can remotely activate the transmitter. They can then determine its precise location and track its subsequent movements.

The owner of the car benefits because the 95 percent retrieval rate on cars with the Lojack system is higher than the 60 percent retrieval rate for cars without the system. But, according to a study by Ayres and Levitt, the benefit to the car owner is only 10 percent of the total benefit. Ninety percent of the total benefit is external; it is a spillover benefit to other car owners in the community.

There are two sources of this positive externality. First, the presence of the Lojack device sometimes enables police to intercept the car while the thief is still driving it. For example, in California the arrest rate for cars with Lojack was three times greater than for cars without it. The arrest puts the car thief out of commission for a time and thus reduces subsequent car thefts in the community. Second, and far more important, the device enables police to trace cars to "chop-shops," where crooks disassemble cars for resale of the parts. When police raid the chop-shop, they put the entire theft ring out of business. In Los Angeles alone, Lojack has eliminated 45 chop-shops in just a few years. The purging of the chop-shop and theft ring reduces auto theft in the community. So, auto owners who do not have Lojack devices in their cars benefit from car owners who do. Ayres and Levitt estimate the marginal social benefit of Lojack—the marginal benefit to the Lojack car owner plus the spillover benefit to other car owners—is 15 times greater than the marginal cost of the device.

We saw in Figure 15-4a that the existence of positive externalities causes an insufficient quantity of a product and thus an underallocation of scarce resources to its production. The two general ways to correct the outcome are to subsidize the consumer, as shown in Figure 15-4b, or to subsidize the producer, as shown in Figure 15-4c. Currently, there is only one form of government intervention in place: provincially mandated insurance discounts for people who install auto retrieval systems such as Lojack. In effect, those discounts on insurance premiums subsidize the consumer by lowering the price of the system to consumers: the lower price raises the number of systems installed. But based on their research, Ayres and Levitt contend that the current levels of insurance discounts are far too small to correct the underallocation that results from the positive externalities created by Lojack.

Source: Based on Ian Ayres and Steven D. Levitt, "Measuring Positive Externalities from Unobservable Victim Precaution: An Empirical Analysis of Lojack," *Quarterly Journal of Economics*, February 1998, pp. 43–77. The authors point out that Lojack did not fund their work in any way, nor do they have any financial stake in Lojack.

Question

Explain how a global positioning antitheft device installed by one car owner can produce positive externalities to thousands of others in a city.

CHAPTER SUMMARY

15.1 ▶ PUBLIC GOODS

- Public goods are distinguished from private goods. Private goods are characterized by rivalry (in consumption) and excludability. One person's purchase and consumption of a private good precludes others from also buying and consuming it. Producers can exclude nonpayers (free riders) from receiving the benefits. In contrast, public goods are characterized by nonrivalry (in consumption) and non-excludability. Public goods are not profitable to private firms because nonpayers (free riders) can obtain and consume those goods. Only government is willing to provide desirable public goods, financing them through taxation.

- The collective demand schedule for a particular public good is found by summing the prices each individual is willing to pay for an additional unit. Graphically, that demand curve is therefore found by summing vertically the individual demand curves for that good. The resulting total demand curve indicates the collective willingness to pay for (or marginal benefit of) the last unit of any given amount of the public good.

- The optimal quantity of a public good occurs where the society's willingness to pay for the last unit—the marginal benefit of the good—equals the marginal cost of the good.

15.2 ▶ EXTERNALITIES

- Externalities or spillovers are costs or benefits that accrue to someone other than the immediate buyer or seller. Such costs or benefits are not captured in market demand or supply curves and therefore cause the output of certain goods to vary from society's optimal output. Negative externalities (or spillover costs or external costs) result in an overallocation of resources to a particular product. Positive externalities (or spillover benefits or external benefits) are accompanied by an underallocaton of resources to a particular product.

- The Coase theorem suggests that private bargaining is capable of solving potential externality problems where (a) the property rights are clearly defined, (b) the number of people involved is small, and (c) bargaining costs are negligible.

- Clearly established property rights and liability rules permit some negative externalities to be prevented or remedied through private lawsuits. Lawsuits, however, can be costly, time-consuming, and uncertain as to their results.

- Direct controls and specific taxes can improve resource allocation in situations where negative externalities affect many people and community resources. Both direct controls (e.g., smokestack emission standards) and specific taxes (e.g., taxes on firms producing toxic chemicals) increase production costs and hence product price. As product price rises, the externality and overallocation of resources are reduced, because less of the output is bought and sold.

- Government can correct the underallocation of resources that results from positive externalities in a particular market either by subsidizing consumers (which increases market demand) or subsidizing producers (which increases market supply). Such subsidies increase the equilibrium output, reducing or eliminating the positive externality and consequent underallocation of resources.

- Markets for pollution rights, where firms can buy and sell the right to discharge a fixed amount of pollution, put a price on pollution and encourage firms to reduce or eliminate it.

- The socially optimal amount of externality abatement occurs where society's marginal cost and marginal benefit of reducing the externality are equal. This optimal amount of pollution abatement is likely to be less than a 100 percent reduction. Changes in technology or changes in society's attitudes toward pollution can affect the optimal amount of pollution abatement.

- A growing body of scientific evidence suggests that accumulation of carbon dioxide and other greenhouse gases in the Earth's atmosphere is contributing to a climate-change problem. In addressing the problem, society needs to assess the costs and benefits of reducing greenhouse gases as well as the costs and benefits of allowing the emission to rise and then mitigating the effects. Two distinct policies for reducing greenhouse gases are (a) a carbon tax on such emissions, and (b) a cap-and-trade system that places a lid on the emissions and allows for trading of the pollution rights.

15.3 ▶ INFORMATION FAILURES

- Asymmetric information between sellers and buyers can cause markets to fail. The moral hazard problem occurs when people alter their behaviour after they sign a contract, imposing costs on the other party. The adverse selection problem occurs when one party to a contract takes advantage of the other party's inadequate information, resulting in an unanticipated loss to the latter party.

15.4 ▶ THE ECONOMICS OF HEALTH CARE

- Special characteristics of the health care market include (a) ethical and equity considerations; (b) an imbalance of information between consumers and suppliers; (c) the moral hazard problem; (d) the adverse selection problem; (e) the presence of positive externalities, and (f) the payment of most health care expenses by public insurance.

TERMS AND CONCEPTS

private good, p. 349
public good, p. 349
free-rider problem, p. 350
cost–benefit analysis, p. 351
marginal cost = marginal benefit
    (MC = MB) rule, p. 353

externalities, p. 354
Coase theorem, p. 355
tragedy of the commons, p. 358
market for externality rights, p. 358
optimal reduction of an externality,
    p. 360

climate-change problem, p. 361
asymmetric information, p. 363
moral hazard problem, p. 364
adverse selection problem, p. 365

STUDY QUESTIONS

15.1 1. **KEY QUESTION** Based on the following three individual demand schedules for a particular good, and assuming these three people are the only ones in the society, determine (a) the market demand schedule on the assumption that the good is a private good, and (b) the collective demand schedule on the assumption that the good is a public good. Explain the differences, if any, in your schedules.

Individual 1		Individual 2		Individual 3	
P	**Q_d**	**P**	**Q_d**	**P**	**Q_d**
$8	0	$8	1	$8	0
7	0	7	2	7	0
6	0	6	3	6	1
5	1	5	4	5	2
4	2	4	5	4	3
3	3	3	6	3	4
2	4	2	7	2	5
1	5	1	8	1	6

15.1 2. **KEY QUESTION** Use your demand schedule for a public good, determined in question 1, and the following supply schedule to ascertain the optimal quantity of this public good. Why is this the optimal quantity?

P	**Q_s**
$19	10
16	8
13	6
10	4
7	2
4	1

3. **KEY QUESTION** The following table shows the total **LO 15.1** costs and total benefits in billions for four different anti-pollution programs of increasing scope. Which program should be undertaken? Why?

Program	Total cost	Total benefit
A	$ 3	$ 7
B	7	12
C	12	16
D	18	19

4. **KEY QUESTION** Why are spillover costs and spillover **LO 15.2** benefits also called negative and positive externalities? Show graphically how a tax can correct for a negative externality and how a subsidy to producers can correct for a positive externality. How does a subsidy to consumers differ from a subsidy to producers in correcting for a positive externality?

5. An apple grower's orchard provides nectar to a neighbour's **LO 15.2** bees, while the beekeeper's bees help the apple grower by pollinating the apple blossoms. Use Figure 15-2b to explain why this situation of dual positive externalities might lead to an underallocation of resources to apple growing and to beekeeping. How might this underallocation get resolved via the means suggested by the Coase theorem?

6. Explain: "Without a market for pollution rights, dumping **LO 15.2** pollutants into the air or water is costless; in the presence of the right to buy and sell pollution rights, dumping pollution creates an opportunity cost for the polluter." What is the significance of this opportunity cost to the search for better technology to reduce pollution?

7. **KEY QUESTION** Explain the following statement using **LO 15.2** the MB curve in Figure 15-6 to illustrate: "The optimal amount of pollution abatement for some substances, say, water from storm drains, is very low; the optimal amount of abatement for other substances, say, cyanide poison, is close to 100 percent."

LO 15.2 8. Assume the atmosphere of an urban area is able to reabsorb 8000 tonnes of pollutants per year. The schedule below shows the price polluters would be willing to pay for the right to dispose of 1 tonne of pollutants per year and the total quantity of pollutants they would wish to dispose of at each price.

Price (per tonne of pollutant rights)	Total quantity of pollutant rights demanded (tonnes)
$ 0	13,000
1000	12,000
2000	11,000
3000	10,000
4000	9,000
5000	8,000
6000	7,000
7000	6,000

a. If there were no emission fee, how many tons of pollutants would there be and how much greater would this amount be than the capacity for re-absorption?

b. What pollution fee should the urban authorities charge to solve the problem?

c. What would happen in this market for pollution rights if quantity demanded increased by 1000 tonnes at each price?

LO 15.2 9. Explain the tragedy of the commons as it relates to pollution.

10. What is the climate-change problem? Using an example other than those given in the text, explain how climate change might hurt one industry, particular region, or country but help another. Distinguish between a carbon-tax and a cap-and-trade strategy for reducing greenhouse gases. Which of the two strategies do you think would have the most political support in an election in your home province? Explain your thinking. **LO**

11. Explain how marketable emission credits add to overall economic efficiency, compared to across-the-board limitations on maximum discharges of air pollutants by firms. **LO**

12. Why is it in the interest of new homebuyers and builders of new homes to have government building codes and building inspectors? **LO**

13. **KEY QUESTION**   Place an "M" beside those items in the following list that describe a moral hazard problem and an "A" beside those that describe an adverse selection problem. **LO**

a. A person with a terminal illness buys several life insurance policies through the mail.

b. A person drives carelessly because he or she has automobile insurance.

c. A person who intends to torch his warehouse takes out a large fire insurance policy.

d. A professional athlete who has a guaranteed contract fails to stay in shape during the off-season.

e. A woman who anticipates having a large family takes a job with a firm that offers exceptional childcare benefits.

14. **KEY QUESTION**   Explain how insurance can lead to overconsumption. How does Canada's publicly funded health care system help to resolve the adverse selection problem? **LO**

INTERNET APPLICATION QUESTIONS @

1. **What Can Government Do to Reduce Water Pollution?** Government can use direct controls in the form of legislation to reduce negative externalities such as water pollution. Go to the McConnell-Brue-Flynn-Barbiero Web site (Chapter 15) to access the Environment Canada Web site. Environment Canada is responsible for getting environmental results on clean water. What success has Environment Canada had? What is it doing now?

CHAPTER 16

Public Choice Theory and the Economics of Taxation

In Chapter 15 we saw that private markets can occasionally produce *market failures,* which impede economic efficiency and justify government intervention in the economy. But the government's response to market failures is not without its own problems and pitfalls. Perhaps that is why government policies and decisions are the focus of hundreds of radio talk shows, television debates, and newspaper articles each day.

In this chapter, we explore a number of *government failures* that impede economic efficiency in the public sector. Our spotlight is first on selected aspects of **public choice theory**—the economic analysis of government decision making—and then on the economics of taxation.

16.1 | Revealing Preferences through Majority Voting

In some manner, society must decide which public goods and services it wants and in what amounts. It must also determine the extent to which it wants government to intervene in private markets to correct externalities. Decisions needed to be made about how much regulation of business is necessary, how much income redistribution is desirable, and other such choices. Furthermore, society must determine the set of taxes it thinks is best for financing government. How should the total tax burden be apportioned (divided) among the public?

Decisions such as these are made collectively in Canada through a democratic process that relies heavily on majority voting. Candidates for office offer alternative policy packages, and citizens elect the people they think will make the best decisions on their collective behalf. Voters retire officials who do not adequately represent their collective wishes. Citizens also periodically have opportunities at the provincial and municipal levels to vote directly on public expenditures or new legislation.

IN THIS CHAPTER
YOU WILL LEARN:

16.1 The difficulties of conveying economic preferences through majority voting

16.2 About "government failure" and why it occurs

16.3 The different philosophies on—and ways to distribute—a nation's tax burden

FIGURE 16-1   **Inefficient Voting Outcomes**

Majority voting can produce inefficient decisions. Panel (a): Majority voting leads to rejection of a public good that has greater total benefit than total cost. Panel (b): Majority voting results in acceptance of a public good that has a higher total cost than total benefit.

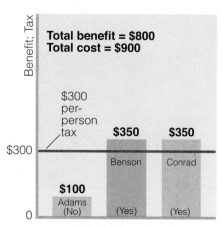

(a) Inefficient majority "no" vote   (b) Inefficient majority "yes" vote

ORIGIN 16.1
Public Choice Theory

public choice theory
The economic analysis of collective and government decision making.

Although the democratic process does a reasonably good job of revealing society's preferences, it is imperfect. Public choice theory demonstrates that majority voting can produce inefficiencies and inconsistencies.

Inefficient Voting Outcomes

Society's well-being is enhanced when government provides a public good whose total benefit exceeds its total cost. Unfortunately, majority voting does not always deliver that outcome.

ILLUSTRATION: INEFFICIENT "NO" VOTE

Assume that the government can provide a public good, say, national defence, at a total expense of $900. Assume there are only three individuals—Adams, Benson, and Conrad—in the society and that they will share the $900 tax expense equally, each being taxed $300 if the proposed public good is provided. And assume, as Figure 16-1a illustrates, that Adams would receive $700 worth of benefits from having this public good; Benson, $250; and Conrad, $200.

What will be the result if a majority vote determines whether this public good is provided? Although people do not always vote strictly according to their own economic interest, it is likely that Benson and Conrad will vote no because they will incur tax costs of $300 each while gaining benefits of only $250 and $200, respectively. Adams will vote yes. So the majority vote will defeat the proposal even though the total benefit of $1150 (= $700 for Adams + $250 for Benson + $200 for Conrad) exceeds the total cost of $900.

ILLUSTRATION: INEFFICIENT "YES" VOTE

Now consider a situation in which the majority favours a public good even though its total cost *exceeds* its total benefit. Figure 16-1b shows the details. Again, Adams, Benson, and Conrad will equally share the $900 cost of the public good; they will each be taxed $300. But since Adams's benefit now is only $100 from the public good, she will vote against it. Meanwhile, Benson and Conrad will benefit by $350 each. They will vote for the public good because that benefit ($350) exceeds their tax payments ($300). The majority vote will provide a public good costing $900 that produces total benefits of only $800 (= $100 for Adams + $350 for Benson + $350 for Conrad). Society's resources will be inefficiently allocated to this public good, and there will be too much of it.

IMPLICATIONS

The point is that an inefficient outcome may occur as either an overproduction or an under-production of a specific public good and, therefore, as an overallocation or underallocation of resources for that particular use. In our examples, each person has only a single vote, no matter how much he or she might gain or lose from a public good. In the first example (inefficient no vote), Adams would be willing to purchase a vote from either Benson or Conrad if buying votes were legal. That way Adams could be assured of obtaining the national defence she so highly values. But since buying votes is illegal, many people with strong preferences for certain public goods may have to go without them.

When individual consumers have a strong preference for a specific *private good,* they usually can find that good in the marketplace even though it may be unpopular with the majority of consumers. But a person cannot easily buy a *public good* such as national defence once the majority has decided against it.

Conversely, a consumer in the marketplace can decide against buying a particular product, even a popular one. But although you may not want national defence, you must "buy" it through your tax payments when it is favoured by the majority.

Conclusion: Because majority voting fails to incorporate the *strength* of the preferences of the individual voter, it may produce economically inefficient outcomes.

Interest Groups and Logrolling

Some, but not all, of the inefficiencies of majority voting get resolved through the political process. Two examples follow.

INTEREST GROUPS

Those who have a strong preference for a public good may band together into an interest group and use advertisements, mailings, and direct persuasion to convince others of the merits of that public good. Adams might try to persuade Benson and Conrad that it is in their best interest to vote for national defence—that national defence is much more valuable to them than their $250 and $200 valuations. Such appeals are common in democratic politics. Sometimes they are successful; sometimes they are not.

POLITICAL LOGROLLING

logrolling
The trading of votes by legislators to secure favourable outcomes on decisions concerning the provision of public goods and quasipublic goods.

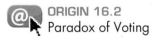

ORIGIN 16.2
Paradox of Voting

Perhaps surprisingly, **logrolling**—the trading of votes to secure favourable outcomes—can also turn an inefficient outcome into an efficient one. In our first example (Figure 16-1a), perhaps Benson has a strong preference for a different public good, for example a new road, which Adams and Conrad do not think is worth the tax expense. That would provide an opportunity for Adams and Benson to trade votes to ensure provision of both national defence and the new road. That is, Adams and Benson would each vote yes on both measures. Adams would get the national defence and Benson would get the road. Without the logrolling, both public goods would have been rejected. Logrolling will add to society's well-being if, as was true for national defence, the road creates a greater overall benefit than cost.

Logrolling need not increase economic efficiency. Even if national defence and the road each cost more than the total benefit they produced, both might still be provided because of the vote trading.

Paradox of Voting

paradox of voting
A situation in which paired-choice majority voting fails to provide a consistent ranking of society's preferences for public goods or services.

Another difficulty with majority voting is the **paradox of voting,** a situation in which society may not be able to rank its preferences consistently through paired-choice majority voting.

TABLE 16-1	Paradox of Voting		
Preferences			
Public Good	**Adams**	**Benson**	**Conrad**
National defence	1st choice	3rd choice	2nd choice
Road	2nd choice	1st choice	3rd choice
Weather warning system	3rd choice	2nd choice	1st choice

Election	**Voting outcomes: winner**
1. National defence vs. road	National defence (preferred by Adams and Conrad)
2. Road vs. weather warning system	Road (preferred by Adams and Benson)
3. National defence vs. weather warning system	Weather warning system (preferred by Benson and Conrad)

PREFERENCES

Consider Table 16-1, in which we again assume a community of three voters: Adams, Benson, and Conrad. Suppose the community has three alternative public goods from which to choose: national defence, a road, and a weather warning system. We expect that each member of the community prefers the three alternatives in a certain order. For example, one person might prefer national defence to a road, and a road to a weather warning system. We can attempt to determine the preferences of the community through paired-choice majority voting. Specifically, a vote can be held between any two of the public goods, and the winner of that vote can then be matched against the third public good in another vote.

The three goods and the assumed individual preferences of the three voters are listed in the top part of Table 16-1. The data indicate that Adams prefers national defence to the road and the road to the weather warning system. This implies also that Adams prefers national defence to the weather warning system. Benson values the road more than the weather warning system and the weather warning system more than national defence. Conrad's order of preference is weather warning system, national defence, and road.

VOTING OUTCOMES

The lower part of Table 16-1 shows the outcomes of three hypothetical decisions of the majority vote. In the first, national defence wins against the road because a majority of voters (Adams and Conrad) prefer national defence to the road. In the second election to see whether this community wants a road or a weather warning system, a majority of voters (Adams and Benson) prefer the road. We have determined that the majority of people in this community prefer national defence to a road and prefer a road to a weather warning system. It seems logical to conclude that the community prefers national defence to a weather warning system, but the community does not!

To demonstrate this conclusion, we hold a direct election between national defence and the weather warning system. Row (3) shows that a majority of voters (Benson and Conrad) prefer the weather warning system to national defence. As listed in Table 16-1, then, the three paired-choice majority votes imply that this community is irrational: it seems to prefer national defence to a road and a road to a weather warning system, but would rather have a weather warning system than national defence.

The problem is not irrational community preferences but rather a flawed procedure for determining those preferences. We see that the outcome from paired-choice majority voting may depend on the order in which the votes are taken up. Under some circumstances majority voting fails to make consistent choices that reflect the community's underlying preferences. As a consequence, government may find it difficult to provide the "correct" public goods by acting in accordance with majority voting. One important note: this critique is not meant to suggest that some better procedure exists. Majority voting is much more likely to reflect community preferences than decisions made by, say, a dictator or a group of self-appointed leaders. *(Key Question 2)*

Median-Voter Model

median-voter model
The theory that under majority rule the median (middle) voter will be in the dominant position to determine the outcome of an election.

One other aspect of majority voting reveals further insights into real-world phenomena. The **median-voter model** suggests that, under majority rule and consistent voting preferences, the median voter will in a sense determine the outcomes of elections. The median voter is the person holding the middle position on an issue: half the other voters have stronger preferences for a public good, amount of taxation, or degree of government regulation, and half have weaker or negative preferences. The extreme voters on each side of an issue prefer the median choice rather than the other extreme position, so the median voter's choice predominates.

EXAMPLE

Suppose a society composed of Adams, Benson, and Conrad has reached agreement that as a society it needs a weather warning system. Each independently is to submit a total dollar amount he or she thinks should be spent on the weather warning system, assuming each will be taxed one-third of that amount. An election will determine the size of the system. Because each person can be expected to vote for his or her own proposal, no majority will occur if all the proposals are placed on the ballot at the same time. Thus, the group decides on a paired-choice vote: they will first vote between two of the proposals and then match the winner of that vote against the remaining proposal.

The three proposals are as follows: Adams desires a $400 system; Benson wants an $800 system; Conrad opts for a $300 system. Which proposal will win? The median-voter model suggests it will be the $400 proposal submitted by the median voter, Adams. Half the other voters favour a more costly system; half favour a less costly system. To understand why the $400 system will be the outcome, let's conduct the two elections.

First, suppose that the $400 proposal is matched against the $800 proposal. Adams naturally votes for her $400 proposal, and Benson votes for his own $800 proposal. Conrad, who proposed the $300 expenditure for the weather warning system, votes for the $400 proposal because it is closer to his own. So Adams's $400 proposal is selected by a 2-to-1 majority vote.

Next, we match the $400 proposal against the $300 proposal. Again the $400 proposal wins. It gets a vote from Adams and one from Benson, who proposed the $800 expenditure and for that reason prefers a $400 expenditure to a $300 one. Adams, the median voter in this case, is in a sense the person who has decided the level of expenditure on a weather warning system for this society.

REAL-WORLD APPLICABILITY

Although our illustration is simple, it explains a great deal. We do note a tendency for public choices to match most closely the median view. Political candidates, for example, take one set of positions to win the nomination of their political parties; in so doing, they tend to appeal to the median voter within their party to get the nomination. They then shift their views more closely to the political centre when they square off against opponents from the opposite political party. In effect, they redirect their appeal toward the median voter within the total population. They also try to label their opponents as being too liberal, or too conservative, and out of touch with mainstream Canada. They then conduct polls and adjust their positions on issues accordingly.

IMPLICATIONS

The median-voter model has two important implications:

1. *At any point in time, many people will be dissatisfied by the extent of government involvement in the economy.* The size of government will largely be determined by the median preference,

leaving many people desiring a much larger, or a much smaller, public sector. In the market-place you can buy no zucchinis, two zucchinis, or 200 zucchinis, depending on how much you enjoy them. In the public sector you get the public health funding the median voter prefers.

2. *Some people may "vote with their feet" by moving into political jurisdictions where the median voter's preferences are closer to their own.* They may move from one province to another where the level of government services, and therefore taxes, is lower. Or they may move into an area known for its excellent but expensive school system. Some may move to other provinces; a few may even move to other countries.

For these reasons, and because our personal preferences for publicly provided goods and services are not static, the median preference shifts over time. Moreover, information about people's prefer-ences is imperfect, leaving much room for politicians to misjudge the true median position. When they misjudge, they may have a difficult time getting elected or re-elected. *(Key Question 3)*

16.2 | Government Failure

As implied in our discussion of voting problems, government does not always perform its economic functions effectively and efficiently. Public choice theory suggests that inherent shortcomings within the public sector can produce inefficient outcomes. Such shortcomings result in **government failure**—inefficiency because of certain characteristics of the public sector. Let's consider some of these characteristics and outcomes.

Special Interests and Rent Seeking

Casual reflection suggests that "sound economics" and "sound politics" are not always one and the same. Sound economics calls for the public sector to pursue various programs as long as marginal benefits exceed marginal costs. Good politics, however, suggests that politicians support programs and policies that will maximize their chance of getting elected and staying in office. The result may be that the government will promote the goals of groups of voters that have special interests to the detriment of the larger public. In the process, inefficient economic outcomes may result.

SPECIAL-INTEREST EFFECT

> **government failure**
> Inefficiencies in resource allocation caused by problems in the operation of the public sector (government).

Efficient public decision making is often impaired by the **special-interest effect.** This is any out-come of the political process where a small number of people obtain a government program or policy that gives them large gains at the expense of a much greater number of persons who individually suffer small losses.

> **special-interest effect**
> Any result of government promotion of the interests (goals) of a small group at the expense of a much larger group.

The small group of potential beneficiaries is well informed and highly vocal on the issue in question, and they press politicians for approval. The large number of people facing very small individual losses, however, are generally uninformed on the issue. Politicians feel they will lose the campaign contributions and votes of the small special-interest group that backs the issue if they leg-islate against it but will not lose the support of the large group of uninformed voters, who are likely to evaluate the politicians on other issues of greater importance to them.

The special-interest effect is also evident in so-called *pork-barrel politics,* a means of securing a gov-ernment project that yields benefits mainly to a single political district and its political representative. In this case, the special-interest group comprises local constituents, while the larger group consists of relatively uninformed taxpayers scattered across a much larger geographic area. Politicians clearly have a strong incentive to secure public goods ("pork") for their local constituents.

Finally, a politician's inclination to support the smaller group of special beneficiaries is enhanced because special-interest groups are often quite willing to help finance the campaigns of right-minded politicians and politicians who "bring home the pork." The result is that politicians may support special-interest programs and projects that cannot be justified on economic grounds.

RENT-SEEKING BEHAVIOUR

rent seeking
The actions by persons, firms, or unions to gain special benefits from government at the taxpayers' or someone else's expense.

The appeal to government for special benefits at taxpayers' or someone else's expense is called **rent seeking.** To economists, rent is a payment beyond the amount necessary to keep a resource supplied in its current use. Corporations, trade associations, labour unions, and professional organizations employ vast resources to secure favourable government policies that result in rent—higher profit or income than would occur under competitive market conditions. The government is able to dispense such rent directly or indirectly through laws, rules, hiring, and purchases. Elected officials are willing to provide such rent because they want to be responsive to key constituents, who in turn help them remain in office.

Here are some examples of "rent-providing" legislation or policies: tariffs on foreign products that limit competition and raise prices to consumers, tax breaks that benefit specific corporations, government construction projects that create union jobs but cost more than the benefits they yield, occupational licensing that goes beyond what is needed to protect consumers, and large subsidies to farmers by taxpayers. None of these is justified by economic efficiency (see this chapter's Last Word).

Clear Benefits, Hidden Costs

Some critics say that vote-seeking politicians will not weigh objectively all the costs and benefits of various programs in deciding which to support and which to reject. Because political officeholders must seek voter support every few years, they favour programs that have immediate and clear-cut benefits and vague or deferred costs.

Such biases may lead politicians to reject economically justifiable programs and to accept programs that are economically irrational. For example, a proposal to construct or expand mass-transit systems in large metropolitan areas may be economically rational on the basis of benefit–cost analysis, but if (1) the program is to be financed by immediate increases in highly visible income or sales taxes and (2) benefits will occur only years from now when the project is completed, then the vote-seeking politician may oppose the program.

Another example of possible political bias is the distribution of health care expenditures by both the federal and provincial governments in Canada. Certain government health care expenditures on a relatively small number of Canadians may lead to much media attention, but may not be the most efficient expenditures of health care resources from society's standpoint. But it is this kind of positive and visible front-page coverage that politicians desire in their attempts to get re-elected.

Limited and Bundled Choice

Public choice theorists point out that the political process forces citizens and their elected representatives to be less selective in choosing public goods and services than they are in choosing private goods and services.

In the marketplace, the citizen as a consumer can exactly satisfy personal preferences by buying certain goods and not buying others. However, in the public sector the citizen as a voter is confronted with, say, only two or three candidates for an office, each representing a different bundle of programs (public goods and services). None of these bundles of public goods is likely to fit exactly the preferences of any particular voter, yet the voter must choose one of them. The candidate who comes closest to voter Smith's preference may endorse national health insurance, increases in Old Age Security benefits, subsidies to tobacco farmers, and tariffs on imported goods. Smith is likely to vote for that candidate even though Smith strongly opposes tobacco subsidies.

Parliament is confronted with a similar limited-choice, bundled-goods problem. Appropriations legislation combines hundreds, even thousands, of spending items into a single bill. Many of these spending items may be completely unrelated to the main purpose of the legislation, yet members of Parliament must vote the entire package—yea or nay. Unlike consumers in the marketplace, they cannot be selective. *(Key Question 4)*

Bureaucracy and Inefficiency

Some economists contend that public agencies are generally less efficient than private businesses. The reason is that the market system creates incentives and pressures for internal efficiency that are absent from the public sector. The market system imposes a very obvious test of performance on private firms: the test of profit and loss. An efficient firm is profitable and therefore successful; it survives, prospers, and grows. An inefficient firm is unprofitable and unsuccessful; it declines and in time goes bankrupt and ceases to exist. But no similar, clear-cut test exists with which to assess the efficiency or inefficiency of public agencies.

Furthermore, economists assert that government employees, together with the special-interest groups they serve, often gain sufficient political clout to block attempts to pare down or eliminate their agencies. Politicians who attempt to reduce the size of huge federal bureaucracies such as those relating to agriculture, education, and health and welfare incur sizable political risk because bureaucrats and special-interest groups will team up to defeat them.

Finally, critics point out that there is a tendency for government bureaucrats to justify their continued employment by looking for and eventually finding new "problems" to solve. It is not surprising that social problems, as defined by government, tend to persist or even expand.

Imperfect Institutions

Such criticisms of public-sector inefficiency shatter the concept of a benevolent government that responds with precision and efficiency to the wants of its citizens. The market system of the private sector is far from perfectly efficient, and government's economic function is mainly to correct that system's shortcomings. But the public sector too is subject to deficiencies in fulfilling its economic function.

Because the market system and public agencies are both imperfect, it is sometimes difficult to determine whether a particular activity can be performed with greater success in the private sector or the public sector. It is easy to reach agreement on opposite extremes: national defence must lie with the public sector, while automobile production can best be accomplished by the private sector. But what about health insurance? Parks and recreation areas? Fire protection? Garbage collection? Housing? Education? It is hard to say absolutely that it should be assigned to either the public sector or the private sector. After all, the goods and services just mentioned are provided in part by *both* private enterprises and public agencies.

QUICK REVIEW

▸ Majority voting can produce voting outcomes that are inefficient; projects having greater total benefits than total costs may be defeated and projects having greater total costs than total benefits may be approved.

▸ The paradox of voting occurs when voting by majority rule does not provide a consistent ranking of society's preferences for public goods and services.

▸ The median-voter model suggests that under majority rule and consistent voting preferences, the voter who has the middle preference will determine the outcome of an election.

▸ Government failure occurs as a result of pressure by special-interest groups, rent seeking, shortsighted political behaviour, limited and bundled choices, and bureaucratic inefficiency.

16.3 | Apportioning the Tax Burden

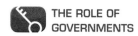
THE ROLE OF GOVERNMENTS

We now turn from the difficulties of making collective decisions about public goods to the difficulties of deciding how those goods should be financed.

It is difficult to measure precisely how the benefits of public goods are apportioned among individuals and institutions. We cannot accurately determine how much citizen Raheed Singh benefits from military installations, a network of highways, a public school system, the national weather bureau, and municipal police and fire protection.

The situation is different when it comes to paying for those benefits. Studies reveal with reasonable clarity how the overall tax burden is apportioned. (By "tax burden" we mean the total cost of taxes imposed on society.) The overall level of taxes is important, but the average citizen is much more concerned with his or her part of the overall tax burden.

Benefits Received versus Ability to Pay

Two basic philosophies coexist on how the economy's tax burden should be apportioned.

BENEFITS-RECEIVED PRINCIPLE

benefits-received principle
The idea that those who receive the benefits of goods and services provided by government should pay the taxes required to finance them.

The **benefits-received principle** of taxation asserts that households and businesses should purchase the goods and services of government in the same way they buy other commodities. Those who benefit most from government-supplied goods or services should pay the taxes necessary to finance them. A few public goods are now financed on this basis. For example, money collected as gasoline taxes is typically used to finance some highway construction and repairs. Thus people who benefit from good roads pay the cost of those roads. Difficulties immediately arise, however, when we consider widespread application of the benefits-received principle.

- How will the government determine the benefits that individual households and businesses receive from national defence, education, the court system, and police and fire protection? Recall that public goods provide widespread spillover benefits and that the exclusion principle does not apply. Even in the seemingly straightforward case of highway financing, it is difficult to measure benefits. Owners of cars benefit in different degrees from good roads, but others also benefit. For example, businesses benefit because good roads bring them workers and customers.

- The benefits-received principle cannot logically be applied to income redistribution programs. It would be absurd and self-defeating to ask poor families to pay the taxes needed to finance their welfare payments. It would be ridiculous to think of taxing only unemployed workers to finance the unemployment compensation payments they receive.

ABILITY-TO-PAY PRINCIPLE

ability-to-pay principle
The idea that those who have greater income (or wealth) should pay a greater proportion of it as taxes than those who have less income (or wealth).

The **ability-to-pay principle** of taxation asserts that the tax burden should be apportioned according to taxpayers' income and wealth. In Canada this means that individuals and businesses with larger incomes should pay more taxes in both absolute and relative terms than those with smaller incomes.

In justifying the ability-to-pay principle, proponents contend that each additional dollar of income received by a household yields a smaller amount of satisfaction or marginal utility when it is spent. Because consumers act rationally, the first dollars of income received in any period will be spent on high-urgency goods that yield the greatest marginal utility. Successive dollars of income will go for less urgently needed goods and finally for trivial goods and services. This process means that a dollar taken through taxes from a poor person who has few dollars represents a greater utility sacrifice than a dollar taken through taxes from a rich person who has many dollars. To balance the sacrifices that taxes impose on income receivers, taxes should be apportioned according to the amount of income a taxpayer receives.

This argument is appealing, but application problems arise here, too. Although we might agree that the household earning $100,000 per year has a greater ability to pay taxes than a household receiving $10,000, we don't know exactly how much more ability to pay the first family has. Should the wealthier family pay the same *percentage* of its larger income, and hence a larger absolute amount, as taxes? Or should it be made to pay a larger *fraction* of its income as taxes? How much larger should that fraction be? Who is to decide?

There is no scientific way of making utility comparisons among individuals and thus of measuring someone's relative ability to pay taxes. That is the main problem. In practice, the solution hinges on guesswork, the tax views of the political party in power, expediency, and how urgently the government needs revenue.

BENEFITS RECEIVED VERSUS ABILITY TO PAY AND HEALTH CARE

In the ongoing debate about Canada's publicly funded national health care system, one of the options is to pursue a taxation policy based on the benefits-received principle. Canadians who use the health care system more frequently would be expected to pay more taxes than Canadians who use it rarely. Those in favour of funding the health care system along these lines do so at least partly because they believe this will reduce inefficient usage of health care services. Critics of this scheme point out that it violates the universality principle: very sick people who cannot afford to pay higher taxes would not be able to access essential health care services. The benefits-received principle of taxation in the case of health care amounts to user fees for medical services. There appears to be a consensus among Canadians that the universality principle in health care should not be violated.

Progressive, Proportional, and Regressive Taxes

Any discussion of taxation leads ultimately to the question of tax rates. Note that an *average tax rate* is the total tax paid divided by some base against which the tax is compared.

DEFINITIONS

progressive tax
A tax whose average tax rate increases as the taxpayer's income increases.

regressive tax
A tax whose average tax rate decreases as the taxpayer's income increases.

proportional tax
A tax whose average tax rate remains constant as the taxpayer's income increases or decreases.

Taxes are classified as progressive, proportional, or regressive, depending on the relationship between average tax rates and taxpayer incomes. We focus on incomes because all taxes, whether on income or on a product or a building or a parcel of land, are ultimately paid out of someone's income.

- A tax is **progressive** if its average rate increases as income increases. Such a tax claims not only a larger absolute (dollar) amount but also a larger percentage of income as income increases.

- A tax is **regressive** if its average rate declines as income increases. Such a tax takes a smaller proportion of income as income increases. A regressive tax may or may not take a larger absolute amount of income as income increases. (You may want to derive an example to confirm this conclusion.)

- A tax is **proportional** if its average rate *remains the same* regardless of the size of income.

We can illustrate these ideas with the personal income tax. Suppose tax rates are such that a household pays 10 percent of its income in taxes regardless of the size of its income. This is a *proportional* income tax. Now suppose the rate structure is such that a household with an annual taxable income of less than $10,000 pays 5 percent in income taxes; a household with an income of $10,000 to $20,000 pays 10 percent; one with a $20,000 to $30,000 income pays 15 percent; and so forth. This is a *progressive* income tax.

Finally, suppose the rate declines as taxable income rises: you pay 15 percent if you earn less than $10,000; 10 percent if you earn $10,000 to $20,000; 5 percent if you earn $20,000 to $30,000; and so forth. This is a regressive income tax.

In general, progressive taxes are those that fall relatively more heavily on those with high incomes; regressive taxes are those that fall relatively more heavily on the poor. *(Key Question 7)*

APPLICATIONS

Let's examine the progressivity, or regressivity, of several taxes. In Table 16-2 you will find the yields of the main taxes in Canada and what these yields are as a percentage of gross domestic product.

- ***Personal Income Tax***   The federal personal income tax is progressive, with the marginal tax rate (those assessed on additional income) ranging from 15 to 29 percent. In 2009 the federal income tax was 15 percent on the first $40,726; 22 percent for income between $40,726 and $81,452; 26 percent for income between $81,452 and $126,264; and 29 percent for income above $126,264. Rules that allow individuals to deduct from income contributions to their

TABLE 16-2	Tax Revenue Sources of Canadian Governments, 2008	
	Billions of dollars	**Percentage of GDP**
Personal income taxes	193.5	12.1
Corporation income taxes	67.6	4.2
Sales taxes	72.1	4.5
Consumption taxes	111.7	7.0
Property and related taxes	54.0	3.3
Other taxes	101.7	6.3
Total tax revenues	600.6	37.4

SOURCE: Statistics Canada. For updates go to http://www40.statcan.ca/l01/cst01/govt01a-eng.htm.

registered retirement saving plan (RRSP) tend to make the tax less progressive than these marginal rates suggest. Nevertheless, average tax rates rise with income. Table 16-2 shows that the personal income tax is the largest source of government revenue.

- **Sales Taxes**   At first thought, a general sales tax with, for example, a 5 percent rate would seem to be proportional, but in fact it is regressive with respect to income. A larger portion of a low-income person's income is taxed than is the case for a high-income person; the rich pay no tax on the part of income that is saved, whereas the poor are unable to save. For example, "low-income" Goldstein has an income of $15,000 and spends it all. "High-income" Jones has an income of $300,000 but spends only $200,000 and saves the rest. Assuming a 5 percent sales tax applies to all expenditures of each individual, we find that Goldstein pays $750 (5 percent of $15,000) in sales taxes and Jones pays $10,000 (5 percent of $200,000). But Goldstein pays $750/$15,000 or 5 percent of income as sales taxes, while Jones pays $10,000/$300,000 or 3.3 percent of income as sales tax. The general sales tax, therefore, is regressive.

- **Corporate Income Tax**   The federal corporate income tax is essentially a proportional tax with a flat 21 percent tax rate in 2008. But this assumes that corporation owners (shareholders) bear the tax. Some tax experts argue that at least part of the tax is passed through to consumers in the form of higher product prices. To the extent that this occurs, the tax is like a sales tax and is thus regressive.

- **Property Taxes**   Most economists conclude that property taxes on buildings are regressive for the same reasons as are sales taxes. First, property owners add the tax to the rents that tenants are charged. Second, property taxes, as a percentage of income, are higher for low-income families than for high-income families because the poor must spend a larger proportion of their incomes for housing. The regressivity of property taxes may be increased by differences in property-tax rates from municipality to municipality.

The LAST WORD   Rent Seeking

The French economist Frédéric Bastiat (1801–50) is remembered for his wit and his capacity to point out absurdities in the arguments of his opponents. In the following passage, he satirizes appeals to government for special benefits at someone else's expense, or what today we call "rent seeking." His message is timeless: When rent-seekers succeed, it is often at the expense of the general interest.

When, unfortunately, one has regard to the interest of the producer, and not to that of the consumer, it is impossible to avoid running counter to the general interest, because the demand of the producer, as such, is only for efforts, wants, and obstacles.

I find a remarkable illustration of this in a Bordeaux newspaper. M. Simiot proposes this question: Should the proposed railway from Paris to Madrid offer a solution of continuity at Bordeaux?

[Mr. Simiot argues that] the railway from Paris to Bayonne should have a break at Bordeaux, for if goods and passengers are forced to stop at that town, profits will accrue to bargemen, pedlars, *commissionaires*, hotel-keepers, etc.

Here we have clearly the interest of labour put before the interest of consumers.

But if Bordeaux has a right to profit by a gap in the line of railway, and if such profit is consistent with the public interest, then Angoulême, Poitiers, Tours, Orleans, nay, more, all the intermediate places, Ruffec, Châtellerault, etc., should also demand gaps, as being

for the general interest, and, of course, for the interest of national industry; for the more these breaks in the line are multiplied, the greater will be the increase of consignments, commissions, transhipments, etc., along the whole extent of the railway. In this way, we shall succeed in having a line of railway composed of successive gaps, and which may be denominated a *Negative Railway*.

The *principle of restriction* is the very same as the *principle of gaps*; the sacrifice of the consumer's interest to that of the producer, in other words, the sacrifice of the ends to the means.*

---

*Bastiat, Frédéric, *Economic Sophisms*. Arthur Goddard, trans. The Foundation of Economic Education, Inc., 1996.

Question

If self-interest is one of the main driving forces of the market economy why does Bastiat, a proponent of the market system, take objection to the expressions of self-interest by the various groups in the construction of the French railway?

CHAPTER SUMMARY

16.1 ▶ REVEALING PREFERENCES THROUGH MAJORITY VOTING

- Public choice theory examines the economics of collective and government decision making, politics, and elections.

- Majority voting creates a possibility of (a) an underallocation or an overallocation of resources to a particular public good, and (b) inconsistent voting outcomes. The median-voter model predicts that, under majority rule, the person holding the middle position on an issue will determine the outcome of an election involving that issue.

16.2 ▶ GOVERNMENT FAILURE

- Public choice theorists cite reasons why government might be inefficient in providing public goods and services: (a) There are strong reasons for politicians to support special-interest legislation; (b) Politicians may be biased in favour of programs with immediate and clear-cut benefits and difficult-to-identify costs and against programs with immediate and easily identified costs and vague or deferred benefits; (c) Citizens as voters and governmental representatives face limited and bundled choices as to public goods and services, whereas consumers in the private sector can be highly selective in their choices; (d) Government bureaucracies have less incentive to operate efficiently than does private businesses.

16.3 ▶ APPORTIONING THE TAX BURDEN

- The benefits-received principle of taxation states that those who receive the benefits of goods and services provided by government should pay the taxes required to finance them. The ability-to-pay principle states that those who have greater income should be taxed more, absolutely and relatively, than those who have less income.

- The federal personal income tax is progressive. The flat-rate corporate income tax is regressive. General sales, excise, and property taxes are regressive.

TERMS AND CONCEPTS

public choice theory, p. 374	government failure, p. 378	ability-to-pay principle, p. 381
logrolling, p. 375	special-interest effect, p. 378	progressive tax, p. 382
paradox of voting, p. 375	rent seeking, p. 379	regressive tax, p. 382
median-voter model, p. 377	benefits-received principle, p. 381	proportional tax, p. 382

STUDY QUESTIONS

16.1 1. Explain how affirmative and negative majority votes can sometimes lead to inefficient allocations of resources to public goods. Is this problem likely to be greater under a benefits-received or under an ability-to-pay tax system? Use the information in Figure 16-1a and b to show how society might be better off if Adams were allowed to buy votes.

16.1 2. **KEY QUESTION** Explain the paradox of voting through reference to the accompanying table, which shows the ranking of three public goods by voters Larry, Curley, and Moe:

Public good	Larry	Rankings Curley	Moe
Courthouse	2nd choice	1st choice	3rd choice
School	3rd choice	2nd choice	1st choice
Park	1st choice	3rd choice	2nd choice

16.1 3. **KEY QUESTION** Suppose there are only five people in a society and each favours one of the five highway construction options from Chapter 15 (see Table 15-2; include no highway construction as one of the options). Explain which of these highway options will be selected using a majority paired-choice vote. Will this option be the optimal size of the project from an economic perspective?

4. **KEY QUESTION** How does the problem of limited and **LO ▶ 16.2** bundled choice in the public sector relate to economic efficiency? Why are public bureaucracies alleged to be less efficient than private enterprises?

5. Explain: "Politicians would make more rational economic **LO ▶ 16.2** decisions if they weren't running for re-election every few years."

6. Distinguish between the benefits-received and the ability- **LO ▶ 16.3** to-pay principles of taxation. Which philosophy is more evident in our present tax structure? Justify your answer. To which principle of taxation do you subscribe? Why?

7. **KEY QUESTION** Suppose a tax is such that an individual **LO ▶ 16.3** with an income of $10,000 pays $2000 of tax, a person with an income of $20,000 pays $3000 of tax, a person with an income of $30,000 pays $4000 of tax, and so forth. What is each person's average tax rate? Is this tax regressive, proportional, or progressive?

8. What is meant by a progressive tax? A regressive tax? A **LO ▶ 16.3** proportional tax? Comment on the progressivity or regressivity of each of the following taxes, indicating your assumption concerning tax incidence: (a) the federal personal income tax, (b) a 7 percent general sales tax, (c) a federal excise tax on automobile tires, (d) a municipal property tax on real estate, (e) the federal corporate income tax.

INTERNET APPLICATION QUESTIONS @

1. **Bureaucracy and Inefficiency—The Post Office versus Federal Express.** Some economists contend that public agencies are generally less efficient than private businesses. Federal Express competes directly with Canada Post for delivery of express mail and packages. Assume you need to send an express letter and a package from your address to either Halifax or Vancouver.

Access the Web sites of Federal Express and Canada Post through the McConnell-Brue-Flynn-Barbiero Web site (Chapter 16). Based on their interactive rate and options calculators, which service is more competitive as to price and delivery? Does a lower rate with greater delivery options mean greater efficiency? Why or why not?

CHAPTER 17

International Trade

Backpackers in the wilderness like to think they are "leaving the world behind," but, like Atlas, they carry the world on their shoulders. Much of their equipment is imported—knives from Switzerland, rain gear from South Korea, cameras from Japan, aluminum pots from England, sleeping bags from China, hiking boots from Italy, and compasses from Finland. Moreover, they may have driven to the trailheads in Japanese-made Toyotas or German-made BMWs, sipping coffee from Colombia and snacking on bananas from Honduras.

International trade and the global economy affect all of us daily, whether we are hiking in the wilderness, driving our cars, listening to music, or working at our jobs. We cannot leave the world behind. We are enmeshed in a global web of economic relationships—trading of goods and services, multinational corporations, cooperative ventures among the world's firms, and ties among the world's financial markets.

In this chapter we provide an analysis of the benefits of international trade and an appraisal of the arguments for protectionism.

17.1 | The Economic Basis for Trade

International trade enables nations to specialize their production, improve their resource productivity, and acquire more goods and services. Nations, like individuals and the regions of a nation, can gain by specializing in those products they can produce with greatest relative efficiency and trading them for those goods they cannot produce as efficiently. A more complete answer to the question "Why do nations trade?" hinges on three facts:

- The distribution of natural, human, and capital resources among nations is uneven; nations differ in their endowments of economic resources.

- Efficient production of various goods requires different technologies or combinations of resources.

- Products are differentiated as to quality and other nonprice attributes. Some people may prefer certain imported goods to similar goods made domestically.

To recognize the character and interaction of these three facts, think of different countries in the world. China, for example, has a large and well-educated labour force and therefore relatively inexpensive skilled labour. As a result, China can produce efficiently (at low cost) a variety of **labour-intensive goods** such as cameras, video game players, and video recorders, the design and production of which require much skilled labour. In contrast, Australia has vast amounts of land and can inexpensively produce such **land-intensive goods** as wheat, wool, and meat. Brazil has the soil, tropical climate, rainfall, and the ready supply of unskilled labour that are needed for the efficient, low-cost production of coffee. Industrially advanced economies with relatively large amounts of capital can produce inexpensively those goods that require much capital to produce, including such **capital-intensive goods** as automobiles, agricultural equipment, machinery, and chemicals.

All nations, regardless of their labour, land, or capital intensity, can find special niches for individual products that are in demand worldwide because of their special qualities. Examples include fashions from Italy, luxury automobiles from Germany, software from the United States, watches from Switzerland, and ice wine from Canada.

The distribution of resources, technology, and product distinctiveness among nations, however, is not forever fixed. When that distribution changes, the relative efficiency and success with which nations produce and sell goods also changes. For example, in the past few decades South Korea has upgraded the quality of its labour force and has greatly expanded its stock of capital. Although South Korea was primarily an exporter of agricultural products and raw materials a half-century ago, it now exports large quantities of manufactured goods.

As national economies evolve, the size and quality of their labour forces may change, the volume and composition of their capital stocks may shift, new technologies may develop, and even the quality of land and the quantity of natural resources may be altered. As such changes occur, the relative efficiency with which a nation can produce specific goods will also change.

Specialization and Comparative Advantage

Let's now use the concept of comparative advantage to analyze the basis for international specialization and trade.

The Basic Principle

The central concept underlying comparative advantage can be illustrated by posing a problem. Suppose that Madison, a chartered accountant (CA), is also a swifter house painter than Mason, the professional painter she is thinking of hiring. Also assume that Madison can earn $50 per hour doing accounting and must pay Mason $15 per hour. And suppose that Madison would need 30 hours to paint her house but Mason would need 40 hours. Finally, assume Madison receives no special pleasure from painting.

Should Madison take time off from accounting to paint her own house or should she hire the painter? Madison's opportunity cost of painting her house is $1500 (= 30 hours × $50 per hour of sacrificed income). The cost of hiring Mason is only $600 (= 40 hours × $15 per hour paid to the painter). Although Madison is better at both accounting and painting, she will get her house painted at a lower cost by specializing in accounting and using some of the proceeds to hire the house painter.

Note that Madison has an **absolute advantage** in both accounting and painting; she can do accounting and paint more efficiently than our hypothetical house painter. Despite this, Madison should hire a house painter because of her "comparative advantage."

Similarly, Mason can reduce his cost of obtaining accounting services by specializing in painting and using some of his income to hire Madison to prepare his income tax forms. Suppose Mason would need 10 hours to prepare his income tax return, but Mason could handle this task in 2 hours.

labour-intensive goods
Products that require a relatively large amount of labour to produce.

land-intensive goods
Products that require a relatively large amount of land to produce.

capital-intensive goods
Products that require a relatively large amount of capital to produce.

All nations, regardless of their labour, land, or capital intensity, can find special niches for products that are in demand worldwide.

absolute advantage
When a region or nation can produce more of good Z and good Y with less resources compared to other regions or nations.

Mason would sacrifice $150 of income (= 10 hours × $15 per hour of sacrificed time) to get a task done that he could hire out for $100 (= 2 hours × $50 per CA hour). By using Madison to prepare his tax return, Mason *lowers his cost of getting the tax return prepared.*

What is true for our CA and house painter is also true for nations. Specializing enables nations to reduce the cost of obtaining goods and services they desire.

With this simple example in mind, let's turn to an international trade model to understand the gains from specialization and trade.

Two Isolated Nations

Suppose the world economy has just two nations, Canada and Brazil. For simplicity, we assume the labour forces in Canada and Brazil are of equal sizes. Each can produce both steel and soybeans, but at differing levels of economic efficiency. Suppose Canadian and Brazilian domestic production possibilities curves for soybeans and steel are as shown in Figures 17-1a and 17-1b. Note especially three characteristics of these production possibilities curves:

- *Constant Costs* The "curves" are drawn as straight lines, in contrast to the concave-from-the-origin production possibilities frontiers introduced in Chapter 1. This means the law of increasing costs has been replaced with the assumption of constant costs. This substitution simplifies our discussion but does not change our analysis and conclusions. Later we will consider the effect of the more realistic increasing opportunity costs.

- *Different Costs* The production possibilities curves of Canada and Brazil reflect different resource mixes and levels of technological progress. Specifically, the differing slopes of the two curves tell us that the opportunity costs of producing steel and soybeans differ between the two nations.

- *Canada Has Absolute Advantage in Both* In view of our assumption that the Canadian and Brazilian labour forces are of equal size, the two production possibilities curves show that

FIGURE 17-1   Production Possibilities Curve

The two production possibilities lines show the amounts of soybeans and steel (a) Canada and (b) Brazil can produce domestically. The curves for both countries are straight lines because we are assuming constant costs. The different cost ratios, 1 steel = 1 soybean for Canada, and 1 steel = 2 soybeans for Brazil are reflected in the different slopes of the two lines.

(a) Canada

(b) Brazil

Canada has an *absolute advantage* in producing both products. If Canada and Brazil use their entire (equal-size) labour forces to produce either steel or soybeans, Canada can produce more of either than Brazil. There are greater production possibilities in Canada using the same number of workers as in Brazil. So output per worker—labour productivity—in Canada exceeds that in Brazil in producing both products.

CANADA

In Figure 17-1a, with full employment, Canada will operate on its production possibilities curve. Canada can increase its output of steel from 0 to 30 tonnes by forgoing an output of 30 tonnes of soybeans. This means the slope of the production possibilities curve is –1 (= –30 soybeans/+30 steel), implying that 1 tonne of steel can be obtained for every tonne of soybeans sacrificed. In Canada the domestic exchange ratio or **opportunity-cost ratio** for the two products is 1 tonne of steel for 1 tonne of soybeans, or

opportunity-cost ratio
An equality showing the number of units of two products that can be produced with the same resources.

$$1S_t = 1S_{oy}$$

Canada can internally "exchange" a tonne of steel for a tonne of soybeans. Our constant-cost assumption means this exchange or opportunity cost equation prevails for all possible moves from one point to another along Canada's production possibilities curve.

BRAZIL

Brazil's production possibilities curve in Figure 17-1b represents a different opportunity cost ratio. In Brazil 2 tonnes of soybeans must be given up to get 1 tonne of steel. The slope of the production possibilities curve is –2 (= –2 soybeans/+1 steel). This means that in Brazil the domestic cost ratio for the two goods is 1 tonne of steel for 2 tonnes of soybeans, or

$$1S_t = 2S_{oy}$$

Self-Sufficiency Output Mix

If Canada and Brazil are isolated and are to be self-sufficient, each must choose some output mix on its production possibilities curve. It will choose the mix that provides the greatest total utility, or satisfaction. Assume point *A* in Figure 17-1a is the optimal output mix in Canada. The choice of this combination of 18 tonnes of steel and 12 tonnes of soybeans equates the marginal benefit and marginal cost of both goods. Suppose Brazil's optimal product mix is 8 tonnes of steel and 4 tonnes of soybeans, indicated by point *B* in Figure 17-1b. These choices are reflected in column 1, Table 17-1.

TABLE 17-1

International Specialization According to Comparative Advantage and the Gains from Trade (in tonnes)

Country	(1) Outputs before specialization	(2) Outputs after specialization	(3) Amounts exported (–) and imported (+)	(4) Outputs available after trade	(5) Gains from specialization and trade (4) – (1)
Canada	18 steel	30 steel	–10 steel	20 steel	2 steel
	12 soybeans	0 soybeans	+15 soybeans	15 soybeans	3 soybeans
Brazil	8 steel	0 steel	+10 steel	10 steel	2 steel
	4 soybeans	20 soybeans	–15 soybeans	5 soybeans	1 soybeans
Total output (steel and soybeans)	42	50		50	8

Specialization Based on Comparative Advantage

Although Canada has an absolute advantage in producing both goods, gains from specialization and trade are possible. Specialization and trade are mutually beneficial or "profitable" to the two nations if the *comparative* opportunity costs of producing the two products within the two nations differ, as they do in this example. The **principle of comparative advantage** says that total output will be greatest when each good is produced by that nation that has the lowest domestic opportunity cost for that good. In our two-nation illustration, Canada's domestic opportunity cost is lower for steel. Canada need only forgo 1 tonne of soybeans to produce 1 tonne of steel, whereas Brazil must forgo 2 tonnes of soybeans for 1 tonne of steel. Canada has a comparative (cost) advantage in steel and should specialize in steel production. The "world" (that is, Canada and Brazil) is not economizing in the use of its resources if a high-cost producer (Brazil) produced a specific product (steel) when a low-cost producer (Canada) could have produced it. Having Brazil produce steel would mean that the world economy would have to give up more soybeans than is necessary to obtain a tonne of steel.

Brazil has the lower domestic opportunity cost for soybeans; it must sacrifice only ½ tonne of steel in producing 1 tonne of soybeans, whereas Canada must forgo 1 tonne of steel in producing a tonne of soybeans. Brazil has a comparative advantage in soybeans and should specialize in soybean production. Economizing requires that any particular good be produced by the nation with the lower domestic opportunity cost, or a comparative advantage. Canada should produce steel and Brazil soybeans. Note that this conclusion holds even though Canada has an absolute advantage in both steel and soybeans.

In column 2 of Table 17-1 we verify that specialization allows the world to get more output from fixed amounts of resources. By specializing completely in steel, Canada can produce 30 tonnes of steel and no soybeans; Brazil, by specializing completely in soybeans, produces 20 tonnes of soybeans and no steel. The world ends up with 4 more tonnes of steel (30 tonnes, compared with 26) *and* 4 more tonnes of soybeans (20 tonnes, compared with 16) than where there is self-sufficiency or unspecialized production.

Terms of Trade

But consumers of each nation want *both* steel and soybeans. They can have both if the two nations trade or exchange the two products. But what will be the **terms of trade**? At what exchange ratio will Canada and Brazil trade steel and soybeans?

Because $1S_t = 1S_{oy}$ in Canada, Canada must get *more than* 1 tonne of soybeans for each tonne of steel exported or it will not benefit Canada to export steel in exchange for Brazilian soybeans. Canada must get a better "price" (more soybeans) for its steel in the world market than it can get domestically, or there is no gain from trade and it will not occur.

Similarly, because $1S_t = 2S_{oy}$ in Brazil, Brazil must get 1 tonne of steel by exporting some amount *less than* 2 tonnes of soybeans. Brazil must pay a lower "price" for steel in the world market than it must pay domestically, or it will not want to trade. The international exchange ratio or terms of trade must lie somewhere between

$$1S_t = 1S_{oy} \text{ (Canada's cost conditions)}$$
and
$$1S_t = 2S_{oy} \text{ (Brazil's cost conditions)}$$

But where between these limits will the world exchange ratio fall? Canada will prefer a ratio close to $1S_t = 2S_{oy}$, say, $1S_t = 1\frac{3}{4} S_{oy}$. Canada wants to get the most soybeans possible for each tonne of steel it exports. Similarly, Brazil wants a rate near $1S_t = 1S_{oy}$, say $1S_t = 1\frac{1}{4} S_{oy}$. Brazil wants to export the least soybeans possible for each tonne of steel it receives in exchange.

The actual exchange ratio depends primarily on world supply and demand for the two products, but also the relative competitiveness of world markets for soybeans and steel. If overall world demand for soybeans is weak relative to its supply and the demand for steel is strong relative to its supply, the exchange ratio will settle nearer the $1S_t = 2S_{oy}$ figure Canada prefers. If overall world

principle of comparative advantage
When a region or nation can produce a good at a lower domestic opportunity cost compared to a potential trading partner.

terms of trade
The rate at which units of one product can be exchanged for units of another product.

demand for soybeans is great relative to its supply and if the demand for steel is weak relative to its supply, the ratio will settle nearer the $1S_t = 1S_{oy}$ level favourable to Brazil. (We will take up the topic of equilibrium world prices later in this chapter.)

Gains from Specialization and Trade

trading possibilities line
Shows the different combinations of two products that an economy is able to obtain when it specializes in the production of one product and exports it to obtain the other product.

Suppose the international exchange ratio or terms of trade is $1S_t = 1\frac{1}{2} S_{oy}$. The possibility of trading on these terms permits each nation to supplement its domestic production possibilities line with a **trading possibilities line.** This can be seen in **Figure 17-2 (Key Graph).** Just as a production possibilities line shows the amount of these products a full-employment economy can obtain by shifting resources from one to the other, a trading possibilities line shows the amounts of two products a nation can obtain by specializing in one product and trading for another. The trading possibilities lines in Figure 17-2 reflect the assumption that both nations specialize based on comparative advantage: Canada specializes completely in steel (point W in Figure 17-2a) and Brazil completely in soybeans (at point c in Figure 17-2b).

IMPROVED OPTIONS

Specialization according to comparative advantage results in more efficient allocation of world resources.

Now Canada is not constrained by its domestic production possibilities line, which requires it to give up 1 tonne of steel for every tonne of soybeans it wants as it moves up its domestic production possibilities line, say from point W. Instead, Canada, through trade with Brazil, can get 1½ tonnes of soybeans for every tonne of steel it exports to Brazil, so long as Brazil has soybeans to export. Trading possibility line WC' thus represents the $1S_t = 1\frac{1}{2} S_{oy}$ trading ratio.

Similarly, Brazil, starting at, say, point c, no longer has to move down its domestic production possibilities curve, giving up 2 tonnes of soybeans for each tonne of steel it wants. It can now export just 1½ tonnes of soybeans for each tonne of steel it wants by moving down its trading possibilities line cw'.

Specialization and trade create a new exchange ratio between steel and soybeans, reflected in a nation's trading possibilities line. This exchange ratio is superior for both nations to the self-sufficiency exchange ratio embodied in the production possibilities line of each. By specializing in steel and trading for Brazil's soybeans, Canada can obtain more than 1 tonne of soybeans for 1 tonne of steel. By specializing in soybeans and trading for Canada's steel, Brazil can get 1 tonne of steel for less than 2 tonnes of soybeans. In both cases, self-sufficiency is undesirable.

ADDED OUTPUT

By specializing according to comparative advantage and trading for those goods produced in other nations with greater domestic efficiency, Canada and Brazil can realize combinations of steel and soybeans beyond their production possibilities boundaries. *Specialization according to comparative advantage results in a more efficient allocation of world resources, and larger outputs of both steel and soybeans are therefore available to both nations.*

Suppose that at the $1S_t = 1\frac{1}{2} S_{oy}$ terms of trade, Canada exports 10 tonnes of steel to Brazil and in return Brazil exports 15 tonnes of soybeans to Canada. How do the new quantities of steel and soybeans available to the two nations compare with the optimal product mixes that existed before specialization and trade? Point A in Figure 17-2a reminds us that Canada chose 18 tonnes of steel and 12 tonnes of soybeans originally. But, by producing 30 tonnes of steel and no soybeans, and by trading 10 tonnes of steel for 15 tonnes of soybeans, Canada can obtain 20 tonnes of steel and 15 tonnes of soybeans. This new, superior combination of steel and soybeans is shown by point A' in Figure 17-2a. Compared with the non-trading figures of 18 tonnes of steel and 12 tonnes of soybeans, Canada's **gains from trade** are 2 tonnes of steel and 3 tonnes of soybeans.

gains from trade
The extra output that trading partners obtain through specialization of production and exchange of goods and services.

Similarly, recall that Brazil's optimal product mix was 4 tonnes of soybeans and 8 tonnes of steel (point B) before specialization and trade. Now, by specializing in soybeans and trading—producing 20 tonnes of soybeans and no steel and exporting 15 tonnes of its soybeans in exchange for 10 tonnes of Canadian steel—Brazil can have 5 tonnes of soybeans and 10 tonnes of steel. This new position is indicated by point B' in Figure 17-2b. Brazil's gains from trade are 1 tonne of soybeans

KEY GRAPH

FIGURE 17-2
Trading Possibilities Lines and the Gains from Trade

As a result of international specialization and trade, Canada and Brazil both can have levels of output higher than those attainable on their domestic production possibilities curves. Panel (a): Canada can move from point A on its domestic production possibilities curve to, say, A' on its trading possibilities line. Panel (b): Brazil can move from B to B'.

(a) Canada

(b) Brazil

Quick Quiz

1. **The production possibilities curves in graphs (a) and (b) imply:**
   a. increasing domestic opportunity costs.
   b. decreasing domestic opportunity costs.
   c. constant domestic opportunity costs.
   d. first decreasing, then increasing, domestic opportunity costs.

2. **Before specialization, the domestic opportunity cost of producing 1 unit of steel is:**
   a. 1 unit of soybeans in both Canada and Brazil.
   b. 1 unit of soybeans in Canada and 2 units of soybeans in Brazil.
   c. 2 units of soybeans in Canada and 1 unit of soybeans in Brazil.
   d. 1 unit of soybeans in Canada and ½ unit of soybeans in Brazil.

3. **After specialization and trade, the world output of steel and soybeans is:**
   a. 20 tonnes of steel and 20 tonnes of soybeans.
   b. 45 tonnes of steel and 15 tonnes of soybeans.
   c. 30 tonnes of steel and 20 tonnes of soybeans.
   d. 10 tonnes of steel and 30 tonnes of soybeans.

4. **After specialization and international trade:**
   a. Canada can obtain units of soybeans at less cost than before trade.
   b. Brazil can obtain more than 20 tonnes of soybeans, if it so chooses.
   c. Canada no longer has a comparative advantage in producing steel.
   d. Brazil can benefit by prohibiting soybean imports from Canada.

Answers: 1. c; 2. b; 3. c; 4. a

and 2 tonnes of steel. *As a result of specialization and trade, both countries have more of both products.* Table 17-1, which summarizes the transaction and outcomes, merits careful study.

WORKED PROBLEM 17.1
Gains from Trade

The fact that points A' and B' are positions superior to A and B is enormously important. We know that a nation can expand its production possibilities boundary by (1) expanding the quantity and improving the quality of its resources or (2) realizing technological progress. We have now established that international trade can enable a nation to get around the output constraint imposed by its production possibilities curve. The effects of international specialization and trade are the equivalent of having more and better resources or discovering improved production techniques.

Trade with Increasing Costs

To explain the basic principles underlying international trade, we simplified our analysis in several ways. For example, we limited discussion to two products and two nations. But multiproduct/multinational analysis yields the same conclusions. We also assumed constant opportunity costs (linear production possibilities curves), which is a more substantive simplification. Let's consider the effect of allowing increasing opportunity costs (concave-from-the-origin production possibilities curves) to enter the picture.

Suppose Canada and Brazil are initially at positions on their concave production possibilities curves where their domestic cost ratios are $1S_t = 1S_{oy}$ and $1S_t = 2S_{oy}$, as they were in our constant-cost analysis. As before, comparative advantage indicates that Canada should specialize in steel and Brazil in soybeans. But now, as Canada begins to expand steel production, its $1S_t = 1S_{oy}$ cost ratio will *fall*; it will have to sacrifice *more than* 1 tonne of soybeans to get 1 additional tonne of steel. Resources are no longer perfectly shiftable between alternative uses, as the constant-cost assumption implied. Resources less and less suited to steel production must be allocated to the Canadian steel industry in expanding steel output, and this means increasing costs—the sacrifice of larger and larger amounts of soybeans for each additional tonne of steel.

17.1 | GLOBAL PERSPECTIVE

The top 12 globalized economies, 2007

Foreign Policy magazine publishes an annual list of the world's most globalized economies, based on 13 key indicators such as foreign trade, cross-border travel, Internet use, and international investment flows. Here is the magazine's list, in descending order, for 2007.

1. Singapore
2. Hong Kong
3. Netherlands
4. Switzerland
5. Ireland
6. Denmark
7. United States
8. Canada
9. Jordan
10. Estonia
11. Sweden
12. United Kingdom

Source: A.T. Kearney, *Foreign Policy*, www.foreignpolicy.com.

Similarly, Brazil, starting from its $1S_t = 2S_{oy}$ cost ratio position, expands soybean production. But as it does, it will find that its $1S_t = 2S_{oy}$ cost ratio begins to *rise*. Sacrificing a tonne of steel will free resources that can be used to produce something less than 2 tonnes of soybeans, because these transferred resources are less suitable to soybean production.

As the Canadian cost ratio falls from $1S_t = 1S_{oy}$ and Brazil's rises from $1S_t = 2S_{oy}$, a point will be reached at which the cost ratios are equal in the two nations, perhaps at $1S_t = 1\frac{3}{4}\,S_{oy}$. At this point, the underlying basis for further specialization and trade—differing cost ratios—has disappeared. Most importantly, this point of equal cost ratios may be reached where Canada is still producing *some* soybeans along with its steel and Brazil is producing some steel along with its soybeans. *The primary effect of increasing costs is to make specialization less than complete.* For this reason we often find domestically produced products competing directly against identical or similar imported products within a particular economy. *(Key Question 3)*

The Case for Free Trade Restated

The case for free trade reduces to one compelling argument. Through free trade based on the principle of comparative advantage, the world economy can achieve a more efficient allocation of resources and a higher level of material well-being than without free trade.

Since the resource mixes and technological knowledge of each country are somewhat different, each nation can produce particular commodities at different real costs. Each nation should produce goods for which its domestic opportunity costs are lower than the domestic opportunity costs of other nations, and exchange these specialties for products for which its domestic opportunity costs are high relative to those of other nations. If each nation does this, the world can realize the advantages of specialization. The world and each free-trading nation can obtain a larger real income from the fixed supplies of resources available to it.

One side benefit of free trade is that it promotes competition and deters monopoly. The increased competition from foreign firms forces domestic firms to adopt the lowest-cost production techniques. It also compels them to be innovative with respect to both product quality and production methods, thereby contributing to economic growth. And free trade provides consumers with a wider range of product choices. The reasons to favour free trade are the same reasons to endorse competition.

A second side-benefit of free trade is that it links national interest and breaks down national animosities. Confronted with political disagreements, trading partners tend to negotiate rather than make war.

QUICK REVIEW

▸ International trade has always been important to Canada, and it is becoming increasingly so.

▸ International trade enables nations to specialize, improve the productivity of their resources, and obtain a larger output.

▸ Comparative advantage means total world output will be greatest when each good is produced by that nation having the lowest domestic opportunity cost.

▸ Specialization is less than complete among nations because opportunity costs normally rise as any particular nation produces more of a particular good.

17.2 | Supply and Demand Analysis of Exports and Imports

world price
The international market price of a good or service, determined by world demand and supply.

domestic price
The price of a good or service within a country, determined by domestic demand and supply.

Supply and demand analysis reveals how equilibrium prices and quantities of exports and imports are determined. The amount of a good or service that a nation will export or import depends on differences between equilibrium world and domestic prices. The interaction of *world* supply and demand determines **world price,** the price at which the quantities supplied and demanded are equal globally. *Domestic supply* and demand determine the equilibrium **domestic price**—the price that would prevail in a closed economy. It is a price at which domestic supply and demand are equal.

In the absence of trade, domestic prices in a closed economy may or may not equal world equilibrium prices. When economies are opened for international trade, differences between world and domestic prices motivate exports or imports. To see how, let's now look at the international effects of such price differences in a simple two-nation world consisting of Canada and the United States, which are both producing aluminum. We assume there are no trade barriers, such as tariffs and quotas, and no international transportation costs.

Supply and Demand in Canada

Figure 17-3a shows the domestic supply curve S_d and domestic demand curve D_d for aluminum in Canada. The intersection of S_d and D_d determines the equilibrium domestic price of $1.25 per kilogram and the equilibrium domestic quantity is 100 million kilograms. Domestic suppliers produce 100 million kilograms and sell them at $1.25. So there are no domestic surpluses or shortages of aluminum.

FIGURE 17-3   Canadian Export Supply and Import Demand

In panel (a) world prices above the $1.25 domestic price create domestic surpluses of aluminum. As shown by the export supply curve in panel (b), these surpluses are exported. Domestic shortages occur when the world price is below $1.25 (a). These shortages are met by importing aluminum (b). The export supply curve shows the direct relationship between world prices and Canadian exports; the import supply curve portrays the inverse relationship between world prices and Canadian imports.

(a) Canadian domestic aluminum market

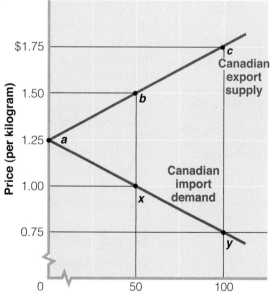

(b) Canadian export supply and import demand

But what if the Canadian economy is opened to world trade and the *world price* of aluminum is above or below this $1.25 domestic price?

CANADIAN EXPORT SUPPLY

If the world aluminum price exceeds $1.25, Canadian firms will produce more than 100 million kilograms and export the excess domestic output to the rest of the world (United States). First, consider a world price of $1.50. We see from the supply curve S_d that Canadian aluminum firms will produce 125 million kilograms of aluminum at that price. The demand curve D_d tells us that Canadians will purchase only 75 million kilograms at $1.50. The outcome is a domestic surplus of 50 million kilograms of aluminum. Canadian producers will export these 50 million kilograms at the $1.50 world price.

What if the world price is $1.75? The supply curve shows that Canadian firms will produce 150 million kilograms of aluminum, while the demand curve tells us that Canadian consumers will buy only 50 million kilograms. So Canadian producers will export the domestic surplus of 100 million kilograms.

In Figure 17-3b we assign the quantity of surplus or shortage to the horizontal scale. The domestic surpluses—the Canadian exports—occurring at world prices above the $1.25 domestic equilibrium price are plotted in red. When the world and domestic prices are equal (= $1.25), the quantity of exports supplied is zero (point *a*). There is no surplus of domestic output to export. But when the world price is $1.50, Canadian firms export 50 million kilograms of surplus aluminum (point *b*). At a $1.75 world price, the domestic surplus of 100 million kilograms is exported (point *c*).

export supply curve
An upward-sloping curve that shows the amount of a product domestic firms will export at each world price that is above the domestic price.

The Canadian **export supply curve,** found by connecting points such as *a, b,* and *c,* shows the amount of aluminum that Canadian producers will export at each world price above $1.25. This curve *slopes upward,* revealing a direct or positive relationship between the world price and amount of Canadian exports. *As world prices increase relative to domestic prices, Canadian exports rise.*

CANADIAN IMPORT DEMAND

If the world price is below $1.25, Canada will end up importing aluminum. Consider a $1.00 world price. The supply curve in Figure 17-3a reveals that at that price Canadian firms will produce only 75 million kilograms of aluminum. But the demand curve shows that Canadians want to buy 125 million kilograms at that price. The result is a domestic shortage of 50 million kilograms. To satisfy that shortage, Canada will import 50 million kilograms of aluminum.

At an even lower $0.75 world price, Canadian producers will supply only 50 million kilograms. Because Canadian consumers want to buy 150 million kilograms, there is a domestic shortage of 100 million kilograms. Imports will flow to Canada to make up the difference. That is, at a $0.75 world price Canadian firms supply 50 million kilograms and 100 million kilograms will be imported.

import demand curve
A downward-sloping curve that shows the amount of a product an economy will import at each world price below the domestic price.

In Figure 17-3b we plot the Canadian **import demand curve** from these data in blue. This *downward-sloping curve* shows the amounts of aluminum that will be imported at world prices below the $1.25 Canadian domestic price. The relationship between world prices and imports is inverse or negative. At a world price of $1.25, domestic output will satisfy Canadian demand; imports will be zero (point *a*). But at $1.00 Canadians will import 50 million kilograms of aluminum (point *x*); at $0.75, they will import 100 million kilograms (point *y*). Connecting points *a, x,* and *y* yields a *downward-sloping* Canadian import demand curve. *As world prices fall relative to domestic prices, Canadian imports increase.*

Supply and Demand in the United States

We repeat our analysis in Figure 17-4, this time for the United States. (We have converted U.S. dollar prices to Canadian dollar prices via an assumed exchange rate.) Note that the domestic supply curve S_d and demand curve D_d for aluminum in the United States yield a domestic price of $1.00, which is $0.25 lower than the $1.25 Canadian domestic price.

FIGURE 17-4   U.S. Export Supply and Import Demand

In panel (a) domestic production of aluminum in the United States exceeds domestic consumption at all world prices above the $1.00 domestic price. These domestic surpluses result in U.S. exports (b). When the domestic price falls below $1.00, domestic shortages occur (a) and imports flow to the United States (b). The U.S. export supply curve and import demand curve depict these relationships.

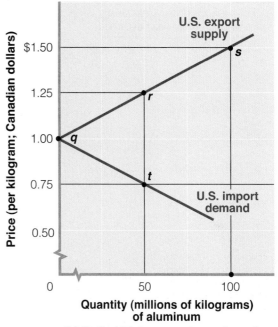

(a) United States domestic aluminum market

(b) United States export supply and import demand

The analysis proceeds exactly as for Canada. If the world price is $1.00, Americans will neither export nor import aluminum (which gives us point *q* in Figure 17-4b). At world prices above $1.00, U.S. firms will produce more aluminum than U.S. consumers will buy. The surplus will be exported. At a $1.25 world price, Figure 17-4a tells us that the United States will export a domestic surplus of 50 million kilograms (yielding point *r*). At $1.50 it will export a domestic surplus of 100 million kilograms (point *s*). Connecting these points yields the red, upward-sloping U.S. export supply curve that reflects the domestic surpluses (and thus exports) occurring when the world price exceeds the $1.00 U.S. domestic price.

At world prices below $1.00 domestic shortages occur in the United States. At a $0.75 world price, Figure 17-4a shows that U.S. consumers want to buy 125 million kilograms of aluminum but U.S. firms will produce only 75 million kilograms. The shortage will bring 50 million kilograms of imports to the United States (point *t* in Figure 17-4b). The blue U.S. import demand curve in that figure shows U.S. imports at world aluminum prices below the $1.00 U.S. domestic price.

Equilibrium World Price, Exports, and Imports

equilibrium world price
A price determined by the intersection of exporting nations' supply of a product and importing nations' demand for the same product.

We now have the tools to determine the **equilibrium world price** of aluminum and the equilibrium world levels of exports and imports. Figure 17-5 combines the Canadian export supply curve and import demand curve in Figure 17-3b and the U.S. export supply curve and import demand curve in Figure 17-4b. The two Canadian curves proceed rightward from the $1.25 domestic price; the two U.S. curves proceed rightward from the $1.00 U.S. domestic price.

FIGURE 17·5   **Equilibrium World Price and Quantity of Exports and Imports**

In a two-nation world, the equilibrium world price (= $1.125) is determined at the intersection of one nation's export supply curve and another nation's import demand curve. This intersection also decides the equilibrium volume of exports and imports. Here, the United States exports 25 million kilograms of aluminum to Canada.

International equilibrium occurs in this two-nation model where one nation's import demand curve intersects another nation's export supply curve. In this case Canada's import demand curve intersects America's export supply curve at *e*. There, the world price of aluminum is $1.125. The U.S. export supply curve indicates that the United States will export 25 million kilograms of aluminum at this price. Also at this price Canada will import 25 million kilograms from the United States, indicated by the Canadian import demand curve. The $1.125 world price equates the quantity of imports demanded and the quantity of exports supplied (= 25 million kilograms). Thus there will be world trade of 25 million kilograms of aluminum at $1.125 per kilogram.

Note that after trade, the single $1.125 world price will prevail in both Canada and the United States. Only one price for a standardized commodity can persist in a competitive market. With trade, all consumers can buy a kilogram of aluminum for $1.125 and all producers can sell it for that price.

WORKED PROBLEM 17.2
Equilibrium World Price, Exports, and Imports

Why would the United States willingly send 50 million kilograms of its aluminum output to Canada for consumption? After all, producing this output uses up scarce U.S. resources and drives up the price of aluminum for Americans. Americans are willing to export aluminum to Canada because they can gain the means—the earnings of Canadian dollars—to import other goods, say telecommunications equipment, from Canada. *(Key Question 5)*

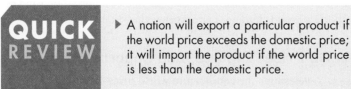

QUICK REVIEW

▶ A nation will export a particular product if the world price exceeds the domestic price; it will import the product if the world price is less than the domestic price.

▶ In a two-country model, equilibrium world prices and equilibrium quantities of exports and imports occur when one nation's export supply curve intersects the other nation's import demand curve.

17.3 | Trade Barriers

No matter how compelling the case for free trade, barriers to free trade *do* exist. Let's expand our discussion of trade barriers.

Excise taxes on imported goods are called **tariffs;** they may be imposed to raise government revenue or to protect domestic firms. A **revenue tariff** is usually applied to a product that is not being produced domestically—examples for Canada are tin, coffee, or bananas. Rates on revenue tariffs are modest; their purpose is to provide the federal government with revenues. A **protective tariff** is designed to shield domestic producers from foreign competition. Although protective tariffs are usually not high enough to stop the importation of foreign goods, they put foreign producers at a competitive disadvantage in selling in domestic markets.

A **nontariff barrier** refers to either a licensing requirement that specifies unreasonable standards pertaining to product quality and safety, or to unnecessary bureaucratic red tape that is used to restrict imports. Japan and the European countries frequently require their domestic importers of foreign goods to obtain licences. By restricting the issuance of licences, imports can be restricted. Great Britain used this barrier in the past to bar the importation of coal.

An **import quota** specifies the maximum amount of a commodity that may be imported in any period. Import quotas can slow down international commerce more effectively than tariffs. A product might be imported in large quantities despite high tariffs; low import quotas completely prohibit imports once quotas have been filled.

A **voluntary export restraint (VER)** is a trade barrier by which foreign firms "voluntarily" limit the amount of their exports to a particular country. Exporters agree to VERs—which have the effect of import quotas—in the hope of avoiding more stringent trade barriers. In the late 1990s, for example, Canadian producers of softwood lumber (fir, spruce, cedar, pine) agreed to a VER on exports to the United States under the threat of a permanently higher U.S. tariff. In section 16.5 we consider the arguments protectionists make to justify trade barriers.

Economic Impact of Tariffs

Once again we use supply and demand analysis to examine the economic effects of protective tariffs. Curves D_d and S_d in **Figure 17-6 (Key Graph)** show domestic demand and supply for a product in which a nation, say Canada, has a comparative *dis*advantage—for example DVD players. (Disregard $S_d + Q$ for now.) Without world trade, the domestic price and output would be P_d and q respectively.

Assume now that the domestic economy is opened to world trade and that the Chinese, who have a comparative advantage in DVD players, begin to sell them in Canada. We assume that with free trade the domestic price cannot differ from the world price, which here is P_w. At P_w domestic consumption is d and domestic production is a. The horizontal distance between the domestic supply and demand curves at P_w represents imports of ad. Thus far, our analysis is similar to the analysis of world prices in Figure 17-3.

DIRECT EFFECTS

Suppose now that Canada imposes a tariff on each imported DVD player. This will raise the domestic price from P_w to P_t and has four effects.

1. ***Decline in Consumption***   Consumption of DVD players in Canada declines from d to c as the higher price moves buyers up and to the left along their demand curve. The tariff prompts consumers to buy fewer DVD players and to reallocate a portion of their expenditures to less-desired substitute products. Canadian consumers are injured by the tariff, since they pay $P_t - P_w$ more for each of the c units they now buy at price P_t.

---

tariff
A tax imposed by a nation on an imported good.

revenue tariff
A tariff designed to produce income for the federal government.

protective tariff
A tariff designed to shield domestic producers of a good or service from the competition of foreign producers.

nontariff barrier
All restrictions other than tariffs that nations erect to impede international trade.

import quota
A limit imposed by a nation on the quantity (or total value) of a good that may be imported during some period of time.

voluntary export restraint (VER)
Voluntary limitations by countries or firms of their exports to a particular foreign nation.

ORIGIN 17.1
Mercantalism

2. **Increased Domestic Production** Canadian producers—who are *not* subject to the tariff—receive higher price P_t per unit. Because this new price is higher than the pre-tariff or world price of P_w, the domestic DVD player industry moves up and to the right along its supply curve S_d, increasing domestic output from *a* to *b*. Domestic producers thus enjoy both a higher price and expanded sales, which explains why domestic producers lobby for protective tariffs. But from a social point of view, the expanded domestic production of *b* instead of *a* means that the tariff permits domestic producers of DVD players to bid resources away from other, more efficient, Canadian industries.

3. **Decline in Imports** Chinese producers are hurt. Although the sale price of DVD players is higher by P_t-P_w, that amount accrues to the Canadian government, not to Chinese producers. The after-tariff world price, and thus the per-unit revenue to Chinese producers, remains at P_w, and the volume of Canadian imports (Chinese exports) falls from *d-a* to *c-b*.

4. **Tariff Revenue** The shaded rectangle indicates the amount of revenue that the tariff yields. Total revenue from the tariff is determined by multiplying the tariff, P_t-P_w per unit, by the number of imported DVD players, *c-b*. This tariff revenue is a transfer of income from consumers to government and does *not* represent any net change in the nation's economic well-being. The result is that government gains a portion of what consumers lose by paying more for DVD players.

INDIRECT EFFECTS

Tariffs have a subtle effect beyond what our supply and demand diagram can show. Because China sells fewer DVD players in Canada, China will earn fewer dollars with which to buy Canadian exports. Canadian export industries must then cut production and release resources. These are highly efficient industries, as evidenced by their comparative advantage and ability to sell goods in world markets.

Tariffs directly promote the expansion of inefficient industries that do not have a comparative advantage; they also indirectly cause contraction of relatively efficient industries that do have a comparative advantage. We know that specialization and world trade lead to more efficient use of world resources and greater world output. But protective tariffs reduce world trade. Therefore, tariffs also reduce efficiency and the world's real output.

Economic Impact of Quotas

The economic impact of quotas is similar to that of a tariff with one salient difference: Although tariffs generate revenue for the Canadian government, a quota transfers that revenue to foreign producers.

Suppose in Figure 17-6 that, instead of imposing a tariff of P_t-P_w per unit, Canada prohibits any Chinese imports of DVD players in excess of *bc* units. In other words, an import quota of *bc* DVD players is imposed on China. We have deliberately chosen the size of this quota to be the same amount as imports would be under a P_t-P_w tariff so we are comparing "equivalent" situations. As a consequence of the quota, the supply of DVD players is $S_d + Q$ in Canada. This consists of the domestic supply plus the constant amount *c-b* $(= Q)$, that importers will provide at each domestic price. The $S_d + Q$ supply curve does not exist below price P_w because Chinese producers would not export DVD players to Canada at any price *below* P_w; instead, they would sell them to other countries at the world market price of P_w.

Most of the economic results are the same as with a tariff. DVD player prices are higher (P_t instead of P_w) because imports have been reduced from *d-a* to *c-b*. Domestic consumption of DVD players is down from *d-a* to *c-b*. Canadian producers enjoy both a higher price (P_t rather than P_w) and increased sales (*b* rather than *a*).

The difference is that the price increase of P_t-P_w paid by Canadian consumers on imports of *c-b*—the shaded area—no longer goes to the Canada Revenue Agency as tariff (tax) revenue, but flows to those Chinese firms that have acquired the quota rights to sell DVD players in Canada. The economic effects of a tariff are better for Canadian taxpayers than are those of a quota, other things being the same. A tariff generates government revenue, which can be used to cut other taxes or to finance public goods and services that benefit Canadian citizens. In contrast, the higher price created by quotas results in additional revenue for foreign producers. *(Key Question 6)*

KEY GRAPH

FIGURE 17-6   The Economic Effects of a Protective Tariff or an Import Quota

A tariff that increases the price of a good from P_w to P_t will reduce domestic consumption from d to c. Domestic producers will be able to sell more output (b rather than a) at a higher price (P_t rather than P_w). Foreign exporters are injured because they sell less output (bc rather than ad). The shaded area indicates the amount of tariff paid by domestic consumers. An import quota of bc units has the same effect as the tariff, with one exception: The amount represented by the shaded area will go to foreign producers rather than to the domestic government.

Quick Quiz

1. **At world price P_w:**
   a. domestic quantity demanded equals quantity supplied.
   b. domestic quantity demanded is less than quantity supplied.
   c. domestic quantity demanded is greater than quantity supplied.
   d. domestic quantity supplied is greater than quantity demanded.

2. **At world prices above P_d Canada would:**
   a. import.
   b. export.
   c. stop producing.
   d. none of the above.

3. **A protective tariff:**
   a. increases domestic production.
   b. decreases domestic production.
   c. does not affect domestic production.
   d. decreases government revenue.

4. **A quota:**
   a. decreases government revenue.
   b. increases government revenue.
   c. has no effect on government revenue.
   d. lowers domestic price.

Net Costs of Tariffs and Quotas

Figure 17-6 shows that tariffs and quotas impose costs on domestic consumers but provide gains to domestic producers, and, in the case of tariffs, revenue to the federal government. The consumer costs of trade restrictions are calculated by determining the effect they have on consumer prices. Protection raises the price of a product in three ways: (1) the price of the imported product goes up, (2) the higher price of imports causes some consumers to shift their purchases to higher-priced domestically produced goods, and (3) the prices of domestically produced goods rise because import competition has declined.

Study after study finds that the costs to consumers substantially exceed gains to producers, workers, and other suppliers of resources in the protected industry, and government. A sizable net cost or efficiency loss to society arises from trade protection. Furthermore, industries employ large amounts of economic resources to influence politicians to pass and retain protectionist laws. Because these rent-seeking efforts divert resources away from more socially desirable purposes, trade restrictions impose these additional costs on society as well.

The LAST WORD — Fair-Trade Products

As a university or college student, you may be aware of fair-trade-certified products, such as those offered at Starbucks. On some campuses, proponents of fair-trade consumption are highly active in encouraging fellow students to purchase only fair-trade goods. What is fair trade all about? And how effective is it as an economic development strategy?

Imports of goods by high-income nations from low-income nations increase the demand for labour in low-income nations. Other things equal, increases in labour demand raise wages and incomes. Some observers, however, conclude that the benefits that low-income countries derive from increased production—especially increased exports of agricultural commodities—accrue mainly to large corporations in those countries, some of which are owned by shareholders from high-income nations. Because workers in many low-income countries are highly immobile, have few employment options, and are not unionized, the large dominant sellers can supposedly keep an undeservedly large portion of the proceeds from added exports for themselves (in the form of profits) while simultaneously denying a fair share to their workers (by keeping wages low).

To counter this purported problem, consumer organizations in some of the high-income countries have tried to bypass the usual distribution channels and buy imported goods directly from producers or producer cooperatives that agree to *fair-trade standards*. Such standards guarantee the producers higher-than-market prices if they agree to pay their workers higher-than-market wages and to abide by rules regarding working conditions and workplace safety. Producers and products that meet the fair-trade standards are certified as fair-trade employers and fair-trade products. Fair-trade advocates in the rich nations then strongly urge consumers to purchase products—for example, coffee, wine, bananas, tea, fresh fruit, and cocoa—only from certified fair-trade producers. When pressure is sufficient, some corporate

buyers of these products conclude that it may be more profitable to provide fair-trade products to customers than to risk being labelled an exploiter of third-world labour. Because of the higher-than-market prices and wages, fair-trade goods usually are more expensive than noncertified products.

In economic terms, the purpose of the fair-trade movement is to redistribute more of the total gains from international trade directly to low-income producers and workers by increasing the demand for fair-trade imports relative to otherwise identical imports. Do these efforts succeed? Economists agree that the efforts of fair-trade advocates do channel purchases away from otherwise identical substitutes and toward fair-trade goods—and that these increases in product demand do, in turn, increase the demand for the labour used to produce fair-trade goods. These increased demands and the increases in prices and wages that result suggests that the fair-trade strategy "works" insofar as it raises prices and wages for *some* sellers and *some* workers in low-wage countries—namely those involved with fair-trade programs.

Nevertheless, most economists question the overall effectiveness of the fair-trade approach as an economic development strategy. They say that price and wage setting by advocacy groups is based on highly subjective views of fairness that may be at odds with economic realities. Distortions of market prices and wages invite inefficiency and unintended consequences. (Recall our discussion of government price floors in Chapter 3.)

The consensus among economists is that fair-trade purchasing in the high-income nations simply shifts demand within low-wage countries (or among them). It does not increase the *average* pay of the workers within a particular low-wage nation. Sustainable increases in average pay require economy-wide gains in labour productivity—output per hour of work. Unlike increases in education, more and improved capital goods, and improved technology, fair-trade purchasing in high-income nations does little, if anything, to affect a nation's overall productivity and wage level.

Some economists say that other action by people in high-income nations might benefit the low income nations more effectively than fair-trade purchasing. For example, pressing for the removal of agricultural subsidies in high-income areas such as Canada, the United States, and the European Union would reduce the overproduction of agricultural output that floods international markets and depresses international agricultural prices. Those low prices keep agricultural producers in low-income countries impoverished and unable to pay for the upgrades that would allow them to profitably diversify their agriculture into higher-profit food products. Instead, they tend to be stuck overproducing low-profit agricultural commodities such as coffee, bananas, and cocoa—keeping those prices artificially low. Ironically, those very low prices (and the low agricultural wages that result) are precisely what the fair-trade movement tries to increase.

Helping people in low-income nations improve their lot in life is certainly admirable. But figuring out the best way to achieve that goal is not always as easy as it may at first seem.

Question

How does a fair-trade product differ from an otherwise identical imported good? What is the purported benefit of fair trade certification and purchases of goods such as chocolate, coffee, bananas, and tea? Do fair-trade goods improve average wage and level of income in low-income nations? Why or why not?

CHAPTER SUMMARY

17.1 ▶ THE ECONOMIC BASIS FOR TRADE

- World trade is based on three considerations: the uneven distribution of economic resources among nations, the fact that efficient production of various goods requires particular techniques or combinations of resources, and the differentiated products produced among nations.

- Mutually advantageous specialization and trade are possible between any two nations if they have different opportunity cost ratios for any two products. By specializing based on comparative advantage, nations can obtain larger real incomes with fixed amounts of resources. The terms of trade determine how this increase in world output is shared by the trading nations. Increasing (rather than constant) costs limit specialization and trade.

17.2 ▶ SUPPLY AND DEMAND ANALYSIS OF EXPORTS AND IMPORTS

- A nation's export supply curve shows the quantity of product it will export at world prices that exceed the domestic price—the price in a closed, no-international-trade economy. Its import demand curve reveals the quantity of a product it will import at world prices below the domestic price. In a two-nation model, the equilibrium world price and the equilibrium quantities of exports and imports occur where one nation's import supply curve intersects the other nation's export demand curve.

17.3 ▶ TRADE BARRIERS

- Trade barriers take the form of protective tariffs, quotas, nontariff barriers, and "voluntary" export restraints. Supply and demand analysis reveals that protective tariffs and quotas increase the prices and reduce the quantities demanded of affected goods. Sales by foreign exporters diminish; domestic producers, however, enjoy higher prices and enlarged sales. Consumer losses from trade restrictions greatly exceed producer and government gains, creating an efficiency loss to society.

TERMS AND CONCEPTS

labour-intensive goods, p. 387
land-intensive goods, p. 387
capital-intensive goods, p. 387
absolute advantage, p. 387
opportunity-cost ratio, p. 389
principle of comparative advantage, p. 390

terms of trade, p. 390
trading possibilities line, p. 391
gains from trade, p. 391
world price, p. 395
domestic price, p. 395
export supply curve, p. 396
import demand curve, p. 396

equilibrium world price, p. 397
tariff, p. 399
revenue tariff, p. 399
protective tariff, p. 399
nontariff barrier, p. 399
import quota, p. 399
voluntary export restraint (VER), p. 399

STUDY QUESTIONS

LO 17.1 1. Distinguish among land-, labour- and capital-intensive commodities, citing an example of each. What role do these distinctions play in explaining international trade?

LO 17.1 2. Suppose nation A can produce 80 units of X by using all its resources to produce X and 60 units of Y by devoting all its resources to Y. Comparative figures for nation B are 60 of X and 60 of Y. Assuming constant costs, in which product should each nation specialize? Why? What are the limits of the terms of trade?

LO 17.1 3. **KEY QUESTION** The following are hypothetical production possibilities tables for New Zealand and Spain.

New Zealand's Production Possibilities Table (millions of bushels)

Product	A	B	C	D
Apples	0	20	40	60
Plums	15	10	5	0

Spain's Production Possibilities Table (millions of bushels)

Product	R	S	T	U
Apples	0	20	40	60
Plums	60	40	20	0

Plot the production possibilities data for each of the two countries separately. Referring to your graphs, determine:

a. Each country's cost ratio of producing plums and apples.

b. Which nation should specialize in which product.

c. The trading possibilities lines for each nation if the actual terms of trade are 1 plum for 2 apples. (Plot these lines on your graph.)

d. Suppose the optimum product mixes before specialization and trade were B in New Zealand and S in Spain. What are the gains from specialization and trade?

4. "Canada can produce product X more efficiently than can Great Britain. Yet we import X from Great Britain." Explain.

5. **KEY QUESTION** Refer to Figure 3-6 on page 61. Assume the graph depicts Canada's domestic market for corn. How many bushels of corn, if any, will Canada export or import at a world price of $1, $2, $3, $4, and $5? Use this information to construct Canada's export supply curve and import demand curve for corn. Suppose the only other corn-producing nation is France, where the domestic price is $4. Why will the equilibrium world price be between $3 and $4? Who will export corn at this world price; who will import it?

6. **KEY QUESTION** Draw a domestic supply and demand diagram for a product in which Canada does not have a comparative advantage. Indicate the impact of foreign imports on domestic price and quantity. Now show a protective tariff that eliminates approximately one-half the assumed imports. Indicate the effects of this tariff on price and on quantity to (a) domestic consumers, (b) domestic producers, and (c) foreign exporters. How would the effects of a quota that creates the same amount of imports differ?

17.3 7. Answer the following question based on the data below.

Quantity demanded domestically	Price	Quantity supplied domestically
700	$6	1100
800	5	1000
900	4	900
1000	3	800
1100	2	700
1200	1	600

a. What would price and quantity be if the market were closed to international trade? What would the domestic and foreign quantity supplied be if it were open to international trade and the world price was $2?

b. If the world price was $2 and a tariff of $1 were placed on the product, what would be the total revenues going to domestic producers, foreign producers (after-tax), and the government? Explain.

c. Given a world price of $2, what would be the difference in the total revenue received by foreign producers with a $1 per unit tariff compared with a quota of 200 units?

17.3 8. "The potentially valid arguments for tariff protection are also the most easily abused." What are these particular arguments? Why are they susceptible to abuse? Evaluate the use of artificial trade barriers, such as tariffs and import quotas, as a means of achieving and maintaining full employment.

17.3 9. Evaluate the following statements:

a. "Protective tariffs limit both the imports and the exports of the nation levying tariffs."

b. "The extensive application of protective tariffs destroys the ability of the international market system to allocate resources efficiently."

c. "Unemployment can often be reduced through tariff protection, but by the same token inefficiency typically increases."

d. "Foreign firms that 'dump' their products onto the Canadian market are in effect presenting the Canadian people with gifts."

e. "In view of the rapidity with which technological advance is dispersed around the world, free trade will inevitably yield structural maladjustments, unemployment, and balance of payments problems for industrially advanced nations."

f. "Free trade can improve the composition and efficiency of domestic output. Only the Volkswagen forced Detroit to make a compact car, and only foreign success with the oxygen process forced Canadian steel firms to modernize."

g. "In the long run foreign trade is neutral with respect to total employment."

LO 17.3 10. Suppose the Japanese agreed to a voluntary export restraint that reduced Canadian imports of Japanese automobiles by about 10 percent. What would you expect the short-run effects to have been on the Canadian and Japanese automobile industries? If this restriction were permanent, what would be its long-run effects in the two nations on (a) the allocation of resources, (b) the volume of employment, (c) the price level, and (d) the standard of living?

LO 17.3 11. In 2005, manufacturing workers in Canada earned an average wage of $21.55 per hour. That same year, manufacturing workers in Mexico earned an average wage of $2.63 per hour. How can Canadian manufacturers possibly compete? Why isn't all manufacturing done in Mexico and other low-wage countries?

INTERNET APPLICATION QUESTIONS @

1. **Trade Liberalization—The WTO.** Access the World Trade Organization (WTO) Web site from the McConnell-Brue-Flynn-Barbiero homepage (Chapter 17) and retrieve the latest news from the WTO. List and summarize three recent news items relating to the WTO.

2. **Canada's Main Trading Partners.** Statistics Canada lists Canada's main trading partners. Go to the McConnell-Brue-Flynn-Barbiero Web site (Chapter 17). Which country is our largest trading partner? What is Canada's biggest export sector? What sector is a close second?

Credits

TEXT CREDITS

Chapter 1
Page 8, www.worldbank.org.

Chapter 2
Page 34, The Heritage Foundation (www.heritage.org) and *The Wall Street Journal.* Page 43, *CIA World Fact Book*, 2008, www.cia.gov. Page 46, Abridged from Donald J. Boudreaux "Mutual Accommodation" *Ideas on Liberty*, May 2000 pp. 4–5.

Chapter 8
Page 207, Compiled from the Fortune 500 listing of the world's largest firms, Fortune Global 500, www.fortune.com © 2007 Time Inc. All rights reserved.

Chapter 9
Page 221, Statistics Canada, *Industrial Organization and Concentration in Manufacturing, Mining and Logging Industries*, Catalogue No. 31C0024, 1997. Page 230, Statistics Canada, *Industrial Organization and Concentration in Manufacturing, Mining and Logging Industries*, Catalogue No. 31C0024, 1997. Page 237, OPEC www.opec.org. Page 240, http://adage.com/images/random/datacenter/2008/globalmarketing2008.pdf. Page 241, Interbrand, www.interbrand.com. Page 243, Based on Kenneth G. Elzinga, "Beer," in Walter Adams and James Brock (eds.), *The Structure of American Industry*, 9th ed. (Englewood Cliffs, NJ: Prentice-Hall, 1995), pp. 119–151; Douglas F. Greer, "Beer: Causes of Structural Change," in Larry Duetsch (ed.), *Industry Studies*, 2nd ed. (New York: M. E. Sharpe, 1998), pp. 28–64; authors' updates; the Conference Board of Canada, *The Canadian Brewing Industry: Historical Evolution and Competitive Structure* (Toronto: International Studies and Development Group, 1989).

Chapter 12
Page 287, U.S. Bureau of Labor Statistics, www.bls.gov. Page 288, Source: Adapted from Statistics Canada CANSIM database. At: http://cansim2.statcan.ca, Table 383-0008, June 2009. Page 302; Adapted from Statistics Canada CANSIM database, http://cansim2.statcan.ca, Table 281-0027, June 2008. Page 303, Reunion des Musées Nationaux/Art Resource, NY © Estate of Pablo Picasso/Artists Rights Society (ARS), New York. Page 307, Source: "Canada's Highest-Paid CEO Spotlighted in Home Province," by

Brian Banks. *Financial Post Daily Magazine*, November 18, 2008. Material reprinted with the express permission of "The National Post Company," a Canwest Partnership.

Chapter 13
Page 319, Sources: Bank of Canada. Page 321, Organisation for Economic Co-operation and Development, www.oecd.org.

Chapter 14
Page 328, *The World Factbook*, www.cia.gov. Data are 2007 estimates. Page 330, *The Economist* magazine, www.economist.com. Inflation adjustments made using the GDP deflator for the United States calculated by the Bureau of Economic Analysis, www.bea.gov. Page 333, Sources: Cambridge Energy Research Associates, www.cera.com; *The Economist*, April 22, 2006, www.economist.com. Page 340, *State of the World's Forests*, 2005, United Nations Food and Agriculture Organization, www.fao.org. Page 344, Source: The EPI data are from the Yale Center for Environmental Law and Policy, www.yale.edu/epi/. The data on real GDP per person (at purchasing power parity) in 2004 are from *The World Factbook*, www.cia.gov.

Chapter 15
Page 362, OECD environmental data www.oecd.org. Page 369, Based on Ian Ayres and Steven D. Levitt, "Measuring Positive Externalities from Unobservable Victim Precaution: An Empirical Analysis of Lojack," *Quarterly Journal of Economics*, February 1998, pp. 43–77. The authors point out that Lojack did not fund their work in any way, nor do they have any financial stake in Lojack.

Chapter 16
Page 383, Adapted from Statistics Canada CANSIM database, http://cansim2.statcan.ca, Table 385-0002, June 2008. Page 384, Bastiat, Frédéric, *Economic Sophisms*. Arthur Goddard, trans. The Foundation for Economic Education, Inc., 1996.

Chapter 17
Page 393, A. T. Kearney, *Foreign Policy*, www.foreignpolicy.com

PHOTOGRAPHS

Chapter 1
page 2, Arthur S. Aubry/Getty Images; page 20, © James Leynse/CORBIS

Chapter 2
page 46, © Royalty Free/CORBIS

Chapter 3
page 50, Ryan McVay/Getty Images; page 66, Ryan McVay/Getty Images; page 68, Royalty-Free/CORBIS

Chapter 4
page 91, Doug Menuez/Getty Images; page 106, © Tom Prettyman/PhotoEdit

Chapter 5
page 112, Ryan McVay/Getty Images, page 122, © James Paul Photographers; page 131, Courtesy of Maps à la Carte, Inc.

Chapter 6
Page 137, © Creatas/PunchStock; page 141, © BananaStock/PunchStock; page 157, © Digital Vision/PunchStock; page 158, © Jonnie Miles/Getty Images

Chapter 7
page 165, Royalty-Free/CORBIS; page 165, Royalty-Free/CORBIS; page 188, © Tannen Maury/epa/CORBIS

Chapter 8
page 193, Stockbyte/PunchStock Images; page 214, © PhotoLink/Getty Images

Chapter 9
page 220, The McGraw-Hill Companies, Inc./Bob Coyle, photographer; page 242, © Burke/Triolo Production Group/Getty Images

Chapter 10
page 264, © AP Photo/Paul Sakuma

Chapter 11
page 269, © Digital Vision/PunchStock; page 282, © Brand X Pictures/PunchStock

Chapter 12
page 287, Ryan McVay/Getty Images; page 293, © Alistair Berg/Photodisc/Getty Images; page 307, © Peter Weber/Getty Images

Chapter 13
page 323, Royalty-Free/CORBIS; page 324, Royalty Free/CORBIS

Chapter 15
page 350, David Toase/Getty Images. Page 354, © Digital Vision/PunchStock. Page 367, © Image 100/PunchStock

Chapter 16
page 384, Getty Images/Steve Allen

Chapter 17
page 387, Stockbyte/PunchStock; page 391, © Digital Vision/PunchStock

Glossary

A

Ability-to-pay principle The idea that those who have greater income (or wealth) should pay a greater proportion of it as taxes than those who have less income (or wealth).

Absolute advantage When a region or nation can produce more of good Z and good Y with less resources compared to other regions or nations.

Absolute poverty A situation in which the basic material needs of an individual or a family (food, clothing, shelter) are not met.

Adverse selection problem A problem arising when information known to one party to a contract is not known to the other party, causing the latter to incur major costs.

Aggregate A collection of specific economic units treated as if they were one unit.

Agribusiness Large corporate firms in farming.

Allocative efficiency The apportionment of resources among firms and industries to produce the goods most wanted by society.

Appreciation (of the dollar) An increase in the value of the dollar relative to the currency of another nation so that a dollar buys a larger amount of the foreign currency and thus of foreign goods.

Asymmetric information A situation in which one party to a market transaction has much more information about a product or service than the other does; the result may be an underallocation or overallocation of resources.

Average fixed cost (AFC) A firm's total fixed cost divided by output.

Average product (AP) The total output divided by the quantity of that employed resource.

Average revenue Total revenue from the sale of a product divided by the quantity of the product sold.

Average total cost (ATC) A firm's total cost divided by output.

Average variable cost (AVC) A firm's total variable cost divided by output.

B

Barriers to entry Anything that artificially prevents the entry of firms into an industry.

Barter The exchange of one good or service for another good or service.

Benefits-received principle The idea that those who receive the benefits of goods and services provided by government should pay the taxes required to finance them.

Bilateral monopoly A market in which there is a single seller (monopoly) and a single buyer (monopsony).

Bond A financial device through which a borrower (a firm or government) is obligated to pay the principal and interest on a loan at a specific date in the future.

Break-even point An output at which a firm makes a normal profit but not an economic profit.

Budget constraint The limit that the size of a consumer's income (and the prices that must be paid for goods and services) imposes on the ability of that consumer to obtain goods and services.

Budget line A schedule or curve that shows various combinations of two products a consumer can purchase with a specific money income.

C

Canada Pension Plan (CPP) A national retirement plan funded by obligatory employer and employee contributions.

Capital Human-made resources (buildings, machinery, and equipment) used to produce goods and services.

Capital goods Goods that do not directly satisfy human wants.

Capital-intensive goods Products that require a relatively large amount of capital to produce.

Cartel A formal agreement among firms in an industry to set the price of a product and establish the outputs of the individual firms or to divide the market among them.

Change in demand A change in the quantity demanded of a good or service at every price.

Change in quantity demanded A movement from one point to another on a demand curve.

Change in quantity supplied A movement from one point to another on a fixed supply curve.

Change in supply A change in the quantity supplied of a good or service at every price; a shift of the supply curve to the left or right.

Circular flow diagram The flow of resources from households to firms and of products from firms to households. These flows are accompanied by reverse flows of money from firms to households and from households to firms.

Climate-change problem The problem of rising world temperatures that most climate experts believe are caused in part by increased carbon dioxide and other greenhouse gases.

Coase theorem The idea first stated by economist Ronald Coase that externalities may be resolved through private negotiations of the affected parties.

Collusion A situation in which firms act together and in agreement to fix prices, divide a market, or otherwise restrict competition.

Command system An economic system in which most property resources are owned by the government and the economic decisions are made by a central government body.

Comparative advantage When a region or nation can produce a good at a lower domestic opportunity cost compared to a potential trading partner.

Compensating differences Differences in the wages received by workers in different jobs to compensate for nonmonetary differences in the jobs.

Competition The presence in a market of a large number of independent buyers and sellers competing with one another and the freedom of buyers and sellers to enter and leave the market.

Competition policy The laws and government actions designed to prevent monopoly and promote competition.

Competition Tribunal A government body that adjudicates under a civil law framework that permits the issuing of remedial orders to restore and maintain competition in the market.

Complementary goods Products and services that are used together.

Concentration ratio The percentage of the total sales of an industry produced and sold by an industry's largest firms.

Conglomerate merger The merger of a firm in one industry with a firm in another industry or region.

Constant opportunity cost An opportunity cost that remains the same for each additional unit as a consumer (or society) shifts purchases (production) from one product to another along a straight-line budget line (production possibilities curve).

Constant returns to scale The range of output between the output at which economies of scale end and diseconomies of scale begin.

Constant-cost industry An industry in which the entry of new firms has no effect on resource prices and thus no effect on production costs.

Consumer goods Products and services that satisfy human wants directly.

Consumer sovereignty Determination by consumers of the types and quantities of goods and services that will be produced with the scarce resources of the economy.

Consumer surplus The difference between the maximum price consumers are willing to pay for a product and the actual price.

Corporation A legal entity chartered by the federal or provincial government that operates as a distinct and separate body from the individuals who own it.

Cost–benefit analysis Comparing the marginal costs with the marginal benefits to decide whether to employ resources in that project and to what extent.

Creative destruction The hypothesis that the creation of new products and production methods simultaneously destroys the market power of firms that are wedded to existing products and older ways of doing business.

Credible threat A statement of harmful intent by one party that the other party views as believable.

Crop restriction In return for guaranteed prices for their crops, farmers agree to limit the number of hectares they plant in that crop.

Cross elasticity of demand The ratio of the percentage change in quantity demanded of one good to the percentage change in the price of some other good; a positive coefficient indicates the two products are substitute goods; a negative coefficient indicates they are complementary goods.

D

Deadweight loss (See Efficiency loss.)

Decreasing-cost industry An industry in which the entry of firms lowers the prices of resources and thus decreases production costs.

Deficiency payments Subsidies that make up the difference between market prices and government-supported prices; a method of price support.

Demand A schedule or curve that shows the various amounts of a product that consumers are willing and able to purchase at each of a series of possible prices during a specified period of time.

Demand curve A curve illustrating the inverse (negative) relationship between the quantity demanded of a good or service and its price, other things equal.

Demographers Scientists who study trends in human populations.

Dependent variable A variable that changes, as a consequence of a change in some other (independent) variable; the "effect" or outcome.

Depreciation (of the dollar) A decrease in the value of the dollar relative to another currency so that a dollar buys a smaller amount of the foreign currency and therefore of foreign goods.

Derived demand The demand for a factor that depends on the products it can be used to produce.

Determinants of demand Factors other than its price that determine the quantities demanded of a good or service.

Determinants of supply Factors other than its price that determine the quantities supplied of a good or service.

Differentiated oligopoly An oligopoly in which the firms produce a differentiated product.

Diminishing marginal utility As a consumer increases the consumption of a good or service, the marginal utility obtained from each additional unit of the good or service decreases.

Direct relationship The relationship between two variables that change in the same direction, for example, product price and quantity supplied.

Diseconomies of scale Increases in the average total cost of producing a product as the firm expands the size of its plant (its output) in the long run.

Division of labour Dividing the work required to produce a product into a number of different tasks that are performed by different workers.

Dollar votes The "votes" that consumers and entrepreneurs cast for the production of consumer and capital goods, respectively, when they purchase them in product and resource markets.

Domestic price The price of a good or service within a country, determined by domestic demand and supply.

Dominant strategy In game theory, an option that is better than any alternative option regardless of what the other firm does.

Dumping The sale in a foreign country of products below the cost or below the prices charged at home.

E

Economic (opportunity) cost A value equal to the value of other products that cannot be produced when resources are instead used to make a particular product.

Economic growth (1) An outward shift in the production possibilities curve that results from an increase in factor supplies or quality or an improvement in technology; (2) an increase either in real output (gross domestic product) or in real output per capita.

Economic model A simplified picture of economic reality; an abstract generalization.

Economic perspective A viewpoint that envisions individuals and institutions making rational decisions by comparing the marginal benefits and marginal costs associated with their actions.

Economic principle A statement about economic behaviour or the economy that enables prediction of the probable effects of certain actions.

Economic problem The need to make choices because society's material wants for goods and services are unlimited but the resources available to satisfy these wants are limited (scarce).

Economic (pure) profit The total revenue of a firm less its economic costs (which includes both explicit costs and implicit costs); also called above-normal profit.

Economic rent The price paid for the use of land and other natural resources, the supply of which is fixed (perfectly inelastic).

Economic resources The land, labour, capital, and entrepreneurial ability that are used in the production of goods and services.

Economic system A particular set of institutional arrangements and a coordinating mechanism for producing goods and services.

Economics The social science concerned with how individuals, institutions, and society make optimal (best) choices under conditions of scarcity.

Economies of scale Reductions in the average total cost of producing a product as the firm expands the size of plant (its output) in the long run.

Efficiency loss of a tax The loss of net benefits to society because a tax reduces the production and consumption of a taxed good below the level of allocative efficiency.

Efficiency losses Reductions of combined consumer and producer surplus caused by an underallocation or overallocation of resources to the production of a good or service. Also called deadweight loss.

Elastic demand Product or resource demand whose price elasticity is greater than one.

Elasticity of factor demand The percentage change in factor quantity divided by the percentage change in factor price; if the result is greater than one, factor demand is elastic; if the result is less than one, factor demand is inelastic; and when the result equals one, factor demand is unit-elastic.

Employment discrimination Inferior treatment in hiring, promotion, and work assignment for a particular group of employees.

Employment equity Policies and programs that establish targets of increased employment and promotion for women and minorities.

Employment insurance (EI) A program that insures workers against the hazards of losing their jobs.

Empty threat A statement of harmful intent that is easily dismissed by the second party because the threat is not viewed as believable.

Entrepreneurial ability The human talents that combine the other resources to produce a product, make nonroutine decisions, innovate, and bear risks.

Equality–efficiency tradeoff The decrease in economic efficiency that may accompany a decrease in income inequality; the presumption that some income inequality is required to achieve economic efficiency.

Equilibrium position The combination of products that yields the greatest satisfaction or utility; the combination will lie on the highest attainable indifference curve.

Equilibrium price The price in a competitive market at which the quantity demanded and the quantity supplied are equal.

Equilibrium quantity The quantity demanded and supplied at the equilibrium price in a competitive market.

Equilibrium world price A price determined by the intersection of exporting nations' supply of a product and importing nations' demand for the same product.

Excess capacity Plant or equipment that is underused because the firm is producing less than the minimum-ATC output.

Exchange rate The rate of exchange of one nation's currency for another nation's currency.

Exclusive unionism The practice of a labour union of restricting the supply of skilled union labour to increase the wages received by union members.

Expected-rate-of-return curve The increase in profit a firm anticipates it will obtain by investing in R&D.

Explicit costs The monetary payments a firm must make to an outsider to obtain a resource.

Export subsidies Government payments to domestic producers to enable them to reduce the price of a good or service to foreign buyers.

Export supply curve An upward-sloping curve that shows the amount of a product domestic firms will export at each world price above the domestic price.

External benefit (See Positive externality.)

External cost (See Negative externality.)

Externalities Benefits or costs from production or consumption accruing without compensation to non-buyers and non-sellers of the product (see negative externality and positive externality).

Extraction costs All costs associated with extracting a natural resource and readying it for sale.

F

Factor market A market in which households sell and firms buy factors of production.

Factors of production Economic resources: land, capital, labour, and entrepreneurial ability.

Fair-return price The price of a product that enables its producer to obtain a normal profit and that is equal to the average cost of producing it.

Firm An organization that employs resources to produce a good or service for profit and that owns and operates one or more plants.

First-mover advantage In game theory, the benefit obtained by the party that moves first in a sequential game.

Fishery A stock of fish or other marine animal that is composed of a distinct group, for example Newfoundland cod, Pacific tuna, or Alaska crab.

Fishery collapse A rapid decline in a fishery's population because the fish are being harvested faster than they can reproduce.

Fixed costs Costs that in total do not change when the firm changes its output.

Foreign exchange market A market in which the money (currency) of one nation can be used to purchase (can be exchanged for) the money of another nation.

Four-Firm Concentration Ratio The percentage of total industry sales accounted for by the top four firms in the industry.

Freedom of choice The freedom of owners of property resources to employ or dispose of them as they see fit, and of consumers to spend their incomes in a manner that they think is appropriate.

Freedom of enterprise The freedom of firms to obtain economic resources, to use these resources to produce products of the firm's own choosing, and to sell their products in markets of their choice.

Free-rider problem The inability of potential providers of an economically desirable but indivisible good or service to obtain payment from those who benefit.

Full employment (1) Use of all available resources to produce want-satisfying goods and services. (2) The situation when the unemployment rate is equal to the full-employment unemployment rate and there is frictional and structural but no cyclical unemployment (and the real output of the economy equals its potential real output).

Full production Employment of available resources so that the maximum amount of (or total value of) goods and services is produced; occurs when both productive efficiency and allocative efficiency are realized.

Future value The amount to which some current amount of money will grow if the interest earned on the amount is left to compound over time.

G

Gains from trade The extra output that trading partners obtain through specialization of production and exchange of goods and services.

Game theory model A means of analyzing the pricing behaviour of oligopolists using the theory of strategy associated with games such as chess and bridge.

Generalizations Statements of the nature of the relation between two or more sets of facts.

Gini ratio A numerical measure of the overall dispersion of income.

Goods and Services Tax (GST) Federal tax that replaced the federal sales tax in Canada; it is 5 percent on a broad base of goods and services (the only exemptions are agricultural and fish products, prescription drugs, and medical devices); businesses remit the difference between the value of their sales and the value of its purchases from other firms.

Government failure Inefficiencies in resource allocation caused by problems in the operation of the public sector (government); occurs because of rent-seeking pressure by special-interest groups, short-sighted political behaviour, limited and bundled choices, and bureaucratic inefficiencies.

Guaranteed Income Supplement (GIS) Money paid on application, subject to a means test, to those receiving an OAS pension who have an income below a certain level.

Guiding function of prices The ability of price changes to bring about changes in the quantities of products and resources demanded and supplied.

H

Herfindahl index The sum of the squared percentage market share of all firms in the industry.

Homogeneous oligopoly An oligopoly in which the firms produce a standardized product.

Horizontal axis The "left–right" or "west–east" axis on a graph or grid.

Horizontal merger A merger between two competitors selling similar products in the same market.

Household An economic unit (of one or more persons) that provides the economy with resources and uses the income received to purchase goods and services that satisfy material wants.

Human capital Any expenditure to improve the education, skills, health, or mobility of workers, with an expectation of greater productivity and thus a positive return on the investment.

Human capital discrimination Arbitrary restriction of particular groups from productivity-enhancing investments in education and training.

I

Imperfect competition The market models monopoly, monopolistic competition, and oligopoly considered as a group.

Implicit costs The monetary income a firm sacrifices when it uses a resource it owns rather than supplying the resource in the market; equal to what the resource could have earned in the best-paying alternative employment (including a normal profit).

Import competition The competition domestic firms encounter from the products and services of foreign producers.

Import demand curve A downward-sloping curve that shows the amount of a product that an economy will import at each world price below the domestic price.

Import quota A limit imposed by a nation on the quantity (or total value) of a good that may be imported during some period.

Incentive function of price The inducement that an increase in the price of a commodity gives to sellers to make more of it available (and conversely for a decrease in price), and the inducement that an increase in price offers to buyers to purchase smaller quantities (and conversely for a decrease in price).

Incentive pay plan A compensation structure, such as piece rates, bonuses, stock options, commissions, and profit sharing, that ties worker pay directly to performance.

Inclusive unionism The practice of a labour union of including as members all workers employed in an industry.

Income effect A change in the price of a product changes a consumer's real income (purchasing power) and thus the quantity of the product purchased.

Income elasticity of demand The ratio of the percentage change in the quantity demanded of a good to a percentage change in consumer income; measures the responsiveness of consumer purchases to income changes.

Income inequality The unequal distribution of an economy's total income among households or families.

Income mobility The movement of individuals and families from one income quintile to another over time.

Increasing-cost industry An industry in which the entry of new firms raises the prices for resources and thus increases their production costs.

Independent variable The variable causing a change in some other (dependent) variable.

Indifference curves Curves showing the different combinations of two products that yield the same satisfaction or utility to a consumer.

Indifference map A series of indifference curves, each of which represents a different level of utility and together show the preferences of a consumer.

Individual transferable quota (ITQ) A limit on the total number or tonnage of fish that individual fishers can harvest during a particular time period.

Industry A group of firms that produce the same or similar products or services.

Inelastic demand Product or resource demand for which the price elasticity coefficient is less than one.

Inferior good A good or service whose consumption declines as income rises (and conversely), price remaining constant.

Innovation The first successful commercial introduction of a new product, the first use of a new method of production, or the creation of a new form of business organization.

Insurable risk An event that would result in a loss but whose frequency of occurrence can be estimated with considerable accuracy; insurance companies are willing to sell insurance against such losses.

Interindustry competition The competition between the products of one industry and the products of another industry.

Inverse relationship The relationship between two variables that change in opposite directions, for example, product price and quantity demanded.

Investment Spending for the production and accumulation of capital and additions to inventories.

Invisible hand The tendency of firms and resource suppliers seeking to further their own self-interests in competitive markets to also promote the interest of society as a whole.

L

Labour The physical and mental talents and efforts of people that are used to produce goods and services.

Labour-intensive goods Products that require a relatively large amount of labour to produce.

Land Natural resources ("free gifts of nature") used to produce goods and services.

Land-intensive goods Products that require a relatively large amount of land to produce.

Law of demand All else equal, as price falls, the quantity demanded rises, and vice versa.

Law of diminishing marginal utility As a consumer increases the consumption of a good or service, the marginal utility obtained from each additional unit of the good or service decreases.

Law of diminishing returns As successive increments of a variable factor are added to a fixed factor, the marginal product of the variable resource will eventually decrease.

Law of increasing opportunity costs As the production of a good increases, the opportunity cost of producing an additional unit rises.

Law of supply The principle that, other things equal, an increase in the price of a product will increase the quantity of it supplied; and conversely for a price decrease.

Least-cost combination of factors The quantity of each factor a firm must employ to produce a particular output at the lowest total cost.

Legal cartel theory of regulation The hypothesis that some industries seek regulation or want to maintain regulation so that they may form a legal cartel.

Limited liability Restriction of the maximum loss to a predetermined amount for the owners (stockholders) of a corporation, the maximum loss is the amount they paid for their shares of stock.

Loanable funds theory of interest The concept that the supply of and demand for loanable funds determines the equilibrium rate of interest.

Logrolling The trading of votes by legislators to secure favourable outcomes on decisions concerning the provision of public goods and quasipublic goods.

Long run A period of time long enough to enable producers of a product to change the quantities of all the resources they employ.

Long-run farm problem The tendency for agriculture to be a declining industry as technological progress increases supply relative to an inelastic and slowly increasing demand.

Long-run supply curve A curve that shows the prices at which a purely competitive industry will make various quantities of the product available in the long run.

Lorenz curve A curve showing the distribution of income in an economy; the cumulated percentage of families (income receivers) is measured along the horizontal axis and cumulated percentage of income is measured along the vertical axis.

M

Macroeconomics The part of economics concerned with the economy as a whole; with such major aggregates as the household, business, and governmental sectors; and with measures of the total economy.

Marginal analysis The comparison or marginal ("extra" or "additional") benefits and marginal costs, usually for decision making.

Marginal cost (MC) The extra or additional cost of producing one more unit of output.

Marginal factor cost (MFC) The amount that each additional unit of a factor adds to the firm's total (factor) cost.

Marginal product (MP) The extra output produced with adding a unit of a variable factor to the production process.

Marginal productivity theory of income distribution The contention that the distribution of income is fair when each unit of each factor receives a money payment equal to its marginal contribution to the firm's revenue (its marginal revenue product).

Marginal rate of substitution The rate at which a consumer is prepared to substitute one good for another (from a given combination of goods) and remain equally satisfied (have the same total utility); equal to the slope of a consumer's indifference curve at each point on the curve.

Marginal resource cost (MRC) The amount that each additional unit of resource adds to the firm's total (resource) cost.

Marginal revenue The change in total revenue that results from selling one more unit of a firm's product.

Marginal revenue product (MRP) The change in total revenue from employing one additional unit of a factor.

Marginal revenue productivity How much workers contribute to their employers' revenue; usually reflected in their pay level.

Marginal utility The extra utility a consumer obtains from the consumption of one additional unit of a good or service; equal to the change in total utility divided by the change in the quantity consumed.

Market Any institution or mechanism that brings together buyers and sellers of particular goods, services, or resources for the purpose of exchange.

Market failure The inability of markets to bring about the allocation of resources that best satisfies the wants of society.

Market for externality rights A market in which firms can buy rights to discharge pollutants; the price of such rights is determined by the demand for the right and a perfectly inelastic supply of such rights (the latter is determined by the quantity of discharges that the environment can assimilate).

Market period A period in which producers of a product are unable to change the quantity produced in response to a change in its price; in which there is a perfectly inelastic supply.

Market system An economic system in which property resources are privately owned and markets and prices are used to direct and coordinate economic activities.

MC = MB rule For a government project, marginal benefit should equal marginal cost to produce maximum benefit to society.

Median-voter model The theory that under majority rule the median (middle) voter will be in the dominant position to determine the outcome of an election.

Medium of exchange Items sellers generally accept and buyers generally use to pay for a good or service.

Microeconomics The part of economics concerned with such individual units as industries, firms, and households; and with individual markets, particular prices, and specific goods and services.

Midpoint formula A method for calculating price elasticity of demand or price elasticity of supply that averages the two prices and two quantities as the reference points for computing percentages.

Minimum efficient scale (MES) The lowest level of output at which a firm can minimize long-run average costs.

Minimum wage The lowest wage employers may legally pay for an hour of work.

Money Any item that is generally acceptable to sellers in exchange for goods and services.

Monopolistic competition A market structure in which a relatively large number of sellers produce differentiated products, and entry into and exit from the market is relatively easy.

Monopoly A market structure in which one firm is the sole seller of a product or service, for which there are no close substitutes.

Monopsony A market structure in which there is only a single buyer.

Moral hazard problem The possibility that individuals or institutions will change their behaviour as the result of a contract or agreement.

Most-favoured-nation (MFN) clause An agreement by Canada to allow some other nation's exports into Canada at the lowest tariff level levied by Canada, then or later.

MR = MC rule A method of determining the total output at which economic profit is at a maximum (or losses at a minimum).

MRP = MFC rule To maximize economic profit (or minimize losses) a firm should use the quantity of a factor at which its marginal revenue product is equal to its marginal factor cost.

Multinational corporation A firm that owns production facilities in other countries and produces and sells its product abroad.

Mutual interdependence A situation in which a change in strategy (usually price) by one firm will affect the sales and profits of other firms.

N

Nash equilibrium An outcome in a non-cooperative game in which players choose their best strategy given the present strategies the others have chosen.

Natural monopoly An industry in which economies of scale are so great that a single firm can produce the product at a lower average total cost than if more than one firm produced the product.

Negative externality A cost imposed without compensation on third parties by the production or consumption of sellers

or buyers. Example: A manufacturer dumps toxic chemicals into a river, killing the fish sought by sport fishers. An external cost or a spillover cost.

Negative-sum game A game in which the gains (+) and losses (−) add up to some amount less than zero.

Net benefits The total benefits of some activity or policy less the total costs of that activity or policy.

Network effects Increases in the value of a product to each user, including existing ones, as the total number of users rises.

Nominal interest rate The interest rate expressed in terms of annual amounts currently charged for interest and not adjusted for inflation.

Nominal wage The amount of money received by a worker per unit of time (hour, day, etc.).

Noncash transfer Government transfer payments in the form of goods and services rather than money; for example, food stamps, housing assistance, and job training; also called in-kind transfers.

Noncompeting groups Collections of workers in the economy who do not compete with each other for employment because the skill and training of the workers in one group are substantially different from those in other groups.

Nonprice competition A selling strategy in which one firm tries to distinguish its product or service from all competing ones based on attributes other than price.

Nonrenewable natural resources Resources that either are in actual fixed supply or that renew so slowly as to be in virtual fixed supply when viewed from a human time perspective.

Nontariff barrier All barriers other than tariffs that nations erect to impede international trade.

Normal good A good or service whose consumption rises when income increases and falls when income decreases, price remaining constant.

Normal profit The payment made by a firm to obtain and retain entrepreneurial ability.

Normative economics The part of economics involving value judgments about what the economy should be like; concerned with which economic goals and policies should be implemented.

O

Occupational discrimination Arbitrary restriction of particular groups from more desirable, higher-paying occupations.

Occupational licensing The laws of provincial or municipal governments that require a worker to satisfy certain specified requirements and obtain a licence from a licensing board before engaging in a particular occupation.

Occupational segregation Crowding women or minorities into less desirable, lower-paying occupations.

Old Age Security (OAS) A pension paid on application at age 65 to everyone resident in Canada for at least 10 years immediately before turning 65.

Oligopoly A market structure in which a few large firms produce homogeneous or differentiated products.

One-time game A game in which firms select their optimal strategy in a single time period without regard to possible interactions in subsequent time periods.

Opportunity cost The amount of other products that must be forgone or sacrificed to produce a unit of a product.

Opportunity-cost ratio An equality showing the number of units of two products that can be produced with the same resources; e.g., the cost 1 corn = 3 olives shows that the resources required to produce 3 units of olives must be shifted to corn production to produce 1 unit of corn.

Optimal reduction of an externality The point at which society's marginal cost and marginal benefit of reducing that externality are equal.

Other-things-equal assumption The assumption that factors other than those being considered are held constant.

Output effect An increase in the price of one input will increase a firm's production costs and reduce its level of output, thus reducing the demand for other inputs (and vice versa).

P

Paradox of voting A situation in which paired-choice voting by majority rule fails to provide a consistent ranking of society's preferences for public goods or services.

Partnership An unincorporated firm owned and operated by two or more people.

Perfect competition A market structure in which a very large number of firms produce a standardized product.

Perfectly competitive labour market A factor market in which a large number of firms demand a particular type of labour supplied by a large number of nonunion workers.

Perfectly elastic demand Product or resource demand in which quantity demanded can be of any amount at a particular product price; graphs as a horizontal demand curve.

Perfectly elastic supply Product or resource supply in which quantity supplied can be of any amount at a particular product or resource price; graphs as a horizontal supply curve.

Perfectly inelastic demand Product or resource demand in which price can be of any amount at a particular quantity of the product or resource demanded; quantity demanded does not respond to a change in price; graphs as a vertical demand curve.

Perfectly inelastic supply Product or resource supply in which price can be of any amount at a particular quantity of the product or resource demanded; quantity supplied does not respond to a change in price; graphs as a vertical supply curve.

Plant A physical establishment that performs one or more functions in producing, fabricating, and distributing goods and services.

Positive economics The analysis of facts or data to establish scientific generalizations about economic behaviour.

Positive externality A benefit obtained without compensation by third parties from the production or consumption of sellers or buyers. Example: A beekeeper benefits when a neighbouring farmer plants clover. An external benefit or spillover benefit.

Post hoc, ergo propter hoc **fallacy** Incorrectly reasoning that when one event precedes another the first event must have caused the second event.

Present value Today's value of some amount of money that is to be received sometime in the future.

Price ceiling A legally established maximum price for a good or service.

Price discrimination The selling of a product to different buyers at different prices when the price differences are not justified by differences in cost.

Price elasticity of demand The ratio of the percentage change in quantity demanded of a product or resource to the percentage change in its price; a measure of the responsiveness of buyers to a change in the price of a product or resource.

Price elasticity of supply The ratio of the percentage change in quantity supplied of a product or resource to the percentage change in its price; the responsiveness of producers to a change in the price of a product or resource.

Price floor A legally determined price above the equilibrium price.

Price leadership An implicit understanding oligopolists use that has the dominant firm initiate price changes and all other firms follow.

Price supports Government-supported minimum prices for agricultural products.

Price-taker A firm in a purely competitive market that cannot change market price, only adjust to it.

Principal-agent problem A conflict of interest that occurs when agents (workers or managers) pursue their own objectives to the detriment of the principals' (stockholders') goals.

Principle of comparative advantage When a region or nation can produce a good at a lower domestic opportunity cost compared to a potential trading partner.

Principles Statements about economic behaviour that enable prediction of the probable effect of certain actions.

Prisoner's dilemma A type of game between two players that shows the difficulty of cooperating when the two cannot communicate with each other, even when it is in their best interest to cooperate.

Private good A good or service that is individually consumed and that can be profitably provided by privately owned firms because they can exclude nonpayers from receiving the benefits.

Private property The right of private persons and firms to obtain, own, control, employ, dispose of, and bequeath land, capital, and other property.

Process innovation The development and use of new or improved production or distribution methods.

Producer surplus The difference between the actual price producers receive and the minimum acceptable price.

Product differentiation A strategy in which one firm's product is distinguished from competing products by means of its design, related services, quality, location, or other attributes (except price).

Product market A market in which products are sold by firms and bought by households.

Production possibilities curve A curve showing the different combinations of two goods or services that can be produced in a full-employment, full-production economy where the available supplies of resources and technology are fixed.

Production possibilities table A table showing the different combinations of two products that can be used produced with a specific set of resources in a full-employment, full-production economy.

Productive efficiency The production of a good in the least costly way.

Profit-maximizing combination of factors The quantity of each factor a firm must employ to maximize its profits or minimize its losses.

Progressive tax A tax whose average tax rate increases as the taxpayer's income increases and decreases as the taxpayer's income decreases.

Proportional tax A tax whose average tax rate remains constant as the taxpayer's income increases or decreases.

Positive-sum game A game in which the gains (+) and losses (–) add up to more than zero.

Protective tariff A tariff designed to shield domestic producers of a good or service from the competition of foreign producers.

Public choice theory The economic analysis of collective and government decision making.

Public good A good or service that can be simultaneously consumed by everyone, and from which no one can be excluded, even if they don't pay for it.

Public interest theory of regulation The theory that industrial regulation is necessary to keep a natural monopoly from charging monopoly prices and thus harming consumers and society.

Pure rate of interest An essentially risk-free, long-term interest rate not influenced by market imperfections.

Q

Quasi-public good A good or service to which the exclusion principle could apply, but that has such a large spillover benefit that government sponsors its production to prevent an under-allocation of resources.

Quota A restriction on the amount of a product that a farm is allowed to produce in a given period.

R

Rational behaviour Human behaviour based on comparison of marginal costs and marginal benefits; behaviour designed to maximize total utility.

Rationing function of prices The ability of market forces in a competitive market to equalize quantity demanded and quantity supplied and to eliminate shortages and surpluses via changes in prices.

Real interest rate The interest rate expressed in dollars of constant value (adjusted for inflation); equal to the nominal interest rate less the expected rate of inflation.

Real wage The amount of goods and services a worker can purchase with a nominal wage.

Regressive tax A tax whose average tax rate decreases as the taxpayer's income increases.

Relative poverty A situation in which an individual's or a family's income is low relative to others in society.

Renewable natural resources Resources that are capable of renewing themselves if they are harvested at moderate rates.

Rent-seeking behaviour The actions by persons, firms, or unions to gain special benefits from government at taxpayers' or someone else's expense.

Repeated game A game that is played again sometime after the previous game ends.

Replacement rate The birthrate necessary to keep the size of a population constant without relying on immigration.

Revenue tariff A tariff designed to produce income for the federal government.

Reverse discrimination The view that the preferential treatment associated with employment equity constitutes discrimination against other groups.

S

Scientific method The systematic pursuit of knowledge through the formulation of a problem, collection of data, and the formulation and testing of hypotheses to obtain theories, principles, and laws.

Self-interest That which each firm, property owner, worker, and consumer believes is best for itself.

Sequential game A game in which the parties make their moves in turn, with one party making the first move, followed by the other party making the next move, and so on.

Short run A period of time in which producers are able to change the quantities of some but not all of the resources they employ.

Shortage The amount by which the quantity demanded of a product exceeds the quantity supplied at a particular (below-equilibrium) price.

Short-run farm problem The sharp year-to-year changes in the prices of agricultural products and in the incomes of farmers.

Short-run supply curve A curve that shows the quantities of the product a firm in a purely competitive industry will offer to sell at various prices in the short run.

Shutdown case The circumstance in which a firm would experience a loss greater than its total fixed cost if it were to produce any output greater than zero; alternatively, a situation in which a firm would cease to operate when the price at which it can sell its product is less than its average variable cost.

Simultaneous consumption A product's ability to satisfy a large number of consumers at the same time.

Simultaneous game A game in which both parties choose their strategies and execute them at the same time.

Slope of a line The ratio of the vertical change (the rise or fall) to the horizontal change (the run) between any two points on a line. The slope of an upward sloping line is positive, reflecting a direct relationship between two variables; the slope of a downward sloping line is negative, reflecting an inverse relationship between two variables.

Social regulation Government regulation of the conditions under which goods are produced, the physical characteristics of goods, and the impact of the production on society.

Socially optimal price The price of a product that results in the most efficient allocation of an economy's resources.

Sole proprietorship An unincorporated firm owned and operated by one person.

Special-interest effect Any result of government promotion of the interests (goals) of a small group at the expense of a much larger group.

Specialization The use of the resources of an individual, a firm, a region, or a nation to produce one or a few goods and services.

Static economy An economy in which factor supplies, technological knowledge, and consumer tastes are constant and unchanging.

Statistical discrimination Judging individuals on the average characteristic of the group to which they belong rather than on their own personal characteristics.

Stock (corporate) A share in the ownership of a corporation.

Strategic behaviour Self-interested behaviour that takes into account the reactions of others.

Strategic trade policy The use of trade barriers to reduce the risk inherent in product development by domestic firms, particularly that involving advanced technology.

Substitute goods Products or services that can be used in place of each other.

Substitution effect (1) A change in the price of a consumer good changes the relative expensiveness of that good and hence changes the consumer's willingness to buy it rather than other goods. (2) A firm will purchase more of an input whose relative price has declined and use less of an input whose relative price has increased.

Supply A schedule or curve that shows the amounts of a product that producers are willing and able to make available for sale at each of a series of possible prices during a specific period.

Supply curve A curve illustrating the positive (direct) relationship between the quantity supplied of a good or service and its price, other things equal.

Support prices Government-supported minimum prices for agricultural products.

Surplus The amount by which the quantity supplied of a product exceeds the quantity demanded at a specific (above-equilibrium) price.

T

Tacit understandings Any method by which competing oligopolists to set prices and outputs that does not involve outright collusion.

Tariff A tax imposed by a nation on an imported good.

Tax incidence The person or group who ends up paying a tax.

Technological advance New and better goods and services and new and better ways of producing or distributing them.

Terms of trade The rate at which units of one product can be exchanged for units of another product.

Theoretical economics The process of deriving and applying economic theories and principles.

Time value of money The idea that a specific amount of money is more valuable to a person the sooner it is received because the money can be placed in a financial account or investment and earn compound interest over time.

Total allowable catch (TAC) A limit on the total number or tonnage of fish that fishers. collectively can harvest during a particular time period.

Total cost The sum of fixed cost and variable cost.

Total fertility rate The average total number of children that a woman is expected to have during her lifetime.

Total product (TP) The total output of a particular good or service produced by a firm.

Total revenue The total number of dollars received by a firm from the sale of a product.

Total utility The total amount of satisfaction derived from the consumption of a single product or a combination of products.

Total-revenue test A test to determine elasticity of demand between any two prices: Demand is elastic if total revenue moves in the opposite direction as price; it is inelastic when it moves in the same direction as price; and it is of unitary elasticity when it does not change when price changes.

Trade bloc A group of nations that lower or abolish trade barriers among members. Examples include the European Union and the nations of the North American Free Trade Agreement.

Tradeoff The sacrifice of some or all of one economic goal, good, or service to achieve some other goal, good, or service.

Trading possibilities line A line that shows the different combinations of two products an economy is able to obtain when it specializes in the production of one product and exports it to obtain the other product.

Tragedy of the commons Air, water, and public land rights are held in common by society and freely available, so no incentive exists to maintain or use them carefully; the result is overuse, degradation, and pollution.

Tying contract A requirement imposed by a seller that a buyer purchase another (or other) of its products as a condition for buying a desired product.

U

Uninsurable risk An event that would result in a loss and whose occurrence is uncontrollable and unpredictable; insurance companies are not willing to sell insurance against such a loss.

Unit elasticity Demand or supply for which the elasticity coefficient is equal to one.

User cost The cost to the user of extracting a resource; current extraction and use means lower future extraction and use.

Utility The want-satisfying power of a good or service; the satisfaction a person gets from consuming a good or service.

Utility-maximizing rule To obtain the greatest utility the consumer should allocate money income so that the last dollar spent on each good or service yields the same marginal utility.

V

Value-added tax (VAT) A tax imposed on the difference between the value of the products sold by a firm and the value of the goods purchased from other firms to produce the product; used in several European countries.

Variable costs Costs that increase or decrease with a firm's output.

Vertical axis The "up–down" or "north–south" axis on a graph or grid.

Vertical intercept The point at which a line meets the vertical axis of a graph.

Vertical merger The merger of firms engaged in different stages of the production process of a final product.

Very long run A period in which technology can change and in which firms can develop and offer entirely new products.

W

Wage differentials The difference between the wage received by one worker or group of workers and that received by another worker or group of workers.

Wage discrimination The payment of a lower wage to members of a less-preferred group than to members of a more-preferred group for the same work.

Wage rate A price paid per unit of labour services.

World price The international market price of a good or service, determined by world demand and supply.

X

X-inefficiency The production of output, whatever its level, at a higher average (and total) cost than is necessary.

Z

Zero-sum game A game in which the gains (+) and losses (–) add up to zero.

Index